Systems and Decision Making

Systems and Decision Making

A Management Science Approach

HANS G DAELLENBACH
University of Canterbury, Christchurch, New Zealand

JOHN WILEY & SONS

Chichester · New York · Brisbane · Toronto · Singapore

Other Wiley Editorial Offices

John Wiley & Sons, Inc., 605 Third Avenue,
New York, NY 10158-0012, USA

Jacaranda Wiley Ltd, 33 Park Road, Milton,
Queensland 4064, Australia

John Wiley & Sons (Canada) Ltd, 22 Worcester Road,
Rexdale, Ontario M9W 1L1, Canada

John Wiley & Sons (SEA) Pte Ltd, 37 Jalan Pemimpin #05-04,
Block B, Union Industrial Building, Singapore 2057

British Library Cataloguing in Publication Data

A catalogue record for this book is available from the British Library

ISBN 0-471-950947

Produced from camera-ready copy supplied by the author
Printed and bound in Great Britain by Biddles Ltd, Guildford

Contents

Preface

As the subtitle indicates, this text expounds a particular methodology for quantitative analysis using Operations Research or Management Science (OR/MS). It consists of two parts. Part 1 looks in detail at methodological issues proper, while Part 2 explores how to deal with such things as the time element, constraints, uncertainty, and multiple goals.

Borrowing from the Soft Systems Methodologies, particularly the methodology developed by Peter Checkland and his associates of the University of Lancaster, the rather stark traditional OR/MS methodology is expanded to incorporate the tenets of systems thinking more explicitly and more fully than is normally seen in OR/MS texts. The methodology fully recognizes the systems components of OR/MS projects to which most other texts, with a few notable exceptions, such as C.W. Churchman's 1959 *Introduction to Operations Research*, pay only scant lip service. Rather than assuming that the usual starting point for a project is a relatively well-structured problem, with clearly defined objectives and alternative courses of action, the methodology steps back to the inception phase, namely the presentation of a problematic situation, where the issues are still vague, fuzzy, and not yet seen in their proper systems context. It then demonstrates a flexible paradigm for identifying the problem and its relevant system, formulating it so that it is suitable for developing a quantitative model, explores various means for facilitating modeling, and discusses the importance, need, and use of sensitivity and error analysis, and finally ends with looking at crucial aspects of implementation.

Most management scientists view modeling more as an art than a science. This is clearly reflected in OR/MS texts. It is my conviction that the boundary between the art and science of modeling can be pushed considerably farther in favour of science. This texts shows that the 'science' or 'technique' component of modeling can, in fact, be expanded by searching for a suitable system's definition of the problem and then use diagrammatic devices to bring out the structural relationships between the various components that make up the system, leaving mainly the determination of the explicit functional relationships to be developed. But even for these, the text suggests ways of facilitating their discovery. It makes modeling much more accessible to the beginner.

The second part of the text then looks at a number of topics that any successful modeler needs to be familiar with. Most projects involve costs and benefits. These may be of a monetary or intangible nature. Which cost and benefits are relevant for a particular problem? Much decision making involves the time element as an integral component of the problem, either in terms of the incidence of costs and benefits or in terms of a time sequence of decisions. How does this affect the decision process and the models representing it?

A variety of restrictions may be imposed on the decision process, expressing limited resources or properties the solution has to satisfy. What effects does this have on the solution and the process of obtaining it? What kind of insights can we derive from analyzing these effects?

Most decisions are made under various degrees of uncertainty about the outcomes. What is uncertainty? How do we react when faced with uncertainty? A substantial portion of the text studies how this changes the decision process.

Finally, there is a brief discussion on how the decision process needs to be adapted if we explicitly acknowledge the fact that the decision maker may be faced with conflicting goals.

The second part of the book demonstrates a number of OR/MS techniques and related tools, such as the principles of discounting of future cash flows, the insights we obtain from marginal or incremental analysis — a tool borrowed from economics, linear programming, production scheduling, queueing and simulation, and decision analysis. However, the emphasis is not on the tools themselves, but on demonstrating how these tools are used to deal with certain aspects or the insights we can get from their use in terms of the decision process. So, this text is not an introductory text into OR/MS techniques. At an introductory level, although interesting and neat, these techniques are often reduced to triviality, devoid of any practical application.

Rather than discuss concepts in the abstract, they are demonstrated using practical case studies that I have been involved with or that have been reported in the literature. By necessity, some of them had to be trimmed to reduce their complexity and render them amenable for inclusion in the limited space of a text book. But most of them have retained the essentials of their original flavour.

Whenever possible, the quantitative analysis is demonstrated using the power and flexibility of PC spreadsheets. The text uses Microsoft EXCEL©, but this choice is more one of convenience, rather than preference. Any other spreadsheet with optimizer or solver capability and the facility for generating random variates will do. When I use this text in a first-year undergraduate course or at the MBA level, I supplement it with giving the students an introduction to spreadsheets.

The use of spreadsheets implies that the level of mathematics involved remains at a fairly elementary level and does not go beyond high school mathematics and statistics. The emphasis is not on the mathematics, but on the concepts and the process of quantitative decision making. The text contains two starred sections, requiring elementary calculus. These can be skipped without loss. The book lives on the principle of 'never let the mathematics get in the way of common sense'!

By the time the reader has studied this text and digested its wealth of learning, he or she will approach all types of problem solving — not just that suitable for quantitative modeling — from a more comprehensive, more enlightened and insightful perspective. Hopefully, the reader will also have been encouraged to reflect on and become more critical of her or his own way of looking at the world.

The main audience of this text is at an introductory undergraduate or MBA level for a 30 to 50 hour course on quantitative decision making, where the emphasis is on methodology and concepts, rather than mathematical techniques. This is the use we have put it to at the University of Canterbury. It is sufficiently challenging for use at an MBA level, where the emphasis is on insights, rather than techniques anyway. The real-life case studies used in many chapters make the text particularly relevant and attractive to mature MBA students. However, it is also suitable for self-study, for instance as recommended background reading to set the stage for an introductory course in OR/MS techniques. It will be valuable to put the techniques into their proper perspective in the decision making process. They are then seen for what they are, namely powerful tools used for what usually does not make more than a small portion of the effort that goes into any project, rather than the most important core of the project. It is not the tools that 'solve a problem', but the process in which they are used.

For two of the chapters I had recourse to the expertise and help of Dr D. C. McNickle, a dear colleague of mine. I gratefully acknowledge his contribution. I also am thankful to the close to 2000 students who suffered through the early versions of this text and whose useful comments and complaints have greatly improved its presentation and content.

The scholar and teacher, who has undoubtedly shaped my whole approach to systems thinking and OR/MS more than anybody else, is C. West Churchman. I would like to dedicate this text to him.

1 Introduction

This chapter tries to whet your appetite to learn more about how to approach practical decision making situations. I will briefly describe five real-life situations that each involved making recommendations as to the best course of action to take. Three look at commercial situations, while the remaining two deal with issues of public decision making or policy. They are intended to give you a feel for the great variety of decision making problems, in terms of area of application, type of organization involved, the degree of complexity, the types of costs and benefits, as well as their importance, where a 'systems approach' will lead to better decision making.

1.1 MOTIVATION

Telephone Betting

In the mid-80s, the Totalisator Agency Board — the New Zealand organization administrating legal horse race betting — introduced a system for placing of bets by telephone. Any punter who maintains a credit account with the TAB can place bets by phone for any race anywhere in N.Z. up to a few minutes prior to the scheduled start of the race. Any winnings are credited directly to the account immediately after the race. One of the major decisions for the TAB concerned the number of telephone lines required for each TAB phone-betting office.

Since the great majority of all bets are placed shortly prior to the official time for most races, the telephone lines will be particularly busy at around the time when major races are scheduled. If a punter calls and finds a free line, then the punter will place one or several bets. If no line is free, the punter gets the busy signal. Most punters will try again, but some may not or may run out of time to place a particular bet before its closing time. Each bet placed contributes towards the TAB's profit. Any bets lost due to busy telephone lines means profit foregone. The more callers that get through, the more bets are placed, the higher will be the profit — profit used to support the N.Z. racing and breeding industry.

But, telephone lines have to be rented from the Telephone Company at a substantial monthly fee. Most remain unused much of the time, except just prior to major races. If too many are rented, some may remain idle even then.

So we see that there are two opposing costs incurred: (1) the cost of profit foregone on bets lost and (2) the line rentals. The problem facing the TAB management is to determine the number of lines to rent so as to balance these two costs properly.

This is a type of problem faced by many organizations, private or public, referred to as a **waiting line** problem. Here are some other examples:

- the number of tellers a bank, insurance office, or post office should open during various times of the business day; or more recently, the number of automatic bank teller machines to install.

- the number of crews needed by a repair or service outfit, like an appliance service firm or a photocopying machine service firm.

- the number of nurses and/or doctors on duty at an emergency clinic during various hours of the week.

- the degree of redundancy built into equipment where failure may have serious consequences.

Vehicle Scheduling

Pick-up and delivery firms, like courier services or armoured car cash-and-securities delivery firms, have to pick up and drop off goods at a number of places. The locations of these pick-ups and drop-offs may be different daily or even hourly with new locations added to the list of locations to visit. Certain of the customers may specify a given time period or 'time-window' during which the visit must occur. The vehicle used may have a limited carrying capacity. The length of time drivers can be on the road in one shift may be limited. Add to this the problem of traffic density on various city arterials and hence the travel times between locations changing during the day. It is also clear that even for a small problem, the number of distinct sequences to visit each location is very large. For example, for 10 locations, there are $10! = 3,628,800$ different itineraries, while for 20 locations the number of itineraries is about 2,432,902,000,000,000,000. Although a majority can be ruled out as bad, it is still a non-trivial task to select the best combination or sequence of pick-ups and deliveries from those that remain such that all complicating factors mentioned earlier are taken into account. It may even be difficult to decide which criterion should be chosen for 'best'. Is it minimum distance, or minimum time, or minimum total cost, or a compromise between these considerations?

Similar types of combinatorial sequencing problems are faced by airlines for the scheduling of aircraft and air crews, public bus or railroad companies for the scheduling of buses or engines and drivers, or the city rubbish collectors for determining their collection rounds.

Feed Mix Production

In most developed countries, chicken, pigs, and other livestock are fed on specially prepared feed mixes that make the chicken grow faster, lay more eggs, or make the livestock put on more meat with less fat, etc.

A chicken feed manufacturer produces a specially formulated mix intended for laying hens. Nutritional experts are put to work to determine exactly what types and amounts of various nutritional elements, including bulk — even chickens have to be 'regular' — a hen needs to enhance its ability to lay big, thick-shelled eggs with a consistent dark yellow coloured yolk. Do not think that these aspects are left to chance by egg producers! The experts also analyze the chemical make-up of various feed raw materials and ingredients available, like grains, maize, slaughter-house or freezing works by-products, to determine their exact composition in terms of nutritional and bulk components digestible by hens. Naturally, each feed ingredient also has a given cost and may only be available in limited quantities.

The problem faced by the feed manufacturer is to determine a 'recipe' from the available ingredients which meets the nutritional requirements of the hens, while at the same time minimizing its cost per kilogram produced. The problem becomes more complex if the manufacturer produces a number of different feed-mixes and has access to only limited quantities of certain valuable ingredients.

This problem can be solved using linear programming — an optimizing technique that you may have come across when you studied linear algebra in high school. There are numerous problems where a decision maker wishes to allocate scarce resources to a number of different uses, each yielding certain benefits. Linear programming may be used to find this best allocation. Linear programming and its various extensions can be applied to a host of other decision problems. Chapter 13 shows several applications of this tool.

Environmental and Economic Considerations: The Deep Cove Project

In the mid-80s an American firm proposed to capture the pristine waters discharged from the Manapouri Power Station in Fiordland National Park at the bottom of N.Z.'s South Island and transport it with large ocean-going tankers to the U.S. West Coast and Middle Eastern countries. This water is so pure that it does not need any chemicals to neutralize harmful bacteria or other contaminations. The proposal consisted of building a floating dock at the end of Deep Cove Sound, close to the tail race of the power station, where up to two tankers could berth simultaneously. The project would provide employment about 30 people in an economically depressed area of N.Z., and the N.Z. Government would collect a 'water royalty'. The project would thus make a substantial contribution to both the local and national economy.

The firm had shown considerable responsibility in planning the whole operation in such a manner that environmental impact in the fiord would be kept as low as economically feasible. For instance, all staff would be flown into Deep Cove daily, allowing no permanent residence. All rubbish would be removed. No permanent structures would be erected. Tanker speed in the fiord would be reduced to keep swells low. There would be extensive safety measures to avoid oil spills, etc.

Naturally, environmental groups were opposed to this project. Here are some of their reasons: First, it would introduce non-tourist commercial activities in the waters of a National Park which is against the charter of National Parks. They feared that the removal of up to 60% of the tail race water would alter the balance between fresh water and salt water and affect the sound's unique flora and fauna that had evolved over millions of years. The big tankers would speed up the mixing of the fresh water layer on top of the salt water base, affecting the ecological balance even further. Due to the severe weather conditions in that part of N.Z., accidents resulting in oil spills would be difficult to prevent, even with the best of intentions, with potentially disastrous consequences.

The N.Z. Government had the final say in this matter. What should it do? Given the potential environmental impact of this project, a decision for or against it cannot be made on economic grounds only. It requires a careful balancing of important economic and environmental factors. There are conflicting objectives, i.e., maximizing the economic welfare of N.Z., versus minimizing possibly irreversible environmental impacts to preserve a unique wilderness area for the enjoyment of future generations, as well as limiting the intrusion of commercial activities into a national park. Problems of multiple and possibly conflicting objectives occur frequently in the public sector. Chapter 19 takes up this theme again.

Breast Cancer Screening Policies

Breast Cancer is currently the biggest cause of mortality for women in developed countries. The incidence in N.Z. is particularly high. About 1 in 11 women will develop breast cancer and of these 40% will die as a result of the disease. (Although men are not immune, the incidence in men is about 100 times less.) Breast cancer incidence and aggressiveness varies with the age of the patient. It starts usually with a small growth or lump in the breast tissue. In its early stages, such a growth is usually benign. If left untreated, it will enlarge and often become malignant, invading adjacent tissue, and ultimately spread to other parts of the body — so-called metastases. The rate of progression varies from person to person and with age. The age specific incidence of breast cancer rises steadily from the mid twenties through the reproductive years. At menopause there is a temporary drop, after which the rate climbs again.

About 95% of all potentially cancerous growths discovered at a preinvasive stage can be cured. It is thus crucial that such growths can be detected as early as possible. In the 70s screening trials were made in a number of countries, like Sweden, England, and the U.S., in an effort to reduce breast cancer mortality. It is now generally accepted that mammography is the most effective method of detecting abnormal tissue growth. Research shows that for women of age 50 mammography can detect about 85% of all abnormal tissue growths that could be expected to develop into breast cancer within the next 12 months after a screening. This is significantly higher than for other methods of screening. The percentage of potentially cancerous growths detected drops substantially as the time interval between screenings becomes longer.

As the need for the introduction of an effective screening policy has become finally recognized by both health professionals and governments, there is still considerable controversy as to the 'best' screening policy to use. A screening policy is defined by the age range of women to be screened and the frequency of screening, e.g., all women between the ages of 48 and 65 at yearly intervals.

In addition to the medical factors and partially avoidable loss of human lives involved, there are economic aspects to be considered. In 1990, the cost of a screening was between $30 and $70, while the equipment cost was in the range of $150,000 to $200,000. Each machine can perform around 6400 screens per year. As the age range and frequency of screening is increased, the number of machines and trained personnel needed also increases. Acquiring these machines and training the personnel required thus involves an enormous capital outlay. Any new policy can thus not be implemented instantly, but has to be phased in gradually. So, the problem faced by health authorities in many countries is what is the policy that offers the best compromise between economic considerations and human-suffering, and how should the policy finally chosen be implemented. As with the Deep Cove project, these are decisions that will not be devoid of political considerations.

1.2 SYSTEMS THINKING

What do all these problem situations have in common? A number of things! First, all of them deal with a decision problem, i.e., there is a person or a group of individuals that would like to achieve one or several goals, or maintain current levels of achievement. They could be dissatisfied with the current situation or mode of operation and see scope for doing something better or more effectively or see some new opportunity or new options. Second, the answer to their problem, or the solution, is not obvious. The problem situations are complex. They may not know enough about the situation to know all their options or to be able to evaluate the performance of these options in term of their goals. Elements of this are present in the Deep Cove and the Breast Cancer problem. Third, the interactions between various elements or aspects are of a degree of complexity that the limited computational capacity of the human mind cannot evaluate in the detail desirable to make an informed decision. All of the problems discussed above are of this nature.

Finally, the settings within which these problems exist are systems. What is a system? Chapters 2 and 3 explore various systems concepts. So for now, a system is seen as a collection of things, entities, or people that relate to each other in specific ways, are organized, i.e., follow certain rules of interaction, and collectively have a given purpose, or are purposeful, i.e., strive towards some state of balance.

If we are to deal effectively with the complexity of systems and decision making within systems, we need a new way of thinking. This new way of thinking has evolved since about 1940 and could be labelled 'systems thinking'. Operations Research, Management Science, or Systems Analysis are strands of this mode of thinking that are particularly suitable if most of the interactions between the various parts of a system can be expressed in quantitative terms, such as mathematical expressions. They are decision aids which help the analyst to explore such problems in their full complexity, to find the optimal or best compromise solutions to the problems, and to give answers to important 'what if' questions, such as for example

'How is the best solution affected by significant changes in various cost factors?' Thus, they provide the decision maker(s) with much of the information necessary to come to an informed decision, rather than be influenced by intuitive, emotional, or political considerations alone. Although political considerations may be unavoidable and may in the end sway the decision one way or another, the use of such decision aids increases the degree of rationality in decision making, be it in the private or public sector. Note however that they are not intended to replace the decision maker, but only provide the decision maker with crucial information relevant to a decision.

The following chapters will study how operations research or management science, or OR/MS for short, is used for exploring decision situations. We will discuss its strength and weaknesses and what is good and bad OR/MS practice.

1.3 OVERVIEW OF WHAT FOLLOWS

The book is divided into two parts. Part 1 looks at the problem solving philosophy and methodology of operations research, management science, and systems analysis. Since most decision making occurs within a systems framework, Chapters 2 and 3 study systems concepts in some detail. Chapter 4 applies systems concepts to the study of a natural system, namely the 'ozone hole problem'. Chapters 5 to 8 give an overview of the OR/MS methodology and demonstrate its use for a produc-tion/inventory control problem.

Part 2 considers a number of aspects that any modeler needs to have carefully thought about. Some or all of them will be present in most problem situations. Being aware of them — even looking for them actively — and dealing with them explicitly rather than by default leads to a better and more valid decision process.

Most decision making involves the evaluation of costs and benefits. Chapter 9 looks at the various types of costs and how they affect the cost of the organization as a whole. This will allow assessing their relevance for a particular problem situation.

The decision choices are often subject to one or several constraints. These may be in the form of limited scarce resources. What difficulties does this introduce into the decision process? What insights can we gain about the value of such resources? These are the topics of Chapters 12 and 13.

Time enters into many problem situations in various ways. For instance, the costs and benefits may not occur all at the same point in time, but are spread over an extended interval of time. Is the value of a dollar to be received two years from now the same as a dollar in the pocket? Chapter 10 explains how to treat cash flows that occur at different points in time and applies the concepts developed to an equipment replacement decision.

Much decision making is done in a dynamic environment. The decision process consists of a sequence of individual actions at various points in time over a given planning horizon. Decisions taken earlier in time will affect the choices available later in time. Similarly, events happening later in time may affect which decision is best now. How to deal with decision processes over time is discussed in Chapter 14.

Many aspects of real life — events, or outcomes of decisions — cannot be predicted with complete certainty. We will carefully explore the meaning and implication of uncertainty in problem situations in Chapter 15, and explore the behaviour of systems when the future is uncertain. Chapters 16 to 18 look at three different decision aids for systems that exhibit random behaviour.

Finally, some situations exhibit several conflicting and possibly non-commensurate goals or objectives. Dealing with multiple objectives has given rise to a whole new branch of OR/MS. This is discussed, albeit much too briefly, in Chapter 19.

Chapter 20 will wrap up this journey by highlighting the crucial features of the OR/MS methodology presented in this book, briefly study aspects of ethics important for the modeler, and then have a rather cursory look at alternative decision making paradigms in the management sciences.

As our journey through the world of systems modeling for decision making progresses, we shall have the opportunity to look at a number of OR/MS techniques or tools. Since the main theme of the book is on the process of model building, the purpose of looking at techniques is to demonstrate this process, rather than a study of these techniques in their own right. This is not a book on Techniques of OR/MS. It is important that you keep this in mind.

PART 1

OR/MS Methodology

As we have seen, most decision making in today's world deals with complex problem situations. They are often ill-defined, subject to conflicting forces and goals. One of the major reasons for this complexity is that these problem situations occur within a system context. Most of these systems are created and controlled by humans. The human element can therefore not be excluded from the decision process.

Although we are endowed with amazing faculties of reasoning and insight, most of us are unable to cope with more than a very few factors at the same time. Without computers, our computational abilities are slow and limited. We have difficulties tracing complex interrelationships and interactions between various elements or factors. Borrowing a phrase from Professor Herbert Simon, the 1978 Nobel Prize Laureate in Economics, human decision making is limited by bounded rationality. It is therefore all the more important that decision making is guided by a systematic and comprehensive methodology that helps us make effective use of our extensive but still limited powers of reasoning.

You may wonder: 'Since science has been one of the major driving forces of modern civilization, why don't we simply adopt the scientific method which seems to have proved itself so successfully in the physical and biological sciences?' There are a number of reasons! There is very little agreement on what the scientific method really is. There are also serious doubts that successful scientists and researchers make their breakthroughs using the scientific method. But even disregarding these controversies, most real-life decision making does not neatly fall into a pattern of observation, followed by generating hypotheses, which are then confirmed or refuted through experimentation. Most importantly though, while scientific research attempts to understand the various aspects of the world we live in, decision making attempts to change aspects of this world. Furthermore, decision making does not occur under idealized conditions in a laboratory, but out in the real and often messy world. So the methodology has to be able to cope with the complexity of the real world, has to be comprehensive and flexible, while still delivering the results in the often short time frame within which most decision making has to occur. Nor is it so important that the methodology used is scientific; it is more important that it leads to good decision making.

Part 1 explores one such methodology in full detail, namely one version of the OR/MS methodology. It is not a panacea, capable of handling all problematic situations. It has proved to be a successful approach for problem situations that lend themselves to quantification, where many aspects are relatively well conditioned. This means that the decision problem can be clearly identified, the decision maker's objective can be spelled out, and decision choices are known or can be developed.

If the problem situation is unclear and fuzzy, with highly conflicting views between the various stakeholders involved, with goals or objectives not necessarily externalized, with the range of decision choices only partially explored, then one of the soft systems methodologies, such as Checkland's [1981, 1990] SSM or the Strategic Choice Approach by Friend [1987] may well be more appropriate. If you wish to get a comprehensive overview of various decision methodologies you should read the thought-provoking book by Michael C. Jackson, *Systems Methodology for the Management Sciences* [1991], or the collection of methods discussed in J. Rosenhead, *Rational Analysis for a Problematic World* [1989] (see References in Chapter 5).

Since most decision making occurs within a systems setting, we first need to study systems concepts in some detail. This is the task of Chapters 2 and 3. Chapter 4 applies these concepts to the study of a natural system, although caused by human activity, namely the 'ozone hole'. Chapters 5 to 8 then go through my version of an OR/MS methodology. A real-life problem is used as a case study to demonstrate the various steps of the approach. Chapter 5 studies how we go about identifying the right problem and formulate it in systems terms. Chapter 6 and 7 look at how to translate this problem into a mathematical model, how we find the best solution and explore its properties by sensitivity analysis, i.e., how the best solution is affected by changes to various inputs into the model. Sensitivity analysis will be a recurrent theme throughout the text. It is one of the most important and powerful aspects of the OR/MS methodology. Finally, Chapter 8 discusses, albeit only too briefly, important considerations for successfully implementing the recommendations of an OR/MS solution.

2 Systems Thinking

Why is there a need for systems thinking in dealing with many of today's decision situations? Why can the traditional analytic methods used by engineers, economists, and accountants for the last 100 years not come up with the 'right' solution to these decision problems? After reading this chapter you will be able to give a tentative answer to these two questions.

2.1 INCREASED COMPLEXITY OF TODAY'S DECISION MAKING

The 20th century, and more particularly its second half, has been marked by unprecedented technological progress. Untold innovations in agriculture, industrial and chemical processes, engineering, and air travel have encroached on our natural environment on a huge scale, a scale so large and unforeseen that we are only now beginning to realize its potential impact on the future of humankind. Similarly, the communication/information explosion since the introduction of television, computer information processing technology, and satellite communications has revolutionized commercial activities and the world of entertainment. Its cultural impact on both developed and developing countries may well turn out to be the greatest leveller the human race has ever experienced and have profound effects on the values and mores of humanity — maybe equalled only by the advent of the world religions like Christianity or Islam.

Hand-in-hand with these two phenomena has been the creation of huge multinational corporations — names of the industrial giants like Shell, General Motors, Du Pont, Mitsubishi, Nestlé, or the world bankers like Chase Manhattan, spring to mind — with financial and human resources and technical know-how that give them a power base that far exceeds the power and control of all but a handful of national governments. Along with these developments also came the accelerating gap between the rich developed countries, with their ever-increasing demand for energy and raw materials, their consumption and waste mentality, and the poor underdeveloped countries, where traditional subsistence farming has been replaced by large-scale planting of cash crops subject to widely fluctuating world prices, leading to unsustainable indebtedness towards the developed countries and hopeless impoverishment of their rural population.

Add to this the problems of overpopulation, the collapse of the communist power bloc, the resurgence of religious fundamentalism, the legitimate call for women's equality in this male-dominated world, and the looming environmental threat of a world which continues to be exploited and abused for the sake of economic growth and power. Today's world has thus increased in complexity to a point where the traditional methods of problem solving based on the cause-and-effect model cannot cope any longer. Let us study briefly some examples.

Construction of the Aswan High Dam in Egypt

Many of the 'great' technical achievements have not just brought the increased well-being used to justify them, but also unexpected undesirable consequences, some of which may far outweigh the benefits hailed. The construction of the Aswan High Dam in Egypt is cited as a possible example. Hailed as the key to Egypt's entry into the world of plenty, it initially increased agricultural production in the Nile Delta. However, it also caused an unprecedented increase in schistosomiasis — a highly debilitating disease spread by water snails that thrive in the irrigation canals. It is claimed that 60% of Egypt's fellahin (farm workers) are affected. Fertile silt, which prior to the building of the dam annually renewed the fertility of the land it inundated, is now trapped behind the dam. In its place a massive increase in the use of fertilizers is needed to maintain output. That, together with poor drainage, causes salinization, annually rendering large tracts of land unsuitable for agriculture. The loss of the silt previously carried past the Delta into the Mediterranean has caused the sea to encroach onto the land, leading to further loss of land. The loss of the nutrients previously fed into the Mediterranean destroyed the sardine fisheries which provided an essential part of the population's diet. Finally, uncontrollable growth of water hyacinth in Lake Nasser causes excessive loss of water through evaporation. So the erection of the Aswan High Dam had a number of unexpected consequences, some of them disastrous. None were predicted and taken into account when the decision to build the dam was made. That decision, in fact, was largely a political power play between the USA and the old USSR, both hoping to incorporate Egypt within their sphere of influence.

Deterioration of Urban Transport

A second example is the increasing deterioration of urban public transport. In response to the suburban population drift and increased car ownership after world war II, it looked like a very responsible public policy of city planners to improve the road network and city centre parking facilities. It unfortunately also led to reduced patronage of public transport facilities. That in turn resulted in fare hikes and a curtailment of service frequency and coverage, which accelerated the shift from public to private transport, and the story continues. The end result is the virtual demise of public transport in many cities and ever more serious traffic congestion in the access roads used by commuters. Again we see that seemingly good responsible decision making resulted in unexpected outcomes which did only temporarily improve access to the city centre. It is interesting to speculate on what would have happened if the city fathers had chosen to upgrade public transport to bring the people from the suburbs into the city, rather than upgrading the road network.

Assessment of Unit Production Costs

Many firms assess the unit production cost at each machine centre by adding up all material, energy, and labour costs incurred at that machine centre and then dividing the total by the number of parts produced. The efficiency of a machine centre is assessed on the level of its unit production costs: the lower the unit production costs at a machine centre, the higher its efficiency. This rule works fine for simple one-stage production processes, where the firm has no difficulties in selling all its output.

However, the above rule runs into serious trouble when we are faced with complex multi-product production processes, where the final finished products are the end result of a multi-stage process. Commonly, each machine centre produces many different parts — usually in small lots — all or most of which are used as input into later stages in the production process. Consider a typical machine centre several stages removed from the finished product. If the centre supervisor is judged on the basis of unit production costs, then he or she will have a strong incentive to have all machines and operators producing parts all the time. If subsequent machine centres do not require the parts immediately, they will temporarily be stored in a warehouse or on the production floor. The costs of keeping these stocks are normally not attributed to the machine centre that produced them. So the machine centre's efficiency looks good, but the firm ends up with excessive intermediate parts stocks that are costly to finance and maintain and furthermore run the risk of becoming obsolete before they are required.

2.2 EFFICIENCY VERSUS EFFECTIVENESS

Efficiency

The last example demonstrates how the concern with efficiency for a particular operation or division of a firm may lead to an overall deterioration of the performance, in this case profit generation, of the firm as a whole. The firm may be very efficient in the use of its resources, but this efficiency is not put to effective use in terms of the firm's overall objectives or goals.

So what is efficiency and what is effectiveness? Everyday language often confuses these concepts. Using a given set of inputs or resources to produce the maximum level of output or, alternatively, producing a given level of output with the minimum amount of inputs or resources represents efficiency, in fact, technical efficiency. For example, driving a car in a manner which maximizes the ratio of distance traveled to fuel consumption is technically efficient. This may mean that you travel at 60 km per hour, always accelerate very gradually, and plan your speed such as to avoid any unnecessary use of the brakes. If the vehicle is used for commercial purposes, such as a bus service, such a mode of driving the vehicle may be economically inefficient, since it ignores wage costs for the driver as well as the potential earning power of the vehicle. For economic efficiency, in terms of maximizing the difference between revenues and total costs, the vehicle may often have to be driven in a technically inefficient way. The gain in additional revenue may well outweigh the increased costs of a technically inefficient operation.

Effectiveness

Effectiveness, on the other hand, looks at how well the goals or objectives of the entity or activity are achieved. For example, the bus service may be part of a city's public transport system. Its objectives may be to provide convenient, but cost-effective commuter transport, where 'convenient' may be defined as 'no resident having to walk more than one kilometre from their home or work place to catch public transport'. Economically efficient operation of each vehicle is now only one aspect of the system's operation. The choice of bus routes, the frequency of service at various times of the day, the type of vehicles used and how they are maintained, as well as the fare structure all enter into determining the effectiveness of the transport system in terms of its objectives and the resource constraints imposed on it. Trade-off between these variables will affect overall effectiveness of the system.

Operating various parts of a system in their most efficient manner does not necessarily mean the system as a whole is effective in terms of achieving its objectives. Consider the operation of a hospital. The fact that its testing laboratory, its physiotherapy service, its blood bank service, etc., are all operated efficiently in a technical and economic sense is not sufficient for the hospital as a whole to operate effectively. For instance, the tests ordered from the laboratory may be the wrong type, or they may be redundant in the sense of not adding any additional information for correct diagnoses. The fact that they are executed efficiently does not imply that their use was effective. Effectiveness implies that these services are used and coordinated appropriately to achieve the objectives or goals of the system.

Why do managers of all sorts of organizations, profit-making as well as non-profit-making, private and public, seem to be so much concerned with efficiency? Working with a fixed budget — a limited amount of funds to spend over a given period of time — any dollar spent on a given activity means a dollar less for another activity. Hence the overriding concern to make every dollar go as far as possible. Now, most firms or organizations operate with some waste or not fully utilized resources. Most managers' natural reaction is to eliminate such waste or underutilized resources. As we have seen above, the consequences for the firm as a whole may, however, not turn out to be as beneficial as expected. Let us look at another example.

Walk through the premises of any manufacturing firm and you will see spare parts for machinery accumulating dust. These spare parts tie up the funds spent to purchase them. These funds are seemingly 'idle'. Hence, it looks like a good idea to reduce the stock of spare parts, freeing the funds for productive use somewhere else in the firm.

But wait a minute! The reason why these spare parts were purchased in the first place was to keep any down-time resulting from a machine part breaking down as short as possible. If the parts are in stock, no time is lost waiting for them to be ordered and to be shipped by the manufacturer of the parts. If the supplier is overseas, this could easily mean a few weeks or expensive air freighting. So lack of adequate stocks of spare parts may result in prolonged down-time during which the machine is 'idle'. The loss of revenue and profit from the loss of output may far outweigh the cost of funding adequate stocks of spares. So elimination of such seemingly 'idle' spares may not be cost effective. The real problem is not one of being efficient in the sense of eliminating idle resources, but rather one of being effective in terms of the operation of the firm as a whole. In this example, this translates itself into finding the proper balance between the cost of the investment in stocks of spares and the cost of machine down-time incurred if the firm is short of spares.

This same theme occurs with respect to productive capacity of all sorts — machine capacities, runway capacity at airports, employee levels in service industries, to name just a few. The difficult question to answer is: at what point is there real excess capacity in terms of the overall costs for the organization as a whole, rather than in terms of seeming 'idleness' over long periods of time?

Effectiveness and Efficiency

This discussion may have given the impression that efficiency is the enemy of effectiveness. Far from it! It is only the narrow concern with efficiency at the exclusion of the overall goals of the organization which could be detrimental. True efficiency takes the overall goals of the organization into account. Hence, the effectiveness of decisions and policies taken by the decision makers will be enhanced. The goals of the organization will be achieved at lower costs, with fewer resources, or with increased benefits — in other words, more efficiently. The two are thus complementary. Effectiveness deals with 'doing the right things', efficiency with 'doing things right'.

2.3   UNPLANNED AND COUNTERINTUITIVE OUTCOMES

In all these cases we see a common theme emerging: seemingly rational decisions are made on the basis that: 'Action A will cause the desired outcome B to be realized.' But in addition to B the decision also causes C, D, and E to happen. Some of these outcomes are unintended, unpredicted, and may partially or wholly negate the sought for economic or social benefits of the intended outcome B.

Responsible decision making clearly must consider the undesirable and/or additional beneficial effects of unplanned outcomes on the system as a whole. Consideration of these outcomes may well sway the decision. A comprehensive systems analysis is more likely to uncover most of the unplanned outcomes than a narrow cause-and-effect analysis.

Some of the outcomes actually realized, both planned and unplanned, may be 'counterintuitive' — what happens appears to contradict what common sense and intuition tells us should occur. Let me demonstrate this with the following somewhat simplified, but real-life example.

An electric power company operates two power stations connected to a transmission network as shown in Figure 2-1. What is the maximum amount of power that can be transmitted via node C to the consumer network? The station capacities are shown in the squares, the transmission line capacities on top of the links. Transmission on each link can occur in either direction. Hence, power from station A can be sent to node C directly on link 1 or via station B on links 2 and 3. Similarly, power from station B can be sent directly to node C or indirectly via station A. (Obviously, power can only flow either from A to B or vice-versa, but not in both directions!) By Kirchoff's laws, power leaving a node by two different sets of links is split between these links according to the resistance on the links. Assume that from station A, 2/3 will be transmitted to node C via link 1, while 1/3 moves through link 2 to station B and then on through link 3 to node C, together with any power generated at station B. The analogous arrangement holds if power from station B is transmitted to node C via both links 2—1 and 3. Note that any link may be closed down.

Figure 2-1: Power transmission problem.

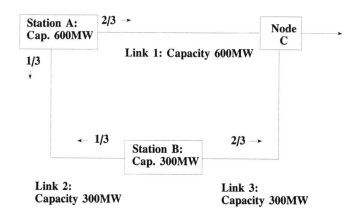

Figure 2-2, parts (a) and (b), shows two possible solutions, with the better of the two transmitting a total of 800 MW via node C. Note that due to transmission link capacities, in both cases one of the power stations cannot generate at full capacity.

There is a generally accepted rule, that introducing additional decision choices into a decision problem will never make the outcome worse, since the previously best solution is still available. On the contrary, additional choices quite often open up the possibility for better decisions. This makes sense intuitively. As a corollary, reducing the decision choices available, can never improve the outcome. Right?

Figure 2-2: Solutions to transmission problem.

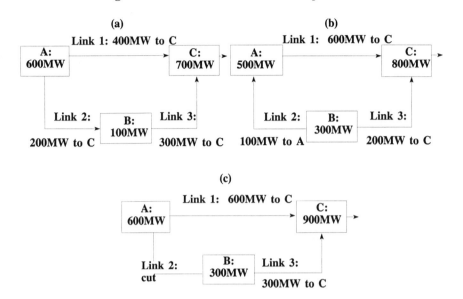

Wrong! Reduce the choices available, by removing link 2. Indirect transmission of power from station A via station B is now excluded. However, the maximum amount that can be transmitted via node C increases to 900 MW, with both stations generating at full capacity, as shown in part (c) of Figure 2-2. This result is counterintuitive to the generally accepted principle that the more variety in decision choices available, the better the outcome!

2.4 REDUCTIONIST AND CAUSE-AND-EFFECT THINKING

How is it that, all too frequently, our decision making process seems to be so singularly linear? There is the desired outcome B — here is action A which will cause B to happen! Russell L. Ackoff — a philosopher, operations researcher, and systems thinker — gives us an answer in his paper 'Science in the Systems Age' [*Operations Research*, May-June 1973]. He says that the intellectual foundations of the traditional scientific model of thought are based on two major ideas. The first is reductionism: the belief that everything in the world and every experience of it can be reduced, decomposed, or disassembled to ultimately simple indivisible parts. Explaining the behaviour of these parts and then aggregating these partial explanations is assumed to be sufficient to allow us to understand and explain the behaviour of the system as a whole. Applied to problem solving this translates into breaking a problem into a set of simpler subproblems, solving each of these individually and then assembling their solutions into an overall solution for the whole problem. 'Division of labour' and 'organizational structure along functional lines', such as finance, personnel, purchasing, manufacture, marketing, and R and D are clear manifestations of this. Even if each is operated with economic efficiency, the sum of the individual solutions does not necessarily produce an overall solution that is best for the system as a whole. The hospital example in Section 2.2 is a clear instance of this.

The second basic idea is that all phenomena are explainable by using cause-and-effect relationships. A thing A is taken to be the cause of B, if A is both necessary and sufficient for B to happen. Hence, 'cause A' is all that is needed to explain 'effect B'. Viewing the world in this way, everything can be explained by decomposing it into parts and looking for cause-and-effect relationships between the parts. But we have seen in the examples above that it may be inadequate to examine the causal relationships one by one. New relationships or properties may emerge through the interaction between the various parts or aspects of a situation — **emergent properties** or relationships that may be unexpected and counterintuitive.

2.5 SYSTEMS THINKING

From about 1940 on, a number of researchers from various scientific disciplines, biology, mathematics, communication theory, and philosophy, started to recognize that all things and events, and the experience of them, are parts of larger wholes. This does not deny the importance of the individual elementary parts or events. But the focus shifts from the parts to the wholes, namely to the **systems** to which the parts belong. This gave rise to a new way of thinking — **systems thinking**. Something to be explained is viewed as part of a larger whole, a system, and is explained in terms of its role in that system.

This new mode of thought has immediate consequences on decision making within a systems context, namely that effective action in terms of the system as a whole can only result from the careful study of the complete system, rather than of individual parts or aspects.

The next chapter defines systems and studies various aspects and properties of systems. Chapter 4 will apply systems thinking to an environmental problem of concern to all of us, namely the ozone depletion in the upper atmosphere.

EXERCISES

1. The University Energy Committee held a meeting discussing ways to save power. The following argument was overheard between two committee members:

    A: 'Clearly, every light turned off means some power saved. Hence, one of the major tasks of this committee is to educate all members of the university, and in particular all staff, to turn off lights whenever they are the last to leave a room, a lecture hall, or a corridor.'

B: 'Admittedly, a policy of turning off lights may generate some immediate power savings. But the greater frequency of turning lights on and off will burn out lights more quickly and result in higher light bulb replacement costs. Furthermore, dark corridors and lecture halls may also increase the incidence of accidents and the potential of crime, imposing higher costs on the university community as a whole.'

A: 'The brief of this committee is to save power. The things you mention are not our concern!'

   (a) What are the desired planned outcomes and what could be the undesired, unplanned and unexpected outcomes of the action proposed by A?

   (b) Discuss the arguments put forth by A and B in terms of efficiency and effectiveness.

2. Consider the Deep Cove Water Export Project briefly described in Section 1.1.

   (a) Contrast the different views, in terms of efficiency and effectiveness, taken by the firm, the Government, and environmental protection groups.

   (b) List the planned outcomes and the unplanned outcomes of the proposal.

3. Consider the Breast Cancer Screening Policy Project described in Section 1.1.

   (a) Contrast the different views, in terms of efficiency versus effectiveness taken, by the Government, health professionals, and the female population in the 50 to 70 age range.

   (b) List the planned outcomes and the unplanned outcomes of the proposal.

4. For each of the following examples discuss the relevance of efficiency versus effectiveness:

   (a) The Aswan High Dam Project in Egypt (Section 2.1)

   (b) The deterioration of urban transport (Section 2.1)

   (c) The Breast Cancer Screening Policies (Section 1.1)

   (d) The Telephone Betting Project (Section 1.1)

5. For each of the following examples list one or more counterintuitive outcomes:

   (a) The Aswan High Dam Project in Egypt (Section 2.1)

   (b) The deterioration of urban transport (Section 2.1)

   (c) The assessment of unit production costs (Section 2.1)

6. Some systems experts stress the importance of the three Es, i.e., efficiency, effectiveness, and efficacy. Look up the meaning of each term in a comprehensive dictionary, and show their relationship and differences. What does 'efficacy' add that is not contained in efficiency and effectiveness?

7. In your own words, discuss the difference between efficiency and effectiveness. Give two real-life practical examples for each. Give an example where a narrow view of efficiency interferes with effectiveness and one where efficiency enhances effectiveness.

REFERENCES

Russel L. Ackoff has written extensively on the need for systems thinking to 'resolve' today's decision problems. He is also of the opinion that OR/MS is not living up to the ideals of its originators during and just after WWII. Controversial but thought-provoking. See for instance:

Ackoff, R. L., 'The Systems Revolution', *Long-Range Planning*, 1974, 2-20.

Ackoff, R. L., 'Science in the Systems Age. Beyond IE, OR, and MS', *Operations Research*, May-June 1973, 661-71.

Ackoff, R. L., 'The Future of OR is Past', *J. of the OR Society*, Feb. 1979, 93-104, and 'Resurrecting the Future of OR', *J. of the OR Society*, March 1979, 189-99.

Ackoff, R. L., *The Art of Problem Solving*, Wiley, 1978. Part 1 deals with various aspects of problem solving, while Part 2 discusses six applications. Includes Ackoff's fables. Enjoyable reading.

Peter Checkland, one of the most articulate proponents of soft systems methodologies, has written numerous articles and two books dealing with systems thinking:

Checkland, P., *Systems Thinking, Systems Practice*, Wiley, 1981. Chapters 1 to 6 have a most authoritative discussion of the systems movement. Important reading.

Checkland, P., and Scholes, J., *Soft Systems Methodology in Action*, Wiley, 1990.

Checkland, P., 'From Optimization to Learning: A Development of Systems Thinking for the 1990s', *J. of the Operational Research Society*, Sept. 1985, 757-67.

C. West Churchman, a mentor and then colleague of R. L. Ackoff, has had a profound impact on my own approach to problem solving. Much of his thinking on the philosophy of OR/MS and the role of the problem analyst has been incorporated in various parts of this text, particularly Part 1. He says that the moment the analyst starts tinkering with a system, he or she becomes part of it. His writings have shaped much of the more recent developments in systems approaches to problem solving, particularly the soft systems methodologies. The flavour of his approach in the form of a 'critical debate among the opposing views of systems protagonists' is well captured in

Churchman, C. West, *The Systems Approach*, Dell Publishing Co., 1968

Churchman, C. West, *The Design of Inquiring Systems*, Basic Books, 1971. A scholarly text on Churchman's thinking.

Other useful and insightful references are:

Flood, R. L., and Carson, E. R., *Dealing with Complexity*, Plenum Press, 1988.

Hill, Percy H., et al., *Making Decisions - A Multidisciplinary Introduction*, Lanham: University Press of America, 1986. This is a delightful little book. Chapters 1 and 2 are particularly relevant for systems thinking.

Jackson, Michael C., *Systems Methodologies for the Management Sciences*, Plenum Press, 1991. A comprehensive and critical review of various systems methodologies. A must for any serious student in systems thinking.

3 Systems Concepts

In Chapter 2 you saw why it is useful to know about systems. This chapter picks up that discussion again. In Sections 3.2 to 3.6 we will look at how to define systems and see what is so special about them and what differentiates them from a mere collection of parts. Section 3.8 studies how system behaviour can be described and introduces the important concept of emergent properties of systems. We then briefly look at various classifications of systems in Section 3.9. In this text, our main interest is the control of systems to achieve certain desired goals. This is the topic of the last section.

3.1 PERVASIVENESS OF SYSTEMS

In the 1950s, with the exception of a few pioneering scientists, the term **system** was hardly used except in words like **systematic**. This is rather surprising, since we are constantly surrounded by systems, belong to various systems, and create new systems. The planet Earth we live on is a part of the **solar system**. Our whole life is spent, shaped, controlled by **social systems**, like the family, the neighbourhood, the school, our work place, and various interest groups we join, participate in, and drop out of. Some of us exploit **political systems** or are frustrated by them. Life without a **telephone system** would be difficult to imagine. In high school or university we learn about **number systems**. Modern management practices would collapse without **information systems**. We expect our rights to be protected by the **legal system.** When our **digestive system** strikes, we suffer. Indeed, the most important part of us, which differentiates us from other animals, is our brain, part of our **central nervous system**.

At first sight, these things seem to have little in common. So, why are they all referred to as systems? The reason is that they are all assemblies of things that are interconnected or stand in clearly defined relationships with each other. They may have evolved to these relationships through natural physical processes, like the solar system or a biological system. These are **natural systems**. Or they have been created by humans, such as **human activity systems**, like most social systems, or **abstract systems**, like number systems or information systems. Figure 3-1 is an excerpt from *Webster's 9th New Collegiate Dictionary*. It lists more than a dozen different meanings or variations of meanings for the word 'system'. Note that in everyday language it is also used for 'procedures' or as a derogatory term for 'the ruling social order' or 'the establishment'.

Our main interest in the term 'system' is as 'an organized assembly of interrela-

Figure 3-1: Excerpt from *Webster's 9th New Collegiate Dictionary*

---

sys·tem *n* [LL *systemat-, systema.* fr Gk *systemat-, systema.* fr. *synistanai* to combine, fr. *syn-* + *histanai* to cause to stand — more at STAND] (1619) **1** : a regularly interacting or interdependent group of items forming a unified whole ⟨a number ~⟩ : as **a** (1) : a group of interacting bodies under the influence of related forces ⟨a gravitational ~⟩ (2) : an assemblage of substances that is in or tends to equilibrium ⟨a thermodynamic ~⟩ **b** (1) : a group of body organs that together perform one or more vital functions ⟨the digestive ~⟩ (2) : the body considered as a functional unit **c** : a group of related natural objects or forces ⟨a river ~⟩ **d** : a group of devices or artificial objects or an organization forming a network esp. for distributing something or serving a common purpose ⟨a telephone ~⟩ ⟨a heating ~⟩ ⟨a highway ~⟩ ⟨a data processing ~⟩ **e** : a major division of rocks usu. larger than a series and including all formed during a period or era **f** : a form of social, economic, or political organization or practice ⟨the capitalist ~⟩ **2** : an organized set of doctrines, ideas, or principles usu. intended to explain the arrangement or working of a systematic whole ⟨the Newtonian ~ of mechanics⟩ **3 a** : an organized or established procedure ⟨the touch ~ of typing⟩ **b** : a manner of classifying, symbolizing, or schematizing ⟨a taxonomic ~⟩ ⟨the decimal ~⟩ **4** : harmonious arrangement or pattern : ORDER ⟨bring ~ out of confusion — Ellen Glasgow⟩ **5** : an organized society or social situation regarded as stultifying: ESTABLISHMENT 2 — usu. used with the *syn* see METHOD — *sys·tem·less*.

---

ted things'. 'Organized' implies that such systems have been created by humans. This excludes natural systems, except in so far as they may have been affected by human activity. Furthermore, it is not the notion of 'systematic', in the sense of carefully using a rational method or following a well laid-out plan, that primarily concerns us here, although we will go about any applications of systems concepts in a systematic way. The emphasis in this text is on **systemic**, i.e., using systems ideas, or viewing things in terms of systems, or 'pertaining to systems'.

3.2 DEFINING SYSTEMS

Out-There and Inside-us View of Systems

One of the prime sources of confusion when calling an organized assembly of things a system is what could be termed the out-there view of systems in contrast to the inside-us view of systems. When I talk about our solar system I have in mind the sun and its nine planets, of which Earth is one, and how the planets are linked to the sun and each other by gravitational forces. Similarly, an electric power system is viewed as the collection of various types of power stations and their equipment, the high tension power transmission grid, the local distribution network, with its transformers and power lines, and the various control stations that regulate the flow of power, as well as what the power system does, i.e., generate electric power and distribute it to its users. A computer information system consists of the pieces of data collected, the rules used to collect the data and their transformation into pieces of information, the storage of this information in computer files, the programs for processing, storing, cross-referencing, manipulating, retrieving, and presenting this information on VDU's or in printed form, and finally the computer equipment needed to perform all these activities. In each of these examples, the system **is seen** as the physical and abstract things that make up the whole assembly, their relationships, and what the system does. This is the out-there view of systems. It is seen as absolute; it exists out there; it is viewed as independent of the observer!

While most informed people today would agree on the same definition of the solar system, no such agreement can be expected for what things make up a particular electric power system or a computer information system. I did not list the hydro reservoirs, the water catchment areas that feed them, and the annual water inflow patterns as part of the system. I made a seemingly arbitrary choice of what I viewed as belonging to that system. Another observer might have included these aspects as integral parts. I guess that one of my colleagues, who is an expert in the efficient operation of such systems, would have included the pricing structure for electricity as part of the system, something partially controllable by the power company. So we see that different people may define the same 'system' in different ways, deliberately choosing what to include and what to exclude. The choice of what to include or exclude will largely depend on what the person viewing something as a system intends to do with this definition, i.e., the purpose of a particular system. The system is now not seen as existing independently of the observer anymore; it is not out there; it has become a mental construct, personal to the observer! This is the inside-us view of systems.

The confusing thing is that in everyday language the word is more often than not used in the out-there meaning. This even happens if the assembly of components is a human construct or view, such as an industrial or business operation. It is described as if it existed independent of the observer. Unfortunately, even systems experts sometimes fall into this trap.

Systems as a Human Conceptualization

In this text, it is the inside-us view of systems that is important. Systems are recognized as human conceptualizations. They do not exist per se. It is only the human observer that may view something as a system. For instance, the grandfather taking his grandchild for a walk along an estuary may see the estuary as a beautiful place to share the many wonders of nature with his grandchild, while the jogger, crossing their path, may be hardly aware of anything more than a few feet away from the path. The biology student studying the estuary will see it as an ecological system, where plants, insects, and all sorts of aquatic life forms interact with each other and are affected by the tides. The engineer working for the local catchment authority will also see it as a system, in fact, a subsystem of a larger water drainage system under her management. The grandfather or the jogger will hardly view the estuary as a system, while the biology student and the engineer each see a different system. But when the engineer takes her windsurfer onto the estuary, she too will not see it as a system, but simply as an enjoyable playground.

The point that systems are human conceptualizations is clearly driven home by the fact that the majority of systems we, as analysts, conceive are not our personal view of some real assembly of things out there in the real world. They are mental conceptualizations of things that do not exist yet, things we plan to realize, or views of major planned changes to an existing operation, still to be implemented.

3.3 SUBJECTIVITY OF SYSTEMS DESCRIPTION

So whether or not some thing or entity is viewed as a system depends on the personal interest of the observer. The purpose of studying an organized assembly of things as a system will determine the type of system seen. However, any two people viewing the same situation with the same purpose in mind may well see surprisingly different systems. The reason for this is that the way an individual views a situation is affected by factors highly personal to that individual.

Figure 3-2: Salvador Dalí's "Slave Market", oil on canvas (1940)

Slave Market with the Disappearing Bust of Voltaire (1940), oil on canvas, 18¼ × 25⅜ in., Collection of The Salvador Dalí Museum, St. Petersburg, Florida, © 1991 Salvador Dalí Museum, Inc.

World View of Observer

These personal factors are such things as the upbringing, cultural and social background, education, practical experience, and values or beliefs of the individual. For example, the three co-owners of a firm may each view their firm as a different system: the first (the materialist) views it as a system to increase his wealth, the second (the idealistic artist) as a system to exercise her creative drive, and the third (the humanitarian) as a system to provide employment for the people in the town he lives in. So one of the skills all budding management scientists have to learn is to see a situation through somebody else's eyes. Hopefully, this will also make them more aware of their own way of looking at the world.

These personal factors are all captured in the concept of **Weltanschauung** of the individual. This German word loosely translates as 'world view'. It operates like a filter that channels a person's view in a given personal direction and allows her or him to attribute a meaning to what he or she observes that is congruent with his or her Weltanschauung or world view.

Effect of Previous Knowledge

Reality is even more diverse and confusing. What we may know or are told about something may affect what we see or observe. Consider the well-known painting by the famous Spanish painter Salvador Dalí, depicting a girl sitting in front of a group of buyers in a slave market. It is reproduced in black and white in Figure 3-2 on the preceding page. What do you see?

Now study Figure 3-3 over the page which shows a photograph of the bust of Voltaire by the 18th century French sculpture Houdon. Turn back to the Dalí painting and observe how the buyers turn into the facial features of the bust of Voltaire. (You may have to go back and forth a number of time to see it!) If I had shown you Voltaire's bust first and given Figure 3-2 its official caption "Slave market and the disappearing bust of Voltaire", your initial perception of the picture might have been quite different. This little exercise neatly demonstrates that what we perceive or observe may be strongly influenced by what we already know.

System's Definitions are Subjective

For all these reasons, the way you view something as a system is to a large extent 'subjective'. It is important for you to recognize that other people, looking at the same thing as a system, may not share your definition. Not only may they attribute a different purpose to the system, they may also include and exclude different things as part of the system. But, and this is an important 'but', one definition cannot be labelled 'right' or 'valid' and another one 'wrong' or 'invalid'. As long as each is logically consistent, each one is valid for the person making it. The only judgment that may be made is that one may be more effective or defensible in terms of the aim or purpose for building it. This is an important aspect of systems thinking that may be difficult for the novice to accept. It is simpler, more comforting, less threatening to think in terms of a single unique answer or solution — the right answer. However, systems thinking is not a matter of black-and-white, but of shades of grey.

Naturally, this discussion deals with the age-old controversy of objective versus subjective. Is there objectivity? From what you have read so far, you must conclude that I am a firm believer that objectivity, at least in its traditional meaning of 'the expression or interpretation of facts or conditions as perceived without distortion by personal feelings, prejudices, in other words, independent of the observer's mind', is an illusion. It is not an operational concept. Our mind can only capture our personal perceptions coherent with our Weltanschauung. The only operational meaning that objectivity may have is what the systems thinker R. L. Ackoff [1974] calls 'the social product of the open interaction of a wide variety of individual subjectivities' — a sort of consensual subjectivity. So, wide consensus of interpretations on many things is thus not excluded. Modern scientific knowledge is based on such consensus. But, as the two examples below show, this is all that it is, a consensus. Or to quote Albert Einstein: 'The only justification for our concepts is that they serve to represent the complex of our experiences; beyond this, they have no legitimacy.'

Figure 3-3: Houdon's Bust of Voltaire
(Courtesy of the Victoria and Albert Museum, London)

Consider the interpretation of 'what is insanity?' We look at past views of 'being possessed by the devil' either with abhorrence or a benign smile. Future generations may think of the current view of 'deep-seated emotional disturbances due to maladjustment to the social environment, particularly in childhood' as rather naive.

Probably the most famous example comes from Physics. Newton's laws of dynamics have been and still are some of the most successful scientific theories of profound theoretical and practical importance ever put forward. Not only were these laws corroborated by countless experiments and observations, but they also proved their practical value in mechanics — the building and working of all machinery on which modern life is based. Yet, at the beginning of the 20th century Einstein showed that, when considering motions with velocities comparable to that of light, or when attempting to analyze the mechanics of atoms and subatomic elements, Newton's laws, seen as inviolate for over two centuries, break down and must be replaced by postulates of relativity and quantum theory. This though in no way diminishes the continued importance of Newton's laws for operations with bodies of ordinary size, as dealt with in industry and much of space science.

3.4 FORMAL DEFINITION OF THE CONCEPT 'SYSTEM'

I choose to define a system as follows:

(1) A system is an organized assembly of components. 'Organized' means that there exist special relationships between the components.

(2) The system does something, i.e., it exhibits a type of behaviour unique to the system.

(3) Each component contributes towards the behaviour of the system and is affected by being in the system. No component has an independent effect on the system. The behaviour of the system is changed if any component is removed or leaves.

(4) Groups of components within the system may by themselves have properties (1), (2), and (3), i.e., they may form subsystems.

(5) The system has an outside — an environment — which provides inputs into the system and receives outputs from the system.

(6) The system has been identified by someone as of special interest.

The crucial ingredients of a system are therefore its **components**, the **relationships** between the components, the **behaviour** or the **activities** or the **transformation process** of the system, its **environment**, the **inputs** from the environment, the **outputs** to the environment, and the **special interest of the observer**.

A system is not a mere collection of parts that do not interact with each other, i.e., it is not a **chaotic aggregate**, such as a pile of rocks.   Adding a few parts to a chaotic aggregate or removing some does not change its nature. Doing so in a system will affect its behaviour. Similarly, a chaotic aggregate does not do anything, while a system does or at least is capable of doing things under specific conditions.

System components do not have to be physical things. They can be abstract things, such as information, numerical variables that measure things, like cumulative costs or levels of achievement, and relationships between physical or abstract things. In fact, most systems of interest in decision making may often consist of abstract things and their relationships alone.

What a system does — its activity — is the aspect of prime interest to the observer or analyst. The system behaviour consists usually of a transformation of inputs into outputs. Examples of such 'activity' are living plants, which when exposed to light transform water and carbon dioxide (inputs) into carbohydrates and oxygen (outputs), or a manufacturing firm which transforms raw materials (inputs) into finished products for sale to customers (outputs).

The system environment is all those aspects that affect the system behaviour and are not in turn significantly affected by it. They are viewed as being outside the system, rather than part of the system. They provide inputs to the system or receive outputs from the system. Inputs are things the system needs to function but does not produce for itself, such as resources, like raw materials and funds or information, or they impose constraints on the behaviour of the system, such as setting quality standards or output restrictions.   Any decisions or decision rules imposed on the system by somebody who has some control over how some aspects of the system function or operate are controllable inputs. Although the system provides outputs to the environment, these outputs are not assumed to affect any aspects of the environment in any significant way. If they were, then they should properly be included in the system itself.

This separation between the system and its environment means that each system has a **boundary**. An important part of a system description is to choose where this boundary should be set.

Finally, the person who views the organized assembly of components as a system has a purpose for doing so. This could be simply to gain a better understanding of the system behaviour or it could be to control the system behaviour in certain ways, e.g., to achieve a maximum output. The purpose for studying a system determines which aspects of the system the person wants to observe and study in detail. Various **measures of performance** or other indicators about the behaviour of the system give rise to abstract outputs of interest to the observer.

3.5 SOME EXAMPLES OF SYSTEMS DESCRIPTIONS

Let's look at some examples to clarify and elaborate on these concepts. For the sake of brevity, the examples used are somewhat coarse. Chapters 4 and 5 each consider real-life situations with all their intricacies.

A Traffic System

A network of roads and their connections, i.e., road intersections, road forks, and highway interchanges, and their physical characteristics which affect their carrying capacity, as well as the vehicles traveling using the roads at any given point in time can be viewed as a traffic system. The relationships between the components consist of their geographic location relative to each other and how they are linked together. Does a traffic system do anything? The road network connects places with each other and thus allows vehicle movement from each point in the road network to all other points. It transforms inputs — vehicles at given source locations — into outputs — vehicles at given destination locations. If a road segment (such as a critical bridge over a river) or a road connection is removed, some places may become isolated from the rest of the system or access to them be made longer. So what the traffic system does or can do changes. The traffic system of, say a country, may contain sub-systems, such as city road networks, that all have these properties.

What constitutes the environment of a traffic system? To answer this question we need to look at the inputs and outputs of the system. The major input consists of the people who want to go from one place to another and the type of vehicles they intend to use. These inputs enter the system and become components of the system. Abstract inputs may consist of the operational settings for various traffic controls at traffic intersections, or green waves, etc. The outputs are people and vehicles discharged from the system at various points on the road network. Note that if the physical inputs (vehicles entering the network) are removed, the road network ceases to be a traffic system, since it lacks one of its major components, namely its users.

The person interested in the system, i.e., the person defining the assembly of components as a system could be a traffic engineer. The aim of studying the road network may be to observe some system performance measures, such as the rate of traffic flow along crucial road segments and the degree to which the road segments' capacities are used during periods of peak traffic. These are some of the abstract outputs of the system. The driver of a vehicle or the scheduler of a fleet of pick-up and delivery vehicles may be another person interested in the road network as a traffic system. The driver's aim is finding the fastest or shortest path from point A to point B. The scheduler's aim is determining the sequence of pick-ups and deliveries for a given vehicle that has the shortest distance.

A Motor Vehicle

A car is often cited as a typical example of a system. It is a complex assembly of thousand of individual parts. Its major components — the engine, its steering, its suspension, the electric parts — are complex subsystems by themselves. Their relationships consist of how they are fitted together and how they interact with each other. It is easy to view this set of parts properly put together as a system — indeed in its out-there meaning, existing independently of the observer. But a car by itself, say parked on the road, in a garage, or exhibited in a car museum, is not a system in a useful sense. It does not and cannot do anything on its own. To become a system more is needed. To assume its intended system role as a means of transporting people and goods, it also needs a driver with some goal about where to go, plus fuel, plus a road network for a road vehicle or some terrain for a cross-country vehicle. The road network or the terrain it drives on and all its properties form the environment of the car-driver system. Without all the components and the environment needed to fulfil its intended activity, a mere assembly of car parts is not a system for a means of transport.

Cars could though form part of different systems. For example, for the car collectors, the cars become a hobby — part of a personal enjoyment system. For the car salesperson, the cars in the sales yard are part of a profit making system.

Viewing a car as part of a transport system, note that a conventional car has many components that do not contribute to its intended purpose. For that it does not need all the trim and much of its interior comforts and conveniences, such as a stereo, or central locking subsystems. It is still part of a transport system without these. (Naturally, if its primary purpose is as a means of self-fulfilment for the owner, these extras may be more important than its ability as a means of transport.) However, remove the wheels, and the car ceases to be a system for a means of transport. If it has an external power pickup link, like some cross-country vehicles or tractors, it may be used as a system to provide motive power for the operation of machinery, such as an electric power generator. Its purpose changes.

A Sawmill

Consider a sawmill, converting logs into various types of wood products for building and carpentry, such as planks, beams, framing materials, and trim, as well as off-cuts and sawdust. An industrial engineer may see it as a production system. The owners of the sawmill may see it as a system for getting a financial return on their invest-ment. A management scientist studying the sawmilling operations may see parts of it as a system for cutting logs into individual products intended to satisfy a given composition of customer demands at the lowest possible cost. Let us now consider each of these views in turn.

An Industrial Engineer's View

Viewing the firm as a wood processing production system, the industrial engineer will be primarily interested in physical components of the operation of transforming logs into a range of finished products, what the components do, and how they interact with each other. These are the different machines and equipment, the buildings and other areas where equipment can be housed and where storage spaces for intermediate products can be located. It also includes the logs as they are fed into the saw, the stockpiles of intermediate products at various stages of processing, and the people needed for operating all machinery. Their activities consist of the various types of operations they perform, such as shifting or moving logs, sawing logs, drying cut timber, and so on. The relationships between the components are given by the sequence of these activities, and the location of fixed components, such as yards and machines, relative to each other.

The physical inputs into the system are logs of various types and grades of quality, and any other supplies needed for operating the machinery. The physical outputs consist of the various types of finished products coming off the final processing stage. Abstract inputs into this system are the rules used for sawing up the logs and the rules used at all subsequent processing stages.

The purpose for studying this system could be to determine good physical layouts for the equipment and storage areas, or good product handling and equipment operating procedures. Hence, abstract outputs are such things as the maximum processing capacity, the location of bottlenecks, and the fraction of time various machines are idle, all with respect to a given combination of inputs, both physical and abstract.

The Sawmill as a Profit Maximizing System

Viewing the firm as a whole as a profit generating system, the owner may not be interested at all in the physical components, but only in the financial consequences of all activities going on in the firm. So the nature of the components changes dramatically. The system is now viewed as an interacting set of subsystems and their relationships. Each subsystem performs a vital task, mission, or function for the firm as a whole to operate. So there is a raw material purchasing subsystem. Its mission is to procure logs of the right quality in the right quantities. To perform this mission it needs information inputs from other subsystems, such as production forecasts. The logs purchased become inputs to one or more production subsystems. There is also a log handling and storage subsystem, a finished goods and warehousing subsystem, a marketing subsystem, and a financial control subsystem. Although there is a physical flow of materials between some of these subsystems, the main relationships or interactions of interest to the analyst are how the various subsystems communicate their needs to other subsystems, what kind of actions are triggered off by the flow of requisitions of goods and the exchange of information on material flow, and what the financial implications of the physical flow of materials are for the firm as a whole. The outputs of one subsystem become thus inputs into other subsystems.

The system's environment consists of the market for sawlogs, the market for finished products, the financial market, the labour market, and the firm's legal environment. These provide various inputs, such as future projections of the various types and grades of logs available and their costs, future projections of the demand for the various finished products as a function of their selling prices, the cost of funds currently invested in the firm, and the availability and cost of funds for future investments in the firm, and so on. Controllable inputs are operating policies now and in the future and future expansion plans. The outputs are projections of sales for the firm's products, projections of operating profits and of cash flows generated.

Note that for a profit generating system, the physical goods supplied to the customers are not the output of prime interest to the analyst. These simply become an input into the financial subsystem through the revenue they generate and how this affects the cash flow of the firm and its profit. The latter two measure the performance of the firm as a profit generating system and are the real outputs of the system. Viewed in this light, the transformation process of the firm is not one of converting logs into finished products, but one of converting wealth at a given point in time, say at the beginning of the financial year, into wealth at a later point in time, say at the end of the financial year.

The Sawmill Operation as a Cost Minimizing System

The management science study for determining the minimum cost operation to meet certain customer orders from the stock of logs available needs a system that has some aspects of both the preceding systems. It retains much of the details on the physical product flow as in the engineering system, but also the financial implications for each activity associated with the multi-stage process of converting logs into finished products as in the profit generating system. Its inputs are the current stock of logs available, differentiated by type, grade, and quality, as well as data on the unit operating cost and processing rate for each piece of equipment for each type of product processed, and a detailed schedule of each type of finished product required to fill a given set of customer orders. Its outputs are the actual amounts of each finished product produced and the total cost of meeting customer orders. Comparing this total cost for various processing rules will allow the analyst to determine the least cost solution. So the output of primary interest to the analyst is the total cost of the operation. The transformation process consists of producing a total cost for a given set of inputs about availabilities of logs and requirements for finished products.

Level of Resolution in System Description

The purpose of studying the firm as a system strongly influences the level of detail or the degree of resolution used for representing the various components, the system's inputs and outputs. For example, if the purpose is to determine the firm's profit potential for its current owners under stable market conditions for both supply of logs and sale of finished products, then the level of resolution can be rather coarse. The conversion of logs into finished products may be shown in aggregate only, using averages for the conversion process and the cost of conversion. Little or no detail on the individual processes within the production subsystem will be included. The main inputs will relate to those essential for the continuation of the current level of operations. The major output of interest will be the return on the owners' investment. In contrast, for the industrial engineering study each operation and its associated equipment, and the flow of materials need to be included in full detail.

Arbitrariness of System Description

These examples together with the discussion in the previous section drive home the point that there is a significant degree of arbitrariness in how a system is defined, where its boundary is placed, and the level of detail or resolution used. As a rule the choice should be the smallest system needed for achieving the purpose for which the system is defined in the first place. But this too is a matter of judgment.

3.6 SYSTEMS AS 'BLACK BOXES'

The complexity of real life may be such that we have no or only incomplete knowledge of the inner workings of a system, even if we are able to identify the physical components. Often the major reason for this lack of knowledge is that the system's behaviour is affected by random aspects. Clearly, how the human brain functions is only partially understood today. So, there is no full understanding of how humans learn. Similarly, in spite of the enormous progress made in meteorology, weather systems are only partially understood. As a result, weather predictions are sometimes wrong. Computers or other machinery fail for a myriad of reasons. It may be impractical to keep track of individual causes. So only aggregate records are compiled.

In each of these examples, the inside of the corresponding system is basically empty. All we know are the inputs into and the outputs from the system. For the lay observer it looks like one of those black control boxes, with lots of wires into and out of the box, but no way of knowing what happens inside. If our aim is to predict the output of such a system in response to various inputs, we may indeed not have to know the details of its inner workings, even if this were possible. In such instances, all we need to discover is the form of the functional relationship between inputs and outputs. Various statistical tools may help in this task. After proper testing, these relationships can then be used to predict the corresponding phenomena, such as the most likely weather pattern resulting from certain meteorological (input) conditions, or the long-run daily breakdown patterns for, say, 24 looms in operation at a carpet or cloth factory — information needed for planning a repair service.

In other situations the transformation process is known exactly. However, rather than represent it in full detail, it may be perfectly adequate to view the inner working as a black box and simply express the various activities of the transformation pro-cess by a single functional relationship. Examples of this are intricate multi-stage chemical processes, like in an oil refinery, where a yield table is used to transform, say, crude oil into a range of refined products. This approach is frequently used as a substitute for the transformation process of a subsystem which receives inputs from and provides outputs to other components of the system. For example, the subsystem for the conversion of logs into finished products in the sawmill profit maximizing system is most likely to be included in the form of a black box.

3.7 HIERARCHY OF SYSTEMS

The purpose of viewing something as a system strongly affects what aspects should be included as part of the system and what aspects are more appropriately placed into the environment, in other words, where to choose the boundary of the system. The two systems for the sawmill, i.e., a profit making system and the cost minimization system, clearly demonstrate this. The value of stocks of logs available and maintained are a component for the profit maximizing system, but become an input for the cost minimization system. The sawmill example demonstrates a further important point. The cost minimization system is completely contained in the profit making system. The fact that the degree of detail shown for the two systems may be different is unimportant. Those aspects of the profit making system not included in the cost minimization system are part of the environment of the latter. So we have a system within a system.

In fact, these are only two of a whole sequence of nested systems related to the sawmill example. The firm itself is embedded in a system of regional sawmills, all sharing the same forest resources. The system of regional sawmills is embedded in the system covering the national wood processing industry. The latter in turn is included in the system for the whole national economy. This nesting of systems within systems within systems is referred to as a **hierarchy of systems**. The containing system becomes the environment of the contained system.

In some instances, the containing system exercises some control over the contained system. The controlling system may set the objectives of the contained system, monitor how well it achieves these objectives, and have control over some of the crucial resources needed by the contained system for performing its mission. The controlling system is then referred to as the **wider system of interest**, while the contained system becomes the **narrow system of interest**. For example, if the sawmill cost minimizing system is the narrow system of interest, then the sawmill profit maximizing system is its wider system of interest.

Some systems theorists distinguish between the wider system of interest and the environment of the narrow system, restricting the latter to only those aspects that affect the narrow system which are not included as part of the wider system. Since these aspects must by necessity be part of the environment of the wider system, I find this distinction rather artificial. I will therefore simply view the wider system as the environment of the narrow system.

The advantage of viewing two systems in a hierarchy of a narrow and a wider system is that their relationships are shown in their correct context. It may show that improvements in the performance of the narrow system may require action to be taken in the wider system. Similarly, the relationships between various inputs into the narrow system are clarified. For example, two inputs originally seen as independent of one another may turn out to be highly related or affected by the same factors when seen in their proper relationship within the wider system. This may lead to a reformulation of the nature of these inputs.

3.8 SYSTEM BEHAVIOUR

System State

As pointed out earlier, the behaviour of the system is of prime interest to the person studying a system. How do we describe the behaviour of a system? We show how various characteristics, properties or attributes of each component change. Consider the road network as a traffic system. The behaviour of this system over a short interval of time is known if we note down exactly for both the beginning and the end of the time interval which road segments and road connections are open for travel and where each vehicle is located and what direction and speed it is traveling. The attribute of interest for each road segment and road connection is thus whether it is open or closed. The attributes of a car consist of its location, its direction of travel, and its speed of travel. We usually refer to these attributes as **state variables**. At any point in time each state variable has a given numerical value (speed and geographical coordinates for two of the car state variables) or categorical value (open or closed for the road segment state variable). The set of values assumed by all state variables as of a given point in time is referred to as the **state of the system**. The behaviour of a system is therefore completely known if we know how the state of the system changes over time.

When we start observing the system the initial values of these state variables are inputs. They change their value in either of two ways:

(1) The change in a state variable is the result of an input provided by the person who has means of affecting the behaviour of the system. For instance, the traffic engineer specifies that at 9 a.m. the road segment between X and Y is to be closed to traffic for 4 hours. Frequently these inputs may be in the form of an automatic decision rule, such as the green phase at a traffic light being triggered by an approaching vehicle between the hours of 8 p.m. and 6 a.m.

(2) The change in a state variable of a component is a consequence of the activity of the component itself or of the relationship with other components. For example, as a vehicle travels in the network it constantly changes the value of some of its state variables, in particular the ones recording its location and speed. Similarly, the speed at which a vehicle can travel is affected by the traffic intensity along that stretch of road or by a bottleneck emerging ahead of it. Both of these aspects will slow down the vehicle's progress.

Variety of System Behaviour

System behaviour can be almost infinitely varied, even for very simple systems. To demonstrate this I borrow the fascinating example in the Open University text *Systems* by J. Beishon (The Open University Press, Milton Keynes, 1971, pp. 16-17). Consider one of those old-fashioned newscaster strips, where advertising and news headlines march across from right to left, each letter being spelled by a specific pattern of on and off light bulbs. They are still seen at many railway stations or city centre squares around the world. Assume that the display panel is 7 light bulbs high and 100 light bulbs long, a rather small newscaster allowing for only 20 letters to be shown at one time. The behaviour of this system is given by the changing patterns of light bulbs on and off. Each possible pattern is one state of this system. How many different states does this system have?

Since each light bulb can either be on or off, the state variable for each light bulb has two values. If there are only two light bulbs, then for each of the two states of the first bulb there are two states for the second bulb, i.e., there are 2 times 2 or 2^2 possible states. For three light bulbs it is 2 times 2 times 2, or 2^3. You now see the pattern. For 700 light bulbs it is 2^{700} different states. This is slightly larger than 10^{210}, i.e., a number consisting of a 1 followed by another 210 zeros. I have great difficulties in grasping how big this number really is. To put it into perspective, consider the number of atomic particles contained in the entire universe. This has been estimated as being in the order of 10^{73}, an infinitesimally small number compared to the number of states for the 700 light bulb newscaster — a rather small one compared to the one on London's Leicester Square which has 30,000 bulbs!

In real-life systems studies we are rarely interested in the minute details of the system behaviour. This would outstrip our cognitive capabilities quite quickly. Our concern is rather with the aggregate or average behaviour of the system. For example, in the road network the traffic engineer is hardly interested in the movement of every vehicle, but rather with 15-minute or half-hour averages of the capacity use or the traffic delays along certain road segments and road intersections over the course of a given day, such as a 'typical' Saturday. This will indicate which road segments and intersections are prone to become traffic bottlenecks. Or the traffic engineer may want to collect information on the number of trips made from a given suburb of the city to various other parts of the city for planning future roading needs. This means that only a few crucial systems variables are kept track of in any detail, and they are usually in the form of summary measures for all state variables of a given class or subgroup of components, like all vehicles traveling past a given location in the road network over a certain interval of time. These summary state variables are especially introduced to monitor the performance of the system as a whole or of various subsystems of it. They are not associated with what would be seen as a natural system component.

Emergent Properties

The behaviour of the road network as a traffic system highlights another important aspect of systems. A traffic bottleneck at a given intersection as a result of high traffic flow cannot be associated with an individual vehicle traveling through that intersection. Similarly the traffic density at a given point in the network is a product of many components acting together. So **the system exhibits behaviours or properties that none if its components individually may exhibit**. Such behaviours or properties are new or different from the behaviours or properties of the individual components. They only emerge from the joint interaction or behaviour of the components that form the system. Such properties are called **emergent properties**. This is often summarized by 'the whole is greater than the sum of its parts'.

Systems are often created or formed in order to produce desired emergent properties. Consider again the car/driver as a system of components (engine, wheels, etc., plus driver, plus road network). This system is more than simply a complementary collection of components arranged in a given pattern; it was created specifically as a mode of transport. None of its parts or a subset of parts has this property by itself.

Similarly, the various subsystems that make up a sawmill, each one viewed by itself, are not capable of producing a profit. Only if their individual activities are properly coordinated does the potential for producing a profit emerge. Again this is a planned emergent property.

Unfortunately, all too often emergent properties are not desirable or even planned. The examples in Chapter 2, such as the Aswan High Dam, the deterioration of urban transport, or the effects of the traditional method of assessing machine efficiencies, clearly highlight this. One of the compelling reasons for using a systems approach to problem solving is exactly to better predict planned desirable and unplanned undesirable consequences of decision making.

3.9 DIFFERENT KINDS OF SYSTEMS

Discrete Systems

In the newscaster light bulb display the state of the system is any one of a huge number of individual states, each characterized by a pattern of on-and-off bulbs. The pattern changes so fast that our eyes are deceived into seeing a continuously moving string of letters. However, that apparent movement consists of a sequence of displays of individual patterns, each one held for a fraction of a second. The patterns do not fade from one display into another. So the state of the system jumps through a sequence of discrete states. Such systems are called **discrete systems**.

Here are a few additional examples of discrete systems: (1) In the telephone betting system discussed in Chapter 1, the number of telephone lines busy is one of the important state variables. It can only be an integer. (2) In a predator/prey system, the state is described by the number of predators and number of preys alive at any point in time. Both are discrete variables. (3) In the loom repair system, two state variables of prime interest are the number of machines operating and the number of machines broken down at any given point in time — again discrete variables.

Continuous Systems

In contrast, the state variables of the road network system change continuously as vehicles move along the road segments or through intersections. The state of the system therefore also changes continuously. Since the state variables are continuous variables, the number of possible states is infinitely large, even if each variable may be restricted to a small range of values. This is an example of a **continuous system**. Many industrial processes, particularly in chemical and petro-chemical plants, should be viewed as continuous systems. Similarly, the process used by warm-blooded animals to maintain the body temperature within a narrow range is also a continuous system.

In practice, rather than observe a continuous system in a continuous manner, its state is observed and recorded only at regular discrete points in time, say, every n minutes. The closer consecutive recordings are in time, the more accurately the system's actual behaviour is approximated.

Deterministic and Stochastic Systems

If the behaviour of a system is predictable in every detail the system is **deterministic**. For example, for most studies the solar system is viewed as a deterministic system. The trajectory of every planet can be predicted exactly. Animated neon advertising signs that go through a regular pattern can be viewed as deterministic systems. A sequence of traffic lights along a one-way street is set at a fixed pattern during certain hours of the day so as to produce a green wave. When operating in this mode, it is a deterministic system.

However, few phenomena in real life, particularly those involving people, behave in deterministic ways. They are generally not completely predictable. Some behaviour may be affected by **random** or **stochastic** inputs. Such systems are called **stochastic systems**. (Stochastic derives from the Greek *stochos*, meaning 'guess'.)

If the variations in behaviour are minor, we may still approximate it by a deterministic system. For example, the Swiss railroads, known for their almost pedantic punctuality, can for most purposes be adequately approximated as a deterministic system.

Closed and Open Systems

The father of General Systems Theory, Ludwig von Bertalanffy, introduced the concepts of **closed and open** systems. A closed system is one that does not receive anything from its environment, nor does it give out anything to its environment. It has no inputs and outputs. A closed system has no interactions with any environment. In fact, it has no environment. In contrast, open systems interact with the environment, by receiving inputs from it and providing outputs to it.

In real life there exist no truly closed systems. Any real-life system has an environment with which it interacts, even if only in a small way. So, the concept of a closed system is a theoretical or laboratory concept. It is used to observe systems under experimental conditions, eliminating as far as possible any interactions with its environment. Its only input is the initial state of the system. By providing different initial states the analyst can observe how the system behaviour responds to each. With no interactions with an environment, this behaviour is regulated entirely by the interactions among the components of the system. These determine to the last detail how the system behaves. Hence, it must be deterministic. If it comes to rest or reaches a final state of internal balance, that final state reached is determined by the initial or starting conditions. This means that, given a particular starting state, a closed system will always follow the same path to the final state if one exists.

Systems defined for decision making purposes are always open systems, since by definition the decisions or the decision making rules are inputs into the system. Stochastic systems are also open systems since the factors that introduce the randomness in the behaviour are the result of outside forces or events.

The Steady State of a Probabilistic System

A stochastic system may exhibit some remarkable and surprising characteristics in its behaviour. It may reach the same final state, if one exists, even if it starts out from different initial conditions or initial states of the system. This 'final state' may in fact be an **equilibrium** or a **steady state** that is independent of the state the system started out from. As we shall see in Chapter 15 when we talk about uncertainty and its meaning, the steady state of a system is not a particular single state, that is maintained in perpetuity once reached. Rather, it is a long-run average behaviour, such as the cumulative average number of lines busy in a telephone exchange or the cumulative average number of machines down in a pool of identical machines. After any large random disturbances, the system may be pushed away from its steady state, but it will gradually approach it again.

3.10 CONTROL OF SYSTEMS

Our reason for viewing something as a system is usually in view of controlling its behaviour. Control is exercised by imposing something on the system in the form of inputs — a set of decisions, or decision rules, or simply an initial state for the system — that will affect some activities in the system and therefore the behaviour of the system in desired ways. We shall refer to them as **control inputs**. Note that if we impose decision rules on the system it may seem, at least superficially, as if the system exercises control by itself. The fact that its behaviour will change if the system is made to obey a different set of rules clearly shows that this apparent self-control is imposed from outside.

Three conditions are needed for exercising control over system behaviour:

(1) A target, objective, or goal for the system to reach. For a deterministic system this may be a particular state of the system. For stochastic systems it may be a desirable steady state.

(2) A system capable of reaching the target or goal. A rather obvious condition! The difficulty is that for stochastic systems there may be no way of guaranteeing that this goal is ever reached.

(3) Some means for influencing the system behaviour. These are the control inputs (decisions, decision rules, or initial states). How these control inputs affect system behaviour is an important aspect of studying systems.

Systems theory distinguishes between three types of controls: **open loop controls**, **closed loop controls**, and **feed-forward controls**.

Open Loop Controls

Open loop controls are inputs imposed on the system based only on the prediction of how the system behaviour responds to them. No account is taken of how the system actually responds to the control inputs. Open loop controls are often in the form of a recipe or a set of rules to follow. For example, in the sawmill cost minimizing system the control inputs will be in the form of a schedule of very detailed cutting patterns to apply for each log to be processed.

We will find that for many OR/MS projects the recommendations derived for controlling the system are in the form of open loop controls. However, for many situations open loop controls are not adequate or effective. Say, I use the following four steps for starting the engine of my Italian sports car:

1. Insert ignition key into ignition lock.

2. Depress clutch pedal and use gear lever to shift into neutral (I always leave the car in gear when the engine is off).

3. Pull choke button half way out.

4. Turn ignition key clockwise to red mark (this engages the starter motor), hold for two seconds, and then return key to black mark.

It is clear that this does not guarantee that I can start my car's engine successfully. For example, the person using my car before me may have left it in neutral. Touching the gear lever will immediately indicate this to me, so I will skip step 2. The engine may still be hot from a previous run, hence no choke is needed; or it may be very cold, and the choke has to be pulled out completely. The engine may start after only one second, so I return the key to the black mark without waiting two seconds. The engine may not start within the two second interval, in which case I may continue holding the key to the red mark for much longer. In fact, what I am doing is adjusting the controls used for starting the engine to how the car responds to my controls. The behaviour of the system becomes a source of feedback to adjust my controls.

Closed Loop Controls

Under this type of control, information about the system behaviour, possibly in response to previous control inputs, is fed back to the controller for evaluation. This may lead the controller to adjust the control signals. The classic example for this is how most people control the temperature of the shower water. Standing safely outside the shower, we turn the shower control valve to a setting somewhere midway between 'cold' and 'hot'. After a few seconds we tentatively put in a hand to test the temperature of the water flowing from the shower rose. This information is interpreted by our brain. We turn the control valve either clockwise to increase the flow of hot water relative to the flow of cold water if the temperature feels too cold or counter clockwise if it is too hot. We then wait again a second or two to check the result. This process continues until the water temperature feels right. The final temperature chosen may not necessarily always be the same. It will be affected by the air temperature and by our internal metabolism.

In systems terms, the controller supplies some initial control inputs to the **feedback control mechanism.** The latter is a component of the system, while the controller itself is outside the system. The initial control inputs are usually in the form of decision rules or a decision strategy (... if such and such is true, do this and that ...). These decisions rules are used by the control mechanism to issue **control signals** that steer the system in a desired direction. Information about the system's resulting behaviour or outputs is then fed back to the control mechanism for evaluation. The latter adjusts the control signals in accordance with the decision rules. So the loop from the control mechanism to other parts of the system is closed by a feedback loop from these parts back to the control mechanism. For this reason, such types of controls are referred to as **closed-loop controls** or **feedback controls**.

Self-Regulation

Feedback loops also occur in many natural systems, particularly biological and ecological systems, where they help regulate the behaviour of these systems. For example, for a given form of tidal action and fresh water inflows, an estuary has a natural state of equilibrium, where the various ecological symbiotic relationships and interdependencies, like predator/prey subsystems, are in balance. If this balance is disturbed it will redress itself slowly over time to its previous equilibrium, provided no new disturbance occurs. Assume, for instance, that a large proportion of the predator population has been wiped out through a natural event, such as a storm. This will lead to an explosion of the prey population. The predator population thus finds very favourable conditions for multiplying beyond its original level. This added pressure will reduce the prey population, with excess predators now also dying off, and so on. Through a series of oscillations of ever decreasing magnitude the previous natural balance will re-establish itself after a while.

This feedback however has nothing to do with control. There are no human input controls for influencing the behaviour of the system. What is happening is a natural self-regulation, which is different from control. Self-regulation returns a natural system to its equilibrium. Human control of natural systems usually has different goals, such as the eradication of some aspect of nature considered a pest or a health menace. In fact, many attempts at human control of natural systems have had disastrous results.

The classical example is the use of DDT for combatting mosquitos and agricultural insect pests. Although DDT admirably accomplished this desirable goal, it also had unplanned consequences, such as weakening the egg shells of a number of predatory birds. As a result, these bird populations crashed almost to the point of extinction. Only last minute banning of DDT use and other rescue measures saved a number of species, like the American eagle, the condor, and the pelican, from being wiped out.

There is obviously a lesson to be learned from such events, namely that a systems approach might have prevented such near-disasters. In fact, state agencies dealing with environmental issues are now very cautious in giving permission for the introduction of new biological controls without having seen sufficient evidence that these controls will not develop into problems themselves.

Feedback Control and Self-Regulation

As Figure 3-4 shows, feedback control and self-regulation differ in important ways. Feedback control receives an extra input of decision rules supplied by a human controller. The rules governing self-regulation are internal, a result of natural evolution.

Negative and Positive Feedback Loops

Feedback loops can act positively or negatively. A positive feedback increases the discrepancy between the future state of the system and some reference state, such as an equilibrium state or some desired target state. In other words, the system state tends to deviate more and more from its reference state. In contrast, negative feedback decreases the discrepancy between the future state and the reference state. (Note that 'positive' and 'negative' are not used in their colloquial meaning of 'good' and 'bad'.)

Positive feedback tends to lead to instability. The system either explodes, for example, by having some of its state variables take on larger and larger values, or it kills itself. In fact, self-regulation in biological and ecological systems is as a rule based on negative feedback. This returns such systems to their natural state of equilibrium.

Although a number of theoretical examples, particularly from mathematics and economics, exhibit positive feedback, human control of systems is usually also based on negative feedback. Human systems are either goal seeking or relationship maintaining. In either case, the control signals are reinforced if they steer the system

Figure 3-4: Feedback control and self-regulation

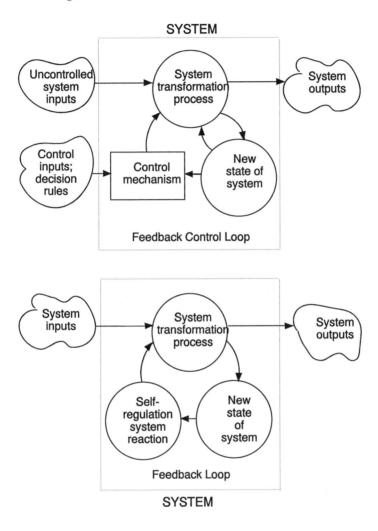

towards the goal or relationship maintaining equilibrium and are weakened or even reversed otherwise.

Feed-forward Control

A feedback control mechanism reacts to changes in some critical state variables or outputs. Rather than react to events after they have happened, a feed-forward control mechanism predicts how changes in uncontrollable inputs are likely to affect system behaviour and then sends control signals that will maintain system behaviour as closely as possible on the desired course, thereby counteracting the effects of input disturbances. This is the type of control used by an experienced driver of a car. It is also commonly used for the control of chemical processes. Similarly, most successful firms attempt to forecast future economic and demand trends in order to take advantage of growth opportunities or avoid potential disasters due to an economic downturn. Again, these are applications of feed-forward control.

Naturally, feed-forward and feedback controls are often combined into a single control strategy.

Response Lags in Systems

Let us briefly return to the temperature control of the shower water. You all have observed that an adjustment of the shower valve does not result in an instantaneous change in the water temperature. In fact, the response is delayed for a short time and then occurs gradually, either increasing or decreasing to a new level. The time delay between the moment when the control signals are applied and their effects have taken full effect is called **lag**.

For example, if the water flow into a canal bringing water to a hydro power station is increased, it may take a few minutes or even hours before the increased water flow reaches the pressure pipes leading to the turbines and an increase in power generation can take effect. Such a lag is a **transport lag**. Such lags are quite common in industry and commerce. For instance, an increase in the production level may take considerable time before it results in increased deliveries from the factory, and even considerably more until it finally leads to an increase in sales from the retail outlets. Most feedback loops are also subject to a transport lag. By the time the information on the state of the system has been processed by the control mechanism that information may already be out-of-date, hence the need for feed-forward controls.

A second kind of lag of great importance is the **exponential lag**. Here, the effect of the control signals is immediate, but gradual in terms of its size. An example of this type of lag is the temperature change in a gas oven. Although the temperature starts rising immediately if the temperature controls are raised, say from 175 C^0 to 250 C^0, the oven will take several minutes to reach that new temperature. Since an increase in the supply of gas has an instant effect in terms of increased heat output, the initial temperature response will be fairly fast as the air in the oven is heated. Some of that heat is lost to heat the oven walls, so the rate of increase in temperature gain will slow down as the temperature approaches its new target level.

Stochastic systems tend to approach their steady state asymptotically. This is an example of an exponential lag response.

The response of a system to control signals may exhibit both a transport lag, as well as an exponential lag. Furthermore, response lags also occur as a consequence of non-controllable inputs, such as the traffic flow response lags as the input of vehicles into the network increases or decreases during certain times of the day.

Natural systems also exhibit response lags to changes in inputs.

EXERCISES

1. Consider a university as a system. Identify a possible relevant world view of the observer, the transformation process of the system, the mission or objective of the system and what systems aspects are used for measuring the system's performance, the inputs into the system, including control inputs, and the outputs from the system, and the major systems components, including possible subsystems, for the following situations:
    (a) From the viewpoint of a student attending the university to acquire theoretical and practical training for a professional career.
    (b) From the viewpoint of an academic staff member who sees the university as a system for pleasant gainful employment.
    (c) From the viewpoint of the chief executive officer of the university who sees the university's major role as one of advancing knowledge.

2. Consider the operation of a small urban fire department as a system. It is funded and operated by local government on behalf of its tax paying residents. Identify a possible relevant world view of the observer, the system's transformation process, its mission or objectives, its measures of performance, its inputs, including control inputs, its outputs, and its major components, from the point of view of
    (a) the local tax payers.
    (b) the chief of the fire department.

3. A local hospital blood bank collects blood from volunteer donors. The donors do not get any compensation for donating blood. Each donor donates one pint of blood one to three times per year. Attrition of blood donors, due to age, illness, or moving away, causes the pool of blood donors to decrease over time. To restore the pool of donors the blood bank periodically organizes a drive to recruit new donors. The amount collected obviously depends on the number of active donors and on the frequency with which they are called up for donations. However, for various reasons the amount collected fluctuates on a daily basis. All blood collected is tested for various diseases. If it is disease free, it is added to the blood bank's stock of blood, available for transfusions to patients. The demand for fresh blood originates either in the hospital's accident and emergency unit or from surgeons' requests for scheduled surgery. Hence, the requirements for blood also fluctuate on a daily basis. Fresh blood has a shelf life of 35 days. Hence, any blood not used within 35 days from its collection is outdated, i.e., removed from stock and destroyed. Some fresh blood is put aside for the production of by-products, such as platelet, plasma, etc., immediately after collection and testing. It is by such withdrawals of fresh blood that the director of the blood bank controls the daily stock of fresh blood. Her objectives are (i) to avoid, as far as possible and reasonable, having to notify surgeons that their requests for blood cannot be satisfied due to stock shortages, and (ii) to avoid having too much blood outdated.
    (a) Identify the various aspects of this system, including a relevant world view.
    (b) The director of the blood bank uses the following rules to control the stock of blood

for each blood type. At the end of each day she determines the amount of fresh blood which is 32 days old. If that amount is larger than some critical number, she withdraws an amount of blood equal to the excess above the critical number, using the most recently collected blood. What type of control is she using? Why do you reach that conclusion?

(c) List some of the state variables used to specify the state of the system.

4. Give an example of a hierarchy of systems
    (a) in a governmental setting.
    (b) in an educational setting.
    (c) in a sports setting.
    (d) in a law enforcement setting.

5. List some of the state variables used to define the state of the system for
    (a) the university as a professional training system (refer to Question 1(a)).
    (b) the fire department (refer to Question 2(a)).

6. In 100 words or less, state what the main reasons are for using a systems approach for problem solving.

7. Give examples of emergent properties for the following types of systems:
    (a) A river system receiving untreated chemical or sewage discharges.
    (b) A computer information system.
    (c) An intersection traffic control system.
    (d) A firm.
    (e) The police department.

8. Give two examples (different from any listed in the text) for
    (a) discrete systems.
    (b) continuous systems.
    (c) deterministic systems.
    (d) closed systems.
    (e) open systems.
    (f) probabilistic systems.

9. For the following situation/systems, identify the type of control/regulation mechanism present:
    (a) Assembly instructions for a kitset.
    (b) Filling air into a car tyre at a service station air pump.
    (c) The driver/car system on a motorway or freeway, where constant speed can be maintained.
    (d) The driver/car system on a curvy, hilly two-lane road with traffic in both directions.
    (e) An automatic wage payment system, where wages are directly credited to the recipients' accounts.
    (f) A firm has the following system to replenish its raw material stocks: whenever the stock level falls below a critical level, called the reorder point, an quantity of X tonnes is ordered.
    (g) The fermentation process for converting the sugar in the grapes into alcohol works as follows: After the yeast starter has been mixed with the grapes, the number of yeast cells multiply manifold and convert the sugar in the grapes into alcohol. As

sugar is depleted or the concentration of alcohol builds up, the growth in the number of yeast cells is inhibited until it stops, and most yeast cells die. At that point, fermentation stops.

(h) A stockbroker constantly watches the price changes in various company shares and tries to predict future price movements. This information is then used to make buying or selling decisions on various shares.

(i) The system used to control filling of the toilet water tank.

10. Identify the types of lags found in the following systems: (Note there may be several types of lags present.)

(a) The system for replenishing products from a supplier who will deliver the goods 10 days after receipt of the order.

(b) The cheque clearing system used by banks, where all checks presented before 4 p.m. on each day are processed over night for credit or debit to the corresponding accounts.

(c) A system of reservoirs used for hydro-electric power generation.

(d) The temperature of an unheated swimming pool.

REFERENCES

See also the references at the end of Chapter 2, in particular the texts by P. Checkland, C. W. Churchman, R. L. Flood, and M. C. Jackson. There are many texts dealing with systems and systems theories (not to be confused with 'systems analysis' of the computer science variety). Most of them tend to be highly abstract and overly mathematical, offering little guidance on how to apply systems concepts to decision making. The major exception is the material published by The Open University Press listed below.

The Open University, Walton Hall, Milton Keynes, MK7 6AA, U.K., offers several courses on systems and systems thinking. The course texts for these courses are available through The Open University Press. Chapters 2, 3, and 4 of this book have been strongly influenced by the writings of several Open University instructors. The relevant texts are:

Beishon, John, *Systems*, Technology Foundation Course T100: Unit 1, The Open University Press, 1971. Although systems thinking has come a long way since this text was published, it still forms a good foundation of the basic ideas. Its major failing is that it does not clearly distinguish between the 'out-there' and 'inside-us' view of systems.

Beishon, John, and Peters, Geoff, editors, *Systems Behaviour*, 3rd ed., Harper & Row, 1981. A collection of articles dealing with systems and systems thinking from a variety of viewpoints. Section 1 is of particular relevance to our discussion.

Hughes, J., and Tait, J., *The Hard Systems Approach - Systems Models*, Technology Course T301: Block 3, The Open University Press, 1984. It is this text that inspired me to write my own book on systems and decision making. It gives a step-by-step account of their version of a hard systems approach. The OR/MS methodology detailed in Chapters 4 to 8 of this book has some parallels, but also differs in several major respects from theirs.

Mayon-White, Bill, and Morris, Dick, *Systems Behaviour - Module 1: Systems and how to describe them,* Technology Course T241, The Open University Press, 1982. The idea of using Salvador Dalí's picture of the 'Slave market with the disappearing bust of Voltaire' to demonstrate the idea of the effect of previous knowledge is borrowed from this text. The major part of the text is devoted to a detailed analysis of two systems.

Naughton, J., *Soft Systems Analysis: An Introductory Guide,* Technology Course T301: Block 4, The Open University Press, 1984. A much more down-to-earth text than P. Checkland's *Systems Thinking, Systems Practice.* Together with its *Workbook* this is one of the best accounts of the use of rich pictures, discussed in Chapters 4 and 5 of this book.

Watson, Lewis, *Systems Paradigms - Studying Systems Failures,* Technology Course T301: Block 2, The Open University Press, 1984. Together with its companion text by Bignell, V., and Fortune, J., *Understanding Systems Failures,* Manchester University Press, 1984, this text applies systems thinking to explore why and how a number of major disasters, such as the Three Mile Island nuclear power station accident, could occur, and what we can learn from such failures.

Other references:

Beer, S., *Diagnosing the System for Organizations,* Wiley, 1985. Stafford Beer is the creator of the 'viable system model', a cybernetic model of organizations, which Beer started to implement for the restructuring of the Chile economy under Allende.

Flood, Robert L., and Carson, E.R., *Dealing with Complexity,* Plenum Press 1988. Chapters 1 and 2 discuss systems concepts from a theoretical point of view.

Flood, Robert L., and Jackson, Michael C., *Creative Problem Solving, Total Systems Intervention,* Wiley 1991. Chapter 1 talks about systems thinking and systems concepts with a number of topical examples.

There is an extensive literature on what is referred to as **general systems theory**, dealing with concepts, principles, properties of systems, and systems behaviour in general terms, not specific to a given field of application. At its inception in the 40s and 50s, there were great hopes placed on the impact that this theory was going to have on our understanding of systems and their use for the betterment of the human race. Unfortunately, general systems theory has not lived up to these expectations. Much of the theory developed is of such a general nature that it is of little practical use. It has also become highly mathematical and abstract.

4 Systems Modeling

In this chapter we will apply the systems concepts and thinking discussed in Chapters 2 and 3 to a real-life problematic situation and define a relevant system for it — relevant for the analysis of a particular issue about the problematic situation. The situation chosen deals with an environmental issue: 'the ozone hole', first discovered over the Antarctic in 1985. Although human caused, it now has a life of its own. We will start out by assembling everything we know about the situation, i.e., we will make a situation summary — a so-called 'rich picture'. This is the topic of the first four sections. In Section 4.6 we will identify some aspect of interest and define a relevant system for it. This will lead us to introduce formally the concept of a model in Section 4.7. Section 4.8 defines the relevant system for 'the ozone hole'. How to represent the relationships in the system in diagrammatic form is the topic of Sections 4.9 and 4.10.

The process of conceptualizing a system of interest is commonly referred to as **systems modeling**. In this chapter and the next, the models used are mainly diagrammatic. In Chapter 6 we will have a first look at mathematical models.

4.1 A SITUATION SUMMARY

The first step when approaching a problem situation is to familiarize yourself with the situation, its processes and structures, the people involved, their aims and desires, the relationships between them, the hierarchy or power structure, the resources available, the sources of data and information — in short, get a 'feel' for anything you discovered that seems relevant for describing the problem situation. An effective way to depict a complex situation is by drawing a **rich picture diagram** — a tool borrowed from Checkland's Soft Systems Methodology [1981].

What is a rich picture diagram? It is a cartoon-like summary of everything (or almost everything!) the observer knows about the situation studied. In some ways, developing such a diagram is similar to brain-storming, except that the aspects are captured in pictorial form. In contrast to a verbal description of a situation, which by necessity has to be sequential, a rich picture diagram shows the situation as a whole in all its complexity at a glance, so-to-speak. It can be 'read' in any direction with all aspects remaining 'present' for instant reference. The information contained in it can be processed in parallel, while a verbal description can only be processed serially. It is thus a much more effective and potent mode of communication.

Note that 'rich picture' does not, in the first place, mean a drawing. It is simply a more colourful term for situation summary. Its cartoon-like representation is called

Figure 4-1: Sample Symbols for Rich Pictures

a rich picture diagram. However, this is rather clumsy and long. So if it is clear from the context I will refer to the diagram also simply as a rich picture.

'But I am no good at drawing!' many of you will object. Neither am I. The representations used are very simple: stick-like figures, clouds, blobs and boxes, some slogan-type writing, and arrows depicting connections or time sequences. Figure 4-1 shows some types of components and symbols that may be used. You will quickly discover that the talent needed is not a good ability to draw, but simply a bit of imagination. In fact, drawing rich pictures is fun.

Although your prime concern may only be with some particular aspect of the situation, it pays to assemble as wide a picture as is reasonably possible within the time frame and resources available to you. Only then will you have some assurance of not missing interactions and relationships that could turn out to be essential for the particular issue that you wish to analyze in detail. Hence, it is advisable to depict all facets you are aware of from your familiarization of the situation and not only those that seem directly related to the original issue that triggered the study. Even so, you will have to use judgment as to what to include and what to leave out, or as to the level of resolution appropriate for depicting details. You will have to strike a sensible balance between the desire for completeness and for parsimony. For instance, you may draw a book, inscribed 'rules', rather than showing these rules in full detail. This serves as a reminder. Slogans (coming out of some person's head) are often highly effective summaries of details.

As you have discussions with other people involved, you may discover new aspects or other angles of the situation. So you add new items, reorganize or discard old material. In some sense, a rich picture is never 'finished'. It will remain a central point of reference during the entire project and a useful reminder for all involved, even after moving on to other things.

Naturally, you can only give your perception of the situation. Hence, be aware that it will be affected by your Weltanschauung. However, you will need to remind yourself as you proceed to keep an open mind, avoid introducing preconceived ideas, refrain from imposing an assumed structure on the situation or viewing it as 'the problem of ...'. The latter is particularly important since other people involved with the situation may each see a different aspect of the situation as 'the problem' to be analyzed. At this point, you do not want to commit the analysis unwittingly into a given direction before you have gained a full understanding of the complexity and crucial interrelationships. All of this is easily said, but more difficult to stick to. We all have a natural tendency to classify problem situations and give them a name. It gives the illusion 'of having the situation under control'. For example, consider truancy at primary school or at high school. 'Oh this is simply a problem of lack of discipline in the home!' The 'problem' has been labelled and hence 'solved' — end of discussion. Taking such a view will severely narrow our focus of attention. It may lead us to overlook the social complexity of truancy and effective means to limit its adverse effects on both the truant, the family, and society.

Most importantly, a rich picture — diagram or concept — is not a system description. The term system implies that any interconnectedness is organized and not coincidental. By assuming such organized interconnections you may impose a structure on the situation which may not be present or, if present, focuses your attention in a given direction, rather than encouraging you to keep a completely open mind. Only once you have identified the aspect of the situation of particular interest to you, or the issue to be analyzed, will you be ready to define a system relevant for that aspect or issue.

Expressing a problem situation in the form of a rich picture diagram is obviously only one mode of making a situation summary. In some instances, a different mode, such as a flow diagram of either material, documents, or information may be more instructive to capture the essence of the situation. For example, a manufacturing operation may best be captured by a flow diagram depicting how material moves from work station to work station, the tasks performed at each station, the quality inspection points, the locations where data are collected about the processes, etc. It may be supplemented by notes about difficulties encountered at various work stations and various options suggested for alleviating them.

4.2 GUIDELINES FOR DRAWING RICH PICTURE DIAGRAMS

There are three major components of the situation represented in a rich picture:

(1) **Elements of structure:** These are all aspects or components of the situation that are all relatively stable or change only very slowly in the time frame implied in the situation. This would include all physical aspects and components, like physical structure, buildings and equipment, and products involved, but also logical, functional, or intellectual structural aspects, like properties of physical and logical components, departmental divisions, information and data, rules of how things should be done, or services rendered.

(2) **Elements of process:** These are aspects of the situation that undergo change or are in a state of flux, like activities that go on within the structure, flow and processing of material or information, and any decision making that goes on.

(3) **Relationship between structure and process and between processes:** How does the structure affect or condition process? How does one process affect or condition other processes? What things or aspects are direct or indirect results of such relationships? For example, if all information on aircraft flight schedules and reservations is stored in each airline's own individual computer data bank (a structure), then booking a flight (a process) necessitates that the customer deals through a travel agent who has access to all these data banks and not just some, or else the flight choice may be drastically reduced.

For human activity systems, the rich picture should include not only 'hard' facts, but also 'soft' facts. Hard facts are the physical structure and processes, data records and their statistical interpretation, information links, anything which is of an 'objective' nature. Soft facts include opinions, gossip, hunches, interpersonal relationships (friendships, hostilities, power, egos) coming to the surface, perceived agendas and sacred cows, synergies, and symbiotic relationships — or what could broadly be called 'the climate' of the situation. This climate is often an important determinant of the various world views held by the people involved in the situation. Unless the climate is sufficiently well understood, essential aspects of these world views may escape the analyst.

All known areas of concern, actual or potential issues or problems should also be shown. This can be done in a number of ways. One is to use the focus symbol of Figure 4-1 pointing at the area of concern. Another is to show a balloon, coming out from an area of concern or a human, containing a question or a short slogan with a questions mark or an exclamation mark. If opposing values, or benefits versus costs have to be weighed, this can be depicted by scales with the baskets containing appropriate words, possibly with a question mark at the top of the scales. Opposing or conflicting views by various people involved can easily be shown by two crossed swords.

The rich picture should also be annotated to define symbols that are not self-explanatory or provide brief footnotes on why certain aspects are excluded or represented only in a cursory way, etc. It may also be interesting and revealing to indicate where you enter into the picture, your interest or role.

The rich picture is basically never finished. As the study progresses, it is updated, enhanced, and amended to reflect new aspects learned or discovered about the problem situation.

4.3 RICH PICTURE FOR 'A PIECE OF SKY IS MISSING'

I now ask you to read the article 'A piece of the sky is missing' by the famous scientist Carl Sagan, reprinted as the Appendix to this chapter, and then return to this section. Although written in 1988, the issues raised are as pressing now as then. In fact, in October 1993 the British Antarctic Research station reported that the hole in the ozone layer over the Antarctic is the deepest yet, with 67% of the ozone destroyed. Nor is this only a Southern Hemisphere problem. Decreases of over 15% have been measured at certain times over far wider areas in the Northern Hemisphere.

First, who is the person looking at the situation? In any real-life problem, this is known. It is usually an analyst, asked to investigate certain aspects of the situation. For 'the ozone hole' it is you and me. Our purpose is to practice systems thinking. We might wish to gain some insights into particular aspects of the situation. This is a perfectly legitimate reason. The most common reason for studying a situation is to come up with some recommendations as to what action should be taken to achieve a certain objective and by whom.

The structural aspects of our situation are given by the current make-up and properties of the Earth's atmosphere, the composition and intensity of the sun's rays reaching the ozone layer in the stratosphere, the Earth surface, the location of the major producers of ozone destroying chemicals, the current major users and uses, and ownership of both producers and users and their employees.

The processes are given by the production of these chemicals, the release into the atmosphere through their use, the release of chlorine through natural processes, the ascent of these chemicals to the ozone layer in the stratosphere and the effects of the prevailing weather patterns on this process, the chemical reaction between them and the ozone, the influx of sun rays and the effect of UV light on living organisms on the Earth's surface and oceans, including humankind, as well as the activities of environmental lobbies, inter- and intra-governmental agencies, the research activities into the effects of these chemicals and the development of safe possible substitutes.

The relationships between structure and process or between processes are given by the rate of destruction of ozone in the stratosphere, etc., the weakening of the food chain, the increase in the rate of cancers, the effect on employment, both in terms of production and industrial uses, of reducing and ultimately abandoning the use of these chemicals, the threat to the health and development of underdeveloped countries if they are deprived of the use of these cheap chemicals without giving them free access to replacement technology, and their reaction to any such moves, the threat to the standard of living of developed countries, etc.

My version of the rich picture for 'the ozone hole' is depicted in Figure 4-2. Note how effective it is to convey a surprisingly accurate and complete picture of the various aspects of this situation and this in spite of its primitive artistic style. In fact, even without any commentator explaining the contents of the rich picture, it can be 'read' like cartoon strip.

The areas of concern and potential issues are shown in various ways, like the human skull, the person calling 'stop', the balloon with the words 'any safer?', etc.

There is no single right version for a rich picture. Naturally we would expect that any well-understood physical process depicted reflects the prevailing theories. But beyond that, different analysts with different social, educational, and cultural backgrounds, training, and world views, will emphasize different aspects of the problematic situation. They may also select a different level of resolution, i.e., show the various aspects at a different level of detail.

4.4 SOME COMMON MISTAKES WHEN DRAWING RICH PICTURES

Some novices mistakenly believe that each item pictured needs to be connected to one or more other items. They end up with a picture where every item is connected directly or indirectly to every other item. Some arrows between some items are useful to indicate relationships, such as cause-and-effect, symbioses, precedence, or processes. However, excessive use of arrows may inadvertently impose a system structure on the rich picture. Remember again, a rich picture is not a system description.

If your rich picture looks like a flowchart, depicting the flow of documents, information, or material (see Figure 13-12 in Chapter 13 for an example), or a prece-

Figure 4-2: A rich picture diagram for the ozone hole

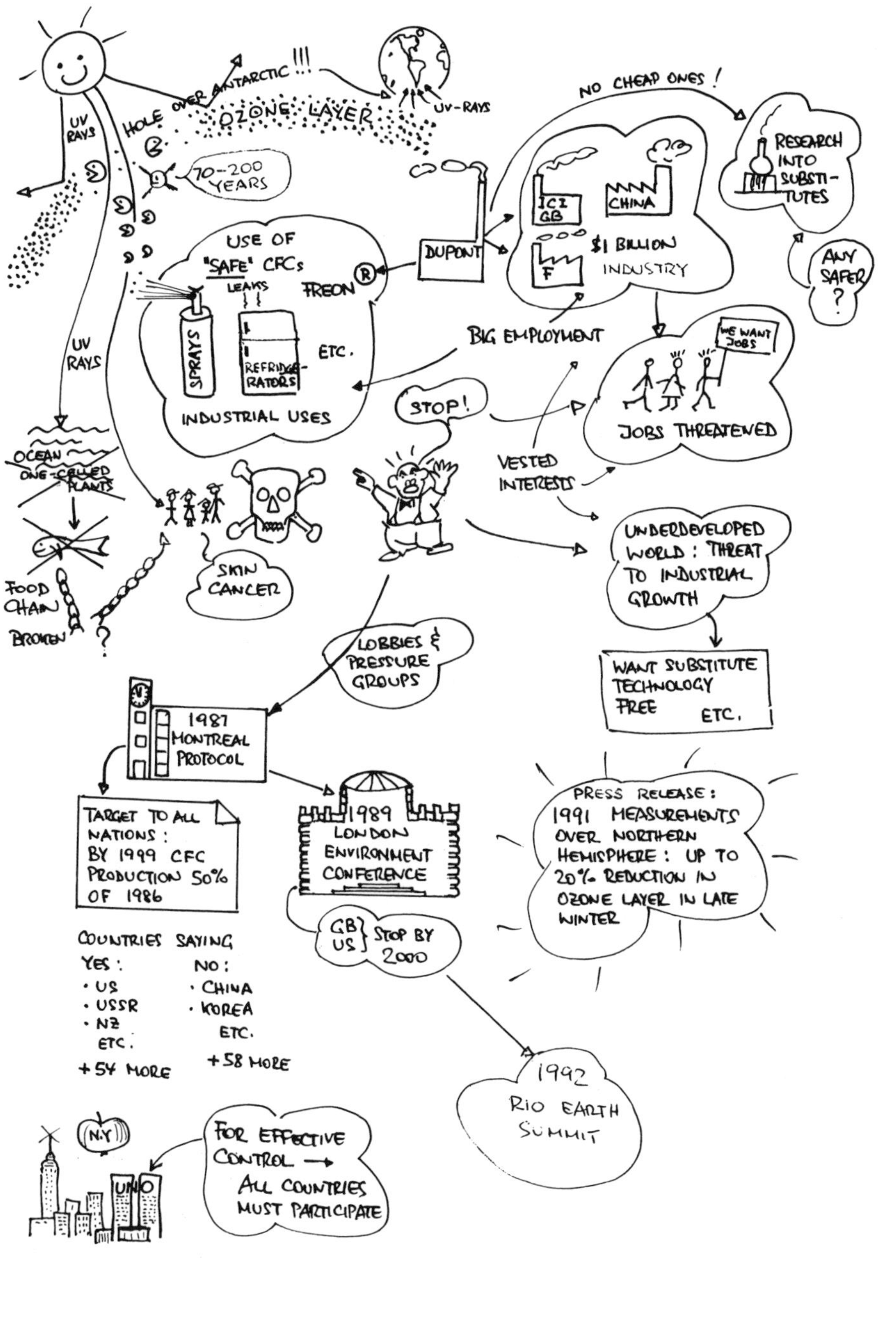

dence diagram of how activities have to be executed (see Figure 4-4 for an example), or like a flowchart of the decision process, you may again have imposed a system structure on it. There could well be some aspects of the problem situation which call for a flow chart of some sort. However, such aspects are usually only one part of the problem situation. For example, the central part of the rich picture in Figure 5-2 of Chapter 5 depicts the flow of material from the refinery, through the mixing and filling plants, to the warehouse, and finally on to the customer. There are, however, many other aspects that show managerial concerns, provide other important information about the situation, or sketch statistical data.

Beginners also tend to neglect including pointers that indicate potential issues. It is important that these are clearly highlighted in one of the ways listed earlier.

4.5 THE USES OF RICH PICTURES

Rich pictures are an ideal vehicle for communicating with other people about complex and problematic situations. The initial reaction of many analysts to rich pictures is one of scepticism. 'Cartoons have no place in serious analysis!' Give the rich picture a chance! You will discover that precisely because they are unconventional, unexpected, and a fun tool, they are more likely to catch and retain your listeners' attention and interest — in fact, have them become active participants.

Interconnections, relationships, and direct and indirect consequences become more clearly visible; understanding is considerably enhanced. Since the whole picture is constantly present, references to aspects previously discussed do not have to rely on the listener's memory, but can be directly pointed out or referred back to. Listener queries can also refer to the picture and hence will be more focused and more precise. Misunderstandings are reduced. Missing aspects become more obvious.

It allows identification of the people who own the problematic situation, the people in positions of power, such as the decision makers, the people who will execute any decisions taken, and the people who will enjoy the benefits or suffer the consequences of the results. It pinpoints the sources and types of data. But most importantly, it will help identify existing or potential issues, conflicts, and problems. It may point out that the particular issue that gave rise to drawing up a rich picture is embedded in other areas of concern that may have to be resolved before the original issue can be tackled. Sometimes, particularly in a learning context, a rich picture is drawn simply to gain a better understanding of a complex situation as a whole. However, more often, the rich picture constitutes the first step towards analyzing a particular issue. It will firm up the choice of the problem to be studied. It will show that problem within its complete context. This will help in selecting the boundaries of the problem and its scope.

With the issue or problem identified, we can then proceed to the next step — defining a relevant system within which the problem exists.

4.6 APPROACHES FOR DESCRIBING A RELEVANT SYSTEM

Why do we need to describe clearly a relevant system for the problem identified for further study? A system description identifies all relevant components, including the structural and process relationships in which the problem is embedded. These will form the basis for building an appropriate formal representation or model for studying and manipulating the problem situation of interest to the analyst. That model constitutes the core of any OR/MS analysis. A careful and sufficiently detailed and complete system description will go a long way towards guaranteeing that all important structural and process relationships are properly taken into account and represented in that model.

A system description consists in specifying

(a) the **transformation process(es)** or activities of the system;

(b) the **boundary** of the system, i.e., what is inside the system — the narrow system of interest — and what makes up its environment or the wider system of interest;

(c) the **components** and **subsystems** of the narrow system of interest, and the stable relationships between them or the **structure**;

(d) the **inputs** into the system from the environment; and

(e) the **outputs** of the system, desired and undesired , planned and unplanned ones.

How should we go about this task? There are two approaches: identifying and fitting an appropriate known basic structure (a structural approach) or analyzing the processes in the system and defining a suitable structure from first principles (a process approach).

A Structural Approach

The issue chosen for detailed study may strongly suggest a typical structure usually found for situations of that sort. For instance, the issue may be the excessive length of time that the customers of a given bank may have to wait for service. This immediately suggests a 'waiting line' structure, as depicted in Figure 4-3, with customers arriving randomly at a service facility, joining the queue in front of the servers, advancing in the queue by one position each time a customer ahead of them has been served, until it is their turn to be served by the next server who becomes free. The system transforms customers in need of service into customers served.

In a waiting line structure the components of the system are the customers waiting in line and the server(s). The structure of the system is given by the manner in which customers pass through the system. After arriving, they wait in line in front of the service facility, i.e., join the queue, are served by the server(s) in a specified sequence or priority, such as first-come first-served, and then depart from the system. The processes are given by the random arrivals of customers from a given 'population' in the environment, the gradual advancement of customers towards

Figure 4-3: Waiting line structure

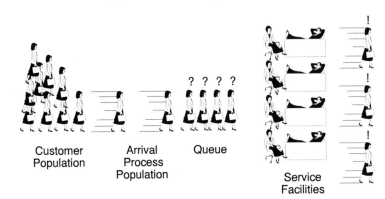

Customer   Arrival   Queue
Population   Process
                Population

                                            Service
                                            Facilities

the front of the queue, and the service activity where both a customer and a server are engaged jointly — a transient relationship. Customer arrivals constitute the inputs into the system. These arrivals obey a given (assumed) known arrival pattern, such as each arrival being independent of all other arrivals and completely random. Once 'arrived', each customer becomes a temporary component of the system. Customer departures are the outputs of the system. Typical performance measures of the system that we may wish to observe are the average waiting time of customers in the queue and the average time the servers are idle.

Using a known basic structure allows fast progress towards a complete system description. Once the basic structure has been identified, the analyst will immediately know which aspects of the situation form the narrow system of interest and which ones are part of the environment, the type of components to look for, the usual relationships between them, the underlying processes, and the usual inputs and outputs of the system, the type of input data needed, and suitable system perform-ance evaluators. The analyst will also have a fair idea which quantitative tools are most appropriate for analyzing the situation. He or she may in fact have access to commercial computer codes or packages specifically written for such problems.

A structural approach is clearly the preferred way to go if the situation is well understood and the Weltanschauung implied by the system performance evaluators of the typical structure chosen fits fairly closely to the one identified in the rich picture. However, for situations with some degree of ambiguity, there is the serious risk that the issue is 'forced' into an inappropriate structure.

A structural approach also presupposes that the analyst is sufficiently familiar with the most common basic structures encountered in systems, and this not simply on a theoretical level, but also through practical experience. The theoretical know-ledge can be acquired through university OR/MS courses. Since you are presumably more of a novice rather than an experienced analyst, this text will put more emphasis on the process approach for defining the relevant system from first principles, in preference to a structural approach.

The experienced analyst, on the other hand, will very quickly be able to recognize which known structure, if any, is an appropriate system description for the problem to be analyzed. If none can be identified, even the experienced analyst will have to fall back on a process approach.

A Process Approach

Here, no assumptions about the possible structure of the problem situation are made. Rather, the observed processes and relationships of interest between the various components of the system are used to discover a good structure for the system. The Weltanschauung dictates which system performance evaluators are to be observed. Often several different possible structures may be suitable. This approach is more challenging, but also more difficult.

What is the best way to go about it? A good starting point is to define the prime transformation process of the system. This points to what inputs the system uses, what outputs it provides, and what system components participate in the transformation process. The following four rules help in identifying the components, the inputs, both uncontrollable and controllable, and the outputs of the system:

(1) Any aspect that affects the system, but in turn is not significantly affected by it, is an input from the environment of the system.

(2) Any aspect that is directly or indirectly affected or controlled by the system, but in turn does not affect any other aspect of the system, is a system output.

(3) Any entity that is either part of the system's structure or its transformation process(es) is a component of the system, unless it is an output of the system. Similarly, if the system or any of its components affects an entity or exercises control over it, then that entity is a component, unless it is a system output.

(4) Any aspect that does not affect the system, or is not affected by it, or not part of its structure or transformation process is irrelevant, and can be ignored.

By rules 1 and 2 there should be no feedback loops between the system and its environment. All aspects in such a feedback loop, except control and data inputs into the feedback control mechanism, should be contained within the system. Any transactions across the system boundary are therefore either inputs or outputs. By rule 3 all entities which are under the control of the system are system components, unless they are in fact system outputs.

These four rules suffer from a bit of circularity. Although this may be undesirable from a purist's point of view, it is of little practical consequence. The real question is 'Is it helpful for identifying the relevant system?'. Most of the circularity can be avoided by identifying all system outputs, including performance measures, first. The application of rule 3 will then not be ambiguous.

Naturally, in the real world things may not be as clear-cut as assumed by these four rules. A given aspect may affect the system only marginally. Similarly, the control may be only partial. The recurrent question is therefore 'At what point does such influence or control become a significant factor that should be taken into account?' If time and funds allow it, the prudent analyst will include rather more than less. If it turns out that the relationship is negligible, it can always be discarded later on.

A simple, effective way of finding out whether an aspect is irrelevant or only marginal relevant is to look at the opposite or absence of that aspect. If it does not change the relevant system definition or its relevant inputs, then that aspect can be ignored.

Section 4.8 uses a process approach to define a system for the ozone hole.

Enriching Parts of the Rich Picture

There is not a one-to-one correspondence between the items shown in the rich picture and the system description. As we have seen, the rich picture does not, indeed should not describe a system. Furthermore, the rich picture may not show the fine detail that is needed for developing a system description. Indeed, once the issue or problem has been identified, the analyst will usually have to fill in additional details, i.e., enrich or blow up the relevant part of the rich picture. This filling-in may call for additional highly focused research into the problem, visits to the 'facilities', and interviews with the people involved. The processes of enriching the rich picture and refining the system description will often be done hand-in-hand — one feeding into the other and vice versa.

4.7 SYSTEM MODELS

At this stage it is useful to remind ourselves that the system description we come up with is an abstract mental construct. It is not the real thing. We call this con-ceptualization **a model**. The activity of building a model is referred to as **systems modeling**.

The word 'model' has many meanings. The one of interest to us now is described in *Webster's Ninth New Collegiate Dictionary* as 'a description or analogy used to help visualize something ... that cannot be directly observed.' This seems to be exactly what we do when defining a system.

A model may be **iconic**, **symbolic**, or **analogous**. Iconic models are reproduc-tions of physical objects, usually to a different scale and with less detail. A car model, or the small-scale aircraft tested in a wind tunnel for the aerodynamics of the real thing, are both iconic models.

Symbolic Models

Symbolic models are representations of the relationships between various entities or concepts by means of symbols. By the time you reached tertiary education, you had encountered and been bombarded with thousands of all sorts of symbolic models: newspapers, magazines, school books in the form of graphs, depicting how a given variable varies as a function of another variable, such as the number of unemployed over time, or statistical charts, such as a pie chart or a bar chart, demonstrating the composition of various aspects of life, like how the Government spends the tax dollars collected. But a geographic map, the hierarchical chart of command of an organization, showing who reports to whom, a flow diagram depicting how material or information flow through an organization, or a diagram depicting the sequence of decisions that need to be made, are all examples of symbolic models. Such models are extensively used for communicating all sorts of data and information.

Symbolic models also turn out to be highly effective means for systematically exploring certain types of decision making situations, as you will discover in a number of subsequent chapters. An example of this — not covered further in this text — is the precedence chart in Figure 4-4. It depicts the sequence in which a complex collection of 26 activities for the construction of a building has to be performed. It shows for instance that once the detailed plans have been drawn up (block 1), an application for a building permit can be prepared and lodged (block 2), while simultaneously steps to finalize all financial arrangements are made (block 3). Task 1 is the predecessor of tasks 2 and 3. Task 2 in turn has to be completed before task 4 (prepare building site). Note that task 10 (erect wall framing) has both task 7 and task 9 as predecessors.

Such precedence diagrams are essential planning tools for any projects that involve a sequence of tasks over time. If the individual task times are also listed in the diagram, it contains all the information needed to determine the earliest time the entire project can be completed.   Critical path scheduling — an MS/OR tool developed in the early 60s — deals with the analysis of such situations. It has found widespread application in the construction industry, in space exploration, in planning exhibitions, the launch of new products, or the shift into new premises, and so on.

Mathematical Models

Another type of symbolic model extensively used in OR/MS is the mathematical model, where the relationships between entities are expressed in the form of mathematical expressions, like functions, equations, and inequalities. You all have come across the mathematical expression for the distance s a free falling object travels in t seconds: $s = 0.5gt^2$, where g is the constant of gravity. This is a mathematical model, although your high school teachers may not have called it that.

Finally, analog models are representations which substitute the properties or features of what is modeled by alternative means such that the model is able to mimic whatever aspect of the real thing is of interest to the modeler. For instance, the constantly updated picture that an air traffic controller observes on a radar monitor is an analog of the air traffic in a given sector of the air space.

In this book we are mainly interested in symbolic models, either diagrammatic

Figure 4-4: A precedence diagram for construction project

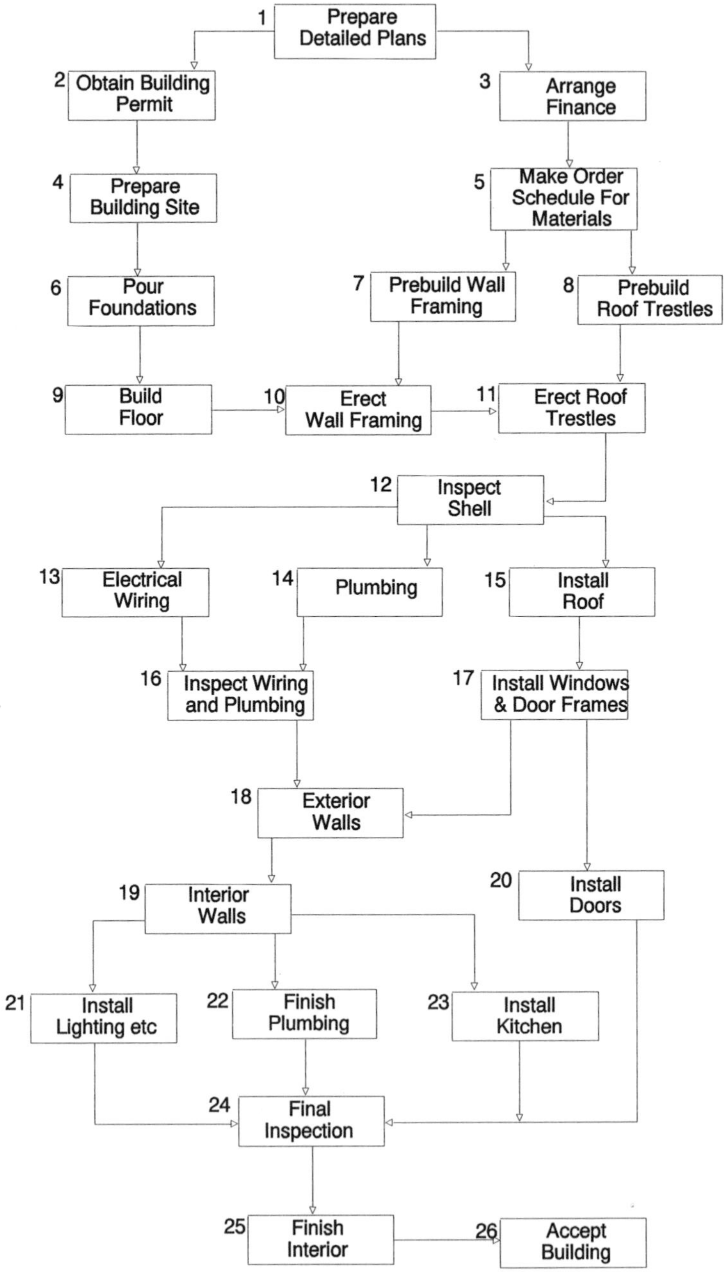

or mathematical, although our first attempt at any symbolic modeling is always in the form of a conceptual model — a mental picture of some object, system, or process. What we call 'experience' is largely a huge memory bank of mental models to which we add new ones daily. This is what allows us to recognize a car, when we see one, and not mistake it for a rubbish container, although closer inspection of what people keep in their cars often makes me wonder whether many cars are in fact used as rubbish containers. A verbal description of a system is also a conceptual model.

Models as Approximations

As Webster's definition states, a model is only a partial representation of reality. It will contain various approximations, some of little, others of great consequence. However, it is essential that the analyst carefully records the form of the approximations made. There are two major reasons for this: one is to insure that any user of the model is aware of its limitations, the other that the effect of these approximations can be explored if this is possible.

The type of approximation made will reflect the training, experience, and personality of the analyst, the resources, particularly in terms of time and funds, available, as well as the purpose of the study. There is always a degree of arbitrariness present Hence, there may be several good models for the same system. However, any model that claims to be a valid representation of the systemic content of a problem must fully specify the boundary of the system, the system's components and structure, its processes, its inputs, and its outputs, as listed at the beginning of Section 4.6.

We are now ready to develop a relevant system for some aspect of the ozone hole from first principles.

4.8 A RELEVANT SYSTEM FOR 'THE OZONE HOLE'

There are a number of potential issues I could choose for further study: (1) the actual process of the ozone hole formation over the Antarctic and its life cycle; (2) the global process of ozone depletion; (3) the environmental effects of global ozone depletion; (4) the world-wide socioeconomic and sociopolitical relationships of gradually abandoning the use of the ozone-destroying chemicals and the issue of international cooperation to 'solve' the problem. I will arbitrarily select the second one for defining a relevant system for further analysis. My objective is gaining a clearer understanding of what is currently known about the process of global ozone depletion. Although it was 'the ozone hole' over the Antarctic that triggered the global concern, in the late 80s and early 90s it has become clear that a similar process is also occurring in the Northern Hemisphere.

The first step is to ascertain my Weltanschauung. My aim is to learn about this process. So the core of my Weltanschauung is 'Learning is useful'. I am also quite concerned about the environment, maybe even the survival of life on Earth in essentially its current form. However, at this point I do not want these concerns to influence my way of looking at this system. Being aware of such aspects and values helps in preventing that they unknowingly bias my system description.

A Verbal Model for the Ozone Depletion System

Here is the description of my mental model for the global depletion of the ozone layer. Most of it is devoted to describing the transformation processes. About one million tonnes of chlorofluorocarbons (CFCs) are produced annually worldwide, adding to the stocks of CFCs in use. Through use, such as for solvents, creation of plastic foam, aerosol propellants, refrigeration, etc., CFCs are released into the atmosphere. Over a period of one to two years, the CFC molecules end up in the ozone layer of the stratosphere. Under the effect of uv-light, CFC molecules gradually break up, releasing chlorine atoms. The average time the CFC molecules survive is about 70 years. The chlorine atoms act as catalysts to destroy ozone molecules, creating ordinary oxygen molecules. This process seems to be highly influenced by unique meteorological conditions over the polar regions during Winter and early Spring. The chlorine atoms will ultimately combine with hydrogen, but only after having assisted in the destruction of about 100,000 ozone molecules first. On the other hand, new ozone is constantly being created under the effect of uv-light passing through the upper levels of the atmosphere, known as the mesosphere. However, from what we know currently, the ozone destruction is progressing faster than the ozone replenishment, resulting in a gradual depletion of the ozone layer. This depletion is particularly pronounced in late Winter/early Spring in the polar regions, producing the 'ozone hole' over the Antarctic (and a severe thinning of the ozone layer in the Northern region of the Northern hemisphere). Under the influence of air turbulence, the ozone hole gradually breaks up in Spring and dilutes ozone levels throughout a large portion of the stratosphere. Finally, the amount of uv-light that reaches the earth's surface increases as the amount of ozone in the atmosphere decreases. This could have serious consequences for life on earth.

I chose to include that last effect as part of the system description. It is this aspect which ultimately is of particular interest and consequence to all life on earth. However, in a narrow sense it already goes beyond the ozone depletion process. Another observer might have chosen to exclude it from the narrow system of interest

All of the processes listed, like the decay of CFC under the influence of uv-light, are in fact complex subsystems. If I were interested in the actual chemical interactions of the depletion process, I would have to do considerable detailed research into atmospheric chemistry and meteorological science. At this point I do not see the need to model these processes in more detail. The information collected to draw the rich picture is sufficient. Note also that all these processes happen over time. So time is an aspect of the system description. Furthermore, the current structure of the atmosphere forms the stable relationship basis for this system.

Summary Definition of Relevant System

Before proceeding to a formal system definition it is useful to summarize the verbal systems description by one or two concise sentences. This summary definition should at a minimum state what the system does, i.e., its transformation process or major activity, and its major inputs and outputs, including the prime performance measure. This helps to keep the analyst better focused. I choose the following summary definition for the global ozone depletion system:

> 'A system for how the ozone layer in the stratosphere is gradually destroyed through the continued release of CFCs into the atmosphere, allowing a greater fraction of the sun's uv-rays to reach the earth's surface.'

The destruction of the ozone layer is the major system activity. The release of CFCs and the sun's uv-light are the major system inputs, while the uv-light reaching the earth's surface is the major system output, as well as its performance measure.

A System Description for the Ozone Depletion Problem

Table 4-1 shows the various aspects and items mentioned in the verbal description and classifies them as system structure, transformation processes, components, inputs, and outputs, using the four rules listed in Section 4.6.

Table 4-1: Identifying system aspects for the ozone depletion problem

Aspect or item	Rule used	Identification
CFC production	1	input (uncontrollable)
uv-light on earth surface	2	output
CFC in use	3	component
Composition and make-up of atmosphere	3	structure
Chemical properties of gases	3	structure
Atmospheric weather conditions	1	input (uncontrollable)
Influx of uv-light from sun	1	input (uncontrollable)
CFC release process	3	subsystem (process)
CFC in stratosphere	3	component
CFC decay process	3	subsystem (process)
Chlorine in stratosphere	3	component
Ozone destruction process	3	subsystem (process)
Ozone in stratosphere	3	component
Chlorine destruction process	3	subsystem (process)
Ozone formation in mesosphere	3	subsystem (process)
uv-light absorption by ozone	3	subsystem (process)
Breaking up of the ozone hole	4	irrelevant
Effect on life on earth	4	irrelevant

I will demonstrate the use of these rules for some items listed. CFC production affects the system, but is not affected by the system. Hence, by rule 1 it is a system input — in fact, a physical system input. The amount of uv-light reaching the earth's surface is affected by the system, but does not affect the system in return (at least in a narrow sense). Hence, by rule 2 it is a system output. CFC in use plays a pivotal part in the CFC release process which is one of the transformation processes of the system. Hence, by rule 3 it is a system component. So are all other relevant gases in the atmosphere interacting in the ozone depletion process directly or indirectly.

The structure of this system consists of the relatively stable physical composition and make-up of the atmosphere and the chemical properties of its gases. The links between these gases in various forms, such as the CFC in use and the CFC in the stratosphere, and their chemical reactions under the influence of uv-light and specific meteorological conditions, such as the decay of CFC molecules into chlorine atoms and other compounds, are the transformation processes over time. They are:

- The release of CFCs into the atmosphere, linking CFC stocks in use with CFC in the atmosphere.

- The decay of CFC molecules and release of chlorine atoms, linking CFC in the atmosphere with chlorine in the atmosphere.

- The destruction of ozone by chlorine atoms, linking ozone levels over time.

- The decay of chlorine atoms, linking chlorine levels over time.

- The creation of ozone in the mesosphere, linking uv-light influx from the sun with ozone levels in the atmosphere.

- The absorption of uv-light by the ozone layer.

Each of these processes is in fact a system in itself. For this reason I show them as subsystems.

In both the verbal systems description and the identification of its components I have made a number of approximations. For instance, I lumped together all CFC in use. The various uses have substantially different characteristics. Some result in almost immediate release, as in spray cans. Others may contains the CFC relatively safely for years, as in refrigerators. If my intention is to use this model to make approximate global predictions about the ozone depletion over the next 100 years or so and I can assume that the current composition of uses remains fairly stable, then this approximation may well be good enough. On the other hand, if the composition of uses changes substantially, say under the influence of a world-wide switch to different technologies and extensive recovery of CFC in use, then I may have to represent the major types of uses individually.

The ozone depletion system is in turn one of several subsystems embedded in a much larger containing system in a hierarchy of systems. The environmental chain of effects is another such subsystem, one of whose inputs is the amount of uv-light reaching the earth's surface — the output of my narrow system of interest. The containing system would also include the socioeconomic infrastructure of CFC production and its various industrial, commercial, and home uses. Going up the hierarchy, it in turn is embedded in an international sociopolitical system.

As a novice, you may find the exercise of compiling such a complete list difficult and sometimes confusing. With some experience, it becomes easier. In fact, the experienced analyst may never formally compile such a list. It is only kept implicitly in her or his mind. However, the novice should not be tempted to skip it. It is a valuable aid towards making sure that all relevant aspects of the system have been taken into account and the relationships between components and the structural framework in which they occur are properly understood.

Rather than define all relevant aspects of the system using the four rules, you may find it easier to do it only after having completed the next step, namely drawing an influence diagram for the system modeled. This is the topic of the next section.

4.9 INFLUENCE DIAGRAMS

As a rich picture diagram is able to convey the complexities of an unstructured situation more effectively than prose, so can various diagrammatic representations help in clarifying both structure and process for many systems. We have already seen a precedence diagram in Figure 4-4. A **decision diagram** is another type of diagram particularly useful for depicting the detailed steps of a decision making process, involving open-loop as well as feedback control mechanisms, of a quantitative as well as qualitative nature.

We will find **influence diagrams** particularly insightful for bringing out the transformation process of the system in terms of the structural and causal relationships between systems components. Influence diagrams share some similarities with the cause-and-effect diagrams used in systems dynamics, a methodology developed by Forrester in the 60s for the study of the dynamic behaviour of complex systems with lagged feedback and feed forward loops [J. Forrester, *Industrial Dynamics*, MIT Press, 1969]. Their use here is more inspired by Eden's concepts [C. Eden, et al., *Messing about in Problems*, Macmillan, 1983].

An influence diagram depicts the influence relationships (a) between the inputs into a system and its components, (b) between the components of the system, and (c) between the components and the outputs of the system, including system performance measures. In OR/MS projects, these influence relationships can usually be measured in quantitative terms. For example, a given density of the ozone layer filters out a given fraction of the uv-light reaching the mesosphere. However, influence diagrams are equally effective for depicting non-quantitative relationships, such as the presence of virgin forests increasing the enjoyment experienced by tourists visiting an area, or the severity of pain suffered by a patient affecting the timing of the relieving surgery required.

If the system's processes lend themselves to being captured quantitatively, a

Figure 4-5: Influence diagrams

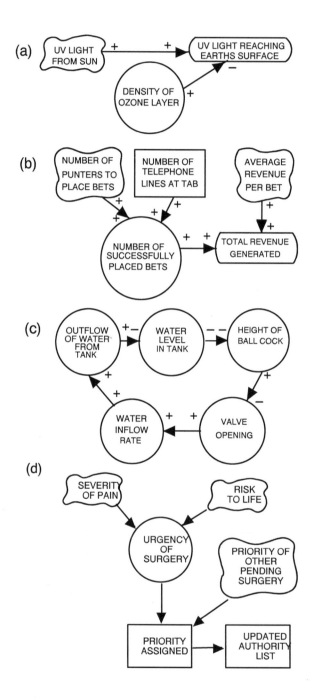

systems component is usually represented by its corresponding state variable(s) or other numerical measures in the form of **time integrated averages** or the **cumulative sum** of state variable values over time. Rather than being a simple average of observed values, for a time integrated average each observed value is weighted by the relative length of time the system holds that value. We shall refer to the representation in the influence diagram of systems components or their associated state variables as **system variables**. Each one gives rise to a separate element. A system variable is always affected by inputs, controls, or/and other system variables. Hence, it does not 'appear' by itself.

Figure 4-5 shows four examples. The volume of uv-light that reaches the mesosphere from the sun (an uncontrollable input into the ozone depletion system) and the density of the ozone layer (the state variable associated with the ozone in the stratosphere) jointly affect the amount of uv-light that reaches the earth's surface (an output of the system). This is depicted in Part (a) of Figure 4-5. Note that the state variable for the ozone density would have some arrows leading into it.

Part (b) looks at parts of the transformation process in a telephone betting system. The number of punters who wish to place telephone bets during a certain interval of time (an uncontrollable input into the telephone betting system) together with the number of phone lines rented (a controllable input into the system) affect the number of punters who place bets successfully (the system variable for the punters in the system), which in turn, together with the average revenue generated by telephone bets (a data input into the system) determines the total revenue generated (a performance measure of the system). Part (c) depicts the feedback influence relationship in a system to control the level in a water tank. Finally, Part (d) shows an example of qualitative relationships. The decision on the level of priority to be assigned to a new patient is influenced by the urgency of the surgery for the new patient (a system variable) and the priority assignments made for all other pending surgery (an input). The urgency of surgery, in turn, is affected by the severity of pain suffered by the new patient and the risk to life, both inputs.

The arrows indicate the direction of the influence relationships. However, they do not show the strength of the relationships. Referring to the diagram in part (c), the outflow from the tank lowers the water level. But the diagram is not intended to tell us by how much, i.e., it does not indicate the exact quantitative relationship between these two variables.

Influence diagrams can easily depict feedback loops in the transformation process, such as in part (c), which are part of the dynamic aspects present in the system.

Notational Conventions

A **cloud** depicts an uncontrollable or a data input from the environment or the wider system. The arrival pattern of punters who wish to place bets is such an uncontrollable input. The average revenue for bets placed is a data input. Such inputs can be deterministic, e.g., they are equal to a known constant like the unit purchase price for a given type of log, or follow a given known pattern, like the flight arrival pattern at an airport. The inputs may fluctuate or vary in an unpredictable way, like the actual number of punters that will call in between 4 and 5 p.m. next Saturday just prior to the race scheduled at Auckland. The input is not known with certainty, but is random. Random inputs are flagged by a tilde shown above the input. By the definition of an input, a cloud can only have arrows leading away from it.

A control input is denoted by a **rectangle**. System variables for system components are shown as **circles**, while system outputs and system performance measures are shown as **ovals**. Any system variable, system output, or performance measure influenced by a random input will also be random, and so will all other system variables and system outputs farther down that influence chain. A circle needs at least one arrow leading to it and one arrow leading away from it. Ovals can only have incoming arrows. A rectangle standing for a control input will only have arrows leading away from it, while a rectangle standing for a feedback control mechanism will have both incoming and outgoing arrows.

The amount of information contained in the diagram can be enhanced by indicating whether the influence relationship is positive, an increase (decrease) in the influencing variable leading to an increase (decrease) in the influenced variable, or negative, an increase in the influencing variable leading to a decrease in the influenced variable and vice-versa. This can be shown by attaching plus or minus signs to the issue and destination points of the arrows. For example, an increase in the amount of water in the tank (+) increases the height of the float (+), while an increase in the height of the float (+) decreases the opening in the valve (−).

Influence diagrams are not intended to show the flow of material or information between various components of a system, or the various steps of a decision process, nor are they precedence charts indicating the sequence in which certain activities have to be performed (like in Figure 4-4), unless these features naturally coincide with the influence chain. They only depict in detail what affects what — the chain of impacts from controllable and uncontrollable inputs via state variables to system output and performance measures. Presented with an influence diagram, an analyst should be able to describe the system model that underlies the transformation process from system inputs, uncontrollable and controllable, to system outputs. He or she should be able to make statements of the form 'system variable X is a function of or affected by input variable A and/or control input P and/or system variable Y.' Without further analysis, this description can only be qualitative. However, as we shall see in Chapter 6, an influence diagram is an ideal starting point for developing a quantitative model of the transformation process.

Like rich pictures, they allow the exploration of complexity in a system. As mentioned earlier, an influence diagram is often a very effective means to define a relevant system for the issue studied. In such instances it can thus be used as a substitute for a more formal system definition using the four-rule scheme described in the previous section. Although we shall see in Chapter 6 that drawing an influence diagram is a helpful first step for building a mathematical model, influence diagrams are also a useful diagrammatic aid for depicting qualitative relationships. Furthermore, influence diagrams facilitate and clarify the communication process between modelers, and between modelers and clients. However, there are situations where an influence diagram may not be a suitable vehicle for unambiguously and clearly bringing out the structure of a decision problem. Other diagrammatic aid, such as material flow diagrams, decision flow diagrams, precedence charts, or a simple schedule of the time sequence of events may be able to shed more light on the problem and its structure.

4.10 AN INFLUENCE DIAGRAM FOR THE OZONE DEPLETION SYSTEM

Figure 4-6 shows an influence diagram for the transformation process in the ozone depletion system. It represents my particular version. You may come up with a somewhat different version, possibly showing a higher degree of resolution with additional state variables. As long as the underlying structure of the process is the same, either one is a valid representation.

Figure 4-6: An influence diagram for ozone depletion

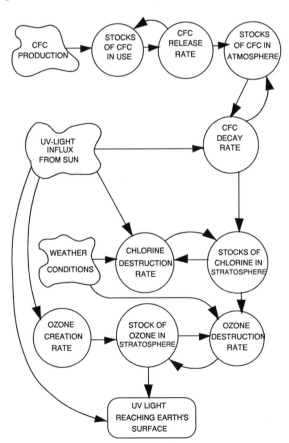

Note that I do not depict the passage of time explicitly. The whole system is shown as an ongoing process with activities occurring simultaneously everywhere.

The system does not include any decisions. In fact, the only aspect that is controllable in a wide sense is the production of CFCs, but the control is scattered over many producers. Hence, for a system modeling global ozone depletion, CFC production has the nature of an uncontrollable input. Obviously, we would most certainly wish to explore how global ozone depletion will be affected by changing the level of CFC production over time. To do this we would need to express all relationships between the variables in quantitative form.

The system variable associated with CFC in use is the 'stock level of CFC in use'. The system variable for the CFC release subsystem is the 'rate of CFC release', and so on.

The diagram contains four feedback loops. These also implicitly reflect the passage of time, or the dynamic aspects in this system. For example, the CFC stock in the atmosphere feeds the CFC decay subsystem. Its state variable is the rate of CFC release. The higher the stock level of CFC, the higher the release rate. But the latter in turn reduces the CFC stock. The uv-light absorption subsystem is not shown explicitly. It is subsumed by the fact that the amount of uv-light reaching the earth's surface is a function of both the uv-light influx from the sun and the density of the ozone layer.

A number of the inputs are in fact random. The production rate of CFC varies over time, so does the weather, and even the influx of uv-light from the sun. Similarly the various subsystem processes are not deterministic, but involve random effects. Hence, the system output is random. I have not shown this aspect explicitly, as it does not enhance the understanding of the transformation process depicted by the influence diagram in this case.

Note that there is a correspondence between the system description in Table 4-1 and the corresponding influence diagram in Figure 4-6. The influence diagram can thus be viewed as another way of describing the system. As pointed out at the end of Section 4.8, rather than identifying the various aspects of the system in an abstract manner, as in Table 4-1, you may find it easier to express the relevant system directly in the form of an influence diagram. The arrow connections represent the structure of the system, implied by the system's transformation process. The components are represented by system variables. Together with the system inputs and system outputs, all aspects of the system descriptions are depicted in the influence diagram.

4.11 THE NEXT PHASE — QUANTITATIVE MODELING

The influence diagram completes the description of the system. The next phase in studying the ozone depletion problem is to build a mathematical model to explore the behaviour of the system over, say, the next 100 years. The relationships shown in the influence diagram need to be translated into a mathematical form. It requires in-depth knowledge of the physical properties of the various processes involved. This is beyond the scope of this text. As an example, scientific analysis indicates that a decrease of 10% in the density of the ozone layer results in a 20% increase in the amount of uv-rays reaching the earth's surface.

The mathematical model in turn is programmed for a computer. This computer program is used to explore the behaviour of the system in response to various possible scenarios of phasing out the use of CFCs and other chlorine releasing products. These steps involve the use of fairly sophisticated computer simulation techniques. As of the time of writing this text, such models seem to indicate that, if the major manufacturing and user countries stick to the plans agreed upon at international conventions in the early 90s, the influx of uv-light in the heavily populated middle latitudes of the earth's surface would increase by about 12% by the year 2000 and then gradually return to the 1970 level by about 2050.

4.12 SOME CONCLUSIONS

As we have seen, how an analyst goes about describing the problem situation by a rich picture has a fair degree of arbitrariness — and so does her or his formal system description and its diagrammatic representation. All are strongly affected by the purpose of the analysis, the Weltanschauung of the analyst, and the resources (time, funds, people) available for the job. You should therefore not be surprised if different people may give very different descriptions of 'their system'. This disparity of views is to be expected and is perfectly valid. **There is no one unique right answer**. Any answer may only be judged as 'right' in the sense that it is derived in a logically correct way from the world view used by the analyst and is internally consistent.

In fact, it may be highly instructive to try several different system descriptions, differing in the level of resolution as well as possibly their assumed Weltanschauung. Such new ways of looking at the problem situation may provide additional insights that contribute towards a more comprehensive understanding of and more productive ways of dealing with the problem situation.

We developed this system description methodology as a first step towards building a mathematical model — a mathematical model which would guide us in either gaining a better understanding of or improving the performance of the system studied. However, the principles involved in defining a relevant system and depicting the influence relationships are also highly useful first steps for problem solving in general. They can as easily be applied to problem situations that do not lend themselves to quantification, but to other analytical approaches for problem solving or problem resolution used in the social sciences.

For example, some years ago OR/MS was taught in a separate department of operations research at the University of Canterbury where I teach. There was another university department teaching marketing, human resource management, production management, and business strategy. In view of a number of common interests, as well as overlapping teaching and research activity, we explored the possibility of a merger between these two departments. I used the methodology discussed in this chapter to develop an approach for analyzing how we should go about making a decision about merging the two departments, i.e., a system for finding a good decision process for the merger decision, not the merger decision itself. This did not contain any quantitative aspects. It highlighted that our original approach of compiling a list of advantages and disadvantages — a balance sheet of pluses and minuses — left out an important aspect, namely how current and prospective students would perceive MS/OR within this new setting.

EXERCISES

1. Draw a rich picture diagram for the telephone betting situation described in Section 1.1 of Chapter 1.

2. Draw a rich picture diagram for the breast cancer screening situation described in Section 1.1 of Chapter 1.

3. Consider the situation summary in exercise 3 of Chapter 3. Draw a rich picture diagram for it.

4. Draw a rich picture diagram for the staff scheduling situation described below. Assume that it will be used to provide feedback to the sponsor of the proposed project on the understanding gained by the consultant about the situation. Note that you may have to make a judgment as to the level of resolution (i.e., detail) that may be appropriate for such a presentation.

    Introduction: In late 1987 the supervisor of customs at the Christchurch International Airport (or CIA for short), Bill Dodge, became increasingly concerned about a number of aspects of the customs operations under his control, namely
    -   excessive overtime of staff, with some officers working up to 70 hours a week.
    -   excessive number of special call-outs, particularly on weekends.
    -   regular inability to process all arriving passengers within the maximum time guidelines set by the Minister of Customs.
    -   insufficient manpower to undertake, what he considers the custom officers' primary role, namely border protection work, such as the prevention of importation of illegal goods (like drugs, pornographic material, etc.), prevention of entry into N.Z. of prohibited aliens, and full and proper assessment of import duties.

    He was also worried about how his staff would be able to cope with the new computerized arrival processing system (CAPS), scheduled to be introduced in early 1988. Although headquarters in Wellington expected that this system should in fact speed up processing of arriving passengers, he had serious doubts that this would materialize. Currently, arriving passengers were processed at a rate of about 65 seconds per person. Even assuming fast response times on the computer, he estimated that with CAPS processing time could increase to over 90 seconds per person. Unless sufficient additional staff and an enlarged arrival processing hall were provided, it was clear that arriving passengers on most 767 and 747 aircraft would experience excessive delays, well outside Government guidelines. In view of these concerns, he was able to get Wellington approval to commission a consultant report on staffing, staff shift scheduling and shift rostering. Tenders were called and the contract awarded to CANTOR CONSULTANTS.

Description of Duties Performed by Customs at CIA: Customs has the following duties:

(1) Processing of passengers arriving on scheduled commercial airliners: All international customers disembarking at CIA have to go through customs. Prior to CAPS the procedure was as follows: After leaving the aircraft, arriving passengers proceed to 'immigration'. All passengers queue in front of the immigration booths, where passports (or other identification documents) for N.Z. and Australian residents, and passports and immigration visas for all other passengers are inspected by a customs officer, who will also do spot checks on the documents of certain passengers or passengers from certain nationalities. Passengers who do not hold a valid visa are directed to the senior customs officer's booth for the issue of a visa. The officer also inspects the passengers' customs declaration and 'entry card' (a questionnaire for statistical purposes) and directs the arriving passengers to the appropriate customs import duty and/or agricultural inspection station, referred to as secondary processing. Once through immigration, the passengers pick up their luggage, which by then should have been unloaded from the aircraft and put on the circular conveyor belt. (Note that sniffer dogs are commonly used now to 'pre-inspect' the luggage of arriving passengers for narcotics. Passengers of any suspected luggage get 'special treatment'.) Passengers then proceed through secondary processing, which for many arrivals, simply means leaving the customs arrival hall.

Government guidelines specify that the time interval between the aircraft being ready for disembarkation and the last passenger being dismissed from secondary processing should not exceed 30 minutes for arrivals of up to 250 passengers and 45 minutes for more than 250 passengers. Naturally, this excludes processing of any arriving passengers who for one reason or another have been caught in the net of 'border protection', such as attempting to import prohibited materials, or making false customs declarations, or being in possession of improper arrival documents, or being on the list of 'suspected' persons.

All customs officers working at the arrival of an aircraft form a 'team'. Depending on the expected number of passengers on the aircraft, the team strength could be anywhere from 10 to 16 officers, including one senior customs officer. The entire team assembles in the customs arrival hall by the time the arriving aircraft has landed. Usually two thirds of the team is engaged with immigration, the rest with secondary processing and border protection. Note that agricultural inspection is not performed by customs, but by officers from the Ministry of Agriculture and Fisheries. They are not part of the customs team.

With the introduction of CAPS and 'self-declaration', immigration processing is done with the help of remote terminal access to a central computer in Wellington. The immigration officers key in the name and passport number of the arriving passenger(s). For N.Z. and Australian passports, the validity of the passport is checked by the computer, while for all other passengers their name is checked with a list of known criminals or suspected persons from information provided by Interpol. With the introduction of self-declaration, the immigration officer will not direct passengers to the appropriate secondary treatment station. Instead passengers will decide for themselves whether they have 'nothing to declare for import duty assessment and agricultural inspection' and then proceed to exit from the customs hall, or 'something to declare for import duty assessment' or 'for agricultural inspection' or both and then proceed to the appropriate inspection station, with agricultural inspection being done first. It is believed that this procedure, which is common in most European countries, will considerably speed up both immigration and secondary processing. Naturally, as an incentive[§] for honesty, a certain proportion of passengers opting for the 'nothing to declare' option will be redirected to one or both of the other two stations, where their luggage will be searched, etc. The officer in charge of this re-directing will receive special training to look for behaviour and other characteristics of the arriving passengers that give clues for possible attempts at cheating. Some passengers will also be redirected on a completely random basis. Furthermore, fines for wilful misdeclarations will be set sufficiently high to discourage most cheating.

(2) Processing of passengers departing on scheduled commercial airliners: Two customs officers process departing passengers over a 30-minute interval prior to the departure of the aircraft. This processing consists largely of collecting the departure card and stamping the passport with an exit stamp.

(3) Processing of non-scheduled commercial airliners: same as above.

(4) Processing of private aircraft arrivals and departures, as well as aircraft of the U.S. Deep Freeze Program: The various steps are roughly the same as for commercial airliners. However, the team size is adjusted to the number of passengers on the plane. It may consist of only two officers. Note that most Deep Freeze aircraft tend to arrive in the middle of the night. This usually will necessitate calling up a small team of officers on overtime.

(5) Processing of mail for the Deep Freeze Program: Once or twice daily two to four officers are seconded to the Deep Freeze premises to process incoming mail from abroad and Antarctica. This operation takes anywhere from 30 to 60 minutes.

(6) Staffing of the airport freight office: Two officers process incoming freight during the hours from 10 a.m. to 4 p.m.

(7) Clerical and administrative duties at the CIA customs office: While not processing passenger arrivals and departures, customs officers perform a variety of clerical duties, including answering of letters dealing with customs matters and inquiries, and assessment of import duties for imports through the Port of Lyttelton by local firms and private individuals. Senior customs officers also perform a certain amount of administrative work, like preparation of detailed work assignment schedules for each customs officer in their team for the coming week, including scheduling of vacations, and other leave, like attendance at training workshops, as well as making arrangements for overtime and special overtime call-outs, as well as covering for emergencies, like unplanned absence from work due to illness, etc.

Current Shift Schedule and Shift Roster: The shift schedules and rosters followed at the end of 1987 had been in use for over 6 years without any major change, and this in spite of a considerable increase in volume of traffic and a substantial change in the time pattern of aircraft arrivals, particularly a large increase in arrivals around and shortly after midnight, since Christchurch has become an end of run point. Three shifts are used: Shift 1: 8.30 a.m. to 5 p.m.; Shift 2: 6 a.m. to 2:30 p.m.; Shift 3: 2 p.m. to 10:30 p.m. Each shift includes a 1/2 hour (unpaid) meal break in the middle of the shift. The shift time includes 15 minutes at the start and at the end of the shift for change of clothing into or out of uniform. This explains the overlap between shift 2 and 3. Shift 1 operates every day, while shifts 2 and 3 are only used from Monday through Friday. Any aircraft arrivals or departures outside these shift times have to be met either by overtime attached to the beginning or end of a shift, or by special call-outs. The latter have to be at least of a 3-hour duration, regardless of the actual time needed for aircraft processing.

The officers are organized into teams of 15 officers, including one senior customs officer. Each team follows a work roster which cycles the team through all three shifts over a three-week period. While on shift 1, half the team is off on Tuesday and Wednesday, and the other half of the team is off on Thursday and Friday. The shift 1 team is fully staffed only on Saturday, Sunday, and Monday. Each officer has thus two out of three weekends off, at least in theory. In practice, up to 2/3 of all officers are called in on overtime to meet the processing requirements of aircraft arrivals and departures outside the shift 1 times.

Work Load Information and Government Guidelines: Each airline using CIA provides the local customs department with a time schedule of arriving and departing aircraft. This schedule tends to undergo major changes twice a year, resulting in a so-called summer schedule and a winter schedule. There are some 40 international flight arrivals and an equal number of international departures per week. Customs is also notified of all minor alterations within each schedule several weeks ahead of time. These schedules not only give the time of arrival and departure, but also information about all points of call where arriving passengers could board the aircraft for a CIA destination, the next point of call for departing aircraft, the type of aircraft, and its capacity. No such information is available for non-scheduled flights. Each airline is also required to provide a status report at least one week in advance for each scheduled arrival showing the number of passengers booked on that aircraft for disembarkation or embarkation at CIA at that time, as well as any planned deviations from the normal time schedule. However, due to booking changes the actual number of passengers on each flight may vary slightly from the number notified. In rare instances, such variations may be major, e.g., due to the cancellation of a major tour group.

Customs has also compiled data on the exact number of passengers arriving for each scheduled flight for the preceding summer and winter schedules. This gives some indication as to the variability of passenger numbers. The notification of passenger numbers by the airlines allows customs to adjust the team size required for processing all passengers of an arriving aircraft within the Government guidelines. Due to changes in the passenger numbers subsequent to the airlines' notifications it is still possible that the team size is too small to meet Government guide-lines. Although these guide lines are set in the form of 'maximum time allowed', they have to be interpreted in an operational way. Due to unforeseen circumstances, it is not realistic nor desirable to attempt meeting the guidelines 100% of the time, except at the cost of having excess personnel standing around doing nothing for most flight arrivals. An operational criterion would be to plan manning levels which allow customs to satisfy these guidelines 90 or 95% of the time. This is in fact the way the rules are interpreted unofficially in practice, if not in theory.

From past experience, customs is also able to forecast the load for all other tasks, particularly Deep Freeze mail, CIA freight processing, and all clerical tasks. Although data is available on all past non-scheduled commercial, private, and Deep Freeze flights, this information is not of much use for planning purposes. These flights exhibit no predictable pattern and are highly variable, with the exception of two weekly Deep Freeze flights, whose arrival tends to occur at set times, plus or minus several hours. During the busy Southern Summer period, as many as 10 flight arrivals have been recorded in certain days.

Processing of flights always gets priority, with departure having the highest priority. Commercial flights also get priority over non-commercial flights. The CIA freight office has regular opening hours which must be met. However, all other tasks can wait within certain limits. For instance, Deep Freeze mail should be processed within 4 hours of its arrival. Clerical tasks should be processed within 48 hours of their arrival, although this rule is sometimes violated for answering of letters, particularly if the answer requires some research to be done. Clerical tasks always have lowest priority.

Employment Conditions for Customs Officers: Customs officers have a regular working week of 40 hours. This includes a 15-minute allowance at the beginning and end of each shift for a change of clothing. They also must have a 1/2 hour meal break no later than 5 hours after the start of the shift. They get a 25% penalty rate for the time in excess of 5 hours they have to wait for the meal break. Overtime worked within the hours from Sunday midnight to Saturday noon incur a 50% penalty rate. Any time worked between Saturday noon and Sunday midnight, regardless of whether it is regular shift time or overtime, is paid at a 100% penalty rate. Overtime as an extension to the regular shift time, either prior to or after the shift, can be of any duration with a minimum of 1/2 hour. Overtime worked on special call-outs has to be paid for at least 3 hours, even if the actual time worked is less than that. The time between leaving work (either a shift or overtime) and the start of the next period of work (either a shift or overtime) has to be at least 9 hours. Each officer has the right to four weeks of paid vacation, plus 7 statutory holidays. Each officer also has the right to attend up to 2 weeks of training courses per year.

Informal Talk to the Union Representatives: The union representatives indicated that they also were concerned about a number of factors. A large portion of the customs officers had volunteered to work at CIA because of the opportunity for a substantial increase in take-home pay due to the high incidence of overtime. However, after a year or so at CIA, many officers begin to dislike the disruption to their private life caused by this high incidence of overtime, particularly the special call-outs on weekends. So on the one hand, the increase in pay due to overtime is highly appreciated, but the resulting disruption to private life is also highly disliked—a catch-22 situation. The representatives indicated that current levels of overtime were excessive, but that the opportunity for some overtime should be retained by any change in staffing, shift schedule and shift rosters. The representatives also reacted strongly negatively when asked about their opinions on flexible shift patterns (i.e., shifts with changing start and finish times every day), short shifts of 4 to 6 hours, and part-time officers (particularly to man short shifts).

Brief of CIA Customs Supervisor to Consultants: The consultants were to come forth with recommendations as to desirable staff size, shift patterns, and shift rosters. What was requested was not a single 'best' solution, but a set of good alternative solutions that differed in terms of their structure (staff size, amount of overtime, shift patterns, total cost, etc.). Some of the solutions evaluated should also include the features like flexible shift start times and short shifts. The consultants were not to take the role of mediators or facilitators between the customs department and the union. Negotiations between the department and the union would follow after the receipt of the consultants' report, based on the evaluation of the various solutions presented by both management and the union. The possibility should be there to easily and quickly evaluate and cost out alternative solutions put forth by either management or the union at that stage.

5. Use a process approach to define a suitable system for exploring how many telephone lines the TAB should hire, so as to maximize the operation's profit contribution (see the situation summary in Section 1.1 of Chapter 1).

6. Use a process approach to define a suitable system for exploring the consequences of different breast cancer screening policy choices on the various conflicting goals (see the situation summary in Section 1.1 of Chapter 1).

7. A blood bank received various types of blood from a central blood collection agency. Fresh blood has a limited shelf life of between 35 and 49 days, depending on the preservatives used. Any blood not used within this period has to be discarded. Fresh blood is used for transfusions in scheduled and emergency surgery. If not enough blood of the correct type is available, scheduled operations have to be postponed, while emergency operations will increase the risk to the patient and may result in death. Hence, management has to find a suitable policy which keeps discarding of outdated blood as low as possible, but at the same time provides enough blood for scheduled operations and enough extra blood for emergencies, so as to avoid shortages as much as possible. Naturally, shortages can be avoided entirely if an excessive amount of blood is always kept on hand. But this would be very wasteful. Use a process approach to define a suitable system for the management of the blood bank, so as to find a good compromise between the two objectives of minimizing shortages and minimizing outdating of blood.

8. Use a process approach to define a suitable system for the staff scheduling problem in exercise 4 above.

9. Draw an influence diagram for exploring the best number of telephone lines the TAB should hire so as to maximize the operation's profit contribution (see the situation summary in Section 1.1 of Chapter 1).

10. Draw an influence diagram for exploring the best breast cancer screening policy (see the situation summary in Section 1.1 of Chapter 1).

11. Draw an influence diagram for the blood bank management system, defined in exercise 7 above. It should clearly show the direct or indirect effects of the controllable actions and decisions on the two performance measures of shortages and outdating.

12. Draw an influence diagram for measuring the total annual cost, the degree of meeting Government flight processing standards, and the degree of equity in staff working hours

for the staff scheduling problem described in exercise 4 above.

REFERENCES

The Open University Press texts, listed in the references to Chapter 3, by (1) J. Hughes and J. Tait, (2) Bill Mayon-White and Dick Morris, (3) J. Naughton, and (4) Lewis Watson all deal with systems modeling. Naughton's *Soft Systems Methodology* and its *Workbook* have an excellent and more extensive treatment on 'rich picture' and their uses. The following workbook shows detailed examples of about a dozen different diagrammatic ways to depict systems or aspects of systems:

Martin, John, *Block I Introduction Workbook*, Technology course T301: Complexity, Management and Change; Applying a Systems Approach, Unit 1/2, The Open University Press, 1984.

R. L. Ackoff, *The Art of Problem Solving*, Wiley, 1978. Many valuable lessons can be gleaned from Ackoff's accounts on problem solving. A clear must, but more useful as a reminder for an analyst with some practical experience. The emphasis is on 'Art', largely learned from experience, and consequently somewhat lost on the beginner.

Bodily, S. E., *Modern Decision Making*, McGraw-Hill, 1985. Most of the book demonstrates the use of the IFPS (Interactive financial planning system) computer package for solving business problems. That part is now out-of-date. However, the first three chapters deal with modeling in general. Chapter 3 is entirely devoted to 'influence diagrams'.

Checkland, P., *Systems Theory, Systems Practice*, Wiley, 1981. Chapters 6 and 7 show how his version of the soft systems methodology is used for systems modeling. Conceptually more difficult and requiring a considerable dose of experience in organizational decision making than this book or Naughton's.

Cooke, Steve, and Slack, Nigel, *Making Management Decisions*, 2nd ed., Prentice-Hall, 1991. Somewhat broader coverage, including behavioural aspects of management, in part at the expense of systems modeling proper. Relevant chapters are 1 to 5 and 8 to 10.

Flood, Robert L., and Carson, E.R., *Dealing with Complexity*, Plenum Press, 1988. Chapter 2 is devoted to various diagrammatic techniques useful for systems analysis.

Flood, Robert L., and Jackson, Michael C., *Creative Problem Solving, Total Systems Intervention*, Wiley, 1991. Chapters 1 and 2 are relevant for this chapter. At a more advanced level.

Forrester, Jay W., 'Understanding the counter-intuitive behaviour of social systems', in J. Beishon and Geoff Peters, editors, *Systems Behaviour*, 3rd ed., Harper & Row, 1981, pp. 270-287. This paper shows a systems analysis for a socioeconomic-environmental problem, based on **systems dynamics**, a technique largely developed by Forrester. This is the type of further quantitative analysis that needs to be done for the ozone depletion problem. (See *Industrial Dynamics*, MIT Press, 1969, and *World Dynamics*, Wright-Allen Press, 1972.)

Appendix to Chapter 4: A Piece of Sky is Missing

by Carl Sagan

reprinted with permission from *PARADE*, copyright © 11/9/1988

I always wanted an electric train, but it wasn't until I was 10 that my parents could afford to buy me one. What they got me, secondhand but in good condition, wasn't one of those bantamweight, finger-long, miniature scale models you see today, but a real clunker. The locomotive alone must have weighed 5 pounds. There was also a coal tender, a passenger car and a caboose. The all-metal interlocking tracks came in three varieties: straight, curved and one beautifully crossed mutation which permitted the construction of a figure-eight railway. I saved up to buy a green plastic tunnel, so I could see the engine, its headlight dispelling the darkness, triumphantly chugging through.

My memories of those happy times are suffused with a smell — not unpleasant, faintly sweet and always emanating from the transformer, a big black metal box with a sliding red lever that controlled the speed of the train. If you had asked me to describe its function, I suppose I would have said that it converted the kind of electricity in the walls of our apartment to the kind of electricity that the locomotive needed.   Only much later did I learn that the smell was made by a particular chemical and that the chemical had a name — ozone.

The air all around us, the stuff we breath, is made of about 20% oxygen — not the atom, symbolized as O, but the molecule, symbolized as O_2, meaning two oxygen atoms chemically bound together. This molecular oxygen is what makes us go. We breathe it in, combine it with food and extract energy. Ozone is a much rarer way in which oxygen atoms combine. It is symbolized as O_3, meaning three oxygen atoms chemically bound together.

My transformer had an imperfection. A tiny electric spark had been sputtering away, breaking the bonds of oxygen molecules as they happened by: O_2 + energy becomes O + O. But solitary oxygen atoms are unhappy, chemically reactive, anxious to combine with adjacent oxygen molecules to form ozone, i.e., $O + O_2 + M$ becomes $O_3 + M$. Here, M stands for any third molecule; it doesn't get used up in the reaction, but is required to help it along. M is a catalyst.

That is what was going on in my transformer to make ozone. It also goes on in automobile engines and in the fires of industry, producing reactive ozone down near the ground, contributing to smog and industrial pollution. It doesn't smell so sweet to me anymore. But the real ozone danger is not too much of it down here, but too little of it up there.

It was all done responsibly, carefully, with concern for the environment. The problem was to find a material that would do no harm. You want to sell, say, a deodorant in a can, press the button, out it comes in a fine mist, and your customer is ready for a big date. You need a safe propellant to carry the deodorant out of the can. Or you are manufacturing a refrigerator and you need a coolant, liquid under the right conditions, that will circulate inside the refrigerator, but won't hurt anything if the refrigerator leaks or is converted to scrap metal. For these purposes, it would be nice to have a material, neither poisonous nor flammable, that doesn't corrode, burn your eyes or attract bugs. The industrial chemists worked hard and developed a class of molecules called chlorofluorocarbons (CFCs), made up of one or more carbon atoms to which are attached some chlorine and/or fluorine atoms. They are used in air-conditioning, refrigeration, spray cans, insulating foams and plastics, and industrial solvents. The most famous brand name is FREON, a trademark of the Du Pont Company. Safe as safe could be, everybody figured. That is why, these days, a surprising amount of what we take for granted depends on CFCs.

So, it's a few years ago, and you are standing in your bathroom, spraying under your arms. The propellant CFC molecules don't stick to you. They bounce off into the air, swirl near the mirror, careen off the walls. Eventually, some of them trickle out the window or under the door and, as time passes — it may take days or weeks — they find themselves in the great outdoors. The CFCs bump into other molecules in the air, off buildings and telephone poles and, carried up by convection, are swept around the planet. With very few exceptions, they do not fall apart and do not chemically combine with any of the molecules they encounter. After a few years, CFC molecules find themselves in the high atmosphere.

Ozone is naturally formed up there at an altitude of around 25 kilometres. Ultraviolet light (uv) from the Sun — corresponding to the spark in my imperfectly insulated electric train transformer — breaks O_2 molecules down into O atoms. They recombine and reform ozone.

A CFC molecule survives at those altitudes on the average for a century before giving up its chlorine. Chlorine is a catalyst that destroys ozone molecules, but is not destroyed itself. It takes a couple of years before the chlorine is carried back into the lower atmosphere and washed out in rainwater. In that time, a chlorine atom may preside over the destruction of 100,000 ozone molecules.

So what? Who cares? Some invisible molecules, somewhere high up in the sky, are being destroyed by some other invisible molecule manufactured down here on Earth. Why should we worry about that?

Ozone is our shield against uv-light from the Sun. If all the ozone in the upper air were brought down to the temperature and pressure around you at this moment, the layer would be only 3 millimetres thick — about the height of the cuticle on your little finger if you are not fastidiously manicured. It is not very much ozone. But that ozone is all that stands between us and the fierce and searing long-wave uv-light from the Sun.

The uv danger we often hear about is skin cancer. Light-skinned people are especially vulnerable; dark-skinned people have a generous supply of melanin to protect them. (Suntanning is an adaptation whereby whites develop more protective melanin when exposed to uv.) There seems to be some remote cosmic justice in light-skinned people inventing CFCs, which then give skin cancer preferentially to light-skinned people, while dark-skinned people, having had little to do with this wonderful invention, are naturally protected. In fact, if things get worse, as without doubt they will, light-skinned people may be required to use special protective clothing during routine excursions out-of-doors.

But increasing skin cancer, while a direct consequence of enhanced uv and threatening millions of deaths, is not the worst of it. Probably more serious is the fact that uv injures the immune system — the body's machinery for fighting disease — but, again, only for people who go out unprotected into the sunlight. Yet, as serious as this seems, the real danger lies elsewhere.

When exposed to uv-light, the organic molecules that constitute all life on Earth fall apart or make unhealthy chemical attachments. The most prevalent beings that inhabit the oceans are tiny one-celled plants that float near the surface of the water. They cannot hide from the uv by diving deep because they make a living through harvesting sunlight. They live from hand to mouth (a metaphor only, they have neither hands nor mouths). Experiments by Sayed El-Sayed of Texas A&M University show that even a moderate increase in uv harms the one-celled plants common in the Antarctic Ocean and elsewhere. Larger increases can be expected to cause profound distress and, eventually, massive deaths.

But if increasing uv falls on the oceans, the damage is not restricted to these little plants, because they are the food of one-celled animals, who are eaten in turn by little shrimp-like crustaceans, who are eaten by small fish, who are eaten by large fish, who are eaten by dolphins, whales, and people. The destruction of the little plants at the base of the food chain causes the entire chain to collapse. There are many such food chains, on land as in water, and all seem vulnerable to disruption by uv. For example, the bacteria in the roots of rice plants that grab nitrogen from the air are uv sensitive. Increasing uv may threaten crops and possibly even compromise the human food supply.

In permitting the ozone layer to be destroyed and the intensity of uv at the Earth's surface to increase, we are posing challenges of unknown severity to the fabric of life on our planet. We are ignorant about the complex mutual dependencies of the beings on Earth, and what the sequential consequences will be if we wipe out some especially vulnerable microbes on which larger organisms depend. We are tugging at a planet-wide biological tapestry and do not know whether one thread only will come out in our hands, or whether the whole tapestry will unravel before us.

No one believes that the entire ozone layer is in imminent danger of disappearing. We will not, even if we remain wholly obdurate about acknowledging our danger, be reduced to the antiseptic circumstance of the martian surface, pummeled by unfiltered solar uv. But even a worldwide reduction in the amount of ozone by a few percent — and many scientists think that is what the present dose of CFCs in the atmosphere will eventually bring about — looks to be very dangerous.

Who discovered that CFCs might endanger the ozone layer? Was it atmospheric chemists employed by the principal manufacturers, such as Du Pont, as a means of safety-testing their products? Was it some laboratory associated with the U.S. Environmental Protection Agency or the U.S. Department of Defense? (Discovering such a danger would unambiguously be defending us.) No, this danger was first pointed out by two university scientists pursuing pure, ivory-tower, abstract, 'impractical' science. Everybody else missed it.

In 1974, Sherwood Rowland and Mario Molina of the Irvine Campus of the University of California first warned that CFCs might seriously damage the ozone layer. Subsequent experiments and calculations by scientists all over the world have supported their findings.

The Du Pont Company, which sells CFCs to the tune of U.S.$600 million a year, took out ads in newspapers and testified before Congressional committees that the danger of CFCs to the ozone layer was unproven, had been greatly exaggerated, or had been based on faulty scientific reasoning. Sometimes they seemed to argue that they would stop CFC manufacture as soon as the ozone layer was irretrievably damaged.

Berkeley, California, has banned the white CFC-blown foam insulation used to keep fast foods warm. McDonald's has pledged replacement of the most damaging CFCs in its packaging. Facing the threat of government regulations and consumer boycotts, Du Pont finally announced in 1988 that it would phase out the manufacture of CFCs — but not to be completed until the year 2000. Other American manufacturers have not even promised that. But the United States accounts for only 30% of worldwide CFC production. Clearly, since the long-term threat to the ozone layer is global and the manufacture and use of CFCs is global, the solution must be global as well.

In September 1987, many of the nations that produce and use CFCs met in Montreal to consider the possible agreement to limit CFC use. At first, Britain, Italy, and France, influenced by their powerful chemical industries, participated in the discussions only reluctantly, and such nations as South Korea were altogether absent. The Chinese delegation did not sign the treaty. Interior Secretary Donald Hodel (U.S.), a conservative averse to government controls, reportedly suggested that, instead of limiting CFC production, we all wear sunglasses and hats. This option is unavailable to the micro-organisms at the base of the food chains that sustain life on Earth, and the U.S. signed the Montreal Protocol despite this advice.

Now 37 nations, including the USSR, have agreed to a schedule of cutbacks in CFC production, so that by 1989 production reverts to 1986 levels, and by 1999 to about 50% of that. The trouble is, we will have to stop producing **all** CFC and then wait a century or two before the atmosphere cleans itself. The longer we dawdle, the greater the danger.

Clearly, the problem will be solved if a cheaper and more effective CFC substitute can be found that does not injure us or the environment. But what if there is no such substitute? What if the best substitute is more expensive? Who pays for the research, and who makes up the price difference — the consumer, the government, or the chemical industry that got us into this mess? What if we need 20 years to be sure that the substitute doesn't cause cancer? What if it is no good for refrigerators? What about the uv now pouring down on the Antarctic Ocean? What about the newly manufactured CFCs rising towards the ozone layer between now and whenever the stuff is completely banned?

The Montreal Protocol is important not for the magnitude or speed of the changes agreed to but for their direction. The Montreal conference was sponsored by the United Nations Environment Programme, whose director, Mostafa K. Tolba, described it as 'the first truly global treaty that offers protection to every single human being'.

But not enough protection! What is needed is a worldwide ban on CFCs as rapidly as possible, greatly enhanced research to find safe substitutes and monitoring of the ozone layer all over the globe at least as conscientiously as we would watch over a loved one suffering from heart palpitations. If we must make a mistake, let it be in the cause of the human species. That is what I call being conservative.

The central elements of the ozone story are like many other environmental threats — the CO_2 greenhouse effect, for example, or nuclear winter. We pour some substance into the atmosphere (or prepare to do so). Somehow we do not thoroughly examine its environmental impact, because it would be expensive, or it would delay production and cut into profits, or those in charge do not want to hear counterarguments, or the best scientific talent has not been brought to bear on the issue. Then, suddenly, we are face-to-face with a wholly unexpected danger of worldwide dimensions that may have its most ominous consequences decades or centuries from now. The problem cannot be solved locally, or in the short term.

In all these cases, the lesson is clear: We are not always smart or wise enough to foresee the consequences of our actions. Because of these human limitations, we must be much more careful and much less forgiving about polluting our fragile atmosphere.

We must develop higher standards of planetary hygiene and significantly greater resources for monitoring and understanding our world. And we must begin to think and act not merely in terms of our nation or generation (much less the profits of a particular industry), but in terms of the entire vulnerable planet Earth, and the generations of children to come.

The hole in the ozone layer is a kind of skywriting. Does it spell out a newly evolving ability to work together on behalf of our species, or our continuing complacency before a witch's brew of deadly perils?

Once CFCs are in the atmosphere, there is no way to scrub them out (or to pump ozone pollution high up, where it is needed). The effects of CFCs, once introduced into the air, will persist for about a century. Thus Sherwood Rowland, other scientists, and the Washington-based Natural Resources Defense Council urged the banning of CFCs. By 1978, CFC propellants in aerosol spray cans were made illegal in the U.S. and some other countries. But most world CFC production does not go into spray cans. Public concern was temporarily mollified, attention drifted elsewhere and the CFC content of the air continued to rise. The amount of chlorine in the atmosphere is now twice what it was when Rowland and Molina sounded the alarm and five times what it was in 1950.

For years, the British Antarctic Survey, a team of scientists stationed at Halley Bay in the southernmost continent, had been measuring the ozone layer high overhead. In 1985, they announced the disconcerting news that the springtime ozone had diminished to nearly half of what they had measured a few years before. Two-thirds of the springtime ozone over Antarctica is now (1988) missing. There is a hole in the Antarctic ozone layer. It has shown up every spring since the late 1970s. While it heals itself in winter, the hole seems to last longer each spring. No scientist had predicted it.

Naturally, the hole led to more calls for a ban on CFCs, as did the discovery that CFCs add to the global warming caused by the carbon dioxide greenhouse effect. But industry officials seemed to have difficulty focusing on the nature of the problem. Richard C. Barnett, chairman of the Alliance for Responsible CFC Policy, a body formed by CFC manufacturers, complained: 'The rapid, complete shutdown of CFCs that some people are calling for would have horrendous consequences. Some industries would have to shut down because they cannot get alternative products. The cure could kill the patient!' But the patient is not some industries, the patient is life on Earth.

The Chemical Manufacturers Association believes that the Antarctic hole 'is highly unlikely to have global significance ... Even in the other most similar region of the world, the Arctic, the meteorology effectively precludes a similar situation'. However, recently, enhanced levels of reactive chlorine have been found in the ozone hole, helping to establish the CFC connection. At northern midlatitudes, where most people on Earth live, the total amount of ozone has been found to have declined by several percent between 1969 and 1988 (mainly in winter). Balloon measurements near the North Pole, compiled by Canadian researchers, suggest that an ozone hole is developing over the Arctic as well.

5   OR/MS Methodology

The ozone depletion problem studied in Chapter 4 is a natural system, although its apparent cause is human. Systems thinking allowed us to gain a better understanding of the various processes that govern its behaviour over time.

The ozone problem did not contain any aspects over which one person or one decision making body could exercise control. Production of CFCs and their use is worldwide and any action requires the voluntary cooperation of many private organizations and governments. Although management scientists may be asked to study such systems, the majority of the OR/MS projects deal with controllable human activity systems. This book studies how systems thinking is incorporated into the OR/MS methodology to deal more effectively with controllable systems where quantitative analysis is an appropriate approach.

This chapter starts out with a brief overview of the OR/MS methodology and then applies its first phase — the problem formulation — to a real-life problem. In Chapter 6 we study how to build a mathematical model for the problem, while Chapters 7 and 8 discuss the remaining phases of the methodology. Conceptually, Chapter 5 is the most difficult of this book. Its aim is to convey the various logical steps, rules, and principles of the process of the OR/MS methodology — together with points of practical experience. Since we are dealing with a real-life process and not some theoretical construct, things are not clear-cut. Each rule will have provisos and exceptions. There is no one right way. What would be altogether obvious to the seasoned practitioner may be bewildering to the novice. So do not expect that everything will be clear after the first reading. It may take several goes before things fall into place. I also suggest that you go back to this chapter after you have studied most of the other chapters in the book.

5.1 ROLES OF PARTICIPANTS IN OR/MS PROJECTS

Any form of problem solving involves the following stakeholders, roles or actors:

- The **problem owner** who is the person or group who has control over certain aspects of the problem situation, in particular over the choice of action to be taken. Most often, the problem owner is the decision maker. In many situations there may be several levels of problem owners: those who have the ultimate power over all controllable aspects of the situation, but may have delegated that power to others, and those who have been given limited powers within a subsystem to make decisions and initiate change.

- The **problem user** who uses the solution and/or executes the decisions approved by the problem owner or decision maker. He or she has no authority to change the decision or initiate new action. Any apparent decision making is simply an application of prescribed rules. If any discretionary power is given, it is very limited in scope.

- The **problem customer** who is the beneficiary or victim of the consequences of using the solution; there may be many problem customers.

- The **problem solver** or analyst who analyzes the problem and develops a solution for approval by the problem owner.

All roles are always defined in terms of the narrow system of interest. Definite identification of who the various stakeholders of a problem situation are becomes fully clear only once the relevant system has been defined, although the analyst may have a fair idea about who most of them are very early in the analysis.

Some examples might help to clarify these roles. Recall the telephone betting problem of Chapter 1. The General Manager of the TAB was the problem owner. This person had the final say over any decision made and hence assumed the role of the ultimate decision maker. The general manager may have delegated the implementation and continued day-to-day management of that aspect of the business to the technical supervisor, who then assumed the role of problem user, with a limited amount of discretionary power, such as setting the best staffing levels at various times of the day. The customers were the punters placing bets. They were the beneficiaries or victims of the service quality and access offered. Finally, the TAB hired the services of a specialist in waiting line problems — a university lecturer — to study the problem and make a recommendation. That person assumed the role of problem analyst.

In the TAB project, each role was assumed by a different person. For many situations, the same individual may act in different roles. Assume that you are considering the replacement of your current car. You have limited finance and borrowing capacity, a wish list of desirable and absolutely essential features that your new car should meet, and a wide choice of options: a range of new cars, as well as suitable second-hand cars. In this case, you are the problem owner, the problem user, the problem customer, as well as the problem analyst — all roles coincide.

The names problem owner, user, customer, and analyst thus do not refer to actual people, but to roles various people involved play. As we have seen, one person may assume more than one role simultaneously or consecutively.

Importance of Clear Role Definition

Why are we concerned about role definition? Firstly, any one of these roles can in fact be the sponsor or initiator of an OR/MS project. The role of the sponsor will colour the nature of the project, i.e., stamp it with a corresponding focus or framework. If initiated by the decision maker, the project will usually be of a substantive nature, leading to real change, with a relevant system for the project clearly defined within the span of control of the decision maker. The relevant Weltanschauung is the one held by the decision maker. If it is initiated by any of the other roles, its nature is usually descriptive. Its initiator will tend to use it as a means of educating or persuading other actors of the problem situation. It will only become substantive if its findings are adopted and acted upon by the problem owner. The appropriate choice of the relevant system for such projects and an appropriate Weltanschauung may be more problematic and possibly controversial. Unless the problem analyst is fairly clear about the roles of the various participants in the problem situation to be studied, the project may be off in the wrong direction from the very start. It goes without saying that the analyst must attempt to see the problem situation through the relevant world view of the sponsor, and not her or his own!

Consider the breast cancer study, discussed in Chapter 1. If the study is initiated by the Director of Public Health, the highest level of decision maker for health issues in the governmental administrative structure, the prevailing Weltanschauung is likely to be 'the effective allocation of public funds'. This would ultimately lead to evaluating tradeoffs between allocating funds to breast cancer screening and other uses of funds, with the entire health system being the potential relevant system. The output of the study would be a given screening policy and a schedule for its implementation. In contrast, if initiated by a group of medical practitioners — a problem users' group, or by the 'Women for Health' — a problem customer group, the relevant Weltanschauung would be achieving the greatest reduction in breast cancer mortality, with the relevant system limited to the relationship between screening policies and breast cancer mortality. Wider issues of allocation of public funds would hardly be considered. The study would be used as evidence to persuade the Health Department to fund a national screening policy.

Similarly, identification of the problem user is essential for effective implementation of any recommendations. The recommendations should be appropriate to the training and educational level of the user. Furthermore, unless the user perceives implementation as being in her or his interest, he or she may easily sabotage the project or the implementation of the recommendations, regardless of how successful the technical aspects of the project turn out to be — a case of 'the operation was successful, but the patient died!'

5.2 OVERVIEW OF THE OR/MS METHODOLOGY

Any OR/MS project that has a happy ending goes through three major phases: (1) problem formulation, (2) mathematical modeling, and (3) implementation of recommendations. Each phase consists of several steps, as depicted in Figure 5-1. The next few sections will discuss each of these steps. Since this chapter deals mainly with the problem formulation phase, the modeling and implementation phases will only be briefly touched upon.

Figure 5-1: OR/MS methodology

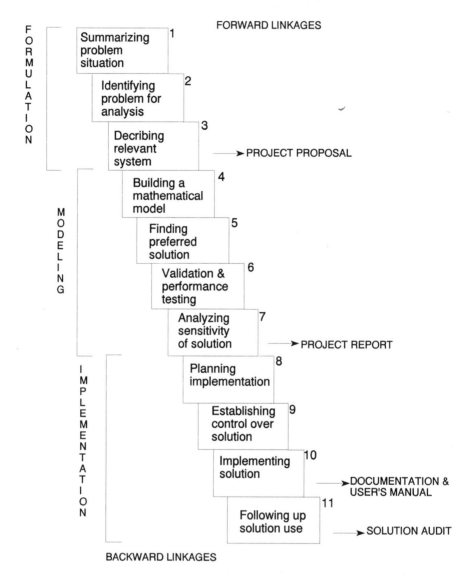

5.3 THE PROBLEM FORMULATION PHASE

You are already somewhat familiar with the three steps of the problem formulation from our discussion of the ozone depletion problem in Chapter 4. The first step — summarizing the problem situation — was done by means of a rich picture. The rich picture helped us in the identification of the problem — the second step of the problem formulation. For the third step, we used a process approach to identify the structure, transformation process(es), components, inputs, and outputs of the relevant system, which we then formalized by an influence diagram.

When dealing with human activity systems, identification of the problem and the relevant system involves an additional dimension, namely establishing who are the various stakeholders of the problem. In particular, the problem owner or decision maker becomes the core reference point of the entire analysis. This becomes immediately clear when we ask: 'What is a problem?'

Conceptual Definition of 'A Problem'

For a problem to exist there must be an individual (or group of individuals), referred to as the decision maker who

- is dissatisfied with the current state of affairs, or has some unsatisfied need, i.e., has some goals or objectives to be achieved;

- knows when these goals or objectives have been achieved to a satisfactory degree; and

- has control over aspects of the problem situation that affect the extent to which goals or objectives can be achieved.

The elements of a problem are thus (1) the **decision maker**, (2) the decision maker's **objectives**, (3) the **performance measure** for assessing how well the objectives have been achieved, and (4) **alternative courses of action** or decision variables for achieving the objectives. Step 2 of the problem formulation, namely the identification of the problem consists in defining these aspects of the problem situation. Step 3 defines the system relevant for the problem identified. This shows the core position that the problem owner or decision maker assumes in the problem formulation phase.

Complexities of Problem Definition

In real life, determining these four elements of a 'problem' may not be simply obtained by questioning the decision maker. The dissatisfaction felt by the decision maker may just be a vague feeling that things could be better. The analyst's job is then to explore and clarify the problem situation with the various stakeholders in the problem situation so that a clear issue can be identified. If this is not possible, a different problem analysis methodology, such as the **problem structuring methods** discussed in J. Rosenhead, *Rational Analysis for a Problematic World* [1989] may be more suitable.

One of the difficulties sometimes encountered at this stage is that the currently existing assignment of 'stakeholder roles' is inappropriate. For example, the person having the control over the decision process may not have access to the necessary information for effective decision making, while the person with the information may have no decision making authority. For effective decision making it may be necessary first to change the organization's structure, leading to a re-assignment of decision making roles. Only then will the climate of the organization be conducive to embarking on an OR/MS study proper. One of the soft systems methodologies may be useful for bringing about the appropriate organizational structure.

The decision maker may also be vague or fuzzy about objectives and, consequently, about performance standards. The analyst will then have to help the decision maker to externalize objectives and preferences. Setting of realistic performance standards may have to wait until the modeling phase is well under way, because only then will it become possible to explore the range of possible solutions. Furthermore, the decision maker may not be aware of the full range of alternative courses of action open. Discovery or development of new decision choices is one of the exciting and rewarding aspects of OR/MS work. Finally, the problem may be of a descriptive nature with the initiator of the project in the role of problem user or problem customer, like in the breast cancer project. In such instances, the real decision maker is not involved in the project. Her or his role is then 'simulated' with the obvious danger that the role may be misrepresented.

In most real-life applications, the problem formulation will not be achieved in a single pass through the three steps. The initial formulation usually goes through a series of progressively more detailed reformulations and refinements, as deeper insights into the problem are gained. In fact, it continues until the project ends. It is, however, in this phase where the ultimate success or failure of most projects has its roots!

5.4 THE PROJECT PROPOSAL

Once the analyst has obtained a sufficiently good understanding of the problem and the relevant system, he or she has to make a judgment about whether OR/MS modeling can successfully be applied to find a 'solution' to the problem. The analyst must weigh the following questions:

(a) Can the problem be expressed in quantitative terms?

(b) Are the required data available or can they be generated at a reasonable cost?

(c) Does the cost of the analysis justify the likely benefits to be derived from the implementation of the results? To what extent can the project sponsor's expectations be met?

Note that to answer some of these questions, the analyst must give cursory considerations to the modeling and implementation phases. Obviously, previous OR/MS experience will be of great help here — little comfort to the tyro management scientist. If the analyst is reasonably satisfied that the answer to all these questions is affirmative, the formulation phase concludes with a project proposal. The problem owner will base the decision on whether or not to give the go-ahead for a full-scale study largely on this document.

The project proposal is easily the most critical piece of work in any study. The quality of its presentation and soundness of the reasoning used often make the difference between acceptance or rejection of the project proposal. In some sense, it is the analyst's sales pitch. However, in contrast to most sales transactions, where the relationship between seller and buyer is often terminated with the goods passing hands, the acceptance of a project proposal by the problem owner signals the beginning of an even closer relationship. It is therefore important that the analyst gains the confidence of the problem owner by being scrupulously honest, both in terms of the likely benefits and the likely costs. The analyst should not promise more than he or she knows can be delivered with the resources likely to be available. If the analyst is an external consultant, the client may in fact hold the analyst to the promises made at the analyst's cost. Major potential difficulties that could derail the project should be brought into the open, discussed, and responsibilities for action clearly assigned. This is particularly true if the sponsor's expectations as to the likely benefits and desired time-table for completion cannot be reasonably met. Since OR/MS modeling claims to have much in common with scientific investigations, it should also be guided by the ethics of scientific research.

Estimation of Project Cost and Likely Benefits

Whether or not a project is undertaken will largely depend on whether its likely benefits will justify its costs and whether the sponsor's expectations can be reasonably met. If both benefits and costs can be expressed in monetary terms, a project is beneficial if some appropriate measure of its benefits over the useful life of the project exceed its total cost. Commercial projects generally have an objective that involves revenues and costs. Hence, they can usually be expressed in monetary terms. This is also the case for many projects in the public sector, particularly at a regional or municipal level, such as flood protection projects.

For projects dealing with environmental, health, or social issues, some or most of the benefits cannot be adequately captured in dollars and cents. Take the preservation of nature, scenic beauty, or the prevention of fatal accidents. How much is it worth to prevent the destruction of some wild life habitat? Similarly, the monetary evaluation of the benefits of noise abatement or pollution control, or the social benefits of pre-school education are controversial. A comparison of benefits and costs may therefore be far from simple. Chapter 19 will take up some of these issues when we look at how to deal with multiple and possibly conflicting objectives.

But even if we restrict ourselves to monetary benefits, providing any reliable answer for what the likely benefits are going to be may be far from simple. At this point in the life of a project, the analyst may have only scant information about the potential size of the benefits. In fact, one of the aims of the project may be to get a clearer answer to that question. Hence, the analyst may propose a preliminary study for assessing the economic feasibility of the project. Such projects are similar in nature to research and development activities. These have to be funded based on vague potential rather than hard facts. Some will succeed and reap great benefits, others will fail. The expectation is that on balance long-term benefits will outweigh long-term costs.

However, the analyst should make a serious and honest attempt at predicting the likely benefits beyond mere guesses. It may require developing a simplified model of the proposed operation or system. This can then be used to compute approximate estimates of benefits. It will also give a better picture of the likely costs for undertaking the project, although these are usually easier to estimate.

The answers to questions (a), (b), and (c) above, require that the analyst will have to do some preliminary thinking about the other two phases of the MS/OR approach, namely mathematical modeling and implementation. In other words, there are forward linkages from the first phase to the subsequent phases, as indicated in Figure 5-1.

Frequently, the sponsor of the project may have certain expectations about what the project should achieve and the time frame within which it should be completed. Even if the project is beneficial from a cost/benefit point of view, it may not meet these expectations. The sponsor should be made aware of this. It could well be that the expectations or the time frame offered are unreasonable. The analyst may then attempt to alter these expectations through reasoned arguments, based on a preliminary study or comparison with similar projects. The analyst must also be aware that he or she may, in fact, encourage the formation of unreasonable expectations unadvertently. Proper and diplomatic management of the sponsor's expectations is an important aspect of any project. Inappropriate expectation may result in implementation failure.

Format of Project Proposal

The project proposal should be relatively short — three to six pages — and presented to a professional standard. It should have correct spelling, grammar and syntax, and concise, clear language. Its line of thought should be logically developed and complete, with one point leading to the next. Its language should not contain OR/MS jargon. Writing a report with correct spelling, grammar and syntax, and proper complete sentences is an integral part of the professional image you wish to convey to the problem owners. One of the most common causes for complaints I hear from employers of novice OR/MS analysts is the often abysmal writing skills of many fresh graduates. It is difficult to come across as credible and professionally competent if your boss has to rewrite your reports before they can be presented to the sponsor of a project. In fact, it is the quickest way to lose your job. The bibliography of this chapter lists three excellent primers for effective report writing. It is worth putting three to four hours of time into studying one of them. The following format has proved successful:

(1) An introductory statement about the background of the project, its context and purpose, and how it came about.

(2) An executive summary of the recommendations.

(3) A more detailed statement of the problem situation and the issue(s) of concern identified, motivating the proposed approach of analysis. For complex issues, it is often a good idea to include a simplified version of the rich picture, stripped of irrelevant details and any sensitive personal aspects.

(4) A brief non-technical description of the major steps of the analysis, properly motivated where their inclusion is not self-evident.

(5) A list of the type and form of data required and their sources, if known.

(6) A qualitative statement about the nature of the benefits to be derived from the project and the form of the likely results, such as the form of the policy to be derived, and, if possible and relevant, a rough estimate (maybe in the form of a range or lower bound) of any financial benefits likely to be derived from the implementation of the results, as well as an indication whether any prior sponsor expectations are likely to be met, and if not, why not.

(7) A list of the resources — mainly inputs of time by the problem analyst and other staff, including those of the problem owner, and funds — required to bring the project to a successful completion.

(8) A detailed time-table in terms of elapsed time for completion of the major steps of the project as proposed.

(9) A statement with supporting evidence of the ability and competence of the project analyst(s) and other project team members to carry out the project as proposed. If the relationship between the sponsor(s) and the analyst(s) is long-standing and close, there may be less need for such a statement.

(10) A statement dealing with aspects of data confidentiality, such as whether data may be removed from their source location and in what form, etc. This may also cover aspects of professional ethics, such as whether permission has to be obtained for contacting external data sources, such as actual or potential problem customers. These aspects are of particular importance for projects in the health or social welfare sector. They are also important for student-type projects.

The written project proposal is often supported by an oral presentation to the problem owner(s) and problem user(s). Questions, doubts, and anxieties — which invariably crop up — can be dealt with, clarified, and alleviated on the spot.

If the decision maker finds that the likely results meet the desired performance standards and has confidence in the analyst's competence to bring the project to a successful completion, he or she will normally give the go-ahead for the second phase — the modeling phase. As mentioned earlier, for most commercial applications, the performance standards are met if the predicted benefits justify the cost incurred for the project analysis and implementation.

5.5 THE PROBLEM MODELING PHASE

We only had a cursory glance at the modeling phase for the ozone depletion problem. It is this phase that distinguishes the OR/MS methodology from other problem solving approaches. Often OR/MS is viewed as synonymous with a collection of powerful mathematical tools and techniques, such as linear programming or computer simulation. We shall see that this is a rather limited view which I find unhelpful, even detrimental to achieving the full potential of OR/MS.

The modeling phase starts out in step 4 by expressing the systems description, as it relates to the problem chosen for further analysis, in quantitative terms. This could consist of simply developing a spreadsheet for the quantitative relationships between the various system variables identified earlier. Often, it may be useful to translate the influence diagram into a set of mathematical relationships between the system variables and those aspects of the system that measure its performance in terms of desired system outputs.

In step 5 we manipulate this quantitative model to explore the response of the system performance to changes in controllable and uncontrollable inputs, i.e., we explore the solution space. The aim is to find the preferred solution in terms of the problem owner's objectives. If the problem owner is interested in one major objective, this means finding the optimal solution. For example, if profits are the performance measure, the optimal solution is the one that maximizes profits.

Step 6 establishes the model's credibility. Is it a valid representation of reality? How well do the model and its solution perform. What improvement in terms of benefits or cost savings does it offer over the current mode of operations? If the project deals with a future proposed system, what is the range of the potential benefits that can be expected? The answers to these questions will determine whether the project is abandoned, re-oriented, or allowed to continue on its current course.

Finally, step 7 consists of systematically asking 'what if' questions. How is the preferred or optimal solution affected by individual or simultaneous changes of uncontrollable inputs into the system? How costly are errors in the inputs in terms of reduced benefits achieved? Both are referred to as **sensitivity analysis**. Sensitivity analysis is without doubt the single most important step of most OR/MS analyses. The insights into the problem gained by sensitivity analysis may be more valuable than finding the optimal solution. Doing sensitivity analysis must become second nature for any operations researcher or management scientist.

Project Report

At the end of the modeling phase, the analyst prepares a detailed project report on the analysis done, its findings, and the analyst's recommendations about implementation. The problem owner's decision about further action on the project will largely depend on this document. Its suggested format is similar to the one followed for the project proposal. The language in the main body of the report should again avoid any OR/MS jargon. Its technical content should be at the appropriate level for the intended audience, namely the problem owner(s) and problem user(s).

5.6 THE IMPLEMENTATION PHASE

If the problem owner agrees that the performance standards are likely to be met, the project enters its last phase — solution implementation. Its first step (step 8) prepares a detailed plan of the various implementation tasks, their assignment to individuals, and a schedule for their coordination.

Step 9 establishes procedures for maintaining and establishing controls over the recommended solution. For example, it will specify for what range of values for various uncontrollable inputs the current solution remains valid and the exact procedure for updating the solution when inputs stray outside these ranges.

Step 10 makes the changes required to switch from the current to the proposed mode of operation. Preparation of complete documentation of the model, any software developed for its use, and self-contained user's manuals form an integral part of the implementation process.

Finally, after the new solution has been in use for an appropriate length of time, the analyst returns and performs an audit of the solution (step 11). This consists of establishing the extent to which the solution fulfils its promises in terms of the benefits achieved and the costs incurred, as well as checking for continued proper use of the solution and recommending possible changes in the light of the practical experience gained. This may give rise to a final project audit report.

As pointed out in earlier chapters, the aim of OR/MS is to improve the effectiveness of the system as a whole. Such improvements can, however, only be secured if the solution to the problem is implemented as fully as possible. Securing implementation of the solution is thus the prime concern underlying the formulation and modeling phases. All measures that increase the chances of full implementation have to be initiated and planned for right from the outset of the project. To some extent, the concern and planning for implementation starts right from the very beginning of a project and is carried through all other steps of the OR/MS methodology.

5.7 THE NATURE OF THE OR/MS PROCESS

Forward and Backward Linkages

The various steps are usually initiated in the sequence shown, but each step may overlap with both the preceding as well as the subsequent steps. For example, when we start identifying the problem to be analyzed, we may need to gather more specific and more detailed information about the problem situation which is then added to the rich picture, i.e., we return from step 2 to step 1 of the problem formulation. By the time we get to the project proposal (end of step 3), we may already have explored, at least tentatively, a general form of the mathematical model (step 4) which we judge to be most suitable for this problem. Not only may this allow us to determine some rough estimates of potential benefits, but it may also affect the boundaries and the level of resolution for the relevant system, thus linking phase 1 and 2.

The choice of the most suitable mathematical model should be influenced by how costly both its detailed development and ultimate implementation is expected to be. For example, if its use presupposes a level of training and skills which goes far beyond the norm for the type of employee in that position, we may opt for a simpler model. It is likely to capture less of the potential savings or benefits, but will have a better chance of successful implementation. The methodology has thus forward and backward linkages between phases, as well as between steps within a phase. The experienced analyst will constantly be on the look-out for such linkages.

Iterative Process

The methodology is also iterative. This means that the analyst may go back to previous steps and redo or modify part of the analysis already done. For example, describing a relevant system may point to contradictions or missing aspects in the rich picture. Before proceeding further with developing a relevant system, these issues should be resolved. This in turn may lead to changes in the relevant system. Sometimes during the solution step, the analyst discovers that the amount of computer time needed to find the optimal solution is excessive and hence the solution procedure too costly. Implementation of the model could therefore not be justified on a resource use basis. The analyst may have to return, or iterate back to the model building step and build a computationally less demanding model. Unfortunately, it may even happen that during implementation, crippling oversights in the problem formulation are discovered which render part or most of the model irrelevant or even change the nature of the issue. If the problem owner agrees, the analyst may have to start almost from scratch with a new problem formulation.

Few projects sail through all the various steps without iterating back once or several times to earlier steps in the analysis. You should therefore clearly keep in mind that even if we will discuss the steps separately in their natural sequence, the steps overlap. The analyst will at various times attempt to foresee potential difficulties in later steps, and may have to iterate back to earlier steps for changes.

Need for Full Documentation of Process: Keeping a Project Diary

During all phases, it is crucial to record for future reference all assumptions and simplifications made, and all data used, including their sources. This point cannot be stressed enough. As a project progresses through its various steps, it invariably undergoes minor or major revisions and changes. Assumptions, simplifications, and shortcuts introduced earlier have to be rechecked for their validity. They are easily overlooked or forgotten, unless they have been properly documented. Documentation is a prerequisite for establishing effective maintenance procedures over the solution. It is also part of proper professional ethics. An effective procedure is to keep a detailed project diary — a small note book that accompanies the analyst everywhere.

The Scientific Method and the OR/MS Process

OR/MS is often referred to as the application of the scientific method to problem solving. It is thus instructive to contrast briefly the three phases of an OR/MS project with the 'scientific method', as commonly professed in the natural sciences. It consists of the following. Based on past observations, logical deduction, or hunches, scientists formulate hypotheses about a phenomenon. They then devise experiments for collecting data which will either confirm or refute each hypothesis.

A priori there seems to be some analogy between the scientific method of the natural sciences and the OR/MS methodology. Formulating the problem may be akin to forming hypotheses; building a model would correspond to devising experiments; while implementing the solution could be seen as confirming or refuting the hypotheses. However, the resemblance is more apparent than real.

One of the prime reasons for this is that the use of the scientific method in the natural sciences is aimed at advancing knowledge in a given scientific discipline, usually under highly controllable laboratory conditions, while the OR/MS methodology is geared towards problem solving out here in the real world with its full complexity. So, one is to understand the world, the other is to change it. Another important tenet of the scientific method is that experiments should be fully repeatable and verifiable, so that the hypotheses are open to refutation by other researchers. This is practically never possible for OR/MS projects, which more often than not are unique and relate to an ever changing organizational setting in a turbulent environment. The prime criterion is 'Does it improve the system's operation?' Few OR/MS solutions would hold up to a rigorous test of refutation.

Whether the OR/MS approach is a scientific method is, in my opinion, not important. What is important though is whether the analyst follows some basic scientific principles, such as:

(1)   Have all important assumptions of the model been identified?

(2)   Has it been verified that they are not in conflict with the best available theoretical knowledge?

(3)   Are they supported by empirical observations about the system modeled?

(4)   Has the sensitivity of the model's behaviour to changes in these assumptions

and the input data used been tested?

(5)   Has a serious attempt at verifying and validating the model been made, e.g., by testing if the model is capable of reproducing satisfactorily the system's behaviour based on historical data?

Data Collection

Note that there is no step for 'Collecting data' in Figure 5-1. This is not an oversight! The reason why there is no separate step for data collection is quite simple — it does not occur at a given point in the analysis as a separate step. We start collecting and assessing data and identify data sources when we meet the problematic situation for the first time. As we proceed, we may need considerably more data for describing the relevant system. For some projects, the major part of the data has to be available when building a mathematical model. The specific form of the quantitative relationships may only be assessed if we know the major characteristics of the data, such as 'Are the relationships linear?', 'Is the probability distribution approximately normal?' In some cases, the data has to be directly incorporated into the mathematical relationships. In other instances, the bulk of data collection can wait until the model is ready for implementation, i.e., for step 10. Identifying sources of data, and collecting and evaluating data are activities that may occur in parallel with any of the 11 steps. Even the solution audit at step 11 requires data collection.

In some instances, the data may not be available in the form required or not at all. It is important that the analyst ascertains very early, but at the latest in step 3, whether the required data sources exist and in what form. If the data is missing or not available in a useful form, action has to be initiated to start the collection of the data in the form required. Furthermore, an assurance by various stakeholders that all the data is available and easily accessible should be treated with a healthy degree of scepticism. Indeed, I always show a lively interest in personally inspecting the data sources, check that they are in a useful form or can be easily transformed into such and verify the size and completeness of all data files. I have seen many instances where volumes of past data existed, but were in a state that did not lend itself to being manipulated into the required form, or had very crucial bits missing, or were in a useful form, but related to a mode of operation which had just recently undergone a substantive change. As a result, only the most recent few weeks or months of data were relevant for the current mode of operation — not enough for a proper analysis. In such cases, the major portion of the analysis or the implementation of the model may have to wait for sufficient data to become available.

Interviewing and Interpersonal Skills of the Analyst

In the initial three steps of the OR/MS methodology, the analyst will have to talk to or interview the various stakeholders, in particular the problem owner(s) and the problem user(s), but also people who have the information needed to get a complete problem situation summary and who may control data sources. Much depends on getting the needed relevant information. Inappropriate interviewing techniques can easily contribute to vital information not being unearthed and remaining hidden, only to be discovered at the implementation stage at a considerable additional cost.

Often such information is best elicited by having a very open interviewing style; by a frame of reference that conveys empathy, interest and curiosity of learning what the other person knows, rather than by coming across as the expert who knows everything — just remember that before you can teach somebody something new, you need to learn what that person knows; by asking questions that cannot be answered by a 'yes' or 'no', but are open-ended; by not asking two questions at the same time; by asking for clarifications, preferably with an example, if anything is not fully understood; and by feeding back the information gathered, so that the other person can verify the interviewer's understanding. Also, nothing can be more intimidating to a person with little or no OR/MS background than the use of technical OR/MS jargon. If several people are involved in the interviewing, avoid competitiveness. You are in it together, not to see who asks the most searching questions. Make sure the respondent has finished with an answer before going on to the next question. It is also important to watch out for non-verbal communications and respond to body-language of the people interviewed.

Rather than take detailed notes that may be disruptive and interfere with the interview, it may be a good practice to tape-record the sessions with the approval of the interviewee. If this is not possible, only minimal reminders should be noted down, and then expanded and completed from memory immediately after the interviews.

Information-seeking interviewing is an essential skill for any analyst. Unfortunately, an adequate treatment of such skills is beyond the scope of this text and the reader is referred to the references on this topic listed at the end of this chapter.

5.8 THE LUBRICATING OIL DIVISION — A SITUATION SUMMARY

The rest of this chapter will now apply the three steps of the problem formulation phase to a real-life project I was involved in some years ago. The modeling phase for this project is the topic of Chapter 6.

How Was the Project Initiated?

The project deals with the operations of the Lubricating Oil Division (LOD) of a major multi-national oil company. The LOD is in charge of producing about 400 types of automotive and industrial lubricating oils and greases, and storing the mixed product in the LOD's warehouse for ultimate sale to over 1000 customers — wholesalers, retailers, and large industrial or governmental organizations. The impetus for the project was a report by the firm's internal auditors to the Vice-

President of Finance of the company that in their judgment the current average stock turnover of 12 times per year achieved by the LOD on their products was well below the company's target of 24. (The stock turnover is equal to the ratio of sales over the value of the goods in stock.) As a result, the average level of inventories, and hence the funds tied up in inventories, was judged as excessive. This concern was passed on from the Vice-President of Finance to the Vice-President of Manufacture who, in turn, informed the manager of the LOD with a request to report to him in due course. The manager of the LOD approached the OR/MS group in the company for help. That is where I came in.

Learning the Stakeholders' Technical Jargon

My first action was to arrange for a guided tour of the offices and facilities of the LOD. Remembering people's names is one of my weaknesses. So, whenever I met a new person, I immediately wrote down their name and function on my note pad. I made a conscientious effort to understand, learn, and use the largely unfamiliar technical terms which I constantly encountered. If I did not understand or catch something, I was not ashamed to ask — even at the risk of looking a bit dumb. Furthermore, do not assume that somebody else's technical meaning of a term is necessarily the same as yours. Check it! It is indeed important to have a clear understanding of all technical terms used so as to ensure clear communications. Much confusion, needless misunderstanding, and frustration can be eliminated.

Details of the Operations

If I had been familiar with rich pictures at that time, I would have drawn up something like Figure 5-2 shown on the next page. Starting in the top left-hand corner, I show what triggers off the study and the implied Weltanschauung, namely a concern for economic efficiency of investments. The core of the picture describes the various operations of the LOD and its relationships with other parts of the re-finery operation and its customers. Here are some additional comments.

Production of lube oils and greases is done in batches varying in size from 400 litres to 100,000 litres, depending on the oil or grease type, the sales volume, and the type of customer. Many products are sold in a range of container sizes — 200-litre drums, 5, 1, and 1/2 litre cans. Defining a product as a given oil or grease packed in a particular size container, the LOD carries 804 different products. As shown in the rich picture, some customers are such large users that each order they place for a given product is satisfied by making a special production run and shipping the goods directly to the customer, rather than taking them from stock. Orders from smaller customers are met from stocks held in the warehouse. Obviously, as these stocks are sold off, they are replenished by an appropriately sized production run. The LOD follows a policy of shipping any goods to the customer within two days after receipt of the order, i.e., the delivery lead time is two days.

Figure 5-2: A Rich Picture for the LOD

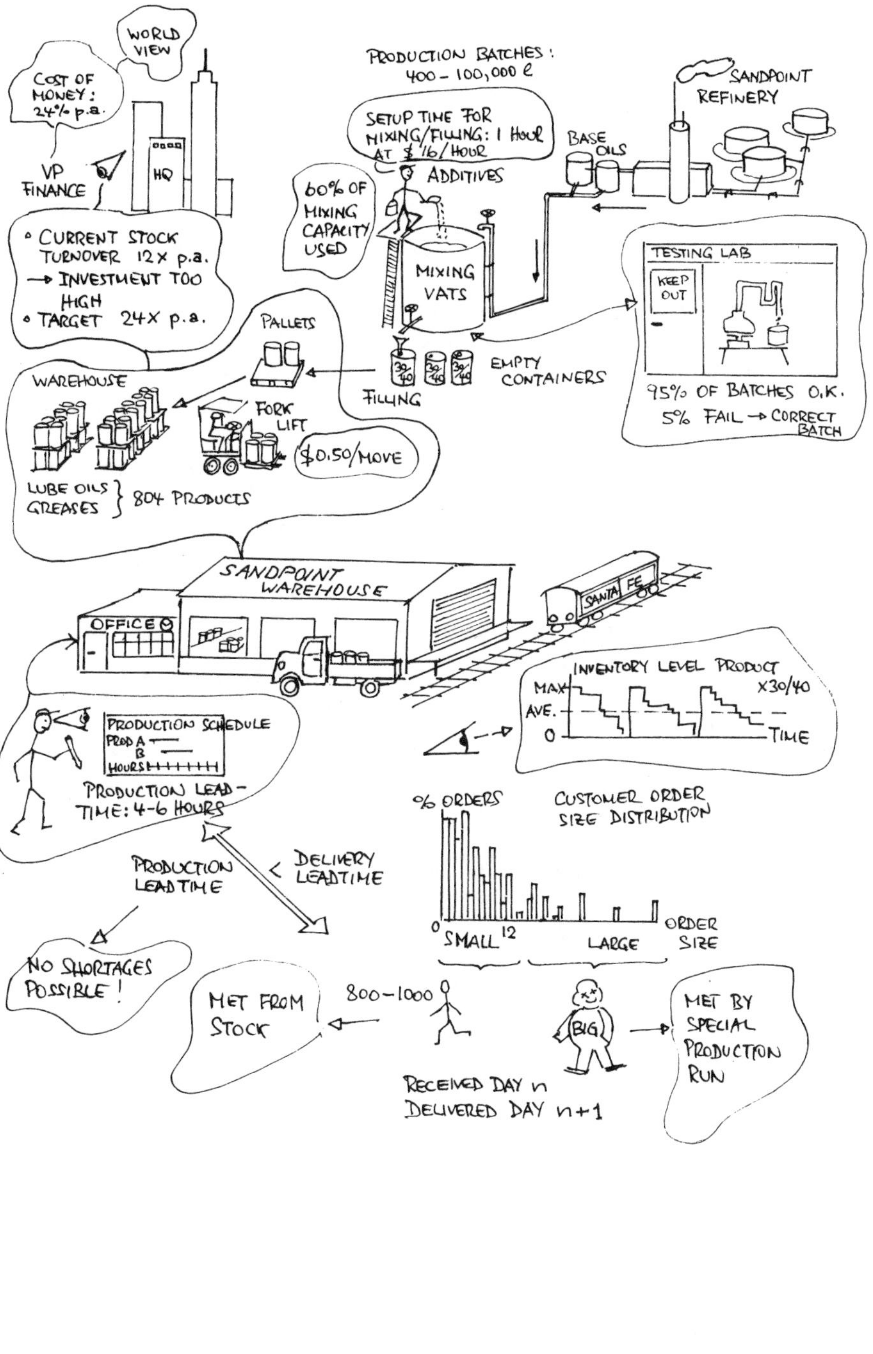

Various base oils and additives are mixed to specified recipes. The vat size chosen depends on the size of the mixing batch. The base oils are drawn from storage tanks, fed from the refinery. After mixing, the finished product is tested to ensure that it meets the desired specifications. Once a batch has passed the tests, the finished lube oil is filled into containers, usually within 4-6 hours. The pattern for grease production is similar.

The LOD's current mixing and filling capacity is sufficiently large so that with rare exceptions all production runs are completed within 24 hours, i.e, the production lead time is one day. It is this aspect which makes it possible to schedule special production runs for large customers after receipt of their orders and still have the shipments ready for dispatch within the planned two-day delivery cycle.

The same aspect also means that a stock replenishment has to be scheduled only once sales have depleted stocks to a level too small for meeting the last small customer order received. All customer orders are thus always met within the planned delivery lead time. Unsatisfied demand or shortages of products can never occur.

Note that packaged goods are moved from one location to another by forklifts. Goods supplied from stock, i.e., for meeting small customer orders, have to be moved twice, once from the production facilities to the stock location in the warehouse and a second time from there to the shipping docks. Goods for big customer orders, in contrast, are only moved once from the production facilities to the shipping docks. Hence, the total workload for forklift operators and the corresponding wage bill can be decreased by having more goods by-pass the inventory stage. The larger the fraction of customers classified as big, the lower the wage bill for forklift operators.

Suitable warehouse space is currently at a premium. On the other hand, ample production capacity is available in both the mixing and filling plants.

Assessing Document Flows and Data Sources

As a sequel to the guided tour of the operating facilities, I had an extended visit to the offices of the LOD. I carefully noted how customer orders and stock replenishment were processed. I took copious notes and drew diagrams of document and information flow for processing customer orders, from receipt to shipment, and for initiating and processing of stock replenishment. I had them verified on the spot by the people involved in the various activities.

Naturally, my 'intense curiosity' in seeing all data files was interpreted as enthusiasm for the project. I asked for photocopies or samples of all documents associated with customer orders and shipment of goods, stock replenishment orders, and stock records. I checked how far into the past data files were kept and whether during that period any major operational or procedural changes in processing information had occurred. I was relieved to find that all customer orders for the current and the most recent past two years were kept on file in an easily accessible form.

Once back in my office, I immediately organized all information gathered in a systematic form, filling in any gaps from memory, and highlighting aspects that needed further clarification or verification on subsequent visits.

5.9 IDENTIFYING THE PROBLEM TO BE ANALYZED

Identifying the Issue to be Analyzed

The rich picture indicates a number of possible issues, such as the process of scheduling production runs, which includes the coordination of mixing and filling; or the decision of which customer orders are classified as big and which ones as small; or whether it would be advantageous to allow a lengthening of the production lead time from the current 1-day period.   The latter would allow for better smoothing of the mixing and filling workload and could possibly reduce the number of operators needed to perform the same tasks.   The constraint on maintaining the current level of customer service clearly precludes the latter course of action.

The stimulus for raising this problem situation in the first place is the concern voiced by the Vice-President of Finance.   Her statement about the inadequate average turnover of stocks in the LOD implies too many funds tied up in stocks. The average stock turnover for the LOD as a whole is simply a weighted average over all products.   As shown in the rich picture, the normal inventory behaviour over time for each product has a typical saw-tooth pattern.   Each tooth corresponds to one stock replenishment and represents one complete stock turnover for that product. The fewer stock turnovers per year, the larger must be the stock replenishment.   For example, if the demand for a given product is 120,000 litres per year and the size of each stock replenishment is 5,000 litres, the stock turnover is 24 times per year. If the stock turnover is reduced to 12 times per year, then each stock replenishment must be equal to 10,000 litres.   So we see that the stock turnover for each product is directly linked to the size of the corresponding stock replenishment, which is controllable by the LOD.   This issue is taken as the focus of our project.

Discussions with the LOD manager indicated that he essentially shares the Weltanschauung revealed by the Vice-President of Finance, namely the most efficient use of the LOD's resources.   The Vice-President of Finance sees funds tied up in stocks as lying idle, whereas a high stock turnover is interpreted as a sign of efficiency.   From this narrow perspective, reducing the size of stock replenishment will increase the stock turnover.   This would allow meeting the Vice-President's goal or prior expectation of a stock turnover of 24 times per year, thereby reducing the total investment in stocks.   However, from the rich picture we see that every mixing and filling run also involves a setup — the time one or several operators spend to prepare a mixing and filling run and the time the lab technician needs to test the mixed products.   Increasing the turnover rate for a given product means that more stock replenishment and hence more production setups have to be made.   As a consequence, the time spent by operators on setups will also increase.   At $16 per hour, this can well mean that any savings made by reducing investments in stock may be lost by higher annual labour costs.

Similarly, lowering the cutoff point, below which customer orders are defined as small, reduces the total demand met from stock. Consequently smaller stock replenishments are needed for maintaining the same stock turnover. This in turn translates into a reduction in the investment in stocks. But such an action also increases the number of special production runs, and increases the annual production setup costs.

A narrow efficiency approach may thus not be in the best interest of the firm (unless for other reasons the firm wishes to reduce its investments regardless of its effect on operating costs). We need to consider all costs that are affected by a change in the inventory replenishment policy. In other words, we are looking for the most effective production/inventory control policy — a policy that keeps the total cost of the operations as low as possible, while at the same time maintaining or even improving the current level of customer service. Even if our relevant system is confined to the production/inventory control operations, the perspective taken is the one that looks at the effects on the firm as a whole, rather than just the narrow (sub)system involved. (Recall our discussion on efficiency in Section 2.2.) If this also meets the Vice-President's target stock turnover, all the better. But it should not be the driving force. The sponsor/problem owner should though fully understand the reasons for this and agree with them. Hence, some management of prior expectation may be required right at the start of the project.

The Narrow System of Interest

There is a whole hierarchy of systems involved in this problem situation. The widest system is the company as a whole, with the refinery as one of its subsystems. The LOD in turn is a subsystem of the refinery system. Within the LOD system, the production/inventory control operations form one of its major subsystems. It is the latter which is the narrow system of interest here. Since the LOD operation as a whole has control over the resources needed by the narrow system of interest, as well as having the final say in terms of the project, it becomes the wider system of interest. A suitable one-sentence definition for this relevant system is 'A system for the replenishment and stock control of packaged finished goods which keeps the total operating costs for the LOD as low as possible while maintaining the current level of customer service'.

Stakeholders

With the narrow system of interest tentatively chosen, we know enough about the situation for identifying the various stakeholders of the problem situation. These are defined with respect to this narrow system of interest. Obviously, I take the role of problem analyst. There seem to be several levels of problem owners or decision makers. This is typical of problem situations involving a hierarchy of systems, as is the case here. At the top is the Vice-President of Finance who coordinates the use of funds within the firm. She states the criteria by which investments of funds are to be evaluated. The Vice-President of Manufacture (refinery system) operates subject to these criteria. He has delegated the authority for making day-to-day operational decisions on production and stock control for packaged products to the manager of the LOD (LOD system). For projects that do not involve any major investments, the latter is the immediate decision maker of the situation. However, he will have to refer the decision on large investments to the Vice-President of Manufacture.

A priori, the only use of new funds is the cost of the project itself. Once the project has been completed, the analyst may recommend a change in the level of investment in inventories. Any such recommendations will then be evaluated in terms of the investment criteria specified by the Vice-President of Finance. At this point in the analysis, the project cost is the only use of funds which has to be evaluated. As it turns out, even that exceeds the manager's authority and hence has to be referred higher up. But once approved, any changes to the day-to-day operation of the LOD are under the control of its manager. He is viewed as the problem owner. It is his Weltanschauung that the problem solver must use as a basis for determining the goal or aim of the project.

It is important to confirm that the Weltanschauung of the various levels of problem owners, corresponding to the hierarchical systems levels, are compatible. If not, the analyst should point this out and strongly suggest that any conflicts are resolved prior to proceeding with the problem formulation. Resolution of such conflicts is usually beyond the scope of an MS/OR project. It deals with basic organizational issues and requires a soft systems methodology geared towards conflict resolution. The persistence of conflicting world views between various levels of decision makers is likely to result in serious suboptimization, i.e., the benefits gained may be wholly or partially negated by additional costs inflicted elsewhere in the organization, e.g., in another subsystem at the same or at a different level. In our case, we have already ascertained that there is basic agreement between the Weltanschauung of the Vice-President of Finance and the LOD manager in terms of profit maximization. However, one source of conflict could arise if the optimal solution does not meet the stock turnover target set by the Vice-President of Finance. This issue should be resolved at an early date.

To determine the problem users, we need to identify who is in charge of ordering production runs for stock replenishment or large customer orders. These 'decisions', within the policy defined by the problem owner — the LOD manager — are made by the stock officer. Naturally, she also has been the major store of information, knowledge, and experience for the rich picture. Any changes to the rules of the inventory/production control policy will have to be such that she is capable of applying them. She has some basic training in using computer work stations, but little tertiary education beyond high school. This aspect is a relevant input for the modeling phase. The complexity of the model should not require much training beyond what the problem user currently has or can obtain with a reasonable effort.

The customers for the LOD's products are the problem customers. One of the first points raised by the LOD manager is that any new policy will have to maintain or improve the current level of service offered to all customers.

In addition to the requirement for maintaining at least the current level of customer service, there is another constraint that any proposed production/inventory control policies will have to meet. The warehouse space and production capacity requirements of any new policy have to remain in the medium term within the current capacities available.

Problem Elements

In summary, the four elements of the problem are:

- the immediate decision maker: the LOD manager;

- the objective: keeping the cost of the LOD's operation as low as possible, subject to maintaining the same level of customer service;

- the performance measure for evaluating any control policy: the total operating costs of the LOD;

- the alternative courses of action: the size of stock replenishment batches and the cutoff point for classifying customer orders as big or small.

This listing of the problem elements may also serve as a substitute for the summary system definition of the problem. It again puts a clear focus on what the analysis is supposed to achieve.

5.10 THE COMPONENTS OF THE STOCK REPLENISHMENT SYSTEM

Step 3 of the problem formulation determines the system relevant for the decision problem identified above. Recall again from Section 4.6 why it is important to carefully define a relevant system with sufficient detail. It forces the analyst to formally recognize all important structural and process relationships in which the problem is embedded and which form the basis for the ensuing mathematical model. It is the major guarantee that they are properly represented in the model the analyst is going to build.

Whereas gaining a better understanding of the system interactions is the aim in the ozone depletion problem, effective control is the reason for analyzing the stock replenishment system. The emphasis of the system description is thus to explore how the system's performance, as measured by its total costs, responds to changes in the controllable inputs. Hence, the relevant aspects of the problem situation are all those that directly or indirectly affect total costs. Any aspect which does not affect the costs of the decision system can, indeed, should be ignored as irrelevant, even if it is directly or indirectly associated with the system.

Furthermore, we are not really interested in the total cost for a particular year, say the most recent 12-month period. Instead, our aim is to devise decision rules for the future. Since that future is unknown we assume it will maintain a pattern similar to the past. So we take the total long-run average cost as a measure of performance. It is the system output of prime importance to us.

The total annual cost is a direct consequence of the behaviour of the system, characterized by the saw-tooth pattern of finished stocks over time, as depicted in the rich picture in Figure 5-2. This pattern is the result of periodic replenishments and the steady trickle of stock withdrawals to satisfy customer orders. The latter are one of the major inputs into the system. Hence, the transformation process of the relevant system is converting a customer demand pattern for a given product into a total cost of meeting that demand.

So where should the boundary of the relevant system be placed? An experienced analyst will be tempted to use the typical inventory/production control structure for defining the system. The usual inventory/production control aspects are all present. But the problem situation includes aspects not normally found in such a structure, in particular, the different rules to meet big and small customer orders. It is thus a good idea to use a process approach for defining the system and start from first principles. The first point to keep in mind is that the system is made up of some 800 different products, each going through the same process of mixing, filling, warehousing, and shipment. So when we apply the four rules for identifying the systems aspects (listed under the Process Approach in Section 4.6), most of the answers refer to individual products. Table 5-1 lists these answers.

Note that orders from big customers by-pass the inventory stage. They are met by scheduling a special production run for immediate shipment to the customer. Does this then imply that this part of the operation is also outside the narrow system of interest dealing with inventory control? The answer depends on whether the decision as to what constitutes a big or a small customer order is viewed as part of the narrow system or not. If it is seen as a policy decision imposed on the system, then that whole part of the operation can be excluded. However, is this a good way of looking at the system? If the cutoff point at which a customer order is classified as big is increased, fewer customer orders are met by special production runs, but more of the demand has to be met from stock. This clearly will decrease the number of special production runs, but increase the number of stock replenishment runs, as well as the workload for the forklift operators. Hence, this aspect affects the inventory/production control system of the LOD in several ways. It is more appropriately seen as a decision that affects the narrow system of interest. This is the approach taken here. So, the cutoff point for classifying customer orders as small or big is one of the two decision variables for each product in this system.

As a footnote, it is interesting to study what type of controls — open loop or feedback controls — these two sets of decision variables give rise to. The customer order classification is an open loop control. Each incoming customer order (an input to the system) is simply classified as big or small depending on whether or not it is

Table 5-1 Identification of LOD system

Aspect of entity	Rule used	Identification
Cutoff point for large customer orders	1	control input
Stock replenishment quantity	1	control input
Total operating costs of LOD	2	performance output
W'house space excess/shortage	2	global output
Mixing capacity excess/shortage	2	global output
Filling capacity excess/shortage	2	global output
Customer order size classification	3	decision subsystem
Stock level review	3	decision subsystem
Demand small customers	3	component
Demand large customers	3	component
LOD production setup (layout, sequence)	3	structure
Production process for stock replenishments	3	subsystem (process)
Production process for large cust. orders	3	subsystem (process)
Batch testing process	3	subsystem (process)
Production setup cost	3	component
Total value of products produced	3	component
Warehousing	3	subsystem (process)
Stocks of filled products	3	component
Investment in stocks	3	component
Warehouse space use	3	component
Stock holding cost	3	component
Product handling process	3	subsystem (process)
Product handling cost	3	component
Delivery of customer orders	4	ignored
Refinery operation	1 (remotely)	ignored
Base oil availability	1 (remotely)	ignored
Product specifications	1	data input
Product cost/unit	1	data input
Customer demand pattern	1	data input
Setup and mixing time/batch	1	data input
Capacity of mixing plant	1	global constraint
Setup and filling time/batch	1	data input
Capacity of filling plant	1	global constraint
Testing cost per batch	1	data input
Container cost	1	data input
Warehouse space/stock unit	1	data input
Mix/fill setup cost/batch	1	data input
Unit product handling costs	1	data input
Cost of funds invested	1	data input
Warehouse capacity	1	global constraint
Delivery lead time	1	constraint
Production lead time	1	constraint

equal to or larger than the cutoff point. In Table 5-1 it is listed as 'Customer order size classification', a decision subsystem. On the other hand, the stock replenishment review forms part of a feedback control mechanism. Whenever the stock of goods (a component of the system) has been depleted so that the balance remaining is less than a given small customer order (also a component of the system), a stock replenishment is triggered. Each stock replenishment is thus initiated by feedback received from the system itself. In Table 5-1 it is listed as 'Stock level review', another decision subsystem.

I find that the easiest way to compile such a table is to start out by listing the control inputs, the performance outputs, and any other system outputs. This is then followed by the system structure and the transformation processes, and the system component. Studying each of the components usually helps in identifying the inputs required, particularly data inputs, such as various costs.

Two potential inputs are shown as only 'remotely' affecting the stock replenishment system and hence ignored for that reason. For instance, any breakdowns in the operation of the refinery or a fundamental change in the output of base oils from the refinery will affect the operations of the LOD. However, we can safely assume that the stocks of base oils are always maintained at a sufficiently high level to insulate the LOD from short refinery breakdowns, or that any fundamental output changes will be planned with the LOD needs in mind.

Some inputs, like the various production capacities, have the character of constraints on each product individually or the system as a whole. They are labelled accordingly. Their effect is to restrict the decision choices either individually or globally. For instance, the warehouse space required to store a product is proportional to the size of the stock replenishment. The total amount of warehouse space needed is the sum over all products. That amount cannot exceed the warehouse space available. So we see that the constraint on warehouse space limits the choice of replenishment sizes that can be used. If the relevant system were enlarged to allow changes in these constraints, then they would become control inputs (decisions) of the system.

5.11 INFLUENCE DIAGRAM FOR STOCK REPLENISHMENT SYSTEM

Figure 5-3 is my version of an influence diagram for the stock replenishment system of the LOD. Remember that an influence diagram shows the transformation process of the system, i.e., how the control inputs and other inputs affect the system variables for various system components, and how these in turn affect the system outputs, in particular the performance outputs. It does not show the flow of material or information or the sequence of tasks and/or the steps of the replenishment decisions.

The LOD system defined analyzes cost relationships within a decision framework. Therefore, the influence diagram must not include the objective, i.e., the minimization of total costs. It should only show the relationships that affect the

Figure 5-3: Influence diagram for LOD stock replenishment system

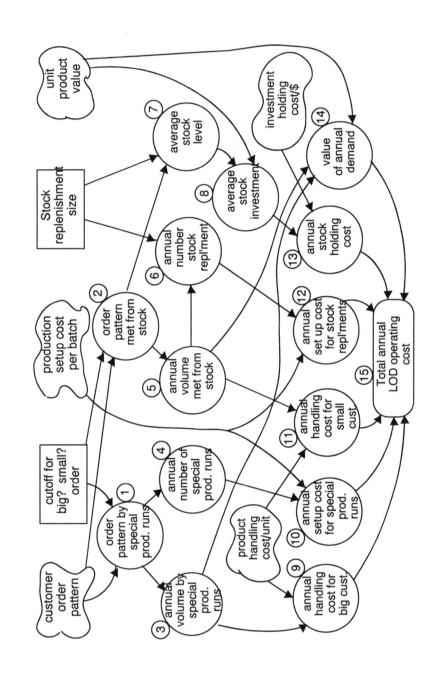

measure of performance of the system defined, namely total cost. I chose to look at total annual cost — a logical choice, but essentially arbitrary. Monthly costs would be equally valid.

To reduce the complexity of the diagram any relationships affecting the remaining three outputs dealing with warehouse, mixing, and filling capacity usage are not shown. Furthermore, the total cost for all products together is simply equal to the sum, over all products, of the individual total costs. These two simplifications allow me to view the influence relationships on an individual product basis, rather than globally. This is the approach taken in Figure 5-3.

I find that the easiest approach to draw an influence diagram is to go from control and other inputs via state variables to system outputs in a logical top-down sequence. For example, the customer order pattern (an input) and the cutoff point for classifying customer orders as small or big (a decision) determine each of the order patterns met from stock or via special production runs. Each customer order pattern in turn determines the annual volume of orders processed via that option, i.e., the annual volume met from stock for small customers, and the annual volume of orders met by special production runs for large customers. The order pattern for special production runs determines the annual number of setups needed for this option. The latter together with the cost of a production setup (an input) determines the annual cost of production setups for special production runs, and so forth.

Once you understand the conventions of influence diagrams, you will find that they bring forth much more clearly and unambiguously the pattern of influence relationships between the various inputs, components, and outputs of the system than is possible with a verbal description. Furthermore, we shall see in Chapter 6, influence diagrams are also a useful step towards building a mathematical model for expressing the quantitative relationships between the various inputs, decisions, state variables, and the outputs of the system.

5.12 PROJECT PROPOSAL FOR LOD

We are now ready to answer the three questions whether to proceed or not, listed in Section 5.4. The answers are all affirmative. The problem can easily be quantified. All required data is readily available or can be determined at little cost. The LOD has a complete computer data base on all customer orders processed for at least the last two years, from which customer order patterns can be determined. Cost data on products and the production and warehousing operations can be either obtained directly from cost accounting data or computed without major expenses by observing operators' time and materials required for various tasks.

The question about potential benefits and costs of the analysis is somewhat more difficult to answer. Crude computations done for a few products using a simplified model indicate that the total operating costs could be reduced by $30 to $200 per product stocked per year, or an average of about $115. (For the time being, you will have to accept these numbers on faith. The next chapter shows what basic model was used to get these estimates. The model used is part of the very basic tool box familiar to all OR/MS analysts.) For a total of over 800 different products, the potential savings could amount to about $92,000 per year. A rough estimate as to the time input by analysts, computer programmers, and LOD staff is guessed to be about 200 days. At an average internal charge-out rate of $300 per day, the cost of the analysis would be recovered within less than one year from implementation of the results.

However, a more prudent approach is to undertake first a preliminary study for only a sample of products and extrapolate the findings for the LOD operations as a whole. If the results confirmed the above guesstimates, then a recommendation for a full-scale study can easily be supported. On the other hand, if a more detailed preliminary study shows that the potential savings are much smaller than the initial guesstimates, then this fact is discovered before an expensive full-scale commitment has been made — clearly a more sensible approach.

In this project much of the ground work done in a preliminary study can also be carried forward to a full-scale study. As a consequence, the total expense of a preliminary study followed by an extension to all products will not be appreciably higher than undertaking a full-scale study from the start. This is due to the fact that a substantially larger portion of the total cost of a full-scale study is incurred for data collection, computation of the optimal policies, and their implementation, while the cost of the modeling phase is relatively small.

A further reason for opting for a preliminary study is that we are dealing with a fairly large number of products. Had it been only a few products, most of the justification for a preliminary study would have disappeared. The cost of a full-scale study would then only have been a little higher.

The choice of whether to go for a preliminary or a full-scale study depends on which phase of the OR/MS methodology incurs the most substantial portion of the cost of the analysis. If it is the modeling phase, the tendency would be to opt directly for a full-scale study. If it is the implementation phase, as in the LOD case, a preliminary study is the less risky approach.

The prior expectations of the Vice-President of Finance about the annual target stock turnover of 24 times has already been discussed earlier. However, this aspect may need to be resolved before the project proposal is submitted. It may also be advisable to pick up this aspect in a diplomatic way in the project proposal.

The Appendix to this chapter contains a project proposal for a preliminary study of the LOD production/inventory control problem. The rich picture is not shown. The relatively low degree of complexity of the LOD problem does not justify its inclusion. Also, the statement of the problem and the brief description of the major steps (points 3 and 4 in Section 5.4) already indicate the nature and form of the expected result; hence point 6 can be omitted. Similarly, points 9 and 10 are usually not relevant for an internal consultant. Keep the pointers given in Section 5.4 clearly in mind when reading the Appendix.

If this project proposal were written by external consultants, a short description of the mathematical model proposed would be included as an appendix

5.13 CONCLUSIONS

How an analyst goes about describing the problem situation by a rich picture has a fair degree of arbitrariness — and so does her or his formal system definition and its diagrammatic representation. All are strongly influenced by the purpose of the analysis, the Weltanschauung of the problem owner as well as the one of the analyst, and the resources (time, funds, people) available for the job. You should therefore not look for a unique right answer. In highly complex or somewhat controversial problem situations, it may be highly instructive to try several descriptions and system definitions, differing in the level of resolution as well as possibly their assumed Weltanschauung. This could bring about new ways of looking at the problem situation. The additional insights gained may contribute towards successfully dealing with the problem situation.

When reading about how to do a problem formulation, the tyro management scientist is often somewhat impatient: 'This seems to be all obvious — let's get down to the really interesting mathematical modeling phase! That is real OR/MS!' Unfortunately, unless the groundwork for the modeling phase is properly done in the formulation, the risk is great that, although challenging, the modeling may address the wrong problem. Not only can this have serious consequences for the analyst, it also puts OR/MS into disrepute.

EXERCISES

1. Draw a rich picture diagram, which shows the various issues and the world view of the project owner, for the following situation: E. Lim E. Nate, or Lim for short, recently joined STEEL FABRICATORS, INC. (SF) as their new production manager. Two years ago, after successfully completing an MBA, Lim had taken up a position as production planner for a sizable steel mill. He had liked that job since it allowed him to practice some of the theory he had encountered during his studies. After a year, the planner's job lost its challenge. It became largely a repetitive routine. Although SF is a much smaller outfit, he felt ready for a change, particularly since it seemed to be a step up in responsibility.

    SF produces a variety of steel products, mostly to special customer specifications. It had acquired a reputation for its high quality work and its ability to meet promised delivery dates. So, in spite of the general economic downturn facing the steel processing industry, SF has been able to attract enough new work to operate close to full capacity. In particular, its machine tool shop No. 3 has maintained a four-week order book up to now, while still keeping its high profit contribution in contrast to most other machine centres. However, it is only a question of time before the considerably lower prices offered by the competition will force SF to lower its prices also in the No. 3 shop. Furthermore, some competitors are offering delivery lead times of three weeks or less compared to SF's 6 to 8 weeks. There is therefore considerable pressure on Lim to remain competitive both in terms of price and delivery lead times. Lim's concerns are being heightened when he reviews the latest report on the rate of defectives produced by the various machine centres. The No. 3 shop sticks out like a sore thumb, with an average rate of over 8%. This is way beyond what could be expected from the type and age of machines operated there. He figures that if the rate of defectives could be reduced to a reasonable 2%, SF could afford to lower prices by 5% without affecting profits, and also trim a few days from its delivery lead times. He therefore decides to have a closer look at the No. 3 shop operation and pick the brains of the shop foreman and some of the operators for possible ideas on how to reduce the rate of defectives.

An extended visit to the No. 3 shop turns up some interesting facts. Most of the defectives seem to come from two particular machines. In fact, their rates regularly reach 1/3 of the machines' total output, while the remaining machines are not out of line with the rest of the plant with rates of around 1.5 to 2%. Although the foreman is well aware of the problem, he assures Lim that the operators are following the guidelines for maintenance and machine adjustments issued by the machine's manufacturer to the last bloody detail. He says that he regularly checks that this is so. Indeed, some months ago when he had been promoted to foreman at the No. 3 shop and had discovered that the rate of defectives of these two machines was around 25% he had called up the technical service of the machine's manufacturer for advice. For the particular job the machines were doing then, they tended to get out of adjustment with time, with a resulting increase in the rate of defectives. Re-adjusting the machine at regular intervals should therefore keep the rate of defectives at a reasonable level, still considerably higher than for other machines and other work. At that time, the machine operators adjusted the machines whenever they thought that the rate of defectives was getting too large, somewhere between every 40 and 50 minutes. The manufacturer's guidelines call for an adjustment every 60 minutes. Lim also finds out that each adjustment takes on average 6 minutes to perform — the time needed to produce three parts. Since the product mix has remained essentially the same, this is the rule that is still followed, however, without any success in lowering the rate of defectives. In fact, it has since increased to an average of over 30%. The foreman thinks that machine age can be the only logical explanation. He recommends that the machines be replaced.

Lim also finds out that about half of the defective parts can be reworked on another machine. So the loss of output from defectives is not 30% or more, but only about 15 to 16%. If this could be lowered substantially, delivery lead times from this machine could be reduced by at least a week.

Back in his office, Lim checks the files for the date of purchase of these machines. They are currently five years old. He also finds in the same folder the latest update on the range of machines offered by this manufacturer. To his consternation he discovers that no changes have been made to the specifications for this particular type of machine and the manufacturer indicates that its average productive life is still around 12 years. This essentially ruled out advanced age as a serious reason for the problem. A call to the cost accounting office shows that the cost of the raw materials used is $16 per part, the cost of reworking defective parts amounts to $4 per part, and the parts sell for a net price of $21. The labour cost for the machine, including all fringe benefits is $18.00 per hour. One operator is needed for each machine.

Taking stock of his finding, he notes down the following major points: The high rate of defectives of the No. 3 shop is exclusively due to two identical machines, with rates of over 30% defectives, half of which could be reworked at a cost. The manufacturer's guidelines on maintenance and hourly adjustment for these machines are followed strictly. The manufacturer has no other advice to offer. Solving the No. 3 shop defectives problem could only justify price decreases and shorter delivery lead times for the parts produced on these two machines, but not for the remainder of the machines. The output of these two machines amounts to just over 20% of the No. 3 shop total output. Pressure for increasing shop efficiencies for other products still remains. He is rather frustrated. This morning he was all fired up to tackle the defectives problem of the No. 3 shop. And now the situation looks rather hopeless, particularly since the manufacturer seems to be of no help!

2. (a) Give a one- or two-sentence summary definition for a suitable system for determining the best time between adjustments of the two problem machines in the No. 3 machine shop in exercise 1 above. The objective is to maximize their profit contribution.

    (b) Identify the stakeholders of the problem.

    (c) Use a process approach to define a detailed system for this problem.

3. Draw an influence diagram for determining the best time interval between machine adjustments, so as to maximize the profit contribution of the two machines in question. See exercise 1 above for details.

4. Mr. Lim Nate from exercise 1 has approached your QM instructor and offered his 'problem' as a student project. You have been assigned to it.

    (a) Identify all stakeholders of this problem.

    (b) Define the four elements of this problem (see Section 5.3 for help!).

    (c) Your first assignment is to come up with a short project proposal, outlining how you would go about 'solving' this problem. Both your QM instructor and Lim realize that without an almost complete analysis, you will not be able to give an estimate of the potential savings that can be obtained. So they do not expect you to estimate the potential savings. (But you should point this out!) Note that the situation summary does not allow you to determine a quantitative relationship between the rate of defectives and the time between adjustments. So you have to think about how you would go about estimating such a relationship in a simple, but still reliable way. In terms of estimating the time required to analyze the problem, armed with all necessary data, the problem can be solved by hand in a few hours or on a spreadsheet in less than an hour, using only simple numerical calculations.

5. The Continental Bakery bakes fresh bread every night for sale in its downtown store next day. Each loaf baked costs $0.75 in ingredients and sells for $1.60 in the store. The bakery employs several bakers. They earn $18 per hour. Each baker can bake 480 loaves of bread per 8-hour shift. Bakers have to be hired for a full 8-hour shift, even if they are not fully occupied. However, up to 1 hour of overtime per day can be scheduled for each baker. All bread baked during the night is delivered by truck to its store by 8 a.m. Naturally, the demand for bread varies from day to day. It is a random variable. So on some days too much bread is baked and some is left unsold at the end of the day, while on other days the store runs out and could have sold more. Any unsold bread from the previous day is picked up in the morning and returned to the bakery, where it is eventually converted into bread crumbs, sold to a fish processing plant. Unsold bread returned incurs a handling cost of $0.12 per loaf, while the value

of the bread crumbs produced is $0.28 per loaf. The owner of the bakery is in business mainly to make a profit. To maximize his profit he has to answer three questions: (1) How many bakers should he employ? (2) How much overtime should he schedule? and (3) How many loaves of bread should he have baked each day? Note that the answers to these questions are not necessarily independent of each other. Clearly, the number of bakers employed must be sufficient to enable production of the desired number of loaves to be baked, either during their regular 8-hour shift or with overtime of up to 1 hour for some or all bakers.

(a)   Give a short summary definition for a suitable system.
(b)   Using the four-rule process, define a detailed system appropriate for exploring the three questions.
(c)   Define the four elements for this problem (see Section 5.3 for help!).
(d)   Draw an influence diagram that shows the connection between the controllable aspects, the uncontrollable aspects, and the performance measure for this problem.

(Note that you are NOT asked to give a numeric answer to these three questions, but only define a relevant system or influence diagram for deriving them.)

6.   Read the Mushrooms Galore Situation Summary in the Appendix to Chapter 9. That case is used in Chapter 9 as an exercise for identifying various types of costs. Here we want to use it for the purpose of identifying a suitable system, etc.
   (a)   Draw a rich picture diagram for this situation summary, showing all issues and the world view of the problem owner.
   (b)   Give a brief summary definition for a suitable system to determine the best number of flushes per mushroom growing cycle. Bob Moss's objective is to maximize profits.
   (c)   Use a process approach for defining in detail a suitable system for this problem.
   (d)   Draw an influence diagram relating system inputs and decisions to the system performance measure.
   (e)   Define the four elements for this problem (see Section 5.3 for help!).
   (f)   Assume that you have been asked to look into this problem and prepare a project proposal for finding the optimal policy concerning the number of flushes. Note that the problem can be solved by hand or using a spreadsheet without any special OR/MS techniques. Assume that at the time you write the project proposal no detailed cost data, nor yield and picking rate data have been collected yet. Such collection is therefore part of undertaking the project. Also, based on the situation summary no estimates of potential savings can be derived.

7.   A firm produces ceramic tiles in its factory near Redding, California, close to the source of raw materials. Production occurs at a more or less constant rate, 24 hours a day seven days per week. The daily production amounts to 2 tonnes of tiles. The tiles produced are stored temporarily in the factory's warehouse in Redding, prior to being shipped to the firm's Oakland Distribution Centre. The current practice is to ship the entire production every Monday from Redding to Oakland. A special-purpose box rail car is used for this purpose. Its capacity is the equivalent of 28 tonnes. So the current practice is to fill the box car only partially. The cost of hiring the box car and having it hauled from Redding to Oakland and returned empty is $1195, regardless of the size of the load. Each tonne of tiles produced has a production cost of $12,000, including all raw materials used. The cost of holding tiles in inventory amounts to 30% of the

average value in inventory per year. The new production manager of the firm questions whether the current practice of weekly shipments is optimal. Obviously, the firm's objective is to make profits.

(a) Use a process approach to define a suitable system for evaluating the economics of shipping the tiles from the factory to its distribution warehouse. (It may help to draw a diagram depicting the behaviour of the tile inventory at the Redding plant.)

(b) Define the four elements of this problem (see Section 5.3 for help!).

(c) Draw an influence diagram for this problem.

8. Chicken farmer Angel Byrd is pondering whether to switch to a newly promoted chicken feed programme. The test results displayed in the advertising brochure seem rather impressive. They show the average weight distribution of chickens by week from hatching to 16 weeks of age. Obviously, the older the chickens, the heavier they become. However, as they get older they also eat more. Their efficiency of converting feed into meat declines. At age 7 weeks chickens have a commercial value. They reach their greatest value in terms of dollars per kg of weight at around a dressed weight of 1.1 kg. The problem is that out of a brood, not all chickens reach that weight at exactly the same age. Some grow faster, some slower than average. Hence, there is a dressed weight distribution for each age. Unfortunately, all chickens of a given brood have to be killed and dressed at the same time. The handling cost of sorting chickens by live weight is too high to be economical. Before Angel is willing to take the plunge for the new feed, she wants to make sure that her annual profit will in fact increase. The new feed promises faster growth, but it also is quite a bit more expensive than the feed she is currently using. So the number of broods per year must increase sufficiently to recover the increased cost of the new feed and also increase the annual profit.

(a) Define the four elements of this problem (see Section 5.3 for help!).

(b) Develop an influence diagram for this problem.

9. Read exercise 7 in Chapter 6 and develop an appropriate influence diagram, showing the relationship between the speed setting of the machine and the performance measure of total costs.

10. Consider the Customs Department case described in exercise 4 of Chapter 4. Identify the stakeholders of the problem and state their likely world view and their resulting aims or objectives.

REFERENCES

See references to Chapters 3 and 4. The problem formulation phase is discussed in detail in (1) J. Hughes and J. Tait, (2) J. Naughton, (3) R. L. Ackoff (*The art of problem solving*), (4) S. Cooke and N. Slack (particularly chapter 4, and 8 to 10), and (5) S. E. Bodily. The following little booklet displays a cartoon-like account of the problem formulation phase:

Carter, Ruth, Martin, John, Mayblin, Bill, and Munday, Michael, *Systems, Management and Change*, Harper & Row, 1984.

See also

Hill, Percy H., et al., *Making Decisions - a Multidisciplinary Introduction*, University Press of America, 1986. Chapter 3 is relevant here.

Hyman, Ray, and Anderson, Barry, 'Solving problems', *Science and Technology*, Sept. 1965, 36-41. Lists eight useful rules for successfully coming to grips with problem formulation and solving.

Pounds, William F., 'The process of problem finding', *Industrial Management Review*, Fall 1969, 1-19. Reviews some empirical and theoretical principles of problem identification — the first step of the OR/MS methodology.

The reader interested in alternative views on problem solving methodologies should consult some of the following texts:

Eden, C., Jones, S., and Sims, D., *Messing about in Problems*, Macmillan, 1983.

Flood, R., and Jackson, M.C., *Creative Problem Solving — Total Systems Intervention*, Wiley, 1991.

Jackson, M.C., *Systems Methodology for the Management Sciences*, Plenum Press, 1991.

Rosenhead, J., *Rational Analysis for a Problematic World*, Wiley, 1989.

Keeney, R.L., *Value-Focused Thinking: A Path to Creative Decision Making*, Harvard University Press, 1992.

References for report writing skills:

Anderson, Richard, *Writing that works*, McGraw-Hill, 1989. Well worth fun reading, with hints on how to overcome blocks in writing, includes a section of business writing.

Dumaine, Deborah, *Writing to the Top: Writing for Corporate Success*, Random House 1989. Step-by-step guide from getting started to final editing.

Sussams, John E., *How to Write Effective Reports (2nd Ed.)*, Gower, 1991. Comprehensive on all facets of report writing, including planning, researching, presentation of data, design, and reproduction.

References for interviewing skills:

Sidney, E., Brown, M., and Argyle, M., *Skills with People — A Guide for Managers.* Hutchinson 1973.

Mackay, I., *A Guide to Asking Questions*, BACIE 1980.

Downs, C.A.L., Linkugel, W., and Berg, D.M., *The Organisational Communicator*, Harper and Row 1977.

Appendix to Chapter 5: LOD Project Proposal

It is good professional practice to submit the written project proposal with a short covering letter.

PURAIR OIL COMPANY INC.
Management Science Group
SAN FRANCISCO, CA 94123

April 11, 199X

INTERNAL MAIL

Trevor Black
Manager, Lubrication Oil Division
Sandpoint Oil Refinery
PURAIR OIL COMPANY INC.

Dear Mr. Black,

   Re. Production/Inventory Control Project Proposal

Please find enclosed two copies of the project proposal for a preliminary production/inventory control study, covering packaged goods in the LOD warehouse at Sandpoint. I would be happy to answer any queries you might have. You can reach me on extension 7707.

I would also welcome the opportunity to make an oral presentation to you, supervisors, and other staff that might be associated with the project. This presentation could be arranged at two days notice and held in the Sandpoint Refinery board room.

In view of my current commitments, I would be able to start on the preliminary study by the end of May. I look forward to hearing from you in due course.

Sincerely yours,

   (signed)
Hans G. Daellenbach
Analyst, Management Science Group

Enclosure: 2 copies of Project Proposal

1

PROJECT PROPOSAL

PRODUCTION/INVENTORY CONTROL STUDY - PACKAGED GOODS
LUBRICATION OIL DIVISION, SANDPOINT REFINERY

Table of Contents

1. INTRODUCTORY STATEMENT

Middle of March, Mr. Black, Manager of the LOD, approached the Management
Science Group at the Company's Headquarters with a request to do a preliminary
investigation of the LOD production/inventory operations of packaged goods. It is
my understanding that this request is a follow-up on remarks in the Company's
internal auditors' report about the current level of investments in stocks at the LOD.
In particular, the auditors pointed out that the LOD's stock turnover of packaged
goods was well below the Company's target of 24 times per year, resulting in a level
of funds tied up in packaged goods judged as excessive.

I arranged for a visit to the LOD's production and warehousing facilities at
Sandpoint on March 27 and 28, during which I had extensive discussions with Mr.
Black, Mary Clarke, the stock control clerk, Bill Quick, the data processing
supervisor, and all four operations supervisors. I also consulted with the Cost
Control Department at Headquarters. The following report outlines my recommendations for a preliminary study, briefly motivates and describes the proposed
analysis, and lists the resources required and a time-table for the proposed study.

2. RECOMMENDATIONS AND EXECUTIVE SUMMARY

It is recommended that the Management Science Group undertakes a preliminary
study of the production/inventory operations with the aim of establishing whether a
full-scale investigation is justified. In view of the unique form of the LOD opera-

2

tions, a suitable model has to be developed and tested first. A crude approximation suggests that the potential annual cost savings range between $30 and $300 per product.

The preliminary study would develop a mathematical model for determining policies that minimize the total operating costs associated with the production and warehousing operations of the LOD. This model would be applied to a representative sample of packaged goods and the results extrapolated to the LOD operations as a whole. If the findings support the conclusion that all further costs for a full-scale study will be recovered within the first year of changing over to the new policy, i.e., within the Company policy payback period normally required for such projects, a recommendation for undertaking such a full-scale study will be made.

At the current internal analyst charge-out rate of $400, the cost of the preliminary study amounts to $8,000. Its recommendations would be submitted within 6 weeks after its commencement.

3. STATEMENT OF THE PROBLEM SITUATION

The auditors' report states that the LOD's stock turnover rate over the last two years averaged 12 times per year and hence is well below the company's target rate of 24. As a result, they conclude that the amount of funds tied up in stocks is about twice as high as the target level corresponding to the turnover rate of 24.

What are the cost implications of a given stock turnover rate? For the current customer delivery policy and production lead time, the average amount of funds tied up in stocks and hence the cost of carrying this investment for any given product is proportional to the size of its stock replenishment batches. On the other hand, the annual production setup cost is inversely proportional to the size of replenishment batches. Any reduction on the annual cost of carrying the investment can therefore only be achieved by increasing the annual production setup cost. It can easily be shown that there is a best size for each replenishment batch for which the sum of these two costs is at its lowest possible level. This also implies a best turnover rate for each product, which is likely to be different from product to product. Only by coincidence will the average turnover rate over all products be equal to the target rate of 24. A target turnover rate of 24 may thus be far from optimal in the sense of achieving lowest total setup and stock carrying costs.

If the objective is reduce total investment in inventories, it is preferably to set an upper limit, rather than a target turnover rate. The models can then be used to find the least expensive policy to stay within this limit. This recognizes the fact that the best turnover rate is different from product to product.

3

The current customer delivery policy offers the possibility for scheduling special production runs for direct delivery to customers, with the goods by-passing the inventory stage. They will then only be handled once, rather than twice. This is currently done for those products where large customer orders occur frequently. A decrease in the cutoff point for which customer orders are met by special production runs reduces the fraction of the total demand satisfied from inventories. This in turn will reduce the best replenishment size and hence the average investment in stocks, decrease product handling costs, but increase the annual number of setups incurred for special production runs and hence the annual setup cost. It will also affect the best stock turnover ratio for the portion of the total demand met from stock.

The best policy is the one which sets a cutoff point for special production runs and a stock replenishment batch size so as to minimize the sum of all the costs affected. The aim of this study is to estimate the potential savings in operating costs that can be achieved by using such a policy for all products and recommending what further steps should be taken.

4. BRIEF DESCRIPTION OF PROPOSED ANALYSIS

Rather than embark on a full-scale study right away, the proposal is to do a preliminary analysis intended to establish beyond doubt if the potential savings of a full-scale study are justified by the cost of such a study. The reasons for recommending a preliminary study are that (1) at this stage it is difficult to make any reliable estimates of the potential savings that could be achieved without substantial additional effort and data collection, and (2) the cost of extending the analysis to all products is roughly proportional to the number of products. The development of a suitable model is relatively simple. It constitutes a small portion of the overall project cost.   Hence, the preliminary analysis will be done for a representative sample of products. The results are then extrapolated to all products carried by the LOD. The preliminary study consists of the following major phases:

(a) **Development of model:** After further on-site study, a suitable model for the total annual relevant cost as a function of the two decision variables will be developed.   In order to keep development costs to an absolute minimum, the model will be prepared in the form of a computer spreadsheet.

(b) **Sample selection and data collection**: In view of increasing the accuracy of potential savings estimates for the new policy, products are grouped according to annual sales and a representative sample selected from each, making up about 5% of all products. Demand and cost data are estimated for all products in the sample using readily available data from the LOD data base of customer orders and costing data from the Cost Control Department.

4

(c) **Estimation of total savings**: Using a spreadsheet, the best combination of cutoff point and stock replenishment batch size is determined for each product with its corresponding total annual cost. These costs are then extrapolated for each product group and finally to the entire product line. This extrapolation is an estimate of the total annual cost of using the best policy for all products. This estimate is compared with the annual costs incurred for the current policy. The difference represents the potential annual savings. It is expected that the office costs of running the new policy are the same as for the current policy.

(d) **Estimation of further expenses for a full-scale study**: The expense in terms of internal employee charge-out rates, materials, and computer running costs for undertaking a full-scale study are estimated.

(e) **Forming of recommendations and preparation of project report**: The recommendation will state whether a full-scale study should be undertaken, based on the normal company criterion that all expenses for such a study must be re-covered by the savings generated within one year after implementation of the recommendations. If appropriate, the project report will also present a detailed budget of resources required and a time-table for undertaking the full-scale study.

The principal analyst has extensive exposure to production and inventory control and has been involved in such projects prior to joining our company. He will also have access for advice to the company's retainer consultant on policy and operational matters, Professor Carol Smart.

6

5. RESOURCES REQUIRED AND TIME-TABLE

Task	Analyst time	Other staff time	Elapse time
(a) Model development	4 days	1 day	
(b) Sampling design	2 days	2 days (LOD staff)	1 week
(c) Data collection	5 days	3 days (cost control) 3 days (LOD staff)	2 weeks
(d) Savings estimates	5 days	1 day (cost control) 2 days (LOD staff)	2 weeks
(e) Expense estimates	1 day		
(f) Recommendations	3 days		1 week
Totals	20 days	4 days (cost control) 8 days (LOD staff)	6 weeks

Chargeable costs: 20 days at $400/day $8,000.

Date: April 11, 199X   Project analyst:
                                        H. G. Daellenbach
                                        Management Science Group

6 Mathematical Modeling

In this chapter we pick up the modeling phase of the OR/MS methodology, in particular, how to capture the relationships between various elements of the relevant system in a mathematical model and explore its solution. We first define what a mathematical model is, argue why it may be advantageous to build a mathematical model, and then describe how a novice may go about the process of building one. This process is demonstrated with the LOD problem studied in Chapter 5. The chapter concludes with a general discussion on various formal approaches used for finding the optimal solution. One of these is then applied to the LOD problem.

6.1 WHAT IS A MATHEMATICAL MODEL?

A mathematical model expresses, in quantitative terms, the relationships between the various components, as they were defined in the relevant system for the problem identified in the formulation phase. Often it may be possible to represent these relationships in a relatively simple table using a PC spreadsheet. Sometimes, it may be more convenient or necessary to formulate the relationships by a mathematical expression or a whole set of mathematical expressions, like equations (e.g., $Q=ax+by$), inequalities (e.g., $ax+by \leq c$), or functions (e.g., $f(x)=ax+[b/x]$). The term mathematical model is thus used in a fairly broad sense, since it could be in the form of a table, as well as formal mathematical expressions.

Before proceeding, it will be useful to define some terminology. The controllable aspects of a problem are referred to as the **decision variables** or the alternative courses of action, the latter term being mainly used if the choices available are discrete and usually few in number. For example, when you consider replacing your car with another one, the alternatives may be: do nothing (i.e., keep the current car), replace it with a car of type A, B, C, ..., or Z. A decision variable, on the other hand, can be any integer or any real valued variable in a given range. In the LOD problem the size of the replenishment run or the cutoff level for classifying customer orders as big or small both have the character of decision variables. Both can assume any integer value (number of containers, e.g., drums, or cases of containers, e.g., cartons of litre cans) of a given product.

Those aspects that measure how well the objectives of the decision maker are achieved are called the **performance measure** or **measure of effectiveness**. If the measure of effectiveness can be expressed as a function of the decision variables, then we usually call it the **objective function**. As we have seen in Section 5.11, the total annual cost of the production/inventory policy for a given product carried by the LOD is an appropriate measure of effectiveness for this problem. Sections 6.5 and 6.7 show how it can be expressed in terms of the two decision variables above; hence this is the objective function of the problem.

Our aim may be to find values for the decision variables that maximize or minimize the objective function, whichever is relevant. In the LOD case, we want to minimize the total annual cost.

The uncontrollable inputs of a decision problem are often referred to as **parameters, coefficients**, or **constants**. For example, the initial purchase price and the fuel consumption per 100 km are input parameters into the car replacement decision, while the value of a product, or the production setup cost are input parameters in the LOD problem.

Mathematical expressions that limit the range of values that a decision variable can assume are called **constraints**. For instance, you may impose conditions on the minimum number of horse power or on the maximum rate of fuel consumption that a car must satisfy to be a possible candidate. Similarly, the amount of warehouse floor space available to store all products in the LOD problem is limited to 2000 square meters. Any solution that requires more than that is not viable or **feasible.**

Since the early 1950s researchers and practitioners of OR/MS have developed a number of general types of mathematical models, each with its own solution method, such as linear programming and its numerous extensions, network models, like critical path scheduling, and waiting line models, etc. They are commonly referred to as OR/MS techniques and form the core of most OR/MS teaching and textbooks. Each such **general-purpose model** has a well defined structure in terms of the nature of the decision variables and the functional form of the underlying relationships. Any problem that satisfies the assumptions of a particular general-purpose model can be cast into this structure and solved by its solution method. A number of chapters later on in the text will discuss some of these techniques in some detail.

For problems which do not fit a particular OR/MS technique, the analyst has to build a **special-purpose model** with a structure unique to the problem in question. He or she will also have to devise a suitable solution technique. Such problems are often more difficult to formulate and to solve, but may also be more challenging.

If all inputs and all relationships are known with certainty, the model is **deterministic**. If certain inputs or outcomes resulting from given actions are subject to uncertainty, i.e., the inputs or outcomes are subject to probabilistic influences, the model is called **probabilistic** or **stochastic.**

6.2 WHY BUILD MATHEMATICAL MODELS?

A pharmaceutical company which does research to develop a medicine for a given ailment will test a large number of compounds or combination of compounds on laboratory animals, and then the one or two that have shown exceptional promise also on humans. In contrast, when a management scientist wants to determine the best mode of operation for an existing process, there are no convenient guinea pigs available, nor is experimentation on the existing facilities a viable option. It would be far too disruptive, often too risky, and usually too expensive. Frequently, the problem deals with potential projects that are still on the drawing board. Hence, real-life tests are not possible. But even if real tests could be done, the time delay caused by testing one, let alone several dozen different configurations, means that real-life testing is out of question. In most cases such tests may take several months or years to become conclusive. The final answer may only be available when the problem has long become irrelevant! Mathematical models are thus be the only way to obtain answers to such problems quickly and reasonably inexpensively.

With today's interactive mathematical modeling packages, such as GAMS or AMPL, such models can be developed fairly easily — often within a few hours or days of analysis. The exception may be models that attempt to represent the entire operation of a firm, such as an entire oil company: the production of crude oil in oil fields, the transportation to the refineries, the detailed operation of each refinery, and finally the distribution of the refined products. Such a project may take several person-years to complete. The major costs are the salary of the analysts and main-frame computer user costs.

Mathematical models are usually easy to manipulate. This allows for quick exploration of the effects of changes in the inputs on the objective function, particularly with the help of computers. In contrast to real-life experiments, a new or updated answer can often be found within a few seconds of computer time, although there are some notable exceptions. It is these attributes which make mathematical models the workhorse of OR/MS.

6.3 ESSENTIAL PROPERTIES OF GOOD MATHEMATICAL MODELS

According to J.D.C. Little ['Models and Managers: Concepts of Decision Calculus', *Management Science*, April 1970], for a mathematical model to be useful it should be

(1) **Simple**: Simple models are more easily understood by the problem owner or decision maker, who is often mathematically untrained. The decision maker will more easily follow the logic of a spreadsheet than of a complicated set of equations, which may do little more than the computations performed in a spreadsheet — admittedly more elegantly. However, sometimes the analyst may have no choice but to build a complicated mathematical model. In such cases, the decision maker will gain confidence in the model if he or she has the opportunity to experiment with it, e.g., by exploring whether changes in the input parameters produce intuitively reasonable changes in the best solution and, if not, whether counterintuitive results can be explained convincingly. To get simple models, the analyst may have to make suitable approximations to the real situation or even delete certain significant aspects, which may later have to be

taken into account in different ways.

(2) **Complete**. The model should include all significant aspects of the problem situation that affect the measure of effectiveness. The problem here is to know, before the model is built, whether an aspect is likely to affect the optimal solution in a significant way. Experience will obviously help. It may though be necessary to build two models, one with these aspects present, the other without them, compare their answers, and then only make a judgment as to the significance of a particular aspect.

(3) **Easy to manipulate**. It should be possible to obtain answers from the model, such as the best solution, with a reasonable amount of computational effort. I am reminded here of the situation faced by meteorological services in the 70s, where they could produce accurate 7-day weather forecasts only by having very fast mainframe computers churn away for 5 days!

(4) **Adaptive**. Usually, reasonable changes in the structure of the problem situation do not completely invalidate the model. If changes invalidate the model, it should be possible to adapt to the new situation with relatively minor model modifications only. This is more likely, if the model consists of a sequence of small modules that each perform a reasonably separable task or set of computations. Any structural changes in the problem situation may then only require modifications to one or a few modules of the model. An adaptive model is often referred to as a **robust** model.

(5) **Easy to communicate with**. It should be easy for the analyst and/or the user to prepare, update, and change the inputs and get answers quickly. In today's world of interactive user-friendly computer programs and software, this property has become one of the standard selling points.

These are properties that the analyst will find particularly useful in a model, although the user will appreciate some of them also, such as (5). However, they may not be sufficient for the problem owner and user to actually implement and use a model. That depends to a large extent on the **confidence** the latter has in the model's ability to produce useful information, or loosely speaking in the model's **credibility**. But credibility and confidence are not attributes of the model, but of its user. The decision maker and user's perceptions of the model and the modeling process will in the end determine the model's fate. This adds a new dimension to the notion of desirable properties of models. In fact, it may not be useful to talk about desirable properties of models, but of **desirable properties of the modeling process**, since user credibility and confidence are more related to that process and the interactions with the modeler than to the model itself. Looking beyond the process of modeling, what are some of the crucial aspects that help building up the 'credibility' of a model?

(6) **The model is appropriate for the situation studied**. By this is meant that the model produces the relevant outputs **at the lowest possible cost** and **in the time**

frame required for effective decision making. For example, a simple financial spreadsheet may well be the appropriate choice of model if our objective is to provide a quick estimate of the company's profits for the next quarter, whereas a simulation study which models the movement of every single widget along the production line will not, unless it also produces suitable financial variables. And even then, its level of detail may be excessive and hence inappropriate for the situation studied. On the other hand, if our objective is to estimate the maximum possible rate of production, or the size of buffer space we need between machines, the simulation model will be appropriate, whereas the financial spreadsheet will not. There are two conclusion from this: (a) A 'good' OR/MS model may not necessarily show details of or resemble the physical system we are trying to optimize, and (b) the model must enable the analyst to measure how well the objectives of the decision maker have been achieved.

(7) **The model has to produce information that is relevant and appropriate for decision making.** This means that the output of the model has to have direct bearing on the decision process, has to be useful for decision making, and has to be in a form that it can be used directly as input for decision making, without the need for further extensive translation or manipulation. This does not imply that the decision maker may not have to use judgment in interpreting the information provided. But the information should lead to insights that the decision maker could not easily obtain by other means.

If the model satisfies these two properties and the analyst can demonstrate this to the decision maker and intended user, then this will considerably increase the likelihood that the latter will judge the model as **useful**. This will enhance the decision maker's confidence in the model and willingness to use it.

As mentioned earlier, confidence in and credibility of the model are not necessarily the result of a logical analysis of the model or even of an understanding of how the model works. It may be largely intuitive, based on a demonstration that the model gives usable, sensible, expected, and explainable answers in a timely fashion and with a reasonable expense. Furthermore, it will be strongly influenced by the working relationship between the modeler and the problem owner/user and the latters' involvement in the modeling process itself.

Note that some of these properties, and in particular the first five, put conflicting demands on the modeling process. A simple model may be unable to capture all significant aspects of the problem situation. A robust model may not be simple. A model that includes all significant aspects may not be easy to manipulate. The model builder will have to balance these conflicting demands and come up with a suitable compromise. This compromise will by necessity reflect not only the training of the analyst, but also the amount of resources in terms of time and funds available for the analysis. It should also reflect the likely benefits that can be achieved. It may be economically more advantageous to use simple quick-and-dirty rules that only capture 50% of the potential benefits, rather than develop a sophisticated and expensive model that may capture 90%. The costs of developing a mathematical model, collecting the required input data, computing the best solution, implementing the model, and finally operating and maintaining it all increase much more than proportionately as the sophistication of the model increases, while the additional benefits go up less than proportionately. All mathematical models are thus to varying degrees approximation to the real situation as perceived by the analyst.

6.4   THE ART OF MODELING

One of the aims of this text is to make mathematical modeling largely a scientific process. However, there still remain aspects of modeling which are more akin to art than science. This means that some people will discover that they possess a natural talent for modeling, while others find it hard going. So how should one go about modeling?

There are a few useful guidelines. Some are little more than common sense when approaching any new task, but, surprisingly, they are often ignored by the inexperienced.

Ockham's Razor

William of Ockham, a 14th century English philosopher stated a useful heuristic rule: 'Things should not be multiplied without good reason'" (Since Ockham was reputed to have a sharp and cutting mind, this heuristic has become known as Ockham's razor!) In terms of modeling it means that the modeler has to be highly selective in including aspects into a model. All aspects that are not absolutely essential or that contribute little to the 'accuracy' or 'predictive power' of the model should be excluded. A good model is a model that is as parsimonious as possible in terms of the variables/aspects included. In other words, it should be simple.

The experienced modeler will often slice through the messy situation confronting her or him and be selective in including all essential aspects in the model and only those. But how should the novice go about applying Ockham's razor? Once you have digested Chapter 6 and 7, you will have a better idea of how to do it and determine whether an aspect is significant or can safely be ignored. So, bear with me!

An Iterative Process of Enrichments

Successful analysts confirm that building a mathematical model is a process of successive rounds of enrichment. We begin with a very simple model — possibly quite removed from reality — and move in an evolutionary fashion toward more elaborate models which more nearly reflect the complexities of the actual problem situation. This advice seems harmless enough, yet it does require a certain amount of 'guts' to back off from the real problem situation in its full complexity, and knowingly commit the sins of omitting or distorting certain aspects. The aim is to discover how much of reality can be captured by the simple model.

On the second round, we enrich the model by incorporating additional aspects of the problem. In other words, we add bells and whistles to the simple model and see how far we get. This will allow us to discover how significant the effect of including other aspects into the model is. If all significant interrelationships have been taken care of, we are home and dry. Otherwise we build a more complex model and go through another round of comparing the new model with reality and of enriching it. Sooner or later we will reach a point where adding further aspects adds little to the accuracy or predictive power of the model, or where the additional complexity of the model puts it out of reach in terms of computational difficulties or renders its successful implementation questionable.

Working out a Numerical Example

Another piece of advice, which I regularly apply myself, is to construct an example with representative numbers and play around with them. I carefully observe how variables of interest behave. Often I discern certain regular patterns. I may also find analogies with other problems that I analyzed another time. It may suggest reasonable approximations or assumptions which make it easier to translate the relationships or the average behaviour over time into mathematics. These insights may suggest a suitable mathematical structure for the problem and allow me to proceed to the next step of formulating a corresponding mathematical model. But even if nothing earth-shattering is discovered, working through a numeric example provides the starting point for defining necessary notation and formulating corresponding mathematical expressions.

Diagrams and Graphs

If you are a visual person like me, you will find it helpful to see things in the form of graphs or other drawings that express relationships or patterns. Typical patterns are more readily visible from a graph than from sequences of numbers. For example as we shall see shortly, tracing the approximate behaviour of the amount of goods for a product held in stock by the LOD shows a strikingly regular behaviour over time. The analogy of a saw-tooth pattern immediately springs to mind. This may allow the analyst to infer something about the average stock level.

The shape or pattern in the graph may suggest analogies with possible completely unrelated problem situations familiar to you. The same approach as used there may turn out to be suitable or can be suitably adapted. Often breakthroughs in finding a suitable model are made from such analogies.

6.5 MATHEMATICAL MODEL FOR THE LOD: FIRST APPROXIMATION

I will now demonstrate some of the above guidelines for developing a first version of a mathematical model of the LOD problem defined in Sections 5.10 and 5.11. I will make frequent reference to the influence diagram for the LOD problem depicted in Figure 5-3.

We already discovered there that the same influence diagram is applicable individually for each product carried. The only connection between products is given by the constraints on warehouse space and mixing and filling capacities. The first obvious simplification to introduce is to ignore these constraints. If the collection of individual best unconstrained solutions for all products satisfies the constraints, then these are not restricting and ignoring them was a good guess. If any one of the constraints is violated, i.e., more than the available production capacity or warehouse space is needed by these solutions taken together, we try to enrich the model by appropriately amending the unconstrained solutions or by embarking on a new round of building a more comprehensive model.

In the influence diagram we identified two decision variables, the cutoff point for what customer order size is classified as big and the size of the stock replenishment. As a first approximation, we would rather deal with only one decision variable per product. Note that the original issue raised by the manager of the LOD — the decision maker — deals with the size of the investment in stocks. That investment is affected by the average stock level. The latter is a function of the stock replenishment size and the order pattern of small customers whose demand is met from stock. Thus, using the stock replenishment size as the only decision variable is a good starting point. However, rather than simply ignoring the decision variable for the cutoff point, we fix it to some arbitrary value. In other words, we do not use it as a decision variable, but treat it as another input. Together with the over-all customer order pattern it determines the order pattern for demand met from stock. Verify that now all inputs needed to find the cost associated with a given stock replenishment policy are given. Furthermore, the left-hand side of the influence diagram (circles 1, 3, 4, 9, and 10) is not affected by the stock replenishment policy and can be ignored for the time being.

We are now ready to build the first approximation of a mathematical model for the LOD. Using the influence diagram in Figure 5-3, I will build it up stepwise by expressing each system variable or outcome in terms of those inputs or other system variables with arrows terminating at that variable or outcome. I arbitrarily start with the annual number of stock replenishments, labelled circle 6 in Figure 5-3. The influence diagram shows that two arrows terminate at this system variable, one originating from the annual volume of demand met from stock (a system variable, labelled circle 5) and the other originating from the stock replenishment size (a decision variable). In mathematical language we say that the annual number of stock replenishments is a function of the annual demand met from stock, denoted by D_l, and the stock replenishment size, denoted by Q, i.e., $f(D_l, Q)$. To discover the form of this function we work out a simple numeric example: if the annual demand from small customers is 12,000 cartons of product X, and each stock replenishment is of size 1500 cartons, then 12,000/1500 or 8 stock replenishments, evenly spaces over time, each of 1500 cartons, are needed to meet the annual demand. In general:

$$
\begin{bmatrix} \text{Annual number of} \\ \text{stock repl'ments} \end{bmatrix} = \begin{bmatrix} \text{Annual demand} \\ \text{met from stock} \end{bmatrix} \div \begin{bmatrix} \text{size of stock} \\ \text{replenishment} \end{bmatrix}
$$

$$
= \quad D_I \quad / \quad Q
$$

The annual volume of demand met from stock (circle 5) is a consequence of the order pattern from small customers (circle 2). This is a system variable in the original influence diagram, but, for an arbitrarily fixed cutoff point, it assumes here the character of an input. It is simply equal to the sum of all small customer orders less than the cutoff point L. It is thus a function of L.

The influence diagram shows that the annual setup cost for stock replenishments (circle 12) is a function of the annual number of stock replenishments (circle 6), which we just determined as D_I / Q, and the production setup cost per batch, s:

$$
\begin{bmatrix} \text{Annual setup cost} \\ \text{for stock repl'ment} \end{bmatrix} = \begin{bmatrix} \text{Setup cost} \\ \text{per batch} \end{bmatrix} \times \begin{bmatrix} \text{Annual number of} \\ \text{stock repl'ments} \end{bmatrix}
$$

$$
= \quad s \quad \times \quad D_I / Q
$$

The influence diagram shows the average stock level (circle 7) as a function of the order pattern from small customers (circle 2) and the stock replenishment size. To discover the quantitative form of the average stock level, I again resort to a numerical example. Fixing the cutoff point to the level currently used by the LOD, namely 12, any customer order of 11 or less is classified as small. Assume that over a period of 12 days the following demands from small customers are received for a given product Y:

day	1	2	3	4	5	6	7	8	9	10	11	12
orders	10	8	0	6	4	1	9	6	10	6	1	5
(in drums)	8	8		5	3		8	5	6	3		3
	5	1		2			1		6	1		

Let us now observe what happens to the stock level for product Y as these orders are met by stock withdrawals. We also assume that we start on day 1 with a beginning stock of 60 and that, whenever the stock level has been reduced to zero, a new replenishment of size 60 drums is added to stocks:

day	1	2	3	4	5	6	7	8	9	10	11	12
beginning stock	60	37	20	20	7	0	59	41	30	8	-2	57
plus replenishment	-	-	-	-	-	60	-	-	-	-	60	-
equals available	60	37	20	20	7	60	59	41	30	8	58	57
less withdrawal	23	17	0	13	7	1	18	11	22	10	1	8
equals ending stock	37	20	20	7	0	59	41	30	8	-2	57	49

Note that the beginning balance on day t is equal to the ending balance on the preceding day t–1. The negative balance on day 10 means a temporary shortage which is immediately met from the new replenishment. A graph of the beginning stock over time gives a more revealing picture of the inventory behaviour. This is shown in Figure 6-1.

Figure 6-1: Stock behaviour over time

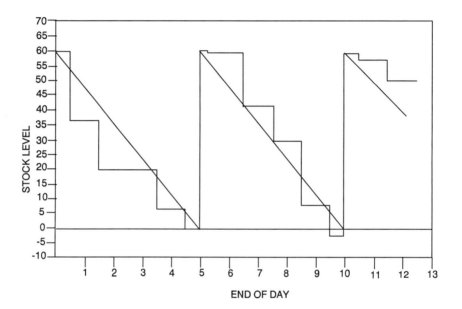

The stock level decreases in discrete steps from around 60 to zero in regular cycles of about 5 days. The broken line shows the average stock behaviour over time. The actual stock level is sometimes above, sometimes below the that line. The deviations tend to compensate each other. Each cycle, the stock level, on average, decreases linearly from its maximum, equal to the stock replenishment size, to its minimum of zero. This saw-tooth pattern is very typical for inventory situations.

The average stock level is simply equal to the average height of each triangle. This is given by

(maximum stock level + minimum stock level)/2 = $(Q + 0)/2 = 0.5Q$

Proceeding in this manner for other intermediate results and outputs, we get the following expressions:

Circle 8:

$$\left[\begin{array}{c} \text{Average stock} \\ \text{investment} \end{array}\right] = \left[\begin{array}{c} \text{Average} \\ \text{stock level} \end{array}\right] \times \left[\begin{array}{c} \text{Unit product} \\ \text{value} \end{array}\right]$$

$$= 0.5Qv$$

where v denotes the unit product value.

Circle 13:

$$\left[\begin{array}{c} \text{Annual stock} \\ \text{holding cost} \end{array}\right] = \left[\begin{array}{c} \text{Average stock} \\ \text{investment} \end{array}\right] \times \left[\begin{array}{c} \text{Holding cost/} \\ \text{\$/year} \end{array}\right]$$

$$= 0.5Qvr$$

where r is the holding cost per dollar invested per year.

Circle 11:

$$\left[\begin{array}{c} \text{Annual handling} \\ \text{cost small cust.} \end{array}\right] = \left[\begin{array}{c} \text{Product handling} \\ \text{cost per unit} \end{array}\right] \times \left[\begin{array}{c} \text{Annual volume} \\ \text{met from stock} \end{array}\right]$$

$$= h_l \, D_l$$

where h_l is the handling cost per unit for demand supplied from stock.

Circle 14:

$$\left[\begin{array}{c} \text{Annual product} \\ \text{value} \end{array}\right] = \left[\begin{array}{c} \text{Unit product} \\ \text{value} \end{array}\right] \times \left[\begin{array}{c} \text{Annual volume} \\ \text{of demand} \end{array}\right]$$

$$= v \, D_l$$

Summing up these intermediate results gives the total annual relevant cost for the LOD operation, based on the first approximate model:

$$\left[\begin{array}{c} \text{Total annual} \\ \text{relevant cost} \end{array}\right] = \left[\begin{array}{c} \text{Annual stock} \\ \text{holding cost} \end{array}\right] + \left[\begin{array}{c} \text{Annual setup cost} \\ \text{for stock repl'ment} \end{array}\right]$$

$$+ \left[\begin{array}{c} \text{Annual hand-} \\ \text{ling cost} \end{array}\right] + \left[\begin{array}{c} \text{Annual product} \\ \text{value} \end{array}\right]$$

$$T(Q) \quad = 0.5Qvr + (sD_l/Q) + h_l \, \mathrm{D_1} + v\mathrm{D_1} \tag{6-1}$$

We denote this total annual cost as $T(Q)$. It is shown as a function of the decision variable Q. Naturally, it is also a function of other inputs in the form of cost and demand parameters. It is customary not to show these explicitly as arguments in $T(Q)$. However, it would be useful to indicate that $T(Q)$ is in fact expressed for a given fixed cutoff point L. This would be shown by the notation $T(Q \mid L)$, read as T of Q given L. For simplicity we will not adopt this notation here.

6.6 EXPLORING THE SOLUTION SPACE FOR $T(Q)$

We now apply this model to one of the high volume products carried by the LOD, product Y. How does the total cost vary as we change the value of Q ? I set up a simple computer spreadsheet to explore this. Figure 6-2 shows the computations in some detail. It is always a good practice to reproduce the input data used somewhere on the spreadsheet, as shown in the top portion here. The cost parameters are those that would be obtained either from cost accounting information and/or by actual measurements of the time taken for various tasks. (Chapter 9 studies in more detail the nature of various costs.) The demand data for product Y are summarized in the frequency table of Table 6-1. It is based on 1266 customer orders received over one year.

The spreadsheet computations are based on a special production run cutoff point of $L=12$, i.e., only customer orders of 11 and fewer drums are supplied from stock, while all those of 12 or over give rise to a special production run. This implies that

Table 6-1: Frequency table of customer orders for product Y

Order size	Number of orders	Cumulative number
1	134	134
2	356	490
3	95	585
4	186	771
5	34	805
6	112	917
8	91	1008
9	15	1023
10	56	1079
12	85	1164
15	12	1176
16	48	1224
20	23	1247
24	19	1259
36	5	1264
48	2	1266

the annual volume of demand met from stock is equal to 4140 drums, while another 2992 drums are supplied by special production runs. These numbers are simply obtained as the sum of products of the order size and the corresponding number of orders in Table 6-1, i.e., the entry in column 1 times the entry in column 2. Verify, for example, that 1×134 + 2×356 + . . . + 10×56 = 4140.

I briefly demonstrate the computations for a particular row, say the row for $Q = 60$. The number of replenishments per year is 4140/60 = 69. Hence the annual setup cost is 69×$18.00 = $1242. The average stock level is ½×60 = 30. This results in an annual holding cost of 30×$320×0.18 = $1728. The annual handling cost is 4140×$1.10 = $4554. The product value of demand met from stock is 4140×$320 = $1,324,800. The last column, labelled 'Total relevant cost' is given as the sum of the two costs which change as a function of the decision variable Q, i.e., the sum of the annual setup and annual holding costs, $1242 + $1728 = $2970. More on its significance in the next paragraph!

Figure 6-2: Spreadsheet printout for $T(Q)$-model

LOD FIRST MODEL FOR STOCK CONTROL							
	Decision variable:	Stock replenishment size					
INPUT DATA							
	Demand met from stock			4140	drums/year		
	Product value			$320.00	/drum		
	Production setup cost			$18.00	/production run		
	Product handling cost			$1.10	/drum via storage		
	Investment holding cost			$0.18	/dollar invested per year		
COMPUTATION OF T(Q)							
Size of repl'ment	Number of repl. per year	Annual setup cost	Average stock level	Annual holding cost	Annual handling cost	Product value of demand	Total relevant cost
4140	1.0	$18	2070.0	$119,232	$4,554	$1,324,800	$119,250
2070	2.0	$36	1035.0	$59,616	$4,554	$1,324,800	$59,652
1035	4.0	$72	517.5	$29,808	$4,554	$1,324,800	$29,880
500	8.3	$149	250.0	$14,400	$4,554	$1,324,800	$14,549
250	16.6	$298	125.0	$7,200	$4,554	$1,324,800	$7,498
125	33.1	$596	62.5	$3,600	$4,554	$1,324,800	$4,196
60	69.0	$1,242	30.0	$1,728	$4,554	$1,324,800	$2,970
51	81.2	$1,461	25.5	$1,469	$4,554	$1,324,800	$2,930
50	82.8	$1,490	25.0	$1,440	$4,554	$1,324,800	$2,930
40	103.5	$1,863	20.0	$1,152	$4,554	$1,324,800	$3,015
30	138.0	$2,484	15.0	$864	$4,554	$1,324,800	$3,348
20	207.0	$3,726	10.0	$576	$4,554	$1,324,800	$4,302
10	414.0	$7,452	5.0	$288	$4,554	$1,324,800	$7,740
5	828.0	$14,904	2.5	$144	$4,554	$1,324,800	$15,048

The first interesting feature in the results shown in Figure 6-2 is that the two columns referring to the total annual handling cost and the product value of the annual demand met from stock remain constant. They are not affected by the size of stock replenishments. Since they are constants, they can in fact be ignored for this simple model. Only the annual setup cost for stock replenishments and the annual stock holding costs vary as a function of Q. Verify that this is in fact confirmed from the form of the total cost expression (6-1), where the last two parts do not involve Q. Those costs that vary as a function of the decision variable are referred to as the **relevant costs**. Ignoring constant parts, expression (6.1) can now be simplified to

$$T(Q) = 0.5Qvr + sD / Q \qquad (6\text{-}1A)$$

Any search for the best values of decision variables can be done on the basis of expression (6-1A) only. Costs that remain constant, regardless of what values the decision variables assume, can be ignored.

Again, a graph of the two relevant costs and their sum as a function of Q shows much more clearly how each behaves. This is depicted in Figure 6-3, produced by the spreadsheet program from columns 1, 3, 5, and 8.

Figure 6-3: Graph of costs as a function of Q

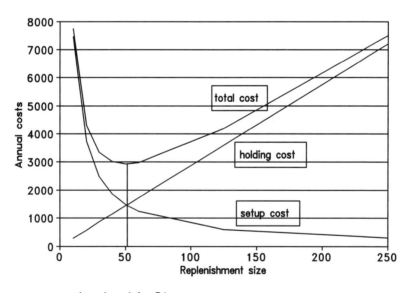

lowest cost for 51

Note that the annual holding cost increases linearly with Q, while the annual setup cost decreases in a highly nonlinear fashion as Q increases. The sum of these two costs has its lowest value of \$2,930 for a stock replenishment of size of about 50 or 51 drums. The value of Q for which the total relevant cost has its minimum is called the **optimal value** of Q. One of the aims of building a mathematical model is to determine the optimal value of all decision variables.

The graph shows that the minimum relevant cost occurs where the annual holding cost is equal to the annual setup cost. As we shall see in Section 6.11, this is not by coincidence. For this simple stock replenishment model, the lowest total annual holding and setup cost is always obtained where the two are equal to each other. This property can be used to find a simple expression for the optimal value of Q in terms of the input parameters. Setting the annual holding cost equal to the annual setup cost and rearranging terms, we get expression (6-2):

$$0.5Qvr \ = \ sD_1 \,/\, Q$$

$$Q^2 \ = \ sD_1 \,/\, 0.5vr$$

or

$$Q \ = \ \sqrt{2sD_1/vr} \tag{6-2}$$

Expression (6-2) is known as the **Economic Order Quantity Formula (EOQ)**. It is the simplest OR/MS inventory control model, but also the most widely used one. In fact it is the model incorporated in most inventory control software packages commercially available. Applied to our example, we get:

$$EOQ \ = \ \sqrt{2(4140)(18)/(320)(0.18)} \ = \ 50.87$$

Since the replenishment has to be an integer number of drums, we would round the answer to the nearest integer. Verify that inserting $Q=51$ into expression (6-1A) the minimum total relevant cost amounts to:

$$T(EOQ) \ = \ 0.5(51)320(0.18) + 18(4140/51) \ = \ \$2,930$$

The optimal solution for this first approximation, given a cutoff point L equal to 12, is to schedule a stock replenishment run of size 51 whenever the stock level has been depleted to zero (or more precisely, whenever the amount left in stock does not cover the last customer order received). Such runs would be made about every $(51/4140)\times250$ or 3 working days (assuming customer orders are only received Monday through Friday each week with 250 such working days per year).

I have doubts that the problem user in the LOD would want to use a replenishment size of 51. First, 51 is an inconvenient size. Second, drums are stored on pallets, each containing 4 drums. No warehouse space is saved by having fewer than 4 drums on a pallet. So it makes sense to have a replenishment size that is a multiple of 4. Third, as we shall see in the next chapter, the increase in costs for deviating slightly from the optimal Q is small. For all these reasons, the LOD would want to round the replenishment size to the nearest multiple of 4. This is 52 in our case. Verify that the total relevant cost would increase by less than one dollar. So, once the optimal value of a decision variable has been found, common sense may dictate to round the solution to some convenient multiple of a base number.

How does this solution compare with the current policy used? The LOD uses currently the same cutoff point of 12, but a stock replenishment size of 80 drums, covering about one week of demand. Note that this results in a turnover for that product of 52 times per year — well above the company target level. The reason for this high turnover is that product Y is one of the highest volume motor oils sold by the LOD. (Note that there must be some products that have a very low turnover to get an average for the LOD as a whole of about 12.) Using expression (6-1A), check that the total relevant cost of the current policy is $3,235, compared to $2,931 for the best $Q=52$ (rounded up) found by the above model — a difference of $304. Obviously, the savings for lower volume products could not expect to be that high.

6.7   SECOND APPROXIMATION FOR THE LOD MODEL

For the first approximate model, we fixed the cutoff point for classifying customer orders arbitrarily at $L = 12$. This allowed us to discover that the EOQ formula could be used to find the optimal stock replenishment size Q. The annual volume of demand met from stock, D_1, is one of the input parameters of the EOQ formula. That formula is still applicable even if D_1 changes, for instance, as a result of a change in the cutoff point L. Is it then not possible to find the best joint values of Q and L by a simple process of enumeration? Right! For all possible values that L can assume we determine the optimal value of Q and also compute the total cost associated with the corresponding combination of L and Q. The lowest of these total costs will allow us to identify the jointly optimal values of L and Q.

An interesting feature emerges. The first simple model developed for finding the optimal stock replenishment size becomes a submodel of the new model. Such nesting of one model inside another model occurs reasonably often. The total cost now also has to include those associated with special production runs. Since it is a function of two decision variables, L and Q, we will denote it as $T(L,Q)$. The influence diagram in Figure 5-3 shows that there are two additional costs associated with L, the annual setup cost for special production runs (circle 10) and the annual handling cost for big customer orders (circle 9). Here are the corresponding expressions:

Circle 9:

$$\left[\begin{array}{c} \text{Annual handling} \\ \text{cost for big cust.} \end{array} \right] = \left[\begin{array}{c} \text{Annual volume by} \\ \text{special prod. runs} \end{array} \right] \times \left[\begin{array}{c} \text{Product handling} \\ \text{cost per unit} \end{array} \right]$$

$$= D_2 \, h_2$$

Figure 6-4: Spreadsheet printout for T(L,Q)-model

LOD SECOND MODEL FOR STOCK CONTROL

| Decision variables: | Stock replenishment size |
| | Special production run cutoff size |

INPUT DATA

Total Demand	7132	drums/year
Product value	$320.00	/drum
Production setup cost	$18.00	/production run
Product handling cost	$1.10	/drum via storage
	$0.45	/drum by special production run
Investment holding cost	$0.18	/dollar invested per year

COMPUTATION OF T(L,Q) (base period: one year)

cutoff point	Demand from stock	Demand by special prod. runs	Number of special prod. runs	Setup cost special prod. runs	Total handling cost	Corresp. EOQ	Corresp. relevant EOQ cost	Total relevant cost
1	0	7132	1266	$22,788	$3,209	0.0	$0	$25,997
2	134	6998	1132	$20,376	$3,297	9.2	$527	$24,200
3	846	6286	776	$13,968	$3,759	23.0	$1,324	$19,052
4	1131	6001	681	$12,258	$3,945	26.6	$1,531	$17,734
5	1875	5257	495	$8,910	$4,428	34.2	$1,972	$15,310
6	2045	5087	461	$8,298	$4,539	35.8	$2,059	$14,896
8	2717	4415	349	$6,282	$4,975	41.2	$2,374	$13,631
9	3445	3687	258	$4,644	$5,449	46.4	$2,673	$12,765
10	3580	3552	243	$4,374	$5,536	47.3	$2,725	$12,635
12	4140	2992	187	$3,366	$5,900	50.9	$2,930	$12,196
15	5160	1972	102	$1,836	$6,563	56.8	$3,271	$11,670
16	5340	1792	90	$1,620	$6,680	57.8	$3,328	$11,628
20	6108	1024	42	$756	$7,180	61.8	$3,559	$11,494
24	6568	564	19	$342	$7,479	64.1	$3,690	$11,511
36	6856	276	7	$126	$7,666	65.5	$3,770	$11,562
48	7036	96	2	$36	$7,783	66.3	$3,820	$11,638
49	7132	0	0	$0	$7,845	66.8	$3,846	$11,691

CUSTOMER DEMAND DATA

Cust. order size	Number	Cumulative number
0	0	0
1	134	134
2	356	490
3	95	585
4	186	771
5	34	805
6	112	917
8	91	1008
9	15	1023
10	56	1079
12	85	1164
15	12	1176
16	48	1224
20	23	1247
24	12	1259
36	5	1264
48	2	1266
49	0	1266

where D_2 denotes the annual volume of demand met by special production runs, and h_2 is the handling per drum supplied by special production runs. Note that D_2 depends on the cutoff point L. It is simply equal to the sum of all customer orders equal to or larger than L.

Circle 10:

$$
\left[\begin{array}{l} \text{Annual setup cost} \\ \text{for spec.prod'n runs} \end{array}\right] = \left[\begin{array}{c} \text{Production setup} \\ \text{cost per batch} \end{array}\right] \times \left[\begin{array}{l} \text{Annual number of} \\ \text{special prod'n runs} \end{array}\right]
$$

$$
= s\,N
$$

where N denotes the annual number of special production runs for big customer orders. It is equal to the number of customer orders equal to or larger than L. N is thus also a function of L. Both D_2 and N can easily be determined for any product from a frequency table for customer orders.

The total relevant cost for $T(L,Q)$ is therefore as follows:

$$
\left[\begin{array}{c} \text{Total cost} \\ \\ \end{array}\right] = \left[\begin{array}{c} \text{Annual setup cost} \\ \text{for special p'runs} \end{array}\right] + \left[\begin{array}{c} \text{Annual handling} \\ \text{cost for big cust.} \end{array}\right]
$$

$$
+ \left[\begin{array}{c} \text{Associated annual} \\ \text{EOQ cost given } L \end{array}\right] + \left[\begin{array}{c} \text{Annual handling} \\ \text{cost for small cust.} \end{array}\right]
$$

$$
\mathrm{T}(L,Q) = [sN] + [h_2\,D_2] + [0.5Qvr + sD_1/Q] + [h_1\,D_1] \qquad (6\text{-}3)
$$

Note that the annual handling cost for small customers increases or decreases depending on whether the cutoff point L increases or decreases. In contrast to the simple EOQ model, this cost is now affected by one of the decision variables and becomes now part of the total relevant cost.

6.8 EXPLORING THE SOLUTION SPACE FOR $T(L,Q)$

Figure 6-4 shows the output from a spreadsheet for product Y. It calculates, for a range of values of L, the associated optimal value of Q (using the EOQ formula), and the various cost components, as well as the total relevant cost.

Note that the annual product value remains constant for all combinations of L and Q. It is thus not a relevant cost even for this more complete model and not shown explicitly in the spreadsheet. The lowest cost of $11,494 is obtained for the combination of $L = 20$, and $Q = 61.8$ or 60 when rounded to the nearest multiple of 4. The optimal policy is therefore to meet all customer orders of size $L = 20$ or larger by scheduling a special production run, supply customer orders of less than 20 from stock, and schedule a stock replenishment of size $Q = 60$ whenever the stock on hand is insufficient to supply the last small customer order received. This happens about every third day. The volume of demand supplied from stock is 6108 drums, while the balance of 1024 is supplied by special production runs.

Figure 6-5 shows the total relevant cost as a function of L. Note that it is fairly flat. Hence, small adjustments to the optimal values of L and Q, so as to have more 'appealing' numbers, will cause only negligible cost increases above the minimum total relevant cost.

Figure 6-5: Total relevant cost for $T(L,Q)$

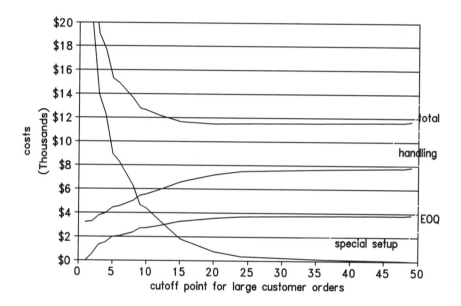

How does the second model compare cost-wise to the policy of $L=12$ and $Q=80$ currently used by the LOD? By expression (6-3), the total relevant cost of the current policy is equal to

$$T(L=12,\ Q=80) = (18)187 + (0.45)2992$$
$$+ [0.5(80)320(0.18) + (18)4140/80] + (1.10)4140 = \$12{,}502$$

or about $1008 higher than the optimal policy (adjusted to $Q=60$) for the second model — a rather substantial saving. Furthermore, the average investment in stock is reduced by $3,200, a reduction of 25%. (Test your understanding and verify these numbers by using expression (6-3).)

Are there any aspects that the second model has not captured? Since it deals with each product separately, it obviously still ignores the constraints on productive capacity and warehouse space. But as I have already outlined, those will only be considered once the optimal policy has been found for all products. At that point the overall effect on capacities can then be assessed. I will come back to this issue in Chapter 12. Otherwise, the model seems to be a good representation of the real situation.

Whether it can be implemented depends on the availability of all required data. There should be little difficulty in obtaining relevant cost data. The only question mark is whether the demand data are in an appropriate form. We need not simply a single figure for the annual demand, but a frequency distribution of the customer orders by size. Fortunately, records for each customer order are kept for at least one year before they are erased. The frequency distribution for product Y in Table 6-1 was extracted from these files. Although one year's data is a bit short, it will do to get started. For later years, procedures can be initiated to accumulate customer order data over a longer period for use in updating the best policies.

There are still some possibilities to streamline the model. Some of you may have wondered whether the LOD would make more than one special production run if more than one customer order of size L or larger is received on the same day. Why not combine them into one larger run and thereby save production setup cost? This leads to a new idea. If one or more small customer orders are also received on the same day as large customer orders, they could all be combined into a single large special production run. Hence, even some small orders will in such cases be met without the goods going through the inventory stage. The effect of this is that a slightly larger fraction of the total demand is supplied by special production runs, leading to a further small decrease in stock investments.

The logical extension to this idea becomes now quite obvious. Rather than look at individual customer orders to decide whether or not to schedule a special production run, all customer orders for a given day are totalled up, regardless of size. If this total is equal to or larger than the cutoff point, all orders received on that day are supplied by a special production run. If the total is less than the cutoff point, they are supplied from stock. (Note that the optimal cutoff for this modified policy may not be equal to the cutoff point found best for the original model.)

This is an example of generating a new form of policy — always an exciting aspect of OR/MS modeling. This extension was in fact adopted. The fortunate aspect is that the same model can handle this extension. Only the demand data now had to be compiled in the form of a daily demand frequency distribution, rather than an order size distribution. So as not to further complicate the issue, we shall, however, ignore this extension here and base all further discussions on the original $T(L, Q)$-model developed earlier.

Another possibility would be to take advantage of special production runs to also replenish stocks for that product. This would further reduce production setup costs and at the same time also lower the size of stock replenishments. This third model was explored and abandoned, because the computational effort required to find the optimal solution became prohibitive.

6.9 SOME REFLECTIONS ON THE PROCESS OF MODELING

We have seen that mathematical modeling is both an art and a science. Some people may discover a natural talent for modeling; others may build up some talent through experience. Little can be said about the 'art' component except some simple rules. This text puts its main focus on the 'science' component of modeling. We have seen that in this instance the influence diagram serves as a basis for mathematical modeling. It indicates the existence of relationships between the system environment and system components, between system components themselves, as well as system components and system outputs. The mathematical model expresses the form of these relationships. So the usefulness of influence diagrams goes beyond clarifying the existence of relationships during the problem formulation phase, but extends to mathematical modeling.

As we shall see in later chapters, there are other types of systems diagrams, such as precedence charts and flow diagrams, which may also serve as an intermediate step between the problem formulation and building a quantitative model.

The process itself may go through a sequence of models, from simple to more sophisticated, through a process of enrichment, until the analyst is satisfied that the right balance of simplicity and completeness has been achieved. It is here where real-life work exposure and modeling experience help in making a confident judgment. In the LOD problem, the first relatively simple EOQ model did not capture all essential aspects. Hence, we went to a second round of model building with two decision variables. In real life this model was modified by having a cutoff point for a total daily demand, rather than one applied to individual customer orders. So we went through another enrichment phase.

A third even more sophisticated model was considered. It explored the possibility of topping up inventory whenever a special production run was scheduled. However, it was abandoned as computationally too complex. The second model was judged as providing the best balance between simplicity and completeness.

6.10 DERIVING A SOLUTION TO THE MODEL

For the LOD problem we could derive the optimal solution by trial-and-error using a computer spreadsheet. For many mathematical models more powerful approaches are needed. This section gives a rather brief general overview of the various approaches used in OR/MS modeling.

Enumeration

If the number of alternative courses of action is relatively small, say in the tens rather than the hundreds, and the computational effort to evaluate each alternative is relatively minor, like in the LOD case, then finding the optimal solution by simply evaluating the performance measure for each alternative course of action or each discrete value of the decision variable may be simple and fast. The 'best solution' is the one which achieves the best value of the performance measure — a minimum or a maximum value, whichever corresponds to the objective.

Enumeration is commonly used if the problem deals with a one-off situation. Rather than spend considerable resources in time and funds to develop a more elegant and efficient solution approach, enumeration may be the cheapest way to find the best alternative. We used this approach in the LOD problem to determine the best cutoff point for supplying customer orders by special production runs. However, this is in fact not a good example for the use of enumeration. The reasons for this are that the model formulated will be applied to some 800 different products and updated solutions will have to be computed regularly, say at least once each year, to reflect changes in demand patterns as well as costs. In this particular instance, it may be preferable to develop a more efficient solution method, both in terms of computational effort and ease of data input.

Search Methods

If the performance measure to be optimized is in the form of an objective function in one or several decision variables, various search methods may reduce the computational effort to find the optimal solution. Several successful search methods are based on the idea of eliminating successively more and more of the solution space which has been identified as not containing the optimal solution, until an arbitrarily small interval remains which will contain the optimal solution. For this reason they are called interval elimination methods. Some of the more famous interval elimination methods developed by mathematicians have been given colourful names, like 'golden-section search'. Interval elimination methods, however, only work if the objective function is so-called well-behaved. If the objective function contains only one decision variable, this implies that the function is either U-shaped or unimodal, i.e., has only one single maximum (for a maximization problem) or one single minimum (for a minimization problem), as depicted in Figure 6-7 further on in this section.

Algorithmic Solution Methods

The most powerful solution methods are based on an **algorithm**. This is a set of logical and mathematical operations performed repeatedly in a specific sequence. Each repetition of the rules is called an **iteration**. To start off the algorithm, an initial or incoming solution has to be supplied. At each iteration, the incoming solution is improved upon, using the rules of the algorithm. The new solution so generated becomes the incoming solution for the next iteration. This process is repeated until certain conditions — referred to as **stopping rules** — are satisfied. These stopping rules either indicate that the optimal solution has been found, or that no feasible solution can be identified (if the initial solution supplied was also infeasible), or that a certain maximum number of iterations has been reached or maximum amount of computer time has been exceeded. Most search methods are based on some algorithm. Figure 6-6 summarizes this approach as a flow diagram.

For an algorithm to be a practical solution method, it has to have certain properties: (1) each successive solution has to be an improvement over the preceding one; (2) successive solutions have to converge, i.e., get closer and closer to the optimal solution; (3) convergence arbitrarily close to the optimal solution should occur in a reasonable number of iterations; and (4) the computation effort at each iteration has to be sufficiently small to remain economically acceptable. What upper limit to the number of iterations is viewed as reasonable depends on the importance and the potential benefits of the problem. What may be reasonable for finding the optimal expansion strategy for a large corporation may be excessive for a problem of finding the best itinerary for a delivery van delivering parcels to various addresses in a city. The former may promise huge benefits, while the potential savings in costs for the latter are likely to be small.

Figure 6-6: General flow diagram for an algorithm

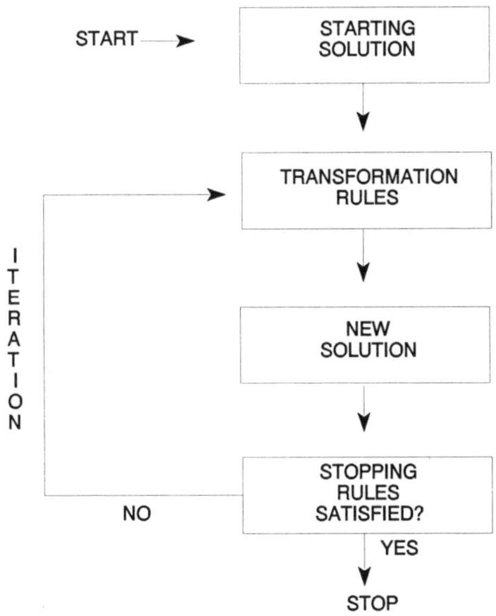

For practically all real-life problems, the computations invariably have to be performed by computer. Many of the general-purpose OR/MS techniques use algorithms for finding the optimal solution. Becoming thoroughly familiar with these algorithms is usually part of an OR/MS university curriculum.

Classical Methods of Calculus

In some instances, classical methods of mathematics, in particular differential calculus, can be used to find the optimal solution. This is often the case for problems involving an objective function with one or two decision variables that can assume any real-valued number. The basic idea can easily be grasped graphically. Consider the U-shaped function $f(x)$ in the variable x in Figure 6-7.

Figure 6-7: A function and its derivative

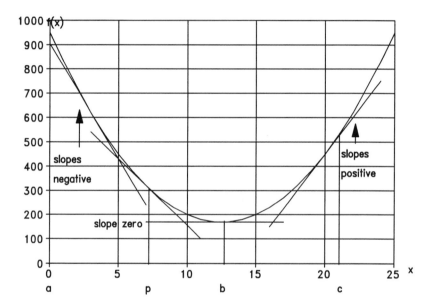

It first decreases as x increases from a to b and then increases as x increases further. Additional insight is gained by studying how the slope of the function changes as x increases. The slope of the function at any point $x=p$ is simply given by the tangent to the function at the point p. Observe that as x increases from a to b, the tangent is downward sloping, i.e., the slope is negative. As x increases beyond b the tangent becomes upward sloping, i.e., the slope is now positive. Furthermore, the slope of $f(x)$ becomes less and less negative as x approaches b. At b itself, the tangent is horizontal, i.e., the slope is 0. As x moves away from b the slope becomes more and more positive. The minimum of $f(x)$ is assumed at b. So we can conclude that the minimum of the function occurs there where the slope of the function is zero. (Note, there may be other points where the slope of the function is zero and where no minimum or maximum occurs, but this will not concern us here!)

All we need for finding the value of x where the function $f(x)$ assumes its minimum value is to discover where the slope of $f(x)$ is zero. The key to this puzzle is given by the **derivative** of $f(x)$. The slope of a function is measured by its derivative. It is denoted by $df(x)/dx$ or simply by $f'(x)$.

So we proceed as follows: Determine the derivative $f'(x)$ of the function $f(x)$. Find the value of x_0 for which $f'(x) = 0$. Check that the function actually has a minimum at x_0. That can be done by verifying that for a value of x just less than x_0 the derivative is negative, while for a value of x just larger than x_0 the derivative is positive.

The analogous reasoning can be used for finding the maximum of a function that has the shape of a U upside down. I leave it up to you to work out the details.

Heuristic Solution Methods

Some models are of such a degree of complexity or computationally so intractable that it is impossible to find the optimal solution with the computational means currently available. There are also instances, where it is possible to find the optimal solution, but the potential benefits do not justify the computational effort needed. Heuristic solution methods may then be the only feasible alternative.

Heuristic methods use the human mind's ingenuity, creativity, intuition, and experience to find good solutions or to improve on an existing solution. It is an informal process of learning how the objective function responds to various solution strategies and then using the insight gained to devise or discover better solution rules. Sometimes it may be possible to find explanations why the rules are successful for finding a good or even the best solution. At other times, they may be adopted simply because trials show that they work.

We all use heuristic problem solving in our daily lives. For example, if I want to travel from point A to point B, I know that in general the shortest way to reach my destination is traveling on a route that is as close to a straight line as possible. However, I also know from experience, that if that shortest route leads through the centre of town, where the traffic is usually slow, it is faster, although longer, to make a detour around the city centre, usually using one-way traffic streets. I may also discover some side streets with little traffic which allow me to travel faster.

When packing boxes of various sizes into containers you will discover after some trials that unless you first put the biggest boxes into the containers you may not be able to fit them in any more later on. So the insight gained from that experience is that it is best to put the biggest boxes into the containers first, and then fill the space with smaller ones.

Although it may be possible sometimes to prove that a given heuristic solution method finds the optimal solution, this cannot be guaranteed. The analyst may have to be satisfied with finding a good, rather than the optimal solution. The famous American Nobel Laureate for Economics, Herbert Simon, coined the word 'satisficing' for this. So, heuristic solution methods are usually associated with satisficing, rather than optimizing.

Simulation

As we have seen in Chapter 3, the behaviour of a system can be accurately described by how the state of the system changes over time. Keeping a detailed record of these state changes and extracting statistics about the average value of critical variables can give useful information about the performance of the system in response to different operating policies. Collecting such data from the observation of the 'real' system may not be possible for a number of reasons — it may be too costly or too time consuming, or the system may not exist yet, etc. So we imitate step by step how the system would behave over time. This can be done with paper and pencil, but is usually more efficient by computer. Such an imitation is called **simulation**. For complex dynamic systems, particularly if they also involve stochastic aspects, simulation may be the only way to collect information about how the system performs under various policies. Again, as for heuristic problem solving, all the analyst can expect is to be able to identify good policies, rather than the optimal one.

As we shall see in Chapter 17, simulation is an important tool for the OR/MS analyst. It is not only used for identifying good, if not optimal solutions, but it is the ideal vehicle for verifying how well the solution derived by other methods is likely to perform in the real world.

6.11*[1] DERIVING THE EOQ FORMULA BY DIFFERENTIAL CALCULUS

I will now demonstrate how the classical methods of calculus can be used to derive the EOQ formula discussed in Section 6.6. Consider again expression (6-1):

$$T(Q) = 0.5Qvr + (sD_1/Q) + h_1 D_1 + vD_1 \qquad (6\text{-}1)$$

It is a differentiable function, i.e., its derivative $dT(Q)/dQ = T'(Q)$ can be determined and has the following form:

$$T'(Q) = 0.5vr - (sD_1/Q^2) \qquad (6\text{-}4)$$

Note that the two constant parts of expression (6-1) do not contribute towards the derivative. In fact, the derivative of expression (6-1A) is also given by expression (6-4). This confirms the fact that these constant parts can be ignored when searching for the optimal value of Q.

Setting the derivative (6-4) equal to zero and solving for Q, we get:

$$T'(Q) = 0.5vr - (sD_1/Q^2) = 0$$

---

[1] Starred sections contain optional material which can be omitted without loss of continuity. This one requires college calculus.

or

$$0.5vr = sD_1 /Q^2 \qquad (6\text{-}5)$$

or

$$Q^2 = 2sD_1 /vr$$

Taking the square root on both sides we derive again (6-2). Note that multiplying both sides of expression (6-5) by Q, we get the equality of annual holding and annual production setup costs, observed from the graphical solution in Figure 6-3.

EXERCISES

1. Consider the machine adjustment problem described in exercises 1 - 4 of Chapter 5. The objective is to find the time between adjustments or the number of adjustments per hour so as to maximize the hourly net profit contribution.

(a) Use the influence diagram developed in exercise 3 of Chapter 5 to formulate a mathematical model. Build it up step by step by finding the expression corresponding to each state variable and output variable in the influence diagram. Once completed, combine them into a single expression which shows hourly net profit contribution as a function of the decision variable. You will need the following additional information to determine the relationship between defectives produced and the running time of the machine. Lim orders the operator to make 5 test runs of one hour each, recording the cumulative number of defectives produced at regular intervals. Prior to each run the machine was properly adjusted. The results obtained are as follows:

Machine running time	Cumulative number of defectives for test				
	1	2	3	4	5
6 minutes	0	0	1	0	0
12 minutes	1	1	2	0	0
24 minutes	2	3	3	1	1
36 minutes	5	5	5	4	2
48 minutes	8	7	9	7	4
60 minutes	11	11	13	12	8

(b) Develop a table with one row for each system variable and output variable and columns for machine adjustments after every 12, 18, 24, 36, 48, and 60 minutes. This includes the time needed for each adjustment. If you have access to a computer spreadsheet, develop it in the form of a spreadsheet. Plot the net profit contribution as a function of the time between adjustments. Indicate the range where the optimal solution seems to lie.

(c) By trial and error or systematic search, find the time between adjustments that maximizes the net profit contribution per hour. In the spreadsheet simply use one of the columns for these trials, such as, e.g., the 60-minute column. Determine this time accurate to one decimal place. Determine the loss in net profit for rounding the optimal time to a convenient number, such as a multiple of 5 minutes.

(d) List all major approximations made for the model developed in (c) above. How reasonable are they?

2*. For the combined expression derived in 1(a) above, use classical methods of calculus (Section 6.11*) to derive an expression for the optimal time between adjustments, evaluate it, and determine the maximum net profit contribution per hour.

3. Consider the ceramic tile problem of exercise 7 in Chapter 5. The objective is to determine the optimal size of each shipment from the factory to the distribution warehouse, so as to minimize the total relevant cost per year.

(a) On the basis of the influence diagram developed in exercise 7 of Chapter 5, find a mathematical expression for each system variable and the output variable. It may be helpful to draw a diagram of the behaviour over time of the inventory of tiles produced at the factory. Note its similarity with the EOQ model developed in Section 6.6. Combine all expressions into a single expression for the total cost as a function of the size of the shipments.

(b) Develop a table or spreadsheet similar to the spreadsheet in Figure 6-2 for shipments of multiples of daily production quotas. Which of these shipments has the lowest relevant cost?

(c) List all major approximations made for the model developed in (c) above. How reasonable are they?

4*. For the combined expression derived in 3(a) above, use classical methods of calculus (Section 6.11*) to derive an expression for the optimal shipment size, evaluate it, and determine its minimum cost. Note again the similarity with the EOQ model.

5. ELMO, a manufacturer of electric motors, has just purchased a machine tool for winding coils of electric motors. Initial trials with the machine indicate that the number of rejects produced varies with the running speed of the machine. The result of the six trials for various speed settings are as follows:

machine speed	30	40	50	60	70	80	90 coils/hour
trial 1	1	2	3	5	6	8	11 rejects
2	0	1	4	6	7	9	10 rejects
3	1	3	4	4	5	7	9 rejects
4	2	3	2	4	5	7	11 rejects
5	2	1	2	4	7	10	10 rejects
6	1	2	3	5	6	7	10 rejects

Rejects have to be scrapped. The material cost of each coil is $2.60. The machine operator is paid at a rate of $22/hour. It costs $6 to operate the machine for one hour. 10,000 good coils have to be produced for a given type of motor. The total cost of producing this batch is used as the performance measure for setting the machine speed. Note that to end up with 10,000 good coils more than 10,000 coils will have to be wound. The size of the batch that needs to be scheduled is equal to 10,000/(1 - fraction of rejects). The fraction of rejects is a function of the machine speed.

(a) Develop an influence diagram showing the relationship between the running speed of the machine and the total cost of producing the batch of 10,000 coils.

(b) Use that influence diagram to derive mathematical expressions for each system variable and the performance measure of total costs. Combine these expressions into a single expression for total costs as a function of the machine speed setting.

(c) Develop a table or a spreadsheet containing one row for each variable and one for the total cost and columns for the running speeds listed above. Graph the results and identify the range where the lowest cost is likely to lie. Use the table to determine the best speed setting.

(d) List all major assumptions made for the model in (c) above. How reasonable are they?

6. (a) Develop a spreadsheet to reproduce the content of Figure 6-2, using the same data.
   (b) Develop a spreadsheet to reproduce the content of Figure 6-4, using the same data.

7. One of the products in the LOD is only sold in multiples of 4 drums. A total of 120 orders were received last year as follows:

Order size	4	8	12	16	20
Number of orders	70	32	11	5	2

   They were evenly spread over the entire year with very few days having more than one order. The sales pattern for the coming year is expected to be fairly similar. The combined mixing and filling setup cost is $15. The product handling cost is $1/drum for orders supplied from stock, and $0.40/drum for orders met by a special production run. Each drum has a value of $400. The stock holding cost is $0.18/$1/year. (For answering the following parts, it is suggested that you develop a spreadsheet similar to Table 6-4.)

   (a) Assume that all orders of more than 8 drums are met by a special production run. What is the optimal inventory replenishment size, its total annual cost, and the overall total annual cost for meeting the entire demand?

   (b) Find the combined optimal policy for meeting customer demand, i.e., an optimal cutoff point for special production runs and an optimal stock replenishment policy. What is the minimum cost associated with the optimal policy?

8. Consider the following data for another LOD product: product value $180/drum, production setup cost $12/setup, product handling cost $1.50/drum via storage, $0.30/drum via special production run, investment holding cost 25% on the value invested per year; and the demand distribution as follows over a period of one year covering 250 working days:

demand	0	2	4	6	8	12	16	20	24	32
days	82	65	32	23	17	10	8	5	4	4

   (a) Develop a spreadsheet similar to Figure 6-2 to find the optimal stock replenishment size if the cutoff point for direct replenishments is set at 12 drums. Note that the demand is not given as a frequency distribution by customer order size, but by total demand for each day. The implication is that special production runs are made to cover all customer orders for a given day, rather than individual customer orders. (This is the extension briefly mentioned in Section 6.8.)

   (b) Develop a spreadsheet similar to Figure 6-4 for finding the joint optimal values for the stock replenishment size and the special production run cutof point.

9. A liquid is mixed in a mixing vessel and then packed into one-litre cans on an automatic filling machine. It takes the mixing technician 2 hours to mix the liquid, regardless of the amount to be mixed. The cost of the ingredients used is $1.60/litre. Two machine operators take 30 minutes to prepare the machine for a filling run. Cans are filled at a rate of 60/minute. Both machine operators have to

be present while the machine is filling cans. The cost of a can, including its label, is $0.15. The labour cost for the technician and the machine operators, including the cost of fringe benefits earned, amount to $18 per hour worked.

(a) Determine the cost of preparing a batch of 3600 cans for the product in question.

(b) The annual demand for that particular product is 180,000 cans. Use the EOQ formula to find the optimal batch size and its associated relevant total annual cost.

(c) The cans are packed into cartons of 48 cans each. Cartons are stored on pallets. Each pallet holds 24 cartons. The practice is to always produce a batch which results in a multiple of full pallets, i.e., a multiple of 24 times 48 cans. If this practice is to be continued, what batch size would you recommend as best in terms of total costs?

10. Last year, Q-Imports sold 750 sets of stainless steel cutlery, imported from Germany at a cost of $60 per set, including airfreight and customs duty. The firm sells the sets to retailers at $96. Sales occur at a fairly steady even rate throughout the year. The sets were imported in two shipments, the first of 250, the second of 500. For each shipment, the firm incurs clerical costs, bank charges, and custom agent clearing charges, totalling $200. Q-imports usually finances most of its purchases by bank overdrafts. The current overdraft rate is 18% per year. There are also insurance costs for storing goods in inventory amounting to 2% of the value of the goods. The manager of Q-Imports expects that sales this coming year will be about 1/3 higher than last year's. He therefore plans to place two orders of 500 sets each.

(a) What would be the total annual cost of the proposed ordering policy?

(b) Could he do better? Why and how?

11. Q-Electronics sells about 2000 of its new 8-sim chips per month at a price of $35/chip. The production cost are $25/chip. The current policy is to replace any chips that fail within the first six months of installation. The dealer doing the replacement also gets $10 to cover the labour cost for the replacement. The competition has recently increased its guarantee period from 6 to 9 months. Q-Electronics is now under pressure to follow suit or even go to a 12-months guarantee period. The engineering department has collected extensive data on replacements of chips, both under guarantee and after the guarantee period. They show the following picture, where time refers to the number of months after the initial installation of the chip:

Time	3	4	5	6	7	8	9	10	11
Replacements	0	1	2	2	5	5	6	6	9
Time	12	13	14	15	16	17	18		
Replacements	9	13	14	18	22	23	27 per 1000 chips		

(a) Management would like to know the increase in annual costs of extending the guarantee period from six months to 9, 12, 15, or 18 months. You need to find a functional relationship between the time and the number of replacements to answer this question. What approximation do you make?

(b) By how much would monthly sales have to increase to recover the increase in guarantee costs?

Answer both questions by building an appropriate spreadsheet.

12. A manufacturer assembles pumps from parts purchased from subcontractors. For a particular type of pump, it takes a technician 8 hours to set up the assembly line. His

pay, including all fringe benefits, is $24/hour. Other production set-up costs, such as picking up the required number of parts from subcontractors, amount to $80. Once the technician has set up the assembly line, four people perform the actual assembly of the pumps. They can assemble 24 pumps per day. The value of the assembled pump, including all parts and labour costs, is $216. The firm estimates that its stock holding cost is 25% per year on the average stock investment. The annual demand for that pump is about 1250. The replenishment policy used is to start a new assembly run of Q pumps whenever the stock for that pump has been depleted. Hence, the technician will prepare a new assembly run one or two days prior to the time the inventory for that pump has been sold. Once assembly has been started, each day's production of 24 pumps is added to the inventory of that pump. These pumps are then available for sale. In other words, during production, some of the pumps are sold. As a result, once a batch of size Q has been completed, fewer than Q pumps still remain in stock. (Note that this situation is slightly different from the EOQ model developed in this chapter, where the entire batch Q is added to stock as a single lot.)

(a) Adapt the influence diagram of Figure 5-2 for this situation. Note that there is no special production run option, so that whole section is not relevant. On the other hand, the section dealing with the average inventory investment is now more complex and needs more detail.

(b) Using this influence diagram, develop a set of expressions that will ultimately culminate in a total relevant annual replenishment and inventory cost.

(c) List the approximations that you made to develop the total cost expression.

(d) Using a spreadsheet similar to Figure 6-2, find the optimal replenishment size and its relevant annual cost.

13*. Using calculus, find an expression for the optimal Q which minimizes the total relevant annual cost developed in exercise 10 (b).

REFERENCES

Ackoff, Russell L., *The Art of Problem Solving*, Wiley, 1978. Entertaining book full of good advice and wisdom on problem solving and modeling.

Churchman, C. West, Ackoff, Russell R., and Arnoff, E.L., *Introduction to Operations Research*, Wiley, 1957. First comprehensive text on O.R., outdated now in terms of technique coverage, but the extensive coverage of the systems approach and modeling principles are still important reading. Chapter 2 gives an insightful account of a complete case history of an inventory control project.

Morris, William T., 'On the art of modeling', *Management Science*, August 1967, B707-17. This paper demonstrates that modeling is a process of discovery, analogy, enrichment and successive refinements. Highly recommended reading for any novice in modeling.

Polya, G., *How to Solve It*, 2nd ed., Doubleday Anchor Books, 1957. This is the classic in how to go about modeling. Although most examples come from geometry, the principles of heuristic reasoning are of universal applicability.

Rivett, Patrick, *Model Building for Decision Analysis*, Wiley,1980. 'Model construction is an amalgam of theory and practice . . . When theory is dominant, elegance of mathematical exposition may lead to consequences which are incapable of implementation. On the other hand, hurried problem solving which conceals within it a technical ineptitude may mean that insight into the structure is lost.' (Quote from text.) Rivett tries to keep to the middle ground. Short, easy reading, but assumes some background in OR/MS.

Starfield, Anthony M., Smith, Karl A., and Bleloch, Andrew L., *How to Model It - Problem Solving for the Computer Age*, McGraw-Hill, 1990. A modern version of Polya's book. Demonstrates various aspects of modeling skills by examples that require no technical background. The emphasis is on interactive learning by doing it. A fascinating book for both students and teachers. Assumes a background in college algebra and calculus.

Urban, Glen L., 'Building models for decision makers,' *Interfaces*, May 1974. The papers draws on the literature along with practical experience to propose a process of building models that have an enhanced likelihood of getting implemented.

European Journal of O.R., Special Issue: Model Validation, April 1993. Guest Editors: M. Landry and M. Oral. This issue looks at theoretical and practical aspects of model validation. However, much of the discussion is equally relevant for model building. Several papers stress the importance of model credibility to get the model accepted by the problem owners. This is also one of the themes of good model building in this chapter.

7 Model Testing and Sensitivity Analysis

The last two steps of the modeling phase deal with model validation, solution performance testing, and sensitivity analysis. The aim of validation is to establish whether the model is mathematically correct, logically consistent, and a sufficiently close approximation to reality. In solution performance testing for an existing operation or system, the analyst estimates the increase in benefits or the savings in costs that the solution offers over the current mode. If the project involves planning some future operation of a system yet to be realized, performance testing provides the estimates of future benefits. In either case this information is needed to make a rational decision about whether or not to implement the proposed system. Sensitivity analysis evaluates the response of the best solution to changes in various inputs.

These are the first three topics of this chapter. They provide essential input into the preparation of the project report which supports the analyst's recommendations to the problem owner about implementation and/or further analysis. Guidelines on how to go about writing the project report is the last topic of this chapter. The LOD problem will be used as the example.

7.1 MODEL VALIDATION AND SOLUTION PERFORMANCE TESTING

Model validation has two facets: checking internal validity, and establishing external validity. Checking internal validity is often referred to as **verification**, while establishing external validity is referred to as **validation**.

Internal validity

Is the model mathematically correct and logically consistent? This means carefully verifying that all mathematical expressions correctly represent the assumed relationships. The best method for validating the model as mathematically correct and logically consistent is by numerically checking the results by hand for a sufficiently wide range of inputs. This also involves verifying that each expression is dimensionally consistent. For example, if the right-hand-side of an equation is in terms of kilograms per hour, so must be the left-hand-side. The correctness of all numerical constants should be verified. In spreadsheets this is simplified if all such constants are provided as input into unique data cells, referenced by all formulas that use them, rather than being inserted as numbers separately into each formula. This ensures that any changes will automatically be carried forward to all formulas where that constant is used.

The prudent analyst does much of the checking for internal validity while developing the model. Establishing internal validity can thus not be divorced from the actual model building — a clear example of how various steps overlap or happen concurrently, at least in part. Not only is it easier to do when everything is still fresh, but it also avoids using erroneous intermediate results as input into further analysis. If the calculations are performed by computer, then each step of the program should be numerically verified for correctness.

Complex models consisting of many separate but interrelated mathematical expressions also have to be checked for logical consistency. Have the parts been fitted together correctly? Again, numerically tracing the results for various inputs through the whole chain of such interrelated relationships is the best way of verifying correctness. For very complex models, this may have to be done using highly simplified inputs, rather than the real data. There are instances where numerical verification, even using simplified data, may computationally not be feasible. It is then all the more crucial that the logic of the model is carefully scrutinized.

External validity

Is the model a sufficiently valid representation of reality? This is far more difficult to establish than internal validity. 'What is or is not a close enough approximation?' is largely a question of judgment. The answer should depend on the purpose for building the model and the intended use of its solution. A rough approximation may well be good enough for an exploratory planning model, while a model intended for daily detailed decisions may need to be a fairly accurate representation of reality. So again we see that validation overlaps with both the definition of the relevant system (step 3 of the OR/MS methodology) and the model building (step 4) (see M. Landry et al., 1983).

All stakeholders, i.e., analyst, problem owner and user, should be clear that it is not possible to prove a model to be externally valid. It is only possible to show it wrong. Hence, external validation is largely a question of establishing the 'credibility' of the model. The importance of a model's credibility and appropriateness were already stressed in Section 6.3 dealing with essential properties of good mathematical models. If the model is credible, the user will have confidence in it. Viewed from this angle, external validation requires that the model's output is carefully scrutinized by people intimately familiar with the situation modeled, such as the problem owner and problem user. But more about that when we talk sensitivity analysis.

External validity can often be assumed if the model is able to accurately mimic reality. Hence, the analyst needs to ascertain the responses of the model to changes in inputs — are they as expected and if not, why are they different? Complex systems often exhibit counterintuitive behaviour. A model's validity is put into question unless convincing explanations can be found for such behaviour. The analyst should at least recheck that such results are not due to errors in the mathematical expressions or the internal logic of the model. Counterintuitive results may often be explained satisfactorily upon careful reflection on the various interactions within the system. If they turn out to be due to factors not included in the model, the model may need to be partially reformulated.

'Ongoing' Evaluation of Modeling Process and Model

Validation and Verification is often viewed as a task performed once the modeling phase is essentially completed. As S. I. Gass, one of the pioneers in O.R., particularly known for his work in linear programming, points out, this view is wrong [S.I. Gass, 'The many faces of OR', *J. of the OR Soc.*, January 1991, pp. 3-16]. Not only is it much more costly to revisit the model at that time. As mentioned earlier, various details of the model may not be fresh in the mind of the analyst any more, it may be difficult or impractical to get access to other key people involved in the original analysis, and if errors or questionable assumptions are discovered at that time, much of the subsequent work done may have been wasted. 'Post-evaluation of the model is like locking the stable door after the horse has been stolen.' Evaluation of all aspects of the model should be ongoing and continual. S. I. Gass suggests that analysts operate under the assumption that their work is continually reviewed and scrutinized. Only then will all the necessary steps about documenting why a certain model is chosen, why others are rejected, about recording of all assumptions and simplifications made, data included and excluded and data analysis done, and numeric verification of any computer programs, including spreadsheets, etc., developed, be done completely and on time. It is thus essential that analysts make time available for this ongoing evaluation and resist the pressure of producing results fast by skipping this important aspect of the modeling phase. This is another example of the iterative nature of the OR/MS process.

7.2 TESTING THE SOLUTION FOR PERFORMANCE

The main aim here is to determine the expected benefits, such as net profits or net savings, that implementation of the solution can produce.

If the project deals with an existing system, testing could be done by running both the existing policy and the proposed policy in parallel. The actual operation would be based on the existing policy, while the proposed policy is simulated on paper alongside. This would permit the most realistic comparisons of the two policies. The drawback is that it would result in an unreasonably long delay before any conclusions can be reached. For this reason, testing is usually done by computer simulation alone. Both the existing and the proposed policies are simulated by computer on the same set of input data.

For example, the project may deal with finding shortest-time itineraries for a delivery vehicle. Each trip visits a number of customers in a given metropolitan area and no two trips are identical, except by coincidence. The schedule has to be developed just prior to departure of the vehicle from the home location, with departures scheduled four times a day. The proposed model is applied to each set of customers visited over a period of say the last four weeks — a total of 4 departures times 5 weekdays times 4 weeks, or 80 sets of data. Travel time between consecutive customers is simulated based on traffic flow data used as input into the model. The actually used itineraries are simulated using the same traffic flow input data. The results of the two policies can then easily be compared. (It is not a valid test to use the actual travel times incurred for the existing policy, since the traffic flow data used as input is only an approximation to the real situation. For a valid comparison, both policies should be tested on the same form of data.)

For systems that are still on the drawing board, no comparison with an existing system needs to be made (although comparisons between competing alternatives may be desirable). Testing is then used to observe the behaviour of the proposed system and to get estimates of potential benefits. Since no actual operational data are yet available, data on future events for the system are artificially generated based on the input data used to derive the best policy. If the proposed model is a deterministic approximation to an inherently stochastic situation, such a simulation should also be stochastic — but more on this in Chapter 17.

Consider for example the Deep Cove fresh water export proposal, briefly outlined in Chapter 1. One of the controllable aspects is the number of tanker ships that should be used on a round trip basis for the transport of water from Deep Cove to the possible destinations in Asia, the Middle East, and the U.S. West Coast. Assume that the model indicates that approximately one tanker would be loaded each day. The question to be answered is, given the weather pattern regarding fog and high winds that could prevent ships from entering or leaving the fiord, is such a policy feasible. So, based on past data on the weather pattern in Deep Cove, the analyst would generate a long sequence of varied but typical daily weather conditions and tanker arrivals at the entrance of the fiord, say covering 10 years of operations, and determine the number of ship-days lost for tankers being delayed due to the weather conditions.

Rules for Testing Validity

Here are some rules for valid testing:

(1) The evaluation of the proposed policy has to be based on observations of actual (simulated) performance. It is invalid to substitute the optimal values of the decision variables into the measure of effectiveness. For instance, substituting the optimal order quantity for the LOD problem obtained from expression (6-2) of Section 6.6 into the associated total cost given in expression (6-1) of Section 6.5 would not yield a valid answer for the total cost of using the proposed policy. The reason for this is that the total cost expression (6-1) is an approximation and hence reflects an idealized and simplified reality. Its answer is possibly biased. The true cost should be determined by simulating the use of

the proposed policy over a sufficient length of time. If the incidence of customer demand is stochastic, the simulation should also mimic this aspect as well as possible. The observed average inventory and number of replenishments would then be substituted into expression (6-1) to get a valid cost estimate.

(2) The data used for the test should be independent of the data used to derive the best policy. For example, if the demand data for the last two years were used as input to derive the optimal policy for the second approximation to the LOD problem (Section 6.7 and 6.8), then using the same data also to test the performance of the model would not be an independent test. Since the policy derived is supposedly optimal for that set of demand data, it should by definition perform better than the present policy on that data. Either some data should be set aside specifically or new demands should be generated artificially for testing. (How to do this is the topic of Chapter 17.)

(3) The tests should not just give expected performance, but also some measure of its variability, such as the standard deviation of the average cost.

By now you have got the message that valid testing of the proposed policy can often only be done by simulation. Unfortunately, building a valid simulation model can be a costly exercise. But it is one that could well prevent faulty policies from getting implemented. The analyst should, therefore, not give in to the temptation to take shortcuts here, unless he or she is dealing with a model that has proven itself conclusively for other systems with similar characteristics.

7.3 SHOULD THE PROJECT CONTINUE OR BE ABANDONED?

The analyst has built a mathematical model that he or she judges is capturing the essential aspects of the problem, and has also developed a method for finding the best solution. Both the model and solution method are still in experimental form — without any bells or whistles. In this form they may be quite unsuitable for implementation. But this is so by design. Before the analyst devotes any more time and funds for upgrading the model for implementation and making the solution method more efficient, it is essential that he or she first establishes whether these additional costs are justified by the likely benefits that implementation of the model and its solution will generate. Further resources should only be allocated to the project if there is a reasonable assurance that the cost of these resources can be recovered within a sufficiently short time by the potential benefits from the use of the solution. If this is not the case, then the analyst's advice to the problem owner must be to either abandon the project as a failure or to devote additional resources to the project if there is a reasonable expectation that a better model and/or solution method can be developed. But the problem owner must be made aware that there is no guarantee that these additional resources will be recovered. (Chapter 10 shows how such evaluations should be done.)

Note that this evaluation does not take into account the cost of all resources spent up to this point, but only those that still will have to be devoted in the future for bringing the project to a successful conclusion. Why do we ignore the costs already spent? The reason is that nothing can be done about them anymore. If implementation of the project produces sufficient benefits to recover any further costs, then it is worth proceeding. Not doing so would forego the excess of the expected benefits over the additional costs projected to procure these benefits. If by proceeding the project is also able to recover some or all of any costs already spent, this is a bonus, but irrelevant for making the decision to allocate more resources. (Chapter 9 will study this argument in more detail.)

Many people may find this form of reasoning difficult to accept. They will argue that each project should recover all costs incurred. There is no fundamental disagreement with this argument. No analyst will be able to justify continued employment unless in the long-run all costs and more are recovered. However, for any particular project only additional costs count.

The lesson we should get from this discussion is that the evaluation of any project should be made as early as possible in the analysis. This will allow culling projects with little prospect of achieving sufficiently high benefits before large amounts of resources have been devoted to them. This was the major reason for opting for a preliminary study for the LOD project. Rather than commit the resources for a full-scale study right from the beginning, it was considered prudent to first test the waters some more. Should the initial expectation about potential savings not be justified, then the project could be abandoned at only a fraction of the cost of a full-scale study.

There is also some similarity between OR/MS type projects and projects for research and development of new products. A certain amount of funds has to be spent initially before anything is known about the potential success of the project. At the time of committing these funds, there is no guarantee that they will ever be recovered.

7.4 TESTING OF LOD MODEL

The LOD model is based, at least in part, on well tested inventory control theory. Hence, there is little doubt about its external validity. Internal validity was tested by verifying the spreadsheet calculations for a typical product by hand.

Testing of the solution of the second LOD model for its performance pretty much followed the steps outlined in the project proposal (Appendix to Chapter 5, Section 4). The 804 products were grouped into four classes, three classes for lubrication oils and one for all greases. Classification of oils was based on the distribution by annual-dollar-sales-volume — the method commonly used to group products for production/inventory control purposes. This classification is analogous to the fairly universally observed 20-80 phenomenon, i.e., 20% of all cases account for 80% of the total volume, like 20% of all income earners earning 80% of all declared income.   The high-volume or A Class products comprise the group of the biggest selling products that make up about 50% of total annual sales, the low-volume or C Class products comprise the slowest selling products that make up about 10% of total sales.   All other products fall into the medium-volume or B class. Usually, the breakdown in terms of number of products in each class is roughly 10% for A, 40% for B, and 50% for C.   These percentage break-downs are only used as rough guidelines and for practical applications may be adjusted to suit the data.

A sample of about 5% of all products was to be chosen.   The number of products to be sampled from each class was proportional to the total dollar sales volume of each class.   The products in each subsample were selected using standard statistical sampling techniques.   The choice of using a sample of about 5% of all products is a compromise between the desire for accuracy (requiring a fairly large sample) and the amount of work involved in data collection and testing.   Using the dollar sales volume of each class as a basis for setting the size of each subsample recognizes the fact that the larger the sales volume of a given product the larger are the potential savings likely to be.   Table 7-1 summarizes the results obtained.

Table 7-1: Estimation of potential annual savings

Class of oils	high volume	medium volume	low volume	greases
Overall:				
Percent of total volume	45%	35%	12%	8%
Number of products	64	205	411	124
Subsample size	20	15	5	4
Ratio (number in class/subsample)	3.2	13.67	82.5	31
Per product:				
Average cost difference	$431	$147	$74	$39
Standard deviation	$125	$26	$21	$19
Extrapolation to class:				
Cost difference	$27,584	$30,135	$30,414	$4,836
Standard error (of estimate)	$1,000	$372	$425	$212
Estimate of total cost difference:		$92,969		
Standard error (of total estimate):		$1,168		

How were the cost differences obtained?   As mentioned in the last section, it is not a valid test to simply substitute the optimal values of the decision variables into the theoretical cost expression (6-3) and compute the cost of the proposed policy for each product.   An estimate of these costs should be obtained by simulating the use of both the proposed and current policy for a sufficient length of time, say 10 years, computing for each the average stock level, the average annual number of replenishments, the average annual number of special production runs, and the average annual volume of demand supplied from stock and by special production runs each. These averages are then fed into expression (6-3) in place of the theoretical values. This was the procedure followed. The computer simulation program needed for this analysis was developed using the computer simulation language SIMSCRIPT. (Detailed discussion of the simulation program goes beyond the scope of this text.) The standard errors of the estimates were computed using standard statistical principles.

Since testing was done on an individual product basis, other aspects of some importance, such as the variations in the daily workload in the mixing and filling plants and total warehouse space usage, could not be observed. However, rough extrapolations of capacity usage on an annual basis indicated a workload similar to the current one. This was due to two opposing changes in the pattern of operations which cancelled each other quite closely. The proposed policies in general had higher cutoff points and hence less capacity usage for special production runs. But it had smaller stock replenishment and hence higher capacity usage for that part of the operations.

These results are used in the project report (Appendix to this chapter).

7.5 ANALYSIS OF SENSITIVITY OF SOLUTION OF THE LOD MODEL

Once the optimal solution has been found, two important issues have to be addressed: (1) 'How does the optimal solution respond to changes in the input parameters?', and (2) 'What is the error, in terms of loss of benefits or savings, incurred for using the model with wrong values for input parameters?' Although both of these are some-times loosely referred to as **sensitivity analysis**, I would like to reserve this term for the first of these issues, while the second is more appropriately referred to as **error analysis**. Both, sensitivity and error analysis are usually performed for each input parameter separately, with all other inputs remaining at their original, most likely value.

Sensitivity Analyses

Sensitivity analysis explores how the optimal solution responds to changes in a given input parameter. I will demonstrate this using the first model approximation for the LOD problem, given by the total cost expression (6-1A) and the EOQ formula (6-2):

$$T(Q) = 0.5Qvr + sD/Q \qquad (6\text{-}1\text{A})$$

and

$$EOQ = \sqrt{2Ds/vr} \qquad (6\text{-}2)$$

where for simplicity the subscript for D has been dropped. D refers thus to the demand from small customers.

Before demonstrating the sensitivity of this model, it is useful to substitute the right-hand side of (6-2) for Q in expression (6-1A) as follows:

$$T(Q) \;=\; 0.5vr\,\sqrt{2Ds/vr} \;+\; sD/\sqrt{2Ds/vr} \qquad\qquad (7\text{-}1)$$

A few algebraic manipulations give the following result:

$$T(Q) \;=\; \sqrt{0.5Dsvr} \;+\; \sqrt{0.5Dsvr} \;=\; 2\sqrt{0.5Dsvr}$$

which simplifies to

$$T(Q) \;=\; \sqrt{2Dsvr} \qquad\qquad (7\text{-}2)$$

How do expressions (6-2) and (7-2) respond to changes in the input parameters D, s, v, and r? Both respond to changes in the demand, D, and the production setup cost, s, proportionately to the square root of the change in these two inputs. If the demand is changed by a factor k, $T(Q)$ and the EOQ change by a factor of $\sqrt{k}$. So, a doubling ($k=2$) of the demand or the setup cost will increase both the EOQ and its total cost by a factor of $\sqrt{2}$ or by about 41%. The response of the total relevant cost (7-2) is identical for the other two inputs, the product value, v, and the holding cost per dollar invested per year, r. But by (6-2), the EOQ responds to changes in v and r inversely proportional to the square root of k. So a 50% increase in the product value ($k=1.5$), results in reduction in the EOQ by a factor of $1/\sqrt{1.5} = 0.8165$, i.e., the EOQ is reduced by 18.35% (100% - 81.65%). These are relatively large changes. An increase of 5% in the demand only results in an increase of about 2.5% in the EOQ and its cost.

Sensitivity analysis has three main purposes:

(1) If the optimal solution is relatively insensitive to reasonably large changes in input parameters, then the decision maker and user can place more confidence in the validity and usefulness of the model (assuming that the model is appropriate). It increases the credibility of the model. This clearly seems to be the case for the EOQ model. Minor changes or shifts in the inputs will not immediately affect the validity of the solution in any significant way.

(2) For inputs into a model that are in the form of scarce resources, sensitivity analysis provides information about the value of additional amounts of each scarce resource. The value of additional scarce resources is called the **shadow price** of the resource. It is a very important concept, both in economics and OR/MS. To demonstrate its usefulness, consider the feed mix problem described in Chapter 1. If some of the feed raw materials, such as slaughterhouse by-products, are available only in limited quantities, the shadow price of that scarce resource would indicate to the feed mix manufacturer the maximum price premium that should be paid to procure additional amounts from other sources, such as by incurring additional freight costs from out-of-town sources. Chapters 12 and 13 take up this concept in detail and study its use for decision making.

(3) There may be considerable uncertainty about the value of some input data. Sensitivity analysis is used for exploring how the optimal solution changes as a function of such uncertain data. If the best solution remains unchanged or is only slightly affected for large departures of these data from their most likely range, then the decision maker can put much confidence into the solution. On the other hand, high sensitivity of the best solution to minor changes in these data would be a signal for caution. Either greater effort must be expended to obtain more accurate estimates for them or a play-safe policy is implemented instead. For example, the average waiting time and queue length in a waiting line situation is very sensitive to the ratio of the rate of arrivals and the rate of service. Particularly, if the service facility is working close to full capacity, the average waiting time rises sharply for even a small increase in the rate of arrivals. Take the case of an accident and emergency clinic at a hospital. If there is considerable uncertainty about the arrival rate of accidents, say, during weekends, a play-safe policy would be to overstaff the clinic. This would allow for coping with a rush of emergencies, without running a serious risk to the health of potential accident victims.

Sensitivity analysis can only be performed with respect to those parameters that have actually been included in the model.

7.6 ERROR ANALYSIS

Many of the input parameters are estimated on the basis of past data. These parameters are then used to optimize the operation in the future. There is no guarantee that the future will be similar to the past. For instance, demand for a product may increase or decrease appreciably. The holding cost may increase due to a world-wide rise in interest rates, etc. The analyst may also have been supplied with wrong data or made a mistake. So the wrong input parameters have been used in the model. The 'optimal' solution derived on that basis is only optimal on paper, but not in reality. I will refer to it as 'pseudo-optimal'. How much does a wrong demand forecast or an error in other input data cost in terms of a loss in potential benefits or potential cost savings? Error analysis explores this aspect.

An Example

Error analysis seems to be a concept that many students find difficult to grasp. Although error analysis is performed prior to implementing the solution, it is easier to think of it initially as something done at some later time. I will demonstrate the steps of error analysis again for the EOQ model.

(1) Using the input data listed in Table 6-2, the EOQ formula of expression (6-2) yields an 'optimal' order quantity of

$$q = \sqrt{2Ds/vr} = \sqrt{2(4140)18/320(0.18)} = 50.87$$

This solution is now implemented.

(2) A year later it is discovered that the actual demand is not 4140, but only 2875. The original demand forecast of 4140 overestimated the true demand by 44%. Hence, the answer derived in (1) is not the optimal solution. It is only 'pseudo-optimal'. By expression (6-2) the true optimal order quantity we should have used is

$$EOQ = \sqrt{2(2875)18/320(0.18)} = 42.4$$

If we had implemented this solution, the minimum relevant cost, by expression (7-2), would have been

$$T(EOQ = 42.4) = \sqrt{2(2875)18/320(0.18)} = \$2442$$

(3) Instead, we implemented the pseudo-optimal solution, and by expression (6-1A) we incurred an actual cost, based on the correct demand level of 2875, of

$$T(q) = 0.5qvr + sD/q$$

or $T(q=50.87) = 0.5(50.87)320(0.18) + 18(2875)/50.87 = \$2482$

(4) The difference between the actual cost of \$2482 incurred and the minimum cost of \$2442 is the loss in potential benefits suffered for using the pseudo-optimal order quantity $q=50.87$, rather than the true optimal $EOQ=42.4$. Expressed as a percentage of the true minimum cost $T(EOQ)$, this loss amounts to

$$[T(q) - T(EOQ)]/T(EOQ) \times 100\% = [2482 - 2442]/2442 \times 100\% = 1.64\%$$

Although we made a 44% error in forecasting the demand, the actual cost incurred was only 1.64% higher than the minimum cost achievable, had the correct demand figure been known and used. The increase in the true cost for a sizable forecast error of 44% is thus surprisingly small.

General Procedure of Error Analysis

Error analysis is not performed after errors in input parameters are discovered. It is done before the solution is implemented. It is part of testing the solution for robustness. When we perform error analysis we do not know whether any input parameters are wrong. If we knew, we would hardly use them. We would make all reasonable effort to ascertain their correct values. So, keep in mind that when error analysis is performed, it is in some sense 'make believe' — 'What would be the effect if a given input parameter were off by a certain amount?'

In general, error analysis follows the four steps listed below:

(1) Determine the optimal policy based on the best estimate values for all input parameters. Assume now that one of these parameters, say p, is in error. The solution derived is, therefore, only pseudo-optimal.

(2) Assume that the value of the input parameter p used in (1) differs from the (unknown) correct value, say P, by a factor of k, i.e., the value used is equal to k times the correct value, or $p=kP$. $k = 1$ means that the value used for the parameter is at its correct value, $k < 1$ means it is smaller, and $k > 1$ means it is larger than the correct value. Find the optimal policy and its associated objective function value, using the (assumed) correct value P for the parameter in question.

(3) Compute the actual value of the objective function if the pseudo-optimal policy determined in (1) were implemented, but using the (assumed) correct value P for the parameter in question. If the objective is to minimize costs, the actual value of the objective function for the pseudo-optimal policy cannot be lower than the one of the truly optimal policy and is usually larger. (To test your understanding spell out the analogous comparison for a benefit or profit function to be maximized.)

(4) Find the difference between the optimal objective function value for the (assumed) correct input parameter value (as determined in (2) above) and the actual objective function value for the pseudo-optimal policy (as determined in (3) above). Express that difference as a percentage of the optimal objective function value computed in (2) above.

This analysis is done for maybe 10 to 20 different values of k, over a reasonable range of k (e.g., for k from 0.2 to 5), to explore how sensitive the solution is to input errors. It is usually helpful to plot the result on a graph.

As is the case with sensitivity analysis, error analysis is usually done individually for each crucial input parameter, with all other inputs remaining at their original best estimate values.

Example Continued

Repeating the earlier analysis for a range of values of k and hence true (unknown) possible values of $D = 4140/k$, we find the following percentage increases in the actual cost over the true (potential) minimum cost:

error in demand	-80%	-50%	-20%	0	+20%	+50%	+100%	+400%
k		.2	.5	.8	1	1.2	1.5	2	4
D implied (4140/k)	20700	8280	5175	4140	3450	2760	2070	1035
$T(EOQ)$ based on D	6552	4144	3276	2930	2675	2392	2072	1465
$T(q=50.87)$ based on D	8790	4395	3296	2930	2686	2442	2198	1831
cost increase		34%	6.1%	0.6%	0	0.4%	2.1%	6.1%	25%

Figure 7-1 shows how the percentage cost increase varies as a function of k. Observe that underestimating the demand causes a higher increase in actual costs than overestimating the demand by the same percentage.

Figure 7-1: Percentage error in cost for deviations from true demand

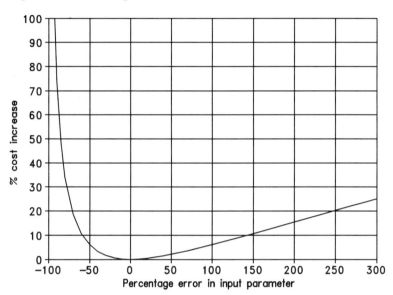

As will be shown in the optional section below, the increase in costs of the EOQ model in response to errors in all other input parameters is equally small. The EOQ model is thus very insensitive to fairly large errors in the input parameters. There is little need for highly sophisticated and hence very accurate demand forecasts when using the EOQ model, nor is there a need to estimate the various cost parameters to a high degree of accuracy. Similarly, once implemented, substantial shifts in demand or changes in cost parameters of 50% or more have to happen before it may be advisable to recompute the optimal policy.

Purpose of Error Analysis

From the above discussion it follows that error analysis is done for two main reasons:

(1) To determine the accuracy required for estimating input data; the more sensitive the solution is to input errors, the more accurate should the input parameters be.

(2) To establish control ranges for changes in input parameters over which the current optimal policy remains near-optimal; as long as the input parameters stay within these limits, there is no need to recompute the optimal policy. The

gain in benefits or savings is too small to warrant the cost of updating. This is an important input for step 1 of the methodology, namely, control and maintenance of the solution (see Chapter 9).

Some Conclusions on Sensitivity and Error Analysis

Both sensitivity and error analysis explore the effect of changes in the inputs parameters on the solution of the model. Sensitivity analysis shows how the optimal solution, i.e., the optimal value of the objective function and the optimal values of the decision variables, respond to changes in the inputs. So, we compare changes in optimal solutions. Error analysis, on the other hand, finds the loss of potential benefits due to changes in the input parameters, say as a consequence of errors in their assessment or due to changes in their values subsequent to the implementation of the 'optimal' solution. So, we compare what could have been, had we used the correct values, and what was actually achieved, given the values used.

In either case, if the solution is not sensitive to reasonable changes in the input parameters, we say that the solution (and hence the model) is **robust**. The decision maker can place more confidence and credibility in robust solutions. **Robustness** is a highly desirable property of any model.

Note that both types of analyses are usually done separately for each input parameter. However, simultaneous changes in several parameters can also be explored in a similar manner. In fact, analyzing changes in several parameters at the same time may be a more useful exercise.

7.7* GENERALIZATION OF ERROR ANALYSIS FOR EOQ MODEL

This section extends the analysis done above to all input parameters of the EOQ model. Assume that the various input parameters are in error by a factor k as follows, i.e., the ratio of the four input parameters Ds/vr in expression (6-2) was incorrectly evaluated as $k(Ds/vr)$. For example, the setup cost s could be in error by a factor of k, or the ratio s/r could be in error by a factor of k. Then the pseudo-optimal replenishment size q is equal to

$$q = \sqrt{2kDs/vr} = (\sqrt{2Ds/vr})\sqrt{k} = EOQ\sqrt{k} \qquad (7\text{-}3)$$

Its true cost by expression (6-1A), in terms of the correct values of the input parameters, is

$$T(q) = 0.5vrq + sD/q = 0.5vr(\sqrt{2Ds/vr})\sqrt{k} + sD/(\sqrt{2Ds/vr})\sqrt{k}$$

The analogous algebraic manipulation as applied to (7-1) above reduces this expression to

$$T(q) = [(k+1)/2\sqrt{k}]\sqrt{2Dsvr} = [(k+1)/2\sqrt{k}]\,T(EOQ) \qquad (7\text{-}4)$$

Note that $(k+1)/2\sqrt{k}$ is equal to 1 if $k=1$. It will always be larger than 1 if k is larger or smaller than 1. This is what we would expect. If due to errors in the input parameters, we do not use the optimal policy, the true cost of the policy actually used will be higher. The percentage increase of the true cost over the minimum cost is derived from the ratio of $T(q)$ and $T(EOQ)$, i.e.,

$$\{[(k+1)/2\sqrt{k}] - 1\} \times 100\% \qquad (7\text{-}5)$$

A rather surprising fact emerges. This percentage error is only a function of k and not of the actual values of the various input parameters. The graph in Figure 7-1 is thus only a function of k and is of general validity for the EOQ model. Its shape is not dependent on the actual values of the input parameters, but only on the combined error factor k in the ratio Ds/vr.

7.8   PROJECT REPORT

The mathematical modeling phase culminates in the preparation of a project report. This is the document that informs the problem owner about the results of the project analysis and presents the analyst's recommendation about implementation. Therefore, the project report requires that the analyst has already thought carefully about what would be involved in implementing the results of the analysis. This needs to be done even before a decision on whether or not implementation should proceed.   This is another case of the forward linkages ever present in OR/MS projects. Although implementation is the topic of the next chapter, the logical place for dealing with the project report is here.   Once you have studied Chapter 8 it would be advisable to return to this section once more.

Format

Here is a suggested format for the project report:

(1)   An introductory statement about the background of the project with reference to the project proposal.

(2)   An executive summary of the findings and major recommendations.

(3)   A brief restatement of the problem investigated, with reference to the project proposal. This is followed by a motivation for the model used and a short non-technical description of the model. It is also important that you include here a brief discussion of the major assumptions made and how the real

situation was simplified for modeling purposes and why, including the possible effects of these simplifications. Only then will the problem owner and user be able to assess how 'good' or realistic the model is. Any detailed technical discussion of the model and technical assumptions made should, however, be relegated to appendices, where appropriate.

(4)   A brief description of the major steps of the analysis, including data collection and analysis. Any technical aspects that require a reasonable degree of OR/MS training for proper understanding should be relegated to appendices rather than be contained in the main body of the report.

(5)   The major findings of the analysis, including important aspects of the sensitivity analysis performed, and the form of the best policy or solution. The importance of including sensitivity analysis in your reported findings cannot be stressed enough. OR/MS is as much about providing insight to the decision maker/problem owner, as it is about providing 'solutions'. Sensitivity analysis is one of the major inputs to such insight. If the solution recommended for implementation differs from the optimal solution of the model, the reasons for deviating from the optimal solution should be fully motivated and explained.

(6)   An estimate of the potential benefits, such as the increase in monetary returns or savings, or the decrease in costs, that are likely to result from the implementation of the recommended solution.

(7)   A brief description of further work to be done for full implementation and estimates of the additional resources required in terms of time and funds.

(8)   The analyst's recommendation about whether implementation should proceed in the light of the decision maker's performance standards and the implementation costs estimated; and

(9)   A detailed plan and time-table for implementing the solution, if appropriate.

(10)   Appendices giving details on
        • assessment of cost parameters and other inputs, such as demand distributions;
        • any statistical tests or statistical analysis performed, such as a test for goodness-of-fit, analysis of variance, or regressions;
        • inputs into analysis done by computers (or hand computations) and the outputs of such computations, e.g., reproductions of the spreadsheets, analysis on sensitivity, or simulation run summaries; if the computations involve a large number of cases, like the 44 products tested in the LOD case, it may be preferable to list detailed inputs, computations, and outputs for only a few products, rather than for all of them; sufficient explanations should be provided so the reader can make sense of what is presented;
        • the model used with adequate explanations, addressed to a person with some basic familiarity with OR/MS, etc.;

- any technical assumptions made;
- if appropriate, reasons why other models or approaches were discarded as unsuitable.

Obviously, the format and style of presentation may need to be adjusted to the nature and type of project. For example, if the project was undertaken as part of an advocacy process, such as an exploratory analysis of an effective breast cancer screening policy initiated by a lobby group, the emphasis of the report may be different.

Presentation Pointers

Few guidelines as to the appropriate length of the project report can be given. It is usually not the final documentation on the project. Hence, it should contain no more than is needed for the problem owner to be able to come to an informed decision as to whether the recommendations contained in it should be implemented.

Since it is addressed to the problem owner, its language should be at a level appropriate for her or his technical background. This usually means that it may contain terminology related to the activities of the organization or industry, but normally not of an OR/MS nature. If OR/MS terminology needs to be used, it should be clearly defined the first time it is used. Unless the definition can be easily understood by people with little or no OR/MS background, technical concepts and terms used may need to be explained. The reasons why they arise and are needed for a proper understanding of the model used have to be properly motivated. Even so, any highly technical details, whether related to the project content or to OR/MS methodology, should be relegated to appendices.

Basically, the project report must be complete to stand on its own. You cannot assume that the recipients of the report will refer back to the project proposal prior to reading the report. They may even not have any access to the project proposal. Hence, some aspects of the project report, such as the motivation for the project and its objectives and other crucial concepts, may have to be restated here.

Any assumptions made must be justified as being reasonable or of minor consequence. Claims made must be backed up with evidence. Both strengths and weaknesses of the analysis made and conclusions reached should be spelled out.

The technical standards of appendices are usually not intended for the problem owner, but her or his advisers or personnel who may need to review, modify, or update the project and its results. For this reason it must be written to a higher technical and scientific standard. It should include references to results of technical or scientific papers used. Modifications made to the methods proposed in such papers need to be stated. The reasons for rejecting their use as inappropriate must be spelled out. Most importantly, any assumptions and simplifications have to be fully documented. Conscientiously following these rules is also for the protection of the analyst. He or she can then not be accused of having done a slipshod job or of negligence.

Most of these aspects, in fact, form part of the analyst's professional ethics!

Note that the suggested format is such that the problem owner can stop after having read the executive summary, either   convinced that the recommendations should be implemented, or alternatively, that the project should be abandoned. The problem owner only proceeds to the main body of the report, if either he or she has not reached a conclusion yet or wishes to read on out of interest. Normally, any problem owner who has little or no training in OR/MS will not read the appendices.

As was true for the project proposal (see Section 5.4), the project report must also be to a high professional standard if it is to taken as a credible document. So I want to stress again the importance of correct spelling, syntax, grammar, and of writing complete logical sentences. Consult the references at end of Chapter 5 for help on report writing skills.

The format, structure, and amount of technical detail given in a report should be appropriate for the problem situation analyzed. The above format is highly suitable for a project dealing with a substantive problem, i.e., one to be implemented in the problem owner's sphere of control. If the project sponsor is not the problem owner or user, such as a project undertaken as part of an advocacy process, e.g., as part of submission made to governmental organizations, more emphasis will have to be put into items 3 and 5, while items 7 and 9 may not be relevant.

The Appendix to this chapter contains the project report for the LOD study.

EXERCISES

The following computational exercises on sensitivity and error analysis are most convenient-ly done using the spreadsheets developed for the original exercises in Chapter 6.

1. For the example used in Figure 6-2, explore the effect on the optimal *EOQ* and its cost for the following changes in input parameters:
    (a) Changes in the replenishment setup cost from $18 to $12, 24, and 36.
    (b) Changes in the investment holding cost from 18% to 12%, 24%, and 30%.

2. For the optimal solution to the machine adjustment problem derived in exercise 1 of Chap. 6 perform the following sensitivity analysis:
    (a) Changes in the net selling price of -10%, -20%, and +25%.
    (b) Changes in the fraction of defectives that can be reworked from 0.5 to 0.4, 0.6, and 0.75.
    (c) Changes in the slope of the function of defectives from the current 10 to 8, 6, and 12/hour.

3. For the optimal solution to the ceramic tile problem derived in exercise 3 of Chap. 6 perform the following sensitivity analysis:
    (a) Changes in the value of the product of -20%, +25%, and +50%.
    (b) Changes in the return hauling cost for the railcar of -20%, +25%, and +50%.
    (c) Changes in the cost of holding tiles in stock at the factory of -20%, +25%, and +50%.

4. For the optimal solution to the ELMO coil production problem in exercise 5 of Chap. 6 do the following sensitivity analysis:
   (a) Changes in the size of the order from 10,000 to 5,000, 20,000, and 40,000.
   (b)   Changes in the rate of defectives per hour, which currently runs at about $0.0075 \times$(running speed of the machine)^2, to 0.005, and 0.01 times the square of the running speed.

5. For the example discussed in Figure 6-2, perform error analysis for the following cases:
   (a) A true replenishment setup cost of $12 and $24, rather than the $18 used.
   (b) A true investment holding cost of 12% and 24%, rather than the 18% used.
   (c) The graph shown in Figure 7-1 is not only valid for errors in the annual demand, but for errors in the replenishment setup costs or the ratio of replenishment setup costs and investment holding cost. Hence, estimate the approximate effect of the following errors:
   - an error of -60%, -25%, +50%, and +100% in the setup cost;
   - true setup costs and investment holding cost penalties of [$12 and 12%], [$15 and 25%], and [$24 and 15%].

6. For the machine adjustment problem of exercise 1 in Chap. 6, perform the following type of error analysis (note that the results of exercise 2 above will be useful):
   (a) An error in the net selling price of -20%.
   (b) An error in the rate of defectives that can be reworked of +25%, -33.33%.
   (c) An error in the slope of the function for the rate of defectives of +25%, - 16.67%.

7. For the ceramic tile problem of exercise 3 in Chap. 6, perform the following type of error analysis (note that the results of exercise 3 above will be useful):
   (a) A true value of the product of $9,600 rather than $12,000.
   (b) A true value of the return hauling cost for the railcar of $956 rather than $1195.
   (c) A true value of the inventory holding cost at the factory of 24% rather than 30%.

8. For the ELMO coil production problem of exercise 5 in Chap. 6, perform the following type of error analysis (note that the results of exercise 4 above will be useful):
   (a) A true value of the order size of 20,000 rather than 10,000.
   (b) A true coefficient value in the function for the rate of defectives of 0.01 rather than 0.0075.

9. Rewrite the general procedure for error analysis in Section 7.6 for the case of maximizing a benefit function (such as profits), rather than minimizing a cost function.

10. Discuss the following apparent contradiction: If at the start of an OR/MS project all costs and potential benefits were known accurately, the project would not get off the ground. However, if the total costs and potential benefits can only be ascertained with some confidence after the model has been tested for performance, but prior to its implementation, the correct decision is to proceed with implementation. What implications does this have for evaluating costs and benefits of OR/MS projects?

11. Based on your analysis in exercise 1 of Chap. 6 and exercises 2 and 6 of this chapter, as well as additional analysis as to the potential savings of the best solution over the current policy, write a short project report, following the guidelines given in Section 7.8.

12. What information/insights is the (a) manager or decision maker, and (b) the problem analyst looking for in sensitivity and error analysis? Say it in your own words.

13. Why is establishing internal and external validity important for (a) the decision maker/user of the solution, and (b) the analyst of the problem.

REFERENCES

Unfortunately, little has been written on sensitivity and error analysis of a general nature. Extensive coverage of this topic is only given with reference to linear programming and other mathematical programming techniques (covered in Chapter 13). See, however, the brief review of various approaches to sensitivity analysis by

Blanning, Robert W., 'The sources and uses of sensitivity information', *Interfaces*, August 1974

A much broader and insightful view of robustness is taken by J. Rosenhead:

Rosenhead, J., *Rational Analysis for a Problematic World*, Wiley 1989. This text contains two chapters on robustness analysis by J. Rosenhead.

The literature on validation is much more extensive, raising similar issues as in other disciplines. An excellent starting point is to study the highly readable article by

Landry M., Malouin, J.-L., and Oral, M., 'Model validation in operations research', *European Journal of Operational Research*, 14/3, Nov. 1983, 207-20.

Landry, M., and Oral, M., Special Issue: Model Validation, *European Journal of Operational Research*, 66/2, April 1993. This issue contains a series of articles dealing with various aspects of model validation. The first article by Landry and Oral gives a comprehensive and comparative survey of the other six articles. Some of their conclusions reached show that the validation issue cannot be divorced from the questions of 'What is science?' and 'Is OR/MS science?' These papers contain extensive bibliographies on validation and the process of science.

For references on report writing, see Chapter 5.

Appendix to Chapter 7: LOD Project Report

PURAIR OIL COMPANY INC.
Management Science Group
SAN FRANCISCO, CA 94123

July 10, 199X

INTERNAL MAIL

Trevor Black
Manager, Lubrication Oil Division
Sandpoint Oil Refinery
PURAIR OIL COMPANY INC.

Dear Mr. Black,

Re. Production/Inventory Control Project Report

Please find enclosed two copies of the project report for
the preliminary study of the production/inventory control
operations of packaged goods in the LOD warehouse at
Sandpoint. I suggest that we arrange for an oral presentation of our findings to the same group of people who
attended the project proposal meeting on April 18. This
would allow a full discussion of our findings. Any questions concerning the model, its operation, and its implementation can then be answered in person. Please contact
me on my new extension 7747.

Sincerely yours,

Hans G. Daellenbach
Senior Analyst, Management Science Group

Enclosure: 2 copies of Project Report

1

PROJECT REPORT

PRODUCTION/INVENTORY CONTROL STUDY FOR PACKAGED GOODS
LUBRICATION OIL DIVISION, SANDPOINT REFINERY

Table of Contents

1. INTRODUCTORY STATEMENT

This report contains the findings of a preliminary study covering the production/inventory control operations for packaged goods in the LOD warehouse at Sandpoint Refinery. Mr. Black, Manager of the LOD, approved this study on April 18, on the basis of the project proposal submitted to him by the Management Science Group on April 11. We undertook the preliminary study during the period from May 27 to July 5.

The aim of the study was (1) to develop a mathematical model for finding the best production and stock replenishment policy which minimizes the sum of all costs affected by the choice of policy, and (2) to estimate the potential savings in operating costs that can be achieved by using such a policy for all products.

2. EXECUTIVE SUMMARY OF FINDINGS AND RECOMMENDATIONS

The following major findings were made:

(a) Implementation of the policy proposed in this report for the entire product line of the LOD is estimated to result in annual savings of operating and investment

2

costs of over $90,000. It will increase the average stock turn over to about 32 times per year.

(b) The additional cost for developing the necessary computer software for implementing the policy and assuring its continued updating, and for actual implementation of the policy amounts to about $32,000 at internal charging rates.

(c) The new policy could be fully implemented within 14 weeks.

In view of this highly favourable ratio of savings to costs, it is recommended that the LOD immediately proceeds with implementing the proposed model.

3.   STATEMENT OF THE PROBLEM

The current production and stock replenishment policy for packaged goods followed by the LOD distinguishes between two groups of products: group 1 includes only high-volume products with frequent large customer orders, and group 2 includes all other products. Group 1 covers currently 78 products (all packaged in drums of 200 litres). Group 2 covers the remaining 726 products. Each group accounts for about 50% of the total dollar throughput of packaged goods. The production and stock replenishment policy is characterized as follows:

(1) Group 1: any customer order equal to or larger than a given cutoff point is supplied by scheduling a special production run, while any customer orders below the cutoff point are supplied from stock. Stock is replenished periodically by a given amount. Currently, the cutoff point for all products is 12 drums, while the stock replenishment size varies from product to product and covers between 2 to 6 weeks of customer orders supplied from stock.

(2) Group 2: all customers orders are supplied from stock. Stock replenishments vary in size with the sales volume and cover 3 and 12 weeks of sales.

Our analysis indicates that, in principle, the policy followed for group 1 products can be applied to all products, drums as well as products packaged in other containers. Furthermore, the choice of the best cutoff point depends not only on the customer order pattern, but also on the various production and warehousing costs. Rather than classify products arbitrarily into these two groups, we decided, after discussions with Mr. Black and other LOD staff, to build a model that allows all products to follow the group 1 policy, but with individually determined cutoff points and stock replenishment sizes. If the cutoff point for a product is set at a level larger than the

3

largest customer order likely to be received, the policy for that product corresponds to the entire demand being supplied from stock.

Although some products exhibit a mild seasonal pattern, the model is based on the assumption that the average demand remains constant over the entire year. The effect of this simplification is negligible, as long as the optimal policy is updated regularly, say once each year.

As a result of opting for a uniform policy for all products, the problem becomes one of developing a model which determines for each product an individual cutoff point and stock replenishment size so as to minimize the sum of all operating costs affected by the choice of these two variables. The relevant costs turn out to be (a) the product raw material and production cost, (b) the mixing and filling operation setup costs, (c) the product handling costs, and (d) the cost of holding products in stock, the latter consisting mainly of the cost of funds invested in stocks.

The second aim of the study, namely the estimation of the potential savings that would accrue if the model is applied to all packaged goods, was to be done by extrapolating the results obtained from a sample to all products.

4.   MAJOR STEPS OF ANALYSIS

These followed the steps outlined in the project proposal.

(a) **Developing a suitable model:** My initial visits to the LOD on March 27 and 28 were followed up by further visits on May 26 and 27. After extensive discussions with Mr. Black and a number of his staff we concluded that a model based on the group 1 policy should be used, in principle, for all products. A computer spreadsheet program was developed to perform the required computations for finding the best policy. The details of the model and a sample output from the spreadsheet are shown in the Appendices to this report.

(b) **Data collection for sample of products to be analyzed:** In view of the large number of products, the model was applied to a sample of about 5% of all products, with the results to be extrapolated to all products. In order to increase the accuracy of the estimate, the products were grouped into relatively homogeneous classes. The usual distribution by annual dollar sales volume was applied, with three classes: high, medium, and low dollar volume. Since the production setup costs of greases are considerably higher than for oils, a fourth class for all greases was   created. The composition of the classes and the subsample sizes is summarized in the top portion of Table 1 below.

4

Products to be analyzed were selected by random sampling methods. The customer order pattern for each sample product was extracted from the 199X customer order file, the most recent complete year of customer data available. Figures for all relevant cost factors were supplied by the Cost Control Department or were computed based on rough time trials.

(c) **Estimation of total savings:** For each product in the sample, the best policy, consisting of the cutoff point for large customer orders and the stock replenishment size, was computed using the spreadsheet developed.

A simple simulation program was written to simulate the performance of the proposed and of the current policy for a given product. This program was used to estimate the total cost difference between the two policies for each product in the sample. This in turn provided all the input required for extrapolating the results obtained to the entirety of all products. The findings are summarized in Table 1.

5.   MAJOR FINDINGS

Table 1 below summarizes the results of extrapolating the savings to the entire packaged goods product line carried by the LOD.   It shows that implementation of the best policy for each product would generate savings over the current operating costs of over $90,000 per year.

A more detailed comparison of the current and proposed best policy indicates the following pattern:

(a) As expected, the best cutoff point differs from product to product. As a rule, it tends to be between 3200 and 4400 litres per order - somewhat higher than the current 2400 (which is equivalent to 12 drums). Hence, a larger proportion of all sales are supplied from stock than is the case currently.

(b) For most products, the best stock replenishment size is also smaller than the current policy and this in spite of the higher cutoff point.

(c) A consequence of (b) is a substantial reduction in total investments, as well as warehouse space needed. This could well ease the current shortage of easily accessible warehouse space suffered by the LOD.

(d) The average stock turnover ratio associated with the best policy seems to be substantially higher than the company target of 24 times per year. A rough esti-

5

mate is around 32 times per year.

(e) The proposed best policy is relatively insensitive to reasonable shifts in the total annual demand and in most cost factors, i.e., changes in any of these of up to 25% that occur after implementation of the best policy for a given product will only result in a small reduction in the potential savings. As a consequence, it will in most instances be adequate to update the best policy once each year, unless a given product is subject to major changes.

Table 1: Estimation of potential annual savings

Class	high volume oils	medium volume oils	low volume oils	greases
Overall:				
Percent of total volume	45%	35%	12%	8%
Number of products	64	205	411	124
Subsample size	20	15	5	4
Ratio (class #/subsample)	3.2	13.67	82.5	31
Per product:				
Average cost difference	$431	$147	$74	$39
Standard deviation	$125	$26	$21	$19
Extrapolation to class:				
Cost difference	$27,584	$30,135	$30,414	$4,836
Standard error (of estimate)	$1,000	$372	$425	$212
Estimate of total cost difference:	$92,969			
Standard error (of total estimate):	$1,168			

6. RECOMMENDATIONS FOR IMPLEMENTATION

Implementation of the model to all products will require computationally efficient programs to be developed for finding the best joint values of the cutoff point and stock replenishment. Furthermore, the format currently used for re-cording customer order data requires substantial data manipulation. Hence, considerable time savings can be gained in the future when the control variables are updated, if some small additions are made to the existing pro-grams for recording customer orders and storing them in an annual data base. Implementation involves therefore mainly staff

6

time, with all other costs being negligible. Table 2 shows the staff time for the various tasks. According to this schedule, the new policies could be in use by the end of October.

The estimate of potential annual savings indicates that the cost of full implementation would be recovered by using the new policies for less than four months. However, it should be noted that the savings will only rise to their full potential level after a transition period. During this period excess stock levels are reduced to their new lower levels. The savings in investment costs will, therefore, only become fully realized once the new lower levels have been achieved. This may take up to 6 months.

Based on this analysis, I recommend that the model developed is implemented.

Table 2: Staff resources required for full implementation

Task	(time in days)	Analyst time	Other staff	Completion date
(a) Programs for use of model		12	1 (LOD)	week 4
(b) Alterations to data files		3	30 (EDP)	week 9
(c) Data collection		5	20 (LOD) 10 (cost control)	week 8
(d) Computation of policies		5		week 12
(e) Preparation of implementation plan		2	2 (LOD)	week 12
(f) Instruction of users		3	5 (LOD)	week 13
(g) Change-over to new policy		2	2 (LOD)	week 14
(h) Follow-up monitoring		8		week 26
Totals		40	30 (LOD) 40 (other)	

Chargeable cost: 80 days at $400/day $32,000.

Date: July 10, 199X   Project analyst:
                            H.G. Daellenbach, Management Science Group

7

APPENDIX: SPREADSHEET COMPUTATIONS FOR FINDING OPTIMAL POLICY FOR PRODUCT Y

(Figure 6-2 of Chapter 6 reproduced here)

APPENDIX ON COMPUTATIONS PERFORMED

(Not shown here in detail.) This appendix gives full details for each product on input parameters used for finding optimal policies and the resulting solution in a table form. It also shows the results of the simulation runs and the cost incurred for the current policy. These form the basis for estimating the potential savings in Table 1. Details on sensitivity analysis performed are included also.

APPENDIX: DETAILED DESCRIPTION OF MODEL

The model has two decision variables for each product:

— The cutoff point L for classifying customer orders into small and large: Any customer order equal to or larger than this cutoff point is supplied by scheduling a special production run and shipping the goods directly to the customer. All other customer orders are supplied from stock.

— The stock replenishment size Q : Whenever the stock has been depleted through deliveries and the amount left on hand is less than the last customer order received, replenish stock by Q.

The total annual relevant cost for $T(L, Q)$ consists of the following four components:

```
┌───────┐   ┌────────────────┐   ┌──────────────────┐
│Total  │ = │Annual setup cost│ + │Annual handling   │
│cost   │   │for special p'runs│   │cost for big cust.│
└───────┘   └────────────────┘   └──────────────────┘

        ┌────────────────┐   ┌────────────────────┐
      + │Annual associated│ + │Annual handling     │
        │EOQ cost given L │   │cost for small cust.│
        └────────────────┘   └────────────────────┘
```

$$= [sN] + [h_2 D_2] + [0.5Qvr + sD_l/Q] + [h_l D_l] \tag{1}$$

where s is the production setup cost per batch,

N is the annual number of stock replenishments,

h_2 is the product handling cost for large customer orders,

8

D_2 is the amount of goods supplied by special production runs,

v is the product value per unit in stock,

r is the cost of carrying goods in stock per dollar invested/year,

D_1 is the amount of goods supplied from stock, and

h_1 is the product handling cost for small customer orders.

The optimal solution for the two decision variables can easily be found by recognizing that for any given amount of goods supplied from stock, $D_1 = D$, the optimal value of Q is given by the EOQ formula:

$$EOQ = \sqrt{2Ds/vr} \qquad (2)$$

with its associated annual cost of $T(EOQ) = \sqrt{2Dsvr}$. Using this result, the total cost in expression (1) is easily evaluated for each values of L and its associated value of D_1 . The optimal combination of L and Q corresponds to the one which achieves the lowest value for expression (1).

Assumptions of the $T(Q,L)$ Model

The model is based on the standard assumptions underlying the EOQ model, i.e., for each product: a constant average demand, a fixed replenishment cost independent of Q and L (although it can be different for stock replenishment and special production runs), a linear holding cost on the average stock investment, a linear handling cost for stock replenishments and special production runs, and no shortages. Furthermore, it is assumed that the daily demand distribution for each product remains the same over time. Obviously, this distribution could change. However, any changes are expected to be gradual. Hence, regular updating of the policy for each product will capture any changes that occurred since the last update.

It is also assumed, that there are no capacity constraints on the equipment, or on the available warehouse space, or maximum allowable investment. This allows the policy for each product to be optimized independently. If such constraints turn out to be binding, once the optimal policies for all products have been computed, suitable adjustments would need to be made. It seems that only the warehouse capacity might become limiting A simple scheme of incremental analysis for reducing warehouse space required by multiples of full pallet areas could be used to quickly determine the optimal constrained solution.

Additional savings could be achieved if the stock level is reviewed whenever a special production run is scheduled for a given product, and topped up at the same time. This would have increased the complexity of the model substantially at only modest further saving. However, no tests were made to confirm this conclusion.

8 Implementation of Solution

The majority of OR/MS projects are aimed at improving the operation of an existing system or finding the best mode of operations for a new proposed system. The potential benefits of such a project can, however, only be secured if the solution to the problem is implemented. Contrary to the belief of most novice OR/MS analysts, implementation is not something tacked on to the end of the modeling phase. Rather it must be a prime concern underlying all earlier steps in the analysis. Planning for implementation starts right from the outset of any project. This is the topic of the first two sections of this chapter.

Once a solution has been implemented, procedures and rules have to be put into place for the continued control, updating and maintenance of the solution. Section 3 takes up that subject, while Section 4 discusses following-up the project to make sure that implementation is as complete as possible and that the solution is correctly applied.

Unfortunately, this whole discussion has to remain largely in general descriptive terms only. Although the LOD proposals were successfully implemented, it would be rather boring to give a step-be-step account of what went on during implementation. It would also cover many pages, without conveying significantly more of a substantive nature.

8.1 IMPLEMENTATION

Implementation of an OR/MS project is putting the tested solution to work. This means translating the mathematical solution into a set of easily understood operating procedures or decision rules for each person involved in preparing inputs for the model, performing any computations, by hand or with the help of computer programs, and using or applying the solution. This is followed by training all people involved for the proper application of these rules, executing the transition from the existing to the proposed mode of operation, and preparing complete documentation for future reference. These sound like fairly straightforward tasks that are easily handled by a systematic approach, good organization and coordination. Unfortunately, the process of implementation is fraught with difficulties that are largely of a human nature. This is particularly pronounced for projects that deal with improving an existing operation.

To get a better 'feel' for one of these human aspects, just put yourself into the position of the stock control officer in the LOD who is controlling the day-to-day replenishments of stocks, or into the position of a dispatcher in charge of scheduling deliveries for an urban parcel delivery service. You have done these tasks for a number of years and considered that you did a competent job. Along comes this OR/MS analyst, called in by your boss or even sent in by somebody higher up in the hierarchy. Few people will not see this as a sign of lack of confidence in their ability to do the job properly and hence perceive it as a threat. What may make it even worse is that this whiz kid is probably fairly young, university trained, but with seemingly little real understanding of the intricacies of your job. It would be rather surprising if you did not view any 'solution' that this analyst proposes with a fair degree of suspicion.

Problems of implementation can stem from three causes:

(1) Those relating to the physical task of implementation, such as the complexity of the solution, the sensitivity of the benefits or costs to deviations from the formally prescribed rules, and the extent to which the proposed solution deviates from current practice. The greater any of these, the greater the problems which have to be overcome.

(2) Those relating to the problem user and other individuals affected by the solution, such as their personalities, their motivation and pride in the job (e.g., does the proposed solution restrict their freedom of action, take away their responsibility, reduce their importance relative to others, transform a challenging job that required years of experience into one of merely feeding data into a computer terminal which then feeds back what action to take?), their ages (routine becomes more entrenched with age, change is more difficult to accept), their background and level of education, and the importance of the tasks associated with the proper use of the solution in relation to their other job activities (the less important they perceive these tasks to be, the less attention these tasks will receive).

(3) Those relating to the environment of the project, such as the support given to the project and its solution by the problem owners or other people at higher echelons in the hierarchy (the less visible and explicit the support given to the project, the less cooperation the project will receive from the problem users), the organizational implications of the solution (if the problem user department become more dependent on another department, or the problem users see the solution as a threat to their job security, the less support the solution will receive from them).

Generally, the OR/MS analyst pays full attention to the first factor, which is a question of technology, largely devoid of human aspects. The tendency is to neglect and overlook the human factors of (2) and (3). They are qualitative in nature and evade the formal treatment that can be given to the technological factors, but can nevertheless act as serious constraints on implementation. It should come as no surprise that neglecting these human constraints in a system can easily lead to a 'solution' that is one on paper only and is not workable in practice. From this point of view, implementation can be viewed as a problem of relaxing the human constraints versus adjusting the technical solution.

The human constraints may be relaxed in a number of ways. More involvement of problem user(s) from the outset of the project and more training may both increase the understanding of the solution. Individuals who could become obstacles to proper implementation could be transferred to other jobs of equal importance or status. The technical solution can be adjusted by simplifying the policy or solution rules, e.g., by going to quick-and-dirty rules that capture the major part of the benefits, but are much easier to use and implement.

The literature on implementation is unanimous on one point — implementation and continued use of a solution are almost guaranteed if the problem owners and problem users 'own' the results of the OR/MS analysis. They will develop this feeling of ownership if they can contribute to the project in meaningful ways with their experience and in-depth knowledge of the operations. The wise analyst will therefore keep them constantly informed, submit all or most ideas to their scrutiny, and solicit their advice. If they feel that they have contributed in significant ways to the project and that their inputs have been valued, they will wish to see the solution put into practice and will take an active role in the implementation process.

In the LOD project, the stock clerk was viewed as the most important stakeholder from the users' group. She was pulled in as an active project team member from the outset and given the responsibility of liaising with all other potential problem users and problem customers. Similarly, the LOD manager was kept fully informed and regu-larly consulted during the project. Rather than have the analyst present the proposed solution to the staff of the LOD and interested refinery personnel, the LOD manager was briefed to give that presentation. The whole project conveyed a strong im-pression of active LOD participation and management support.

8.2   PLANNING FOR IMPLEMENTATION

Planning for implementation starts at the outset of any project, when the first contacts are established with the sponsor of a potential project. As the project progresses, the groundwork for implementation is laid through-out all other phases. This truth cannot be overemphasized. It is not sufficient to start planning for implementation once the solution to the model has been tested and the project report submitted to the sponsor. Not only could this result in serious delays in getting the solution implemented, because crucial input data may not be available, but the human aspect discussed in the previous section will most certainly have been neglected.

Planning for implementation consists of the following elements:

(1)   **Identifying all stakeholders** of a problem situation, in particular the problem owners and problem users: the first because they will ultimately have to give approval for implementation, the second because their full cooperation is needed for continued use of the solution.

(2)   **Establishing effective lines of communication** with the problem owners and
       problem users. Which channels, formal or informal, does the analyst use to
       communicate with various people in the sponsor organization? Who are the
       liaison people? To be effective, the lines of communication must be open, and
       there must be mutual respect and trust between the problem owners and users
       and the analyst.

       If the project is the first contact that the analyst has with them, trust and
       respect must be explicitly established and nurtured, because, as discussed in
       the previous section, the problem owners and problem users are likely to feel
       threatened by the project. Any attitude revealing condescension or superiority
       by the analyst will only reinforce mistrust on the part of the problem users, in
       particular. The analyst has to be aware that such messages are more often than
       not conveyed by non-verbal body language, such as signals of impatience or
       'knowing smiles'.

       As a rule, the problem users have done their best, based on their training,
       education, and resources available. The analyst may know more about OR/MS
       modeling, but they know much more about the problem, not only those aspects
       that are easily visible, but also those that may require extensive experience and
       exposure to the problem situation. It is easy to withhold such information,
       which will then become an obstacle to proper implementation. So, at least
       initially, it is the analyst who has to rely on them and learn from them, before
       he or she can start contributing to the problem.

(3)   **Exploring and managing the prior expectations for the project.** As
       discussed in Section 5.3, a problem owner and/or problem user may have
       formed prior expectations about what the project will deliver in terms of
       benefits or in terms of the time frame for its execution. If these expectations
       cannot be met, these stakeholders may withdraw their support from the project,
       either actively or passively. This may jeopardize implementation of the
       results. For this reason, the prudent analyst will explore and evaluate all prior
       expectations. If they are unrealistic or difficult to meet within the time and
       resources available, they should be confronted in a diplomatic manner. The
       analyst must also be aware, that he or she could unwittingly contribute to the
       formation of unrealistic expectations by indirectly promising more than can be
       delivered.

(4)   **Keeping the problem owners and problem users regularly informed** about
       the progress of the project. Get feedback from them on new ideas and solicit
       ideas from them.

(5)   **Checking out availability and sources of all input data needed.** Are the
       data available in the form, quantity and quality needed? It may take months
       to accumulate missing data, like demand for products, etc. Unless such data
       collection is initiated right at the start of the project, undesirable delays in
       implementation of any results will be unavoidable. What is to be done with

bad data?

(6) Ordering of special equipment and commercial computer software may have to be done well in advance of implementation. This includes the computer hardware, including cabling for a networking, if proper use of the model needs it.

(7) Developing all software needed for implementation and continued use of the new solution.

(8) Planning and executing the actual process of implementation. Planning and executing the various steps of changing over from the current mode of operation to the new mode of operation requires a detailed timetable of which tasks are scheduled to happened when, and their assignment to the people best equipped to execute them. This includes:

- Preparation of all data base in the exact format needed for implementation and continued use of the solution.

- Preparation of special stationery or forms needed for the use of the solution, users' manuals, and material for training sessions with problem users. Special care needs to be given to users' manuals, particularly those involving the use of computer software. They have to be complete, covering not only the normal operations, but also how to handle exceptions, as well as all procedures for updating, controlling, and maintaining the solution (see the next section). The importance of complete users' manuals cannot be stressed enough. Incomplete or inaccurate users' manuals are a prime cause for implementation failure or a rapid deterioration in the proper use of the implemented solution.

- Training sessions with problem users for manual and software-based operations.

- 'Physical' change-over to new mode of operation: for large projects this may be scheduled to occur in stages rather than in one go in order to avoid straining the resources and facilities.

(9) Regular following-up sessions with problem users during the early stages of the use of the new mode of operation to eliminate or overcome any problems that may arise and could threaten the proper use of the solution.

Planning for implementation may call for the use of an OR/MS technique, called the project evaluation and review technique (PERT) or the critical path method (CPM), which is a topic of most texts on OR/MS techniques and texts on production management.

8.3 CONTROLLING AND MAINTAINING THE SOLUTION

The environment in which most organizations operate is constantly undergoing change. This means that inputs into the system which the model represents are also changing. Such change may be quantitative or structural. Any changes that only affect the magnitude of inputs into the model, such as the volume of the annual demand for the LOD problem or the travel time from point A to B in the delivery problem, say due to road alterations, are referred to as quantitative. In most cases, the model remains a valid representation of the system. However, the optimal solution derived from the model usually changes. If the changes in the inputs are sufficiently large, then the current solution may need to be adjusted. Sensitivity and error analysis will provide guidelines as to when such an adjustment may be desirable, hence the importance of performing systematic sensitivity and error analysis with respect to all important inputs into the model.

A change in the form or nature of an input is called structural if it affects the influence relationship between this input and one or more intermediate variables in the model. The original model may not be a valid representation of the system any more. Certain functional relationships in the model may have to be reformulated. For example in the LOD problem, installation of new mixing and filling equipment may result in substantial savings in production setup costs if stock replenishments are scheduled in such a way that all container sizes of the same oil are filled from one single mixing batch, rather than having separate mixing setups for each container size. The current model deals with each oil/container size combination individually. This structural change requires a new model that finds a joint optimal policy for several related products.

Procedures have to be set up to monitor such quantitative and structural changes in the environment, so that corrective action is initiated when the changes become significant. These form an important part of the users' manuals. A change is judged significant if the improvement in the benefits that can be gained by adjusting the solution exceeds the cost of making the adjustment. If the solution is regularly updated, say once every six months, the improvement in benefits only covers the period remaining until the next regular adjustment.

Establishing controls over the solution consists of:

(1) Listing for each input (parameters, constraints) — both for those that are explicitly included in the model as well as for those that have been excluded as insignificant — the quantitative change in values for which the present solution remains optimal or near-optimal. Rather than indicate such permissible changes in absolute terms, it is more useful to show permissible percentage changes. Percentage changes often remain valid even after successive updates of the solution, while absolute changes could become out of date already after one or two updates. For example, for the LOD project, any change in the rate of demand for a given product in excess of 50% became a signal for an update of the control parameters, unless an annual update was less than three months away.

(2) Listing of the structural form of all influence relationships between inputs and intermediate variables, and intermediate and outcome variables assumed by the

current version of the model, again both for those explicitly included and those excluded. Any OR/MS analyst will then be able to judge whether a given subsequent structural change in relationships invalidates the current version of the model. For the LOD project, any changes in equipment and processing procedures for customer orders could imply structural changes.

(3) Specifying in detail how each input has to be measured to assess if a change is significant, how frequently such measurements should be made, and specific events that may call for such measurements to be taken. For the LOD project, the customer demand distribution was updated monthly by computer using a forecasting method called **exponential smoothing**. The updated monthly average computed by that method was the input measured. The introduction of possible substitute products also was used as a trigger for a possible update.

(4) Assigning responsibility for the control of each item and who is to be notified if significant changes have been detected. Rather than name a specific individual, such responsibilities should be part of a job description for a given position. This will avoid the procedures becoming lost if personnel changes occur. For the LOD project, the stock clerk was responsible for the majority of the control tasks, except those of a purely financial nature, like changes in the cost of capital or changes in labour costs. Control of these was assigned to a position in the Cost Control Department.

(5) Specifying in detail how the solution has to be adjusted in response to quantitative changes in inputs and by whom, and what action has to be initiated to deal with possible structural changes detected. For the LOD project, the stock clerk was put in charge of updating the solution for quantitative changes in the input parameters. She was also in charge of updating all control parameters once each year. She would notify the head of the Management Science Group at headquarters if events occurred that could imply structural changes.

8.4 FOLLOWING UP IMPLEMENTATION AND MODEL PERFORMANCE

Monitoring Implementation

The job of the OR/MS analyst is not finished once the solution has been implemented. There is always the danger that, after some time, enforcement of the rules for using the solution becomes somewhat lax. Shortcuts may have been taken by the users without any visible deterioration of the performance, but with repeated use will ultimately lead to problems. The reasons for this may be that certain rules have been misunderstood or misinterpreted. Even with the most comprehensive planning and greatest care, events unforeseen by the analyst will occur and remedial action be taken by individuals who do not have the right information or training to make the proper changes. For all these reasons, it is essential that the analyst keeps monitoring the performance of the model for some time after implementation.

If any misapplication or misinterpretations of the solution show up, corrective action must be initiated. This may consist simply of again going over the rules for using the solution correctly with the individuals in question, or issuing or making corrections to the users' manuals, organizing follow-up training sessions, or even adjusting the solution rules to circumvent a recurrence of errors. It is crucial that the analyst does not underestimate the importance of such follow-ups. Neglecting this aspect of implementation could well result in the actual operation reverting back to the previous mode within a few weeks or months, with the new solution being 'shelved'. Resurrecting it at that time may be quite difficult, due to the negative attitude that most users will have developed towards it by then. It is quite natural that they will blame the solution or the analyst for the failure, rather than the improper use of the solution.

For example, follow-up monitoring revealed that the supervisor of the grease operation at the LOD continued using the old replenishment rules. He had worked in that plant for over 40 years and was not going to 'take orders from anybody who had not the slightest idea of how to make grease', as he put it to the LOD manager. In the end, implementation of the solution for the grease plant could only be obtained by shifting the supervisor of the grease operation to another job. Sadly, he could not adjust to the new job either and was offered early retirement at full pension, which he accepted.

Performance Audit

One of the final duties of the analyst is to make a performance audit on the solution. This means checking the extent to which the projected benefit or cost savings have been realized. The benefits actually generated by the use of the new solution are computed or estimated, based on the solution's actual performance. These are then compared with performance of the old solution. To be valid, the comparison should be made using the same input data. If no or only small changes have occurred since the implementation of the new solution, then a comparison of the benefits actually achieved before and after the implementation will give a sufficiently accurate picture. However, if significant changes in the environmental inputs have occurred, the comparison may have to be made by simulating the performance of the old solution for the same actual data used to estimate the benefits generated by the new solution. Any serious discrepancy between the projected and the actual benefits should be fully examined and properly explained.

This audit is not only important for the sponsor of the project, but also for the analyst. Only then does the analyst get valid quantitative and qualitative feedback on her or his own performance.

The final audit for the LOD project was undertaken one year after implementation. The costs savings based on one full year of operations were estimated at $72,000. Given that the new policy only became effective for a substantial portion of the products after the initial large stocks had been drawn down, this fairly well confirmed the original savings estimates. However, the costs of implementation were slightly more than $40,000. This was largely due to significant additions to the software produced, in particular, a demand forecasting system.

8.5   CONCLUSIONS

Full implementation of all recommendations of an OR/MS project is rare. It is more useful to talk about the degree of implementation achieved. The aim of the analyst should be to achieve a sufficiently high degree of implementation to capture the major portion of the potential benefits.   The principle encountered when we discussed model building, namely that for any additional effort the returns obtained should exceed the cost, applies here too.

EXERCISES

1. Prof. Churchman, after reviewing the introductory chapter of another OR text I co-authored, casually observed to me :'Don't you know that implementation is the first phase of any OR/MS project?' This initially startled me, particularly since Churchman's own text shows implementation as the final step of the analysis. However, as I let this remark sink in I came to agree with it.   In the light of the coverage you have seen of the 11-step OR/MS methodology critically discuss Churchman's statement. It may be helpful to clearly distinguish between the physical process of implementing the results and the substantive issues involved in implementation.

2. Do you see any parallels between the major OR/MS implementation principle of 'get the problem owners and problem users to own the project' and your own personal experiences of getting family members or friends to go along with some new activity or way of dealing with recurrent daily problems or being at the receiving end of such pressures coming from family members or friends?

3. Assume that your project report (exercise 11 of Chap. 7) convinced E. Lim E. Nate to implement the results of the analysis.   Prepare a detailed list of steps to implement, maintain, and audit your recommended solution. Note that the problem users, i.e., the machine operators, are trained mechanics, but have no other tertiary education.

4. When we looked at desirable properties of models in Chapter 6, Section 6.3, and validation in Chapter 7, Section 7.1, the concept of model 'credibility' was mentioned. I also pointed out that it may be more useful to talk about 'desirable properties of the modeling process', rather than of the model alone. Integrating this with the material in Chapter 8, develop a list of such desirable properties that enhance the likelihood of full implementation and facilitate implementation.

REFERENCES

Implementation has given rise to a substantial literature. The claimed widespread lack of securing implementation for OR/MS projects is one of the main reasons for some of the more recent 'softer' decision-aiding methodologies, such as the various soft systems methodologies (see references in Chapters 2, 3, and 4). With computer information systems becoming the data base for OR/MS projects, the implementation debate has again assumed greater prominence. Some of the earlier material includes:

Churchman, C.W., and Schainblatt, A. H., 'The researcher and the manager: A dialectic of implementation', *Management Science*, Feb. 1965. A philosophical analysis of the activities and attitudes by analysts and problem owners which are most appropriate for bringing about a climate conducive to proper implementation. See also the October 1965 issue of *Management Science* for a follow-up discussion on this very provocative paper, particularly the comments by W. Alderson.

Schultz, R. L., and Slevin, D. P., eds, *Implementing of Operation Research/Management Science*, Elsevier, 1975. A collection of papers on various facets of implementation. Read the paper by A. Reisman and C.A. de Kluyver 'Strategies for implementing systems studies' for a pragmatic view of how to improve the chances for successful implementation.

Urban, G. L., 'Building models for decision makers', *Interfaces*, May 1974. Looks at the process of building implementable models.

More recent publications include:

Interfaces, May-June 1987 Special Issue: Implementation. The entire issue is devoted to implementation with particular emphasis on management information systems.

PART 2

How to Deal with Costs, Benefits, Constraints, Time, Uncertainty, and Multiple Goals?

Most OR/MS analyses involve costs and benefits, expressed in monetary terms. A good understanding of the nature of costs and benefits is thus essential. Only then will the analyst be able to identify those which are relevant and incorporate them properly in the analysis. Briefly expressed, the relevant costs and benefits are those which, for the system as a whole, are affected by the decision choice. Chapter 9 studies the nature and types of costs.

Often costs and benefits occur over time. How can we aggregate costs and benefits that occur over several years? This leads us to study discounting and expressing future cash flows in terms of their present value — the topic of Chapter 10.

Decision choices often involve tradeoffs between opposing costs or costs and benefits. As the level of activity, e.g., the level of output, is increased, certain costs go up more than proportionately, while other costs decrease less than proportionately. Can economics teach us something about how to view tradeoffs of this sort. This will lead us to marginal analysis — the topic of Chapter 11. It is one of the most pervasive concepts in economics. Many OR/MS techniques are off-shoots of this idea.

Limited resources often put constraints on the decision choices. Chapter 12 explores the allocation of scarce resources to various uses. How should such resources be valued? This topic is continued in Chapter 13, which looks at linear programming -a powerful optimization tool. It has proven its usefulness not only for more complex situations involving the allocation of scarce resources, but also for a host of other optimization problems.

The problem situations considered so far all assumed a stable environment. Chapter 14 allows the environment to change over time and looks at how this affects the decision process.

The meaning and implications of uncertainty are taken up in Chapter 15, while Chapters 16 to 18 study various approaches to incorporate uncertainty into the decision making.

Chapter 19 introduces you into some of the basic aspects of how to deal with multiple objectives, which may be conflicting or non-commensurate.

Chapter 20 will wrap up our journey. We will critically review the OR/MS methodology presented in this text and then consider a number of other issues. One of these deals with ethics — both in terms of an alternative approach to decision making and as an issue the analyst will have to deal with when faced with world views in conflict with her or his own. Finally, alternative problem resolution or problem structuring methods are considered briefly. One of them — Checkland's soft systems methodology — is discussed in some detail.

9 Relevant Costs and Benefits

If the word 'system' is used in various different ways, the word 'cost' has even more varied uses in our language. Business people speak of the cost of goods and materials purchased for production or resale, the cost of equipment, the cost of operating the equipment, and the cost of workers and employees — referring to wages and salaries paid. It is relatively easy to put an exact dollar figure to each of these. But business people also talk of the cost of delivering goods late to customers, the cost of a strike, either within their own organization or that of a supplier or a big customer, or the cost of rescheduling production to meet a rush job to a major customer. It is usually not possible to assess the exact dollar amount such events 'cost' the firm.

In everyday language, the use of the word 'cost' becomes even more fuzzy: the social cost of unemployment in terms of despair, low self-esteem, increased suicide rate, increased crime, increased family breakups; or the environmental cost of pollution; or simply the cost of a missed opportunity! The possibilities for ambiguity are compounded by the differing use and classification of costs by the two major professions dealing with costs, namely accountants and economists.

This chapter first looks at how accountants and economists each define and use various types of costs. Section 9.3 studies which costs are relevant for decision making. In OR/MS modeling, we are usually concerned with how costs and benefits change in response to a change in policy or the mode of operation. Hence, like managerial economists, management scientists are interested in incremental changes in costs and benefits.

These concepts will be explored for a real-life case in Sections 9.4 to 9.8.

9.1 EXPLICIT, IMPLICIT, AND INTANGIBLE COSTS

Some of the ambiguity when dealing with costs concepts arises from the fact that some costs involve an 'out-of-pocket' transfer of funds from one party to another, while others do not. The first are called **explicit costs**, the second **implicit costs**. The payment by a firm for goods or equipment purchased from a supplier is an example of an explicit cost. The annual reduction in the value of a piece of equipment, called depreciation, recorded by accountants, is an example of an implicit cost. No funds change hands. It is simply a convention used by accountants to reflect the fact that through use and aging that piece of equipment has lost some of its original value. By the time the firm disposes of this equipment, its 'book' value recorded in the accounts is expected to have been reduced from the original purchase price to its current disposal value, say as scrap or second-hand machinery.

Several of the instances of 'costs' mentioned in the introduction, like the cost of late delivery, the cost of reduced productivity and disruption caused by rescheduling production in response to some emergency, the social cost of unemployment, etc., are also examples of implicit costs.

The difference between these examples and depreciation is that it is relatively easy to put an exact dollar figure on the amount of depreciation, while it is usually very difficult to assess the 'cost' of a late delivery. If a late delivery is a very exceptional occurrence, happening for reasons beyond the control of the firm, and the customer has been notified prior to the delivery due date, there is probably no cost. However, if late deliveries occur several times for the same customer, the firm runs a high risk of ultimately losing that customer. The 'cost' for the firm is the possible loss of profits that future sales to that customer could have generated. The potential for future profits through sales is also called 'goodwill'. So the firm may suffer a loss in goodwill with its ensuing financial impact. Such costs are also referred to as **intangible costs**. Their assessment is often based on guesswork and therefore highly subjective to the assessor.

The amount of depreciation assessed on a piece of equipment will usually have no effect on decision making, except in so far as it affects the timing of taxes paid (given that depreciation reduces the taxable income). On the other hand, intangible costs clearly should be taken into account in decision making.

As a footnote, it should be pointed out that accountants also refer to intangible costs, particularly goodwill and reserves for doubtful accounts receivables (credit customers who are seriously in arrears in their payments). The balance sheet item 'goodwill' usually arises from the acquisition of a going concern where the purchase price exceeds the net value of the assets acquired. This excess is seen as representing the growth in potential earnings of the firm. It is recorded as an asset. It is depreciated in the same way as most other fixed assets. Similarly, the reserve for doubtful accounts receivable is recorded as a form of asset reduction or liability in the balance sheet. Although accountants refer to these items as intangible assets or intangible costs, their use of the term 'intangible' is somewhat different from OR/MS. They refer to actual entries in the accounts of the firm. In OR/MS, we refer to potential future costs or loss of benefits that should be recognized as relevant for the correct evaluation of decision alternatives. However, no cash transaction or entry in the accounts of the firm is implied or will occur if a decision is implemented.

9.2 ACCOUNTING VERSUS ECONOMICS CONCEPTS OF COSTS

Accountants' View

In general, accountants are historians. They record costs in terms of the amount of cash expended to acquire goods and services, like raw materials and supplies needed for a manufacturing operation, goods for resale, employees' time, equipment and facilities, and the use of funds. This then allows them to determine the financial position of a firm as of a given point in time, i.e., what the firm owns in the form of various assets, and what the firm owes to its creditors. The difference between these two represents the equity position of its owners. These three aspects are summarized in the **balance sheet**. Furthermore, accountants record in detail how this equity position changes over time, usually over a 12 months period. This gives rise to the **profit-and-loss statement**.

The balance sheet and the profit-and-loss statement allow current and potential investors in the firm (this includes its current owners) to assess how well their investment is doing. Producing these two documents is also a legal requirement for all firms, for assessment of taxes as well as for the protection of creditors of the firm. These are the main purposes for financial accounting.

In order to help management in pricing decisions, and monitoring and control of costs, accountants have extended the concept of costs to the notion of **standard costs** — a measure indicating what it should cost on average to produce a given item or service under normal operating conditions. Actual historical costs vary from standard cost in the short run due to unexpected events, like price fluctuations of raw materials or varying productivity of the work force. Significant deviations (or what cost accountants call 'variances') from standard costs are flagged and brought to the attention of management. In the absence of inflation (or deflation, if this 'curiosity' should ever happen again), actual average historical cost will approximate standard costs in the long run, since the latter are in fact derived from the former.

Economists' View

In contrast, economists measure the cost of a resource in terms of the earnings power or the opportunities foregone by not applying the resource in question to some other potentially available use — in fact, the best alternative use of the resource. Economists thus argue that the implicit cost of a resource is equal to what it could 'earn' if used for its best alternative use now or at some future point in time. This cost is called the **opportunity cost** of the resource. Being an implicit cost, no funds change hands. For resources already owned by the firm it is not the original cost of acquiring the resource that is relevant any more, but the return on its best alternative use that counts.

Economic theory shows that applying this principle consistently will lead to the optimal use of all resources available to a firm and hence to the maximum possible profit. If all firms behave in this manner, this should, in theory, lead to the optimal allocation of resources for the economy as a whole. In practice, the world is not quite that simple. Individuals and firms do not pay the true cost of the use of many resources, particularly for so-called 'free goods' like the environment (air, water, land), by polluting it, and for 'public goods' paid through taxes, like the road network (damage to road surfaces by trucks exceeding heavy vehicle road taxes), or the public health system (the health cost of alcohol or smoking far exceeding the tax revenue on such goods).

The most common application of the opportunity cost concept in decision making concerns situations in which a particular resource enjoys several potential uses at the same point in time. Using the resource for one purpose precludes its use for any other purpose.

Accountants' Classification of Costs

Accountants classify costs either by product identification or by variability. In the first classification (by product identification), costs are grouped into **prime or direct costs** and **overhead or indirect costs**. Prime costs are those directly identifiable with a specific end product or service. This includes the purchase costs of goods or materials used in the production process and the costs of all labour directly attributable to the production of that product or service. Prime costs tend to increase or decrease (often proportionately, but not necessarily so) with the volume of output. It is fairly obvious that if the level of output doubles, the amount of materials needed to produce the goods also doubles. Similarly, a doubling of the level of service offered will in most cases also double the labour input and its cost.

Overheads cover the cost of all support activities that are not directly attributable to a particular product or service or are shared by all or a given group of products or services. Examples of overheads are the cost of salaries and fringe benefits of executives, managers, supervisors; various support staff, like maintenance, personnel and other administrative services, including vacation and holiday pay for these employees. The cost of borrowed funds, like loans or mortgages, are also overheads.

Most overheads, but not all, remain fixed over a wide range of output levels. For example, the same administrative support staff may be needed even if the output level of the firm decreases or increases within a fairly wide range around the current level. Only a change in output level beyond that range may result in a change in overheads, e.g., by requiring additional administrative staff or additional shared production facilities which need to be financed. The interest cost of loans taken up to finance the purchase of plant and equipment will have to be paid regardless of the level of output of the plant.

For product costing purposes, all overheads will ultimately be allocated on some suitable basis to the individual products or services. This allocation by necessity involves a varying degree of arbitrariness. The most commonly used basis for allocating overheads is in proportion to the amount or the cost of direct labour involved in producing each product or service.

The distinction between prime cost and overheads is often not clear cut, particularly if the costs do not vary proportionately with output. Furthermore, some costs may be classified as overheads because the efforts or 'cost' of identifying which portion is directly attributable to each product or service may be excessive, while increasing the accuracy of their unit costs in only a minor way.

Economists' Classification of Costs

The main classifications used by economists are **fixed costs** and **variable costs**, on the one hand, and **short-run costs** and **long-run costs** on the other. Fixed costs are those that are not affected by changes in output level, but variable costs are. There is thus some analogy between the accountants' distinction of direct costs and overheads and the economists' distinction of variable and fixed costs. However, the analogy is far from perfect. Direct costs may include charges which can be directly attributed to a given product, but are essentially fixed in character. For example, a given machine may be exclusively dedicated to the production of a single product or an office may solely be used for providing a given service. The cost of either may remain constant over a wide range of output levels. The cost associated with their use (depreciation or decrease in disposal value for the machine, rental of the office) may be constant per period (say a year). They are classified as direct costs by accountants, but as fixed costs by economists.

In the short-run, investments in capital goods, such as equipment, buildings, land, etc., are taken as given. They are not easily changed without often substantial new investments of funds. They restrict the firm's output to a given range. Hence, the cost of using these resources is fixed. On the other hand, other aspects of a firm's operations, such as the amount of raw materials and labour used, usually vary in proportion to the output level. Hence they are variable costs.

In the long-run, however, the composition of all inputs into a firm's operation can be altered. The number and type of machines, the number and size of facilities, and so on, can all be changed. Hence, in the long-run all costs become variable.

In general, economists use costs to derive normative statements about how a firm should operate under market conditions. Economists' view of costs is thus more akin to the prescriptive focus of the management scientist. Hence, we will find the economists classification of costs more useful for decision making.

9.3   RELEVANT COSTS AND BENEFITS

Which costs and benefits should the decision maker take into account when evaluating the monetary effects of alternative decision choices? The short answer is: **All those that change as a consequence of any of the decision choices! Any cost or benefit now or in the future that remains the same in total terms, regardless of the decision choice, is irrelevant.** As is true for most short answers, this only tells part of the story. In many instances it may be difficult to determine which costs and benefits change until the analysis has been completed. Fortunately, any costs included in the analysis that are not affected by the decision choice will not influence which decision is best, provided such costs are included in the correct manner. It is obvious that if the same constant is added or subtracted from the monetary outcome of each decision choice, the ranking of these choices is not changed. (If you have doubts about this principle, test it with a practical example.

Alternatives A and B have outcomes of 8 and 5, respectively. The outcome for A is highest. Adding the number 3 to both does not affect that ranking.) Viewed in this light, it is more important to include costs in the correct manner, rather than worrying about whether a cost item should be included or not.

Having said this, I will nevertheless review which costs and benefits are relevant. I hope that this discussion will clarify grey areas and improve your understanding. For each cost and benefit we attempt to answer the following question: **Does this cost item (in terms of its current or future impact for the project or entity as a whole) increase or decrease if any of the decision choices is implemented or does it remain the same, regardless of which decision choice is taken? If it changes, it is a relevant cost item; if it remains the same, it can be ignored.** Let us consider a few examples!

Explicit Costs

It is quite obvious that explicit costs incurred by a decision choice, whether fixed capital investments or variable with the output level, are relevant costs. However, this does not tell us what the correct way is of including explicit costs, particularly if they are of a fixed nature — more about that later. Any explicit cost, incurred regardless of the decision choice, is not relevant. But what about costs incurred in the past and clearly associated with the project or activity in question?

Sunk Costs

To answer this question, I will pick up our discussion in Chapter 7 on whether or not the results of a MS/OR project should be implemented. The LOD manager has received the final project report. For discussion's sake, assume that this report states that the potential cost savings amount to $35,000 per year (considerably smaller than the figure quoted in the Appendix to Chapter 7) and that a further $30,000 will have to be spent for implementation of the new policy. This is in addition to the $8000 already charged to the LOD for the project so far. Recall that the firm's criterion for accepting any investment of that nature requires that the estimated first-year benefits must exceed the cost of the project. Should the LOD manager give the go-ahead for implementation or not?

One line of reasoning is to state that the results of the project should not be implemented, since the total cost of the project (consisting of the initial $8000 for the preliminary study plus the additional $30,000 for implementation of the results) exceeds the estimated first-year savings of $35,000 by $3000. The firm would be worse off by $3000 if it proceeded. What is wrong with this reasoning? It is true that the total cost for the project is $3000 larger than the estimated first-year savings. On the other hand, the expenditure of a further $30,000 will provide estimated first-year savings of $35,000, a gain of $5000. Hence, within one year of implementation the firm would be better off by this amount compared to abandoning the project now. So, if the LOD manager uses as the criterion for accepting new projects 'the recovery of all further costs within one year', then he should go ahead with implementing the recommendations.

The fallacy in the first line of reasoning is that the $8000 has already been spent. Nothing can be done about it. None of the decision choices available to the LOD manager will be able to recover the funds already spent. They are a so-called **sunk cost**. Sunk costs are irrelevant for decision making. Had the LOD manager known prior to engaging in the preliminary study that the total cost would be $38,000, while the estimated first-year's savings would only come to $35,000, the project would never have got off the ground. The $8000 cost of the preliminary study would not have been spent. However, the manager did not know this at that time. He made the best choice on the basis of the information available at that time. Hindsight shows that this was the wrong choice. Taking the funds already spent into account again now would only lead to making another error in choice — one that can be avoided!

Sunk costs may sometimes be hidden in cost data derived from accounting records. Depreciation charges on a machine included in the unit production costs for a given item may be a case in point. On the one hand, reasoning from a short-run perspective, if the depreciation charge does not reflect an equivalent lowering of the machine's disposal value as a direct consequence of using the machine for the production of the item, such as wear-and-tear, rather than simply accounting for the loss in value due to the aging of the machine, it is not a relevant cost item. The initial purchase price of the machine is a sunk cost and hence is irrelevant. The loss in value of the machine due to aging may be relevant for a different decision problem, such as whether or not the machine should be kept for a further time given its earning potential or should be disposed of right now and possibly replaced by a more efficient machine.

This is not to deny that, in the long-run, the continued survival of the firm depends on whether it can generate enough funds to replace all existing equipment and buildings at the end of their productive life. Hence, even the loss in value due to aging becomes a cost that has to be recovered from the sale of the products or services produced by that capital goods item. As is often the case in OR/MS, answers are not clear-cut, but depend on the circumstances and purpose of the analysis. This reminds me of that firm that advertised for a 'one-armed' operations researcher. When the chief executive was asked why the firm wanted a 'one-armed' operations researcher, he answered that he was sick and tired of getting answers to OR/MS problems which said 'on the one hand, you should do this; on the other hand it may be advantageous to do that!'

Opportunity Costs

Firms own or are in control of many resources, such as raw materials, machinery, buildings, and funds. These resources may have been bought or been created by the firm's own operations. They may be used currently for some purpose or the firm may be considering putting them to an alternative use. In either case, how should these resources be valued? What is the 'cost' of their use? These are important questions. Their correct answer will determine whether these resources are put to their best use or not.

Consider again the LOD problem, and, in particular, the investment of funds in finished goods. What is the cost of these funds? You may say that this depends on the source of these funds. You could reason that if they are raised through loans from a bank, the cost of these funds is the interest charged by the bank. On the other hand, if they come from retained earnings (profits accumulated and not paid out as dividends to the shareholders), there is no cost. What is wrong with this reasoning?

It ignores the return the firm could earn on these funds from alternative uses. Assume the firm has alternative investment opportunities, such as the acquisition of shares of another company that earn a high return or the purchase of a machine that can produce a highly marketable and profitable product, thus raising the firm's profits. Using the funds for investment in finished goods means that these same funds cannot be used for the best of these alternative investments. Therefore, the firm foregoes the return on this lost opportunity. The return foregone becomes the 'real' cost of using these funds for investment in finished goods.

Since the assessment of this cost is based on the best alternative opportunity foregone, it is called an **opportunity cost.** All resources available to the firm or, for that matter, to any organization should always be valued at their opportunity cost. This will assure that these resources are used efficiently.

Here is another example. What is the 'cost' of the current warehouse space available to the LOD? As for funds, this item is relevant for assessing the cost of holding goods in stock for future sale. The cost accountant would claim that the cost of warehouse space is equal to the total maintenance costs incurred for the warehouse, the operating costs, such as electricity, cleaning, and heating, depreciation on the warehouse, and the cost of the funds originally invested in its construction. The opportunity cost, on the other hand, depends on the return that could be earned for the best alternative use of the warehouse. This cost is not recorded in the accounting records which only show historical costs. The latter may be more or less than the opportunity cost.

Assessing opportunity costs requires that the analyst goes beyond accounting records. It may need some research into potential alternative uses. In the LOD case, some analysis may show that due to its location, there is no alternative use for the warehouse as such, only for its land. The best alternative use for this land is as parking space for refinery employees, which currently has to be rented from the city at $240 per parking space per year. This cost, expressed on an equivalent square metre basis (say 12 m² per parking space) would then correspond to an opportunity cost for warehouse space at the LOD of $20 per square metre per year. Alternatively, if another division of the firm currently has to rent warehouse space adjacent to the refinery at $36 per square metre per year, and the LOD warehouse would be a suitable alternative, the opportunity cost would amount to $36 per square metre.

Should maintenance and operating costs be added? The answer is yes if these costs are incurred as a consequence of the LOD's use of the warehouse and no if they are incurred regardless of the level of usage. In general, interest charges on the funds invested in the warehouse land and building are irrelevant since they do not depend on the level of usage of the warehouse. If no alternative use exists for the warehouse, including its possible disposal, and maintenance and operating costs do not depend on the level of usage, the opportunity cost of warehouse space could well be zero.

Replacement Costs

The historical cost paid for a resource or for goods recorded by the accountants is not a relevant measure for the value of this resource or these goods. Rather, it is the replacement cost which is relevant. For example, a cable manufacturer purchased a large quantity of copper wire at $1.63 per kilogram. A few weeks later, the price of copper wire increased to $1.84. It would then be incorrect to value the copper wire still in inventory at its original purchase price of $1.63. Any copper wire used up would have to be replaced right now at the higher value of $1.84. Furthermore, copper being a world commodity, any stock on hand presumably could be sold also at the new higher price of $1.84/kg. Replacement costs are thus a type of opportunity costs.

Future Costs and Benefits

Opportunity costs could well be in the form of the value of the resource for use at some future point in time. Future costs may, however, often occur as explicit costs. For example, at the end of the productive life of a piece of equipment, a plot of land used for mining, or a facility built on some rented land, a substantial removal, disposal, or restoration cost may have to be incurred. This cost is a direct consequence of the decision choice and hence is a relevant cost. The huge decommissioning costs of nuclear power stations are a case in point.

The converse could also be true, i.e., the resource has some residual value at the end of the planning horizon for the project in question. This is particularly true for land and buildings, but also for equipment, if they have a positive disposal or salvage value.

Intangible Costs

As pointed out earlier, the intangible costs may significantly reduce the worth or effectiveness of a decision alternative. For example, in terms of explicit costs (wages, etc.) alone, it is clearly much cheaper for a bank to have few tellers to serve customers. But excessive waiting times for customers will ultimately cause some customers to switch to another bank. This potential loss of future business may be far more costly for the bank in the long run, than the cost of additional tellers. The decision choice of the best number of tellers for the bank may thus be significantly affected by intangible costs.

Given the difficulty and ambiguity in assessing intangible costs, the analyst may be tempted to ignore them. This is not advisable. Every effort should be made to determine a valid monetary equivalent for these costs. **If this is not possible, the analyst should perform extensive sensitivity analysis to ascertain how the best decision changes as the (assumed) value of intangible costs varies.** If intangible costs have been ignored, this fact should be clearly stated in any report on the project. This will forewarn the decision maker that her or his final conclusion should take the possible presence of intangible factors into account in other qualitative ways. Armed with extensive sensitivity analysis, the decision maker will find that this task is greatly facilitated.

9.4 MUSHROOMS GALORE, LTD — PROBLEM FORMULATION

The next few sections are an account of a MS/OR project, where the major effort of the analysis was the correct assessment and use of various costs, and their presentation in a convincing form. I now ask you to carefully study the situation summary in Appendix to this chapter. It is crucial that you get a clear understanding of the MUSHROOMS GALORE situation. This may require more than one reading. If you have not done so yet as part of exercise 6 in Chapter 5, it will be helpful to represent the situation as a rich picture diagram, identifying the various issues to be analyzed, and defining a relevant system for each.

Problem Definition

I will confine the discussion to only one of the options considered by Bob Moss, namely the reduction of the number of flushes in each production cycle from the current five to either 4, 3, 2, or 1. The aim is to learn if this will increase the annual output of mushrooms, and its effect on the firm's profits. In accordance with this option, Bob Moss would like to know the best number of flushes to use. We shall assume that he interprets 'best' as that policy which maximizes annual profits for the current production facilities available. To investigate this we will have to find out exactly what the relationship is between the number of flushes, the total annual output and the associated revenue, and the total annual cost. This will lead us to study in detail the nature of the various costs involved and to identify which ones are affected by any change in the number of flushes, i.e., which costs are 'relevant'. Finally, we want to establish how the annual profit varies as the number of flushes decreases. The relationship between these two variables is the main piece of information the analysis should produce.

The above paragraph talks about relationships between various operating characteristics, costs of inputs and producing outputs, and overall profits. Influence diagrams are the ideal tool for establishing these relationships. So, I will now formally define the problem, summarize the relevant system, and then construct the associated influence diagram.

Referring to Section 5.3, the essence of the problem is defined by identifying the decision maker, her or his objectives, the measure(s) of performance, and the alternative courses of action. The decision maker is Bob Moss. His objective is to maximize annual profits. Hence, the measure of performance is the annual profit. Finally, the alternative courses of action are the number of flushes in each cycle. To keep things simple, we will assume that none of the potential constraints, like the size of the market and the availability of raw materials, particularly straw, will become effective.

Systems Description

The firm's annual profit is mainly affected by how the various costs of inputs into the process (raw materials, labour, etc.) and revenues from the outputs produced change as a function of the number of flushes. The systems description thus only needs to focus on these relationships. Little additional insight will be gained by expanding the systems description to also include the biological details of mushroom growing. We will simply treat those aspects as 'black boxes'. As a consequence, the system can easily be divided into a number of subsystems, each concerned with a given task or operation and its associated costs and revenues. My choice is:

(1) Subsystem 1: the operations of phase 1 (composting and tray preparation). Its major external inputs are raw materials and supplies for compost making, power, and labour, and the unit costs of all external inputs. The empty trays after they have been removed from the sheds and cleaned (an output of subsystem 2) are also an input. Its outputs are trays ready for the growing phase, and tray preparation costs. I will include peak heating as part of that subsystem. Trays are the major systems component relevant to this subsystem.

(2) Subsystem 2: the operations associated with loading and emptying the sheds. Its major inputs are the trays prepared by subsystem 1 (output of subsystem 1), sheds having completed the harvesting phase (output of subsystem 3), supplies, compost packing material, and labour, and the unit costs of all external inputs. Its outputs are sheds ready for the harvesting phase, empty trays, and spent compost, ready for sale, the costs of its operations, and the revenue from sale of spent compost. The systems components of prime concern to us are trays and sheds.

(3) Subsystem 3: the harvesting operation. Its major inputs are sheds ready for harvesting (output of subsystem 2), labour picking rates for each successive flush, and labour pay rates. Its outputs are mushrooms (measured in kilograms), ready for sorting, the cost of picking mushrooms, and sheds having completed a full cycle. Sheds and kilograms of mushrooms are its major systems components of interest to us.

(4) Subsystem 4: the sorting and packing operations. Its inputs are mushrooms

(output of subsystem 3), packing material and supplies, and labour, and the unit cost of all external inputs. Its outputs are mushrooms delivered to customers and the canning factory, the cost of its operations, and the revenue of mushrooms sold. Its major systems components are mushrooms.

(5) Subsystem 5: the biological and climate control subsystem. Its inputs are some supplies and power, and labour. Its outputs are sheds climatically controlled for best growth and harvesting, and the cost of this control. The latter is the only part of interest to us. Sheds are its major systems components.

Each subsystem receives external inputs and provides some outputs. Some of these outputs becomes inputs to other subsystems. These form the links between the subsystems. They are also linked together by the decision variable which affects the system as a whole, namely the number of flushes in each harvesting cycle. Furthermore, various subsystems are subject to biological factors, such as the length of time needed to produce compost, the duration of the growing phase, and the duration of each flush.

A Suitable Influence Diagram

You need to clearly keep in mind that the influence diagram only depicts the systems relationships relevant for the actual problem defined. It is not a diagrammatic representation of the system and its various subsystems, as summarized above. For the systems description, I listed aspects and relationships which reflect the tasks a given subsystem performs. For the influence diagram I am only concerned with those aspects that directly or indirectly affect the measure of performance defined for the system. The annual profit is the measure of performance for the MG problem. This is therefore the output for the system as a whole in the influence diagram. Hence, the system variables for only those aspects of the system which have a direct bearing on annual profits will be shown explicitly in the influence diagram.

Before you study my version of a suitable influence diagram for the MG problem, I strongly recommend that you draw up your own. Not only will this be a valuable exercise in becoming more proficient in this useful tool, but it will also force you to thoroughly think through the problem. Only then should you compare your diagram with the one in Figure 9-1 shown on the next page.

Note that I chose to show each of the first four subsystems as a separate sequence of relationships, each receiving external and internal inputs and having costs and/or revenues as the output to the system as a whole. While the cost relationships of each subsystem are fairly straightforward, the relationship between the decision variable, i.e., the number of flushes in each cycle and other systems variables, such as the length of each cycle, the number of cycles per year, and the output per cycle, may need some explanation.

Figure 9-1: Influence diagram for the MG problem

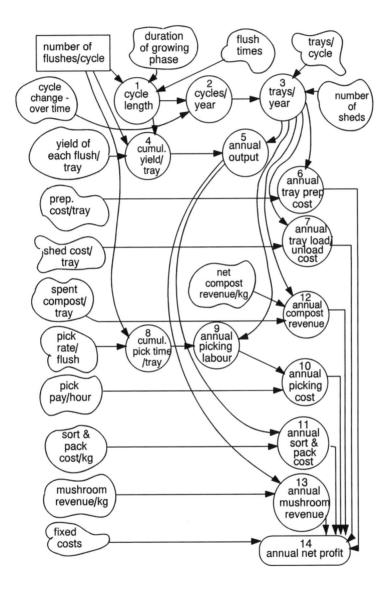

Recall that the duration of the growing phase is 28 days, while each flush takes on average 7 days. Together these two determine the length of a complete cycle (circle 1). The shorter each cycle, the more cycles can be scheduled per year for each shed. With each of the 65 sheds constantly in use carrying 400 trays per cycle, the number of cycles per year (circle 2) then determines the annual number of trays needed per year (circle 3). The latter is one of the internal inputs into subsystems 1 and 2. Similarly, the length of each cycle (circle 1), together with the yield of mushrooms of each successive cycle determines the cumulative yield per cycle per tray (circle 4). This in turn, together with the annual number of trays (circle 3), fixes the annual output of mushrooms (circle 5), the output variable of subsystem 3.

Try to explain the relationship between system variables for the length of the cycle, the picking efficiency, and the amount of picking time required per tray.

The next task is to examine all cost and revenue items listed in the description of Appendix and associate them with the inputs to the various subsystems shown in the influence diagram.

9.5 MUSHROOMS GALORE — ANALYSIS OF COSTS

To determine which costs are relevant, we answer, for each cost factor separately, the question: Does the annual cost for the firm as a whole change if the decision variable changes from its current value of 5 flushes per cycle? If the answer is 'yes', that particular cost factor is relevant, if 'no', it can be ignored. Note that we may still wish to add it in as a cost that remains constant for all decision choices. We then get a complete picture of the net profit. However, including or excluding such fixed costs in the measure of performance will not affect which decision choice is optimal.   As is clear from the influence diagram, the effect of the number of flushes on the annual cost for the firm as a whole may not be direct, but indirect via other system variables.

Table 9-1 states the relevance of each cost factor listed in the Appendix to this chapter, its nature, and the corresponding input parameter that captures its effect.

Table 9-1: Analysis of MG cost factors

Section	Relevance	Nature of effect	Input parameter
Compost/tray preparation:			
raw materials	yes	prop./tray	prep. cost/tray
electricity	yes	variable/tray	prep. cost/tray
diesel fuel	yes	prop./tray	prep. cost/tray
maintenance on veh.	yes	variable/tray	prep. cost/tray
vehicle depreciation	no	constant	fixed cost
yard/build. maint.	no	constant	fixed cost
yard workers wages	yes	prop./tray	prep. cost/tray
salary J.Brownsey	no	constant	fixed cost
Shed loading and maintenance:			
supplies	yes	prop./tray	shed cost/tray
compost pack material	yes	prop./tray	shed cost/tray

Section	Relevance	Nature of effect	Input parameter
tray repair & maint.	yes	prop./tray	shed cost/tray
diesel fuel	yes	prop./tray	shed cost/tray
vehicle maintenance	yes	variable/tray	shed cost/tray
vehicle depreciation	no	constant	fixed cost
shed workers' wages	yes	prop./tray	shed cost/tray
salary of M.McTrae	no	constant	fixed cost
Climate control:			
electricity	no	approx. constant	fixed cost
materials	no	approx. constant	fixed cost
lab. maintenance	no	constant	fixed cost
equipment depreciation	no	constant	fixed cost
new equipment	no	sunk cost	excluded
salaries	no	constant	fixed cost
Picking, sorting, packaging:			
packing materials	yes	prop./kg	sort/pack. cost/kg
supplies	yes	variable/kg	sort/pack. cost/kg
electricity	yes	variable/kg	sort/pack. cost/kg
new equipment	no	sunk cost	excluded
maintenance equip.	yes	variable/kg	sort/pack. cost/kg
equip. depreciation	no	constant	fixed cost
diesel fuel trucks	yes	prop./kg	sort/pack. cost/kg
maintenance trucks	yes	variable/kg	sort/pack. cost/kg
depreciation trucks	no	constant	fixed cost
wages sort/pack	yes	prop./kg	sort/pack. cost/kg
wages for drivers	yes	variable/kg	sort/pack. cost/kg
salary J.Bloom	no	constant	fixed cost
wages picking	yes	variable/hour	pick pay/hr
vacation/sick pay	yes	variable/hour	pick pay/hr
Local marketing:			
salary J. Sellers	no	constant	fixed cost
travel J. Sellers	no	approx. constant	fixed cost
Other costs:			
office supplies	no	approx. constant	fixed cost
new equipment	no	sunk cost	excluded
company cars running cost	no	approx. constant	fixed cost
depreciation company cars	no	constant	fixed cost
office salaries	no	approx. constant	fixed cost
gardener	no	constant	fixed cost
maintenance office	no	constant	fixed cost
depreciation office bldg	no	constant	fixed cost
mortgage interest	no	constant	fixed cost
property insurance	no	constant	fixed cost
salaried employees accid. insurance, pension fund	no	constant	fixed cost

Section	Relevance	Nature of effect	Input parameter
worker accident insurance & pension fund	yes	prop./$ paid	prep. cost/tray & shed cost/tray & sort/pack. cost/kg & pick cost/hour
salary B. Moss	no	constant	fixed cost
travel B. Moss	no	approx. constant	fixed cost

There is little question that such costs, like raw materials and wages, are proportional to either the number of trays prepared per year or the mushroom output in kg per year. Fringe benefits, like vacation and sick pay, accident insurance and pension fund contributions, on wages vary in proportion with the wage payment. As the wage bill changes, so will such items. Hence, they are a variable cost. Note that accountants may include such costs for reasons of convenience and tradition as part of various overheads. You may thus have to analyze the composition of overheads for such items and re-allocate them properly.

Other costs, like the purchase of equipment, are clearly irrelevant and must be excluded from consideration. Salaries, including the associated fringe benefits, in general are constant, at least over the variation in the output level considered. Hence, they are fixed costs. Depreciation, insurance, and mortgage interests on buildings, etc., are not affected by the level of activity. Hence, they are fixed costs. Depreciation on equipment and vehicles depends on whether it is mainly affected by usage or by age. In the first case, it is a variable cost, while in the second it is fixed. Given the relatively small amounts involved, I shall arbitrarily assume for simplicity that such depreciation is a fixed cost.

Most supplies and electricity usage are affected by the level of activity, but not necessarily in a proportional fashion. Again, to keep things simple, I will assume that these costs are approximately proportional to the level of activity, i.e., either the number of sheds prepared or the output of mushrooms. The exception is the section dealing with climate control. The sheds are in constant use for either the growing or harvesting phases, except for the 2 days of change-over from one cycle to the next. But even during the change-over, the cooling of the sheds continues. Hence, the annual power cost is constant. Since the firm cultivates its own mycelium, the annual cost of supplies, etc., is not affected by fairly large variations in the output level. All costs of the climate control section can thus be treated as constant.

Maintenance of yard equipment and vehicles, and of the sorting and packing equipment is likely to be affected by the level of activity. Hence, it is viewed as a variable cost, for simplicity approximated as proportional to the output level.

The travel costs of both the marketing manager and Bob Moss are likely to be partially affected by the mushroom output. The more mushrooms available, the larger must be the selling effort. This may require more travel. However, it would be very difficult to determine a suitable mathematical relationship between output and travel cost. Again, given the small amounts of funds involved, we simply take them as fixed costs.

The tray maintenance, repair, and replacement costs are proportional to the level of activity. Most damage to the trays occurs during handling, so it is assumed to be proportional to the number of trays prepared.

The mushroom picking costs clearly are affected by the output level of mushrooms. But the relationship is somewhat complex, since the picking rate decreases somewhat with each additional flush. We shall analyze this aspect in more detail when we look at the mathematical model of total costs.

The two revenue sources are sales of mushrooms and sale of spent compost, both proportional to the volume of output of each.

9.6 MATHEMATICAL MODEL FOR ANNUAL PROFIT

I will now list the mathematical form of the relationships represented in the influence diagram of Figure 9-1. Rather than using mathematical notation, the relationships are shown in plain English. Most of the expressions are simple enough to be self- explanatory. If you have doubts about any of them, I suggest that you check it by working out a few examples using trial numbers. That usually helps.

All expressions are defined for a decision choice of n consecutive flushes in each cycle, where n can be 5, 4, 3, 2, or 1. The expressions are labelled by the numbers shown in each circle or output.

1. Length of each cycle:

   [cycle length] = [growing phase duration]+[average flush length] $\times n$

   $$= 28 + 7\,n$$

2. Number of cycles per year:

   [cycles/year] = [days in year]/([cycle length] + [cycle change-over time])

   $$= 365/([\text{cycle length}] + 2)$$

3. Number of trays prepared per year:

   [trays/year] = [number of sheds] $\times$ [trays/shed] $\times$ [cycles/year]

   $$= 65 \times 400 \times [\text{cycles/year}]$$

4. Mushroom output per cycle per tray: The data collected by Jennifer Bloom for sheds 5 and 6 allow us to compute the average yield for each consecutive flush. In practice, it would be advisable to collect data on about a dozen cycles, rather than just two. Verify from the data listed that a new flush seems to start at regular intervals of about 7 days. (A graphical representation highlights this regularity clearly.) So we add up the amount picked for each consecutive 7-day interval for both sheds and divide this sum by two. This gives the average yield for each flush per shed. Dividing these numbers by 400 gives the following

average yields and cumulative average yields per tray for each consecutive flush:

flush $n =$	1	2	3	4	5	
average yield	9189	6432	2841	1711	1044	kg/shed
or	22.97	16.08	7.10	4.28	2.61	kg/tray
cumulative yield	22.97	39.05	46.15	50.43	53.04	kg/tray

5. Annual output of mushrooms:

    [annual output] = [trays/year] × [cumulative yield/tray for n flushes]

6. Annual tray preparation cost:

    [annual tray preparation cost] = [preparation cost/tray] × [trays/year]

7. Annual shed loading and unloading cost:

    [annual shed cost] = [shed cost/tray] × [trays/year]

8. Mushroom picking time per tray: The picking time per kg increases with each consecutive flush. As for the yield, Jennifer's figures allow us to compute an average picking rate for each consecutive flush. To test your understanding of the relationship, compare the answers you compute with the ones shown below:

flush	1	2	3	4	5
kg picked/hour	10.804	9.629	6.938	5.085	4.176
hours per tray	2.126	1.670	1.024	0.841	0.625
cumul. hrs/tray	2.126	3.796	4.820	5.661	6.286

9. Annual number of hours required for picking mushroom output:

    [annual picking labour] = [trays/year] × [cumulative hours/tray]

10. Annual cost of picking labour:

    [annual picking cost] = [annual picking labour] × [picking pay/hour]

11. Annual sorting and packing cost:

    [annual sorting & packing cost] = [annual output] × [sort. & pack. cost/kg]

12. Annual compost revenue:

    [annual compost revenue] = [spent compost/tray] × [trays/year]

    × [net compost selling price/kg]

13. Annual mushroom revenue:

    [annual mushroom revenue] = [annual output] × [mushroom revenue/kg]

14. Annual net profit: total revenue less total costs

[annual net profit] = [annual mushroom revenue]

+ [annual compost revenue]

- [annual tray preparation cost]

- [annual shed cost]

- [annual picking cost]

- [annual sorting & packing cost]

- [annual fixed cost]

To apply this model, we now have to compute the various cost factors used in expressions 6, 7, 10, and 11.

9.7 COMPUTATION OF COST FACTORS FOR EACH SUBSYSTEM

I will now demonstrate how some of the cost coefficients are computed for use in the mathematical model. It is important to remember that all costs compiled by the accountant, reported in the Appendix, refer to the preceding financial year. During that year, the policy used was to let each harvesting cycle go through five flushes, i.e., $n=5$. We shall also assume that there is no inflation. This implies that the cost factors derived will remain valid for the future.

Preparation Costs per Tray

This covers all costs of the compost making and phase 1 tray preparation that vary proportionally with the number of trays prepared per year. They are thus best expressed in the form of an average preparation cost per tray.

For $n=5$ flushes per harvesting cycle, the cycle length is $28 + 7(5) = 63$ days. The number of cycles per year is then $365/(63 + 2) = 5.6154$ cycles on average. With 65 sheds in constant use and each shed carrying 400 trays, the annual number of trays required is $65(400)(5.6154) = 146,000$ trays.

Applying the classification of Table 9-1 to the data listed for tray preparation in the Appendix, the costs that vary proportionally to the number of trays prepared amount to $6,243,310. This includes $428,211 for wages. The total cost of waged labour also has to include the cost of any fringe benefits, such as vacation pay, sick pay, accident insurance and pension fund contributions, paid by the employer. We can assume that the figure on the total wage payments compiled by the accountant includes vacation and sick pay. So no adjustment for this is needed any more. However, the accountant also lists under other costs accident insurance and pension fund contributions, totalling $784,906. These contributions are incurred on the totality of all wages paid. The percentage contribution rates for each are 2.5% for accident insurance and 4% for employer's pension fund contributions, or a total of 6.5%. This amounts to $27,834 on the $428,211 wages paid for this section. The total variable cost for this section is thus

Materials, power, fuel, etc.		$5,815,099
Waged labour	$428,211	
Fringe benefits 6.5%	$ 27,834	
Total waged labour cost		$ 456,045
Total variable cost for 146,000 trays		$6,271,144

This gives an average tray preparation cost of $42.96.

Shed Cost per Tray

Using the classification of costs in Table 9-1 for this section, verify that the analogous reasoning as for the tray preparation leads to a shed cost per tray of $5.40.

Mushroom Pickers Gross Pay per Hour

The accountant lists the hourly pay rate for mushroom pickers at $9.20. This is again exclusive of all fringe benefits supported by the employer. The accountant also quotes that the vacation and sickness pay is limited to the equivalent of 8% of the total annual pay of a picker. Adding to this the accident insurance and pension fund contribution, fringe benefits of 14.5% have to be added to the hourly pay rate. The hourly cost to the firm is thus $10.53.

Sorting and Packing Costs per Kilogram of Mushrooms Produced

The total variable cost for materials, etc., and labour, including the 6.5% cost of fringe benefits amount to $6,353,911. The annual output is equal to the cumulative yield per tray multiplied by the number of trays per year, i.e., 53.043(146000) or 7,744,205 kg. This gives a sorting and packing cost of $0.8205 per kilogram of mushrooms produced. (It is important to use this cost with sufficient decimal places, since it will be multiplied by numbers in the millions. Any small rounding error will thus be highly magnified.)

9.8 ANALYSIS OF MUSHROOMS GALORE BY SPREADSHEET

The spreadsheet to evaluate the mathematical model shown in Section 9.6 is shown in Figure 9-2. As usual, I show all the inputs in a separate part of the spreadsheet. The evaluation of the net profit as a function of the decision variable is shown in the second part of the spreadsheet. It first computes the various intermediate variables as a function of the number of flushes per cycle. These are then used in the cost and revenue computations. Finally, it shows the difference in annual profits in comparison with the current policy of five flushes per harvesting cycle.

Figure 9-2: Spreadsheet evaluation for MG problem

MUSHROOMS GALORE LTD.			
INPUT DATA:			
Picking cost:			
Labour/hour		9.20	
Fringe benefit 14.5%		1.33	(incl. 8% vacation pay,
Total/hour		10.53	2.5% acc.ins., 4% pension funds)
Tray preparation:			
Materials		5815099	
Labour	428211		
Fringe benefit 6.5%	27834	456045	(incl. 2.5% acc. ins.,
Total for 146,000 trays		6271144	4% pension fund)
per tray		42.9560	
Shed cost:			
Materials, etc.		588343	
Labour	188231		
Fringe benefit 6.5%	12235	200466	(as above)
Total for 146,000 trays		788809	
per tray		5.4032	
Processing cost:			
Materials, etc.		4121198	
Labour	2096444		
Fringe benefit 6.5%	136269	2232713	(as above)
Total for 7,744,205 kg		6353911	
per kg		0.8205	
SUMMARY INPUT DATA:			
Number of trays/shed	400	Flush Yield (kg) Picking hrs	
Number of sheds	65	1 9189 850.5	
Revenue/kg	$3.60	2 6432 668.0	
Sort & Pack cost/kg	0.82047	3 2841 409.5	
Picking cost/kg	$10.53	4 1711 336.5	
Preparation cost/tray	$42.96	5 1044 250.0	
Shed cost/tray	$5.40		
Fixed cost/year	$2914294		
Compost revenue/tray	$8.40		

Figure 9-2: MG problem (continued)

EVALUATION					
Tray and Volume computations					
Flushes per cycle	1	2	3	4	5
Cycle length in days	37	44	51	58	65
Number of cycles/year	9.865	8.295	7.157	6.293	5.615
Yield/tray in kg	22.973	16.080	7.103	4.278	2.610
Cumul. yield/tray in kg	22.973	39.053	46.155	50.433	53.043
Picking hours/tray	2.126	1.670	1.024	0.841	0.625
Cumul. picking hr/tray	2.126	3.796	4.820	5.661	6.286
Number of trays/year	256,486	215,682	186,078	163,621	146,000
Total output/year in kg	5,892,136	8,422,914	8,588,450	8,251,800	7,744,205
Revenue and cost computations					
Mushroom revenue	21,211,689	30,322,491	30,918,420	29,706,482	27,879,138
Compost revenue	2,154,486	1,811,727	1,563,059	1,374,414	1,226,400
Tray preparation cost	11,017,629	9,264,824	7,993,182	7,028,487	6,271,573
Shed cost	1,385,840	1,165,366	1,005,414	884,071	788,863
Picking cost	5,744,763	8,625,051	9,447,924	9,757,619	9,668,026
Sort & Pack cost	4,834,338	6,910,773	7,046,591	6,770,379	6,353,911
Fixed cost	2,914,294	2,914,294	2,914,294	2,914,294	2,914,294
Net profit	(2,530,689)	3,253,910	4,074,075	3,726,045	3,108,871
Difference with 5 flushes	(5,639,560)	145,040	965,204	617,174	0

Postscript: When this solution was submitted to the management for consideration, the chief executive's response was disbelief. His answer was the one attributed in the case write-up in the Appendix to the father of Bob Moss. However, three years later, the firm nevertheless went ahead and reduced the flushes per harvesting cycle, a delay that could have cost them up to three million dollars!

The annual profit is higher for 2, 3, and 4 flushes than for the current policy. The highest profit increase is obtained for 3 flushes per harvesting cycle. The increase is almost 1 million dollars per year. It also results in an increase in mushroom output of 844,245 kg or slightly more than 10%. The interesting aspect is that a policy of 3 flushes per cycle also achieves a higher mushroom output than any other policy. Based on this analysis, Bob Moss would be advised to reduce the number of flushes from 5 to 3 per harvesting cycle. This would achieve his objectives of both increasing output and profits at the same time. The increase in output is about the equivalent of 7 additional sheds if the current policy of 5 flushes were continued. Any decision as to adding more sheds can thus be postponed by another few years.

EXERCISES

1. Compare opportunity costs and intangible costs and discuss their differences and similarities, if any.

2. Discuss why opportunity costs are a form of implicit costs.

3. Why are opportunity costs relevant for decision making?

4. Give an example of explicit costs, implicit costs, fixed costs, variable costs, opportunity costs, sunk costs, and intangible costs for each of the following types of entities:
   (a) An industrial firm, such as a manufacturer of household appliances.
   (b) A merchandising firm, such as a department store chain.
   (c) A service industry firm, such as a restaurant.
   (d) A public service organization, such as a hospital.
   (e) A local government agency, such as the water supply authority.
   (f) An educational institution, such as a university or a polytechnic.

5. The following questions all refer to the Mushrooms Galore case and the classification of costs in Table 9-1:
   (a) The depreciation for yard vehicles is currently classified as a fixed cost. Assume now that MG adopts the optimal cycle length of three flushes. The number of trays to be prepared increases from 146,000 to 186,078, a 27% increase. When Jeff Brownsey hears this, he casually mentions to Roger Munny that this implies that the yard vehicles may have to be replaced earlier than under the previous scheme. What effect has this on the relevance of depreciation?
   (b) Jeff Brownsey also points out that, while the compost stacking machine can easily cope with the increased workload, this is not the case for the current assortment of forklift tractors. In fact, he reckons that at least one additional forklift tractor will have to be purchased. Its operating and maintenance costs, as well as its depreciation, would be identical to the ones for the current tractors. What is the effect of purchasing another tractor on the costs under the new system?
   (c) The amount of work for climate control is considerably more intensive during the 26-28 day growing phase than during the harvesting phases. Under the new system, the number of cycles per year also increases by 27%. Carl Sharp worries that he and Tina Trott will not be able to handle the increased workload without getting a part-time assistant. How does this affect the relevance of costs for climate control?
   (d) The increase in the level of operations due to the higher volume of mushrooms requires additional working capital (funds invested in inventories of all sorts, increase in the level of outstanding customer bills, increased bank account balances required for daily operations, etc.). Bob Moss proposes to raise the additional funds by getting a short-term bank loan of $300,000 at an interest rate of 15%. How does this affect the imputation of costs?

6. A firm produces various types of adhesive tapes, like flesh coloured vinyl for bandages, electrical insulating tape, etc. Depending on the type of tape, it is either produced on the older and more expensive Classic line or the newer and more efficient Modern line. Both lines are currently used for about 1.5 shifts per day. In an effort to reduce production costs, the production engineer experiments with various different setups and comes up with a proposal, which he claims will reduce production costs substantially. The proposal implies that the equivalent of about 1/2 shift of work is moved from the Classic line to the Modern line. This would increase the workload of the Modern line by about 1/4 shift. He presents the following summary of savings for switching bandage vinyl from the Classic to the Modern line:

	Classic line	Modern line	Savings
Speed of production (m²/hr)	600	1200	
Adhesive applied (kg/m²)	0.275	0.25	
Adhesive cost/year at $15/kg for 140,000 m²	$577,500	$525,000	$52,500
Machine hours for production	233.33	116.67	
Size of batches in m²	5000	10000	
Annual setup time in hrs	28	14	
Total machine hours required (hrs)	261.33	130.67	
Labour cost at $20/hr + 25% fringe ben.	$6533	$3267	$ 3,266
Overhead* allocation rate per mach. hour	$102	$78	
Total overhead allocation	$26,656	$10,660	$15,996
Total net savings			$71,762

* Overhead also includes recovery of the initial cost of the machine, i.e., machine depreciation.

Upon seeing this statement, the accountant reports that switching production from the Classic line to the Modern line would result in the overhead allocation rate changing. Reducing the work load on the Classic line by 1/2 shift would increase its overhead rate to around $123 dollars. Given the greater efficiency of the Modern line, its overhead rate would decrease by about 14% only. As a result, all the remaining products produced on the Classic line would increase substantially in cost, either reducing the profitability of these products or forcing corresponding price increases, with a potential drop-off in sales. The firm might even have to stop production of some of the previously profitable products due to decreased sales. The increased profitability of products produced on the Modern line would probably not justify any price reductions in these products or if prices were reduced marginally, this was unlikely to increase sales noticeably. He therefore recommended against this move. When asked if the overhead allocation rate on the Classic line could not simply be left at its present level, he was quite adamant that this would violate company policy that each machine had to recover all its costs, including its proper overhead allocation. If this were done in this instance, then pressure would build to use this kind of ploy in other instances also. This would invalidate all attempts to properly cost products.

Analyze these costs and discuss their relevance for the decision to switch production lines. Discuss the accountant's arguments.

Are there any relevant costs that the engineer missed?

7. A firm sells a range of chemical products in a variety of containers: 0.3 litre plastic bottles, 1 litre plastic bottles, 1 litre cans, 5 litre cans, etc.. Each product goes through

the following production process. The first stage is mixing the basic ingredients. This is done in vats of 100, 500, 1000, 4000, and 10000 litres. An operator measures out the ingredients according to a specification sheet and adds them to the vat chosen for mixing in a prescribed sequence, with the mixing blades activated at various times. The ingredients are stored in the basic chemical warehouse, which is just adjacent to the mixing vats. However, for safety reasons each ingredient has to be handled individually, i.e., removing the desired quantity from the stock of ingredients if it comes in containers of the correct size, or else bringing a drum or bag from the storage area to the scales and measuring out the required amount, and then returning the balance to the stock of ingredients. Measuring out each ingredient takes, on average, the same length of time, regardless of the quantity to be measured out. Most products require between 5 and 20 ingredients, but some are made up of up to 50 different ingredients. Once mixed, some of the products have to go through a homogenization process, i.e., the mixing vat is covered and the mixing blades rotated at extremely high speed. The entire mixing operation can take anywhere from 1 to 6 hours.

Once mixing is completed, a 0.5 litre sample is removed and brought to the testing lab, where it undergoes a series of tests. About 5% of all batches mixed fail one or several of these tests. If this happens, the lab technician returns an upgrading report to the mixing operator. That report spells out exactly what additional quantities of ingredients have to be added to bring the batch up to specifications. The time taken for this is on average about 60% of the original mixing setup time. It occasionally also means that the size of the batch becomes larger than originally ordered. Naturally the upgraded batch has to be retested. Over the last 5-year period no batch has failed a test twice. Test results are usually available within 30 minutes.

Once a batch has been cleared, it is then ready for filling into containers. Direct plastic or rubber lines can be hooked up to connect the mixers to each of the three filling machines: one for each size container. To eliminate any contamination which could potentially be hazardous to the operators and the users of the products, these lines have to be thoroughly cleaned after each use. Furthermore, these lines deteriorate with use and can only be used about 80 times before they have to be discarded. A new line has a cost of $60.

Prior to the start of filling a new batch, the containers have to be made ready, the labels inserted into the machine, the filling machine adjusted for the viscosity of the product filled (this controls the quantity filled), and the lines from the mixer hooked up to the filling machine. Two operators are engaged in these preparations for a total of 15 minutes each. A trial batch of 12 containers is then filled and inspected. The last three containers are tested for weight. One of the containers is also returned to the testing lab for confirmation of its content. This container is then labelled by the batch number and date, and stored for 8 months, after which it is discarded. The time taken for these final tests is about 15 minutes during which time the filling machine is stopped. Although the two machine operators keep busy, such as making final readjustments to the machine, the production engineer views this time as essentially unproductive. Once the sample can has been cleared by the lab, filling takes place at full machine speed. The containers are packed into cardboard boxes by hand by up to four labourers. The boxes are sealed, labelled and then placed on pallets, which are stored in the finished goods warehouse. During the machine setup and testing, these labourers are kept busy by other productive work. Their wages during setup are therefore not chargeable to the product being filled. Filling time depends on the batch size. The 1 litre machines can fill up to 300 cans or 180 bottles per minute.

Consider a particular product X. Its ingredients have a value of $5.50 per litre of finished product. Preparation for mixing takes 2 hours. This includes the cleaning of the vat. The actual mixing operation is proportional to the size of the batch and takes 20 minutes for every 1000 litres of mix. The two laboratory technicians test 20 - 40 products each day. They also spend some 2 hours per day testing raw materials, as these come in from suppliers. Hooking up the mixers to the filling machine takes 5 minutes. This is done by the mixing operator. The actual filling occurs at a rate of 200 cans per minute. Four packers are needed for packing the cans into boxes, etc. Cleaning the filling machine and the hookup lines after a run takes another 10 minutes for two people. Cleaning is done using cleaning solvents and neutralizers. For this particular product it takes 12 litres of fresh cleaning solvents to clean the vat, filling machine and hookup lines. Furthermore, the first two cans filled cannot be used, since even after thorough cleaning, there may still be some small amounts of residues left in the filling mechanism, which is washed out by the flow of chemicals to fill the first two cans. Consumption of power during all these operations is about $0.16 per 1000 litres of product. Can labels cost 2 cents/can, while a carton for 24 cans has a cost of 60 cents, including the label.

The wage rate for the mixing operator and the two filling machine operators is $16 per hour, while the packing labourers at the filling machine are paid $12 hour. The lab technicians are on a weekly salary of $800 for a 40 hour week. Any increase in the lab workload of more than 10% would either require overtime or the addition of a part- or full-time technician.

Other costs involved in inventory control include clerical costs at the accounting department. Currently about 3 persons are fully occupied in maintaining computerized inventory records, including the processing of customer orders, preparation of customer delivery documents, preparation and processing of stock replenishments. It is estimated that each stock replenishment takes about 20 minutes of clerical time for all processing involved. Only about 20% of their time is taken up by processing stock replenishments. Clerks are on monthly salaries of $2,000 and work a 40-hour week.

There are two types of overhead charged to the plant. Plant overhead is charged at 50% of direct labour cost. General overhead is assessed at a rate of 64% on direct labour cost. General overhead also includes fringe benefits of 30%, such as vacation pay, pension fund contributions, health and accident insurance, cafeteria subsidies, etc. The company wishes to earn a return on its investment of 15% after taxes. The current marginal tax rate is 33%.

The company rents its premises. The cost accountant has figured out that each square metre of floor space has an annual cost of $40. One pallet stored in the warehouse requires 1.44 square metres of floor space. Pallets are stored three high. For each pallet area, 0.56 square metres of floor space is needed for access aisles. The filling machine requires a floor space of 10 by 15 metres, while a vat needs about 9 square metres of floor space. The premises consist of a separate building. It is not subdividable and has to be rented as a whole unit. Currently, there is ample floor space available for expansion. Maintenance of the plant area has an annual cost of $12 per square metre.

The current inventory replenishment policy used by the firm is based on the economic order quantity model. Identify all costs relevant for determining the EOQ for the product in question. Develop a Table similar to Table 9-1 for classifying all costs mentioned. You may wish to review some of the material in Chap. 6 dealing with the EOQ model. Recall that there are two types of relevant costs for the EOQ model, those that are fixed for each replenishment, regardless of its size, and those that are associated with the cost of holding goods in stock, usually assessed on the average inventory level.

8. For the cost factors developed in exercise 7 above, find the optimal replenishment size and its total annual cost, using the EOQ model of Chap. 6.

REFERENCES

Most texts on business economics or micro-economics, and engineering economics have a chapter on costs. Their treatment will be similar to the treatment in this chapter, although somewhat more theoretical. Texts on production and operations management also have some coverage of the various types of costs, particularly as relevant for production and operations decisions. A more complete treatment of costs and their incidence can be found in cost accounting texts, although their emphasis will be more in terms of allocation of costs to products and services, rather than their relevance for project type decision making. Unfortunately, few OR/MS texts have any comprehensive coverage of costs, their incidence, and their relevance to decision making. Most simply assume that the reader is fully conversant on this topic.

Appendix to Chapter 9: Mushrooms Galore — Situation Summary

MUSHROOMS GALORE LTD. (MG) grows mushrooms on a commercial basis all year long. Cultivated mushrooms are grown under carefully controlled climatic and hygienic conditions, usually in complete darkness in caves, cellars, or specially constructed sheds. MG uses sheds.

The Production Process

Mushrooms are grown on a base of specially prepared compost. MG makes its own compost. It buys straw from the surrounding farms and wheat growers. In fact, MG buys well over 50% of all straw locally available. This straw is mixed with animal manure and other organic materials. The mixture is stacked into long snakes or rows of about 2 by 2 metres diameter. This operation is done by a special-purpose stacking machine. Once stacked, the mixture naturally undergoes a fermentation from inside out which transforms it slowly into compost. This creates a substantial amount of heat which further contributes to the process. Outside temperatures and the amount of natural rain can affect the speed of fermentation. Sprinkler systems are used to control the humidity level of the mixture. After 1 to 2 weeks when the insides of the stacks have become compost, the stacking machine turns the stacks inside out. This speeds up complete fermentation of all material. The whole process takes anywhere from 2 to 4 weeks, depending on the time of the year and the outside temperature. New stacks of compost are started at regular intervals to guarantee a constant supply of fresh compost for the production process.

The mushroom production itself consists of three phases. In phase 1 the compost is put into 30-centimetre deep wooden trays. These are topped with peat. The trays and their contents are then sterilized to kill any diseases or unwanted seeds, etc. Once sterilized, the trays are injected with laboratory grown mycelium (mushroom spawn), covered with casing soil, and treated in a process called 'peak heating'. Phase 2 is the mycelium growing stage. The trays are stored on shelves in growing sheds. The inside of the sheds is almost completely dark and kept within carefully controlled temperature and humidity ranges. The growing phase lasts about 26 to 28 days. During this time the mycelium invests the entire bed in each tray. The third phase is the cropping stage. The mushrooms which are the fruiting bodies of the plant appear in a sequence of 'flushes' at intervals of 6 to 8 days. Within 1 to 2 days of breaking through the casing soil, the mushrooms are harvested. The yield of the first two flushes is substantially higher than for the subsequent flushes. Also, the size of the mushrooms becomes smaller for the later flushes. As a result, the amount of labour needed to pick the mushrooms appearing in the later flushes increases markedly over the first two flushes. The reason for both these phenomena is that each flush reduces the nutrient content of the compost until, after about 5 to 6 flushes, it has been almost exhausted. At that point, the trays are removed from the sheds, the 'spent' compost packed into bags for resale as mulch to home gardeners or commercial vegetable growers, the trays cleaned and returned to the compost filling station, ready for use in a new production cycle. Emptying a shed, preparing it for the next cycle, and loading it with a fresh batch of trays takes about 2 days.

Like the composting operation, phase 1 of the production process is done on a continuous basis, with new trays prepared daily for phase 2. With the number of sheds currently in operation, a new shed starts on phase 2 practically every day. As a consequence the sheds are on a continuous rotation, with each shed at a different stage in the process. This provides a fairly constant output level for the operation as a whole.

Picking of mushrooms is done by hand. For this reason, the width of the trays and their spacing on the shelves in the sheds is such that a picker can easily reach to the middle of each tray, working either from the floor for the lowest shelf or from a ladder that rolls along the shelves for the upper two shelf levels. In order to maintain strict hygiene, any person entering a growing shed has to pass through a lock where shoes and clothing are automatically sterilized. The freshly picked mushrooms are sorted by size and quality. The very small ones are used by a canning factory, operated by MG at a different site. Most of the high-quality product is exported to Australia and Singapore, while the second grade mushrooms are sold on the local NZ market or used in the canning operation.

The firm currently operates 66 sheds, each capable of storing 400 trays. All but one of these sheds are continuously in use for the growing and harvesting phases, except for the 2 days needed to clean a shed after each cycle and prepare it for the next cycle. The one shed not in use is undergoing major maintenance and repair work which takes 5 to 6 days per year. Trays also need regular repairs and replacement. On average a tray last about four years.

The People

Bob Moss is the principal owner of the firm, having taken over from his father as managing director two years ago. Before that he was the firm's marketing manager. He has six people in supervisory positions reporting to him. Roger Munny is the chief accountant and also serves as office manager. The compost and tray preparation sections are managed by Jeff Brownsey. It is said of him that with his super sensitive nose, which is a most striking feature in his face, and by sticking his right index finger into the fermenting stacks he is able to judge the correct temperature and humidity level of the stacks as well and with less effort than the scientific tests Bob Moss tried to convince him to use. His portion of the operation is highly mechanized, using the rather expensive compost stacking machine, forklift tractors, the automatic sprinkler system, the tray filling machine, the sterilization and peak heating ovens. Mike McTrae is in charge of the gangs filling and emptying the sheds, shed maintenance and cleaning, repair and maintenance of trays, as well as disposing of the spent compost. Carl Sharp and his laboratory assistant, Tina Trott, are responsible for the climatic control of the sheds. They are by far the most scientifically trained employees of the firm. Picking and sorting of the mushrooms and the dispatch to the customers, all highly labour intensive operations, are managed by Jennifer Bloom. Jack Sellers has recently been hired as the marketing manager in charge of domestic sales, with him as the sole member of that department. Bob Moss retained control over international marketing contracts and promotion.

The Problem

When Bob Moss took over control of the firm after his father's retirement, his initial efforts went mainly into developing the export markets in Australia and Singapore. This led to increasing requirements for top-quality product. To meet the additional demand, ten new sheds were added to the original 56 in operation at the time Bob assumed the top position. Otherwise, Bob did not make any major changes to the operation or its management. The exception was hiring Carl to improve quality control. It may also be worth mentioning that, as one of his first actions after taking over the management of the firm, he upgraded the staff cafeteria and the staff changing facilities — a deed that earned him the respect and loyalty of his waged and salaried staff and strongly contributed to staff morale and productivity.

Given the potential for increased export sales, Bob now sees upgrading the production capacity for top-grade product as one of his priorities. The firm's current facilities do not really allow the construction of more sheds, unless the firm adopted the rather expensive two-level sheds. A plot of land, two kilometres to the South of the existing plant and suitable for a maximum of 32 sheds, had recently been offered for sale. This opens up the option of going to a two-site growing operation, with the composting and phase 1 done on the current premises for both sites. Bob doubts that the firm will need more than about 10 to 16 additional sheds within the next five years. Hence, only a small portion of the site would be used productively. However, this option would provide the firm with sufficient breathing space for further expansion for a long time. The increase in transportation cost for trays and mushrooms is an added disadvantage of the two-site option.

Bob wonders whether it would be possible to increase the output of top-grade mushrooms at the current site without the need to construct new sheds. He has always wondered about the reasons why his father had used a 5-flush harvesting cycle, although he was aware that practically all commercial mushroom growers, using the same system as MG, seemed to follow this policy. In fact, he recently discussed this issue with his father when he visited him with his young family at a weekend. His father was very sceptical that any gains could be made by adopting a policy with a smaller number of cycles. His main argument was that if this were advantageous, the mushroom industry would have adopted it long ago. Bob was not convinced by this argument, since the mushroom industry was hardly known for its initiative in researching anything else but how to grow the perfect mushroom.

Being a cautious businessman, he decides to cost out the three options for increasing the output of top-grade mushrooms. He remembers bumping into his old university buddy, John Smart, at a recent function, where he discovered with some envy that John Smart had continued his university study, completing a Ph.D. in Operations Research at an American university. He had just recently accepted a teaching position at his old Alma Mater. John had mentioned that he was always looking for potential student projects. Would this problem not be an ideal project? He contacts John who seems very interested. John asks him to gather some data on various aspects of the operation, like costs of various tasks and the yield for each consecutive flush.

Data Collected

Bob asks Roger Munny to compile a preliminary list of various cost items incurred in the production of mushrooms. Jennifer willingly agrees to keep an exact tally of the quantity of mushrooms harvested each day over the entire harvesting cycle for sheds 5 and 6 which where just coming on-stream for producing mushrooms. It turns out that Jennifer goes a step further by also recording for each day the number of hours worked by the pickers harvesting mushrooms in these two sheds.

Here is a list of the various items of data compiled or collected:

Cost data compiled by Roger Munny, based on the preceding financial year:

1. **J. Brownsey's Section** (Composting and Tray Preparation):
   - $5,493,557 for raw materials (straw, manure, peat, casing sand, sterilization agents, etc.). Most raw materials were purchased regularly, some like straw almost daily, with raw material stocks being small and remaining fairly constant over the entire year.
   - $267,844 electricity for peak heating, and operation of tray filling equipment, etc.
   - $27,911 diesel fuel for yard vehicles.
   - $25,787 maintenance and repair costs on yard vehicles.
   - $123,000 depreciation on yard vehicles and equipment.
   - $86,520 yard ground and building maintenance and repair costs.
   - $428,211 for yard workers' wages, including vacation pay.
   - $36,400 salary of J. Brownsey.

2. **Mike McTrae's Section** (Shed loading and unloading):
   - $51,333 for supplies (sterilization and cleaning chemicals for sheds).
   - $219,102 packing material for spent compost.
   - $24,451 for diesel fuel.
   - $12,211 for vehicle maintenance and repairs.

- $35,600 depreciation on vehicles.
- $44,898 repairs and maintenance of sheds
- $281,346 for replacement, repairs, and maintenance of trays.
- $188,231 wages, including vacation pay.
- $31,200 salary of M. McTrae.

3. **Carl Sharp's Section** (Climate control):
   - $37,866 electricity for climate control.
   - $34,613 for materials (mycelium, laboratory supplies, etc.).
   - $12,452 laboratory maintenance, cleaning, etc.
   - $33,200 depreciation on climate control and lab equipment.
   - $55,800 new climate control and lab equipment.
   - $68,400 salary of C. Sharp and Tina Trott.

4. **Jennifer Bloom's Section** (Picking, sorting, and packaging):
   - $4,071,758 for packing materials.
   - $14,881 for supplies.
   - $6,554 for electricity.
   - $24,600 for new sorting machine.
   - $4,212 for sorting and packing equipment maintenance.
   - $14,600 depreciation on sorting and packing equipment.
   - $5,602 maintenance and repair of sorting and packing shed.
   - $18,006 for diesel fuel for trucks.
   - $5,787 for truck maintenance and repairs.
   - $37,800 depreciation on trucks.
   - $2,044,324 wages for sorting and packing staff only, including vacation pay.
   - $52,120 wages for drivers.
   - $36,000 salary of J. Bloom.
   - Hourly wage rate for pickers: $9.20.
   - Vacation and sick pay allowance for pickers: 8% on wages paid.

5. **Local marketing:**
   - $34,800 salary of J. Sellers.
   - $26,922 travel and daily allowances.

6. **Other costs:**
   - $48,766 for office supplies.
   - $32,688 for new office equipment and computers.
   - $3,435 for office building electricity.
   - $12,111 fuel and maintenance costs for two company cars.
   - $6,600 depreciation on company cars.
   - $288,420 salaries of office staff.
   - $22,600 gardener.
   - $8,688 office building maintenance.

- $190,000 depreciation on all buildings and sheds.
- $1,360,000 mortgage interest.
- $124,005 fire and property insurance.
- $301,887 accident insurance on waged workers (2.5%).
- $8,517 accident insurance on salaried employees (1.5%).
- $483,019 pension fund contribution on waged workers (4%).
- $34,069 pension fund contribution on salaried employees (6%).
- $72,000 salary of B. Moss.
- $35,210 travel cost for B. Moss.

Yield and picking data collected by Jennifer Bloom:

day		kilograms picked in		hours pickers spent in	
		shed 5	shed 6	shed 5	shed 6
Feb	2	452	576	45	66
	3	912	797	78	83
	4	1463	1620	124	140
	5	2043	1304	191	119
	6	2495	2710	220	241
	7	1302	2003	129	176
	8	496	205	55	34
	9	0	298	0	48
	10	983	1160	94	103
	11	1224	1567	131	172
	12	1498	1364	161	129
	13	1373	1112	141	120
	14	1057	761	118	71
	15	467	0	48	0
	16	0	421	0	65
	17	232	365	36	64
	18	786	613	109	81
	19	848	907	123	112
	20	595	426	81	61
	21	264	225	46	41
	22	0	0	0	0
	23	0	289	0	43
	24	323	180	69	35
	25	368	423	71	81
	26	404	407	80	82
	27	301	198	61	42
	28	115	172	25	34
Mar	01	242	0	50	0
	02	0	0	0	0
	03	175	204	39	44

| day | kilograms picked in | | hours pickers spent in | |
	shed 5	shed 6	shed 5	shed 6
04	238	153	49	36
05	98	311	24	54
06	307	144	56	34
07	118	121	26	27
08	94	87	23	21
09	56	69	15	17

Current revenue, net of sales commissions:
| Mushrooms | $3.60/kg |
| Spent compost | $8.40/tray |

10 Discounted Cash Flows

Many OR/MS projects involve costs and benefits, occurring not just at a single point in time, but spread over a number of time periods. For example, a project may involve initial investments in plant and equipment, followed one or two years later by a stream of cash inflows over many years, as that plant and equipment produces goods or services to meet customer demands. Should this project be undertaken?

You have already come across another example of a similar nature. The project report in Chapter 7 recommended that a full-scale study be undertaken to find the optimal replenishment and stocking policies for all finished products carried by the Lubricating Oil Division of Purair. That recommendation entailed spending some $32,000 now, with the promise of generating annual total savings in costs of about $93,000 for several years. The decision for going ahead with this study hinged on whether the flow of promised savings over several years justified spending the additional development costs. The criterion used there was whether these costs would be recovered in less than a year by the promised savings. For the majority of OR/MS projects, this type of analysis will have to be done as part of the recommendations for implementation.

To determine the net monetary outcome of projects with costs and benefits spread over several years, we have to aggregate the costs and benefits into a summary measure. Is the net monetary outcome of a project simply equal to the difference of total benefits and total costs, regardless of what points in time the individual items occur? The answer to this question depends on whether a dollar received, say, one year from now is worth exactly the same as a dollar received now. If this is so, then the answer is yes; otherwise, adding costs or benefits occurring at different points in time would be like adding apples and oranges.

This chapter studies how costs and benefits, that are spread over several time periods, can be aggregated into a single meaningful measure which allows valid comparisons to be made between different streams of cash flows. In Section 10.1 we will first study the time value of money. This will lead us in Sections 10.2 to the concept of discounting future costs and benefits. Section 10.3 shows how any uneven cash flow can be expressed as an equivalent sequence of equal cash flows. We will find this concept useful when we need to compare projects with different productive lives in Section 10.7. Section 10.4 discusses criteria for accepting or rejecting a project from a purely financial point of view, while Section 10.5 looks at the implications of the choice of a suitable discount rate. The chapter ends with a demonstration of a real-life application dealing with finding the best replacement age for piece of equipment.

All numerical computations — and they can be very laborious — will be demonstrated with the help of spreadsheets.   In fact, nowadays no financial calculations are ever done by hand anymore. However, in order to fully understand the principles involved, we cannot avoid delving into some aspects of 'financial mathematics'.

10.1 THE TIME VALUE OF MONEY

Compounding

Under normal economic conditions, we expect that the money in a savings account will earn interest. Say, the current interest rate is r = 8% per year. Then putting $100 into a savings account and leaving it there for one full year will earn 8% of $100 interest. So after one year the balance of the account will be $108. If we leave this amount in the account for a second year, it will earn another 8% of $108 interest, or $8.64. By the end of the second year, the original $100 will have grown to $116.64.

It is useful to look at this process in a slightly more mathematical way. Let r be expressed as a decimal fraction — in our case r = 0.08. Then at the end of year 1, the investment has grown to $100(1+0.08) = $108, and at the end of year 2 to $108(1+0.08) = $116.64. Substituting $100(1.08) for $108, the balance at the end of the second year can be expressed as [$100(1.08)](1.08) = $100(1.08^2)$.

This growth process of the original investment, as interest gets added to it, is called **compounding**. The original investment of C_0 at time 0, compounded at a rate r per period, will grow by the end of n periods to a future value F_n of

$$F_n = C_0(1+r)^n \qquad\qquad (10\text{-}1)$$

This is depicted graphically in Figure 10-1. (Recall that any number to the power 0 is simply equal to 1. So $1.08^0 = 1$.)

Figure 10-1: Compounding at a rate r

time	0	1	2	3
	$C_0(1+r)^0$	$F_1=C_0(1+r)^1$	$F_2=C_0(1+r)^2$	$F_3=C_0(1+r)^3$
example for	$100(1.08^0)$	$100(1.08^1)$	$100(1.08^2)$	$100(1.08^3)$
r=0.08	$100(1)	$100(1.08)	$100(1.1664)	$100(1.259712)
	$100	$108	$116.64	$125.97

A period can be of any length — a year, 6 months, 1 month, or even 1 day. The compounding rate r is simply adjusted accordingly. For example, if the annual rate is equal to i = 0.08, then rate r is reduced to $i/2$ or 0.04 for a half-year period and to $i/12$ or 0.00667 for a one-month period. (Note that these rates are approximations only, but for most purposes are good enough. The approximation gets worse the shorter the compounding period. For instance, $100 compounded half-yearly at the rate $r = 0.04$ grows to $108.16, i.e., $0.16 more than annual compounding at $r = 0.08$. For monthly compounding the difference is $0.30.)

Discounting

Assume that you have won a cash prize of $108. The snag is that you will receive it only one year from now. But you need the money now. You also know that a friend of yours has some spare cash that she would like to invest for at least one year at the going annual rate of 8%. So you ask her for a swap, namely that she gives you cash in exchange for your prize worth $108 one year from now. How much should she be willing to pay you? We just saw that $100 invested at an interest rate of 8% will grow to $108 by the end of one year. So we can infer from this that $108 received in one year is worth right now $100, namely $108/1.08. Similarly, $116.64 to be received two years from now has a value right now of $116.64/(1.08)^2$ or also $100.

The process of converting a future value into its worth right now — its **present value** — is called **discounting**. It is thus the reverse of compounding. The rate at which the future value diminishes is called the **discount rate**. In our example the annual discount rate was $r = 0.08$ or 8%. In general, the present value, PV, of a payment, C_n, received at the end of n periods, discounted at a rate r per period, is given by

$$PV = C_n \,/\, (1+r)^n \tag{10-2}$$

Expression (10-2) is simply the inverse of (10-1). As for compounding, the discount rate r can refer to any length period, not exclusively to annual periods. Its size is simply adjusted proportionately.

Note that (10-2) can be expressed as $PV = C_n [1/(1+r)^n]$. $1/(1+r)$ is referred to as the **discount factor**, often denoted by the greek letter α. α^n represent the present value of one dollar received at the end of n periods. So $PV = \alpha^n C_n$. I will use this short-hand notation most of the time. The example below demonstrates these concepts for a sum of $100 received at the end of n years:

end of year n	1	2	3	...	8
discount factor	$1/(1+r)^1$	$1/(1+r)^2$	$1/(1+r)^3$	...	$1/(1+r)^8$
or for $\alpha=1/(1+r)$	α^1	α^2	α^3	...	α^8
example for $r=0.08$					
$\alpha=(1/1.08)$	0.925926	0.925926^2	0.925926^3	...	0.925926^8
equals	0.925926	0.857339	0.793832	...	0.540269
PV of $100	$92.59	$85.73	$79.38	...	$54.03

There exist extensive tables for discount rates. Their importance and usefulness has diminished dramatically since the widespread availability of pocket calculators. More recently, the availability of electronic spreadsheets for personal computers has made these tables largely superfluous, at least for commercial use.

Opportunity Cost Concept of Discount Rate

From the above discussion it is clear that the discount rate is an opportunity cost concept. By receiving funds only n periods from now, the recipient foregoes the return that could be earned if the funds were available right now. Hence, these funds are worth less now. Similarly, in order to make a payment n periods from now, a lesser amount needs to be invested now. The amount less is equal to the compounded interest that can be earned during these n periods.

The size of the discount rate depends on the alternative uses available for any funds between now and some future point in time. The higher the earnings potential for funds, the higher is the discount rate. It is also affected by the degree of risk inherent in the 'promise' of the future payment. The riskier the promise, the higher is the discount rate. This explains why a second mortgage carries a higher interest rate than the first mortgage or why loan sharks charge a higher interest rate.

10.2 THE PRESENT VALUE OF A SERIES OF CASH FLOWS OVER TIME

We will now apply these concepts to determine whether a given investment proposal is an attractive proposition from a purely financial point of view. Note that even if this is so, the proposal may still be rejected for other reasons. For instance, it may be riskier than the investor is willing to accept or it may result in a highly uneven and hence undesirable cash flow pattern, etc. The financial analysis developed below only considers the net monetary worth of the proposed investment.

Recall the Mushrooms Galore case in Chapter 9. We explored whether MG should reduce the number of flushes per growing cycle from the current five to less than five. We discovered that by going to three flushes per cycle, the annual profit would increase by about $965,000. Some additional analysis indicates that at least initially, the increased output could only be disposed of by decreasing the selling price, while at the same time increasing sales promotion. This would reduce the annual net savings as follows:

Year	1	2	3	4	5
Profit increase	$320,000	$360,000	$450,000	$600,000	$800,000

Furthermore, the increased output would require the acquisition of additional yard equipment and trays at a total cost of $1,200,000. This additional equipment and the trays would have a productive life of 5 years. In other words, at the end of 5 years, continued increased output would require its replacement. This would give rise to a new evaluation and investment decision at that time.

After consultation with the accountant, the owner of MG, Bob Moss, concluded that any new investments in the firm would have to earn an annual return of at least 18%, otherwise the investment was not attractive financially.

What is the meaning of a required annual return of 18%? It means that if Bob Moss lends somebody $1,200,000 for N years, he would expect, in return, to get annually a payment of 18% of $1,200,000 or $216,000 for the use of the funds, as well as receiving back his initial capital advanced at the end of the N years.

This situation is depicted in Figure 10-2 for $N = 5$ years. The initial loan of $1,200,000 is shown as a cash outflow (a negative number) at the beginning of year 1 (= time 0). It is followed by four payments of $216,000 and a final payment of $216,000 plus the initial capital of $1,200,000 also returned at that time. The row underneath lists the discount factors for converting each payment to its present value. The row labelled PV shows the product of the cash flow and the corresponding discount factors. Each payment is thus expressed in terms of its worth as of the same point in time, namely the beginning of the 5-year period. As required, the sum of the present values for the cash inflows from year 1 to year 5 add up to the initial cash outflow of $1,200,000. At a discount rate of 18%, the initial cash outflow is thus exactly recovered by the present values of the cash inflows.

Figure 10-2: Cash flow pattern earning 18%

end of year n	0	1	2	3	4	5
cash flow	C_0	C_1	C_2	C_3	C_4	C_5
($1000)	−1200	+216	+216	+216	+216	+1416
α^n	1	0.847458	0.718184	0.608631	0.515789	0.437109
PV ($1000)	−1200	+183.05	+155.13	+131.46	+111.41	+618.95

sum of present values of cash inflows   +1200 (thousand $)

The sum of the present values of all cash flows — cash outflows and cash inflows — is called the **net present value** or NPV of the project cash flows. Since in our example the cash flows were fixed such that they exactly meet the required 18% return per year, the $NPV=0$. From this we can conclude that if the NPV is positive at a rate of discount of 18%, the project has a higher return than 18%. If its NPV is negative, then the project returns less than 18%. Therefore, we have now a criterion for deciding whether the proposed expansion of MG returns more or less than 18% per annum, and by extension whether John Moss will find the project financially attractive or not.

Evaluation of the MG Expansion Project

Figure 10-3 shows the computations for finding the *NPV* for the cash flow associated with the MG expansion project, executed in a spreadsheet using the financial functions available in a spreadsheet package, like LOTUS 1-2-3®, Quattro PRO®, or Microsoft EXCEL®.

Figure 10-3: Net present value calculations for MG expansion

MUSHROOMS GALORE EXPANSION PROJECT: DETAILED NPV COMPUTATION						
Year	Cash flow	Discount factor for 18%	Present value for 18%	Present value for 12%	Present value for 24%	Present value for 30%
0	-1,200,000	1.000000	-1,200,000	-1,200,000	-1,200,000	-1,200,000
1	320,000	0.847458	271,186	285,714	258,065	246,154
2	360,000	0.718184	258,546	286,990	234,131	213,018
3	450,000	0.608631	273,884	320,301	236,019	204,825
4	600,000	0.515789	309,473	381,311	253,784	210,077
5	800,000	0.437109	349,687	453,941	272,886	215,463
Net present value			262,777	528,258	54,885	-110,464

The first four columns reproduce the computations for a discount rate of 18%. Recall that under the currency display option, negative numbers are shown in parentheses. The *NPV* for the project is given by the sum of the entries in column 4. It comes to $262,777, i.e., the sum of the present values of the inflows exceeds the initial investment of $1,200,000 by $262,777. This signals that the project has a better return than 18%. It is thus an attractive project.

Columns 5 - 7 repeat the calculations for discount rates of 12, 24, and 30%, respectively. Note that for 12% the *NPV* is substantially larger than for 18%, while for 24% it is substantially smaller. As the discount rate increases, the *NPV* decreases. For 30% it has become negative. This relationship is depicted in Figure 10-4.

The Internal Rate of Return

From Figure 10-4 we see that there is a discount rate for which the *NPV* is exactly equal to zero. Verify that this occurs for a discount rate of 25.84755%, shown as 25.85 in the graph. The discount rate for which the *NPV* is equal to zero is called **the internal rate of return** or **the marginal efficiency of capital** — a concept extensively used by economists.

Figure 10-4: Relationship between discount rate and *NPV*

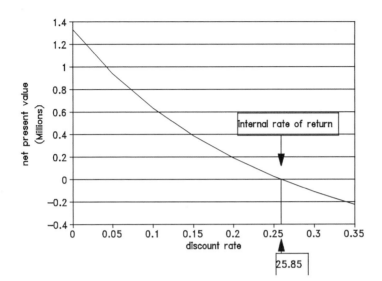

10.3 ANNUITIES AND PERPETUITIES

The computations of the *NPV* are somewhat simpler if the cash flow is the same in each period of the project's productive life. An equal cash receipt or payment at annual intervals is called an **annuity**. By extension, any equal cash flow at regular intervals of any length is referred to as an annuity. For example, assume that at the end of each of the coming five years, you receive a payment of $84,030.40. What is the present value of this annuity at a discount rate of 18%? The table below shows the computations:

period	1	2	3	4	5
amount	$84,030.40	$84,030.40	$84,030.40	$84,030.40	$84,030.40
α^n	0.847458	0.718184	0.608631	0.515789	0.437109

NPV   ($84,030.40) 3.127171 = $262,777

Since the amount is the same each period, the *NPV* is simply equal to the product of this constant amount and the sum of the discount factors.

If the constant cash flow occurs for ever — a so-called **perpetuity**, then the *NPV* is given by this simple formula (which is derived as the sum of a geometric series):

$$NPV_r = C / r$$

C is the amount of the perpetuity occurring at the end of each period. For example, the NPV of a perpetuity of $47,299.90 at a discount rate of $r = 18\%$ is equal to $47,299.90/0.18 = 262,777$.

Equivalent Annuity

These two examples demonstrate an interesting concept. Note that the original cash flow for the MG project has a NPV of $262,777. The annuity of $84,030.40 received at the end of each of five consecutive years also has a NPV of $262,777. These two completely different sequences of cash flows, both covering a 5-year span, have thus the same NPV. They are equivalent to each other in terms of their NPV. This property allows us to express any sequence of unequal cash flows as a sequence of equal cash payments or receipts, or as a so-called **equivalent annuity**, covering the same number of periods. The annuity of $84,030.40 for five years is thus the equivalent annuity for the original stream of cash flows of the MG project.

Similarly, to generate an annual cash payment of $47,299.90 over all future periods, i.e., a perpetuity, all that is needed is an investment of $262,777, earning interest at 18% per year. So this perpetuity is also an equivalent stream of cash flows to the original MG project (although for a different number of periods).

This ability to express uneven cash flows in terms of equivalent annuities turns out to be very useful when we deal with comparison of projects that have different productive lives.

10.4 ACCEPT/REJECT CRITERIA FOR FINANCIAL PROJECTS

The previous discussion provides us with two alternative criteria for deciding whether to accept or reject a project from a purely financial point of view.

> **Given a target rate of return of r^*, accept the project**
> **if $NPV_r{}^* \geq 0$ (Net Present Value Criterion)**
> **or**
> **if $IRR \geq r^*$ (Internal Rate of Return Criterion)**
> **and**
> **reject the project otherwise.**

These two criteria give the same accept or reject decision, if the project's cash flow consists of an initial cash outflow, followed by a string of cash inflows. The MG project has this pattern. So, if the target rate of return is $r^* = 18\%$, then the project is accepted under both criteria, since $NPV = 262,777 \geq 0$ and $IRR = 25.84755\% \geq 18\%$.

Unfortunately, if the cash flow is not so well behaved, having several reversals of cash flows from negative to positive and vice-versa, there may be two or more distinct *IRR* values for which the *NPV* = 0. For example, the cash flow pattern of $–720, $1700, $–1000, has two *IRR*-values, one of 11.11%, the other of 25%. If the target rate of return is 20%, the *NPV* = $2.22. Under the NPV-criterion, we get an unambiguous answer of 'accept this project'. Under the IRR-criterion, we do not know which *IRR*-value the target rate of return should be compared with, if any. For this and other reasons, financial analysts usually recommend the use of the NPV-criterion in preference to the IRR-criterion. We will follow this advice.

10.5   CHOICE OF TARGET RATE OF RETURN

What is the appropriate discount rate to use in evaluating the worth of a project? This is a rather complex problem — it is a topic extensively discussed in the financial theory literature. I shall only give it a rather cursory treatment. Any text on Managerial Finance will fill in the details.

Opportunity Cost Basis

Since the basis for discounting is the opportunity cost associated with the use of funds, the most obvious choice for the correct discount rate is the rate of return foregone on the best alternative use of the funds. Unfortunately, the best alternative use of funds changes over time. It is affected by changes in the range of alternative uses of the funds available at any given point in time. This could result in rather inconsistent choices being made from one project to the next, as the best alternative may change within a short span of time. Furthermore, the decision maker may not really be aware of all possible uses of funds. In real life, the concept of the best alternative use is not a practicable approach for setting a suitable discount rate.

Desired Rate of Return — A Policy Choice

A logical alternative is to ask management or the decision makers to formulate a policy as to what the minimum acceptable rate of return is for investments of a given level of risk in the entity or organization under their control. This minimum acceptable rate is then used as the target discount rate. It will reflect the general economic climate and will therefore be less subject to short-term fluctuations. From an OR/MS point of view, this is the preferred approach. It puts the onus for setting the target rate where it belongs, namely with the decision makers.

Firm's Average Cost of Capital

An alternative approach is based on the concept of the organization's cost of capital. This is the average cost of the funds available for investment in an organization's operations. How do we measure this cost? Any organization has recourse to a variety of different sources of funds. For example, a limited liability company in the manufacturing sector will have somewhere between 40 and 60% of its funds financed by the owners — its shareholders. These so-called equity funds are in the form of share capital and retained earnings (i.e., profits re-invested in the firm, rather than paid out as dividends to the shareholders). The balance will be funds in the form of liabilities, such as mortgages, debentures, short-term bank loans, and trade credit from suppliers. The latter is regularly renewed through new purchases. If the firm wants to be viewed as a good investment prospect for existing and new owners and creditors, it will have to maintain a composition of funds or a capital structure considered appropriate for the type of business it is in. Any significant departure will cause the firm to be perceived as a more risky investment and hence cause its average cost of capital to increase.

For each of these sources of funds we determine the cost to the firm of raising additional capital, i.e., the marginal or incremental cost of funds. This cost is easy to define for liabilities, like a bank loan. It is equal to the interest rate paid to the creditors. Finding the cost of equity funds is a bit more difficult and controversial. Given these individual marginal costs of funds and their long-run (ideal) proportion in the firm's capital structure, we can compute a weighted average marginal cost. These proportions are used as the weights.

This weighted average marginal cost of capital is used as the minimum required rate of return and hence the target discount rate for any project proposal. Any project that has a positive NPV at that discount rate increases the net worth of the firm, since it recovers more than what is required on average for remunerating the firm's combined sources of additional funds.

Note that it would be incorrect to simply use the cost of the funds actually raised for the project as the target discount rate. This would again lead to inconsistent decisions, since this cost would change from project to project, as the firm endeavours to re-balance its capital structure to what investors expect.

Effect of Choice of Target Discount Rate

The choice of target discount rate has a significant impact on the type of project an organization accepts. The higher the target discount rate, the lower is the NPV. But more significantly, this will also give less weight to future cash flows, both positive and negative. It will thus favour projects that have a low initial cost and/or quick recovery of the funds invested. For instance, a high r^* will favour low initial cost rather than high quality and durability. You go for the low cost second-hand car, rather than the Mercedes. It will favour the purchase of cheap equipment and plant, rather than equipment and plant with low running costs but a higher initial investment.

When dealing with environmental problems, a high r^* will favour quick resource exploitation and destruction of our environment rather than conservation. Also abandonment costs which are incurred way in the future will contribute very little to the NPV and hence are practically ignored. This explains why construction of nuclear power stations may be favoured over other power sources, like solar power, in spite of the fact that the cost of decommissioning a nuclear power plant 30 or 40 years in the future and the cost of the storage of nuclear waste material for hundreds of years afterwards may run into the billions. However, discounting reduces these costs to insignificance. Just consider that the present value of a $1 billion cost 40 years from now at a discount rate of 10% amounts to a mere $22 million — a small sum compared to the initial investment for a nuclear power plant. These are some of the reasons why environmentally concerned people argue that the discount rate appropriate for projects with high environmental impacts has to be very low or even zero.

Discounting of costs for public projects, in fact, raises serious ethical questions of equity between generations. Bluntly put, discounting implies that future generations do not count. The interested reader should consult a text like E. J. Mishan, *Introduction to Normative Economics*, Oxford University Press, N.Y., 1981.

10.6 SPREADSHEET FINANCIAL FUNCTIONS

Spreadsheets have built-in financial functions that perform most discounting computations with a few easy key strokes. Some spreadsheets assume that all cash flows always occur at the end of each period. If cash flows occur at the beginning of a period, you need to make some simple adjustments to the functions, such as multiplying the result of the function by an appropriate factor. Other spreadsheets allow the user to specify the timing, with end-of-period timing usually being the default.

The four financial functions which you will need most often are the following (the form shown is for Microsoft EXCEL©; they are similar for other spreadsheet packages; the major difference may be the sequence of the function arguments):

Net present value of a stream of cash flows: NPV(r, Xi:Yj), where [Xi:Yj] indicates the first and last in a row or column of cells containing the sequence of cash flows, occurring at the end of consecutive periods. The initial cash flow at the beginning of the first period is added to the result.

Present value of an annuity: PV(r, number of periods, annuity, fv, type), where the annuity is the constant payment per period, fv and type are optional arguments with a default value of zero. If type = 0, then the annuity is assumed to occur at the end of each period — a so-called **post-paid annuity**, if type = 1, then the annuity is assumed to occur at the beginning of each period — a so-called **prepaid annuity**. (For EXCEL this function assumes that the annuity is a cash outflow, hence it returns a negative value if the annuity is listed as positive.)

Internal rate of return: IRR(Xi:Yj, initial guess for r), where [Xi:Yj] again denotes the first and last cells in a row or column of cells containing the sequence of cash flows, including the initial cash flow at the beginning of the first period. At least one value must be positive (a cash inflow) and one value negative (a cash outflow). This function finds the answer by an algorithm of successive approximations. If no convergence occurs by the end of 20 iterations, a corresponding message is shown. A better initial guess must then be supplied.

Equivalent annuity: PMT(r, number of periods, NPV, fv, type), where NPV is the net present value of the original sequence of irregular cash flows, including the cash flow at the beginning of the first period, with fv = 0 and type = 0 as default values. For type = 0 the equivalent annuity is timed at the end of each period (post-paid), while for type = 1 it is timed at the beginning of each period (prepaid).

Using spreadsheets, most of the computations shown in Figure 10-3 can be done automatically without first computing the corresponding discount factors. Figure 10-5 demonstrates the use of these functions for the MG project. The cell formulas for

Figure 10-5: The use of spreadsheet financial functions

	A	B	C	D	F	G
1	MUSHROOMS GALORE EXPANSION PROJECT EVALUATION					
2						
3	Year	Cash flow				
4	0	($1,200,000)				
5	1	$320,000				
6	2	$360,000				
7	3	$450,000				
8	4	$600,000				
9	5	$800,000				
10						
11		Discount rate	0.12	0.18	0.24	0.3
12		NPV	$528,258	$262,777	$54,885	($110,464)
13		Equiv. annuity	$130,843	$71,212	$16,122	($34,888)
14		IRR	0.258476			
15						
16	Spreadsheet formulas for [0.12] column:					
17	C12	EXCEL:	=NPV(C11,$B5:$B9)+$B4			
18	C13		=PMT(C11,$A9,-C12,0,1)			
19	C14		=IRR(B4:B9,0.5)			
20	C12	LOTUS 1-2-3:	@NPV(C11,$B5..$B9)+$B4			
21	C13		@PMT(C12,C10,$A9)*(1/(1+C11))			
22	C14		@IRR(0.5,$B4..$B9)			

EXCEL and LOTUS 1-2-3 for the present value calculation in a typical column — column C in this case — are reproduced in the bottom portion of the spreadsheet. They refer to the column and row identifiers shown at the margins. The equivalent annuity is computed as occurring at the beginning of each period.

10.7 DEPENDENT, INDEPENDENT, AND MUTUALLY EXCLUSIVE PROJECTS

In evaluating an investment proposal the analyst has to explore possible inter-relationships of the project in question with other potential project proposals. So far we assumed that the cash flow of a given project is not affected by whether any other project is also implemented. If this is the case, the project in question is economically independent. An accept-or-reject decision can be made on its own.

In many instances, the cash flow for a given project is affected by the concurrent or subsequent acceptance of other projects, i.e., several projects together form an interdependent system. For example, the LOD (Chapter 5) was considering the replacement of its main can filling machine with a substantially faster model. For taking full advantage of the increased filling speed, the carton packing equipment also needed upgrading. The savings in operating costs for the new filling machine depended therefore on whether or not the carton packing equipment was also upgraded and if yes, when. The two projects 'purchase of a new filling machine' and 'upgrading of carton packing equipment' are thus interdependent. It could well be that the purchase of the new filling machine is financially unattractive without upgrading the packing equipment, while undertaking both projects is highly attractive.

The interdependence may even be stronger. Project A may be a prerequisite for project B. For example, the purchase of a laser printer has as a prerequisite the availability of a compatible computer, say a PC. Note that the evaluation of the purchase of a PC can be done independently of the purchase of a laser printer, but not the other way around.

At the other extreme, two or several projects are mutually exclusive — only one of them can be accepted. For instance, there may be several filling machines that would have the required hourly filling capacity and would be suitable for the LOD. Each machine may have slightly different characteristics and hence different operating costs. Only one of them will be purchased, if any at all.

It may be helpful to think of these cases as points along a continuum of relationships, as depicted in Figure 10-6. At one extreme there is the complete dependency — one project being the prerequisite of another. On the other extreme, the projects are mutually exclusive. To the right of 'prerequisite' we have decreasing degrees of complementarity. To the left of 'mutually exclusive' we have decreasing degrees of substitutability. At the centre, we have independence.

Mutually exclusive projects may not only differ in terms of the initial investment, but also in terms of their productive lives. To make the correct decision,

Figure 10-6: Range of interdependence of projects

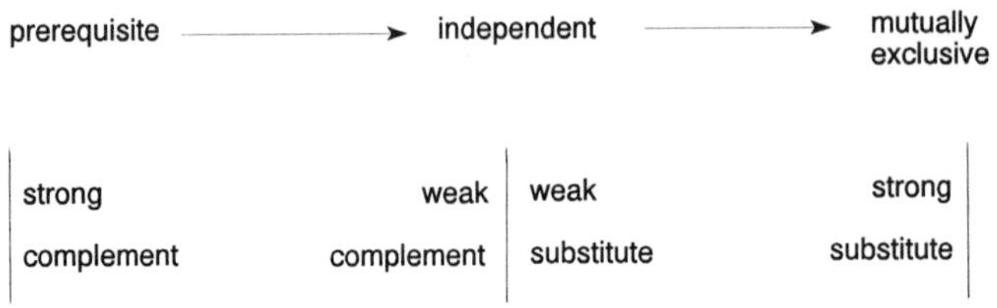

the evaluation has to take these differences properly into account.

Differing Initial Investments

Which one of the following two projects should be accepted, if any?

Project	Cash flows			NPV at
	year 0	year 1	year 2	r = .2
A	$-2000	$1440	$1512	$250
B	$-3000	$1500	$2952	$300

Both projects have a positive *NPV* and are, therefore, acceptable. Project B has the higher *NPV*. Hence it should be selected. By finding the present value of the difference between inflows and outflows, the *NPV* already takes into account that the two projects have a different initial investment. Both projects recover the initial investment plus more. (Project A would only be preferred over project B, if the difference in initial outlay between the two projects could be invested and yield a *NPV* at the same *r* of 0.2 in excess of $50. For instance, assume that there is a third project which can be undertaken jointly with A and which has a cash flow pattern of -1000, 0, +1548 for years 0, 1, and 2, respectively. Its *NPV* at a discount rate of 20% is $75. Hence, the combination of projects A and C yields a combined *NPV* of $325, or $25 more than project B.)

Figure 10-7 shows how the *NPV* of project A and B vary as a function of the discount rate. Note that for discount rates of less than 23.1%, project B has a higher *NPV* than project A. For discount rates of more than 23.1%, this reverses. So for discount rates of less than 23.1% project B is preferred, while for discount rates of more than 23.1% project A is preferred.

Differing Productive Lives

Often mutually exclusive projects have different productive lives. For example, a building contractor may have the choice between purchasing one type utility vehicle

Figure 10-7: Comparison of *NPV*s as a function of the discount rate

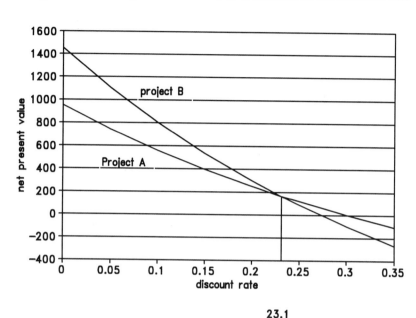

23.1

or leasing it on a fixed-term contract. A purchased vehicle may have a productive life of 5 years for the kind of usage considered, while the fixed-term lease may have to run for 4 years. The cash flow for each choice is shown in the top portion of the spreadsheet printout in Figure 10-8. The buy-option has an initial purchase cost of $44,000 at the beginning of year 1 (= end of year 0), followed by operating costs each year. These increase as the vehicle gets older. At the end of year 5, the vehicle is sold for $14,000. Subtracting the operating cost for year 5 of $7,700 results in a net cash inflow at the end of year 5 of $6,300. Both the buy- and the lease-options involve making some minor alterations to the vehicle at the beginning of year 1 at a cost of $1000. The rental cost for years 1 through 4 is $14,000 per year. The operating costs are identical under both options. Note that all cash flows are assumed to occur at the end of each year, except for the initial outlays.

Management would like to know which option has the lower cost.

This is a cost minimization problem rather than one of maximizing profit or wealth. How should 'costs' be evaluated? Can we simply compute the NPV for each proposal as it stands and then select the one with the lowest NPV cost? The NPV for each option is listed under 'NPV per cycle' in Figure 10-8. The lease-option has by far the lower NPV over its productive life. But note that the two options do not have the same productive life. The lease-option terminates after 4 years, while the buy-option goes to the end of year 5. What happens under the lease-option in year 5?

Figure 10-8: Mutually exclusive projects with different lives

MUTUALLY EXCLUSIVE PROJECTS WITH DIFFERENT PRODUCTIVE LIVES						
Discount rate		0.2				
			Year			
Input data:	0	1	2	3	4	5
Purchase price	$44,000					($14,000)
Operating cost	$1,000	$5,600	$5,800	$6,400	$6,900	$7,700
Leasing cost		$14,000	$14,000	$14,000	$14,000	
Cash flow for options						
Buy	$45,000	$5,600	$5,800	$6,400	$6,900	($6,300)
Lease	$1,000	$19,600	$19,800	$20,400	$20,900	
Evaluation:						
	NPV	Cycle	Repeats	NPV for		Equivalent
Project	per cycle	length		N cycles		annuity
Buy	$58,194	5	4	$94,756		$16,216
Lease	$52,968	4	5	$99,636		$17,051

Two mutually exclusive options that do not have the same productive life cannot be compared without appropriate adjustments to the evaluation. There are several ways of making them comparable. I will look at two. The first is to assume that each option is renewed several times until both options reach the end of the productive life in the same period. There is no implication that this will actually be done in real life. It is only used as a trick to render the two options comparable.

In our example the buy-option would be repeated four times and the lease-option five times. Both options reach the end of their productive life at the end of year 20. This is depicted graphically in Figure 10-9. The *NPV*-cost for the 20-year interval is shown under the heading 'NPV for N cycles' in the spreadsheet of Figure 10-8. Note now that the buy-option has the lower *NPV*-cost, which is the correct answer.

An alternative approach is to express the original cash flow for each option as an equivalent annuity. Each annuity represents the average cash flow in each period — in our case the average cost. Hence, the option with the lowest average cost is the preferred one.

The equivalent annuity for each option is easily computed from the NPV for one cycle, using the PMT function. In Figure 10-8 it is a prepaid equivalent annuity. Note again that the buy-option is cheaper. In fact, the two approaches give identical answers to the decision choice. The equivalent annuity approach is though simpler and intuitively more appealing. The interpretation of an equivalent annuity as a weighted average, with the discount factors as weights, is a more meaningful concept than the *NPV* covering several repetitions of the same project to a common multiple of periods.

Figure 10-9: NPV-calculations for projects with unequal productive lives

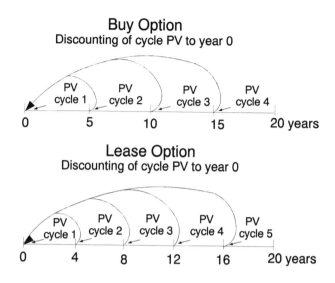

(If you do not have access to a spreadsheet program, the equivalent annuity can be computed using financial tables for **annuity factors**. These are simply multiplied by the NPV for one cycle to yield the equivalent annuity. The PMT function gives the annuity factor for the desired discount rate and number of periods, setting NPV = 1. For EXCEL, setting type=0, the annuity is post-paid, setting type=1 it is prepaid.)

10.8 REPLACEMENT DECISIONS

This section considers an application of discounting concepts to an important optimization problem, namely the optimal time to replace a piece of equipment. The performance of most machines or vehicles deteriorates with age. Aging equipment becomes increasingly prone to breakdowns, repairs become more frequent and more substantial, and the quality and volume of its output decreases. As a result operating and maintenance costs increase, while its potential for profit contributions decreases. Furthermore, its resale or salvage value also decreases, requiring a larger net outlay when it is replaced.   Given these trends, it becomes more cost effective or more profitable to replace it with the latest model, even if the old equipment can still do its intended tasks and meet all capacity requirements adequately. This process is constantly going on — just look at the second-hand car market.

Case Situation Summary of a Replacement Problem

QUIKTRANS is a small regional goods carrier. It currently operates three articulated multi-axle tractor-trailer units. Two are just starting their third year of operation, while one is 3 years old. Carey Bumps, the owner-manager of QUIKTRANS, has just been studying advertising leaflets on the latest model AZ articulated units to become available. He is impressed by the operating cost information provided by the manufacturer. At first glance, these figures look very favourable compared to the operating costs of his oldest unit. Should he upgrade his fleet now or wait another two or three years?

Following the recommendations of the long-haul carrier association, Carey has kept careful records of operating and maintenance costs on his three units. The mileage run by each unit is very similar. Below is a summary of this information on an average per truck basis:

Operating year	1	2	3	approximate timing
Insurance, licence	$8,840	$8,640	$8,440	beginning of year
Maintenance		$11,952	$12,526	$13,048 end of year
Mechanical overhauls	-	-	$3,041	beginning of year
Tyres		$7,962	$8,008	beginning of year
Paint & body work	-	-	$11,951	beginning of year
Repairs	-	$2,044	$2,953	end of year
Variable running cost	$1.62	$1.64	$1.67	per kilometre

The initial purchase cost of the existing units was $255,000. He has some information about the expected costs over the next few years of operations for the various units. In particular, according to his mechanic, each unit will need a new motor every three years. So if the oldest unit is kept on, its motor will have to be replaced right away. This will push up the mechanical overhaul costs for year 4 to $22,000. Similarly, he expects that major body and paint work needs to be done every second year. Naturally, if a unit is sold at the end of a given year, it is put on the market as is without these jobs being done. He has set up a little table, outlining these costs, as well as the variable running costs/km. The latter actually decrease slightly in the year the motor is replaced, but in general accelerate steeply with age.

Predicted costs in	4th	5th	6th	7th	year of operation
variable running cost	$1.64	$1.75	$1.98	$1.85	per kilometre
Repairs	$4,000	$4,000	$8,000	$15,000	
Mechanical overhauls	$22,000	$6,000	$9,000	$28,000	
Paint & body work	-	$15,000	-	$15,000	

The annual pattern for tyre replacement and regular maintenance is expected to continue as during the first three years.

Advertisements in the associations trade journal for second-hand units of a similar type, initial purchase cost of $255,000, and typical annual mileage of between 90,000 and 110,000 km give the following picture:

Age	1	2	3	4	5	6	7	years
Maximum asking price	210	160	118	94	62	29	20	(thousand $)
Minimum asking price	190	140	102	76	38	11	6	(thousand $)

The advertised characteristics for the new model AZ unit list the following variable running costs per kilometre:

Operating year	1	2	3	4	5	6	7
Running cost/km ($)	1.40	1.42	1.45	1.43	1.54	1.73	1.65

First year maintenance costs are predicted at about $10,000. Again replacement of the motor is expected after about 260,000 to 300,000 km. A replacement motor is tentatively priced at $24,000. This is $6,000 more than for the current models. The new unit is priced at $295,000 ready to roll. The insurance premium is expected to be $6,960, declining by $220 each year, while the licence cost remains constant at $2,200, rounded to the nearest $10. Carey's accountant suggests that an appropriate opportunity cost of capital is around 15%.

What should Carey Bumps do?

Approach for Analyzing Replacement Problems

The old equipment should be replaced as soon as the total relevant cost for operating it for another period, say, a year, is higher than the minimum average cost per period for the new equipment. So, the first step in solving a replacement problems is to find the optimal age at which the new equipment should be replaced, if it is acquired, and its corresponding minimum average cost per period.

The second step compares this cost with the total incremental cost incurred for keeping the current equipment for another period. If that cost is lower than the average cost for the new equipment, we retain the old equipment for another period. At the end of that period we again ask the same question: is the incremental cost for operating the old equipment for a further period lower than the minimum average cost for the new equipment? This process repeats itself, until the incremental cost for operating the old equipment for another year becomes larger. At that point, the old equipment is replaced with the new. The only complicating factor is that the various cash flows occur at different points in time. They all have to be converted to a relevant common reference point in time.

Analysis for QUIKTRANS

The manufacturer's advertisement contains estimates of the variable running costs per kilometre, but most other cost information has to be inferred from either the costs incurred or predicted for the current units. It is a fair assumption that many of these costs will be identical or follow a similar pattern. We shall assume that the costs for repairs, tyres, paint and body work, and mechanical overhauls for the new unit are the same as for the current units, except that the motor replacement costs at the beginning of years 4 and 7 are $6,000 higher. We shall assume that, starting from a base of $10,000, the annual maintenance costs increase also by about $500 per year. The resale value of the new unit is assumed to follow the pattern of the current model, but adjusted for the higher initial purchase price. For example, the resale value of a one-year old AZ model truck is set equal to 295/255 times the average of the corresponding maximum and minimum asking price for the old unit, i.e., 0.5($210,000 + $190,000)(295/255), rounded to the nearest $100, or $231,400.

Finding the optimal replacement policy for the new unit boils down to a comparison of several mutually exclusive options, namely replacing the AZ unit after every N years, where $N = 1, 2, 3, ...$. In fact, we shall assume that Carey Bumps will never contemplate keeping a truck for more than 6 years, so $N = 6$ is the highest option. These options all cover different productive lives. Using the equivalent annuity approach, the optimal replacement policy is the one with the lowest equivalent annuity.

Figure 10-10 shows the spreadsheet computations for this analysis. As usual, the top portion of the spreadsheet lists all input data. Each cash flow item is assumed to occur at a given point in time, either at the end (**end/yr**) or at the beginning (**beg/yr**) of a given year. This is indicated under the column 'timing'. In reality, many cash flow items, in particular the variable running costs, are spread throughout each year. However, accounting for this more accurately would complicate matters somewhat. (We would have to go to continuous discounting — a topic not covered in this text.) So I will stick to this simplification, which will only result in small errors. The row for the variable running cost is simply equal to the running cost/km times the annual assumed mileage of 90,000 km.

The beginning and end of year costs are summed separately. These two rows together with the row of resale values form the input into the *NPV* calculations. Each column in these computations refers to one of the 6 replacement options considered. The *NPV* for replacing the truck every N years is obtained as follows:

$NPV(N)$ = (Initial purchase price for new unit) +
$\qquad$ (Cumulative present value of all costs over N years) –
$\qquad$ (Present value of resale value for a unit N years old)

For example, for $N = 2$, the computations are:

$NPV(2)$ = $295,000 +$ $\qquad$ | initial purchase price
$\qquad\qquad$ $127,421 +$ $\qquad$ | *PV* of year 1 costs
$\qquad\qquad$ $16,940(0.869565 +$ $\qquad$ | *PV* of year 2 beg/y cost
$\qquad\qquad$ $140,300(0.869565^2) -$ $\qquad$ | *PV* of year 2 end/y cost
$\qquad\qquad$ $173,500(0.869565^2)$ $\qquad$ | *PV* of resale value end year 2

Figure 10-10: Spreadsheet analysis for optimal replacement period

QUICKTRANS TRUCK REPLACEMENT PROBLEM							
New truck cost	$295,000		Kilometres/year				90000
Discount rate	0.15		Discount factor				0.869565
				Year of operation			
Cost item	timing	1	2	3	4	5	6
Running cost/km		$1.40	$1.42	$1.45	$1.43	$1.54	$1.73
Running cost/yr	end/yr	$126,000	$127,800	$130,500	$128,700	$138,600	$155,700
Maintenance	end/yr	$10,000	$10,500	$11,000	$11,500	$12,000	$12,500
Repairs	end/yr		$2,000	$3,000	$4,000	$8,000	$15,000
Tyres	beg/yr		$8,000	$8,000	$8,000	$8,000	$8,000
Mech. overhauls	beg/yr			$3,000	$28,000	$6,000	$9,000
Paint/body work	beg/yr			$12,000		$15,000	
Annual licence	beg/yr	$2,200	$2,200	$2,200	$2,200	$2,200	$2,200
Insurance	beg/yr	$6,960	$6,740	$6,520	$6,300	$6,080	$5,860
Total cost as of	beg/yr	$9,160	$16,940	$31,720	$44,500	$37,280	$25,060
Total cost as of	end/yr	$136,000	$140,300	$144,500	$144,200	$158,600	$183,200
Resale value	end/yr	$231,400	$173,500	$127,300	$98,300	$57,800	$23,100
Replace after year		1	2	3	4	5	6
PV cumul.costs		$127,421	$248,238	$367,234	$478,941	$579,108	$670,769
PV resale value		$201,217	$131,191	$83,702	$56,203	$28,737	$9,987
NPV of policy		$221,203	$412,047	$578,532	$717,737	$845,371	$955,783
Equiv.Annuity	beg/yr	$221,203	$220,397	$220,334	$218,607	$219,293	$219,611
					BEST		

The cumulative present value of all costs over N years is recursively computed adding the year N present value costs to the N-1 cumulative present value costs. I chose to express the equivalent annuity as occurring at the beginning of each period. For this particular application, this approach seemed to be more natural.

The lowest cost is obtained for $N = 4$. So the optimal policy is to keep the new AZ unit for four years and then replace it by a new one. Naturally, only one decision, namely the first purchase, would ever be implemented based on this analysis. Any subsequent replacement decisions would be based on a new analysis, using the latest up-to-date relevant information about new models and costs.

The somewhat surprising outcome of this analysis is that the equivalent annuity costs for the various options differ by less than $3,000 per year. The cost function is thus fairly flat. The final decision made by Carey may well also reflect other factors not explicitly included in the financial analysis, such as the level of goodwill created by having relatively new trucks and replacing them more frequently than implied by the optimal policy.

The second surprising factor is that the high cost of replacing the motor just one year prior to disposing of the unit does not turn out to be a deterrent for keeping the unit for a fourth year — a counterintuitive result.

When to Replace the Old Units

We are now ready for the second step of the analysis, namely the decision about the timing of replacing the current units. These calculations are shown in the spreadsheet in Figure 10-11. It again lists all inputs in the top portion. This analysis is done for each current unit one period at a time. For example, for the 3-year-old unit, we want to establish whether it is financially more attractive to operate it for a fourth year or replace it straight away. If it is replaced, then the annual cost is equal to $218,607 — the minimum equivalent annuity found in the previous analysis. If the incremental cost of keeping the 3-year-old unit for a fourth year is less than that, then it should be kept, otherwise it should be replaced.

Recall that the equivalent annuities shown in Figure 10-10 are expressed as beginning-of-year annuities, rather than end-of-year annuities. The incremental cost of keeping the old unit should therefore also refer to the beginning of the year. This cost consists of two elements:

> Incremental cost = (Operating cost for another year) +
> (Loss of resale value foregone by not selling now)

Since some of these costs are approximated as occurring at the beginning of the year, while others at the end of the year, all cash flows need to be expressed as of the same point in time, namely the beginning of the year. The operating costs are given by the column labelled year '4' of Figure 10-11. $38,240 of these occur at the beginning of the year, while the balance of $165,100 occur at the end of the year. Discounting the latter by one year and adding the two costs together equals $181,805 — the entry in row 'Total cost/year' and column year '4'.

If the unit were sold right away, it would net $110,000 (the resale value at the end of year 3). Sold one year later at the age of 4 years, it will only bring in $85,000. So the difference in resale value foregone, expressed in dollars as of the beginning of the year, is equal to

> Loss in resale value = (Resale value now) – (PV of resale value 1 period later)

Figure 10-11: (Spreadsheet continued) When to replace current trucks?

QUICKTRANS REPLACEMENT OF CURRENT TRUCKS						
		Year of operation				
Item	timing	2	3	4	5	6
Running cost/km			$1.67	$1.64	$1.75	$1.98
Running cost/year	end/yr		$150,300	$147,600	$157,500	$178,200
Maintenance	end/yr		$13,000	$13,500	$14,000	$14,500
Repairs	end/yr		$3,000	$4,000	$8,000	$15,000
Tyres	beg/yr		$8,000	$8,000	$8,000	$8,000
Mech.overhauls	beg/yr		$3,000	$22,000	$6,000	$9,000
Paint/body work	beg/yr		$12,000		$15,000	
Annual licence	beg/yr		$2,200	$2,200	$2,200	$2,200
Insurance	beg/yr		$6,240	$6,040	$5,840	$5,640
Total cost as of	beg/yr		$31,440	$38,240	$37,040	$24,840
Total cost as of	end/yr		$166,300	$165,100	$179,500	$207,700
Total cost/year	beg/yr		$176,049	$181,805	$193,127	$205,449
Resale value	end/yr	$150,000	$110,000	$85,000	$50,000	$20,000
Incremental cost of running truck one more year	beg/yr		$230,397	$217,892	$234,649	$238,057

or $110,000 - \$85,000(0.869565) = \$36,087.$

The total incremental cost of keeping the 3-year-old unit for a fourth year is
$181,805 + $36,087 = $217,892. This is less than the minimum equivalent annuity.
Hence the 3-year-old truck should be kept for a fourth year.

At the end of its fourth year of operation, this analysis is repeated. Verify that
now the total incremental cost for keeping the (then 4-year-old) unit for a fifth year
is $234,649. This is more than the minimum equivalent annuity. Hence the unit
should be sold at the end of its fourth year of operations.

Although these calculations should normally be done at the appropriate time with
the latest up-to-date cost information, they are all shown in Figure 10-11. Note the
counterintuitive conclusion that the 2-year-old units should be sold right away, while

the 3-year-old unit should be kept running for a fourth year. This result seems to be due to the considerably larger loss in resale value suffered in the third year, given these units are due for a new motor at the beginning of their next year of operations, as well as the higher running costs in year 3 as compared to year 4.

In conclusion, I stress again that this analysis only considers the financial side of things. The decision maker may need to take other factors into account, such as company image, safety, or quality, before reaching a final decision. This may lead to a choice different from the recommended one. However, the decision maker will know exactly the financial effect of this choice.

EXERCISES

All computational exercises should be done with the help of a computer spreadsheet.

1. The local town clerk of a seaside resort is considering two possible options for preventing or alleviating further encroachment of the sea on a newly developed housing estate for vacation houses. The first option is to build a rockwall, reinforced by concrete. It would have an initial cost of $700,000 and would require little maintenance for about 20 years. The property owners would be assessed an annual levy which would bring in $30,000 each year. The second option is to raise the protective sand dunes and plant it with various grasses for stabilization, as well as build several wooden crossings for beach access. This would have an initial cost of $100,000. It would require annual maintenance of $20,000. No levy could be raised in this case. The town can borrow funds from the local banks at 10% per year. Use a planning horizon of 20 years for each option.
   (a) Find the present value of each option. Which one is the preferred option from a purely financial point of view?
   (b) Since the annual levy would be paid by each property owner in two equal instalments and the maintenance costs would be occurred in early Spring and early Fall in roughly equal amounts, the clerk thinks that annual discounting is not accurate enough. He asks you to compute the present value based on half-yearly discounting.
   (c) Find the equivalent annual annuity for each option evaluated under (a).
   (d) Assume now that both options essentially have an infinite lifetime. Find their present value under annual discounting. Which one is the better option now?

2. Consider the following two projects:

Year	0	1	2	3	4	5
Cash flow project A	-1000	-200	400	500	600	300
Cash flow project B	-500	-700	0	800	900	600

   (a) Find the net present value for each for a discount rate of 15%. Which one would you accept, if they are mutually exclusive?
   (b) Find the discount rate for which both projects have the same net present value. Discuss the meaning of this rate.
   (c) Find the internal rate of return for each project. Using the internal rate of return criterion, which one would you accept if the firm wishes to earn at least 15% on its

investments?

3. You consider buying a car that has a cash price of $18,000. The dealer also offers you a monthly payment plan which requires an initial down-payment of $3000 followed by 36 monthly instalments of $525. As it happens, the dealer has offered you $3000 trade-in for your current car. This would just cover the down-payment. You could also take out a loan from your local savings bank. The bank's current interest rate is 15% per year on a declining balance basis. They would also insist that you repay the loan completely within 3 years. The minimum payment each month would be $400, covering both principal and interest. This would give you considerably more freedom in terms of choosing your payment schedule, as long as you repay the loan within three years. Which is the cheaper option?

4. A forest owner has just clearfelled 200 hectares of hillside trees and is evaluating which one of two reafforestation options is the more profitable one. Option A calls for planting at a rate of 1600 seedlings per hectare at a cost of $2000/ha. Thinning is scheduled at age 6 to a density of 800 trees per hectare at a cost of $400/ha. The remaining trees will be pruned at an additional cost of $600/ha. A second pruning is scheduled for age 10 at a cost of $800/ha. All trees will be clearfelled at age 35 at a cost of $3000/ha. Their quality will make them suitable for sawmilling. Hence the estimated revenue is $64,000/ha. Option B calls for planting at a rate of about 1100 seedlings per hectare at a cost of $1500/ha. A thinning is scheduled for age 14 at a cost of $2000/ha. The thinned logs are then suitable for use as roundwood and are estimated to fetch $3,600/ha. All remaining trees will be clearfelled at age 27 for use as pulpwood. The clearfelling cost is $2200/ha. The revenue from the logs is estimated to be $28,000/ha. Note all prices are in terms of current dollars (i.e., either there is assumed to be no inflation, or future dollars have been adjusted to remove inflation effects). Which option is the better one if the forest owner wishes to earn a return of 5% on any investment?

    (a) Build a spreadsheet for finding the present value of all cash flows associated with each option over its productive life. Which spreadsheet functions do you need to use?

    (b) Why can you not determine which option is better on the basis of these two present values? What is the recommended approach for comparing the two options? Do it. Which spreadsheet functions will you use?

5. A firm wants to determine which one of two different machine tools to purchase. The two machines differ in terms of purchase price, annual fixed and variable costs, as well as maximum output capacity. However, the quality of their output is identical. The following data have been prepared:

Model		1	2
Initial purchase price		$30,000	$60,000
Variable operating cost/unit		$1.50	$1.45
Fixed annual operating cost		$18,000	$8,000
Maximum annual output capacity		100,000	120,000 units
Expected resale value end of year 3		7,000	$19,000
Expected sales	year 1	year 2	year 3
amount	60,000	90,000	120,000

Each unit is sold at a price of $2.00. Note that if model 1 is purchased, not all of the demand of year 3 can be met. It is also expected that at the end of year 3, this particular product will become obsolete. It will then be replaced by another product, requiring different machinery. The firm's policy is to accept projects only if they reach a 20% rate of return. Which machine should the firm purchase, if it wants to maximize the net present value of all cash flows?

6. A firm considers buying a new piece of equipment. Its purchase price is $30,000. Its profile for the predicted annual output, predicted operating and maintenance costs, and resale value is as follows:

Year of operation	1	2	3	4	5	6
Annual output	12,000	12,000	11,500	10,800	10,000	9,000
Operating costs	$3,400	$3,600	$3,900	$4,500	$5,400	$6,800
Resale value	$27,000	$24,000	$20,000	$15,000	$9,000	$2,000

Each unit produced brings in a net contribution of $2.50 (= sales price less material and labour costs). The firm works with a rate of return of 20% on its investments.

(a) Assume that all cash flows occur at the end of the year. Develop a spreadsheet for finding the optimal replacement interval. Does it satisfy the firm's criterion of earning at least 20% per year?

(b) For greater accuracy, approximate all continuous cash flows, i.e., the net contribution and the operating costs, by 4 equal amounts spaced at 3-monthly intervals. Adapt your spreadsheet for this change. Does it affect the optimal replacement interval?

7. Management of ABC Printing is considering replacement of its current 4-year-old guillotine. It has seen very heavy use. The production supervisor has looked into various possible options for upgrading the firm's cutting capacity. The two options which look the most promising are:

A   Overhaul the current machine at a cost of $11,000. The machine would then gain at most another 4 - 5 years of productive use before it has to be sold for scrap. The manufacturer of the machine has provided some information on the expected operating cost and resale value of the overhauled machine:

Age of machine	5	6	7	8	9
Operating cost	$6,500	$7,200	$8,500	$10,100	$12,500
Resale value	$22,000	$18,000	$12,000	$6,000	$1,200

B   Buy a new machine which has a current price of $35,000. The manufacturer is willing to take the old machine as a trade-in for $13,000 now. The operating cost and predicted resale value for the new machine are as follows:

Year of operation	1	2	3	4	5
Operating cost	$3,500	$3,600	$4,000	$6,000	$8,000
Resale value	$31,000	$26,000	$20,000	$12,000	$3,000

Naturally, if it is decided to overhaul the current machine, it still can be traded in at the resale values listed under option A for a new machine at a later date. The firm's policy is to require a rate of return of 18% on all new investments.

(a) Determine the optimal replacement interval for the new machine of option (B).

(b) Should the firm overhaul the current machine and only purchase the new machine at a later date, and if so how much longer should the current machine be kept?

8. It is early 1992. Silicone Plastics Ltd is considering the replacement of one of its current injection moulding machines, purchased at the beginning of 1986 for $164,000. The operating log of that machine shows the following picture:

Year	1986	1987	1988	1989	1990	1991
Down-time hours	192	192	192	212	233	260
Reject rate	1%	1%	1%	1%	1.2%	1.6%
Repair costs	0	0	$146	$290	$590	$1180
Overhaul costs	0	0	0	$2867	0	0

Part of the down time includes the weekly cleaning of the machine, which takes about 4 hours. It is expected that a major overhaul will be required every 4 years from the fourth year on, at a cost of around $3000. The production supervisor also thinks that all other operating characteristics of the machine will continue at the same trend as up to now. Whenever possible, the machine is in use, producing at a rate of 78 kg per hour. The firm works one 40-hour shift per week, 48 weeks per year. The output of good parts (exclusive of rejects) required by the machine is 140,000 kg per year. This is expected to continue for the next few years. Overtime is scheduled as needed to meet this target. The amount of raw materials required is equal to the output produced. The current cost of the raw materials is $3640/1000 kg. Three people are needed during the operations: a machine operator and two labourers. The latter are in charge of loading the machine and packing the output produced. The operator is paid at $16/hour, while the labourers get $12/hour. All three are needed for the weekly cleaning of the machine. They also have to be paid during any down-time of the machine due to breakdowns.

The accountant has provided the following breakdown of overheads, all assessed on the direct labour cost: Employee fringe benefits 20%, other factory overheads 28% (building maintenance, building depreciation, general lighting and power, salaried production staff), general company overhead 52% (general administrative staff salaries, building maintenance and depreciation, salaries for research and development and marketing, insurance, interest on loan capital). The firm's current average return on capital is 18%. In the past, new investment projects have usually been accepted if their rate of return exceeded this target.

The latest version of this type of machine has an initial cost of $246,000. According to the manufacturer, its reliability should be substantially better than that of older models. In particular, the reject rate should only be about 80% of the current model. Similarly, down-time other than regular weekly cleaning should also be about 50% less. The machine should be overhauled regularly every 3 years at a cost of about $4000. No information on other repair costs is available, except that most spare parts seem to be about 30% less expensive for the new machine. Information obtained from a second-hand machine dealer indicates the following pattern of prices, as a function of the age of the machine which has had regular overhauls (in $1000):

Age	1	2	3	4	5	6	7	8
Resale value	$144	$132	$122	$112	$88	$64	$40	$14

(a) Construct a spreadsheet to determine the optimal replacement period for the new machine and find the optimal replacement period. This spreadsheet should show sufficient details of how all costs are computed and manipulated.

(b) Add a section to the spreadsheet for determining when the current machine should be replaced. It is now the beginning of 1992. At the beginning of what year should the current machine be replaced?

9. KIWI WINES (KW) produces top class wines. In contrast to most other wines produced in N.Z., some of KW's wines are best aged for several years to bring out their full flavour and rich bouquet. Sue Keller, KW's owner-manager, wonders whether the firm should do the aging of its wines itself or let its customers take responsibility for that aspect. In the past most wines were sold within one year of harvesting the grapes. This is about 3-4 months after bottling. Such wine is referred to as 'new wine'. However, Sue realizes that a substantial portion of those wines are drunk without being properly aged by the customers. The argument for having KW age its wines is really that the reputation of KW's wines will be considerably enhanced by making sure that the wines are properly aged. This can only be guaranteed if KW does the aging itself. However, this would mean that KW would have to build an addition to its bottle warehouse - a fairly expensive proposition, since the warehouse has to be air-conditioned to provide the right storing environment. The cost of building the warehouse extension is estimated at $300,000. It would be able to hold up to 360,000 bottles.

The cost of producing unaged wine is roughly proportional to the volume produced, since most of the costs incurred are the value of the grapes used and the labour of picking and processing the grapes. Although all grapes are produced on KW's own vineyards, Sue is of the opinion that any grapes used for wine making by KW itself should be valued at the going wine grape market price, although she is not sure whether this argument is in fact correct, since no money changes hands. Sue figures that once the wine has been bottled, the remaining cost of aging the wine consists mainly of the interest paid to the bank for the funds invested in the wine, the cost of maintaining the warehouse and running the air-conditioning installation. The current new wine bottle warehouse is owned by KW. There is no mortgage outstanding on it. The addition to the warehouse would need to be financed by a mortgage loan. Hence, Sue thinks that the warehousing cost would now also need to include the repayment of the loan and the interest incurred on it. Naturally, as the wine ages, its selling price goes up consider-ably. So at least some, possibly even all, additional costs might be recovered from the increased revenue generated through aging. However, the best age to offer wine for sale is not necessarily the age when its flavour and bouquet are judged to be at their peak - 4 to 5 years for the wine considered below. So before a decision can be made on whether the warehouse should be built, the question of the best age to sell the wines would also need to be settled.

Sue also realizes that the amount of grapes available each year allows the production of more wine than can be stored in the warehouse addition, except possibly for a one-year aging interval. (Note that since wine making is an annual operation, if the wine is stored for 2 years, only 180,000 bottles of wine can be added to storage each year, given the warehouse capacity of 360,000 bottles. Similarly, storage for 3 years reduces the quantity that can be added to storage to 120,000, and so on.) Naturally the whole harvest would be processed. But the plan is to store as many bottles as either the harvest or the warehouse capacity permits. Any excess bottles that cannot be stored would be sold as fresh wine. Bottles stored for aging are kept on racks. Proper aging requires that they are turned several times per year. Just prior to selling, all wine, fresh or aged, is put into cartons of 12 bottles.

In the past, Sue has not accepted any new project that did not have a rate of return before taxes of 18% per year. The following additional data have been collected:

Warehouse addition:
    Total construction cost: $300,000
    Completion date: 3 months after start
    Financed by a 10-year mortgage of $250,000 at an annual interest rate of 12%
    Annual repayment on principal: $25,000
    Additional storage capacity: 360,000 bottles
    Expected useful life: 20 years
    Air-conditioning running cost: $32,000/year (independent of amount stored)
    Fixed maintenance cost: $10,000/year
    Building insurance: $1,600/year

Wine operation:
    Current market price for grapes: $1800/tonne
    Average size of harvest available: 240 tonnes
    Each tonne produces 920 litres of wine
    Picking cost for grapes: $250/tonne
    Cost of processing grapes, incl. fermentation and initial storage in glass tanks:
        $850/tonne
    Bottling cost, incl. bottle & label: $0.36/bottle
    Each bottle contains 0.7 litre
    Aging cost per year: $0.21/bottle
    Cost of packing, incl. case: $1.18/12 bottles

Wine wholesale selling price:

year sold	Fresh 1	2	3	4	5	6
price/case ($)	72	86	110	136	148	156	160

(a) Determine how long the wine should be aged to maximize the annual contribution to profits. Note that part of the assignment is to identify which costs are relevant and which ones should be ignored as neither affecting the optimal time to age the wines nor whether the warehouse addition should be built. So you need to scrutinize carefully all costs listed to determine whether they are relevant or not. (Hints: You need to determine the total revenue and total relevant cost associated with the grapes harvested each year. Each total consists of cash flows occurring during the year of the harvest and cash flows occurring during the aging interval or at the end of the aging interval.)

(b) In view of the answer about the best age to sell wine, should the warehouse be built or not? Note that the optimal solution from (a) above would be implemented as follows: Say, the optimal age to sell the wines is 2 years (not necessarily the correct answer!). Then 180,000 bottles of the wine pressed from the zero-year harvest would be put into storage at the beginning of the first year, and 180,000 bottles from the first-year harvest would be added at the beginning of the second year to fill the warehouse. From then on, at the beginning of each year 180,000 of aged wine would be removed for sale and replaced with the same quantity of fresh wine for aging. At the end of the productive life of the warehouse addition, the aging process stops. However, simply assume that even the wine added at the beginning of year

20 still is aged for its optimal interval. This obviously slightly overestimates the return obtained, because some end of planning horizon costs are ignored. However, these cash flows, occurring at the end of the productive life of the warehouse, are discounted to the present. Hence, their effect will be negligible. Therefore, simply ignore this complication.

10. Discounting is pretty much the norm for commercial decisions. It is also extensively used for many public projects that have mainly pecuniary effects or effects that lend themselves to be easily expressed in monetary terms, such as flood control projects and similar public works. However, for projects that involve environmental, health, or social aspects there is considerable debate whether discounting is appropriate for evaluating their merit. Examples of this sort are: pre-school education, vaccination and other health promoting programmes, projects that involve prevention of loss of life, road-safety campaigns, conservation and environmental projects, recreational facilities for which charging may be difficult or discriminatory, etc. What are the pros and cons of using discounting in such instances? What alternative criteria may be more suitable for evaluating their merit(s)? It may be interesting to do a limited literature search on this issue. The book by Mishan may be a good starting point.

REFERENCES

Most texts on Finance, Financial Management, Corporate Finance, Financial Theory, Capital Budgeting, or Engineering Economics will contain one or several chapters related to the material of this chapter, under headings, such as Net Present Values, Discounted Cash Flows, or Capital Budgeting. Here is a list of some of the better known ones:

Bierman, Harold, and Smidt, S., *The Capital Budgeting Decision*, Macmillan Publishing Co., 1988. A text with new editions every few years since the mid-sixties. It has an elementary but comprehensive treatment of all aspects of evaluation of projects. Part 1 covers in more detail the material of this chapter. Part 4 looks at decision problems, involving discounted cash flows, such as buy or lease, replacement, and capital rationing decisions.

Brigham, E.F., and Gapenski, L.C., *Financial Management*, 6th ed., The Dryden Press, 1991. Chapter 6 discusses discounted cash flows, Chapter 9 the basics of capital budgeting, both at a fairly elementary level.

Copeland, R.E., and Weston, J.F., *Financial Theory and Corporate Policy*, 3rd ed., Addison-Wesley, 1988. Chapters 2 and 3 look at discounted cash flows and capital budgeting. Somewhat more advanced than Brigham and Gapenski.

Ross, S.A., Westerfied, J.F., , and Jaffe, J.F., *Fundamentals of Corporate Finance*, Irwin, 1991. Introduction to these topics at undergraduate level (Chapters 7 - 9). See also *Corporate Finance*, 3rd ed., Irwin, 1993. MBA level treatment of same topics (Chapters 4, 6, and 7).

11 Marginal and Incremental Analysis

Marginal analysis is one of the most fundamental tools in economics. It forms the theoretical basis for deriving normative rules for a firm's optimal allocation of scarce resources to the production of goods and services, for the optimal output levels, as well as for product and service pricing decisions.

OR/MS problems often deal with decisions about resource allocation for the production of goods and services. Furthermore, a number of OR/MS tools, both simple ones and highly sophisticated ones, have borrowed the mode of thinking underlying marginal analysis. In fact, you already have encountered this type of reasoning in the truck replacement problem of Chapter 10. It is thus essential that you have a clear understanding of the principles of marginal analysis and its extension to incremental analysis.

Sections 11.2 and 11.3 review the typical forms of total costs, total revenues, and total profits as functions of the level of activity or output of a firm. This will lead us in Section 11.4 to a short detour into break-even analysis — a useful tool when these functions are all linear in the level of output. Section 11.5 studies the relationships between marginal costs and revenues and total profits, and derives the basic principle of marginal analysis, which are then demonstrated in Section 11.6. The discussion in Sections 11.2 to 11.6 will, with one exception, be in terms of variables that only assume integer values. Hence, the marginal output is always equal to the incremental output for a unit increase in the input. This will allow us to demonstrate the concepts with simple numerical examples.

Sections 11.7 and 11.8 generalize these concepts to the case of continuous variables. The starred Section 11.7 is somewhat more demanding and assumes a rudimentary understanding of differential calculus.

Sections 11.9 to 11.11 look at incremental analysis. Its usefulness is demonstrated with a transport problem for a leading U.S. manufacturer of ketchup. Chapter 12 extends these concepts to the optimal allocation of scarce resources.

11.1 MARGINAL ANALYSIS VERSUS INCREMENTAL ANALYSIS

The term 'marginal' has a number of meanings. In everyday language, it is usually used to denote being 'just barely acceptable'. In economics, it relates to infinitesimally small changes occurring at the margin — a rather different meaning. For example, a wheat farmer applies 100 kg of fertilizer per hectare of land. This results in an output of 2000 kg of wheat per hectare. If the farmer increases the amount of fertilizer applied per hectare by a very small amount, say 0.5 kg, the wheat output goes up by 4 kg per hectare. This increase in output is called the marginal output. It relates to the change in output associated with a small change in the use of fertilizer from the current level or, in other words, at the margin. It is usually expressed in terms of a unit change in the factor that causes the output to change. For our example, the marginal output of wheat is 8 kg for 1 kg of fertilizer applied beyond the current level of 100 kg per hectare. Viewed in this way, the marginal output is the rate of change in the output of wheat at a level of 100 kg of fertilizer use per hectare. However, that rate may only be valid for a small increase in fertilizer use. Increasing the use of fertilizers by another 0.5 kg may only result in an additional 3.9 kg of wheat. The marginal output has already dropped to 7.8 kg at 100.5 kg of fertilizer use.

These are two important things to keep firmly in mind when using the concept of 'marginal output'. Firstly, it is related to a rate of change, usually expressed in terms of a unit change in some input. Secondly, it is the rate of change at a given level of this input and may only be valid for a very small change in that input.

'Incremental' on the other hand relates to the actual numeric change in an output associated with a given increase of an input from its current level. In the above example, an increase in fertilizer use from 100 kg to 110 kg per hectare will increase the wheat output from 2000 kg to 2050 kg. The incremental output for increasing the use of fertilizers from 100 to 110 kg is therefore 50 kg.

In this example, the inputs and outputs are continuous variables that can assume any real value, integer or fractional. If the input can only assume integer values, such as the number of tellers used by a bank during a given time period, or the number of cars owned by a car rental company, the marginal output is equal to the incremental change in output for an additional unit of input. However, if the input is a continuous variable then marginal output and the incremental output for a unit increase in the input will in many cases be different.

Figure 11-1 depicts the relationship between the marginal output and the incremental output for the wheat production example. The incremental output is measured by the actual achieved increase in output in response to an increase in input from a given level, e.g., 50 kg for a 10 kg fertilizer increase from 100 to 110 kg. The marginal output, on the other hand, is given by the slope of the total output curve at a given level of input. This slope is given by the tangent to the curve. For instance, at an input of 100 kg of fertilizer, the slope of the output curve is 8 kg.

11.2 TOTAL COSTS, MARGINAL AND AVERAGE COSTS

POLYCOMPOUND, INC., or PC for short, produces silicone rubber for specific customer orders. Silicone rubber production is a two step process. In step 1, the various ingredients, mostly PVC resins, plasticiser, fillers, stabilisers, pigments, and various other additives, are mixed in a specified sequence in individual subbatches of 80 kg in a mixer. During mixing the blend is heated to temperatures of up to 140° C. The mixed blend is cooled and dumped into the hopper of a compounding

Figure 11-1: Marginal and incremental outputs

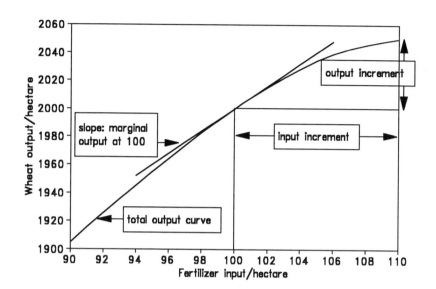

extruder forming PVC granules. These granules are aircooled and then packed into 40 kg bags, shrink wrapped and labelled for delivery to the customer. Customer orders are always in integer multiples of subbatches.

All operations need constant supervision and hence are labour intensive. Processing of the first two subbatches takes much longer than later subbatches, since numerous tests have to be performed to have the mixing and extruding operations properly adjusted. This reflects itself in higher labour costs for the first few subbatches. Up to 8 subbatches can be processed in a regular 8-hour shift. Once a run has been started, it has to be completed, even if this has to be done on overtime. If the extrusion section is stopped for more than 10 minutes, it requires a complete clean-down that results in a down-time of 3 hours — the same as for a new setup.

The setup cost covers the cost of preparing a new run and the cleaning of both the mixer and the extrusion section after completion of a run. This avoids contamination between runs and prevents any residues left in the machines to harden. The latter would require expensive scraping off and possible damage to the machines. Overtime requires the presence of two operators and a supervisor. This explains the rather large increase in labour cost from the ninth batch on. Table 11-1 lists the machine setup, material, and labour costs incurred for a production run requiring up to 12 mixing subbatches for silicone rubber PC312-X.

As expected, the machine setup cost per run remains fixed, regardless of the number of subbatches needed. The material cost increases linearly at a rate of $10 per subbatch. Labour costs decrease from $72 for the first subbatch to a low $12 for the

Table 11-1: Production costs per run

Number of subbatches	Setup cost per run	Material cost	Labour cost	Total cost per run
1	$80	$ 10	$ 72	$162
2	$80	$ 20	$108	$208
3	$80	$ 30	$132	$242
4	$80	$ 40	$144	$264
5	$80	$ 50	$156	$286
6	$80	$ 60	$168	$308
7	$80	$ 70	$180	$330
8	$80	$ 80	$192	$352
9	$80	$ 90	$228	$398
10	$80	$100	$264	$444
11	$80	$110	$300	$490
12	$80	$120	$336	$536

fourth subbatch. Subbatches produced on overtime incur a labour cost of $36.

Figure 11-2 shows the graph of the total costs as a function of the run size. Although costs are only defined for multiples of full subbatches, for greater generality the total cost is depicted as a continuous curve. Starting from the fixed cost of $80, the total cost curve initially increases less than proportionately, then rises at a constant rate of $22 per batch. At a run size of 8 batches, the total cost curve has a kink, increasing at a rate of $46 from then on.

This general shape of the total cost function is fairly typical. Initially, total costs tend to increase less than proportionately due to such aspects as the learning effect — workers becoming more proficient in their tasks — and other economies of scale. Then for operating levels in the normal range of operations, costs rise proportionately with the increase in the level of activity or output. Finally, as the firm starts stretching its capacity levels to the limit, costs begin to increase more than proportionately. The result is a total cost curve in the shape of a stretched-out S.

Marginal Costs

The marginal cost of an activity measures the rate of change in the total cost at a given activity level. As pointed out in Section 11.1, for an activity that assumes integer values only, the **marginal cost** $MC(Q)$ at the level of output Q is equal to the incremental cost, i.e., the difference in total cost for a unit increase in the level of activity, say from $Q-1$ to Q:

$$MC(Q) = T(Q) - T(Q-1) \qquad (11\text{-}1)$$

For our example, a unit of output corresponds to a subbatch. The marginal cost of, say, the second unit (the second subbatch) is $MC(Q{=}2) = T(Q{=}2) - T(Q{=}1) = \$208 - \$162 = \$46$. Verify that for the fourth to the eighth units, the marginal cost is $22, and then increases to $46 from there on. The marginal cost of the first unit includes the fixed setup cost. In terms of Figure 11-2, the marginal cost for Qth unit is equal to the slope of the total cost curve $TC(Q)$ between run size $Q-1$ and Q.

Figure 11-2: The graph of total costs versus run size

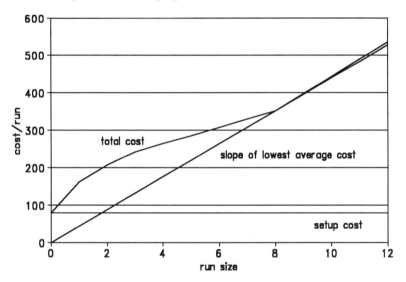

Observe the shape of the rather typical cost curve depicted in Figure 11-2. Recall that the marginal cost is represented by the slope of the total cost curve. As the level of activity increases, the marginal cost first decreases (the slope of the total cost curve becomes less steep), then becomes constant (the slope remains the same), and finally starts to increase again (the slope becomes steeper). These three phases are also referred to as **increasing returns to scale**, **constant returns to scale**, and **decreasing returns to scale**. Obviously, most firms prefer to operate in the range of increasing or constant returns to scale.

In the short run, where only a limited number of input factors can be increased, while others have to remain constant, practically all production and service oper-ations will ultimately exhibit increasing marginal costs for a variety of reasons — the additional output requires overtime, the factory floor becomes more congested, increasing delays and errors, etc. Increasing marginal cost is also seen in marketing. As the advertising budget increases, the gain in additional sales generated will sooner or later fall off. These are all examples of the almost universal **law of diminishing marginal returns**, i.e., as the input of one variable production factor is increased, while all other production factors remain fixed in the short run, the resulting increase in the total output will, after some point, become progressively smaller.

The same result may not hold in the long run. In theory at least, it should be possible to simply duplicate existing operations and run all at their optimum levels of activity. Similarly, it is usually true that, by introducing more sophisticated capital goods, it may even be possible to adopt production processes that have both lower fixed and variable costs than those obtainable through duplication. This may allow the firm to achieve the same or a higher level of activity at lower marginal costs. However, as the scale of operations increases, even more and more sophisticated equipment will ultimately follow the law of decreasing marginal returns. In the long run, we should also expect that further technological developments will from time to time reduce marginal costs at most levels of output.

Average Costs

The **average cost** $AC(Q)$ at the level of activity Q is defined as the ratio of total costs to output: $TC(Q)/Q$. This corresponds to the slope of the straight line from the origin to a given point on the $T(Q)$-curve. This is demonstrated in Figure 11-2 for $Q = 8$. The slope of the straight line from the origin to $T(Q=8) = 352$ is equal to 44, i.e., 352/8.

Table 11-2 lists the marginal, total, and average costs for the PC case. (Ignore for the time being the last three columns of the table.) Observe what happens to the average cost as output or run size increases. Initially the average cost decreases. This must be so as long as the marginal cost of the next unit added is less than the average cost up to then. For instance, the average cost for a run of two units equals

Table 11-2: Marginal, total, and average costs and revenues

1 Run size Q	2 Marginal cost $MC(Q)$	3 Total cost $TC(Q)$	4 Average cost $AC(Q)$	5 Marginal revenue $MR(Q)$	6 Total revenue $TR(Q)$	7 Total profit $TP(Q)$
1	$162	$162	$162	$80	$80	-$82
2	$46	$208	$104	$80	$160	-$48
3	$34	$242	$80.67	$80	$240	-$2
4	$22	$264	$66	$80	$320	+$56
5	$22	$286	$57.20	$80	$400	+$114
6	$22	$308	$51.33	$80 .	$480	+$172
7	$22	$330	$47.14	$40	$520	+$190
8	$22	$352	$44	$40	$560	+$208
9	$46	$398	$44.22	$40	$600	+$202
10	$46	$444	$44.40	$40	$640	+$196
11	$46	$490	$44.56	$40	$680	+$190
12	$46	$536	$44.67	$40	$720	+$184

$208/2 = 104. The marginal cost for the 3rd unit is $34. So the average cost decreases to $(208 + 34)/3 = 80.67. In this example, average costs continue to decrease up to the eighth unit, when they reach $44. The marginal cost of the ninth unit is $46. This is more than the average cost for 8 units. As a result, the average cost for 9 units now increases to $44.22.

Relationships between Marginal and Average Costs

From these observations we can deduce some general principles. First, as long as the marginal cost for another unit of output is less than the average cost up to the previous output level, the average cost continues to decrease as the output increases. This is in part due to the fact that the initial fixed setup cost can be spread over a larger volume. Second, as soon as the marginal cost becomes larger than the average cost, the latter starts to increase. Third, as a consequence, the lowest average cost is achieved just prior to the level of output where the marginal cost becomes larger than the average cost, or for a level of output Q^* where the following relationship holds:

$$MC(Q^*) \leq AC(Q^*) < MC(Q^*+1) \qquad (11\text{-}2)$$

It is instructive to study the graphical representation of these principles in Figure 11-2. Recall that the slope of $TC(Q)$ between two adjacent output levels $Q-1$ and Q is equal to the marginal cost of the Qth unit. For instance, the slope from $TC(Q=7)$ to $TC(Q=8)$ is $352 - 330 = 22$, the marginal cost of the eighth subbatch.

Similarly, the slope of the straight line from the origin to $TC(Q)$ represents the average cost for an output level Q. For output levels of 8 or less, the slope representing the marginal cost is everywhere less steep than the slope representing the average cost (except that both are the same for the first unit). From the ninth unit on, the relationship between these two slopes reverses. The slope representing marginal costs is now everywhere steeper than the slope representing average costs. The smallest (or the least steep) slope for the average cost is achieved when this reversal occurs.

The above explanations are all couched in terms of individual customer orders for a product made to order only. However, the concepts developed have a more general validity. They can be extended to the analysis of the level of a given activity of a firm during a specified time interval of, e.g., one year. Any positive level of output results in annual fixed costs in the amount of F dollars. This covers all those fixed costs (administrative infrastructure and fixed production costs) directly incurred by that activity — cost which falls away if that activity ceases. It does not include other overheads shared with other activities! As the annual level of activity increases, the marginal cost first tends to decrease, then becomes constant over the normal range of operations for that activity, and finally starts to increase beyond that range. The average cost will then be lowest at the level of activity where marginal cost is just equal to or larger than average cost.

11.3 TOTAL REVENUE AND MARGINAL REVENUE

PC is one of the smaller manufacturers for silicone rubber. It tends to follow the prices charged by the bigger manufacturers, competing on quality rather than price. Hence, the price charged for orders of up to 8 subbatches is $80 per subbatch of 80 kilogram. The price drops to $40 per subbatch for any amount in excess of 8 subbatches. This results in the total revenue pattern listed in the sixth column of Table 11-2. It is denoted as $TR(Q)$.

The rate of change of the total revenue at the level of activity Q is called the marginal revenue, denoted by $MR(Q)$. For a discrete variable, the marginal revenue for the Qth subbatch of an order is equal to the difference between the total revenue for an order of size Q and $Q-1$, i.e., $TR(Q) - TR(Q\text{-}1)$. Column 5 in Table 11-2 lists the marginal revenue for the PC example.

These concepts can again be extended to the behaviour of revenues for a product produced on a sustained basis over a specified time period, say one year. Furthermore, in many instances, the unit price a firm charges for its products is constant, regardless of its output level. This is particularly so for standard type products, such as most food staples, but also many manufactured goods. Such products are typically sold by several firms in competition with each other. Each firm taken alone may be too small to affect the market in any significant way. The total revenue over one year is then simply equal to the quantity sold Q during the year times the unit price P, or $TR(Q) = PQ$. The marginal revenue is constant at P.

On the other hand, if one firm dominates the market for a particular product, it may have to reduce the unit price charged for its entire output, and not just for the additional output, if it wants to sell more in any given time period. In this case marginal revenue for selling an additional unit is given by the difference between the additional revenue obtained from that unit and the loss in revenue suffered on the previous output due to the reduction in price. Hence, the marginal revenue tends to decrease by more than simply the reduction in price as the output level increases.

11.4 BREAK-EVEN ANALYSIS

Figure 11-3 superimposes the graphs for total revenue $TR(Q)$ and total cost $TC(Q)$ for the PC example, as listed in columns 3 and 6 of Table 11-2. The difference $TR(Q) - TC(Q)$ between the two curves corresponds to the total profit $TP(Q)$ for an order of size Q — the numbers listed in column 7 of Table 11-2.

Observe what happens as the run size increases. For run sizes of three or fewer subbatches the total cost exceeds the total revenue. The firm is in a loss position. As the run size increases to 3, the size of the loss decreases. At a run size of 4 the firm starts making a profit on the order. Whenever possible, the firm would attempt to convince its customers to order at least 4 subbatches or 320 kg. If the firm could refuse to accept any orders of less than this amount without affecting its long-run sales prospects, it should do so. Alternatively, it could give customers a price incen-

Figure 11-3: Total cost and total revenue curves

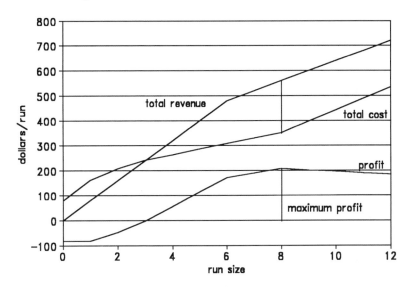

tive to order at least this amount by charging an even higher price for orders of 3 subbatches or less, if market conditions allowed such a pricing policy. For instance, a price structure of $104 for the first two subbatches, decreasing to $56 for the next two and $40 from subbatch 5 on would leave the total price for medium to large customer orders unchanged, only penalizing the very small orders. A loss would then only be incurred for orders of size 1.

The level of activity, Q_0, at which total revenue exactly recovers all fixed and variable costs incurred is called the **break-even point**. At the break-even point the total profit is zero. The firm would want to operate at a level of activity beyond the break-even point. If the level of activity is a continuous variable, then there exists an exact break-even point. In the PC example where the output is discrete, there is no run size where the profit on the customer order is exactly equal to zero. So the run size of 4 subbatches at which the profit becomes positive is then the equivalent of the break-even point. For the alternative price structure, the break-even point would drop to 2 subbatches exactly.

If both the total cost and the total revenue are linear functions of the level of activity, the break-even point can easily be determined mathematically. For linear functions, the total cost is given by

$$TC(Q) = F + VQ \qquad (11\text{-}3)$$

where F is the fixed cost, independent of the level of activity, and V is the variable unit production cost. The total revenue function is given by

$$TR(Q) = PQ \qquad (11\text{-}4)$$

At the break-even point, the total cost is equal to the total revenue:

$$PQ = F + V \qquad (11\text{-}5)$$

Solving expression (11-5) for Q we get:

$$\text{Break-even point} = Q_0 = F / (P - V) \qquad (11\text{-}6)$$

This derivation assumes that the level of activity Q can be varied continuously. If the output is in discrete units, then there may be no value of Q for which total revenue is exactly equal to total cost. This is the case in the PC example. In such instances, the break-even point Q_0 is the first value just larger than the ratio $F/(P-V)$ in expression (11-6).

Obviously, expression (11-6) only makes sense if the unit revenue exceeds the unit variable cost, otherwise that product should not be produced at all.

There is another way of looking at break-even analysis. The denominator of expression (11-5), $(P-V)$, is the difference between the unit revenue and the unit variable cost. This difference is the **contribution** each unit (sold) makes towards covering of fixed costs and profits. The larger the contribution that each unit makes towards the recovery of fixed costs, the lower will be the break-even point.

An Example: Quiktrans

Remember QUIKTRANS from Section 10.8? Carey Bumps would like to know what the break-even point is for the new AZ truck if he sells the 3-year old unit at the end of its fourth year of operation. In the first year, the fixed costs for the new AZ unit consist of the annual license and insurance cost of $9,160, interest cost of 12% on the net investment $210,000 (i.e., cost of AZ truck less resale value of a 4-year old truck of $85,000) equal to $25,200, and that portion of the depreciation of the truck that is attributable to age, rather than mileage, which he estimates as 60% of the loss of $63,600 in resale value (i.e., $295,000 – $231,400) in the first year, or $38,160. These sum up to $75,520.

The output of the truck consists of volume-kilometres carried. If we assume an average load for each trip, the output can be measured in terms of kilometres travelled only. So the variable cost refers to the cost of the truck travelling for one kilometre (with an average load). This consists of the 'running cost' of $1.40, as specified by the manufacturer, the maintenance and tyre costs, and the mileage dependent depreciation. Using the estimates listed in Figure 10-10, and based on an annual mileage of 90,000 km, the latter two amount to $0.156/km for maintenance and mileage (i.e., $10,000 for maintenance plus half of $8000 for tyres divided by 90,000), and $0.283/km for depreciation (i.e., 40% of $63,600 divided by 90,000). All three costs together add up to $1.839/km. It is reasonable to assume that this variable cost remains constant over a fairly large mileage range. Hence, the total cost function is linear over this range.

Carey's accountant tells him that the revenue per kilometre for an average load amounts to $2.78. Again, this unit revenue can safely be assumed to remain constant over a wide mileage range, resulting in a linear revenue function.

From the assumptions about linearity of both costs and revenues, the contribution per 'unit output' towards fixed costs and profits is also constant and equal to $2.78 minus $1.839, or $1.171/km. Note also that number of kilometres travelled is a continuous variable. Hence, expression (11-6) can be used:

$$\text{Break-even point} = \$75,520 \Big/ (\$3.01 - 1.839) = 64,492 \text{ km}$$

This break-even point would change with the age of the truck as additional fixed costs are incurred and as the variable cost increases with the age and mileage.

Expression (11-6) was derived on the assumption that both the total revenue and total cost functions are linear. This assumption made the mathematics simple, but is also the Achilles' heel of break-even analysis. Although the total revenue is quite often proportional to sales, total costs are frequently nonlinear. Expression (11-6) can then not be used anymore. This is the case for the PC example, where both the marginal cost and the marginal revenue vary with the run size and hence the total cost and total revenue are not linear. The computations to find the break-even point usually have to be done by search and enumeration. However, the break-even point still remains a useful concept for the decision maker.

11.5 BASIC PRINCIPLE OF MARGINAL ANALYSIS

In a marginal analysis framework, a decision as to the best level of an activity is based on the comparison of the change in both revenues and costs resulting from a small change in the level of activity. Such a change in activity is desirable if the difference between total revenues and total costs, or in other words the total profit increases. The decision maker should continue making such small changes in the level of activity until no further increase in profit can be achieved. At that point, total profit is maximized.

An Algorithm for Marginal Analysis

We now have to convert this principle into a practical approach for finding the optimal level of activity — an algorithm. We start out with a relatively small level of activity Q. The break-even point provides a good start. Next, we increase the level of activity by a small amount, say one unit. So the level of activity increases to $Q+1$. This yields an increase in revenue, while simultaneously increasing costs. The increase in revenue is equal to the marginal revenue at the level $Q+1$, i.e., $MR(Q+1)$. The increase in cost is equal to the marginal cost at that level, i.e.,

$MC(Q+1)$. If $MR(Q+1)$ is larger than $MC(Q+1)$, then the increase in the level of activity from Q to $Q+1$ increases total profit. We continue this process of increasing the level of activity by 1 as long as the marginal revenue is larger than the marginal cost. We stop when the reverse becomes true, i.e., when for a further increase in the level of activity the marginal cost would be larger than marginal revenue. This would cause the total profit to decrease. At that point we have found the optimal level of activity, maximizing the total profit. In summary, the algorithm of marginal analysis uses the following principle: At the optimal level of activity Q^*

$$MR(Q^*) \geq MC(Q^*) \quad \text{and} \quad MR(Q^*+1) < MC(Q^*+1) \qquad (11\text{-}7)$$

You could visualize this process of successive small changes in the level of activity as resembling the strategy adopted by a myopic mountain climber (or climber trying to scale a mountain in fog conditions) who does not know where or how far away the top of the mountain is. However, the climber is confident that, as long as each step goes uphill, the top will be reached sooner or later. (What assumption is made about the shape or form of that mountain for this process to work?) By analogy to the firm, the height of the mountain is measured in dollars of profits, and the gain in height at each step is the additional profit achieved. As long as further steps go uphill, the direction taken by the myopic climber is profitable. Once the top has been reached, steps in any direction go either on the flat or downhill again, i.e., no further gains in profit can be made.

11.6 SOME APPLICATIONS OF MARGINAL ANALYSIS

Marginal Analysis for the PC Example

Table 11-3 lists again the total revenue $TR(Q)$, the total costs $TC(Q)$, and the total profit $TP(Q)$ for the PC example as a function of the run size. The total profit is computed as $TR(Q) - TC(Q)$. The last three columns show the marginal revenue $MR(Q)$, the marginal cost $MC(Q)$, and the marginal profit $MP(Q) = MR(Q) - MC(Q)$. We wish to find the run size that maximizes the total profit for an individual customer order.

We start this process with the break-even point of 4. For the fifth unit, the marginal revenue is $80, while the marginal cost is only $22 — a net increase in profit of $58. The same pattern repeats itself for unit 6. For units 7 and 8, the marginal revenue drops to $40, while the marginal cost remains at $22 — still profitable. So we continue. For unit 9, the marginal cost increases to $46, or $6 more than the marginal revenue. We now encounter conditions (11-7) for the first time. For a run size of 8 the first part of condition (11-7) is satisfied, while a run size of 9 satisfies the second part. Hence, we stop at a run size of 8 with a maximum profit of $208. Verify that increasing the run size to 9 decreases the total profit.

In many cases, the optimal decision can more easily be found by evaluating the

Table 11-3: Marginal analysis for the PC example

Run size	Total revenue	Total cost	Total profit	Marginal revenue	Marginal cost	Marginal profit
1	$80	$162	−$82	$80	$162	-$82
2	$160	$208	−$48	$80	$46	+$34
3	$240	$242	−$2	$80	$34	+$46
4	$320	$264	$56	$80	$22	+$58
5	$400	$286	$114	$80	$22	+$58
6	$480	$308	$172	$80	$22	+$58
7	$520	$330	$190	$40	$22	+$18
8	$560	$352	$208	$40	$22	+$18
9	$600	$398	$202	$40	$46	-$6
10	$640	$444	$196	$40	$46	-$6
11	$680	$490	$190	$40	$46	-$6
12	$720	$536	$184	$40	$46	-$6

profit function. This is clearly the case here. However, there are many other cases where a marginal analysis offers useful additional insights which remain hidden when looking at profits alone.

What can PC do with this information? The order sizes are controlled by the customers. PC can only exert an indirect influence by steering customers to an order size of 8 subbatches, whenever possible. Marginal analysis on the other hand tells us two things. First, the drop in marginal revenue for an order of size 7 has a serious effect on marginal profits. So, the firm may consider altering its pricing structure to give customers some incentive for placing orders of size 8, e.g., by giving a small discount of 2 - 3 percent for orders of that size alone. Secondly, the increase in the marginal cost of production when an order has to be completed in overtime completely erodes any marginal profit. The firm could attempt to change the marginal cost pattern for larger orders, such as investigating ways to eliminate the need for a supervisor to be on site for runs in excess of 8 subbatches, reducing labour costs.

Is marginal analysis of any help if the total cost and total revenue functions are linear? For the usual case where the unit revenue exceeds the unit variable cost, marginal revenues will always be larger than marginal costs. Hence, the optimal level of activity is theoretically infinity. In practice, it will be equal to the maximum capacity of the operation.

In the discussion so far, I developed marginal analysis in a production framework. The aim was to find the optimal level of a given activity by comparing marginal revenues with marginal costs. However, the principles of marginal analysis have a much wider scope of application. In fact, the majority of OR/MS projects where this approach is useful are of a different type.

For many OR/MS projects the focus may be only on minimizing costs. No revenues are involved. Altering the level of some activity may increase certain costs, while offering savings in other costs. The savings achieved assume the role of 'revenues'. Marginal analysis then involves trading marginal costs for marginal savings. The next application is of that nature.

Finding the Optimal Economic Order Quantity

I suggest that at this point you briefly reacquaint yourself with Model I of the LOD study discussed in Sections 6.5 and 6.6, in particular with the spreadsheet output in Figure 6-2. We derived the EOQ formula of expression (6-2) from the observation that the *EOQ* occurs at that level of Q where the total annual holding costs are equal to the total annual setup costs. We shall now find the *EOQ* using a marginal analysis approach. The product used as an example is packed into drums. The replenishment size is therefore a discrete variable, namely the number of drums produced per run.

The two costs that vary as functions of Q are the annual holding and annual setup costs. Say, we arbitrarily start with a replenishment size of $Q=10$. As Q goes

Table 11-4: Marginal Analysis for the EOQ Model

| Data: | Product value v = $320/unit | | Holding cost penalty r = 0.18/$/year | | |
| | Annual demand D = 4140 | | Setup cost s = $18/setup | | |

Q	Setup cost Ds/Q	Holding cost $0.5Qvr$	$MR(Q)$	$MC(Q)$	Continue?
10	$7452	$288			
11	$6774.55	$316	$677.45	$28.80	yes
20	$3726	$576			
21	$3548.57	$604.80	$177.43	$28.80	yes
30	$2484	$864			
31	$2403.87	$892.80	$80.13	$28.80	yes
40	$1863	$1152			
41	$1817.56	$1180.80	$45.44	$28.80	yes
50	$1490.40	$1440			
51	$1461.18	$1468.80	$29.22	$28.80	yes
60	$1242	$1728			
61	$1221.64	$1756.80	$20.36	$28.80	no
51	$1461.18	$1468.80			
52	$1433.08	$1497.60	$28.10	$28.80	no

to 11, the average inventory increases, and hence we incur additional holding costs. But, at the same time, the number of replenishments decreases, hence we save some setup costs. So the change in holding costs becomes the 'marginal cost' and the savings in setup costs take the role of the 'marginal revenue'. The idea of marginal analysis is to continue increasing Q by small amounts as long as the marginal cost is less than the marginal savings gained. Once this condition reverses, we stop. The value of Q where this occurs is the *EOQ*.

Table 11-4 summarizes the iterations of the algorithm for the starting level of Q = 10. Increasing Q from 10 to 11 gives a marginal savings of setup costs of 4140($18)/10 − 4140($18)/11 = $677.45, while the marginal cost of holding costs is 0.5(11)($320)(0.18) − 0.5(10)($320)().18) = $28.80. The 'marginal revenue' is substantially larger than the 'marginal cost'. So we continue increasing Q. Rather than increasing Q to 12, we make initially bigger jumps and backtrack if the last jump turned out to be too large. This will reduce the number of iterations needed and hence speed up convergence to the optimal solution. Condition (11-7) is next tested for Q = 20 and 21. Again, marginal savings exceed marginal cost. We continue in this vein. At Q = 60 and 61 marginal savings have become smaller than marginal cost. We now backtrack. The test for Q = 51 and 52 shows that even for that level marginal savings are smaller than marginal cost. We now have found the two values for Q which satisfy condition (11-7). The optimal Q is therefore 51.

11.7*[1]   MARGINAL ANALYSIS FOR CONTINUOUS VARIABLES

From the introductory discussion in Section 11.1 it follows that, if the activity is a continuous variable, such as the amount of flour produced by a flour mill, or the output of electricity of a power station, the marginal cost is the rate of change of the total cost function and the marginal revenue is the rate of change of the total revenue function at a given level of output. In graphical terms, they represent the slopes of the total cost or total revenue curves.

In some cases, the exact or approximate algebraic form of these total cost and revenue functions may be known or, at least, assumed to be known. As the next section will show, the marginal cost and marginal revenue may then be computed algebraically. In most instances, however, they must be approximated numerically.

Expression (11-1) is a reasonable approximation to the true rate of change in total cost when a unit change in the activity is relatively small in relation to the normal range of activity, e.g., the latter being in the hundreds or larger. However, when an increase by one unit is relatively large in relation to the normal range of activity, expression (11-1) may be a bad estimate of the true marginal cost. In such cases a better approximation to the true rate of change is obtained by taking the difference between $T(Q)$ and $T(Q-\delta)$, where δ is chosen arbitrarily, but sufficiently

---

[1] Starred sections are optional.

small, say 0.1 or 0.01, and then extrapolating this difference to a unit increase. .
Expression (11-1) then becomes:

$$MC(Q) = [T(Q) - T(Q-\delta)]/\delta \qquad (11\text{-}1A)$$

Condition (11-2) defining at what level of activity the lowest average cost occurs
also changes. Since the change in the level of activity can be made infinitesimally
small, the lowest average cost occurs at the level of output Q^* where marginal cost
and average cost are equal, i.e., where

$$MC(Q^*) = AC(Q^*) \qquad (11\text{-}2A)$$

Similarly, condition (11-7) for the optimal level of activity Q^* also becomes an
equality:

$$\text{At the optimal level of activity } Q^*, \ MR(Q^*) = MC(Q^*) \qquad (11\text{-}7A)$$

Consider again the example in Table 11-4, except that we now allow Q to be a
continuous variable. From Table 11-4 we know that the optimal Q has to be around
51. Setting δ equal to 0.1 and $Q = 51$, expression (11-1A) gives a marginal holding
cost of [$1468.80 − 0.5(50.9)($320)(0.18)]/0.1 = $2.88/0.1 = $28.80. Since the
holding cost is proportional to Q this simply confirms our previous results. The
marginal savings in setup cost are equal to the negative of the marginal setup cost.
We can again use (11-1A): −[$1461.18 − 4140($18)/50.9]/0.1 = $2.87/0.1 = $28.70.
Since marginal savings are just smaller than marginal cost, the optimal Q must be
just below 51.

We now repeat the same analysis for $Q = 50.9$. The marginal cost is constant
at $28.80. The marginal savings are now −[4140($18)/50.9 − 4140($18)/50.8]/0.1
= $28.80, i.e., equal to the marginal cost after rounding to two decimal places. You
should verify that for $Q = 50.8$ marginal savings are just larger than marginal cost.
Hence, the optimal Q is 50.9. Note that this result only differs 'marginally' from
the more accurate value of 50.87 found using the EOQ formula. By decreasing the
value of δ to 0.01, we could have derived the exact answer.

11.8*   MARGINAL ANALYSIS AND DIFFERENTIAL CALCULUS

The graph in Figure 11-4 shows typical total revenue $TR(Q)$ and total cost curves
$TC(Q)$ in the same quadrant. The vertical difference between the two curves for any
level of output Q is the profit $TP(Q) = TR(Q) - TC(Q)$.

Remember that the marginal revenue and marginal cost are given by the slope
of the total revenue and total cost curves. In the general case, the slope of a
function for any given value of its argument, Q in our case, is given by the tangent
of the corresponding curve at Q. But you will also remember that the tangent to a

Figure 11-4: Marginal costs and marginal revenues

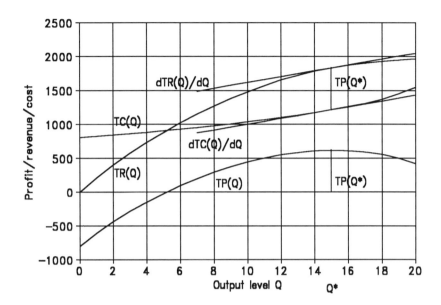

curve is equal to the first derivative of the corresponding function. Putting these two things together, we see that the marginal revenue at any given output level Q' is equal to the first derivative of the total revenue function, evaluated at Q':

$$MR(Q) = dTR(Q)/dQ \text{ evaluated at } Q = Q'$$

By the analogous reasoning, the marginal cost at the output level Q' is equal to the first derivative of the total cost curve evaluated at Q':

$$MC(Q) = dTC(Q)/dQ \text{ evaluated at } Q = Q'$$

For what level of output is the profit maximized? From the graph we see that the difference between the total revenue curve and the total cost curve is largest at the output level Q^*. At that point the tangents to the two curves have exactly the same slope, i.e., $dTR(Q)/dQ = dTC(Q)/dQ$, both evaluated at Q^*, or

$$MR(Q^*) = MC(Q^*).$$

This is again the condition (11-7A) of 'marginal revenue equals marginal cost'.

The stock replenishment example in Table 11-4 will be used to demonstrate this result. Recall again that the 'total revenue' is represented by the savings in annual setup costs. Hence, $TR(Q)$ is the negative of annual setup costs. From expression (6-1A) of Section 6.6, this is $TR(Q) = -sD/Q$, while the 'total cost' corresponds to the holding cost $TC(Q) = 0.5Qvr$. Taking derivatives and setting them equal, we get

$$sD/Q^2 = 0.5vr$$

Solving this expression for Q we obtain, to no surprise, the EOQ formula.

There is an alternative way to derive condition (11-7A), using the total profit function. As we have already seen in Section 6.10, the value of x where the function $f(x)$ assumes its maximum can be found by setting the first derivative of $f(x)$ equal to zero and solving for x. Let us apply this to the profit function $TP(Q) = TR(Q) - TC(Q)$:

$$dTP(Q)/dQ = d(TR(Q) - TC(Q))/dQ$$
$$= dTR(Q)/dQ - dTC(Q)/dQ = 0$$

Re-arranging this last expression we get again that, at the optimum, marginal revenue equals marginal cost:

$$dTR(Q)/dQ = dTC(Q)/dQ$$

Classical methods of differential calculus are often a simple and convenient method for determining the maximum or minimum value of a differentiable function.

11.9   INCREMENTAL ANALYSIS

Incremental analysis deals with the effect on revenue and costs of discrete, and often large, changes in the level of an activity, in contrast to marginal analysis which looks at small changes at the margin. The majority of decisions relating to changes in activity levels call for this type of analysis, rather than marginal analysis.

For instance, the optimal number of long-haul trucks operated by a transport firm has to be an integer, while their activity, measured in terms of tonne-kilometres, can assume any value, not simply a multiple of the basic unit capacity of a truck. Some trucks may not be used to full capacity. Airlines face similar problems in terms of the number of each type of aircraft to have in their fleet.

The number of gasoline pumps installed at a service station, the number of telephone lines rented by the TAB (see Section 1.1), the number of doctors on duty in an accident and emergency clinic, or the number of generators in operation at a power station at a given time, are all examples giving rise to incremental changes.

The next example is a somewhat simplified account of a logistic problem faced by Heinz USA, the leading US manufacturer of ketchup. It is adapted from the paper by Sunder Kerke et al., 'A logistics analysis at Heinz', in the Sep.-Oct. 1990 issue of *Interfaces* (pp. 1-13). *Interfaces* is one of the more readable OR/MS journals.

11.10   A LOGISTICS ANALYSIS

Logistics deals with the transportation and distribution of goods. Many successful OR/MS applications world-wide involve such issues.

Situation Summary

Over 80% of the US tomato crop is grown in California and harvested from early July to mid-October. Part of this crop is immediately processed into various finished tomato products. A large portion, however, is made into tomato paste in factories located close to the growing areas in California. This paste is later converted into various other finished products, with ketchup taking the biggest slice, at a number of plants throughout the US. Sales of finished products are also seasonal, but with a sizable steady demand throughout the year. The production pattern for finished products at the conversion plants tends to follow the seasonal demand.

Assume that this is January 1987. Heinz faces a vast logistics problem of how to transport large quantities of tomato paste from the factories in California to these conversion plants. This transport is done with a specialized fleet of railroad tank cars. These are due to come off lease in early 1988. A team of analysts coming from finance and all major functional operating areas, as well as three academics from Carnegie Mellon University, is set up to identify and analyze various transport strategy options.

Three options stand out:

1. Use a fleet of specialized tank cars only. This involves a substantial initial investment, but low maintenance costs during the long life of the tank cars. On the other hand, Heinz has to pay the return trip of the empty tank cars. Hence, round trip hauling costs for the tank cars are considerably higher than the one-way transport cost for the same volume of goods in regular box cars. The question to be analyzed is the number of such cars needed.

2. Use giant pouches, similar in concept to the single-portion packets of ketchup you get in fast food restaurants, except that these pouches contain 300 gallons of paste (i.e., more than 1 cubic meter). They are called Scholle bags, after the company that commercialized them. They are not reusable, used for one trip only. Only minor investments in filling and unloading equipment are required. Filled Scholle bags can be stored and transported in simple plywood cases which can be reused for up to 5 years. Transportation is done in box cars, and hence is about 40% cheaper per gallon than transport by tank cars. This is though more than compensated by the cost of the bags.

3. A combination of options 1 and 2, with option 1 used for covering the steady transport needs all year round, while option 2 is used to fill the peak transport requirement during periods of high demand for tomato paste at the conversion plants.

Figure 11-5: Spreadsheet evaluation of Heinz transportation problem

TOMATO PASTE TRANSPORTATION PROBLEM

DATA: Rail:			Scholle:			COST EVALUATIONS:	
Investment/railcar	$80,000		Capacity of bag	1.1355	tonnes	Discount rate	0.15
Useful life of railcar	12	years	Cost of bag	$59		Equivalent annuity/car	$14,758
Carrying capacity/railcar	18	tonne	Plywood case cost/case	$73		Rail cost/tonne	$54.00
Railcar roundtrips/year	30	maximum	Useful life of case	40	roundtrips		
Rail hauling cost/ car	$972		Rail hauling cost/case	$43		Bag cost/tonne	$93.20
			Cost of case return	$2			

DEMAND:

Month	January	February	March	April	May	June	July	August	September	October	November	December
Tonnes Total 24000	600	1100	2300	2900	1800	1200	1300	2400	3700	3200	2100	1400

MARGINAL ANALYSIS BY DEMAND LEVEL

Demand level	0	12	11	10	9	8	7	6	5	4	3	2	1
Month at level	none	Jan	Feb	June	July	Dec	May	Nov	March	Aug	Apr	Oct	Sep
Demand for month	0	600	1100	1200	1300	1400	1800	2100	2300	2400	2900	3200	3700
Size of level	0	600	500	100	100	100	400	300	200	100	500	300	500
Additional volume	0	7200	5500	1000	900	800	2800	1800	1000	400	1500	600	500
Total volume	0	7200	12700	13700	14600	15400	18200	20000	21000	21400	22900	23500	24000
Additional railcars	0	14	11	2	2	3	8	7	5	2	11	7	11
Railcars required	0	14	25	27	29	32	40	47	52	54	65	72	83
Marginal rail cost	$82.70	$82.70	$83.52	$83.52	$86.80	$109.34	$96.17	$111.33	$127.79	$127.79	$162.23	$226.18	$378.68
Marginal bag cost	$93.20	$93.20	$93.20	$93.20	$93.20	$93.20	$93.20	$93.20	$93.20	$93.20	$93.20	$93.20	$93.20
					OPTIMUM								

TOTAL COST ANALYSIS

	0	12	11	10	9	8	7	6	5	4	3	2	1
Railcars required	0	14	25	27	29	32	40	47	52	54	65	72	83
Cost by rail	0	595,412	1,054,750	1,138,266	1,216,382	1,303,856	1,573,120	1,773,626	1,901,416	1,952,532	2,195,870	2,331,576	2,520,914
Cost by bags	2,236,800	1,565,760	1,053,160	959,960	876,080	801,520	540,560	372,800	279,600	242,320	102,520	46,600	0
Total cost	2,236,800	2,161,172	2,107,910	2,098,226	2,092,462	2,105,376	2,113,680	2,146,426	2,181,016	2,194,852	2,298,390	2,378,176	2,520,914
					LOWEST								

Note that options 1 and 2 are, in fact, simply limiting cases of option 3. In other words, option 3 includes the other two options. Hence, the analysis only needs to consider option 3, since it allows the optimal solution to either be a true combination or options 1 or 2 as limiting cases.

Input Data

Rather than look at this problem as a whole, I will demonstrate the approach used by considering the transportation of paste from factory X to conversion plant Y. Since the report in *Interfaces* does not contain any real data, all cost and demand figures come from the inexhaustible store of numbers in my brain.

The top portion of the spreadsheet output in Figure 11-5 lists the sample input data used. Since the useful life of the railcars is 12 years, an obvious way of analyzing this problem is to determine the net present value of all costs incurred over that 12-year planning horizon for all possible numbers of railcars. The best solution is then the one that minimizes the NPV. We shall take a more insightful approach, based on marginal analysis.

Usage of Railcars by Demand Levels

The total annual volume to be transported is 24,000 tonnes.   Note that a railcar carries 18 tonnes per trip.   For an average of 30 round trips per year or 2.5/month, one railcar can carry an average of 45 tonnes per month.   If the demand were constant throughout the year at 2000 tonnes per month, then a total of 2000/45 or about 45 railcars could do the job.   However, the demand is unevenly spread over the year, with as little as 600 tonnes in January and a peak of 3700 tonnes in September. To meet the September demand 3700/45 or 83 railcars are needed. The next highest demand month, October with 3200 tonnes, only requires 72 railcars. If Heinz acquired 83 railcars, 11 would be used only for one month per year, remaining idle for the rest of the year. The third highest demand month, April with 2900 tonnes, requires 65 railcars. So, another 7 cars would only be used during two months of each year. To test your understanding, find out how many will be idle 9 months of the year. Only 14 railcars would be used every month of the year. This is depicted graphically in Figure 11-6.

The monthly demands have been ordered in increasing size.   The horizontal bands represent demand levels that persist for $n = 12, 11, 10, ..., 1$ months during the year.   Each band requires an additional number of railcars which see use during n months and are idle during $12-n$ months.   For example, demand level 5 is a band 200 tonnes wide which covers the months of March, August, April, October, and September.   It would require an additional 5 rail cars over the number needed to cover all demand levels up to level 6.   These 5 rail cars would be used in the 5 months listed and idle during the remaining 7.

Figure 11-6: Demand pattern for paste by levels

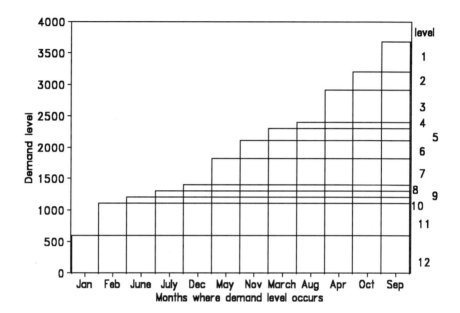

Marginal Reasoning: A Motivation

If a railcar is in use most of the time, its initial investment can be spread over many tonnes. The cost per tonne carried is low. On the other hand, if it is used only a few months of the year, the tonnage carried is low. Hence the initial investment is spread over fewer tonnes and the cost per tonne carried goes up. This means that the marginal cost per tonne carried increases as the number of railcars acquired goes up. In contrast, the cost of transporting paste in Scholle bags remains virtually unchanged, regardless of the volume transported in any month. There is no big initial investment to be spread over the total tonnage served. The major costs are the bags, which can only be used once, and the rail freight charge, which is constant per tonne. The marginal cost per tonne for transport by Scholle bags remains constant.

So we see that one marginal cost increases, while the other remains constant. This insight is the key for finding the optimal solution. We start out with a solution where all paste is transported in Scholle bags. We now consider substituting railcars for Scholle bags. The demand level which has the lowest marginal cost for transport by rail is the one chosen first. This is demand level 12 (which persists all-year round). Demand level 11 would be next and so on. With each additional demand level switched to rail, the cost of transport by railcars may increase, while the cost of transport by Scholle bags remains constant. In terms of the language of marginal analysis, these savings in Scholle bag costs are the equivalent of the marginal revenue as the level of activity — in this case the use of railcars — increases. From condition (11-7) we know that the optimal solution occurs at the point when the marginal costs have increased to a level where any further increase in the number of railcars used would become larger than the (marginal) savings from the reduced use of Scholle bags.

Incremental Analysis

The marginal cost for the use of railcars increases in discrete steps at each demand level. Since there are 12 demand levels, we have to compute at most 12 marginal costs for rail use and compare them with the constant marginal savings in Scholle bag costs. These calculations are performed under the heading 'Incremental Analysis by Demand Levels' in the spreadsheet in Figure 11-5. Figure 11-7 shows the behaviour of marginal costs and marginal savings graphically.

I will demonstrate some of the calculations. First, we need to determine the annual cost implied by the initial investment of $80,000 for a railcar. This is the major cost incurred by Heinz for the use of the railcars over a 12-year productive life. We want to apportion this cost in equal amounts to each year, such that the NPVs of these costs add up to $80,000. This is the same concept we used in the replacement problem of Chapter 10 for comparing different policies, namely the concept of the equivalent annuity. For a discount rate of 15%, the equivalent annuity amounts to $14,758. The other cost incurred for transport by rail is the rail hauling cost of $971 per round trip, carrying 18 tonnes. It is constant at $53.94 per tonne ($971/18). These are the numbers listed under 'cost evaluations' for rail in the top right-hand corner of the spreadsheet in Figure 11-5.

The marginal cost per tonne for transport by Scholle bag based on the sum of the bag cost ($59), the transport cost for full bags in cases ($43), the return freight for the boxes ($2), and a portion of the initial cost for the plywood case. Since that case can, on average, be used for 40 round trips, this is equal to 1/40 of $73. (Forty round trips cover 1.25 years if the case is used all year round. But it could take several years if the case is only used for a few months. A more accurate treatment would express the case cost also in the form of an annuity, as a function of the number of years the case is in use. However, the cost difference would be small. Hence, I opted for a simplified approach.) Adding these costs and dividing them by the weight carried per bag (1.1355 tonnes) results in a constant marginal cost for transport by Scholle bag of $93.20 per tonne.

The marginal rail cost for demand level 12 is then computed as follows. Demand level 12 amount to 600 tonnes for each of 12 months or a total of 7200 tonnes. Rounded to the next highest integer, this requires 14 railcars (600/45 = 13.33, rounded to 14). Hence, the annual investment cost amounts to 14 times the equivalent annuity of $14,758 or $206,612. To express this cost on a per tonne basis, we divide it by 7200 tonnes. The resulting investment cost per tonne carried for demand level 12 is $28.70 ($206,612 / 7200). Adding the constant hauling cost

Figure 11-7: Marginal costs for rail and Scholle bags

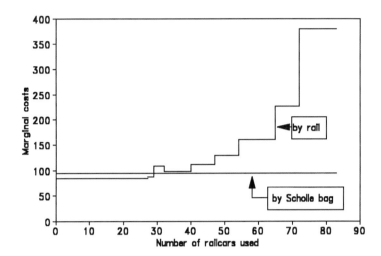

per tonne of $53.94 gives a marginal rail cost of $82.64 per tonne. So, switching demand level 12 from Scholle bags to rail increases rail costs by $82.64 per tonne, but saves $93.20 per tonne by reducing the cost of transport by Scholle bag. Hence, this switch is advantageous.

We now consider switching demand level 11 to rail. Eleven additional railcars are required. These will transport an additional volume of 5500 tonnes (11 times the size of demand level 11). The annual investment cost of 11 times $14,758 is now apportioned to these 5500 tonnes and comes to $29.52. Adding the constant rail hauling cost ($53.94) results in a marginal rail cost for demand level 11 of $83.46. This is still lower than the marginal cost by Scholle bags. Hence, it is cost effective to switch demand level 11 to rail.

This process is continued until the marginal rail cost becomes larger than the marginal cost by Scholle bags. This happens for demand level 8. Hence, the optimal policy is to acquire 29 railcars, capable of transporting all paste included in demand levels 12, 11, 10, and 9, or a total tonnage of 14,600. The balance of 9,400 tonnes is transported by Scholle bags.

Further Discussion of Solution

Again, there is no need to continue these calculations beyond demand level 8. However, it is interesting to see how steeply the marginal rail cost increases, as more and more demand levels are switched from Scholle bags to rail. Since marginal rail costs remain constant within each demand level, the graph of the marginal rail cost is a step function, as depicted in Figure 11-7. The steps become increasingly larger past demand level 4 (54 railcars).

Note also the unexpected dip in the marginal cost for level 7. This dip is caused by the fact that the number of railcars added to cover any given level has to be an integer. The three railcars needed to cover the transport requirement for demand level 8 are not used to 100% capacity during the 8 months that this demand level is maintained. If the demand for December had been 1395, rather than 1400, only 31 railcars would be needed. The marginal cost for demand level 8 would then have been only $92.84, which is still less than the marginal cost by Scholle bags. Increasing the resource use in incremental steps of several rail cars may result in a less than 100% use for part of the increment. It is this aspect that may introduce irregularities of this sort. Had we incremented the resource use in steps of single railcars rather than increments of several railcars to cover each successive demand level, the algorithm would have discovered that the marginal cost of railcars exceeds the marginal cost of Scholle bags for rail car 32. Hence, the optimal solution would have been 31 railcars.

The spreadsheet in Figure 11-5 also shows the total average annual cost as a function of the number of railcars used. It is an average because it includes not only the variable costs, but also the annual equivalent investment cost. Verify it! As inferred from the marginal analysis approach, the minimum total cost is achieved for 29 railcars. The results are graphed in Figure 11-8. The total cost curve is quite flat over the range of 25 to 40 railcars. Given that the demand data used are future predictions which may not be that reliable, management has quite some leeway in the choice of the final decision. A choice somewhere in that range will not affect total costs seriously.

Before making a final decision, management would also want to know something about how robust the solution is with respect to certain important assumptions. One of those is the discount rate. However, the average of 30 round trips per year assumed in all calculations may be more critical. One of the exercises to this chapter will ask you to investigate such aspects.

Again the marginal analysis approach provides insights into the situation that cannot be readily inferred from a total cost approach. For example, the difference in marginal costs is fairly small down to demand level 7 (May), corresponding to a use of 40 railcars. For demand level 7 the difference in marginal cost is $2.97 per tonne in favour of Scholle bags. A price increase for bags of less than $3 makes rail the more attractive option also for May (and by implication for December). Unless Heinz can secure long-term price contracts with the bag manufacturer, the risk of a price increase may well sway the decision to purchase 40 railcars, rather than just 29.

The next example is of a completely different nature. Rather than analyzing the optimal number of identical entities to get for a given activity, we have a set of distinct and different entities, each contributing towards the system's objectives and requiring the input of some shared resource.

Figure 11-8: Total annual average costs for Heinz

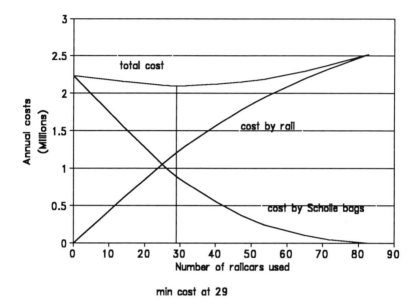

min cost at 29

11.11 AN INVESTMENT PORTFOLIO SELECTION

The Sure-Bet Investment House has just completed the evaluation of 9 potential investment projects. Each one has to be accepted or rejected in its entirety. Table 11-5 lists their ranking in terms of decreasing internal rates of return. Sure-Bet has currently also several firm offers for funds. In contrast to the projects, offers for funds can be taken up partially. These and their costs are also listed in Table 11-5.

Which projects should be accepted? From the analysis in Section 10.4, the temptation is great to say 'all of them', since even the last ranked project has an IRR higher than the cheapest source of funds. If this were done, the annual return would be $5.477 million. Subtracting the annual cost of $3.55 million from the $30 million of funds used gives a net annual profit of $1.927 million. This naive approach, however, leads to the wrong decision. The correct method is to use incremental analysis.

An incremental analysis approach looks at the projects one at a time in order of decreasing IRRs — the equivalent to decreasing marginal revenues as the level of activity increases. The funds, on the other hand, are considered in order of increasing costs — the equivalent to increasing marginal cost as the level of activity increases. The level of activity is the amount of funds invested. This level of activity can only be increased in unequal discrete amounts. So we compare the incremental revenue per year for each additional project with the incremental cost per year of the funds used. Projects are accepted if the incremental revenue exceeds the incremental cost of the funds.

Table 11-5: Investment choices and sources of funds

Project	Initial investment	Internal rate of return
A	$1.8 million	32 %
B	$6.9 million	26 %
C	$2.5 million	23 %
D	$1.1 million	18 %
E	$7.3 million	15 %
F	$3.2 million	14 %
G	$0.9 million	13 %
H	$2.2 million	12 %
I	$4.1 million	10 %

Source	Funds offered	Cost/year
1	up to $10 million	9.5 %
2	up to $ 4 million	12 %
3	up to $ 8 million	12.5%
4	up to $10 million	14 %

Table 11-6 summarizes the steps of the analysis. All dollar amounts are shown in millions. We start with project A. Its incremental annual revenue is 32% of $1.8 million or $576,000. Funded from the cheapest source of funds, the incremental annual cost is 9.5% of $1.8 million or $171,000. So project A is accepted. This reduces the amount of funds available at a cost of 9.5% to $8.2 million.

The second-ranked project B has an incremental annual revenue of 26% of $6.9 million or $1,794,000. It can be funded entirely from the cheapest source at an annual cost of $655,500. This leaves $8.2 - $6.9 or $1.3 of the 9.5% funds. The third-ranked project C has an incremental annual return of $575,000. $1.3 million can be financed at 9.5%, and the balance of $1.2 million at 12%. This results in an incremental annual cost of $267,500. Hence, C is accepted. The 9.5% funds have now been exhausted, and $2.8 million of the 12% funds remain. This process continues until we discover that the next ranked project fails to recover all annual interest costs. This occurs for project G.

The optimal solution is to accept projects A to F for a total annual revenue of $4.686 million. The amount of funds used is $22.8 million. This uses up the 9.5%, the 12%, the 12.5% funds, and $0.8 million of the 14% funds, leaving the balance of $9.2 million unused. The total annual cost of the funds used is $2.542 million, leaving an annual total profit of $2.144 million — $217,000 more than the naive approach.

Note that in view of the order in which both the projects and the sources of funds were considered, there is no need to continue the analysis, once a project has been rejected. Any project farther down in the rank order will stack up even more unfavourably.

Table 11-6: Incremental analysis for an investment portfolio

Project	Funds needed	Marginal revenue	Marginal cost	Accept/ reject	Unused sources of funds			
					9.5%	12.0%	12.5%	14%
A	1.8	0.576	0.171	accept	8.2	4.0	8.0	10.0
B	6.9	1.794	0.6555	accept	1.3	4.0	8.0	10.0
C	2.5	0.575	0.2675	accept	0	2.8	8.0	10.0
D	1.1	0.198	0.132	accept	0	1.7	8.0	10.0
E	7.3	1.095	0.904	accept	0	0	2.4	10.0
F	3.2	0.448	0.412	accept	0	0	0	9.2
G	0.9	0.117	0.126	reject	0	0	0	8.3

EXERCISES

1. What is the practical difference between marginal and incremental analysis and why is the latter more useful for decision making?

2. An electrical goods manufacturer makes industrial transformers which it sells for $840 each. The material used in the manufacture consists of $120 for metal and plastic castings and wire costing $70 per km. The particular type of transformer produced on that machine requires 8 km of wire and 2 hours of labour per unit. The fixed annual cost of operating the machinery and overheads directly associated with the operation amount to $80,000. The machine operator is paid $800 for a 40-hour week.

   (a) Assuming that the operator does other tasks when not working on this machine, determine the break-even point in terms of the number of transformers to produce per year.

   (b) If the machine operator remains idle when not operating the machine, what is the break-even point then?

3. A travel agent is contemplating opening another office in a different part of town. There is little or no overlap in potential clients expected. The cost of setting up a new agency is as follows: refurbishing of the office $24,000; computer equipment and software licences $17,500; initial training of staff $3,600; initial promotion $6,900. The annual operating cost of the office consists of: office rental $10,400; staff salaries, incl. fringe benefits $58,000; various fixed office costs, such as telephone rentals, power, heating, etc. $4,200; subscription to travel data sources, etc. $6000. Commission on travel ticket and accommodation sales, etc., averages 10% of gross sales. Other variable sales costs amount to about 3% of gross sales.

   (a) Determine the break-even point for annual gross sales needed for the agency to remain viable.

(b) The first office opened by the firm was able to operate at a sales level of 80% of the break-even point for the first year, 30% above the break-even point for the second year, 50% above the break-even point in the third year, and has maintained that level on average since then. How many years will it take to recover the initial investment?

4. An electric power company operates a number of hydro and thermal power generating stations. Although the actual variable cost of using hydro stations is essentially zero, power planners impute values for the water stored in hydro lakes based on the most expensive thermal power that they can replace at some later time of the year. The table below lists the power increments available at the various stations and the associated real or imputed generating cost per megawatt hour (MWh) of power produced, valid for a given week:

Station	A			B		C	D			
Power increments	1	2	3	1	2	1	1	2	3	4
Output in MWh	50	50	50	40	40	20	30	30	30	30
Cost in 1000$/MWh	80	80	85	110	112	300	65	65	70	75

The company has firm contracts for supply of electricity of 170 MWh for that week. It can also offer additional power to other power companies at various prices: up to 40 MWh at $120,000/ MWh, up to 50 MWh at $90,000/MWh, and up to 80 MWh at $82,000/MWh. What is the company's best power generating schedule for that week? Use marginal reasoning. It may help setting up a table similar to Table 11-3.

5. Consider exercise 7 of Chapter 5. Compute the optimal number of days each shipment should cover using marginal analysis, as demonstrated in Section 11.6.

6. Earth Care, Inc., sells beauty products through house calls by its 'certified personal advisors', more commonly known as door-to-door salespersons. A recent study revealed the following pattern between the number of "advisors" assigned to urban areas, the total annual sales volume, and the total travel costs reimbursed to the "advisors" for each 200,000 inhabitants: (all in $1000)

'Advisors'	1	2	3	4	5	6	7	8	9	10
Sales	250	500	750	1000	1240	1470	1690	1890	2050	2170
Travel costs	2	4	6	8	10	12	14.5	17	20	23

The reason for the ultimate decrease in additional sales is partially due to the fact that less and less affluent urban areas have to be included. Travel costs increase more than proportionately for similar reasons. Each 'advisor' gets a basic annual salary of $15,000 and a commission of 5% on sales. Earth Care makes 9% gross profit on its sales, after subtracting any sales commissions, but before other selling costs. Use marginal or incremental analysis to determine the optimal number of 'advisors' to assign for each 200,000 inhabitants.

7. A soft drink bottling firm faces a seasonal demand as follows:

Period	Jan/Feb	Mar/Apr	May/June	July/Aug	Sep/Oct	Nov/Dec
Bottles sold	10	15	20	28	22	15 millions

The firm can meet as much or as little of the demand as it wishes. Due to the limited shelf life of bottled soft drinks, no stock can be carried from one period to the next, i.e., production in any two-months period never exceeds demand. The firm is currently modernizing its bottling plant, by acquiring new bottling machines. Each bottling machine has a 2-monthly capacity of 5 million bottles. The predicted total annual cost for each machine is $75,000. This includes all relevant fixed operating costs, as well as the recovery of the initial outlay less the salvage value at the end of its productive life, all expressed in terms of an equivalent annuity, as discussed in Chapter 10. The net contribution to profits is equal to $10,000 for each 1 million bottles sold. Use incremental analysis to determine the optimal number of machines to purchase.

8. Create a spreadsheet to reproduce the results in Figure 11-5.

9. Use the spreadsheet developed in exercise 6 above for the following sensitivity analysis:
    (a) A change in the annual number of round trips from the current 30 to 25.
    (b) An increase in the cost of Scholle bags by 10%.
    (c) An increase in the carrying capacity of railcars from 18 to 20 tonnes.

10*.   Adapt the spreadsheet developed in exercise 8 or create a new spreadsheet so that it overcomes the difficulty caused by some of the carrying capacity of the railcars added at each increment not being used up fully (as occurred for level 8, causing the dip in marginal costs for level 7). It requires that for each level two increments in railcars are tested, namely the one that can carry the entire volume added at each level (the approach used now in Figure 11-5), and one that uses just one railcar less than that level. Any residual volume not carried by railcars is transported by Scholle bag, and then added to the volume carried by railcars for the next volume level tested. This should eliminate the anomaly of dips in the marginal cost curve.

11. A firm has the following indivisible investment opportunities, with the investment in $1000 and the internal rate of return (IRR) in % per year:

Project	A	B	C	D	E	F	G	H	I	J
Investment	20	40	60	30	50	10	20	50	40	30
IRR	28	27	25	22	21	21	18	15	12	10

It has the following sources of funds available, each of which can be taken up in its entirety or only partially:

Funds source	1	2	3	4
Limit in $1000	150	120	90	80
Cost/year %	12	16	20	24

Determine which investment projects should be entered into.

REFERENCES

Unfortunately, few authors of OR/MS texts consider marginal and incremental analysis a legitimate OR/MS technique, although many highly sophisticated mathematical programming approaches are based on this type of reasoning. Texts on Managerial Economics or Business Economics have some coverage of marginal reasoning. Some also have some cursory discussion of incremental analysis.

12 Constraints on Decision Making

So far, the decision problems studied did not involve quantitative restrictions on the values the decision variables could assume or on the combination of alternative courses of action that could be considered. For example, in the LOD problem of Chapters 5 to 8 there was no restriction on the possible combinations of the stock replenishment quantity and the cutoff size for special production runs for the various products (except that negative values were implicitly ruled out). Their optimal values were determined without consideration of any resource constraints. Although the mixing and filling capacity, and the warehouse space, were limited, and had to be shared by all products, we assumed that the total capacities of these resources was ample and would not restrict the decision choices. This simplified the analysis considerably. It made it possible to look at each product individually, ignoring the fact that they shared the same resources. Similarly, when we analyzed in Chapter 10 which investment projects should be accepted we assumed that there was no restriction on the amount of funds available.

This and the following chapter will study the effect of constraints on the decision choices. These constraints can be in the form of limited availability of resources, such as funds, machine capacities, and so on. They could also be in the form of other conditions, such as minimum output requirements, minimum quality standards, or fixed relationships between activities.

To keep things simple, this chapter only considers the case of a single resource constraint. Chapter 13 will look at how to deal with many constraints when the mathematical relationships are linear.

Section 12.1 deals with a single activity using the limited resource. We then study the effect of relaxing the constraint by increasing the amount of the resource marginally, i.e., we perform sensitivity analysis on the resource availability. This will lead us to the concept of the shadow price of a resource — an important theoretical concept of constrained optimization. Section 12.5 shows how the ideas of marginal analysis can be extended to the allocation of the limited resource to several uses. The last section looks at the allocation of a scarce resource when the uses occur in discrete increments.

12.1 RESOURCE CONSTRAINT ON A SINGLE ACTIVITY

In this section, some of the basic concepts of constrained optimization will be explored. Rather than do this in the abstract, I will refer to the simple inventory replenishment model of Chapter 6.

The Optimal Unconstrained Solution

One of the LOD products has to be stored under refrigeration. Any demand for this product is always met from stock. Whenever the stock is depleted, a replenishment of size Q is initiated. The situation thus corresponds to the first model for stock replenishment developed in Section 6.5. The relevant annual cost is given by

$$T(Q) = 0.5Qvr + sD/Q \qquad (6\text{-}1A)$$

where D is the predicted number of cans sold over the coming year, s is the production setup cost, v is the value of the product per can, and r is the annual investment holding cost per dollar invested. This total cost function is so-called well-behaved. In this context this means that it has a nice U-shape. Verify that this is the case in Figure 6-3. Therefore, it follows that it has its minimum value at a single point corresponding to the economic order quantity, given by expression (6-2):

$$EOQ = \sqrt{2Ds/vr} \qquad (6\text{-}2)$$

Figure 12-1 lists the input parameters for this product in the top portion. Verify that the EOQ formula gives an order quantity of 1857.7 cans. Since fractional cans cannot be stored, this is rounded to 1858 cans. Using expression (6-1A), the relevant annual cost amounts to $3,274.

The cans are packed into boxes which are placed on pallets, with 12 cans per box and 8 boxes per pallet. A pallet measures exactly 1 m^2. The pallets in turn are placed on shelves in the cool store. Therefore, 1858 cans require 19.35 pallets. Since any partially used pallet uses the same storage space as a full pallet, an order corresponds to 20 pallets. This is 20 m^2 of storage space. If there is no restriction on the amount of refrigerated space available, then the optimal replenishment policy for this product is to order 1858 cans whenever the inventory is depleted. This occurs, on the average, about 31 times per year, or about every 8 working days (assuming 250 working days/year). By definition, no other policy can have a lower annual cost.

Unfortunately, the current cool store only has a storage capacity of 8 m^2, or the equivalent of 768 cans. In other words, there is a constraint imposed on the values that the decision variable may assume. The unconstrained optimal policy of 1858 cans violates this constraint. Therefore, it is not a feasible solution. It violates the constraint. To have a feasible solution, the stock replenishment has to be decreased. **Any deviation from the unconstrained optimal policy, by definition, results in a higher relevant annual cost.** Hence, the annual cost will increase. For what feasible value of the decision variable is this cost increase the smallest?

Finding the Optimal Constrained Solution

Fractional pallet areas cannot be used as storage space, since a pallet requires a shelf measuring one square metre. It only makes sense to consider reductions in the replenishment quantity equivalent to one pallet area, or 96 cans. We have, therefore, recourse to an incremental type analysis, except that this time we study the effect of decreases in the activity, rather than increases. This is demonstrated in the lower portion of the spreadsheet in Figure 12-1. Starting from the unconstrained optimal solution, we reduce the warehouse required by one square metre. Since the 20th pallet is only partially used, the increase in costs is small — in fact, only one dollar. Further reductions in area imply a reduction in Q by 96 cans and increase costs by larger and larger amounts. They are listed in the column labelled 'Cost increase'.

The constraint limits the stock replenishment to values that require no more than

Figure 12-1: Stock replenishment with limited warehouse space

Limited Warehouse Space						
Annual demand in cans	57600	(D)				
Value per can	$7.05	(v)				
Production setup cost/setup	$52.80	(s)				
Investment holding cost/$/year	$0.25	(r)				
W'house space: cans/square metre	96					
W'house space avail.: square metres	8					
Unconstrained optimal solution:						
Economic order quantity Q in cans	1858					
Total w'house space needed in square metres	20					
Annual cost	$3,274					
Constrained optimal solution:						
Available space	Order quantity		Annual cost		Cost increase	Shadow price
21	1858	(EOQ)	$3,274			
20	1858	(EOQ)	$3,274		$0	0.00
19	1824		$3,275		$1	3.16
18	1728		$3,283		$8	13.18
17	1632		$3,302		$19	25.02
16	1536		$3,334		$32	39.15
15	1440		$3,381		$47	56.20
14	1344		$3,447		$66	77.03
13	1248		$3,537		$89	102.86
12	1152		$3,655		$118	135.40
11	1056		$3,811		$155	177.22
10	960		$4,014		$203	232.20
9	864		$4,281		$267	306.51
8	768		$4,637		$355	410.40
7	672		$5,118		$481	561.93
6	576		$5,788		$670	795.40
5	480		$6,759		$971	1182.60
4	384		$8,258		$1,499	1895.40

8 m^2 of storage space. The only values for the decision variable which satisfy this constraint are those involving a stock replenishment of 768 cans or less. From the 'Annual cost' listed in Figure 12-1 we see that the cheapest feasible solution is the one that uses the entire space available. The optimal constrained replenishment quantity is therefore $Q = 768$ cans at an annual relevant cost of \$4,637. Any lower value for Q results in higher costs, while any larger Q is not a feasible solution.

Generalizing the Results

We can now generalize this result for the case of a single resource constraint. If the unconstrained optimal solution violates the constraint, i.e., is not feasible, then the optimal constrained solution is to choose a value for the decision variable that just satisfies the constraint, i.e., uses up all of the resource available. We then say that **the constraint is binding.** On the other hand, if the unconstrained optimal solution does not violate the constraint, i.e., requires less of the resource than is available, we say that **the constraint has slack.** The amount of slack is the difference between the amount available and the amount used. Slack is the amount of unused resource.

This discussion was couched in terms of a resource constraint. However, the conclusions reached are no different for any other type of constraint. If there is only one constraint and that constraint is violated by the optimal unconstrained solution, then the optimal constrained values of the decision variables just satisfy the constraint, i.e., constraint holds as an equality.

Procedure for Finding the Optimal Solution Subject to One Constraint

This suggests the following procedure for finding the optimal solution if the values of the decision variables are subject to a single constraint:

Step 1: Ignore the constraint and find the optimal (unconstrained) solution.

Step 2: Verify if the constraint is satisfied by this solution. If 'yes', this solution is the optimal solution. If 'no', go to step 3.

Step 3: The optimal constrained solution is the one which has the best objective function value, while satisfying the constraint as an equality.

If there is only one decision variable, step 3 reduces to solving the constraint for the decision variable. For instance, in the LOD example we know that $Q/96 = 8$ m^2. Hence $Q = 8(96) = 768$. If there are two or more decision variables, step 3 is somewhat more challenging, as we shall see in Section 12.5.

12.2 SENSITIVITY ANALYSIS WITH RESPECT TO THE CONSTRAINT

This section demonstrates how incremental analysis may be used for analyzing the effect of changing the constraint.

With only 8 m² of cool store space available, the optimal constrained replenishment is 768 cans, using up all the available space. How much is it worth to acquire additional storage space for this product? This is the type of question regularly asked by a decision maker, faced with limited resources. The worth of additional storage space is given by the decrease in the total annual relevant cost. For example, increasing the available storage space from 8 to 9 m² results in a decrease in the total annual cost of $356, as shown in Figure 12-1 for the entry in column 'Cost increase' and row 'Available space 8'. (Verify this result!) If the cost of an additional square metre is less than $356, then it would be to the LOD's advantage to acquire at least one more square metre of space.

Often a resource can only be acquired or effectively used in a limited range of sizes or quantities. For instance, machine capacity may only be increased by adding further machines of the same type. In the LOD case it is possible to rent refrigerated containers that increase the storage capacity by 6 m² at an annual rental cost of $600 per container. Should the LOD rent one? With the container, the total storage space increases from 8 to 14 m². For 14 m² the optimal constrained order quantity is 1344 cans with a total annual cost of $3,447 — a decrease of $1,190 from the best solution with the space constraint at 8 m². After payment of the container rental, the LOD will still be better off by $590. Hence, this option should be considered seriously if it is technically acceptable.

Should the firm consider renting two refrigerated containers, increasing the total storage space to 20 m² ? A second container reduces the annual cost by another $173. This saving is substantially less than the annual rental of the container. The total combined cost increases. The answer to the question is thus 'No'.

12.3   SHADOW PRICE OF A CONSTRAINT

The Concept of Shadow Price

The rate of change of the optimal value of the objective function in response to a marginal change in a resource constraint is called **the shadow price** of the constraint. Two points are important in this definition. First, the shadow price is **a rate of change valid for a particular value of the constraint**. As the amount of the resource changes, so does the shadow price. Secondly, it refers to the rate of change in the objective function **at the optimal solution** for a given resource availability, not simply at any arbitrary solution.

Note the similarity of this definition with the concept of the marginal costs and revenues, discussed in Sections 11.2 and 11.3. Both refer to the rate of change of some 'output' for a marginal change in some input — a resource in this case. They differ, however, in one respect. The shadow price always refers to the rate of change at the optimal solution, while the marginal costs and revenues can be assessed for any arbitrary 'solution'.

Given this similarity, determining the shadow price of a resource uses the same marginal reasoning as used in Section 11.7 for finding the marginal cost of an activity that is a continuous variable. What is the shadow price of the storage constraint at the present limit of 8 m^2 ?

Procedure for Finding the Shadow Price

Since a shadow price is a marginal concept, the first step is to abandon the assumption that storage space can only be increased in discrete increments of one pallet area, but by any arbitrarily small amount. Assume the storage space is increased by 1/96 of a square metre — just enough to store one additional can. By how much does the minimum cost decrease? Extrapolating this to a unit change in storage space gives an approximate value for the shadow price at the current constraint level of 8 m^2.

The minimum total annual cost for 8 m^2 of storage space (or the equivalent of 768 cans) is \$4,636.80, precise to two decimals. For 8 1/96 m^2 Q increases to 769 cans. Verify that the total annual cost decreases to \$4,632.53. So the cost decrease is \$4.27. Extrapolated to 1 m^2 (or 96 cans) this gives an approximate shadow price of \$4.27/(1/96) = \$409.92. At the current constraint of 8 m^2 the rate of change of the minimum cost is approximately \$409.92 per square metre of storage space. This is though only an approximation. As we shall see later on, there is a more accurate method for computing the shadow price, which was used to find the values listed in the spreadsheet of Figure 12-1.

The shadow price is, however, quite sensitive to the amount of storage space. Consider another increase of 1/96 m^2 to 8 2/96 m^2. This second increase lowers the minimum cost by \$4.25, resulting in an approximate shadow price of \$408. Figure 12-2 shows how the accurately computed shadow price behaves as the storage space available increases. Initially, the shadow price drops quite steeply, as the storage space is increased from 6 m^2 to 20 m^2. At 20 m^2, the unconstrained optimal solution can be implemented. Additional increases in storage space available will not decrease the minimum cost any further. Hence, they have a zero value, i.e., the shadow price drops to zero once the resource is not constraining the optimal solution.

Analytic Method for Finding the Shadow Price of the Storage Constraint

In many problems, the approach demonstrated above is the most efficient way to determine an approximate curve for the shadow price as a function of the resource availability. In some cases, there is a more elegant way. The idea is deceptively simple! The relevant cost in expression (6-1A) only includes the annual replenishment setup cost and the annual inventory holding cost. We now introduce a further penalty in the form of a yet unknown, annual charge π per square metre of storage space used. In our example, this additional charge for a replenishment of size Q amounts to $\pi Q / 96$, since 96 cans can be stored on one square metre. Adding this

Figure 12-2: The shadow price of storage space

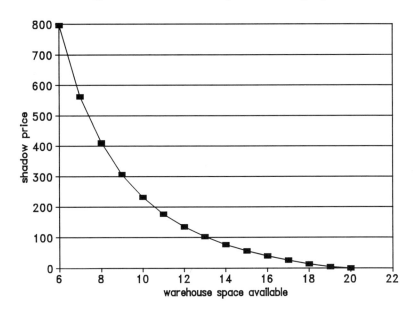

term to the total cost expression (6-1A), we get

$$T(Q) = 0.5Qvr + sD/Q + \pi Q/96 \tag{12-1}$$

Using the method explained in Section 6.11, the optimal replenishment Q^* is now

$$Q^* = \sqrt{2Ds/(vr+(1/48)\pi))} \tag{12-2}$$

Note the similarity with EOQ formula (6-2). There is an additional term of $(1/48)\pi$ in the denominator. If π is set equal to zero, expression (12-2) gives the same answer as the EOQ formula. This must be so, since a zero charge implies that storage space is abundant and hence has no value. However, for any positive value of π, Q^* will be smaller than the EOQ.

Expression (12-2) can now be used to determine the value of this unknown charge π implied by a given amount of storage space available. As we saw in the previous section, if the storage space is restricted, the constrained optimal order quantity is set to a value q which exactly uses up all storage space. We now simply assign π a value such that expression (12-2) yields a Q^* equal to q. We could find the correct value for π by trial and error. However, in this instance, some elementary algebra allows us to find a formula for the value of π we are looking for:

$$\pi = 48([2Ds/q^2] - vr) \tag{12-3}$$

For example, for the current storage restriction of 8 m², we see from Table 12-1 that $q = 768$. Expression (12-3) then yields the following value for π:

$$\pi = 48([2(57600)(52.80)/(768^2)] - (7.05)(0.25)) = \$410.40.$$

Verify that if you insert this value into expression (12-2) you get $Q^* = 768$. This shadow price is an exact value — not an approximation, unlike the one obtained by making small, but discrete changes in the constraint and extrapolating the resulting cost decrease to a full unit of the resource. The difference is though small. The values listed under the heading 'Shadow price' in Figure 12-1 are the exact shadow prices computed by the above formula.

Generalizing the Meaning of Shadow Price

The concept of shadow price can be extended to any type of restriction on the set of activities or values of the decision variables of an optimization problem. The shadow price always refers to the rate of change in the optimal value of the objective function for relaxing the constraint by one unit. Relaxing a constraint means making that constraint less binding or less tight. For a resource constraint this means providing additional amounts of the resource. The optimal constrained solution will then get closer to the unconstrained optimal solution. Hence the value of the objective function should normally improve, i.e., decrease if we minimize costs or increase if we maximize profits.

Relaxing a constraint may take many different forms besides increasing the amount of a scarce resource. Here are a few examples to illustrate this.

The problem may require a given level of output for a product, say the amount of water required for irrigation. Relaxing this output requirement means having more water available for other more profitable uses, such as electric power generation may increase total profits.

The constraint may be in the form of a maximum amount of output of a by-product for a given activity, say the emission of air pollutants at a factory. Relaxing this constraint means allowing higher emissions, hence reducing the cost of emission control.

The constraint may refer to minimum quality standards, such as a minimum breaking strength for a cable. Relaxing this constraint means making it easier to satisfy this quality standard. This implies decreasing this minimum breaking strength required. It hopefully results in a decrease in manufacturing costs.

The shadow price also reflects the rate of change in the objective function for making a constraint marginally tighter, such as decreasing the amount of a resource available. Naturally, making a constraint tighter means that the optimal value of the objective function deteriorates, i.e., just the reverse effect of relaxing a constraint. Minimum costs go up, maximum benefits go down.

12.4 INTERPRETATION AND USES OF SHADOW PRICE

Value of Additional Resources

The discussion in the previous section immediately suggests that the shadow price of a resource constraint can be interpreted as the maximum price the user entity, e.g., a firm, should be willing to pay for additional (but possibly very small) amounts of the resource. So, if the cost of the resource is less than the shadow price at the current constraint level, this is a signal for acquiring additional amounts of that resource. On the other hand, if the cost of the resource is more than the shadow price, this may be an indication that the firm either uses too much of the resource or uses it inefficiently.

Although the shadow price gives a signal whether to acquire more of the resource or dispose of some of the resource, there still remains the question of 'how much?'. The answer to this question is made more difficult by the fact that the shadow price of a resource is a marginal concept and may be highly sensitive to changes in the constraint level.

As a first cut, we can study the curve of the shadow price as a function of the constraint level. For example, assume that the current cost of refrigerated storage space is about $100 per m². Figure 12-2 shows that for storage space of 13 m² or less the shadow price is more than $100. Hence, if storage space can be purchased at that unit price in any arbitrary amount (within reason), the optimal decision for the LOD is to increase the refrigerated storage space to 13 m². So we see that knowing the shadow price at the current constraint level of 8 m² is not sufficient. In fact, we generally need to know part or most of the shadow price curve for answering the question of 'how much'.

If the resource can only be acquired in a limited number of sizes or amounts, 'how much' is not a question of marginal analysis, but one of incremental analysis. Section 12.2 demonstrated this approach for the storage problem. There, additional storage could be obtained in lots of 6 m² at a cost of $600. This is also $100 per m². We concluded that the optimal solution was to increase the storage space to 14 m². This is 1 m² more than the optimal solution derived from marginal analysis. The reason why the two answers differ is that marginal analysis assumes the resource is infinitesimally divisible, i.e., can be acquired in any arbitrary amounts, while incremental analysis is based on the realities of the real world.

Correct Interpretation of Shadow Price

A clear understanding of the distinction between marginal and incremental analysis is the basis for a proper interpretation of the shadow price at a given constraint level. Only then will the use of shadow prices lead to the correct decisions.

There is a second source of potential confusion in the interpretation of shadow prices. If the objective function already includes a charge for the resource, say the going purchase price, the shadow price already reflects this cost. It then only represents the highest additional premium that should be paid for the resource at the current constraint level. For example, the scarce resource is hours of labour during regular work time. The labour cost is already included as a cost component in the objective function. Then the shadow price represents the maximum overtime premium the firm can afford to pay without being worse off. (Note that the question of 'how much' still needs to be answered!)

A shadow price may not necessarily be expressed in monetary terms. In fact, it is always expressed in terms of the measure used in the objective function. If the latter deals, e.g., with maximizing the amount of electric power produced, then the shadow price on the water in the hydro reservoir, which limits the amount of power that can be produced, will also be in terms of units of electric power.

In conclusion, shadow prices provide indicators on whether or not it may be advantageous to change the current constraint level and whether the change should be a relaxation or a tightening of the constraint. However, without further analysis, it does not tell us the best size of any change. To answer that question, we may need to have recourse to incremental analysis.

Shadow prices are one of the more difficult concepts to grasp. You may need to study this and the previous section again. They are a most important practical aspect of sensitivity analysis, providing valuable insights into the solution space. They are also an important theoretical concept in OR/MS. We will demonstrate their usefulness in this as well as several later chapters.

12.5 SEVERAL ACTIVITIES SHARING A LIMITED RESOURCE

When several activities compete for the use of the same scarce resource, the optimal level of each activity cannot be determined individually for each activity. They are now linked together through the resource use. There will be trade-offs. Allocating more to one activity in order to capture high benefits will leave less for the other activities, reducing the benefits there. The optimal combination of activity levels now needs to be determined jointly.

The Heinz Logistics Problem Revisited

At this point, I suggest that you briefly review the Heinz USA logistics case of Section 11.10, and in particular Table 11-5. Using the idea of marginal costs and marginal savings, we found the optimal number of railcars by stepwise increasing their number until their marginal cost became larger than the marginal savings from the reduction in Scholle bag usage. This approach was possible because we only looked at the transport of tomato paste from one factory to one processing plant.

Heinz operates several factories and many processing plants. If there is no constraint on the total number of railcars that can be purchased, then each combination of factory and plant can be solved individually. (We also make the assumption that the demand follows the same pattern of peaks and troughs. This implies that idle railcars cannot be switched to other routes in order to increase their usage and lower the marginal rail cost.) Let us now throw a spanner into the works by assuming that the railcar manufacturer can only supply a total of 60 railcars. Again, to simplify things, we consider only four different combinations of factories and processing plants, each being a separate activity. How should we go about finding the optimal allocation of railcars to each activity?

As is often the case, the basic idea is very simple — it just needed somebody to think of it. Let me demonstrate it with this little story. After having seen the film classic 'Babette's Feast' with a group of friends, you invited them for a special treat. You planned to surprise them with 'caille au sarcophage'— the main course Babette offered to her guests. A crude translation is 'quail in a coffin'. But do not be deceived — it is delicious! Unfortunately you procrastinated in buying the quails. In panic you go to the local farmers' market. A quick check shows that several stalls still have a few suitable birds left and that the prices vary substantially from stall to stall. But no single stall can supply all the quails you need. Being a frugal gourmet — a rather interesting contradiction — you quickly note down prices and the number of quails at each stall. Your purchasing strategy is to start buying as many quails as are available at the stall with the lowest price, then proceed to the stall with the next lowest price, and so on, until you have bought the required number of quails. In other words, true to your character, you use a greedy algorithm. It will guarantee that you spend the least amount of money to buy the number of quails required.

A Greedy Algorithm for Resource Allocation

This same type of greedy algorithm can be applied to the allocation of railcars. All we need is a schedule of the difference between the marginal Scholle bag cost and the marginal rail cost per tonne for each activity. I will call these differences 'the marginal advantage of rail over bags' or MARB for short. You then allocate the railcars sequentially in order of decreasing value of MARBs until all 60 railcars have been allocated to the four activities.

Table 12-1 lists the MARBs for each factory/processing plant considered. Activity 1 is the one we analyzed in Table 11-5. For example, the MARB for demand level 12 is the difference between $93.20 for Scholle bags and $82.70 for rail per tonne transported. Only positive MARBs are shown, since we would never use railcars when the MARBs become negative.

Activity 3 has the highest MARB of $13.12 per tonne, valid for the first 9 railcars used. So, the first 9 railcars are thus allocated to activity 3. There are 51 railcars left to allocate. Activity 2 has the next highest MARB with $11.96 and gets allocated 10 railcars. This leaves 41 railcars. The third allocation is again to activity 3, and so on. (How about testing your understanding by doing the next four allocations?) The numbers in brackets after the MARBs show the order in which the railcars are allocated. After the seventh allocation (to activity 2) there are only 7 railcars left. These are allocated to activity 1. The asterisk flags the fact that the eighth incremental allocation only covers a portion of the 11 railcars which have the MARB of $9.68. The bottom row shows the total number of railcars allocated to each activity.

Table 12-1: MARBs in decreasing value for each activity

Demand level	Activity 1 railcars	MARB	Activity 2 railcars	MARB	Activity 3 railcars	MARB	Activity 4 railcars	MARB
12	14	$10.50 (6)	10	$11.96 (2)	9	$13.12 (1)	12	9.65
11	11	9.68 (8*)	8	10.98 (4)	7	11.63 (3)	9	9.03
10	2	9.68	4	10.02 (7)	1	10.63 (5)	3	9.03
9	2	6.40	1	7.03	2	7.45	2	6.74
8	3	neg.	2	2.61	4	2.92	4	0.49
7			5	neg.	6	neg.	8	neg.
allocation		21		22		17		0

The shadow price of the current constraint level for railcars is given by the MARB for the sixty-first railcar available. That railcar would be used to increase the eighth incremental allocation. It goes to activity 1, increasing that allocation for the eleventh demand level from 7 to 8. Its MARB is $9.68 per tonne, valid for up to 11 railcars. Since the MARB is the difference between the rail cost and the Scholle bag cost per tonne transported, this shadow price must now be interpreted as a premium. It is the highest premium, in addition to the normal rail cost per tonne, HEINZ should be willing to pay to get an additional railcar. In contrast to the inventory control example, this premium remains the same for a total of 6 railcars, rather than changing continuously. Can you figure out why?

The answer to this question can be found in Figure 11-7. It shows how the marginal rail cost increases step-wise with each progressive higher demand level, but remains constant for additional railcars within each demand level. As a consequence, the shadow price for additional railcars also remains constant within a demand level, and increases when stepping to a higher demand level.

There is a close similarity between the greedy algorithm and the algorithm for marginal analysis. As a result, both require that the objective function is well behaved. This means that the marginal costs have to be non-decreasing, i.e., they either stay the same or increase for additional allocations, and the marginal savings have to be non-increasing, i.e., they either stay the same or decrease for additional allocations. As a result, the marginal advantage will ultimately decrease as the amount allocated increases further and further. If costs or benefits do not satisfy this property, then the greedy algorithm fails to find the optimal solution. It may also fail if the allocation has to be done in irregularly discrete chunks. The next section will demonstrate this aspect.

12.6 DISCRETE AND IRREGULAR USE OF A RESOURCE

A firm is considering its investment budget for the coming year. A list of possible candidates has been prepared from the proposals put forward by the various operating departments. Each proposal has been subjected to the accept/reject test in terms of the firm's desired rate of return on new investments, as discussed in Section 10.4. The first three rows in Table 12-2 list the candidate projects, their individual initial investment or cash outflow, and the NPV, i.e., the present value of all cash outflows and cash inflows associated with each project, all expressed in units of $1000.

Table 12-2: Selection of investment portfolio

Project	A	B	C	D	E	F	G	H	J	K
Init. investment	107	201	182	133	82	141	30	37	25	12
NPV	84	50	45	39	35	26	24	9	8	2
Ranking by decreasing NPV:										
NPV rank	1	2	3	4	5	6	7	8	9	10
Cumul. investment	107	308	490	-	572	-	-	-	597	-
Cumul. NPV	84	134	179	-	214	-	-	-	222	-
Ranking by decreasing ratio of [PV of cash inflows / Initial investment]:										
PV cash inflow	191	251	227	172	117	167	54	46	33	14
Ratio	1.785	1.249	1.247	1.293	1.427	1.184	1.800	1.243	1.320	1.167
Ratio rank	2	6	7	5	3	9	1	8	4	10
Cumul. investment	137	578	-	377	219	-	30	-	244	590
Cumul. NPV	108	240	-	190	143	-	24	-	151	242
Optimal solution:										
Cumul. investment	107	-	289	422	82	-	534	571	596	-
Cumul. NPV	84	-	129	168	203	-	227	236	244	-

The firm has an investment budget of $600,000. Which combination or portfolio of projects should be undertaken? The firm's objective is to maximize the NPV of the portfolio selected. A naive application of the greedy algorithm would choose the projects in terms of decreasing NPVs. The second set of rows in Table 12-2 shows that the projects have already been ranked in this order. Hence A, B, and C are the first three projects chosen. They use up $490,000 of the $600,000 available. The fourth ranked project D with an initial investment of $133,000 exceeds the balance of funds left. Hence, it is skipped over. The initial investment of the fifth ranked project E can be accommodated, leaving a balance of unallocated funds of $28,000. Projects F, G, and H again have to be skipped. The final project selected is J, leaving a unused balance of $3000. The sum of the NPVs is $222,000.

This selection method has serious flaws. Just consider the extreme case where there is another candidate L with an initial investment of $600,000 and an associated NPV of $120,000. Since it has the largest NPV it is the first one chosen, exhausting the entire budget. It leads to a substantially inferior return than if project L had been ignored.

Some 40 years ago, two economists (J. Lorie and L. J. Savage) suggested that the projects be viewed in terms of the ratio of the PV of (all cash flows exclusive of the initial investment) to (the initial investment), also referred to as the benefit/cost ratio. A more sophisticated version of the greedy algorithm would then select projects in terms of decreasing values of their benefit/cost ratios. This method is demonstrated in the third set of rows in Table 12-2. Verify that this method selects the first six projects G, A, E, J, D, B in that order. Project C is the seventh ranked one. Its initial investment exceeds the unallocated balance of $22,000. Hence, it is skipped. So are projects F, G, and H. Only project K still fits into the budget. The NPVs of the projects chosen add up to $240,000, a considerable improvement over the first method.

However, even that criterion does not guarantee finding the optimal solution. The reason for this is that funds are allocated in discrete and uneven chunks. The objective function is not well-behaved. As a result, the unused balance may end up to be fairly large. A different choice may use more of the funds budgeted and hence achieve a higher NPV sum. For our example, the optimal solution is shown in the last set of rows. Note that it does not select the projects in terms of their decreasing benefit/cost ratio. However, for large problems with many relatively small projects, the Laurie-Savage criterion often finds the optimal solution or one very close to it.

EXERCISES

1. Using the cost and demand data in Figure 12-1, redo a similar analysis but for a restriction on the average investment in inventories. Reduce the investment limit initially to the nearest multiple of $100 and then by decrements of $100 to a minimum of $5000. Plot the incremental cost change as a function of the average investment, i.e., the x-axis increases from $5000 to the unconstrained optimal average investment. If possible do the analysis on a spreadsheet.

2. For the data in Figure 12-1, find the shadow price for a warehouse constraint of 12 m^2,
   (a) using first the approximation procedure described in the second subsection of Section 12.3.
   (b) using expression (12-3).

3. Using the approximation procedure described the second subsection of Section 12.3,
   (a) find a reasonably accurate shadow price for the situation in exercise 1 above for an average investment limit of $5,500.
   (b) What is the exact interpretation of this shadow price?
   (c) Show that the difference between the constrained optimal solution for an average

investment limit of $5,500 is substantially less than the product of the shadow price and the difference between the unconstrained optimal average investment and $5,500.

4*. Develop an analytic expression similar to expression (12-3) for determining the shadow price on the average inventory investment and use it to evaluate the shadow price for a $5,500 limit.

5. Analyze the differences and similarities between sensitivity analysis, as discussed in Chapter 7, and the concept of the shadow price of a constraint.

6. Determine the shadow price for the data given in exercise 6 of Chapter 11 if the number of 'advisors' is limited to 6.

7*. (Requires a spreadsheet for the Heinz case of Section 11.10, as for Figure 11-5.) The original data had a limit of 30 round trips per year and a railcar capacity of 18 tonnes. Using the approximation procedure demonstrated in the second subsection of Section 12.3, determine the shadow price
(a)   for 30 round trips.
(b)   for railcars of 18-tonne capacity.

8. A chain of supermarkets has just received the last shipment of strawberries of the season, packed in cases containing 24 punnets each. From past observations, the fresh fruit marketing manager is able to develop the following table of total sales revenues (in dollars) for allocating n cases to each of the 6 stores of the chain:

Store		1	2	3	4	5	6
Allocation of	1 case	36	36	32	30	30	28
	2 cases	70	68	64	60	58	57
	3 cases	95	96	96	90	84	84
	4 cases	112	116	128	118	105	104
	5 cases	122	125	152	138	126	118
	6 cases	122	125	172	153	135	125
	7 cases	122	125	181	160	135	125
	8 cases	122	125	181	160	135	125

The difference in revenues is due to differences of location and customer propensity to buy strawberries.   Each case has a cost of $20.   Use a greedy algorithm for the following situation:
(a)   If there is no restriction on the number of cases that can be obtained, how many cases should be purchased to at least break even? How many are allocated to each store? What is the total gross profit (difference between revenue and cost)?
(b)   If the maximum number of cases that the manager can procure is 16, how should they be allocated to the various stores? What is the total revenue? What is the shadow price of case 17?

9. The table below shows the choices of an electric power generating company for generating incremental amounts of power for a given day, where the numbers in the table represent the actual cost of thermal generation or the imputed value of the water used for hydro generation for incremental units of one MWh in $1000.

Source of power	station 1	station 2	station 3	station 4
Type of station	hydro	hydro	thermal	thermal
Incremental output				
1st MWh	56	75	80	110
2nd MWh	72	75	80	110
3rd MWh	84	82	80	110
4th MWh	95	90	96	120
5th MWh	110	110	96	120
6th MWh	110	110	96	120

(a) If the amount of power required is 9 MWh, what is the optimal output for each station, assuming that there are no fixed start-up costs for thermal power stations? What is the total cost? Use a greedy algorithm.

(b) Assume now that there is a start-up cost of $20,000 for each thermal station. This means that the first MWh of power produced costs $20,000 more than listed in the table above, but the cost of further increments is the same as above. Discuss why a greedy algorithm will fail to find the optimal solution.

10. Consider the investment opportunities in exercise 11 of Chapter 11. Assume now that only $270,000 of funds are available for investment (i.e., only the first two sources of funds). Using the ratio method of Section 12.6, find the resulting choice of projects made. By trial-and-error try to determine if you can find a better solution.

REFERENCES

There are a number of fairly sophisticated mathematical algorithms or methods for finding the optimal solution to single-constraint problems. If both the objective function and the constraint are differentiable in the decision variable, the **Lagrange multiplier approach** can be used. See Section 19-7 in H.G. Daellenbach et al. *Introduction to O.R. Techniques*, 2nd ed., Allyn and Bacon, 1983, or any other intermediate level O.R. text for an introductory discussion. If the functions are not differentiable or not well behaved, **dynamic programming** is the most commonly recommended approach. See Chapter 9 of Daellenbach, *opus cited.*

13 Multiple Constraints — Linear Programming

We saw in Chapter 12 that a constraint on the decision choices may force a solution that is less advantageous than the one achievable without a constraint. If the decision choices have to satisfy several constraints simultaneously, this is even more true. This chapter studies a special case of constrained optimization, namely when the relationships between the decision variables are all linear. Although the assumption of linearity may look highly restrictive, there are, in fact, numerous applications in business, industry, agriculture, the public sector, as well as in engineering, where linearity of all relationships between the variables holds or is at least a very good approximation over the normal range of operations.

As an example, consider the construction of a freeway or motorway through a hilly countryside. A lot of soil and rocks will have to be shifted from places where the road cuts through hills to where fill is required to raise the road or to be discarded at suitable sites. The construction firm wants to do this as cheaply as possible. For any two sites, one where excess material is to be removed, called a source of material, and one where material is to be deposited or may be dumped, called a sink of material, the cost of shifting this material is approximately proportional to the amount that is transported. However, this cost does not have to be proportional to the distance between the two sites. The constraints imposed on the schedule for shifting material are, on the one hand, the amounts of excess material to be removed from each source and, on the other hand, the amounts of fill material required at each sink or the capacity of sinks serving as dumps for unwanted material. The schedule for shifting material consists of a detailed list of how much is transported from each source to each sink — the decision variables of the problem. Clearly, the constraints are linear. They simply consist of the sum of material shifted. For instance, if site A has a capacity for receiving 120,000 m^3 of dumped material, then the sum of the amounts transported from all sources to sink A cannot exceed this limit.

This chapter starts out with a short general discussion on optimization in the presence of multiple constraints. Section 13.2 gives a summary of a somewhat simplified, but typical situation and shows the associated influence diagram. The mathematical formulation and its graphical interpretation and solution is given in Section 13.3. In Section 13.4 we gain some insights into the general structure of linear programming problems and the solution algorithm. The ease with which sensitivity analysis can be performed in linear programming is one of the strengths of this tool. This is the topic of Section 13.5. Section 13.6 shows how the optimal solution can be found using the **solvers** or **optimizers** built into some of the more powerful spreadsheets. The chapter concludes with two, albeit somewhat simplified, practical applications of linear programming.

13.1 CONSTRAINED OPTIMIZATION

Section 12.1 suggests a three-step procedure for finding the best solution if there is a single constraint on the decision choices. We first determine the optimal solution ignoring the constraint. If this solution satisfies the constraint, we have found the optimal solution to the problem. If the constraint is violated, then we know that the best solution will satisfy the constraint as an equality, e.g., use up all of the available resource for continuous decision variables or use up as much as possible of the resource if the decision variables can only assume discrete values. Often a greedy algorithm will find the best constrained optimal solution.

New Aspects with Multiple Constraints

Faced with many constraints, often in the hundreds or thousands, more powerful approaches are needed. Over the last 40 years a number of sophisticated mathematical algorithms have been developed. A few are of a fairly general nature, making few assumptions about the mathematical structure of the problem. The majority, however, deal with special classes of problems and take advantage of their special mathematical structure. For instance, as indicated above, if all relationships are linear and the variables are continuous, the solution technique of linear programming can be applied. If all decision variables can only assume values of 0 or 1, then network algorithms are often computationally highly efficient for finding the optimal solution. These algorithms are the topic of advanced university courses in operations research and are beyond the scope of this text. Our interest here is much more modest. We simply wish to get a better understanding of the nature of the difficulties and maybe gain some insights into the general form of the solutions.

   In a multiple constraint decision problem, some of the constraints may be binding on the optimal solution, others will not. If the constraints are all in the form of scarce resources, a binding constraint implies that all of the resource is used up — in other words, the total amount of the resource consumed is equal to the amount available. A constraint that is not binding means that some of the resource remains unused — in other words, the constraint has slack.

   From what we discovered in Section 12.1, we also know that the optimal constrained solution can never be better than the optimal unconstrained solution. In fact, unless all constraints have slack, the best constrained solution will be worse.

   If we knew which constraints are binding on the decision variables, we could simply discard all other non-binding constraints. These will, by definition, have no effect on the optimal constrained values of the decision variables. With fewer constraints to be considered, finding the optimal constrained solution would be computationally simpler. At the optimal constrained solution, all the binding constraints would be in the form of equations. The computational problem would then boil down to solving a system of equations, some or all of which could be nonlinear. Unfortunately, there is no simple way for identifying which constraints are binding and which constraints have slack.

An Algorithmic Analogy — South Sea Island Treasure Hunt

So, how do the majority of these algorithmic methods go about finding the optimal constrained solution to a problem? The easiest way to explain the general principle is to take a geographical analogy. Consider this enchanting South Sea island. Your treasure map only tells you that the treasure is hidden under a round rock at the highest point on this island. You arrive on the island in the middle of a pitch black night. You cannot wait until daylight before starting the ascent to the highest point since one-eyed Jack is in hot pursuit of you. You also know that the island has a very rugged coastline, with high cliffs at various places. In fact, the highest point on the island could well be at some cliff top.

At this point I ask you to quickly review the description of algorithmic solution methods given in Section 6.10.

You reason as follows: You land at some suitable spot where the ground rises slowly from the shore. This is your initial solution. Since you could land there, it must be feasible solution. You now want to move away from this spot. Your aim is to go uphill. You measure your level of success (your objective function) by the height you have reached. But you only consider steps that do not lead you over a cliff. The cliffs are constraints on the direction you can travel. So you only make steps that are feasible (i.e., do not go over a cliff) and at the same time improve your objective function. Once you reach a point where you cannot take another step in a feasible direction that leads uphill, you stop having reached a top.

Local and Global Optima

The question now is 'is this the highest point on the island?' If the island has only a single peak and the ground rises from the shore steadily towards this single peak from every feasible direction, even along the cliff edges, then you can be sure that you have reached the highest point even in pitch darkness. Mathematically speaking, we say that the surface of the island is **well-behaved**. In this case your algorithm will find the optimal solution.

On the other hand, if the island has many high points with peaks of various heights and possibly also some plateaus part way up, we say that the surface of the island is not well-behaved. Then there is no guarantee that this algorithm will lead you to the highest point on the island. You could easily end up at a plateau part way up or at one of the minor peaks, i.e., a local peak rather the highest or global peak. Had you started at some different initial point, you might have reached a different local peak or even the global peak. But in the dark you can never tell!

Back to the discussion of constrained optimization! If the mathematical form of the problem is well-behaved, an algorithm which at each iteration improves the value of the objective function, while remaining feasible, will ultimately find the optimal solution. If a problem does not have a well-behaved mathematical form, then no such guarantee can be given. You might have found a **local optimum** or the **global optimum**. The vexing question is that you will never know which one.

For certain classes of problems we can though ascertain that the mathematical form is 'well-behaved' and, hence, the solution algorithm is guaranteed to find the global optimal constrained solution. Linear programming is one of those.

13.2 AN EXAMPLE

A Situation Summary

For pedagogic reasons, the situation used is highly simplified. The technical manager of a coal-fired electric power generating plant is reviewing the plant's operational setup in the light of the emission standards of the new air pollution control laws coming into force early next year. These specify the following maximum emission rates for airborne particles and sulphur oxides:

- particles: 12 kilograms/hour
- sulphur oxides: 3000 parts per million (PPM)

The plant currently uses the cheap $80 per tonne Longburne coal with high sulphur and particle emissions. These are well above the new maximum limits. The only way to reduce these emissions is to mix Longburne with a less polluting coal. The mixture will have emission rates that are the weighted average for both coals. The only high quality coal available in sufficient volume is the rather expensive $100 per tonne Blackball coal.

The two coals available have the following emissions:

Coal	Sulphur oxides (PPM)	Particles (kg/tonne coal)
Longburne	3800 PPM	1.0 kg
Blackball	1800 PPM	0.5 kg

Longburne can generate 20,000 pounds of steam per tonne, while Blackball generates 24,000 pounds of steam. Coal is injected into the burners in the form of a powder. The plant's pulverizer can handle 24 tonnes of the soft Longburne coal per hour, but only 16 tonnes of the hard Blackball coal. Another restriction is the conveyer belt supplying the pulverizer. It can handle a maximum of 20 tonnes per hour.

The technical manager would like to have answers to two questions:

(1) What is the maximum steam output of the plant under the new emission

standards? This will determine the maximum amount of electricity the plant can contribute towards meeting power consumption in periods of peak usage.

(2) What is the cheapest combination of the two coals that will produce a steam output of 240,000 pounds/hour? This is the steam output required to base load the plant.

We shall consider question (1) first and leave question (2) as an exercise for you.

An Influence Diagram

The influence diagram in Figure 13-1 depicts the chain of consequences associated with various decision choices. The objective of the problem is to maximize the amount of steam that can be produced. Recall though that the influence diagram only traces the effects of an arbitrary combination of inputs, including control inputs on the system outputs. The optimization aspect is not specifically included in the diagram. That aspect is implied by the possibility of altering the control inputs and observing the effect on the performance measure.

What influences the steam output? The amount of each coal burned per hour. This is controllable by the decision maker. Hence, we have two decision variables:

- the number of tonnes of Longburne burned per hour, and
- the number of tonnes of Blackball burned per hour.

In the influence diagram, the control inputs or decisions are represented by the rectangular box, labelled 1. The combination of coals used (box 1), together with the steam output per tonne for each coal (the input cloud, labelled 18) determine the total steam output per hour (result oval 19).

Each combination of coals burned causes a corresponding amount of particle emission. So the system variable for the amount of particle emissions (circle 3) is influenced by the emission rate per tonne for each coal (input cloud 2) and the combination of coals burned (decision rectangle 1). Given the limit on particle emissions (input cloud 4), the feasibility of the particle emission or the lack thereof can be ascertained (output oval 5). In other words, we find out whether or not a given choice of coals satisfies the constraint on particle emissions.

Each of the other three constraints is depicted by a similar connected set of decision variables, inputs, system variables and/or outputs. Verify that the sulphur oxide constraint is given by items 1, 6, 7, 8, and 9.

So we see that, in addition to the measure of performance, each constraint may also give rise to an output. For a solution to be feasible, each one of the constraints must be feasible. Note also that the cost of the coals is not relevant for finding the maximum steam output of the plant.

In this particular example, depicting the relationship via an influence diagram will help us in the mathematical formulation. This is, however, not always so. Other diagrammatic representations, such as a material flow diagram or a network of nodes may be more instructive and useful.

Figure 13-1: Influence diagram for power plant operation

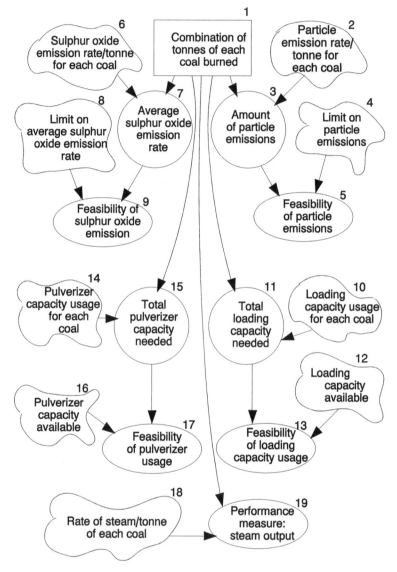

13.3 A LINEAR PROGRAMMING FORMULATION

Decision Variables

The first step is to introduce names for the two decision variables. Rather than denote the variables by symbols, like x_1 and x_2, it is more helpful to use **mnemonic** names, such as LONG and BLACK for the number of tonnes of each type of coal burned per hour. Mnemonic names immediately suggest what the variable stands for. This is particularly useful if the problem involves hundreds of variables.

LONG and BLACK may each assume any value, integer or fractional, that is **non-negative**. In fact, **non-negativity** of the variables is one of the basic assumptions of the linear programming model. This assumption reflects the nature of most activities in the real world, where it rarely makes much sense within an economic or industrial context to talk about negative activities. If an activity may also assume negative values, there is a simple trick to get around this assumption. We simply replace the original variable by the difference of two separate variables, both non-negative, one measuring the positive values of the variable, the other measuring the negative values.

The Objective Function

The influence diagram shows the amount of steam to be produced per hour (output oval 19) as the performance measure to be maximized. Let the variable OUTPUT denote the number of pounds of steam produced per hour. OUTPUT is seen to be a function of the amount of each coal burned per hour (decision box 1) and the rate of steam produced per tonne for each coal (input 18), as shown in Table 13-1.

Table 13-1: Construction of performance measure

Coal	Rate of steam in pounds/tonne	Tonnes of coal/hour	Steam output in pounds/hour
Longburne	20,000	LONG	20000 LONG
Blackball	24,000	BLACK	24000 BLACK
Total steam output/hour: OUTPUT = 20000 LONG + 24000 BLACK			

To indicate that it is the variable OUTPUT that is to be maximized, we show the objective function as follows:

$$\text{Maximize OUTPUT} = 20000 \text{ LONG} + 24000 \text{ BLACK} \qquad (13\text{-}1)$$

The two coefficients multiplying the decision variables are referred to as **objective function coefficients**. Figure 13-2 shows that for any specific value assumed by OUTPUT, equation (13-1) is a straight line. The decision variable LONG is measured along the y-axis, while BLACK is measured along the x-axis. Since the two decision variables can only assume non-negative values, each point in the positive quadrant and along the axes represents a combination of values for the two variables. Remember also that any straight line can be determined by finding two points on it. In this example, the two logical points are easily found by in turn setting each of the variables equal to zero and solving for the other one. So, for OUTPUT=240,000, we find the two points (LONG=0, BLACK=10) and (BLACK=0, LONG=12). The straight line through these two points represents all combinations of the two decision variables that yield an output of 240,000 pounds. **Equal-output** lines for other values of OUTPUT correspond to straight line parallel to this line. Note that, as the value of OUTPUT increases, these equal-output lines move parallel to themselves, up and to the right.

Figure 13-2: The graph of the objective function

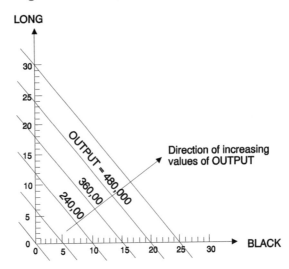

A straight line means that OUTPUT is a linear function of its two decision variables. This is not simply a coincidence, but another of the basic assumptions of linear programming. In fact, in linear programming all relationships are assumed to be linear, hence its name!

Particle Emission Constraint

The total particle emission per hour (circle 3) is a function of the amount of each coal burned per hour (decision box 1) and the rate of particle emission for each coal (input 2). If this total emission does not exceed 12 kg/hour (input 4), then it is technically feasible, otherwise not (output 5). Use a method similar to Table 13-1 for formulating the particle emission constraint. This is what you should get:

(SMOKE)   1 LONG + 0.5 BLACK ≤ 12   (13-2)

This is a less-than-or-equal inequality constraint. It says that the sum on the left-hand side has to be less than or at most equal to the number on the right-hand side. The coefficients multiplying the decision variables in a constraint are called **left-hand-side (LHS) coefficients** (since they appear on the left-hand-side of the inequality sign), while the number on the right-hand side of the inequality sign is referred to as the **right-hand-side (RHS) parameter**. (Note that a LHS coefficient of 1 is usually not shown explicitly, i.e., (13-2) would be shown as LONG + 0.5 BLACK ≤ 12.)

As required, this constraint is also linear. So, the constraint boundary, i.e., the combination of LONG and BLACK that produces exactly 12 kg of smoke, is also a straight line. It is shown in Figure 13-3. Considering the SMOKE constraint alone, only those combinations of LONG and BLACK that fall onto this line or to the left and below it — the area shaded in grey — are technically feasible.

Figure 13-3: The graph of the SMOKE constraint

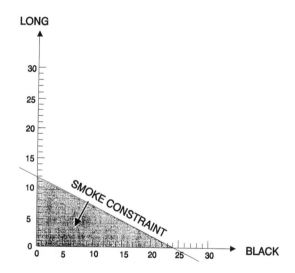

Sulphur Emission Constraint

The two coals are fed into the burners as a homogeneous mixture. As a result, the rate of sulphur emission in the flue gases (circle 7), measured in PPM, is a weighted average of the individual rates of each coal (input 6), where the amounts of each coal burned per hour (decision box 1) are used as the weights. So, if LONG tonnes of Longburne coal and BLACK tonnes of Blackball coal are mixed, then a fraction of LONG/(LONG+BLACK) of this mixture is Longburne, while a fraction of BLACK/(LONG+BLACK) is Blackball coal. These ratios serve as the weights attached to the emission rates of the two coals. The weighted average emission rate cannot exceed 3000 PPM (input 8). We get the following inequality:

3800 LONG/(LONG+BLACK)] + [1800 BLACK/(LONG+BLACK)] ≤ 3000

This does not look like a linear relationship. Fortunately, it can be converted into a linear relationship by a simple trick. We multiply both sides of the inequality by (LONG+BLACK) and cancel the ratios of (LONG+BLACK)/(LONG+BLACK):

3800 LONG + 1800 BLACK ≤ 3000 LONG + 3000 BLACK

Finally, re-arranging this inequality, such that all decision variables are shown on the left-hand-side, we get the sulphur emission constraint in its linear form:

(SULPHUR)   800 LONG − 1200 BLACK ≤ 0   (13-3)

This constraint differs from the preceding one in two respects. First, it is measured in PPM rather than in kilograms. The various constraints may thus be measured in different units. Second, it is a difference, rather than a sum, and has to be less than or equal to zero. Consequently, the usual trick of identifying two points for graphing the inequality only yields twice the same point, namely the origin (LONG=0, BLACK=0). However, a second point can be found by arbitrarily setting, say, LONG=12 and then solve for the value of BLACK such that the difference is zero. This yields the point (LONG=12, BLACK=8). The resulting line is shown in Figure 13-4. Verify that only those combinations of LONG and BLACK are feasible which lie on this line or in the shaded area below it.

Figure 13-4: The graph of the sulphur constraint

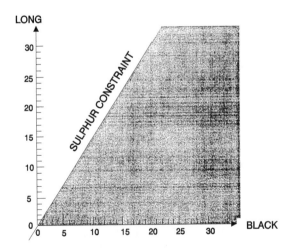

You now have the hang of it. Verify that the remaining two constraints have the following form:

Loading constraint:

(LOADING)   LONG + BLACK $\leq$ 20 (tonnes)   (13-4)

Pulverizer constraint:

(PULVERIZER)   0.041667 LONG + 0.0625 BLACK $\leq$ 1 (hour)   (13-5)

The LHS coefficients for the pulverizer constraint were obtained by realizing that if the pulverizer can process 24 tonnes of, say, Longburne coal per hour, then it takes 1/24 or 0.041666... (rounded to 0.041667) hours for one tonne of that coal.

The Feasible Region

Figure 13-5 shows all constraints on the same graph. To be an admissible choice, only those combinations of the two decision variables that satisfy all constraints simultaneously can be selected.   The set of all these admissible combinations is called the **feasible region**. The feasible region is the shaded area and its boundary

Figure 13-5: The feasible region

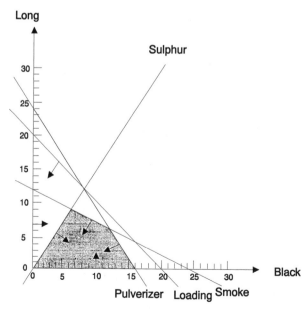

in Figure 13-5. Here, the boundary is given by the two non-negativity constraints on LONG and by segments of the lines for the SULPHUR, SMOKE, and PULVERIZER constraints as equalities. Note that the LOADING constraint has no point in common with the feasible region. Such a constraint is referred to as a **redundant constraint**.

For finding the feasible region we only needed the constraints. The objective function does not enter into consideration. It becomes relevant when we want to find where in the feasible region the optimal solution is located.

Graphical Solution

We now superimpose the graph of the objective function, Figure 13-2, onto the graph of the feasible region, Figure 13-5. The result is shown in Figure 13-6.

Figure 13-6: Graph for finding the optimal solution

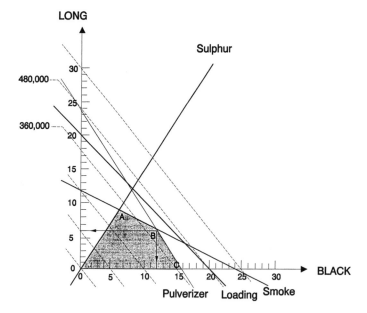

The equal-output lines for OUTPUT of 360,000 or less all have a segment that falls inside the feasible region, whereas the line for 480,000 has no point in common with the feasible region. Since the objective is to maximize OUTPUT, we can conclude that the maximum value of OUTPUT must be larger than 360,000, but less than 480,000. The highest equal-output line for OUTPUT which still has at least one point in common with the feasible region is OUTPUT=408,000, i.e., point B. If we push the it an infinitesimally small amount higher up, it is completely outside the feasible region. Hence, no combination of coals on that line is feasible. On the other hand, if the line is pushed down by an infinitesimally small amount, there is an infinite number of points located inside the feasible region which have a higher value for OUTPUT. So, OUTPUT=408,000 is the maximal value of the objective function. It implies values for the two decision variables of LONG=6 and BLACK= 12. This is the optimal solution to the maximum steam output problem.

Status of Constraints

Which ones of the constraints are binding at the optimal solution and which ones do have slack? Verify the results summarized in Table 13-2.

Table 13-2: Status of constraints

Constraint	RHS	LHS	Status	Amount of slack
Smoke emission (kg)	12	12	binding	zero
Sulphur emission (PPM)	3000	2467	slack	533
Loading capacity (tonnes)	20	18	slack	2
Pulverizer capacity (hrs)	1	1	binding	zero

At point B, the combination of coals used reaches the particle emission limit exactly and uses up all the pulverizer capacity. However, the coal conveyer belt could handle 2 tonnes more coal and the average sulphur emission is below its permissible limit. For determining the amount of slack in the SULPHUR constraint I need to revert back to the original constraint rather than use the transformed inequality (13-3). This gives a more meaningful interpretation. The average sulphur emission is $1800[12/(12+6)] + 3800[6/(12+6)] = 2466.67$. This is 533.33 under the limit of 3000 PPM. (Inequality (13-3) gives a difference between the RHS and the LHS of $0 - [800(6) + 1200(12)] = -9600$. The interpretation of this difference is rather difficult. It is equal to $(12+6)533.33$, i.e., the total amount of coal used times the average amount of slack per tonne in terms of PPM, as defined for the original constraint.)

Recapitulation of Graphical Solution

I now briefly recap what we did to find the optimal solution graphically. We pushed the line for the objective function parallel to itself, up and to the right. We continued pushing as long as any part of that line remained inside the feasible region. We stopped when pushing it any fraction further would have implied leaving the feasible region.

From this process it follows that the optimal solution to a linear programming problem must always lie somewhere along the boundary of the feasible region. It is either a corner point, also referred to as an **extreme point**, such as in this example, or the optimal solution is any point along the segment of a constraint that forms part of the boundary of the feasible region. The latter is the case when the lines for the objective function are parallel to one of the constraints. If this happens, then there is an infinite number of possible optimal solutions to choose from. Any point along the boundary coinciding with the maximum value of the objective function is an optimal solution. But more on that later on.

13.4 SOME GENERALIZATIONS

This example has only two decision variables. The problem and its solution can therefore easily be depicted graphically. Real-life problems may have hundreds or even thousands of variables and constraints. Does what we discovered for a two-dimensional problem still hold then? This section will draw some insights from the simple two-dimensional case and then generalize them to the multi-dimensional case.

A Well-Behaved Problem

In the introduction I briefly talked about the importance of a mathematical problem being well-behaved. Only then can we be sure that a search method that attempts to go uphill at each step will converge on the optimal solution. Linear programming problems are well-behaved. Why?

First, note the shape of the feasible region. For a problem with two decision variables, the feasible region is a polygon, i.e., an area bounded by straight lines — segments of all non-redundant constraints. Any straight line drawn from one point on the boundary to another point on the boundary never leaves the feasible region. This means that the feasible region is well-behaved. Second, from the process of finding the optimal solution, it is also evident that the optimal solution always occurs somewhere on the boundary of the feasible region. Furthermore, it is the slope of the objective function lines that determines where on the boundary this is.

These properties also hold if we have more than two decision variables. We can still picture what happens with three decision variables. Each constraint, satisfied as equalities, is now not a straight line anymore, but a plane, dissecting a three-dimensional space. The feasible region is a polyhedron, a solid form with faces in the form of polygons, corresponding to portions of all non-redundant constraints. Just imagine one of those old-fashioned (or ultra-modern) lamp shades made of odd-shaped coloured glass panes, held together by lead beads. This is very much what the feasible region would look like, except normally with a much more irregular shape. Still, the straight line connecting any two arbitrarily chosen points on the surface of this polyhedron would still remain entirely within the polyhedron or the feasible region. So, again the feasible region is well-behaved. The objective function is also a plane, which moves parallel to itself and up as the value of the objective function increases. Again, it will achieve its maximum value somewhere on the boundary of this polyhedron.

It is these two features, namely the well-behaved shape of the feasible region and the parallel shift of the objective function as its value increases, that make the solution process of linear programs relatively easy, in contrast to ill-behaved problems. Mind you, even so solutions by hand-calculations are generally out of question — they would take months, years, or even centuries to complete. By that time, the solution to the problem would not be relevant any more. In fact, most problems would have been solved by other means. For this reason, linear programming problems are always solved with the help of powerful computer software packages. Section 13.6 will demonstrate how this can be done using one of the modern spreadsheet packages.

Form of Solution Algorithm

Remember the South Sea Island treasure quest! We started with an initial feasible landing spot and then proceeded in an uphill direction until we reached a location where all directions led downhill. How does this translate to the process of finding the optimal solution to a linear programming problem?

In the power generating example, an obvious initial feasible solution is to produce nothing, i.e., set both LOAD and BLACK equal to zero. This corresponds to the origin in Figure 13-6. At the origin OUTPUT=0. We now search for an uphill direction. In linear programming this search is restricted to movements along an edge of the feasible region. In our example there are two edges leading away from the origin. We either move along the x-axis or along the SULPHUR constraint. We also want to choose the steepest uphill direction. So, moving along the x-axis implies increasing BLACK only. For every unit increase in BLACK the value of OUTPUT increases by 24,000 pounds — the objective function coefficient of BLACK. On the other hand, it can be shown that a unit change along the edge of the SULPHUR constraint implies an increase in LOAD of 0.75 and in BLACK of 0.5. Hence, a unit change up along the SULPHUR constraint edge increases output by 20,000(0.75) + 24,000(0.5) = 27,000.[1] Since this is higher, we move along that edge. The farthest we can go is to corner point A. At that point LOAD=9 and BLACK=6, with OUTPUT= 324,000. This completes one iteration of the algorithm. We now have a new solution and restart our search for an uphill direction.

At corner point A we can either move back to the origin, which would decrease

---

[1]For those curious to know how I derived the factors of 0.75 for LONG and 0.5 for BLACK here is how. A unit move along the SULPHUR constraint edge means reducing the slack in the SMOKE constraint by one kilogram. At the origin, the amount of slack in SMOKE is 12 kg. At the corner point A, the SMOKE slack has been reduced to zero, with LONG = 9 and BLACK = 6. Hence, each kilogram reduction in SMOKE implies 9/12 = 0.75 tonnes of Longburne coal and 6/12 = 0.5 tonnes of Blackball coal. You can also verify that at point A, OUTPUT = 324. So each unit reduction in SMOKE increased OUTPUT by 324,000/12 = 27,000 pounds, confirming the result derived above.

the OUTPUT by 27,000 for every unit move along the SULPHUR constraint edge — obviously of no interest, or we can move along the SMOKE constraint edge towards corner point B. For every additional tonne of Blackball coal, we have to decrease the use of Longburne coal by 0.5 tonne in order to remain feasible. But this trade-off is clearly attractive. So, at the second iteration we move along the SMOKE constraint edge to point B. At that point LONG=6 and BLACK=12, with OUTPUT=408,000.

From point B we can either move back to point A, which reduced OUTPUT, or along the PULVERIZER constraint edge on to point C. A move along that edge implies that for every additional tonne of Blackball coal we have to give up 1.5 tonnes of Longburne coal. That also leads to a decrease in OUTPUT. So there is no edge along the feasible region leading away from point B that increases the objective function further. All paths now lead downhill. We have reached the highest point; in other words, point B is the optimal solution.

13.5 SENSITIVITY ANALYSIS

One of the major strengths of linear programming is the ease with which sensitivity analysis can be done with respect to the RHS parameters and the objective function coefficients. This section explores this for the power generating problem.

Alternative Optimal Solutions

The slope of the objective function lines determine where on the boundary of the feasible region the optimal solution occurs. For the original objective function of OUTPUT = 20,000 LONG + 24,000 BLACK the optimal solution occurs at corner point B with a maximal value of OUTPUT = 408,000. Assume now that new tests show that the objective function coefficient for BLACK is in fact 29,000 pounds of steam per tonne. The new objective function reads:

$$\text{Maximize OUTPUT} = 20,000\ \text{LONG} + 29,000\ \text{BLACK} \qquad (13\text{-}6)$$

As you can see in Figure 13-7, the slope of (13-6) is a bit steeper than for the original objective function (13-1). Although the maximal value of OUTPUT increases from 408 to 468, the values of the two decision variables remain the same, namely LONG = 6 and BLACK = 12. The same corner point of the feasible region, i.e., point B, gives the optimal solution.

Assume now that the objective function coefficient for BLACK increases to 31,000:

$$\text{Maximize OUTPUT} = 20,000\ \text{LONG} + 31,000\ \text{BLACK} \qquad (13\text{-}7)$$

The slope of (13-7) is even steeper, as shown in Figure 13-7. OUTPUT obtains

Figure 13-7: Changes in the objective function

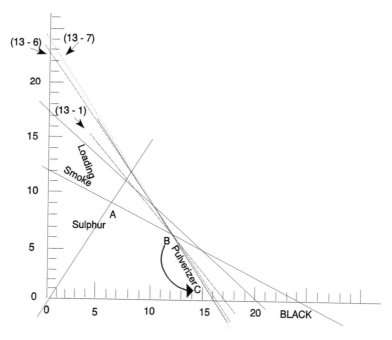

its maximal value not at point B, but at point C. At point C, only Blackball coal is used, i.e., LONG=0 and BLACK=16. The OUTPUT increases to 496,000.

These two examples provide us with some interesting insights. We see that possibly quite large changes in the objective function of a given decision variable, in our example from 24,000 to 29,000, may have no effect on the optimal values of the decision variables, while a much smaller (further) increase from 29,000 to 31,000 caused the optimal solution to jump to an adjacent corner point, with different values for the optimal decision variables. In other instances, a small change may immediately result in a sizable shift in the values of the decision variables, while additional large shifts may have no further effect.

Many decision makers would expect the size of the shift in the optimal values of the decision variables to reflect the size of the change in an input coefficient, with a small change resulting in small shifts and a large change in corresponding larger shifts. The fact that linear programming often responds in a rather unexpected way is disconcerting to many decision makers.

The second insight we get is that there must be a value for the objective function coefficient of BLACK where the switch from point B to point C occurs. This value must be between 29,000 and 31,000. In fact, it is 30,000. For the objective function

$$\text{Maximize OUTPUT} = 20,000 \text{ LONG} + 30,000 \text{ BLACK} \qquad (13\text{-}8)$$

the contour lines for OUTPUT in Figure 13-7 are parallel to the PULVERIZER constraint (13-5). (You can verify this by multiplying (13-5) through on both sides by 1250.) Hence, the highest line for OUTPUT passes through both point B and point C, as well as coinciding with the PULVERIZER constraint edge over this segment. So, any combination of values for LOAD and BLACK represented by that segment is an optimal solution with a maximal OUTPUT value of 480,000.

Sensitivity Analysis with Respect to a RHS Parameter of a Constraint

What happens to the maximal value of OUTPUT if, say, the RHS parameter of the SMOKE constraint is increased from 12 to 13 kg? The size of the feasible region is increased by the dark shaded portion in Figure 13-8.

Figure 13-8: Changes in RHS parameters

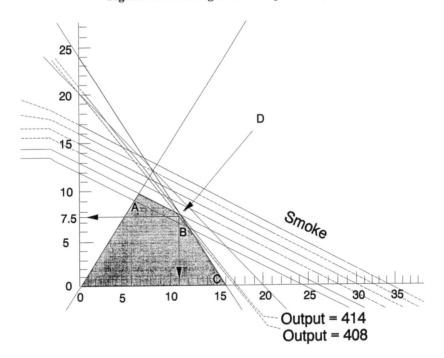

The line for OUTPUT=408,000 — the former maximal value of OUTPUT — has now a short segment entirely inside the enlarged feasible region. The value of OUTPUT can therefore be increased further. It obtains its maximum of 414,000 at point D. So, a 1 kg increase in permissible smoke emission results in an increase of the maximal value of the objective function of 6,000.

Note that the maximal value of OUTPUT continues to increase by 6,000 for further increases of the SMOKE constraint by 1 kg, up to a maximum emission of

16 kg. At that point, further increases in the permissible smoke emission have no effect on the maximal value of OUTPUT any more. The PULVERIZER constraint becomes redundant at that point and the LOADING constraint becomes binding.

You have already encountered the value of relaxing a constraint in Chapter 12. It is nothing else but the **shadow price** of the SMOKE constraint. Recall its interpretation: the shadow price measures the rate of change in the optimal value of the objective function for relaxing a constraint by one unit. However, in contrast to the example in Chapter 12 (which had a nonlinear objective function) the shadow price associated with a linear programming constraint remains constant over a certain interval of the RHS parameter. For the SMOKE constraint the shadow price is equal to 6,000 for any 1 kg change in the RHS parameter between 8 and 16 kg. Note though that the shadow price of a constraint may not be valid for a whole unit change in the RHS parameter. (You can verify this statement by increasing the RHS parameter of the PULVERIZER constraint beyond 1 hour. Once you reach 1.25 hours, equivalent to a processing rate of 20 tonnes of Blackball coal, further increases in time have no additional effect.) This feature (of constant shadow prices over specified intervals) makes the shadow price a more valuable tool for sensitivity analysis (why?).

It is though important to keep in mind that the shadow price measures the change in the objective function for a unit change in the RHS parameter of a constraint under the assumption that all other RHS parameters, all objective function and all LHS coefficients remain unchanged. If changes in more than one RHS parameter occur, the combined change in the objective function may not equal the sum of the shadow prices. If simultaneous changes occur in several inputs, inclu-ding changes in LHS coefficients, then there is little choice but to solve the model again.

13.6 SOLUTION BY COMPUTER

For practically all real-life applications, linear programming problems have to be solved by computers. Small to medium-size problems of up to 1000 variables and up to 1000 constraints are easily within the bounds of a micro-computer, particularly the more high-powered ones. There are numerous suitable and relatively inexpen-sive software packages around. Very large problems with several thousand constraints and possibly tens of thousands of variables need access to a mainframe computer, for which a number of highly sophisticated and rather expensive mathematical programming computer codes exist.

Some of the more sophisticated spreadsheet packages, such as Microsoft EXCEL©, LOTUS© 1-2-3, and QUATTRO PRO©, have built in **optimizer or solver functions** or **add-on mathematical programming routines**. Solvers can handle small problems quite effectively, while problems with more than 100 variables or constraints are well within the capability of the add-on routines. I will now demonstrate how the power generating problem can be solved using the EXCEL Solver.

Input to EXCEL Solver

Any LP computer program, whether in a spreadsheet or as a stand alone program, needs to know the names of the variables, labels for the constraints, the values of the objective function coefficients, the LHS coefficients, the RHS parameters, the form of each constraint ($\le$, $=$, $\ge$), and whether the problem is to be maximized or minimized. This is most conveniently done as a table, like the EXCEL spreadsheet in Figure 13-9. The numerical body of the table has a column for each variable, a column for the form of the constraint, and one for the RHS parameters. It has a row for the objective function and one for each constraint. The row for the objective function lists the objective function coefficient for each variable. The corresponding LHS coefficient is inserted at the intersection of each constraint row and variable column. Such a table is referred to as the **linear program in detached coefficient form.** Multiplying the coefficients of each row with its corresponding variable, and summing across all variables generates the objective function and the LHS of each constraint, respectively. Hence, the table contains all information needed for expressing the mathematical relationships of the corresponding linear program.

Figure 13-9: Microsoft EXCEL spreadsheet for power generating problem

Maximum power output subject to air pollution standards					
Decision Variables		LONG	BLACK	Relation	RHS
Objective function		20000	24000		
Constraints:	Smoke	1	0.5	< or =	12
	Sulphur	-800	1200	> or =	0
	Loading	1	1	< or =	20
	Pulverizer	0.041667	0.0625	< or =	1

Before invoking EXCEL solver it is advisable to do further preparations. First, we add an additional row, for instance at the bottom of the table. In Figure 13-10, I named that row 'Changing cells'. These are the cells where Solver will display the values of the decision variables. Inially, we set all these values equal to zero. The use of EXCEL Solver is made easier if we insert an additional column, preferably directly to the right of the constraint labels. This column contains formulas for the LHS of the constraints and the objective function. These formulas are simply the sum of the products of LHS coefficients and the changing cells for each constraints and the objective function. In EXCEL these sums of products are conveniently obtained by the function

SUMPRODUCT(range 1, range 2),

where 'range 1' refers to the row of LHS or objective function coefficients, and 'range 2' refers to the changing cells. The expanded table is shown in the top portion of Figure 13-10.

Figure 13-10: EXCEL Solver dialog box in power generating problem

	C3		=SUMPRODUCT(D3:E3,D$8:E$8)				
			POWER1.XLS				
	A	B	C	D	E	F	G
1	Maximum power output subject to air pollution standards						
2	Decision Variables				LONG	BLACK	Relation	RHS
3	Objective function	Set cell	0	20000	24000		
4	Constraints:	Sulphur	0	-800	1200	> or =	0
5		Smoke	0	1	0.5	< or =	12
6		Loading	0	1	1	< or =	20
7		Pulverizer	0	0.041667	0.0625	< or =	1
8	Changing cells			0	0		
9			Solver Parameters				
10							
11		Set Cell: A10$B$1				Solve	
12		Equal to: ◉ Max ○ Min ○ Value of: 0				Close	
13		By Changing Cells:					
14		$D$8:$E$8			Guess		
15							
16		Subject to the Constraints:			Options...		
17		$C$4 >= $G$4			Add...		
Enter		$C$5:$C$7 <= $G$5:$G$7					
		$D$8:$E$8 >= 0			Change...	Reset All	
					Delete	Help	

When EXCEL Solver is invoked (as a function in the 'formula' submenu), a **dialog box** appears, shown in the bottom portion of the screen reproduction in Figure 13-10. This dialog box asks the user to specify the 'set cell', i.e., the cell where the optimal value of the objective function is to be stored, whether the objective function is to be maximized or minimized, and the constraints. These can be entered in groups. For this reason it is convenient to regroup the constraints into sets of '≥', '=', and '≤'. This was done in Figure 13-10, where the sulphur constraint is shown first, followed by the other three constraints entered as a group. Each group is entered into another dialog box which opens when 'Add' is clicked. Carefully study how the constraints are shown in the dialog box. Their entry is made so much easier by having added the additional column next to the constraint labels. (By placing this extra column next to the constraint labels, the various reports generated by Solver will refer to these labels, making the interpretation of these reports unambiguous.) The non-negativity constraints on all decision variables also have to be entered specifically, as shown by the highlighted last row in the constraint portion of the dialog box. Note the specific form EXCEL uses for displaying inequality constraints (< = or > = rather than ≤ or ≥).

Clicking 'Options' opens a dialog box for specifying if the model in linear. I suggest that you do this. The output reports use then conventional LP terminology.

Solution Output of EXCEL Solver

EXCEL Solver saves the optimal solution and all sensitivity analysis in three separate reports. These are reproduced in Figure 13-11. The 'Answer Report' lists the maximal value of the 'target or set cell', i.e., the objective function, followed by the optimal values of the 'changing cells' or the decision variables. Note that the optimal values of the decision variables are not exactly equal to 6 and 12, but 6.00024 and 11.99995. This is due to having entered the coefficient for LONG in the pulverizer constraint as 0.041667 rather than an exact 1/24. Rounding errors thus mean that the optimal solution values for the objective function and the decision variables printed out by any optimizer package need to be interpreted with some common sense.

The output then lists the form of all constraints, their status ('binding' or 'not binding'), and the amount of slack.

The second report is entitled 'Sensitivity Report'. Its first part gives the usual sensitivity analysis with respect to the objective function coefficients. The last two columns show the 'Allowable Increase' and 'Decrease' in each coefficient for which the current solution values for all decision variables remain optimal. Recall that sensitivity analysis on any input coefficient or parameter is valid under the assumption that all other inputs remain unchanged at their original values. In our example it indicates that as long as the objective function coefficient for BLACK does not increase by more than 6000 or decrease by more than 14000, i.e., remains within the range of 24000 − 14000 = 10000 and 24000 + 6000 = 30000, the current solution of LONG=6 and BLACK=12 is optimal, all other inputs remaining unchanged.

That portion of the output also lists the **Reduced Costs** associated with each variable. In our example, these are both zero. If the reduced costs are non-zero, then they represent the change in the optimal value of the objective function that would result from increasing the corresponding decision variable by one unit. In a maximizing problem, for a decision variable that has zero optimal value the reduced cost is usually negative. This can be explained as follows: At the optimal solution it is not advantageous to let that variable assume a positive value. If forced to become positive, then by definition it must reduce the value of the objective function. This is signalled by the negative value of the reduced cost. Why? What is the sign of the reduced cost for a cost minimization problem? Why?

What is the interpretation of a zero reduced cost when the corresponding variable is also zero in the optimal solution? It means that the problem has alternative optimal solutions. That particular variable could be given positive values, by adjusting all other positive variables, without changing the optimal value of the objective function.

The Sensitivity Report also lists the shadow prices and the increase and decrease in each RHS parameter for which they remain valid. In fact, what is shown is the value by which the objective function would change, if the RHS parameter is **decreased** by one unit, rather than **increased** by one unit. An increase in the RHS will thus produce a change in the objective function value by the negative of the 'shadow price' listed. For example, if the SMOKE constraint is increased from 12 to 13, the optimal value of the objective function changes from 408,000 to 408,000

Figure 13-11:   Excel Solver Reports

Microsoft Excel 4.0 Answer Report

Target Cell (Max)

Cell	Name	Original	Final Value
$C$3	Set cell	0	407999.328

Adjustable Cells

Cell	Name	Original	Final Value
$D$8	Changing cells LONG	0	6.000024
$E$8	Changing cells BLACK	0	11.999952

Constraints

Cell	Name	Cell Value	Formula	Status	Slack
$C$4	Sulphur	9599.9232	$C$4 > = $G$4	Not Binding	9599.923
$C$5	Smoke	12	$C$5 < = $G$5	Binding	0
$C$6	Loading	17.999976	$C$6 < = $G$6	Not Binding	2.000024
$C$7	Pulverizer	1	$C$7 < = $G$7	Binding	0
$D$8	Changing cells LONG	6.000024	$D$8 > = 0	Not Binding	6.000024
$E$8	Changing cells BLACK	11.999952	$E$8 > = 0	Not Binding	11.999952

Microsoft Excel 4.0 Sensitivity Report

Changing Cells

Cell	Name	Final Value	Reduced Cost	Objective Coefficient	Allowable Increase	Allowable Decrease
$D$8	Changing cells LONG	6.000024	0	20000	28000	3999.872
$E$8	Changing cells BLACK	11.99995	0	24000	5999.760002	14000

Constraints

Cell	Name	Final Value	Shadow Price	Constraint R.H. Side	Allowable Increase	Allowable Decrease
$C$4	Sulphur	9599.923	0	0	9599.9232	1E+30
$C$5	Smoke	12	5999.832	12	3.999936	4
$C$6	Loading	17.99998	0	20	1E+30	2.000024
$C$7	Pulverizer	1	336001.344	1	0.166668	0.249997

Microsoft Excel 4.0 Limits Report

Cell	Target Name	Value
$C$3	Set cell	407999.33

Cell	Adjustable Name	Value	Lower Limit	Target Result	Upper Limit	Target Result
$D$8	Changing cells LONG	6.000024	0	287998.85	6.000024	407999.33
$E$8	Changing cells BLACK	11.999952	4.00002	216000.86	11.99995	407999.33

+ 1($-[-6000]$) = 414,000, as we found from the graphical analysis.

The third report, entitled Limits Report, lists how the objective function varies if each decision variable takes on its lowest and highest feasible value, respectively. For instance, for all constraints to be satisfied, BLACK has to be at least 4, but no more than 12. If BLACK=4, then $z = 216,000$, while for BLACK=12, $z = 408,000$. This gives some indication of the range for the objective function in response to the feasible range of each decision variable.

The theoretical problem size limit that Solver in EXCEL can handle is 200 decision variables and 100 constraints. Computation times for large problems can though be rather long — an hour or longer. EXCEL Solver can also handle problems other than linear programming, such as problems where some or all variables are restricted to assume integer values only, or problems where the objective function or some of the constraints or both are nonlinear, like polynomials. The steep increase in computation times means only relatively small nonlinear or integer problems can be handled.

13.7 A PRODUCT-MIX CASE STUDY

A Situation Summary

PINEAPPLE DELIGHT, Inc., owns its pineapple plantation. Most years it processes its entire harvest in its cannery. Exceptionally, some fruit is sold at the going market price to other processors. The current price for pineapple fruit sold on the market is $440 per metric tonne (= 1000 kg).

This coming season the crop is estimated at 24 000 metric tonnes. For processing, fresh fruit has to be skinned. This produces an average waste of 39.4%. Also the outer part of the skinned pineapple and its core, amounting to another 26.6%, can only be used for juice extraction. Juice is used in the finished pineapple product or sold at cost to beverage manufacturers. The balance of the flesh has traditionally been used for the premium pineapple rings. Offcuts in the form of crushed pineapple are used in fruit salad, and so on. With the market for canned pineapple rings becoming more competitive, Pineapple Delight has started to differentiate its products by marketing some of its output in novel shapes, such as spears and chunky pieces or mixed with passion fruit.

Rings use 81% of the pineapple flesh, while 85% of the flesh can be cut into chunks. Flesh used for spears produces 60% spears and 28% chunks. In each case the balance of the flesh is off-cuts, used for crush. Chunks are canned as chunky pieces or as passion fruit/pineapple chunks. Off-cuts are used in fruit salad, fruit salad catering packs, and crush catering packs. The normal retail can has a net weight of 1 pound or 454 grams, while catering packs have a net weight of 4.54 kg. The actual fruit content of each can is about 70% of the net weight.

Table 13-3 lists the pineapple products marketed by Pineapple Delight, the amount of skinned flesh, the price ex factory, the sum of cutting, canning, and ingredient costs (mainly sugar) for each product. It also lists the upper limit for potential sales of each finished product. Naturally, these are only forecasts. They could be affected by advertising. For simplicity, we will ignore this aspect.

Table 13-3: Pineapple Delight product information

Product	Flesh	Revenue	Cost*	Contribution	Upper limit
Rings Delight	0.31 kg	$0.74	$0.12	$0.62	9 million cans
Spears Delight	0.27 kg	$0.82	$0.13	$0.69	6 million cans
Passion fruit/Pineapple Delight	0.31 kg	$0.88	$0.19	$0.69	4 million cans
Chunky Pieces Delight	0.34 kg	$0.68	$0.10	$0.41	7 million cans
Fruit Salad Catering Packs	1.6 kg	$6.20	$4.05	$2.15	2 million cans
Crush Catering Packs	3.4 kg	$5.10	$0.88	$4.22	unlimited

*exclusive of pineapple fruit cost

Management of Pineapple Delight would like to develop an operating plan for the coming season's crop. Its objective is to maximize profits. This means determining how much of its crop should be processed in its own cannery, how much sold to other processors, and how to allocate the usable flesh from the pineapple processed in its own cannery to the various products it produces.

A Material Flow Diagram

Figure 13-12 shows the material flow associated with selling and processing pineapples. The cloud denotes the input of 24 000 tonnes of fresh pineapples. The first choice is how much to process in the firm's own cannery, with the balance sold to other processors. 34% of the amount of pineapples processed in its own cannery becomes usable flesh, while the rest is either waste or used for juice. We do not keep track of the use of juice. Most is used in the firm's finished products. The balance is sold at cost to beverage manufacturers; hence it does not affect the profit. Pineapple flesh is then allocated to the production of the three main products: rings, spears, and chunks. Each of these allocations is processed into its intended main product, with part of it becoming offcuts. Chunks are also a by-product of spears production. Finally, chunks and offcuts are allocated to the remaining five finished products.

In this material flow diagram each circle represents a variable whose optimal value we wish to determine. (Note that this may not always be the most appropriate diagrammatic representation. Sometimes it may be easier to let the arrows between circles or nodes represent the variables. This will be the case in Section 13.8.) We will refer to all these variables as 'decision variables'. This may not be strictly true, since some of them are simply consequences of another variable, i.e., we do not have the freedom to choose their values independently of each other. For example,

Figure 13-12: Material flow for pineapple processing

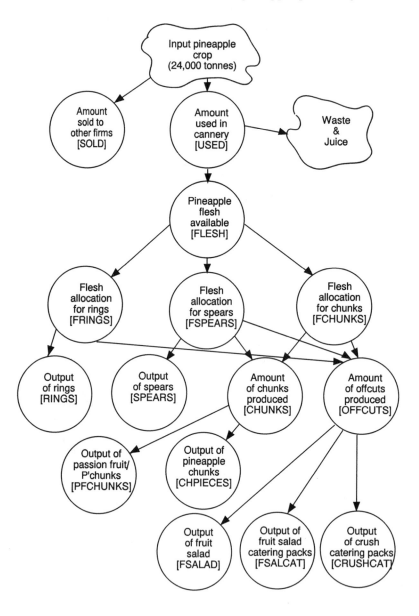

the amount of pineapple flesh we get for any quantity of pineapples used in the cannery is 34%. Choosing the quantity of pineapples used immediately fixes the amount of pineapple flesh available.

Variable Names and Units

The variables names used for formulating the mathematical relationships are the mnemonic labels shown in brackets in the material flow diagram of Figure 13-12. In the formulation all variables are measured in terms of units of 1000, either 1000 kg (= 1 tonne) or 1000 cans. This is referred to as **scaling**. It is done for two reasons. First it avoids writing all the extra zeros. More importantly though the accuracy of the computations performed by the linear programming computer packages increases if all LHS coefficients and RHS parameters are scaled such that they are close to 1, rather than some being extremely small, while others are very large. So, the variables USED, SOLD, FLESH, FRINGS, FSPEARS, FCHUNKS, CHUNKS and OFFCUTS are all measured in 1000 kg, while the variables for the finished products are measured in 1000 cans. Also, all variables are non-negative.

Objective function

The objective is to maximize profits, i.e., the difference between revenues and costs. However, fixed costs can be ignored. They will not affect the optimal operating plans, unless it is better to close down the plant. Revenues consist of the net receipt from selling either fresh fruit or canned products, as listed under revenue in Table 13-3. The variable costs include the cost of preparing the fruit, cutting and canning it, as well as the cost of any ingredients used in the canning operation.

Should the cost of the pineapple fruit also be included? What is, in fact, the cost of the fruit? We could interpret it as the cost of harvesting it. If the entire harvest is used, either internally or sold, then this cost is a constant. Hence, it can be ignored. However, if less than the entire potential harvest is used, either sold or processed, with some fruit left in the fields, then the harvesting cost becomes a function of the pineapple used and must be included. In our case, all fruit is either processed or sold, so we will exclude the harvesting cost.

Alternatively, we could say the cost of the fruit is the opportunity cost of using it for the best alternative use. This is selling it to other processors. But this is one of the options included in the linear programming model, with the receipts from selling fruit added to the total revenue. Hence, including the opportunity cost as part of the production cost would amount to double counting. This is another reason why the 'contribution' in Table 13-3 excludes the fruit cost in this example.

With the relevant variable costs directly allocated to the various finished products, the total contribution towards profit is simply given by the product of the amount of each finished product produced (and presumably sold) and its unit contribution, as listed in Table 13-3. To this we also add the receipts from fresh pineapples sold. The objective function therefore reads as follows:

$$
\begin{aligned}
\text{MAXIMIZE} \quad & 0.44 \text{ SOLD} + 0.62 \text{ RINGS} + 0.69 \text{ SPEARS} \\
& + 0.69 \text{ PFCHUNKS} + 058 \text{ CHPIECES} + 0.41 \text{ FSALAD} \\
& + 2.15 \text{ FSALCAT} + 4.22 \text{ CRUSHCAT}
\end{aligned}
\qquad (13\text{-}9)
$$

Note that since all variables are in units of 1000, the objective function coefficients are in fact also in units of $1000.

Processing Constraints

The material flow diagram also helps us in determining the constraints. We associate one constraint with the set of flows (or arrows) coming out of each cloud or circle and one constraint with each set of flows (or arrows) leading to a circle.

Starting at the top of the diagram we see the cloud for the input of 24,000 tonnes of fresh fruit that can either be SOLD to other processors or USED in the firm's own cannery — the two arrows leaving the cloud. Obviously, some of the crop could also be left over unused. Hence, we get the following inequality constraint:

$$\text{SOLD} + \text{USED} \leq 24,000 \qquad (13\text{-}10)$$

Stepping down the diagram, the next element is the circle for the amount of pineapple flesh, denoted by FLESH, resulting from the decision USED. From the description of the operation, we know that only 34% of fresh pineapple fruit is suitable for further processing into canned products:

$$\text{FLESH} = 0.34\ \text{USED}$$

or expressed in the usual linear programming form:

$$\text{FLESH} - 0.34\ \text{USED} = 0 \qquad (13\text{-}11)$$

This is an accounting type **material balance** or **input-output constraint**.

The next constraint allocates the usable flesh for cutting into finished shapes, i.e., rings, spears, and chunks, represented by the three arrows leaving the circle for FLESH:

$$\text{FRINGS} + \text{FSPEARS} + \text{FCHUNKS} = \text{FLESH}$$

or $\qquad$ $$\text{FRINGS} + \text{FSPEARS} + \text{FCHUNKS} - \text{FLESH} = 0 \qquad (13\text{-}12)$$

The next layer in the diagram has four circles. So with the set of arrows leading into each one we have a separate constraint. The first one deals with the output of rings. Each unit of 1000 cans contains 0.31 tonnes of flesh. But only 81% of the flesh allocated for ring production is rings, the balance is off-cuts. So we get the following relationship:

$$0.31\ \text{RINGS} = 0.81\ \text{FRINGS}$$

or $\qquad$ $$0.31\ \text{RINGS} - 0.81\ \text{FRINGS} = 0 \qquad (13\text{-}13)$$

We get a similar constraint for the output of spears:

$$0.27 \text{ SPEARS} - 0.6 \text{ FSPEARS} = 0 \qquad (13\text{-}14)$$

Chunks are produced as a by-product from spears as well as from the flesh allocated specifically to chunk production, each flow associated with one of the two arrows leading into the circle for CHUNKS:

$$0.28 \text{ FSPEARS} + 0.85 \text{ FCHUNKS} = \text{CHUNKS}$$

or $\qquad 0.28 \text{ FSPEARS} + 0.85 \text{ FCHUNKS} - \text{CHUNKS} = 0 \qquad (13\text{-}15)$

Verify that the amount of offcuts produced yields the following constraint:

$$0.19 \text{ FRINGS} + 0.12 \text{ FSPEARS} + 0.15 \text{ CHUNKS} - \text{OFFCUTS} = 0 \qquad (13\text{-}16)$$

Finally, we have to allocate chunks and spears to their canned products:

$$0.31 \text{ PFCHUNKS} + 0.34 \text{ CHPIECES} - \text{CHUNKS} = 0 \qquad (13\text{-}17)$$

$$0.16 \text{ FSALAD} + 1.6 \text{ FSALCAT} + 3.4 \text{ CRUSHCAT} - \text{OFFCUTS} = 0 \qquad (13\text{-}18)$$

Note that with the exception of (13-10) all these constraints are equalities. They represent the flow of materials. The material issued by a given node, e.g., the circle for 'pineapple flesh available', must be equal to the sum of the material entering the receiving nodes, e.g., the three circles for flesh allocation. Similarly, what is received by a given node, e.g., the circle for 'amount of chunks produced', must be equal to the sum of the material coming from the nodes issuing that material, e.g., the circles for 'flesh allocation to spears' and 'flesh allocation to chunks'.

Marketing Constraints

The output of each finished product, with the exception of crush in catering packs, should not exceed its upper limit listed in Table 13-3. Hence, we get the following so-called **upper bound constraint**:

RINGS ≤ 9000,	SPEARS ≤ 6000,	
PFCHUNKS≤ 4000,	CHPIECES ≤ 8000,	(13-19)
FSALAD ≤ 7000,	FSALCAT ≤ 3000	

Optimal Solution

This linear program was solved using the Microsoft EXCEL Solver. The input was in the form of the linear program in detached coefficient form.

The maximal value of the objective function is 17,662.95. Since the objective function coefficients are in units of $1000, this is a total contribution of $17,662,950.

Information on all variables and all inequality constraints at the optimal solution is listed in Table 13-4. The shadow prices for the equality constraints are not shown. The reason for this is that their interpretation is rather complex and well beyond the level of this text. When interpreting these numbers, remember that they are in units of 1000 kg or cans, respectively. Similarly, the 'Reduced cost' and the 'Shadow price' are in thousands of dollars.

Table 13-4: Optimal solution to Pineapple Delight

Product	Variable	Optimal value	Shadow price	Reduced Cost
Pineapples sold	SOLD	0		−0.1215
Pineapples processed	USED	24000		0
Usable flesh	FLESH	8160		0
Flesh allocated to rings	FRINGS	3444.4		0
Flesh allocated to spears	FSPEARS	2700		0
Flesh allocated to chunks	FCHUNKS	2015.6		0
Chunks produced	CHUNKS	1280.8		0
Rings	RINGS	9000*		0.0856
Spears	SPEARS	6000*		0.2343
Passion fruit chunks	PFCHUNKS	4000*		0.1612
Chunky pieces	CHPIECES	3615.4		0
Fruit salad	FSALAD	7000*		0.195
Fruit salad catering packs	FSALCAT	100.5		0
Crush catering packs	CRUSHCAT	0		−0.3487
Total fresh fruit	13-10	binding	0	0.5615
Upper limit on				
rings	13-19	binding	0	0.0856
spears	13-19	binding	0	0.2343
passion fruit chunks	13-19	binding	0	0.1612
chunky pieces	13-19	slack	4384.6	0
fruit salad	13-19	binding	0	0.195
fruit salad cat. packs	13-19	slack	2899.5	0

*variable at its upper limit

What If Analysis

No catering packs of crush are produced. The output of fruit salad catering packs is only 100,000 cans. It is conceivable that this is too small for effective marketing of this product. The firm may wish to increase its marketing effort for retail cans of fruit salad to absorb the crush allocated to catering packs. It would imply raising the upper limit on fruit salad by about 1000 units of one thousand cans. The shadow price for the upper limit on fruit salad is 0.195, or $195 per 1000 cans. It turns out that this shadow price is valid for any conceivable increase in the upper limit (not shown!). Hence, if the upper limit on fruit salad can be lifted to at least 8 million cans through further advertising at a cost of less than $195,000 (=$195 times 1000), such a switch would be advantageous.

We could have obtained the same answer using the reduced costs. The reason is that the interpretation of the reduced cost is somewhat more complex for decision variables that are upper bounded, as is the case for most of the final products sold. These cannot exceed the limits imposed by marketing considerations. If such a variable has a zero value in the optimal solution, the meaning of the reduced cost is as it was defined for the power generating problem. However, if the variable has an optimal value equal to its upper bound, such as is the case in this problem for RINGS, SPEARS, PFCHUNKS, and FSALAD, the reduced cost (for a maximizing problem) will be positive. It then indicates the improvement in the maximal value of the objective function resulting from increasing this upper bound by one unit. The reduced cost for FSALAD is 0.195 — the same as the shadow price for the upper bound constraint on fruit salad.

All fresh fruit is processed internally. None is sold. The reduced cost coefficient for SOLD indicates that the total profit contribution would decrease by 0.1215 (= $121.50/tonne) for every unit increase (= 1 tonne) of SOLD. It may be useful to ask 'What increase in price for fresh fruit would be required before selling some or all fresh fruit becomes attractive?' The reduced cost for SOLD again provides us with the answer. Its negative is the minimum price increase needed for the variable SOLD to assume a positive value without reducing the objective function. The market price for fresh fruit would need to increase by $121.50/tonne to at least $561.50 (= $440 + $121.50).

This is also the increase in contribution realized by increasing the amount of the available crop by 1 tonne, as indicated by the shadow price of the total fresh fruit constraint (13-10). Hence, if the firm can acquire fresh fruit on the open market for less than $561.50 it could increase its profits by the difference for each additional tonne processed, up to a maximum of 5158.4 tonnes (not shown!).

13.8 A TRANSPORTATION PROBLEM

An application of high practical importance deals with transportation problems. Goods are available in limited quantities at several sources and required in given quantities at various destinations. There is a cost of transporting the goods between sources and destinations. The problem consists of satisfying the requirements at all destinations so as to minimize the sum of all transportation costs. The shifting of soil and rocks in the highway construction problem referred to in the introduction to this chapter is an example of a transportation problem.

A Production/Transportation Problem Situation

Remember the HEINZ Tomato Paste logistics situation in Section 11-10? There the problem consisted in finding the optimal number of railcars for transporting tomato paste from factory X to conversion plant Y. Obviously, HEINZ processes tomatoes at several factories and has quite a few conversion plants scattered all over the United States. Consider the following (hypothetical) example. There are tomato processing plants in Stockton and Riverside, California, and Tuscaloosa, Alabama. There are 5 conversion plants: Los Angeles, Dallas, Chicago, Atlanta, and Newark (New Jersey).

Table 13-5 summarizes the unit transportation cost from each tomato processing plant to each conversion station, the unit processing costs at each processing plant, the production capacity at each processing plant, and the tomato paste requirements at each conversion plant during a given 4-week period. For example, the transportation cost from Stockton to Chicago is $54 per tonne, Stockton's production cost is $524 per tonne, and it has a production capacity of 4600 tonnes for the given 4-week period, while Chicago has a requirement of 1600 tonnes for the corresponding 4-week period. (The 4-week requirement period for the conversion plants is off-set by one week from the 4-week production period for the processing plants to take the transportation time delay into account.) The firm would like to determine the least-cost schedule for production and transportation.

Table 13-5: Input data for a transportation problem

Destination Source	Prod. Cost	L.A.	Dallas	Chicago	Atlanta	Newark	Capacity
Stockton	$524	$25	$48	$54	$67	$75	4600 tonnes
Riverside	$541	$11	$44	$57	$61	$81	2900 tonnes
Tuscaloosa	$612	$57	$33	$32	$10	$36	1700 tonnes
Requirement		2100	1700	1600	1300	2200	tonnes

As in the previous example, a material flow diagram makes the transportation problem much more transparent. The network in Figure 13-13 depicts the flow of goods from the three source nodes to the five destination nodes. Each arrow from a source node to a destination node depicts a shipping option. For instance, the arrow from Stockton to Chicago represents the option of shipping goods from Stockton to Chicago. The amount shipped is denoted by the mnemonic variable STCH, using the first two letters of each name.

Note that, in contrast to Figure 13-12, the flow of material from sources to destinations is represented by the arrows, rather than by the circles in Figure 13-13. If all options are available, then the number of arrows leaving each source is equal to the number of destinations, denoted by n, while the number of arrows entering each destination is equal to the number of sources, denoted by m. The total number of variables is therefore equal to m times n, i.e., 3 times 5 or 15.

Figure 13-13: Goods flow diagram for transportation problem

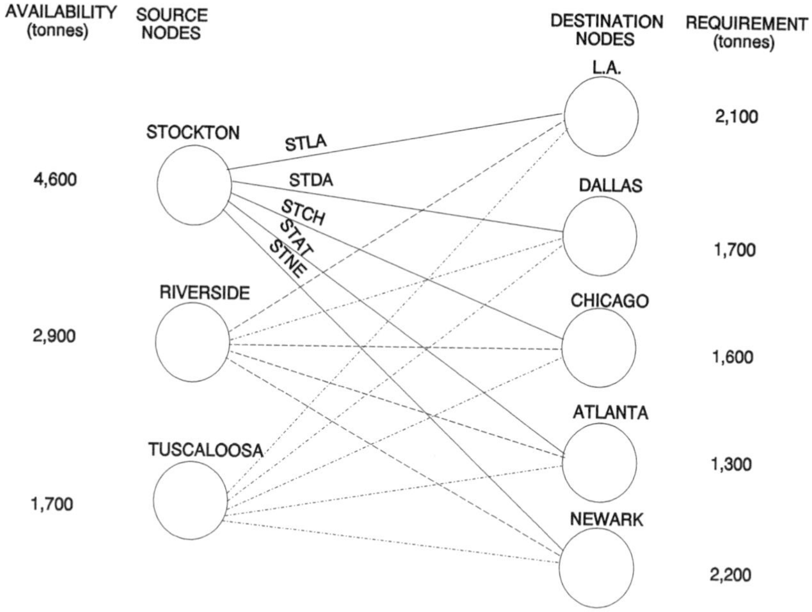

The network flow diagram again helps us in determining all constraints of the transportation model. As in the previous example, we associate a constraint with each set of arrows leaving a source node (the nodes issuing material) and one with each set of arrows entering a destination node (the nodes receiving material).

Availability Constraints

Consider the five arrows leaving the Stockton node. Each one represents the amount shipped from Stockton to one of the five destinations. It is obvious that the total amount shipped from Stockton cannot exceed Stockton's capacity of 4600 tonnes for the 4-week period in question. So we get the following constraint, called **an availability constraint**:

$$STLA + STDA + STCH + STAT + STNE \leq 4600 \qquad (13\text{-}20)$$

Each of the other two sources has a similar constraint on the amount that can be shipped:

$$RILA + RIDA + RICH + RIAT + RINE \leq 2900 \qquad (13\text{-}21)$$

$$TULA + TUDA + TUCH + TUAT + TUNE \leq 1700 \qquad (13\text{-}22)$$

Demand Constraints

The arrows entering the destination nodes represent the amount shipped from each of the three sources. We have to ensure that each destination gets exactly what it requires. So, we get the following **demand constraint** for Los Angeles:

$$STLA + RILA + TULA = 2100 \qquad (13\text{-}23)$$

The demand constraints for the other four destinations are:

$$STDA + RIDA + TUDA = 1700 \qquad (13\text{-}24)$$

$$STCH + RICH + TUCH = 1600 \qquad (13\text{-}25)$$

$$STAT + RIAT + TUAT = 1300 \qquad (13\text{-}26)$$

and $\qquad$ $$STNE + RINE + TUNE = 2200 \qquad (13\text{-}27)$$

Obviously, this problem only has a feasible solution if the total amount available at all sources is at least as large as the total amount required at all destinations. Verify that our problem has an excess capacity of 300 tonnes. (If the total availability is smaller than the total requirement, the nature of the problem changes to one of allocating the goods so as to maximize net profits.)

Objective Function

The objective is to minimize total relevant costs. In a transportation problem the relevant cost includes only the transportation costs. However, in our example the production costs at the three tomato processing plants differ. Furthermore, there is 300 tonnes excess processing capacity. Hence, not all processing plants will operate at full capacity. The total production cost will depend on which plants are left with excess capacity. As a consequence the production costs become a relevant cost. For example, from Table 13-5 it follows that the relevant cost of allocating one tonne of goods from Stockton to Chicago is equal to the production costs at Stockton of $524 plus the transportation cost from Stockton to Chicago of $54, or a total of $578. (Can production costs be ignored if the total availability equals total requirements? Why or why not?)

The total cost is simply equal to the product of the unit allocation cost, computed from Table 13-5, and the amount shipped, summed over all allocation options:

$$
\begin{aligned}
z = \ & 549\ STLA + 572\ STDA + 578\ STCH + 591\ STAT \\
& + 601\ STNE + 552\ RILA + 585\ RIDA + 598\ RICH \\
& + 602\ RIAT + 622\ RINE + 669\ TULA + 645\ TUDA \qquad (13\text{-}28) \\
& + 644\ TUCH + 622\ TUAT + 648\ TUNE
\end{aligned}
$$

Optimal Solution

The problem has $m+n$ or $3+5 = 8$ constraints, plus the 15 nonnegativity constraints on the decision variables. It was solved using Microsoft EXCEL Solver. The optimal solution has a cost of $5,202,300. The production/transportation schedule is listed in Table 13-6. Note that Tuscaloosa ends up with an excess capacity of 300 tonnes.

Table 13-6: Optimal production/transportation schedule

Destination Source	LA	Dallas	Chicago	Atlanta	Newark	Total shipped
Stockton	0	900	1600	0	2100	4600
Riverside	2100	800	0	0	0	2900
Tuscaloosa	0	0	0	1300	100	1400
Total received	2100	1700	1600	1300	2200	

The optimal solution has some interesting features. As expected, the expensive Tuscaloosa plant does not work at full capacity. Far more unexpected though is that the optimal transportation schedule does not necessarily select the cheapest options. For example, Stockton ships nothing to Los Angeles — its cheapest option — but supplies almost the entire Newark requirement — its most expensive option. How can this rather counterintuitive result be optimal?

The answer lies in the relative total unit cost differences between the various shipping options from a given source. If Stockton supplied Los Angeles while Riverside shipped to Newark, there would be a $3 unit cost savings for Stockton shipments, but a $21 additional cost for Riverside shipments, or a net increase of $18.

The third interesting feature is that all decision variables assume integer values, although we did not put any restriction into the formulation, that all shipments had to be in integer tonnes. It turns out that this is a general characteristic of all transportation problem solutions, provided that the availabilities at all sources and the requirements at all destinations are integer also.

Other Problem Situations Disguised as Transportation Problems

The tomato problem above involved transporting goods **over space**, i.e., from given locations to other locations. However, goods can also be 'transported', figuratively speaking, **over time** from a given period to a later period. For example, a firm has a production capacity that fluctuates in a known pattern over time, while it also has to meet a demand that varies in a different pattern over time. So production in, say, March is stored in inventory until it is used in June. Obviously, there is a cost associated with storing goods. Furthermore, the firm may in fact have the option of adding more production capacity by going to overtime, again at a cost. The firm would like to find a production and storage schedule, including the use of overtime, so as to minimize the total relevant cost. That cost includes the cost of storing goods for later use and the cost of regular and overtime production. (Any option that implies meeting demand in a given period by production in a later period is ruled out by simply penalizing it with a prohibitive cost.) This is often referred to as the **regular time/overtime production scheduling problem**.

A related situation is the **assignment problem**. Here we have a number of jobs that need to be done and a number of people to do them. Due to differences in training and experience, the people differ in their aptitude or suitability to do the various jobs. The problem is to find the best match of people and jobs. This can again be viewed as a sort of transportation problem. The people become the sources, the jobs the destinations. Each source has an availability of 1. Each destination has a requirement of 1. The objective function is to maximize the sum of the 'suitability indices' of the people-to-job assignments. With all RHS parameters equal to 1 and the optimal solution being integer, each job is assigned to one person only. There are no split or partial assignments.

(The assignment problem was actually used by the inventor of the first efficient solution algorithm for linear programs, George B. Dantzig, to prove that monogamy is the optimal social structure. When asked at a press conference in the late 40s to explain in layman's terms what the linear programming 'model' was, he used the following allegory. Assume that 100 men and 100 women get ship-wrecked on a deserted island with no hope of any rescue in their lifetime. They decide to pair off men and women. But they wish to find the optimal set of pairs that maximizes happiness for their isolated society. This is an assignment problem. Since its optimal solution will have no split assignments, say several men partially assigned to one women, but only all or nothing assignments, this proves that monogamy is the optimal solution. As in real life, not all matches will be ideal, but viewed overall no other assignment will have a greater total happiness. My difficulty with this little story is 'how did George Dantzig think he would be able to determine the happiness indices for all possible pairings?' Sampling might well take for ever!)

EXERCISES

1. A manufacturer of camping trailers is offered a contract with the leading local distributor for producing two types of trailers, A and B, to the specifications supplied by the distributor. Trailer A offers a net profit per unit of $600, while B's unit profit is $900. A and B would share the same assembly and painting facilities. Type A requires 2 person-weeks of assembly time per unit, B requires 3⅓ person-weeks per unit. There are 20 person weeks of assembly time available per month (=5 people for 4

weeks each). The painting facilities can handle a maximum of 8 trailers per month. The distributor would leave it to the manufacturer to determine the product mix, provided that at least two trailers of type A would be available, and the number of type A is at least ⅓ of the number of type B produced. This is to guarantee an acceptable product mix.

(a) Draw an influence diagram for this problem and use it to formulate this problem as an LP with the objective of maximizing total monthly profits.

(b) Graph the feasible region and the objective function for $3000 and $6000. Is any constraint redundant?

(c) Find the optimal solution graphically and verify that all constraints are satisfied. What is the optimal number of each trailer to produce?

(d) Determine which constraints are binding and the amount of slack of the non-binding constraints.

2. Consider again the situation summary in Section 13.2. Assume now that management of the plant wishes to determine the least-cost mode of operation for an output of 240,000 pounds of steam per hour. The new objective function is now the cost of the coals burned per hour, while the previous steam output performance measure becomes an additional constraint.

(a) Formulate this problem as an LP.

(b) Graph the feasible region and the objective function for total hourly costs of $800, $1600, and $2400.

(c) Find the least-cost solution. How much of each coal is used?

(d) Determine the binding constraints and the amount of slack of non-binding constraints.

3. Consider again exercise 1 above.

(a) Determine the increase in the unit profit of the type B trailer required for any point along the assembly constraint between solution [A = 5, B = 3] and solution [A = 2, B = 4.8] to become an alternative optimal solution.

(b) Determine the shadow price for each of the binding constraints and interpret their meaning. (Note that the unit profit already includes the regular time pay for workers.)

(c) Determine the range for which the shadow price of the assembly time constraint is valid.

For the following exercises you need access to a computer LP package, such as is contained in the EXCEL spreadsheet.

4. A cabinet maker would like to use the current excess capacity in the factory to produce a combination of three different types of bathroom cabinets. The table below lists labour requirements for the various operations per unit and other input data:

Product	Cutting time	Gluing time	Sanding time	Finishing time	Profit/ unit
Modern	24 min.	60 min.	20 min.	160 min.	$60.00
Provincial	36 min.	90 min.	60 min.	120 min.	$60.00
Colonial	48 min.	60 min.	60 min.	180 min.	$56.00
Excess capacity	8 hours	15 hours	8 hours	32 hours	per week

(a) Formulate this problem as an LP, maximizing weekly profits for the additional activity.

(b) Solve this problem. What is the optimal solution?

(c) The cabinet maker considers introducing overtime for some of the operations. Which ones are possible candidates and what is the maximum overtime premium the cabinet maker should consider paying?

(d) The optimal solution does not produce any colonial cabinets. The cabinet maker has been approached by a bathroom dealer to supply at least 1 colonial cabinet per week. Using the information on sensitivity analysis available from the computer printout, how much would the cabinet maker's weekly profit decrease if one colonial cabinet is produced per week? How much larger would the increase in the unit profit for colonial have to be before it would become attractive to produce colonial cabinets?

5. During the construction of a reservoir dam, large quantities of aggregate suitable for concrete mixing have to be prepared at some or all the four possible sites with sufficient quantities of deposits and then transported to the concrete mixing plant near the dam:

Deposit site	Available m^3	Cost/m^3
River-dredge material site A	8,000	$3.20
River-dredge material site B	16,000	$4.50
Island aggregate site C	8,000	$2.80
River bar aggregate site D	6,000	$4.00

The costs listed include preparation and transportation to concrete mixing plant. Three different aggregate blends are required at the quantities and additional costs shown:

Blend	Specifications	Cost/m^3	Requirement
1	(A + B) ≤ 50%, C ≥ 10%, D no limit	$4.80	6,000 m^3
2	(A + B) ≤ 60%, C ≥ 10%, (C + D) ≤ (A + B)	$4.20	15,000 m^3
3	A ≥ 20%, (C + D) ≥ 0.5(A + B)	$5.40	8,000 m^3

Formulate this problem as an LP minimizing total costs. Find the optimal solution.

6. The Western Paper Company (WPC) operates a cardboard plant in Seattle. The plant has been operating at only 75% capacity, producing 2700 tonnes per month at a total cost of $77.33 per tonne. Included in the total cost per tonne is the cost of wastepaper, one of the major raw materials used. For each 100 tonnes of product, 80 tonnes of wastepaper are required. Up to 1440 tonnes of wastepaper per month can be purchased locally at $18.75 per tonne. Additional wastepaper may be purchased through brokers at $27.50 per tonne delivered to the plant. Of the present total monthly costs at the plant, $59,400 is estimated to be fixed costs not dependent on the output level of the plant. The remainder of the cost varies in proportion to the output level. WPC has a second plant in Oregon. That plant is operated currently at 60% capacity, producing 3600 tonnes per month at a total cost per tonne of $85.00. Local wastepaper at the Oregon plant costs $20 per tonne and is limited to 4000 tonnes per month. Again, additional wastepaper can be purchased through brokers at the same conditions as for the Seattle plant. Of the present operating cost at the Oregon plant, $108,000 is fixed cost.

(a) Determine the variable cost per tonne of producing cardboard at each factory.

(b) The firm wants to determine the optimal output at each plant to produce the current combined output of 6300 tonnes per year. The objective is to minimize total combined production costs. Formulate this as an LP.

(c) Find the optimal solution.

(d) Using the information on sensitivity analysis provided by the LP computer printout, answer the following questions:

- What is the additional cost of increasing the combined output to 6400 tonnes per year?
- What are the shadow prices for locally available wastepaper at each plant?
- Due to a slump in demand, the wastepaper broker approaches WPC offering the possibility of a substantial discount on wastepaper. What is the maximum price WPC would be willing to pay for wastepaper bought from the broker at each of the two plants?

7. BULL DIESEL produces two specialized lightweight Diesel trucks. Production is done in four departments: the metal cutting and press department, engine assembly, Model A final assembly, and Model B final assembly. The monthly production capacities are as follows:

- The metal cutting and press department can either produce 1200 Model A or 857.14 Model B, or any corresponding combination of the two.
- The engine assembly department has an assembly capacity that can assemble either 800 Model A engines or 1200 Model B engines or any corresponding combination of the two.
- The two final assembly departments have the following capacities: 800 Model A, 600 Model B. Note that each model can only be assembled on its own dedicated assembly line. .

BULL can currently sell as many trucks as they can produce. However, dealers insist on a balance between the two models. In particular, they want to receive no more than twice as many of Model A as of Model B. This has not been a problem in the last few years. BULL tended to produce considerably more Model B trucks than Model A, since according to the accountants standard cost imputations Model B is much more profitable than Model A, as can be seen from the table below:

	Standard costs of production	
	Model A	Model B
Materials and purchased parts	$7,400	$5,900
Direct labour:		
Metal cutting and press	$1200	$ 900
Engine assembly	$900	$1300
Final assembly	$2400	$1800
total labour	$4,500	$4,000
Overhead allocation:		
Shared manufacturing overhead	$1512	$1584
Final assembly overhead	$4008 $1696	
subtotal	$5520 $3280	
General overhead 25% of above	$1380 $820	
total overhead	$6,900	$4,100
Total cost	$18,800	$14,000
Net selling price	$20,000	$18,450

Overheads for the two shared manufacturing departments (metal cutting and press, and the engine assembly), expected to total $1,404,000 per month, are allocated to the two models in terms of the direct labour costs for these two departments, based on the preliminary plan of producing 300 Model A and 600 Model B trucks each month. Monthly overheads for the two final assembly departments are forecast at $1,202,400 for the Model A assembly department and $1,017,600 for the Model B department. The predicted monthly general overhead of $906,000 is allocated to the two models as 25% of manufacturing overheads. Note that the manufacturing overhead included 20% fringe benefits (vacation pay, pension fund contributions, insurance, etc.) on direct labour costs. The figures shown for direct labour above are exclusive of fringe benefits.

At the regular monthly planning session, the chief executive voiced his concern about the company's profit performance. The marketing manager immediately pointed out that it was impossible to raise the price of Model A trucks to yield a profit comparable to the Model B truck. He suggested that serious consideration should be given to dropping this model from the product line. He asked the production manager by how much the output of Model B could be increased by such a move. The production manager took out his calculator and, after 20 seconds, responded: 'About 200 more, but only if the Model A assembly line is converted to the production of Model B trucks! That would cost roughly $500,000!' The marketing manager nodded and expressed the opinion that most dealers would welcome an increased output of Model B, particularly if they were made aware of the firm's current plans to develop two new models for introduction in about 18 months time. The company's vice-president of finance objected to this suggestion. She pointed out that the seemingly bad profit margin on Model A was caused by trying to absorb the entire fixed overhead of the Model A assembly department with only a small number of units produced. She suggested that the firm should explore the possibility of producing more Model A trucks. The production manager interjected that this would only be possible by reducing the output of Model B trucks, although he thought that it would be possible to buy in engines to the required specifications from another engine manufacturer. This would obviously be considerably more expensive. At this point in the discussions, the chief executive decided that additional information was needed before a decision could be reached. He asked the production manager to inquire about the cost of buying in engines and report to him as quickly as possible. He asked the marketing manager to investigate the response of some of the important dealerships about the possibility of dropping Model A, as well as whether the market could absorb up to 800 Model B trucks, as well as possibly more Model A trucks, without forcing a price reduction in either model. Five days later the production manager reported that engines to the required specifications could be purchased for $5,980 for Model A engines and for $6,910 for Model B engines. Purchasing engines from outside would also reduce material costs by $1600 for each truck. Obviously, no engine assembly costs would be incurred. Assume that you are the chief executive's analytic assistant. He asks you to analyze this situation. In particular, he wants recommendations about the following points:

(a) Should Model A be dropped from the production line and the output of Model B increased to 800 units by converting the assembly line for Model A to Model B assembly?

(b) Should output of Model B trucks even be increased beyond 800 by purchasing engines from outside suppliers? If purchase of engines from outside suppliers is not on the cards at the current prices quoted, he would like to know the maximum price the firm would be willing to pay.

(c) Is the suggestion of the vice-president of finance to increase production of Model A units by reducing the output of Model B trucks or buying in engines a better solution than either of the two above? Again, he also wants to know the maximum price the firm should be willing to pay for engines purchased from outside.

Note that all questions can be answered by using a single model that allows all possible options and letting the model determine the optimal solution. Identification of relevant costs is an integral part of this exercise. (This exercise has been liberally adapted from an example in W.L. Berry et al., *Management Decision Sciences*, Irwin, 1980, pp. 88-91.)

8. One of the earliest successful applications of linear programming deals with diet or feed-mix problems. A feedlot farmer has just bought a herd of 200 young steers for fattening up. He feeds his animals on a carefully chosen combination of various feeds, such that they get just the right combination of nutrients in the form of starch, protein, and fibre. The table below lists the currently available feeds, the percentage by weight of the three nutrients, and their cost per 100 kg:

Feed	starch	protein	fibre	cost
Potatoes	18.8	0.82	0.89	$8.00
Swedes	7.4	0.68	1.12	$5.50
Lucerne	6.9	3.1	6.15	$8.80
Meadow hay	33	3.8	25.5	$10.40
Dried grass	52.4	9.5	19.6	$15.60
Barley	71.1	6.4	5.3	$17.80
Wheat	71.8	9.4	2.2	$18.90
Soya beans	68.9	17.8	4.1	$27.50

The Government farm consultant advises him that if he wants his steers to grow at a rate of 0.5 kg per day, each animal needs a daily nutrient intake of at least 4 kg of starch, 0.5 kg of protein, and 0.5 kg of fibre. The farmer would like to know which combination of feeds to choose so as to meet these requirements at least cost.

(a) Formulate this problem as an LP.

(b) Find the optimal solution by computer. What quantities of each feed does he have to prepare and mix each day to feed the herd? What is the total cost?

(c) How much cheaper would meadow hay have to become before it would become an alternative feed choice to use?

(This exercise has been adapted from J. Hughes and J. Tait, *The Hard Systems Approach - Systems Models*, The Open University Press, 1984)

9. Continental Meats, a Christchurch sausage factory, produces two types of sausages: beef frankfurters and luncheon meat. The firm uses by-products from other company divisions, in particular its chain of butcher stores, as major inputs into sausage production, namely pork trimmings, pork heads, beef trimmings, and mutton. The recipes for beef frankfurters and luncheon meats allow considerable flexibility in the inputs, as long as certain other specifications, such as fat and water content are met. The production manager of Continental Meats is confident that these two products can be produced from a wide range of inputs, while still maintaining product quality in terms of flavour, colour, and texture. The specifications for beef frankfurters require

that: (1) the total fat content cannot exceed 31% of the finished product; (2) the total moisture must not exceed four times the protein content; (3) the amount of pork must be between 20% and 40% of the finished product; (4) the content of mutton cannot exceed 30%; and (5) the content of beef trimmings has to exceed 45%. For luncheon meat the recipe states that it can contain any combination of mutton, beef trimmings, and pork, provided that: (1) the content of pork is at least 15%; (2) fat content cannot exceed 40%; (3) moisture content has to be at most 47%; and (4) the protein content has to be at least 12%; and (4) mutton cannot be more than 35% of the total input into luncheon meat.

Although the different batches of the various inputs used vary slightly in terms of their fat, protein, and moisture composition, the production manager is confident that production plans can be based on past averages. These are as follows:

Input	Content of	Fat	Protein	Moisture
Pork trimmings		61.7%	6.5%	28.9%
Pork heads		70.2%	4.5%	23.8%
Beef trimmings		12.2%	19.1%	66.0%
Mutton		15.3%	18.7%	64.3%

The current selling price per kilogram is $8.60 for beef frankfurters and $5.90 for luncheon meat. Although about 80% of the total inputs used come from other company divisions, with the balance purchased from external suppliers, the production manager considers that the value of the inputs received from other company divisions should be equal to the cost from external suppliers. The latest schedule specifies the following price schedule: pork trimmings $4.80; pork heads $2.85; beef trimmings $5.90; and mutton $2.80. However, the total amount of pork heads available from other company divisions, as well as other external sources is limited to about 2000 kg per week.

Marketing has supplied the following information about average weekly sales requirements: beef frankfurters between 4000 and 8000 kg; luncheon meat between 4000 and 6000 kg. The firm's daily production capacity is 2000 kg. The factory works 5 days per week. The wage cost for the production workers amounts to $4236 per week. This includes variable overheads (fringe benefits) of 18%. Other production costs, such as other ingredients used (salt, pepper, spices, etc.), casings for the sausages, and electricity, etc., amount to $0.27 per kg of output. The production manager's salary, including fringe benefits, is $2800 per month. The sausage production department also employs an office clerk who is paid $586 per week, including fringe benefits. The sausage department is assessed a charge for facility rental and general overhead contribution, totalling $8,800 per week.

(a) The production manager would like to have a detailed weekly production schedule, specifying exact quantities of each sausage type produced, together with an exact schedule of input requirements. Obviously, that schedule should maximize profits. Formulate this problem as an LP and find the optimal solution. Note that identification of the relevant cost factors is an integral part of this exercise.

(b) He would also like to know whether to schedule some overtime. Overtime amounting to up to 20% per week can be scheduled, at a wage premium of 50%. Overtime increases the maximum daily output proportionately. How much overtime should he schedule? Why?

(c) He has just learned from a colleague in Dunedin that there are up to 500 kg of pork heads available in that city on a weekly basis. Pork heads sell for the same price as in Christchurch. However, there would be an additional cost of $0.70/kg incurred for the packing and transport under refrigeration from Dunedin to Christchurch. Should he buy these pork heads? Why?

(d) The product quality supervisor approaches the production manager with the request that some pork trimmings should be used in place of pork heads in the production of beef frankfurters. This would improve the texture of the final product. Since the recent appearance of frankfurters imported from the North Island, such an improvement might be important for Continental to maintain its share of the market. What effect would this have on the weekly profits?

(This exercise was liberally adapted from a case in W.L. Berry et al., *Management Decision Sciences*, Irwin, 1970, pp. 97-103.)

10. A car rental firm projects the following distribution of its most popular rental model for the coming Monday, listed as 'available', in contrast to its ideal planned distribution, listed as 'planned':

Location	A	B	C	D	E	F
Available	18	6	22	11	7	4
Planned	12	9	15	18	6	6

Note that the planned distribution requires fewer cars than are available. Cars can be transferred between locations at the following cost/car:

To		A	B	C	D	E	F
From	A	0	$48	$92	$65	$74	$126
	B		0	$115	$58	$35	$88
	C			0	$50	$78	$105
	D				0	$44	$65
	E					0	$38

(a) Draw a flow diagram similar to Figure 13-13.
(b) Use the diagram to formulate the corresponding LP.
(c) What is the least-cost redistribution schedule? Which location ends up with more cars than planned?

11. A firm faces a seasonal demand for its products. The firm has the policy to maintain a stable workforce, although the workforce can be scheduled to work overtime up to 25% of its regular time capacity. Goods produced in any given month are available for sale in the same months. Any goods produced in a given month can be stored in inventory for sale in a later month at a cost of $4 per unit per month stored, assessed on the ending stock of each month. The regular time capacity of the plant is 6000 units per month. Each unit produced during regular time has a cost of $250, while a unit produced on overtime has a cost of $260. The firm faces the following demands over the coming 6 months:

Month	1	2	3	4	5	6
Demand	3000	4500	6500	9000	7000	6500

Demand cannot be backordered.
(a) Draw a flow diagram similar to Figure 13-13.
(b) Use it to formulate the corresponding LP.
(c) Find the optimal regular time/overtime production schedule.

12. MAINLAND FOREST CORPORATION (MFC) is planning its production schedule for the coming month. MFC is currently logging two forests, F1 and F2. The logs harvested are used either in MFC's sawmill or its pulp mill. Some of the logs can also be exported through Lyttelton (the sea port of Christchurch, N.Z.). The table below lists the average output of each forest per day, the maximum percentage of logs suitable for processing by the sawmill or for export (export logs need to be straight, otherwise they take too much space in the ship's hold), and the cost of harvesting and of transporting the logs from each forest to the plants or to Lyttelton. Logs not suitable for the sawmill can only be used for pulp, except those that can be exported. Export logs fetch $200/cubic metre.

Logs processed by the sawmill are converted into construction timber and dressed timber in the proportions shown below. Offcuts and scraps are transferred to the pulp mill for use there. The conversion proportions shown are fixed and cannot be altered, i.e., they are not decision variables.

Forest		F1	F2
Upper limit to log output in cubic metres		128	192
Maximum percentage of logs harvested			
suitable for sawmill and export		41%	55%
Cost of harvesting logs		$12.40	$13.20/cubic metre
Transport cost to	sawmill	$4.20	$6.60/cubic metre
	pulp mill	$3.20	$4.50/cubic metre
	Lyttelton	$6.20	$5.60/cubic metre
Conversion of logs at sawmill: Construction timber		60%	40%
	Dressed timber	30%	48%
	Scrap and offcuts	10%	12%
Transport cost sawmill to pulp mill		$2.40/cubic metre	

The sawmill has an average capacity of 6 hours per day, the remaining 2 hours for the shift are used for maintenance. Processing one cubic metre of logs into construction timber takes 0.06 hours of sawmill capacity, while processing one cubic metre of logs into dressed timber takes 0.12 hours of sawmill capacity. Obviously scraps and offcuts are simply a by-product of the sawmill process. Construction timber sells for $150/cubic metre, while dressed timber sells for $300/cubic metre. MFC wants to meet the demand for construction timber of at least 32 cubic metres per day, while the output of dressed timber should not exceed 40 cubic metres per day. The processing cost for construction timber is $15/cubic metre and for dressed timber $25/cubic metre.

Logs, scraps, and offcuts are converted into chips at the pulp mill. The chips are then processed into pulp, used for newsprint production. Each cubic metre of wood yields 0.5 tonne of pulp which has a value of $340/tonne and incurs a processing cost of $40/tonne. The pulp mill can process up to 160 cubic metres per day. MFC has to meet firm contracts for pulp of 60 tonnes per day.

Management of MFC would like to know its best daily operating schedule, in terms of allocation of logs to the various uses, and output of final products, so as to maximize net profits. The fixed costs of operating the sawmill amount to $6,000 per day, while they amount to $12,000 for the pulp mill. Administrative overheads run at $5,000 per day. (Note that most integrated forest products processing companies use OR/MS methods to help them determine suitable operating plans. Obviously, their problems are much more complex, involving logs of different qualities with different conversion rates into final products, as well as modeling their operations in greater detail.)

(a) Develop a diagram depicting the material flow for this situation, similar to the one shown in Figure 13-13. However, you may find it easier to have the flows associated with the arrows, with the nodes representing either sources, processes, or uses. This will be helpful for part (b) below.

(b) Formulate this problem as a linear program. Use a formulation that corresponds to your material flow diagram, i.e., showing variables for intermediate and final products, as well as for the log supply. Use and define mnemonic names for the decision variables and label each constraint clearly (such as 'sawmill capacity constraint'). Note that in this example, it may be easier to associate decision variables with the arrows, rather than the circles.

(c) Solve the problem using an LP computer package, e.g., Solver in EXCEL.

(d) Show the numerical values of your solution on the flow diagram developed under (a) above, by attaching to each arrow the value of the corresponding decision variable.

(e) Management is considering the possibility of shifting all or part of the maintenance work on the sawmill work to overtime. What increase in profit can be achieved for an additional hour of capacity? It is also possible to add an additional logging gang to forest F1 at a daily cost of $480. The additional gang would be able to log up to 32 cubic metres of logs per day. Should MFC consider this option? Why or why not? The marketing manager would like to launch a campaign to increase sales of dressed timber, since it seems to provide such a high contribution towards profits. Should he be encouraged to do this? What would be the consequences of it and why?

Note, you can find ample additional LP formulation problems in any OR/MS introductory text held in a university library.

REFERENCES

Any OR/MS introductory text usually has a fairly extensive treatment of the graphical solution to 2-variable LP problems, several formulation examples, as well as full coverage of the Simplex LP solution technique. The latter will require a fair background in linear algebra. The emphasis given to the Simplex method in such introductory texts is, in my opinion, misplaced. The ordinary user of linear programming will never need to know the details of the Simplex method. Instead it is crucial to have some familiarity with a commercial LP computer package, such as LINDO, the spreadsheet based WHATSBEST, or another spreadsheet optimizer, like EXCEL's Solver. Some texts use their own, mostly rather restrictive and limited LP code, supplied with a diskette coming with the text.

There are a few specialized linear programming texts around. Most of them will be beyond your reach, unless you have a good working knowledge of linear algebra, including matrix and vector notation. One of the few exceptions is

Daellenbach, H.G., and Bell, E.J., *User's Guide to Linear Programming*, Prentice-Hall, 1970. Its treatment is at a similar level to this chapter. It contains a number of real-life examples, including a scaled-down version of a planning model for an integrated oil company with several sources of crude oils, two refineries, and several marketing areas. Except for its use of a simple LP computer code, it still is up-to-date in terms of formulation examples and its treatment of sensitivity analysis.

All introductory texts to operations research or management science have at least one chapter devoted to LP formulations.

14 Dynamic Systems

The type of decision processes we have studied so far were concerned with making a single decision at a given point in time, usually the present. For instance, we considered which one of several mutually exclusive investments should be undertaken, or the best allocation of scarce resources to one or several activities. The future, if it is explicitly considered, only enters in so far as it affects the costs and benefits flowing from the decision.

The inventory control problem of the Lubricating Oil Division (chapters 5 to 8) considers a string of decisions, namely the periodic stock replenishment whenever the inventory for a given product has been depleted. At each decision point, the future in terms of the demand for the product and the incidence of costs, however, remains unchanged. In technical terms, the future is said to be **stationary**. As a consequence, each decision is identical to the first one.

In this chapter, the time element is explicitly incorporated into the decision process in several ways. All problems studied involve a sequence of decision points over time. The future is not stationary, but **dynamic**. Hence, the state of the system changes over time. Each future decision point may face a different state of the system — the latter being affected by changing inputs from the environment, as well as by prior future decisions. Hence, consecutive decisions are not identical, but each one is unique.

When the time element enters into the decision process, the first question that must be addressed is 'how long into the future should we look?'. The length of time that the model covers is called **the planning horizon**. We already used the concept of a planning horizon in some of the examples and case studies of previous chapters. For example, for investment and replacement problems we included all costs and benefits over the productive life of the investment in the analysis. Hence, the productive life of an investment became the planning horizon. For the stationary situation of the LOD stock control problem we looked at annual costs. Hence, the planning horizon covered one year. However, the latter choice was arbitrary. The optimal replenishment policy would have been identical, even if the model had used a planning horizon of one month.

For dynamic situations, the choice of the planning horizon becomes more critical. The best sequence of decisions or the **decision policy** derived from the model may be affected by the length of the planning horizon. The analyst is now faced with a new consideration. What is its most appropriate length? Section 14.1 gives some tentative answers to this question. The same theme is taken up again in Sections 14.3 and 14.9. Sections 14.2, 14.4 to 14.7, and 14.8 study two production planning situations. Each one exhibits distinct features and calls for a different approach for choosing the planning horizon and finding the best sequence of decisions.

14.1 THE PLANNING HORIZON

The planning horizon is the length of time — number of weeks, months, or years — covered by the model. What is its most appropriate length for dynamic models? Before trying to answer this question, it is useful to carefully clarify our aim for modeling dynamic situations.

Aim of Modeling Dynamic Situations

One of the rules of good OR/MS practice is to avoid taking any decision or action that will unnecessarily reduce the scope of future decision choices, as far as this is desirable and practical.   In line with this, only those decisions are physically implemented which cannot be postponed any further without affecting costs and benefits unfavourably. No commitment is made on any decision that only has to be implemented at some later point in time. If the future is uncertain, the wisdom of this rule is obvious. The future may turn out to be different than we expected. By keeping our options open, we will be in a better position to respond effectively to unexpected situations.

But even if we pretend that the future is known, following this rule is equally advisable. In most cases the assumption of a certain future is only a simplifying approximation. So, the reason for looking into the future is to determine the best initial set of decisions for which a firm commitment has to be made at the beginning of the planning horizon. This may require us to make tentative choices about decisions at future points in time. However, no steps are undertaken for their implementation until later. At that time, new information about the future may lead us to re-evaluate these tentative decision choices and possibly change some of them if this has become advantageous.

We are now ready to give a general answer about the most appropriate length of the planning horizon. It goes without saying that the longer the planning horizon, the costlier is the data collection and the computation of the optimal policy. Hence, the analyst will want to keep the planning horizon as short as possible. Its minimum length should cover a time interval that includes all those aspects, activities, or events which would lead to different initial sets of firm decisions being optimal when included and when ignored.

Putting this into practice is far from simple. As the length of the planning horizon is extended, events and decisions towards the end of the planning horizon will in general influence initial decisions less and less. This is particularly true for costs and benefits occurring many years in the future, if these cash flows are discounted. Even at a moderate discount rate of 10%, a dollar received in 10 years is worth now only 38 cents, while after 20 years its value now is less than 15 cents.

Furthermore, the reliability of inputs into the system, such as demand, benefit, and cost forecasts also decreases as we look farther into the future. In some rare and special instances, the mathematical structure of the model lends itself to either give a precise minimum interval or specify some conditions which, once satisfied, allow the future to be ignored. In most cases, however, the actual choice of the length of the planning horizon is a compromise between all the factors mentioned and the cost of data collection and computations.

Systematic sensitivity analysis with respect to the time interval covered may help in assessing the effects of future events on the initial set of decisions. This will hopefully lead to a better choice for the most suitable length of planning horizon needed for a particular problem situation. But it will also increase the cost and the time incurred for completing the project. This is justified, if the project offers substantial benefits because of its size and importance. It is also justified if the model developed is intended for repeated and continued use on a regular basis. In either case the cost incurred in getting the length of the planning horizon right will be recouped through lower costs or higher benefits in using the model. In most other situations it pays to be conservative and select a planning horizon on the long rather than short side.

Planning Horizons for Seasonal Processes

For some situations, the nature of the problem may strongly suggest a suitable length for the planning horizon. This is particularly the case for decision problems subject to a seasonal pattern for some of their crucial inputs. For example, a hydro reservoir used for electric power generation may go through a natural annual cycle. Spring snow melt and rainfall will fill the reservoir to its full capacity. The water stored is then used to generate electricity either over the following summer period if the power is used mainly for air conditioning or over the following winter period if power is mainly used for heating. In either case, at the end of the 'season' the reservoir is empty. There is no carry-over from one year to the next. A new cycle starts each year. A planning horizon of one year, starting with the beginning of the snow melt, is the natural and appropriate choice used by many hydro-electric power companies.

However, there are some very large hydro reservoirs, particularly in Quebec (Canada) and in Sweden, that take several years to fill or empty under normal inflow and usage conditions. Substantial volumes of stored water are carried from one year to the next. Although the water inflow into the reservoir and the water usage may be highly seasonal, the planning horizon needs to be substantially longer, covering several years of operations.

These two examples indicate that an annual planning horizon is a suitable choice for seasonal activities, provided that there is a natural break between consecutive seasonal cycles, with no or only insignificant carry-over from one cycle to the next. Such breaks clearly satisfy the conditions stated earlier that events occurring past the end of the planning horizon should not affect the optimality of the initial set of firm decisions. A substantial portion of agricultural production and processing falls into this category. Can you think of other human-created activities which are seasonal with clear breaks between annual cycles?

We may still choose to use an annual planning horizon, even if there is a significant carry-over from one cycle to the next. The trick used is to create an artificial break between consecutive cycles. For example, the consumption of many beverages also has a seasonal pattern, superimposed on a more or less steady base rate. The lowest point of the seasonal cycle is chosen as the starting point of the annual planning horizon. The break between consecutive cycles is created artificially by specifying ending conditions for the state of the system. These then become the beginning conditions for the next planning horizon. Specifying such ending/beginning conditions reduces or even eliminates the influence of later events on the current set of decisions. The size of finished product inventories, stocks of raw materials, and the work force are excellent choices for the ending and starting conditions between consecutive cycles. Again, good levels for these conditions may be determined through sensitivity analysis.

Rolling Planning Horizon

For ongoing processes with no natural breaks or end points, **a rolling planning horizon** approach is used. This is depicted in Figure 14-1. A planning horizon of T periods, e.g., weeks, months, or years, is used to determine the initial set of optimal decisions. These decisions are then implemented and their effects on the state of the system recorded. One period later, the problem is again analyzed based

Figure 14-1: Rolling planning horizon of constant length

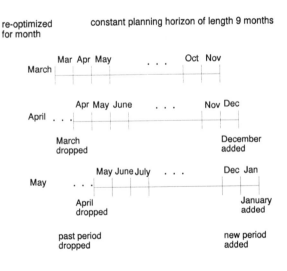

on the updated state of the system. The planning horizon used remains constant at T periods by dropping the period just passed and adding a new period at the end of the previous planning horizon. This scheme of dropping and adding periods at opposite ends of the planning horizon and re-optimizing the problem after each period based on the updated state of the system continues indefinitely. After each period, the planning horizon is, so-to-speak, rolled forward by one period, hence the label 'rolling planning horizon'.

Planning Horizon Lead-up Time

Implementation of the decisions may not be instantaneous, but may consist of a sequence of activities which take several days, weeks, months, or even years to plan in detail and execute. Decisions of this sort, scheduled for implementation early on in the planning horizon, need to be planned prior to the planning horizon. Therefore, such a lead-up time becomes part of the effective planning horizon. Similarly, the time needed for developing the overall plan may for many situations take several months. During this time, no decisions that are part of the plan can normally be implemented. Hence, this development time is also part of the lead-up time.

The effective planning horizon thus consists of two parts. The first part covers the lead-up time. During the lead-up time, firm commitments based on decisions that were part of the previous planning horizon will still get implemented, but they can only be changed with heavy penalties. The second part is the active planning horizon for which decisions can still be made. This second part is the actual focus of the planning exercise. The role of the lead-up time is to update the state of the system to the position it will be in at the beginning of the active planning horizon.

14.2 SITUATION SUMMARY FOR SEASONAL PRODUCTION PLAN

The CRYSTAL SPRINGS MINERAL WATER COMPANY produces carbonized mineral water with various flavours which it sells through supermarkets and corner groceries on the US Westcoast at $3.50 per case. It is a family-owned firm with Sam Spring being the major shareholder. He is also CRYSTAL's general manager, while his daughter and son do the selling. It has a permanent staff of 18 people. Sales of its waters are highly seasonal with demand during the summer months being three to four times larger than in the middle of Winter.   Since bottled water does not store well beyond one or two months, the rate of production has to follow the seasonal demand pattern to a large extent.

CRYSTAL's output is pretty much limited by the capacity of its bottling machine. Normally, during the low season from November to April or May the bottling operation is run with one shift, staffed by a core of 12 employees who in the main have been with the company for many years. During the hot season, when sales soar, a second shift is operated by hiring temporary staff who work alongside the permanent staff. Since temporary staff have to undergo training, they have to be hired about 2 weeks prior to the time the second shift starts producing. Sam Spring estimates that the cost of hiring staff for a second shift, including advertising and interviewing, amounts to about $18,000. Similarly, once the second shift is abandoned, CRYSTAL again incurs a cost of about $15,000 for laying off all temporary staff.

The bottles are sold in cases of 12. Hence, all accounting and planning is in terms of cases, rather than bottles or volume. The production process is rather simple. Water is captured from a pristine natural spring on the firm's premises. Various minerals and flavourings are mixed into the water. The water is piped to the carbonizing machine and immediately filled into bottles which are sealed and labelled, all in one sequence of operations. The bottles are then put into cases. The cost of all ingredients, packing materials and labels, including power to operate the machines, but excluding any labour costs, comes to $3.10 per case.

There is some temporary storage space for about one week's production right next to the bottling machine. The normal mode of operation is to ship cases to the various stores directly off the production floor without storing them first. The temporary storage of up to one week's production is sufficient to absorb the normal daily fluctuations in selling and shipping. However, any excess has to be moved into the cool store warehouse, some 50 metres away. Moving and storing cases incurs a handling and holding cost of about $0.15 per case stored per month. Any cases stored are carefully rotated to avoid storage in excess of one month. Sam Spring reckons that if CRYSTAL is unable to meet all potential sales, unsatisfied potential customers simply buy another brand. As a consequence, any unmet demand is lost. Sam attempts to meet demand whenever physically possible, since he is afraid that lost sales could mean more than simply $0.40 of profits foregone per case. It could imply losing some customers to the competition for good.

Although total annual sales have increased by about 5% in each of the past four years, the percentages of annual sales falling into each month have shown a remarkably stable seasonal pattern. Their averages are:

Month	1	2	3	4	5	6	7	8	9	10	11	12
Sales percentage	3.5	3.1	4.7	8.0	7.4	10.3	13.8	14.4	14.0	9.9	4.7	6.2

The regular time (RT) shift cost is the same regardless of whether the shift works at full or below full capacity. A shift can also work up to 25% overtime (OT). Overtime is paid at a 50% premium above the regular time pay. The capacities for a one and two shift operation, for regular time only and for overtime, and the associated costs are as follows:

Operating mode	Capacity	Cost
1 shift on RT only	288,000 cartons	$24,000/month
OT capacity for one shift	72,000 cartons	$125/1000 cartons
2 shifts on RT only	540,000 cartons	$48,000/month
OT capacity for two shifts	125,000 cartons	$144/1000 cartons

OT capacity for a two-shift operation is less than twice the OT capacity for one shift, due to reduced work efficiency. All other costs incurred are fixed overheads. They are not affected by the production schedule, hence may be ignored.

It is now early December. Reviewing sales this year so far, Sam Spring expects that they will reach about 4,900,000 cartons. He is getting ready to develop a tentative aggregate production schedule for the coming year. The intention is not to implement it blindly, but to use it as a guide for the planning of temporary staffing needs, purchasing of various ingredients, scheduling of bottle and carton deliveries to the plant, and for developing the vacation roster for the permanent staff. Nevertheless, Sam would like an aggregate production schedule that maximizes profits for the year. In the past, he usually planned for an end of December inventory of 50,000 cartons of bottled water. He wishes to continue this practice.

As a useful exercise, I suggest you draw a rich picture for this problem situation. The issue to be analyzed is the development of a production plan that maximizes profits. Next, you should define a relevant system, following the suggestions in Chapters 4 and 5. Armed with these preliminaries, we are ready to formulate a mathematical model which we will explore using a spreadsheet approach.

14.3 CHOICE OF PLANNING HORIZON

This is a typical seasonal planning situation. Each calendar year forms a natural planning horizon. For Sam's intended use of the annual plan it will be sufficient to divide the planning horizon into monthly subintervals. From a planning point of view, any change in shift levels or the production rate are then assumed to occur at the beginning of each month. Later on in the year Sam will break the planned monthly aggregates into detailed weekly production schedules which he will adjust in the light of the demand and shipment pattern actually observed at that time.

Changing the number of shifts needs to be initiated at least one month prior to the actual change, while changes in the production rate can be implemented with only a few days notice. However, it takes only a few hours to develop a new annual production schedule. The first item requires the longest lead-up time. The effective planning horizon should therefore also include a lead-up time of one month — in this case the month of December. However, a second shift has never been introduced prior to April. Hence for all practical purposes, the lead-up time is only a few days. If Sam is able to predict how many cases will be shipped out prior to the end of December, he can adjust the December output such that the inventory of bottled water at the end of December is approximately 50,000 cases. Hence, there is no need for including a lead-up time in the planning horizon.

14.4 INFLUENCE DIAGRAM FOR PRODUCTION PLANNING PROBLEM

Drawing an influence diagram for relationships between inputs, systems variables,

Figure 14-2: Influence diagram for profit for multi-period production planning

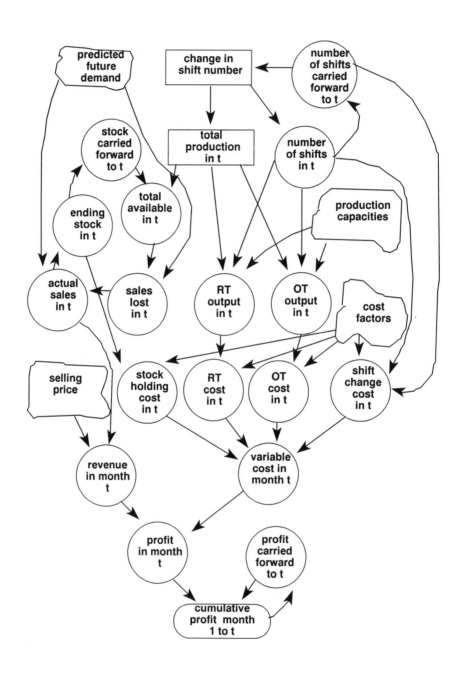

and outputs will facilitate the formulation of a mathematical model from first principles. Figure 14-2 shows my version of such a diagram. The inputs into the system are demand predictions, production capacities for the four shift configurations, and various revenue and cost factors. The major output of interest is the difference between total revenue and total relevant cost for the entire planning horizon, or a measure of the profit. (Note that this difference is not the net profit since all fixed costs have been excluded!)

For each month there are two decision variables: the number of shifts operated and the production level. The latter is restricted by the number of shifts and their production capacities. Given the shift capacity during regular time, these two decision variables also define the amount of the output produced on overtime. A third decision variable for overtime worked each month is not needed.

Each month is usefully viewed as a subsystem. The subsystems are linked by three system variables, namely, the ending stock and the number of shifts operated in month $t-1$, and the cumulative profit from month 1 to $t-1$. In some sense they are pseudo-outputs of the subsystem for month $t-1$ and become pseudo-inputs into the subsystem for month t. This feature calls for inventiveness in drawing the influence diagram. Rather than duplicate the subsystem relationships for each of the 12 months and connecting the subsystems through these pseudo-output/input linkages, I only show the relationships for one typical month t. The subsystem linkages are indicated symbolically by broken lines.

14.5 SPREADSHEET MATHEMATICAL MODEL

The mathematical relationships for this production planning model are relatively simple. Some have the form of accounting equations. Others require a table look-up. They are listed below, and their spreadsheet implementation is shown in Figure 14-3. To test your understanding I suggest that you verify each relationship numerically in the spreadsheet for several consecutive periods. March, April, May and June cover most situations. In accordance with Sam Spring's policy, the beginning stock in January is entered as 50,000. All carton amounts are listed in thousands.

Functional Relations of Model

The ending stock in month $t-1$ becomes the beginning stock in month t (depicted by the feedback loop in the influence diagram). The total stock available for sale is then:

[Total available in t] = [Ending inventory in $t-1$] + [Production in t]

The regular time output in month t is obtained by comparing the total production in month t with the production capacities for the number of shifts scheduled. The

Figure 14-3: Spreadsheet implementation of CRYSTAL production plan — Schedule 1

CRYSTAL NATURAL MINERAL WATER COMPANY
POLICY: Schedule follows demand without shortages

DATA:	Capacity in 1000 cases	Cost/month in $1000
On operations:		
1 shift	288	24
1 shift o/time	72	9
2 shifts	540	48
2 shifts o/time	125	18

Sales most recent year in 1000 cases	4900
Percentage growth next year	5
Sales forecast next year in 1000	5145
Desired ending stock in 1000 cases	50

Other costs:	in
Raw materials/1000 cases	3.1
Holding cost/1000 cases	0.15
Revenue per 1000 cases (in $1000)	3.5

Shift change cost	up 18	down 15

Month:	JAN	FEB	MAR	APR	MAY	JUNE	JULY	AUG	SEP	OCT	NOV	DEC	TOTAL
Sales percent	3.5	3.1	4.7	8	7.4	10.3	13.8	14.4	14	9.9	4.7	6.2	100
Potential sales	181	160	242	412	381	530	711	741	721	510	242	319	5150
Total production	131	160	242	412	424	665	665	665	665	510	251	360	5150
Shift level	1	1	1	2	2	2	2	2	2	2	1	1	
Product transactions:													
Beginning stock	50	0	0	0	0	43	178	132	56	0	0	9	
R/T output	131	160	242	412	424	540	540	540	540	510	251	288	4578
O/T output	0	0	0	0	0	125	125	125	125	0	0	72	572
Amt available	181	160	242	412	424	708	843	797	721	510	251	369	
Potential sales	181	160	242	412	381	530	711	741	721	510	242	319	
Ending stock	0	0	0	0	43	178	132	56	0	0	9	50	
Lost sales	0	0	0	0	0	0	0	0	0	0	0	0	
Variable costs/month:													
Materials	406.1	496	750.2	1277.2	1314.4	2061.5	2061.5	2061.5	2061.5	1581	778.1	1116	15965
R/T shift cost	24	24	24	48	48	48	48	48	48	48	24	24	456
O/T shift cost	0	0	0	0	0	18	18	18	18	0	0	9	81
Shift change cost	0	0	0	18	0	0	0	0	0	0	15	0	33
Holding cost	0	0	0	0	6.45	26.7	19.8	8.4	0	0	1.35	7.5	70.2
Total cost	430.1	520	774.2	1343.2	1368.85	2154.2	2147.3	2135.9	2127.5	1629	818.45	1156.5	16605
Revenue	633.5	560	847	1442	1333.5	1855	2488.5	2593.5	2523.5	1785	847	1116.5	18025
Total revenue minus total variable cost													1419.8

regular output is equal to the total production or the relevant shift level capacity, whichever is smaller. Any excess is then produced on overtime. For example, production in June is 665,000 cases with two shifts in operation. The two-shift capacities are 540,000 on RT and 125,000 on OT. Hence, 540,000 are produced on RT and the balance of 665,000 - 540,000 or 125,000 on OT:

$$[\text{RT output in } t] = \{[\text{RT capacity for number of shifts in } t]$$
$$\text{or } [\text{Production in } t], \text{ whichever is smaller}\}$$

$$[\text{OT output in } t] = \{[\text{Production in } t] - [\text{RT cap. for number of shifts in } t]$$
$$\text{if positive, and } 0 \text{ otherwise}\}$$

Subtracting the total amount available for month t from potential sales (a system input) results in either some stock left over or an amount of lost sales. Lost sales are subtracted from potential sales to give actual sales. Subtracting actual sales from total available gives the ending stock, carried forward to the following month:

$$[\text{Lost sales in } t] = \{0 \text{ if } [\text{Pot. sales in } t] \leq [\text{Total available in } t]$$
$$\text{or } [\text{Pot. sales in } t] - [\text{Total available in } t] \text{ otherwise}\}$$

$$[\text{Actual sales in } t] = [\text{Pot. sales in } t] - [\text{Lost sales in } t]$$

$$[\text{Ending inventory in } t] = [\text{Total available in } t] - [\text{Actual sales in } t]$$

Any stock carried forward to month $t+1$ is penalized in month t by a stock handling and holding cost:

$$[\text{Stock holding cost in } t] = [\text{Unit stock holding cost}][\text{Ending inventory in } t]$$

The RT production cost for one or two shifts is obtained from the production cost table. The OT production cost is proportional to the OT output. In our example for June, the RT output of 540,000 has a RT production cost of \$48,000. The OT production cost for one shift is \$144/1000 cases or \$18,000 for 125,000 cases:

$$[\text{RT production cost in } t] = [\text{RT shift cost for number of shifts in } t]$$

$$[\text{OT production cost in } t] = [\text{OT output in } t][\text{OT cost/unit for shift level}]$$

The shift change cost is only incurred if the number of shifts in month t is different than in month $t-1$. It is allocated to the month in which the capacity change takes effect. For example, an increase in the shift capacity effective for May means that the additional staff is hired and trained in the second half of April, but all costs are allocated to May. This approximation does not affect the total cost incurred over the entire planning horizon, while simplifying the spreadsheet computations. It is computed as follows:

[Shift change cost in t] = {[shift increase cost] if
　　　　　　[number of shifts used in t] ≥ [number of shifts used in $t-1$],
　　　　　　or [shift decrease cost] if
　　　　　　[number of shifts used in t] ≤ [number of shifts used in $t-1$],
　　　　　　and 0 otherwise}

The sum of all these costs is the total variable cost in month t:

[Variable cost in t] = [Stock holding cost in t] + [RT production cost in t]
　　　　　　　　　　+ [OT production cost in t] + [Shift change cost in t]

The revenue in month t is equal to actual sales in t times the unit selling price:

[Revenue in t] = [Actual sales in t][Unit selling price]

The profit in month t (without accounting for any fixed costs) is the difference between revenue and the total variable cost in month t:

[Profit in t] = [Revenue in t] – [Variable cost in t]

Finally, the cumulative profit from month 1 through month t is (another feedback loop in the influence diagram):

[Cumul. profit to t] = [Profit in t] + [Cumul. profit to $t-1$]

In the spreadsheet, the two rows for [Total production] and [Shift level] are the decision variables. They are inserted by the user. The rest of the numbers below the second double line are calculated by the spreadsheet using the expressions listed above. The [Potential sales] volume is computed as the product of [Sales percent] times [Expected sales next year]. The latter is equal to [Current sales] times [1 + Percent growth next year]. (Due to rounding errors, the sum of the monthly sales adds up to 5,150,000 rather than the projected total of 5,145,000.) A number of rows, such as [RT output], [OT output], [Ending stock[, [Lost sales], [RT shift cost], [OT shift cost], and [Shift change cost] use logical spreadsheet functions. It took me about an hour to develop this spreadsheet.

14.6 FINDING THE OPTIMAL PRODUCTION PLAN

Two different optimizing techniques could be applied to find the optimal production plan for this problem. (They are dynamic programming and integer programming.)

However, the computational effort is excessive for both. Having set up a spreadsheet, an obvious approach is to try out various schedules and let the spreadsheet almost instantly compute the corresponding annual profit. Its advantage is that the intended problem owner and user, Sam Spring, will be able to fully understand its logic and can easily verify that it is correct. This is one of the prime selling points for implementation and continued use of this tailor-made tool.

The schedule tried first in Figure 14-3 uses a so-called 'chase strategy'. Production follows sales as closely as possible. Lost sales are avoided. So the analyst will initially set the production level equal to the sales level, adjusting the number of shifts as needed. Since the two-shift capacity with overtime is insufficient to cover the high demands from July to September, the analyst will backtrack and increase production to its maximum capacity level in the months just preceding July, until lost sales are eliminated. Production in June is thus increased to 665,000, needing another 43,000 cases to be produced in May in addition to the May demand. Note the same sort of adjustment is made to cover the December requirements, including the provision of an ending stock of 50,000 cases. This policy has a total annual profit of $1,419,800.

This schedule does not use the RT production capacity efficiently. For instance, the March output is 242,000. This is 46,000 less than the one-shift RT capacity. Similarly, the two-shift RT capacity for May is underutilized by 116,000. By fully using the RT shift capacity in March and also producing 6,000 cases on overtime, it is possible to delay the start of the second shift by one month. This results in a small increase in profits of $6,450. The resulting schedule is shown in Figure 14-4.

Neither of these two schedules allows any lost sales. As a consequence, the amount of stock carried during the months of May to August is quite substantial. That stock is carried to cover demand in the three peak season months of July, August and September, where the maximum production capacity is less than potential sales. The amount carried forward to month $t+1$ never exceeds the potential sales in that month. Hence, the restriction on the limited shelf life of the product is never violated.

Reducing the amount of stock carried implies that some of the demand will not be met, resulting in some lost sales. For instance, if production in May is restricted to 381,000 cases — a reduction of 43,000 from the second schedule — then no stocks are carried forward from May to June, and the stocks at the end of June, July, and August are also reduced by the same amount. However, potential sales for September cannot be met completely, resulting in lost sales of 43,000. The savings in stock holding costs is $150 for each of these four months for every 1000 cases, or $150(43)(4) = $25,800. The loss in profit per 1000 cases is the difference between the sales price and the total material cost, i.e., $3500 - $3100 or $400 per 1000 cases. For 43,000 cases of lost sales this amounts to $17,200, or $8600 less than the cost savings. Clearly, from a purely profit maximizing point of view this trade-off is advantageous. A similar (somewhat smaller) trade-off can be achieved by carrying no stocks from June to September.

The savings potential does not stop here. The new output for May still requires

Figure 14-4: CRYSTAL production plan — Schedule 2

CRYSTAL NATURAL MINERAL WATER COMPANY — POLICY: Delaying 2nd shift by one month, no shortages

DATA:	Capacity in 1000 cases	Cost/month in $1000		
On operations:				
1 shift	288	24		
1 shift o/time	72	9		
2 shifts	640	48		
2 shifts o/time	125	18		

Sales most recent year in 1000 cases	4900	
Percentage growth next year	5	
Sales forecast next year in 1000	5145	
Desired ending stock in 1000 cases	50	

Other costs:		
Raw materials/1000 cases	in	3.1
Holding cost/1000 cases	0.15	
Revenue per 1000 cases	in $1000	3.5
Shift change cost	up 18	down 15

Month:	JAN	FEB	MAR	APR	MAY	JUNE	JULY	AUG	SEP	OCT	NOV	DEC	TOTAL
Sales percent	3.5	3.1	4.7	8	7.4	10.3	13.8	14.4	14	9.9	4.7	6.2	100
Potential sales	181	160	242	412	381	530	711	741	721	510	242	319	5150
Total production	131	160	294	360	424	665	665	665	665	510	251	360	5150
Shift level	1	1	1	1	2	2	2	2	2	2	1	1	
Product transactions:													
Beginning stock	50	160	288	288	0	43	178	132	56	0	0	9	
R/T output	131	160	288	288	424	540	540	540	540	510	251	288	4500
O/T output	0	0	6	72	0	125	125	125	125	0	0	72	650
Amt available	181	160	294	412	424	708	843	797	721	510	251	369	
Potential sales	181	160	242	412	381	530	711	741	721	510	242	319	
Ending stock	0	0	52	0	43	178	132	56	0	0	9	50	
Lost sales	0	0	0	0	0	0	0	0	0	0	0	0	
Variable costs/month:													
Materials	406.1	496	911.4	1116	1314.4	2061.5	2061.5	2061.5	2061.5	1581	778.1	1116	15965
R/T shift cost	24	24	24	48	48	48	48	48	48	48	24	24	432
O/T shift cost	0	0	0.75	9	0	18	18	18	18	0	0	9	90.75
Shift change cost	0	0	0	0	18	0	0	0	0	0	15	0	33
Holding cost	0	0	7.8	0	6.45	26.7	19.8	8.4	0	0	1.35	7.5	78
Total cost	430.1	520	943.95	1149	1186.85	2154.2	2147.3	2135.9	2127.5	1629	818.45	1156.5	16598.75
Revenue	633.5	560	847	1442	1333.5	1855	2488.5	2593.5	2523.5	1785	847	1116.5	18025
Total revenue minus total variable cost													1426.25

two shifts and is only 21,000 cases more than the maximum capacity of one shift with overtime. Delaying the introduction of the second shift until June, at the cost of additional lost sales in May, further increases total profits. These adjustments increase profits by $21,066 over schedule 2, as shown in Figure 14-5.

Given the ease with which such 'what if' questions can be explored in a spreadsheet, I did not actually cost out such changes before trying them out. I simply reduced the production levels by successive small amounts first in May, then in June, and finally in July. If total profits increased I kept these changes. I reversed them if profits decreased. The same 'systematic' search by trial-and-error was used for exploring possible changes for April and May, etc.

It may be that Sam Spring is not willing to accept losing almost 3 percent of the potential sales forecasted (153,000/5,145,000) for an increase in profits of only $21,066. He may prefer the schedule in Figure 14-4 (note that it may be possible to improve upon that schedule without incurring any shortages!), or one that lies between the second and the best schedule, allowing some lost sales in September, but none in August.

14.7 CONSIDERATIONS FOR PRACTICAL IMPLEMENTATION

Seasonal planning horizons have well-defined calendar start and end points. In the CRYSTAL case, January 1 is the start and December 31 the end of the annual planning horizon. The initial planning is done using these dates. As time progresses, more recent information about potential sales and stock levels becomes available and Sam will want to have a new look at the production schedule to see if any adjustments to the plan are advisable. For example, assume that it is now early April. Sales have been somewhat higher than expected, largely due to unseasonably warm weather. Long-term weather predictions indicate that this is likely to continue well into June. Should the second shift now be introduced in May rather than only in June?

To answer this question, Sam will go back to the spreadsheet template, update the sales forecasts from April on, and insert the current stock position at the beginning of April. The starting point of the planning horizon is now April 1. Should the end point also be extended by another three months? Given the rather definite break in the annual cycle at the end of December, the December 31 end point will be maintained. Hence, for subsequent updates of the production schedule, the planning horizon becomes shorter and shorter. So rather than talk about an annual seasonal planning horizon, it is more accurate the refer to it as a fixed date or fixed end point planning horizon.

Only towards the end of the current cycle, e.g., sometimes in the last quarter of the calendar year, may Sam wish to extend the planning horizon by a full annual season, in preparation for mapping out next year's schedule.

Figure 14-5: CRYSTAL production plan — Best schedule

CRYSTAL NATURAL MINERAL WATER COMPANY

DATA: On operations:	Capacity in 1000 cases	Cost/month in $1000	POLICY: Best schedule allowing some shortages	
1 shift	288	24	Sales most recent year in 1000 cases	4900
1 shift o/time	72	9	Percentage growth next year	5
2 shifts	540	48	Sales forecast next year in 1000 cases	5145
2 shifts o/time	125	18	Desired ending stock in 1000 cases	50

Other costs:	in			
Raw materials/1000 cases	3.1			
Holding cost/1000 cases	0.15			
Shift change cost	up 18	down 15	Revenue per 1000 cases in $1000	3.5

Month:	JAN	FEB	MAR	APR	MAY	JUNE	JULY	AUG	SEP	OCT	NOV	DEC	TOTAL
Sales percent	3.5	3.1	4.7	8	7.4	10.3	13.8	14.4	14	9.9	4.7	6.2	100
Potential sales	181	160	242	412	381	530	711	741	721	510	242	319	5150
Total production	131	160	294	360	360	576	665	665	665	510	251	360	4997
Shift level	1	1	1	1	1	2	2	2	2	2	1	1	
Product transactions:													
Beginning stock	50	0	0	0	0	0	46	0	0	0	0	9	
R/T output	131	160	288	288	288	540	540	540	540	510	251	288	4364
O/T output	0	0	6	72	72	36	125	125	125	0	0	72	633
Amt available	181	160	294	412	360	576	711	665	665	510	251	369	
Potential sales	181	160	242	412	381	530	711	741	721	510	242	319	
Ending stock	0	0	52	0	0	46	0	0	0	0	9	50	
Lost sales	0	0	0	0	21	46	0	76	56	0	0	0	153
Variable costs/month:													
Materials	406.1	496	911.4	1116	1116	1785.6	2061.5	2061.5	2061.5	1581	778.1	1116	15490.7
R/T shift cost	24	24	24	24	24	48	48	48	48	48	24	24	408
O/T shift cost	0	0	0.75	9	9	5.184	18	18	18	0	0	9	86.934
Shift change cost	0	0	0	0	0	18	0	0	0	0	15	0	33
Holding cost	0	0	7800	0	0	6.9	0	0	0	0	1.35	7.5	23.55
Total cost	430.1	520	943.95	1149	1149	1863.684	2127.5	2127.5	2127.5	1629	818.45	1156.5	16042.
Revenue	633.5	560	847	1442	1260	1855	2488.5	2327.5	2327.5	1785	847	1116.5	17489.5
Total revenue minus total variable cost													1447.316

14.8   AN EXAMPLE OF A ROLLING PLANNING HORIZON

A rolling planning horizon is suitable when activities are not subject to a pronounced seasonality, but just fluctuate in a predictable pattern. The following example of production planning in a manufacturing setting is a typical application for which a rolling planning horizon approach is highly suitable.

The schedule for the final product assembly for a household appliance manufacturer implies the following requirements for the electric motor type AC230/4 built into some of these appliances:

Week	1	2	3	4	5	6	7	8	9	10	11	12	13	14	15
Number	460	820	220	450	1200	360	80	50	100	750	200	0	550	630	1050

These motors are produced in batches. Each new production run requires that the motor subassembly line is switched from one model of motor to another. That change-over has a cost of $960. No more than one run is made for any motor during any given week. However, a run may well produce enough to cover the requirements for several consecutive weeks. Any motors not used in the week they are produced are stored. The storage cost for the AC230/4 motor is 26% per year on its unit production cost of $80. This amounts to $0.40 per unit per week. All other costs are not affected by the size and timing of production runs. They are either fixed costs or variable costs that only depend on the total amount produced per year, but not on individual run sizes.

At the beginning of week 1 there are 480 motors in stock. The objective is to determine a schedule of production runs for the AC230/4 motor, starting in week 1, so as to minimize the total relevant cost for any given planning horizon.

What would be a suitable length for the active planning horizon? A tentative answer can be obtained from a stationary type analysis. If the requirements for the motor would be the same in each week, then we could use the EOQ model (see Sections 6.5 and 6.6). The average weekly demand over the 15 weeks listed above is 460. Using the EOQ formula of expression 6.2 for a weekly (rather than annual) model, we express all time-dependent inputs in terms of weekly figures. Hence, $D = 460$, $s = 960$, $r = .26/52 = 0.005$, and $v = 80$. The resulting EOQ is 1486, covering 3.23 weeks of average requirements. (Verify that the answer would be identical if all time-dependent inputs had been expressed in annual figures!) In view of the highly fluctuating requirements the planning horizon should be considerably longer than that. In fact, the requirements for several consecutive weeks listed above (weeks 7 to 9) are less than 1/4 of the average. For a weekly average that small (115 units), the run size will cover 6.46 weeks of average demand. This analysis suggests, that a suitably conservative choice for the active planning horizon is somewhere in the range of 6 to 9 weeks. I will settle for 8 weeks.

It takes about one week to prepare a change-over on the motor assembly line. Hence, the lead-up time is one week. This gives an effective planning horizon of 9 weeks. So the first planning horizon will cover weeks 1 through 9. However, due to the one-week lead-up time the first production run can only be scheduled for week 2 or later, but not for week 1.

Remember again that the intention of this planning exercise is to implement only the first decision in the active part of the 9-week planning horizon. In our example this is the decision for week 2 — the first week after the lead-up time. Subsequent decisions can wait. In fact, prior to implementing decisions for later periods, they will be re-evaluated in the light of the updated requirements and costs. The reason why they are evaluated in the first place is simply to make sure that any possible effects they might have on the first decision are properly taken into account. Once the initial decision for week 2 has been implemented, the planning horizon is rolled forward by one week, covering weeks 2 to 10, and so on.

The Silver-Meal Heuristic for Dynamic Replenishment Problems

Rather than use an optimizing model, we will use a heuristic approach (see Section 6.10) — the Silver-Meal heuristic [E.A. Silver and R. Peterson, *Decision Systems for Inventory Management and Production Planning*, N.Y.: Wiley, 1985, pp.232-9]. Extensive tests have shown that it tends to give close-to-optimal, if not optimal solutions. Each replenishment covers the complete requirements for one or several consecutive periods. The basic idea of the Silver-Meal heuristic is that each replenishment should minimize the average cost per period for all periods covered by it. The two costs included are the change-over cost incurred for each replenishment and the holding cost on goods carried forward from the period in which they are produced to later periods.

First Replenishment

Table 14-1 shows the calculations for weeks 1 through 9. No decision can be made for week 1. Hence, no cost calculations need to be made. The week 1 requirement of 460 units is met from the stock of 480 carried into the planning horizon. The last column in Table 14-1 records the ending inventory in each week. Week 2 starts with a beginning stock of 20. These are allocated to the requirement in week 2. This leaves another 800 units to be catered for. We call this the net requirement. Hence, a replenishment has to be scheduled which covers at least the net requirement. Our task is to determine its best size. We do this by an incremental type analysis. Starting with a 'trial' replenishment covering the requirement for one period only, we increase the number of periods covered one period at a time as long as the average cost decreases. When a reversal occurs, i.e., the average cost increases, we stop. We have found the best initial replenishment.

The first 'trial' replenishment for week 2 only covers the week 2 net requirements of 800. Since all units produced are used up in week 2, the only cost incurred is the change-over cost of $960, which is also the total cost as well as the average cost for week 2 for this first 'trial' replenishment. (Ignore the last two columns in Table 14-1 for the moment.)

Table 14-1:   Replenishment schedule for weeks 1 through 9

Week	Require- ment	Trial reple- nishment	Increm'l · Cost	Total Cost	Average Cost	Best run size	Stock on hand at end of week
0			stock carried forward				480
1	460		no decision to be made				20
2	820	800	$960	$960	$960	1470	670
3	220	1020	$88	$1048	$524		450
4	450	**1470**	$360	$1408	**$469**	lowest	0
5	1200	2670	$1440	$2848	$712		
5	1200	1200	960	960	960	1790	590
6	360	1560	$144	$1104	$552		230
7	80	1640	$64	$1168	$389		150
8	50	1690	$60	$1228	$307		100
9	100	**1790**	$160	$1388	**$278**	lowest	0

At the second round, the interval covered by the 'trial' replenishment in week 2 is extended to also include the week 3 requirements of 220. The size of the 'trial' replenishment is now 1020. The costs incurred consist of the change-over cost of $960 plus the cost of carrying 220 units from week 2 to week 3. At $0.40 per unit per week, the holding cost is 220(0.40) or $88. This is also the incremental cost incurred for increasing the 'trial' replenishment from a one-week to a two-week cover. The total cost for the two weeks is $1048, which averages to $524 per week. This is lower than the average cost for the first 'trial' replenishment covering one week only. So the process continues.

The third 'trial' replenishment covers three weeks. It increases by another 450 units to 1470. The incremental cost is the cost of holding the additional 450 units from week 2 to week 4, or $0.40/unit/week for two weeks. This amounts to 450(2)-(0.40) or $360. The total cost for a 'trial' replenishment covering these three weeks is $1408 or $469 per week. This is again lower than for the 'trial' replenishment covering two weeks. So the 'trial' replenishment is increased by 1200 to also cover the week 4 requirement. The incremental cost incurred consists of the holding cost for 3 weeks on these 1200 units from week 2 to week 5, or $1440. The resulting average cost is $712, an increase in costs from the 'trial' replenishment covering the first three weeks only.

We now have found the best run size for the first replenishment in week 2. It is 1470, covering the requirements for weeks 2, 3, and 4. The last column in Table 14-1 shows the inventory position at the end of each week, associated with this replenishment.

Second Replenishment

The process now restarts with finding the best run size for the replenishment to be scheduled in week 5. Verify that the average cost continues to decrease for the remainder of the planning horizon. We now have found the best replenishment schedule for the AC230/4 motor over the initial 9-week planning horizon. It consists of a replenishment of 1470 in week 2 to cover the requirements for weeks 2 to 4, and a replenishment of 1790 in week 5 to cover the requirements for weeks 5 to 9. Again, the last column records the resulting end-of-week inventory position.

Planning Horizon Roll-Forward

Assume that time has advanced to the end of week 1. Week 1 has occurred as planned and the replenishment of 1470 units for week 2 has been initiated for execution in week 2. 800 motors of this first replenishment are still scheduled for use in the final assembly during week 2. This will leave a stock of 670 to be carried into week 3. The planning horizon is rolled forward by one week, covering the interval from week 2 to week 10. Due to a rush order, the final product assembly schedule has been revised for weeks 3 and 4. They are now 320 and 350, respectively. No changes in requirements for weeks 5 through 10 are planned.

Table 14-2 shows the calculations for finding the production schedule covering weeks 2 through 10. As shown in the last column, the planned stock of motors carried into week 3 still covers the revised requirements for week 3 and week 4. It simply confirms the original plan that no replenishment is needed in these two weeks. Although the actual holding costs are different from the original plan, there

Table 14-2: Replenishment schedule for weeks 2 through 10

Week	Require- ment	Trial reple- nishment	Increm. Cost	Total Cost	Average Cost	Best run size	Stock on hand at end of week
1			stock carried forward				1470
2	800		no decisions to be made				670
3	320		previous decision confirmed				350
4	350		previous decision confirmed				0
5	1200	1200	960	960	960	1790	590
6	360	1560	$144	$1104	$552		230
7	80	1640	$64	$1168	$389		150
8	50	1690	$60	$1228	$307		100
9	100	**1790**	$160	$1388	**$278**	lowest	0
10	750	2540	$1500	$2888	$481		
10	750	750	$960	$960	$960	750	0

is no point in computing them, since they are already committed by the original decision. The calculations for finding the best run size for week 5 are identical to the ones in Table 14-1. Adding week 10 confirms that the best replenishment size for week 5 found earlier remains the same, with a new replenishment scheduled for week 10.

The point of redoing these calculations was to find out whether the revised requirements resulted in any change in the planned decision of covering the week 3 requirements from the planned stock to be carried forward from week 2. Table 14-2 confirms that there is no change. In fact, regardless of any changes in requirements, as long as the planned stock carried forward into week 3 is sufficient to cover the week 3 requirements, this same conclusion will be reached. Hence, there was really no need to perform the calculations in Table 14-2. However, if the planned stock to be carried forward were less than the planned requirement for week 3, there would be a need to push the replenishment planned for week 5 forward to week 3. A completely new schedule would then have to be developed.

Time now advances to the end of week 2. The week 2 activities realize as per the revised plan. The planning horizon is again rolled forward by one week, covering weeks 3 to 11, with week 4 the first one where a new decision can be made. Again some changes in the final assembly schedule result in the following revised forecasts for the AC230/4 motor requirements:

Week	3	4	5	6	7	8	9	10	11	12	13	14	15
Number	320	210	1200	360	80	100	630	220	200	0	550	630	1050

The planned requirement for week 3 results in a planned stock of 350 to be carried forward to week 4. Does the smaller requirement in week 4 make it necessary do redo the calculations? The answer is 'No' for the following reasons. The smaller week 4 requirement results in a stock of 140 units carried into week 5. As a consequence the replenishment planned for week 5 will change. However, the decision to have no replenishment in week 4 still stands. It does not affect and is not affected by the planned replenishment for week 5.

Time advances to the end of week 3. The planning horizon is again rolled forward by one week, covering weeks 4 through 12, with the first possible decision affecting week 5. Assume that the planned requirements for weeks 4 through 12 do not change anymore. Hence, the planned stock to be carried forward to week 5 is 140 motors. The net requirement for week 5 is reduced from 1200 to 1060. The original schedule provided for a replenishment in week 5. This is still the case, but its size may be different due to the changes in net requirements. A new production schedule has to be developed. This is done in Table 14-3. The new schedule provides for a run of size 1600 in week 5 and a run of size 1100 in week 9.

This process of rolling the planning horizon forward one week at a time continues. No action is scheduled until the planned stock carried forward does not cover the requirements in the first period of the new active planning horizon. At that point a new shcedule is developed.

Table 14-3: Replenishment schedule for weeks 4 through 12

Week	Require-ment	Trial reple-nishment	Increm. Cost	Total Cost	Average Cost	Best run size	Stock on hand at end of week
3				stock carried forward			350
4	210		no decision to be made				140
5	1200	1060	960	960	960	1600	540
6	360	1420	$144	$1104	$552		180
7	80	1500	$64	$1168	$389		100
8	100	**1600**	$120	$1288	**$322**	lowest	0
9	630	2330	$1008	$1388	$459		
9	630	630	$960	$960	$960	1100	470
10	220	850	$88	$1048	$524		250
11	200	1050	$160	$1208	$403		50
12	50	**1100**	$60	$1268	**$317**	lowest	0

14.9   MINIMUM LENGTH OF PLANNING HORIZON

As briefly mentioned in Section 14.1, in a few special instances, the mathematical structure of the model or the solution method used to solve it may allow identifying a minimum length for the planning horizon or specifying conditions which when satisfied allow the planning horizon to be truncated. The astute reader may have already guessed that this is the case for the solution approach to the replenishment scheduling problem of the previous section.

Recall again that we are only interested in the 'best' initial decision, i.e., whether or not to schedule a replenishment in the first week of the active planning horizon and, if yes, what its best run size should be. For the situation of Table 14-1, the 'best' run size for week 2 is established once the 'trial' replenishment covering the requirements for weeks 2 to 5 had been costed out and found to have a higher average than the 'trial' replenishment covering only weeks 2 to 4. The rest of the incremental analysis for finding the best run size for week 5 did not affect the best run size for week 2. There was, indeed, little point in continuing these computations. Similarly, the computations in Table 14-3 again did not need to go beyond week 9. At that point the best run size for week 5 had been identified as covering the requirements for weeks 5 to 8. Whatever happens after week 9 will not affect this decision.

So we see that for this particular production scheduling problem, in those weeks where a replenishment is needed, the solution method used allows us to truncate the active planning horizon as soon as we have found that the average cost per week starts to increase, while in all other weeks, where the incoming stock is sufficient to cover the week's requirements, the active planning horizon is only one week, covering just the lead-up time.

EXERCISES

1. Consider the Crystal Springs example. Develop a spreadsheet to reproduce the results in Figure 14-3. If you find more elegant ways to handle some aspects, do so.

2. Still with Crystal Springs, assume now that, as indicated in Section 14.7, it is early April. Sales have been somewhat higher than expected. Actual sales and production for the first three months have been as follows:

Month	Jan	Feb	March
Actual sales	179	194	289
% increase over predicted	-1%	+21%	+19%
Actual production	129	206	320

    Given the long-range weather forecast for another summer of heat and drought in California, Sam Spring expects that sales are likely to remain at a higher level well into September and only then revert back to the previous level. Then there is the problem with the union organizers who have been talking to his regular workforce. His workers seem to be unhappy about the way overtime was scheduled as needed. They want, if any overtime is scheduled, that it be for a minimum of at least 1 hour per day (the current maximum is 2 hours per day). In other words, overtime for at least 36,000 cases for a one-shift operation and at least 62,000 cases for a two-shift operation should be scheduled, and any extra up to the maximum of 72,000 and 125,000, respectively. He also expects that due to having to offer higher moving allowances, the cost of adding a second shift would increase to $24,000. Similarly, due to increases in interest rates, the implied cost of holding stock had increased to $180/1000 cases/month. Sam has also been experimenting with the processing speed of his filling machine. He is pretty certain that he can increase the filling speed by 5% without affecting the safety or accuracy of the machine operation. He plans to implement this starting April. Finally, Sam has been advised by his raw material suppliers that, due to inflation, prices will increase in July, adding another 14 cents to the cost of producing a case. Given all these changes, Sam wants to develop a new production/shift schedule for the rest of the year. Use the spreadsheet of exercise 1, making the necessary changes in input data to explore various possible schedules, trying to identify the highest profit solution.

3. A highway construction company rents certain specialized earth-moving equipment from a leasing company as needed during the various phases of a construction job. Such equipment has to be rented for one or more full weeks, even if it might only be required for part of the week. For a particular piece of equipment, the rental cost per week is $2000. Each time a unit is rented, there is a preparation and transport charge of $1200 by the leasing company. Each time a unit is returned, there is a service, cleaning, and transport cost of $1500. As an alternative to renting, the company can farm out some or all work during any given week to a local contractor at a cost of $1000 per unit short per working day. The weekly workload, shown in unit-days, i.e., the number of days

work that needs to be done during each week with this equipment, is as follows:

Week	1	2	3	4	5	6	7	8	9	10
Unit-days	6	10	8	14	7	15	0	4	5	7

Assume that each week has 5 workdays. Hence a requirement of 8, for example, implies there is a need for one full unit and another unit for 3 days. But recall that rental charges cover full weeks only. At the beginning of the planning horizon, the company has one rental unit on hand. It can return it or keep it. There is no need for any units after week 10. Hence, all units rented at that time are returned. Develop a spreadsheet and try to find the optimal renting schedule by trial and error.

4*. Study exercise 4 of Chap. 4 carefully. If you have not done exercise 12 of Chap. 4 yet, it may be advisable to do so now. The brief for the consultant is to propose several good shift patterns and suitable rosters for the staff which differ in terms of amount of overtime, total staff size, and total weekly cost. Consider following additional data:

- Summer schedule of commercial flights: (PAX = estimate of passenger number)

Arrival	Day	Time	PAX	Departure	Day	Time	PAX
1	Mon	00:30	180	1	Mon	07:10	210
2	Mon	16:20	370	2	Mon	17:20	400
3	Mon	18:30	280	3	Mon	20:40	250
4	Mon	23:10	250	4	Tue	06:50	220
5	Tue	09:50	400	5	Tue	11:10	360
6	Tue	14:30	180	6	Tue	17:20	180
7	Tue	19:50	360	7	Tue	21:10	380
8	Tue	20:50	180	8	Tue	22:10	160
9	Wed	10:10	200	9	Wed	11:10	180
10	Wed	15:40	360	10	Wed	17:00	380
11	Wed	23:10	250	11	Thu	06:50	280
12	Thu	01:20	180	12	Thu	07:30	180
13	Thu	15:40	360	13	Thu	17:00	360
14	Fri	09:40	400	14	Thu	11:00	400
15	Fri	14:50	190	15	Fri	16:00	180
16	Fri	16:10	380	16	Fri	17:30	400
17	Fri	17:10	280	17	Fri	18:30	260
18	Fri	22:30	180	18	Sat	06:20	200
19	Fri	23:50	370	19	Sat	06:50	400
20	Sat	00:20	330	20	Sat	07:00	350
21	Sat	05:50	200	21	Sat	07:30	180
22	Sat	06:00	180	22	Sat	08:00	180
23	Sat	14:50	190	23	Sat	16:10	180
24	Sat	16:30	360	24	Sat	18:00	350
25	Sat	23:40	190	25	Sun	06:20	180
26	Sun	05:20	200	26	Sun	07:30	180
278	Sun	15:40	400	27	Sun	17:10	400
28	Sun	18:00	360	28	Sun	19:30	400

- Processing arriving passengers: It takes 1 minute to clear a passenger through immigration or passport control (primary processing). The maximum number of booths available is 10. For secondary processing, there is usually one officer for every 60 passengers arriving. In addition to this, one supervisor and two other customs officers are staffing the observation room which has a bank of TV monitors, one for each remote control camera in the arrival hall, or are roaming around in the arrival hall. Recall also that the officers form a team which assembles 30 minutes prior to the scheduled flight arrival for briefing and preparation of arrival hall.

- Processing of departing passengers: Regardless of the number of passengers on a departing plane, processing of departing customers starts 30 minutes prior to the scheduled departure and involves always just two custom officers. If several flights depart less than 30 minutes apart, no additional staff are scheduled. There is no extra time for briefing and preparation needed for departures.
- Deep Freeze mail schedule: usual arrival time of mail

Day	Mon	Tue	Wed	Thu	Fri	Fri	Sat	Sun
Time	09:00	09:00	09:00	15:00	09:00	15:00	15:00	09:00
Staffing	4	2	2	2	2	1	4	2

Assume that it always takes 60 minutes to process the mail.
- CIA freight office schedule: Daily 10:00 to 16:00, 2 staff required.
- Clerical task load for custom officers: 80 hours/day Monday through Friday,
                                                                    48 hours/day Saturday and Sunday.

(a) Use the following approach for developing a schedule of shifts: Use regular graph paper to indicate the number of people required for processing flights and other regular scheduled duties. For each flight arrival, the number of people required has to be computed from the expected number of passengers on that flight, given the government processing standards, as well as the limitations of immigration booths. Let each square represent one person for 10 minutes. Elapse time is measured along the x-axis, while the number of people required is shown along the y-axis. Use different colours for the various duties. If several duties occur at the same time, the duties are juxtaposed on top of each other. The resulting graph will look like the skyline of a city. You now superimpose onto this pattern a set of shifts. The shifts do not have to start at the same time each day, but it would be highly desirable that each day has the same total number of shifts. Assigning people to shifts will also be considerably simplified if each shift always has the same number of members. For instance, you might have three shifts of 12 people, including one supervisor, and two shifts of 2 people each day. The latter are used for processing departures. Each shift should be 9 hours long. However, only 8.5 hours are working hours, since each officer will take off for a 30 minute break sometime towards the middle of the shift. If a shift is relieved during a time when they are processing a flight, there must be a 30 minute overlap between the two shifts involved to allow for a smooth change-over. Draw the shifts in easy-erase pencil on top of the task schedule. Each shift is shown as a rectangle 9 hours long and up to 20 squares high (= 19 custom officers + one supervisor). If two shifts overlap, then for the duration of the overlap, one shift is shown above the other. Arrange the start times of the shifts in such a way that you can meet most of the flights, as well as the other scheduled tasks. Any flights not covered or only partially by a shift will require the scheduling of overtime. The aim is to minimize the amount of overtime scheduled, while at the same time keeping the total number of staff needed to a minimum. Obviously, there is a trade-off between the size of each shift and the amount of overtime. Note that overtime has a cost that is 50% higher than regular time. Develop two or three different shift schedules, differing in their timing and size of the shifts.

(b) Develop a roster for the staff. A roster assigns staff to shifts. Contractual arrangements require that, on average, each staff member works 4 out of 6 days. The kinds of rostering patterns that seem to work well are cycles such as 4 days on/2 days off, or 5 days on/two days off/5 days on/3 days off. Such patterns have the effect that each staff member has the same number of weekends off. Indicate how many weeks it will take before a given person or whole shift team starts its cyclic pattern anew on the same day of the week.

5. An appliance manufacturer faces the following weekly requirements (in thousands of units) for a given subassembly, produced by the firm itself:

Week	1	2	3	4	5	6	7	8	9	10
Requirement	17	8	12	4	10	20	15	3	6	9

The cost of setting up a production run for this subassembly amounts to $500, while it costs $2 to store 1000 units from one week to the next, assessed on the ending stock on hand. Using the Silver-Meal heuristic, find the resulting schedule of production runs and stock holdings for the entire 10 weeks. (Note that once you find the size of the production run in period 1, you simply start the heuristic anew from the first period not covered by that run.) What is the minimum length of the planning horizon required?

6. Referring back to exercise 5 above, assume now that a production run of 25,000 subassemblies was scheduled for week 1. It is now the beginning of week 3. It turns out that due to a power failure only 22,000 subassemblies were actually produced. Furthermore, the actual usage in weeks 1 and 2 amounted to 20,000 subassemblies only. The revised predicted requirements are now as follows (in thousands of units):

Week	3	4	5	6	7	8	9	10	11	12
Requirement	15	10	20	4	15	3	6	9	2	20

Determine a revised production schedule for this subassembly to the end of week 12, using the Silver-Meal heuristic.

REFERENCES

Although the issues discussed in this Chapter are of a general nature, the examples used are covered in texts on production and operations management. There is an extensive literature under the title 'planning horizon theorems' devoted to finding the minimum planning horizon needed for the initial decision to be optimal. Unfortunately, these theorems are only of limited usefulness. Experimenting with typical cases gives satisfactory results. A reference for the Silver-Meal heuristic is

Silver, E.A., and Peterson, R., *Decision Systems for Inventory Management and Production Planning*, 2nd ed., Wiley, 1985.

15   Uncertainty

The approaches to decision making within systems discussed so far implicitly assumed that if we take a given action, we can predict the resulting effect on the system with (absolute) certainty. In many problems, our knowledge of the situation actually may be good enough to satisfy this assumption, at least in a practical sense, if not in theory. Situations of this sort are called **deterministic**.

For example, XL Bakers has a firm contract with the Big-G chain of supermarkets for delivery of 2000 loaves of white sandwich-sliced bread each day of the week. It enjoys a deterministic demand for that portion of its sales. Accordingly, it can take firm decisions regarding the number of loaves to be baked to meet that demand. On the other hand, XL Bakers also has a firm contract to supply each of the 13 stores of the rival Bargain Barn chain daily with sufficient bread to satisfy customer demand, with the obligation to take back any bread that is not sold within 24 hours after delivery. On some days, all bread delivered to a given store is sold within the 24-hour period. In fact, had XL stocked more, all or a portion of the additional amount stocked would also have been sold. On other days it may have to take back from the same store dozens of unsold (stale) loaves. XL may be able to predict how many loaves are sold on average by each store, but not how many will be sold on any specific day. So, it faces an uncertain demand picture for that part of its daily operation.

Similarly, a firm signs a contract with a highly reputable supplier for the delivery of 10,000 units of a given item three months from now at a firm price of $11.35. It can be pretty sure to receive these goods at that fixed price, barring any major catastrophe beyond the control of the supplier — a highly unlikely event. However, if the firm had decided to produce these items in house, the exact total cost for producing the entire lot would only be known well after the last item has left the production floor. Furthermore, the accuracy with which the cost can be determined will depend on the detail of the data recorded by the cost accountants on each production job. Again, the cost accountant of the firm may be able to make a good educated guess of the cost, based on standards developed from past performance, but only by coincidence will the actual cost turn out to be identical to the prediction.

So, in the real world, while we may be able to make a fair guess as to the long-run behaviour of many systems, we cannot be certain about what will happen in a particular instance. Such situations are referred to as **uncertain, risky, stochastic, or probabilistic**. This has a number of important consequences for how we go about making decisions in such situations, as well as on the form of the decision itself.

The first three sections of this chapter explore the meaning, causes, and types of uncertainty. Section 15.4 then looks at how uncertainty is expressed in everyday language, and how we try to deal with uncertainty through various approaches of forecasting future events. The concepts of objective and subjective probabilities and the difficulties associated with assessing subjective probabilities are the topics of Sections 15.6 and 15.7. Sections 15.8 and 15.9 explore the meaning of a random variables and their measures of central location and variation, while the last two sections address the problems of how to reduce uncertainty and the decision criteria relevant in the face of uncertainty.

The chapter does not deal with the computational rules of probabilities and statistical data analysis. It assumes that you are familiar with elementary operations of probability and statistics. Its aim is to enhance your understanding of the meaning of uncertainty on a conceptual level. This will hopefully lead to a more informed grasp of decision making under uncertainty. The chapter is a complement to, rather than a substitute for, a basic exposure to elementary operations of probability and statistics.

15.1 LINGUISTIC AMBIGUITY ABOUT UNCERTAINTY

Uncertainty is an everyday occurrence. Just consider the large number of words in the English language related to this concept: chance, probability, likelihood, possibility, risk, hazard, fortune, random, stochastic, odds, to expect, believe, feel, or guess that something will or might happen, to name just a few. In fact, this proliferation of words may be an indication of the ambiguity, even of a certain degree of confusion, associated with the notion of uncertainty.

What is the meaning of phrases like 'There is a possibility that . . .' or 'It is very unlikely that . . .'? Table 15-1 shows the responses to everyday language phrases indicating uncertainty to various degrees, with 0 denoting absolute impossibility and 100 absolute certainty. They were obtained from a group of over 500 students in a first year university course. For comparison, a group of 40 older students (average age 33) in an executive type MBA course was also asked the same questions. Their responses are shown in parentheses. The wide range of responses for both groups indicates highly divergent interpretations, even for statements suggesting a very high or a very low likelihood. No wonder that such statements lead to confusing and contradictory interpretations.

Such ambiguity is not only exhibited by the 'person in the street'. 'Experts' and professional people, such as economic advisers or national security advisers to governments, or judges in courts of law, are equally prone to it. C.W. Kelly and C.R. Peterson [*Probability estimates and probabilistic procedures in current-intelligence analysis*. Gathersburg, MD: IBM, 1971, pp. 4-1, 4-2] report on a test involving a group of national security analysts. They were asked to give a numeric probability interpretation for the statement 'The cease-fire is holding, but it could be broken within the next week.' The author, a colleague of the group interviewed, intended the sentence to mean that there was a 30 percent chance of the cease-fire

Table 15-1: Interpretation of statements about uncertainty

Phrase	Assigned probability in percent		
	10th percentile	Median	90th percentile
It is highly likely that ...	75 (50)	90 (80)	95 (90)
There is a much better than even chance that ...	55 (50)	70 (65)	75 (75)
It is improbable that ...	5 (10)	20 (20)	40 (40)
There is a fair chance that ...	40 (35)	50 (50)	65 (70)
It is very unlikely that ...	5 (5)	10 (20)	25 (40)
It is quite possible that ...	30 (50)	60 (60)	80 (75)
It is almost impossible that ...	1 (3)	5 (5)	10 (30)
It was sunny today; it is likely to stay fine tomorrow.	40 (50)	50 (57)	75 (75)
The likelihood of a strong earthquake in the Los Angeles area next year is quite high.	10 (20)	60 (60)	80 (80)
The probability of a serious nuclear power plant accident anywhere is quite small.	2 (5)	10 (18)	40 (50)

being broken. However, most of the other analysts thought that it meant a probability of 50 percent or higher.

Peter Wyden [*Bay of Pigs*. New York: Simon and Schuster, 1979, pp. 89-90] reports on an instance where such divergent interpretation may have led to a serious international incident. In early 1961, President Kennedy ordered the Joint Chiefs of Staff to study the CIA's plan for an invasion of Cuba by expatriate Cubans. The general in charge of the evaluation concluded that its chances of overall success were 'fair'. Interviewed on this affair several years later he revealed that he intended this to mean a 30 percent chance. He recalled 'We thought other people would think that a 'fair chance' would mean 'not too good'.' When the report was sent to the White House, it stated 'This plan has a fair chance of ultimate success'. It is well possible that this misinterpretation of the word 'fair' led President Kennedy to authorize this mission, which ended in disaster for the invaders and humiliation for the US.

Surveys of judges and jurors indicate that the commonly used court-room statement 'beyond a reasonable doubt' is variably interpreted as anywhere from 50 to 100 percent chance of guilt. This is rather alarming for both the innocent accused, as well as the victim of a guilty accused.

The ambiguity of language and the widely differing interpretations given to statements about uncertainty suggest that numeric statements about the probability of an event would lead to clearer understanding and, consequently, to better decision making. Although this will be so in many cases, even probability statements may not be unambiguous, as we shall see in Section 15.7, nor will it necessarily lead to more 'rational' decision making [A. Tversky and D. Kahneman, 'Rational Choice and the Framing of Decisions', *Journal of Business*, 1986, S251-S278; P. Delquié, Inconsistent trade-offs between attributes: New evidence in preference assessment biases, *Management Science*, Nov. 1993, pp. 1382-95].

15.2 CAUSES OF UNCERTAINTY

Uncertainty about the exact nature of some phenomenon, some process, or the precise state of a system at a given point is due to any one or any combination of the following four reasons:

(1) The most common reason is that the process in question is not known or understood in sufficient detail. Many physical phenomena, like the weather, or whether a coin flipped into the air will land head or tail, or the time, strength, and duration of the next earthquake at a given location, are all processes that we do not fully understand yet or for which it would be prohibitively expensive and time consuming to gather all relevant information. Clearly, there is nothing inherently random about the next earthquake in San Francisco or in Wellington (N.Z.), if the processes that cause earthquakes could be understood to their last details. So uncertainty is a result of our ignorance.

(2) The second reason is that statements about a phenomenon or process are based on incomplete information. For instance, a statement about the percentage of all television viewers tuned in to a given station at a given time is, for cost reasons, usually based on a sample of some 500 to 1000 viewers, rather than the entire population of all viewers at that time. It is an estimate and hence it will only be exactly correct by coincidence. In other words its accuracy is uncertain. The uncertainty is again due to ignorance, except that this time it is ignorance by design. This type of uncertainty can be eliminated by surveying the entire population (provided no measurement errors occur).

(3) A third important reason, particularly for economic phenomena, but also for competitive sports and games, is the inability to predict what moves other actors in the real world, like competitors, customers, employees, or the Government, will make, and which could affect the outcome. Such moves may be made completely independently of our own decisions or may be in response or in anticipation of our decisions. Take again the example of bread delivery. If — and this includes many sub-'ifs' — it were possible to ascertain by 6 p.m. today exactly how many loaves of bread each of the supermarkets' potential regular and casual customers will buy over the 24-hour time span starting tomorrow at noon, then the bakery would know how many loaves of bread to supply. It would then also know how many loaves to bake for delivery at noon tomorrow to cover these sales exactly. Clearly, such detailed information is not known, nor can it reliably be collected. Hence, the demand for bread remains uncertain.

(4) The final and increasingly less important reason for uncertainty is measurement error about a phenomenon. Such errors may be due to mistakes made by the observer or improper gauging or functioning of measuring instruments, unknown to the observer. These measurement errors may lead to the conclusion that any variability observed is inherent in the phenomenon measured, rather than a result of the measuring process. But even if it is known that the measuring process may lack accuracy, the results obtained still involve uncertainty. They are estimates of the true values, not the true values themselves.

15.3 TYPES AND DEGREES OF UNCERTAINTY

Most of the uncertainties relevant to systems or faced by individuals or firms deal either with the numerical value (quantity, size, dollar amount, etc.), associated with the phenomenon of interest, or with timing. A firm being uncertain as to the size of the demand for one of its products during a given time period in the future, or at what price raw materials will have to be purchased next month on the commodity market, are examples of uncertainty about the numerical value of a phenomenon. The time between consecutive arrivals of customers at a service station is an example of uncertainty about timing — in this case there may be no uncertainty about the 'size' of each arrival. As customers arrive singly, the associated numerical value is one. Finally, prior to concluding the negotiations for a contract with a customer a firm may be uncertain about both the dollar value of the contract and when payments will be received.

The degree of uncertainty may vary from knowing almost nothing about the process or phenomenon to knowing almost everything. For instance, a firm interested in making a cash flow budget (a plan of the timing and amounts of cash receipts and cash disbursements over a given time interval) may know exactly the timing and amounts of cash needed for disbursements over the first two weeks, have fairly accurate data on disbursements for the next four weeks, with less and less reliable information the further in the future these disbursements will occur. For the far distant future, only rough average guesstimates may be available, since these events are influenced by many other unknown events, like the level of production, etc., which in turn depend on the level of sales in the far future.

When we are dealing with events involving competitors, any predictions about their responses may be even more precarious. We may not even have a complete list of all possible alternative courses of action available to them and their consequences for us. Similarly, for the introduction of a novel product, a firm may have little to go on for predicting how successful it will be. Knowledge about new technology, even just a few years from now, may be hazy or even completely absent — a case of complete uncertainty.

In the decision making literature, we usually talk about **decision making under risk** if all outcomes can be listed and numerical statements made about the likelihood of each. If the second or both conditions are not met, then we talk about

decision making under complete uncertainty. (However, 'decision making under uncertainty' is often loosely used to denote both types!) As we shall see in later chapters, the approaches used to deal with these two cases are radically different.

15.4 PREDICTION AND FORECASTING

Much of the uncertainty faced by decision makers deals with future events. How can we foresee the future? For thousands of years, the search for an answer has given rise to all sorts of professions: shamans, seers and soothsayers, travelling fortune-tellers, and high priests of all sorts, who often exploited their position of power and control over those that believed in their abilities. Economists and treasury officials are the modern version of these gurus (and they are usually highly paid too).

Persistence Prediction

At least a partial answer to 'How do we foresee the future?' is: 'By studying the past!' Even in the turbulent and often chaotic world we live in, there are some threads of continuity and stability. So the first step toward prediction is the identification of characteristics that have persisted and have exhibited some degree of stability over time — hence the name persistence prediction. By far the simplest approach!

Persistence prediction is good for phenomena that remain at the current position or move up or down in a completely unpredictable pattern. It could be likened to the erratic movements of a drunk who, after struggling to his feet, is equally likely to simply fall right over again or take a step in any direction — a so-called **random walk**. For example, the short-term daily fluctuations in share prices or foreign exchange rates, when these markets are in a stable phase, follow a random walk.

In weather forecasting, persistence prediction is almost as good as the forecast developed with highly sophisticated monitoring equipment, complicated air-mass theories, and running computer programs on very large mainframe computers for hours or days. In fact, in many areas with relatively stable weather patterns, comparisons show that the weather office is only about 10% more often correct than the simple prediction that tomorrow's weather will be the same as today's. This is not because the methods used by the weather office are so bad. Rather, it is because persistence prediction is so good.

So, predictions about the number of newspapers sold each day at a location subject to a highly regular and stable pedestrian traffic pattern, such as Grand Central Station in New York, or for that matter in some suburban shopping mall, can safely be based on the average number sold in the most recent past. The prediction 'error' — the difference between the forecast and the actual realization — will on most days be fairly small, particularly if such factors, as the day of the week, etc., are also taken into account.

Trend Prediction

A slightly more sophisticated scheme for forecasting the future is trajectory or trend prediction. This method assumes that, although there is change, the change itself is stable. If sales of bread by XL Bakers in Riverside, California, have shown a fairly regular increase of 8% in each of the past few years, presumably due to the increase in the town's population, it will be fairly safe to assume that this trend will continue, at least for another few years, until most remaining vacant land has been built over.

Trend prediction is without doubt the most successful and most used forecasting approach. Tests have shown that it tends to give more reliable forecasts than much more sophisticated methods based on econometric models. It provides usually good short-run forecasts, but may lead to absurd long-range predictions.

Many phenomena exhibit initially an exponential-type growth. This could, for instance, be observed in the 60s and 70s for consumption of electricity and gasoline, or the creation of household and commercial garbage, and the emission of air pollutants in a number of countries. But it is clear that such processes will ultimately change their pattern fundamentally. Electricity consumption is a case in point. Its growth pattern in the 80s and early 90s did not follow the exponential trends of the 60s and 70s. So the trend predictions for the 80s based on the data of the 60s and 70s overestimated consumptions systematically.

Cyclic Prediction

Cyclic predictions are based on the principle that history repeats itself. Cyclic predictions for seasonal phenomena are highly successful. They may be super-imposed onto a trend prediction and hence give considerably better short-run forecasts. This is the case for demand forecasts for many products subject to seasonal consumption, like beverages, ketchup, and so on. But cyclic predictions are equally fickle when they are based on long-range phenomena, such as business cycles. Just look at the notoriously bad business forecasts made by economic research institutes or banks — fortunately as quickly forgotten by most people as they are issued by the forecasters.

Associative Prediction

This method uses past data from one type of process (usually referred to as an independent factor) to predict another type of process (referred to as the dependent factor). It has given rise to powerful statistical techniques, such as regression analysis, and its extension to econometrics.

Associative prediction is often expressed as the independent factor being the 'cause' of the dependent factor, such as an increase in the amount of money in circulation 'causes' inflation, or a decrease in the number of building permits issued causes a subsequent slump in the construction industry. In these cases, the 'cause' precedes the 'consequence'. However, there are many useful applications of associative predictions where there is no causal relationship between (what is used as) the independent factor and the dependent factor. Both could, in fact, be influenced by a third factor for which no data exists or which is difficult to observe directly. For example, the grade-point average of university students has a strong association with their IQ. But clearly, a high IQ is not the cause of a high grade-point average. Both are in fact a result of high intelligence, which cannot be measured directly. IQ tests are a crude attempt to measure intelligence. Similarly, the fact that some astute observer has discovered that there are remarkable parallels between the increase in university teachers' salaries and the consumption of wine hardly means that the former is the 'cause' of the latter (or is it?).

Associative prediction greatly enlarges the area that is searched for clues. Much of regression analysis deals with discerning which independent clues are helpful — so-called **statistically significant** — for predicting a dependent process or event of interest.

But without doubt the method that uses all data available in the most effective way is hindsight prediction — the prediction of an event after it has already been observed and measured. Historians, news commentators, economists, and politicians use this method to great effect.

Validity of Past Data for Predicting Future

With the exception of hindsight prediction, all approaches mentioned so far use past data to predict future events. The crucial systemic assumption underlying these approaches is that the past is a valid basis for predicting the future. If this is not a valid premise, i.e., there are indications of structural or behavioural changes in the phenomenon observed, the validity of these methods becomes highly questionable. Structural changes could be due to changes in legislation, technology, or economic relationships governing the phenomenon in question. Behavioural changes could be the result of psychological, moral, or life-style changes in the population concerned.

There are though many instances, where there is no known past data that can be used for predicting future events. The occurrence and far-reaching consequences of technological innovations, like the invention of electronic computers, microchips, or laser technology clearly could not be predicted even by experts in the fields, except the very few actually involved in their development. Hence, predictions based on past data without any knowledge of the imminence of such technological break-throughs were badly off. But even for less spectacular events, such as next year's fashion trends or the Christmas sales volume of a given toy, predictions are difficult to make and are often unreliable. This is why fashion and toy stores only stock these goods just prior to the season and only in quantities that they are fairly confident to clear by the end of the season. However, the large number of end-of-season sales, with price reductions to a fraction of the original selling price for fashion items and toys is a clear indication of the difficulty of sales predictions in these areas.

Predictions should not be restricted to single estimates. The only way to assess the reliability of predictions is to also obtain some measure of the degree of variability inherent in the phenomenon predicted. If the predictions are part of an ongoing repetitive process, then it will be possible to compute some measure of the 'prediction error', such as an estimate of the standard deviation of the differences between corresponding pairs of predicted and actual values.

15.5 PREDICTIONS BY EXPERT JUDGMENT

In recent years, several other prediction methods have been developed and are regularly used by big business, market research consultants, and government. Firms test new products on consumer panels to get some indication as to their likely appeal. Larger firms and governments use various techniques involving experts in the field of interest — in an attempt to pool the combined and considered judgment of a group of experts.

Delphi Method

The best known of these is the Delphi method. Consider the example of oil price predictions in the late 70s, needed by the MS/OR group evaluating the economic desirability of the expansion of the only oil refinery operated in New Zealand. A group of economic and energy experts from all over the world was asked to participate in a survey about the likely levels of oil prices over a 30-year span. All participants were given a questionnaire with a precise set of questions. Their responses were collated and expressed in statistical form by a researcher. The results of the first questionnaire were then communicated in summarized form (averages, medium responses, range of responses, etc.) to the experts, who were asked if, in the light of the first round results, they wanted to change their original responses and how. Their new answers were again processed as for the first time. The Delphi method usually repeats this procedure through three or four iterations, with the responses of the last iteration being used as the final predictions. Note that complete anonymity of any responses received is preserved throughout the procedure.

The Delphi method has had many successful applications. It is not a cheap method. Unless the experts are all locally present, it takes considerable time to reach a conclusion. Each iteration can easily take weeks. It is therefore only suitable for relatively important projects. Before embarking in such an exercise, the analyst should perform considerable sensitivity analysis to determine how crucial it is to get a reliable estimate. In the oil price exercise reported above, the price for a barrel of the type of crude oil processed at the refinery in early 1978 was around US$35. The final predictions, made in early 1978, for the price by the end of the 80s covered a range of US$60 to US$95. The analysis for the expansion option chosen established that it would remain economically viable as long as the price remained above about US$29. The actual price in 1989 was well below US$20, reaching lows of US$15 at times. So we see that even judgments by experts may be far off the mark.

Subjective or Judgment Predictions

What can be done for one-off cases, where no recourse to past history or comparable situations is available? In such instances, persons intimately familiar with the situation, usually the decision makers themselves, are asked to make a subjective prediction, based on general relevant experience, assessments obtained by other people, and pure 'gut feelings'. Such a prediction could, for instance, take the form of: 'I estimate that the most likely outcome is x, with a 50-50 chance that the outcome will not deviate from x by more than 10%'. The latter part of the statement provides an indication of the confidence that the respondent puts into the prediction. It can be used as a basis for a measure of the perceived degree of uncertainty in the prediction.

Unfortunately, many decision makers are very reluctant to be pinned down to making a subjective prediction that involves a statement of odds. They are not used to thinking or reasoning in these terms. They may also be unfamiliar with or have forgotten the most basic statistical concepts. Either case will require skilful and sympathetic questioning on the part of the analyst. Furthermore, such judgmental assessments are prone to various biases, as discussed in Section 15.7.

So you may rightfully ask, why bother getting such predictions which smack of spurious accuracy, and then use them as input into some fancy decision model? Remember the principle of GIGO (garbage in, garbage out)! Why not ask the decision maker directly to make the choice of which action he or she considers best? The answer is that the latter course solves nothing and may hide everything. The very process of obtaining subjective predictions will force the decision maker to a more thorough and logical analysis of the situation, and to render many hidden elements explicit. This in itself is of considerable value. The use of the model will allow the situation to be fully explored through sensitivity analysis on the very bones of contention — the subjective predictions — and hence to assess the robustness of the solution(s). Finally, the reason for going through the modeling process is not to relieve the decision maker of the responsibility to make the final decision, but to provide a consistent framework and insights for reaching the 'best' decision.

Judgmental Adjustments to Forecasts Derived by Other Methods

Quantitative forecasting methods, by necessity, are based on past data. As we have seen, there may sometimes be reasons to believe that such past data are not entirely representative of the future, due to events which have not been reflected in the data yet or which are only appearing on the horizon. The seemingly obvious action is to use judgmental inputs to 'correct' the quantitative forecasts obtained on past data. In many instances this is a highly appropriate course of action to take. However, empirical research has shown that such adjustments are prone to bias and that certain rules should be followed (see, e.g., J.S. Armstrong, 'Research needs in forecasting', *Int. J. of Forecasting*, 1988, number 4, pp. 449-65, or S. Makridakis, 'Metaforecasting: Ways of improving forecast accuracy and usefulness', *Int. J. of Forecasting*,

1988, number 4, pp. 467-91). Some of the biases showing up in such adjustments are wishful thinking (more on this in Section 15.7) and the illusion of control, i.e., that making the forecast will, in fact, help reduce the variability of the phenomenon in question, such as sales.

There is fair agreement among experts, that judgmental adjustments should be restricted to only take account of extra information or insider knowledge, but definitely not of 'gut' feelings. Any adjustment made should be fully justified in writing (say, as a footnote). Experience shows that this often reduces the incidence of unjustified adjustments. Furthermore, the person(s) should be made aware of the common types of biases prevalent, as discussed in detail in Section 15.7. Finally, the persons making judgmental forecasts or judgmental adjustments to forecasts should receive timely and personalized feedback on their performance, with emphasis on timely. Again, research has shown that such feedback helps improve forecasting and tends to reduce biases.

15.6 PROBABILITY MEASURES AND THEIR INTERPRETATION

Uncertainty means that one of a number of possible outcomes will occur and that it is not possible to state, with certainty, which one of these outcomes will eventuate. The number of possible outcomes may be small (e.g., the price of IBM shares at the New York Stock Exchange will go up by 0, 1, 2, . . ., U cents or it will go down by 1, 2, 3, . . ., D cents by tomorrow, where both U and D are small numbers, like 5 to 15 cents); it may be large (e.g., the number of air passengers passing through Dulles International Airport in Washington, D.C., in one year is anywhere between 6 and 15 million), or it may even be an infinitely large number (e.g., the time between two successive arrivals of cars at a service station in the two-hour span between 7 and 9 a.m. can be anywhere between 1 second and 480 seconds — time being measured on a continuous scale). In some instances, we may not even know exactly what the range of outcomes is — the case of complete uncertainty.

If we know the range of possible outcomes, the best thing we can do is to make a numeric statement about the likelihood of each possible outcome, if that number is finite, or that the outcome falls into a given subrange, if the number of possible outcomes is infinite.

Say I flip a fair coin. It repeatedly spins in midair and then lands on one of its sides. We all agree that the probability it will show 'heads' is 1/2. Take a more complex problem, like the case of firm A having submitted a tender for a major construction job. A number of other firms have done the same. The manager of firm A estimates the probability that her firm will be awarded the contract to be 0.6. What is the meaning of either of these two numbers and the statements using them?

There are at least four major schools of thought on this subject. Although the literature gives the impression that there are great differences between these schools, the differences are largely of a philosophical nature. (Facetious tongues warn us that in this quest we should be particularly aware of Academitis—a disease characterized by hairsplitting and, eventually, by rigor mortis.) All schools agree on the numerical values for all simple problems (particularly hypothetical ones), the rules of manipulating probabilities, and the broad principles of using them for decision making. So, how do they differ? We shall now examine two of them.

Objective Probabilities

For many simple situations, like games of chance, or any process that may repeat itself in more or less the same form time and again, the numerical value of the probability of a given outcome or event E, denoted by $P(E)$, can be interpreted as the long-run relative frequency with which this outcome occurs. However, for any given repetition of the process, the event E may or may not occur. We cannot state categorically for which repetition event E will occur or will not occur. If the probability $P(E)$ is close to 1, say 0.9, we would be fairly safe to predict that E will occur. In fact, in this situation we always should predict that event E will occur — in the long-run only in about 10% of all predictions would we be wrong. It would be completely illogical to randomly switch our prediction to the outcome that event E will not occur in about 10% of all such predictions. Our betting average would decrease from 90 to 82% correct. (Assume now that the probability of event E is only $P(E) = 0.51$ and you are repeatedly asked to predict the outcome. What sequence of prediction would you make now and why?)

Probability assessments that are either based on physical properties of the phenomenon, such as rolling dice, or based on a vast pool of past experience, such as the number of newspapers sold by a vendor at a given location, can all be given this long-run frequency interpretation. Such probabilities are referred to as **objective probabilities**. Powerful statistical data analysis can be applied to such phenomena.

Subjective Probabilities

Difficulties of interpretation arise if we are dealing with one-shot deals — situations that are sufficiently unique and different from any previous experience. In fact, the majority of strategic decisions in business and government, such as the introduction of a new product, the effect of a given government intervention, or even a core meltdown at a nuclear power station, deal with unique situations. What is now the meaning of 'The probability that outcome X occurs (e.g., sales of the new product exceed the break-even point) is 60%'? The repeatability argument makes little sense — the product launch will not repeat itself ever under the same circumstances. It is in such cases where the **subjective probability** school comes to our rescue. It tells us that the numerical value, referred to as the probability of an event, simply measures the confidence or degree of belief of a reasonable person, who is sufficiently informed about the situation, that the event in question will happen. Hence, two individuals, faced with the same situation, may assign different probabilities to the same event. Their probability assessments are the personal, subjective perception of each individual, and hence both are valid — each for the individual who made it. Nor does that perception necessarily remain the same over even short time intervals of a day or a week.

It also seems obvious that if an event is repeatable and sufficient data on past outcomes have been collected, a reasonable individual's subjective probability assessment will coincide with the observed frequencies.

The use and validity of subjective probabilities sits rather uncomfortably with many people. Interestingly, we use them daily with such statements as 'it's highly probable' (about 0.9?), 'rather unlikely' (0.1?), 'impossible' (0.01?), '50-50'. Punters at the races use intuition or hunches to assess the odds of a horse winning — again subjective probabilities that are never explicitly stated, but still clearly enter into their choices. When you cross an intersection on your bike just in front of the oncoming car, you assess it as highly unlikely (about 0.02?) that you will not make it. So, rather than use such assessments implicitly, it makes good sense to render them explicit. Not only could this lead to a re-assessment of what is the best decision, but it again allows us to do sensitivity analysis on these assessments. This helps in determining over what range of values for the subjective probability the decision remains unaffected. It will also lead to more consistent decision making.

Whether we are dealing with objective or subjective probabilities, the event in question will either occur or will not occur. Since it is a one-shot deal, it would be nonsense to interpret its probability as 'it occurs x% of the time'. The probability measure only reflects our strength of belief in the event occurring. A probability statement is an a priori concept. It is made before the uncertainty has been resolved — before we know which one of the various possible outcomes has occurred. Once 'the die has been cast', one and only one of these outcomes has occurred, and it could well be one which, a priori, had a low probability.

15.7 BEHAVIOURAL RESEARCH ON SUBJECTIVE PROBABILITY ASSESSMENT

Research into how individuals assess uncertainty and make judgments under uncertainty shows up a number of rather disturbing behavioural patterns. G. Miller [*The Psychology of Communications: Seven Essays.* New York: Basic Books, 1967] states that people face severe limits in their capacity for processing information. This is particularly the case for understanding and processing complex multi-faceted relationships. Most people can only cope with about five to nine different uni-dimensional pieces of information at the same time, hence 'the magical number seven, plus or minus two'. Miller noted that once this threshold has been exceeded, people tend to reformulate information into bigger and less detailed chunks. This leads to stereotyping and other gross simplifications.

Simplifying Heuristics for Decision Making under Uncertainty

The Appendix to this chapter reproduces the seminal paper by A. Tversky and D.

Kahneman ['Judgment under uncertainty: heuristics and biases'. *Science*, Vol. 185, Sept. 1974, pp. 1124-31]. They found that research into how the mind copes with uncertainty indicates that people tend to rely on a limited number of heuristic principles, rules, or patterns, which they use for reducing the complex task of assessing probabilities and making predictions into simpler judgmental operations. This process happens most of the time outside their conscious awareness. Although these heuristics are often useful, they may also lead to serious errors in assessment and to systematic bias. For example, asked about the likely profession of a person described as 'very shy and withdrawn, invariably helpful, but with little interest in people, or in the world of reality, a meek and tidy soul with a need for order, structure, and a passion for detail', people tend to have recourse to stereotyping. Since that description is very representative of the mental image most people have about librarians, the likelihood that people will classify a person fitting this description as a librarian rather than as a farmer is much larger. The fact that the proportion of farmers in the population is several times larger than the proportion of librarians does not enter into the assessment. Similarly, the frequency of an event is given a much higher assessment if it is easy to recall or retrieve, or if it is easy to imagine instances or occurrences of that event than when this is not the case.

At this point I ask you to read the paper by Tversky and Kahneman in the Appendix and then only continue reading the rest of the chapter.

Overconfidence and Wishful Thinking

Other research indicates that people tend to be overconfident in their ability to assess probabilities — not justified by their actual performance. They tend to overestimate the probability of rare events and underestimate the probability of highly likely events. People are prone to the gambler's fallacy, expecting that an outcome that has failed to occur for a while is likely to occur in the near future, disregarding the fact that each outcome may be independent of what happened before. People also tend to overestimate probabilities of events that they would like to happen and underestimate those that they do not like.

Experiments with MBA students and executives clearly reveal the existence of this type of wishful thinking. The subjects were presented with a sales history on a new product as shown in part (a) of Figure 15-1. Sales have increased dramatically after the product's launch, but then very recently have shown a small decline. The subjects were put into two groups. Group 1 were told to put themselves into the position of the marketing manager of the firm, while group 2 were told that they were the marketing manager of the firm's major competitor. Each group was then asked to predict the future sales pattern for that product. Most subjects in group 1 predicted that the sales would recover promptly and continue their dramatic increase. In contrast, the subjects in group 2 predicted that the sales downturn would continue. This is depicted by the broken lines in part (b) of Figure 15-1. Clearly, each group seemed to reflect a high degree of wishful thinking.

This type of behaviour is true for the people in the street, as well as for experts and business executives, responsible for important decisions.   Although some learning occurs in response to assessments that are discovered as far off the mark, the degree of learning is hindered by the lack of accurate and immediate feedback about the correctness or otherwise of assessments made. The necessary feedback is often lacking because (a) outcomes are commonly delayed and not easily attributable to a particular action, (b) variability in the environment degrades the reliability of the feedback, especially where outcomes of low probability are involved, (c) there is often no information about what the outcome would have been if another action had been taken, and (d) most decisions for which such assessments are made are unique and therefore provide little opportunity for learning [Tversky and Kahneman, 1986, p. 274, opus cited].

Figure 15-1: Sales predictions by wishful thinking

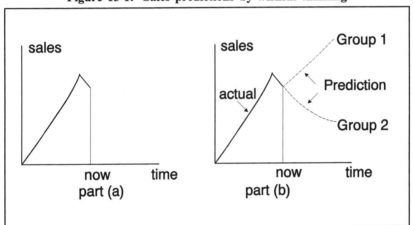

Lessons to be Learned

What lessons can we learn from this research?   First, the individual making subjective probability assessments or predictions must be aware of the potential short-comings of the heuristics of representativeness, availability, and the anchoring effect, as well as the tendency towards biased assessment. It is best not to rush into an initial guess and then try to rationalize its validity. Instead, a good starting point is decomposing the problematic situation and developing as complete a list of all the factors that may affect the situation, how the situation is affected by each one, and weighing them carefully and deliberately against each other. It is also helpful to restate the same situation in a different framework, e.g., expressing a positive statement as the exact equivalent negative statement, and observe if this leads to a different assessment and why.

Rather than settle for a single number, it is more effective to select as the initial anchor or benchmark a fairly wide interval and then attempt to narrow it down in the light of the various influencing factors listed earlier. Pooling the judgment of other people who are sufficiently familiar with the situation is likely to lead to a more balanced and more representative answer. A final assessment in the form of a narrow interval is usually a more honest and more useful piece of information than a single number.

Finally, once the final assessment has been made, it is important that the recommended decision is subjected to extensive sensitivity analysis with respect to all important subjective probability or prediction inputs. This will reveal how important it is to arrive at reliable assessments for each input of this nature.

15.8 RANDOM VARIABLES AND PROBABILITY DISTRIBUTIONS

Random Variables

Assume now that a situation has several alternative outcomes and that with each outcome we can associate a real number. An example will help. Sales for XL Bakers' fruit loaves at supermarket K vary from day to day. On the odd day, none are sold. The largest number ever sold, recorded in recent history, is 12. On most days, sales range somewhere between 4 and 8. Past history thus indicates that daily sales may assume any outcome between 0 and 12. So we can associate with each outcome (= daily sales) one of the integers from 0 to 12. These numbers represent the values that the **random variable** 'daily sales' may assume.

Frequency and Probability Distributions

The historical frequencies with which each sales amount has been observed could be used as an approximate model for the probabilities with which each of these sales amounts will occur in the future. These probabilities are now seen to be a function of the integers from 0 to 12. We call this function a **probability frequency function** of the random variable 'daily sales'. It is also sometimes loosely referred to as a probability distribution, although in probability theory this term has another meaning. The above case is an example of a discrete probability distribution. But remember again, on any given day only one of these outcomes will actually be realized. (By analogy, these concepts can also be applied to one-shot deals. The 'frequency' interpretation is then replaced by 'the strength of belief' or 'the degree of confidence' in each possible value of the outcome.)

A probability distribution conveys considerably more information than does a single-valued prediction. Not only does it show the range of possible outcomes, but also their relative frequency in a reproducible situation, or the subjective strength of belief in each outcome for one-shot deals. It should thus lead to better decisions than those derived from a single-valued prediction. However, it is also more costly to determine and usually leads to more complicated and hence costlier models.

Approximations by Theoretical Distributions

Since the determination of the exact probability distribution is difficult, we often have recourse to approximations. Events that occur singly and are relatively rare, like the breakdown of machines or the arrival of customers within a sufficiently small interval of time, are quite often approximated with a surprisingly good fit by a **Poisson** distribution. The Poisson distribution is completely specified by a single number, the average or expected value of the random variable.

If the outcome is affected by, or the sum of, a large number of independent factors, with no factor having a predominant influence, the **normal distribution** provides an excellent approximation. Demand for bread — mentioned earlier — would be a good example. Daily sales are the result of many individuals independently making a decision to buy one or a few loaves, with no individual buying a very large number and thus having an undue influence over sales, whenever this would occur.

The normal distribution is a continuous distribution, i.e., the random variable may assume any real value from minus infinity to plus infinity. In practice though, the outcomes tend to be clustered more or less tightly around a measure of central tendency, i.e., the average or **expected value** of the random variable. For example, there is a 95% probability that any particular observed outcome of a normal random variable lies within two **standard deviations** of the expected value of the random variable. The position and shape of the normal distribution is completely defined by these two parameters, i.e., the expected value of the random variable and its standard deviation. The meaning of these concepts will be discussed later on.

Note that in the bread demand example, sales are in whole loaves. Hence, daily sales is an integer variable. Still, if sales are sufficiently large, usually about 20 or more, then using a continuous random variable is a suitable and convenient approximation for many decision situations.

For a discrete distribution, each value that the random variable may assume has a positive probability. Not so for a continuous distribution. The probability that a continuous random variable assumes any given value is always zero, although the random variable will ultimately assume a value within its range. This may sound like a contradiction, but a little bit of reasoning shows that this is not so. There is a positive probability that a continuous random variable will assume a value in a specific interval within its range. But since there is an infinite number of possible values in each interval (part of the real line), the probability of any one of them occurring is zero. So for continuous distributions we only associate probabilities for intervals of the random variable, not for any specific value!

15.9   THE EXPECTED VALUE AND STANDARD DEVIATION OF A RANDOM VARIABLE

For any set of numbers we can compute the average or mean value, which gives us an indication of the centre of gravity of these numbers. We can also find the standard deviation which provides us with a measure of how widely the numbers are dispersed, although most of us have difficulties putting any intuitive meaning into a standard deviation. Sometimes comparing the average and the standard deviation helps in getting a better feel for the situation. For example, if the standard deviation is only a small fraction of the average, then the observations will tend to be bunched closely around the average.

The same type of measures can be computed for random variables. The average becomes the expected value of the random variable, while the standard deviation retains its name. The expected value shows where the centre of gravity of the possible outcomes is located. The standard deviation is a measure of the variability or dispersion of the possible outcomes. For discrete distributions, rather than simply take an average of all possible values of the random variable, we find the expected value as a weighted average, with the probabilities serving as the weights. We make the analogous adjustment for computing the standard deviation.

Meaning or Interpretation of the Expected Value

What is the meaning of the expected value of a random variable? As with an average of a set of numbers, only by coincidence will the actual value realized by a random variable ever fall exactly on its expected value. But for a repetitive situation, the average of a large number of observations of the random variable will fluctuate around the expected value. Furthermore, by the **Central Limit Theorem** as the number of observations gets larger, their average value tends to become closer and closer to the expected value of the random variable.

Often we may use the expected value as a convenient substitute for the long-run behaviour of a random variable and base our decisions on this long-run behaviour. However, it is only an approximation — a modeling simplification. It never implies that the random variable will, in fact, assume its expected value. For a discrete distribution, the expected value may not even be one of the possible outcomes, while for a continuous distribution it will be a pure coincidence if the realized value of a random variable falls exactly on top of its expected value.

For subjective probability distributions, particularly for one-shot deals, we do not even have the comfort of a long-run interpretation. By assumption, no averaging can occur then. The expected value has no meaning beyond its mathematical definition. Nevertheless, it can be shown that for many problems, a decision based on the alternative with the highest expected value of the measure of performance is the best decision. But, do not fall into the trap of assuming that the outcome when it occurs will, by necessity, be equal to the expected value. This point cannot be overstressed!

15.10   APPROACHES TO REDUCE UNCERTAINTY

Most decision makers would rather make decisions under certainty than under uncertainty. The higher the uncertainty, the higher their discomfort and anxiety. Hence, it is not surprising that substantial efforts are made to create decision making structures that reduce or avoid uncertainty. This is an important topic for theories in organizational behaviour and strategy. There are four basic approaches: we attempt to reduce uncertainty as such, we attempt to alleviate its effects, we postpone any firm commitments as long as possible, in the hope of dissolving some of the uncertainty as time passes, or we opt for greater flexibility for future responses by creating future options.

Collecting More Information

The obvious approach to reduce uncertainty is to gather more information, and hence improve our predictions, be it in terms of a single-valued guesstimate or a probability distribution. For instance, a firm has experienced a steady growth for one of its main product lines over the last 18 months. If this trend continues, sales will increase by another 40% over the next year. The existing production facilities are now taxed to the limit. Substantial investments in new plant and equipment are needed to increase it. There is though considerable uncertainty about the long-run potential for this product line. Will the growth trend be sustained, and if so, for how much longer? Faced with such a situation, most firms would undertake a serious market research study to obtain a better picture of the market potential for the product line. In other words, they would gather more information to reduce the uncertainty faced.

Gathering more information is costly and time consuming. This is only justified, if the new information gained in fact reduces uncertainty and leads to making better decisions. There is a whole branch of statistical decision theory dealing with these aspects, namely **Bayesian decision analysis**. The underlying mathematics are, unfortunately, beyond an introductory survey. The basic idea though is simple and intuitively appealing. We start with some prior, albeit imperfect, information. This is used for computing an approximation to the potential increase in benefits gained by gathering additional information. The additional information is obtained, if its potential benefits justify its costs, otherwise the decision is based on the information available now.

Often, the conditions for applying this analysis are not satisfied or the analysis is too complicated. At that point, it is our natural creative instinct, more commonly referred to as a hunch, which will lead us to either get more information or make do with what we have. If the information is easy and relatively cheap to get and we judge that it might bring a considerable improvement in the decision process — or at least alleviate our anxiety about it — we collect additional information, otherwise not. There still is a lot of 'art' in decision making, not just 'science'!

Sensitivity Analysis

The second approach is to ascertain how crucial it is to get accurate information about uncertain events. Sensitivity analysis comes to the rescue. We systematically evaluate over what range of values for any uncertain parameters the best decision remains the same as for the guesstimates used to derive it. If that range is small, then this may be an incentive to acquire more accurate information. If the range is wide and we feel fairly confident that the true value of the uncertain parameters lies well within that range, nothing will be gained by spending time and funds to get better information.

Keeping Options Open

The third approach is to select a decision strategy that closes the fewest doors for future action. In other words, any action which commits us firmly into a given direction and eliminates a large number of other possible future actions is either avoided or postponed until more and better information becomes available. Naturally, many decisions will narrow down future choices. It is a problem of finding a good balance between maximizing the benefit of the course of action to be chosen and keeping our options open ——a version of the perennial problem in decision making, namely balancing benefits against costs, neither of which may be fully expressed in numerical terms only.

Creating Future Options

Rather that simply keeping options open, it may be strategically advisable to take actions that create new future options. For instance, a firm located in a growth area where suitable land is becoming scarce may decide to purchase a site now in anticipation of possible future expansion of its production facilities, although no decision or even exploratory planning has been made at the time of the purchase. It simply creates a new option for the future. If no expansion is made within 5 to 10 years, the land may be sold again — hopefully at a good profit.

Similarly, firms investing heavily into basic research clearly do this in anticipation of opening up new future options, i.e., new products.

Any two or all three of these approaches may be used jointly for reducing the degree of uncertainty.

15.11   DECISION CRITERIA UNDER UNCERTAINTY

When the outcome of each alternative course of action is known with certainty, the evaluation of which action is best boils down to identifying the one with the highest net benefit, if the objective is maximizing benefits, or the lowest cost, if the objective is minimizing costs. When the outcomes are uncertain, what criterion should be used for choosing the 'best' decision? The following chapters will explore this question more extensively. The discussion below is only intended as a cursory overview.

The most obvious approach is to adapt the criterion of maximizing benefits or minimizing costs for deterministic situations. Under uncertainty, each action leads to one of a number of possible outcomes. Which particular outcome will be realized is only known in terms of its probability. So, we substitute 'expected benefits' or 'expected cost' for benefits or costs in the above criterion. The 'best' action is the one with the highest expected benefit or the lowest expected cost, whichever is relevant. Economic theory, in fact, shows that under fairly general conditions, this criterion achieves the best possible long-run results.

For repetitive risky situations, the meaning of this statement is the usual long-run frequency interpretation. Applied to one-shot deals, the meaning implied is that, in the long-run, the cumulative benefits achieved on many different, unique one-shot deals are superior to any other criterion. However, for any particular one-shot deal, the outcome could still spell disaster!

In situations with extremely serious possible outcomes, such as large losses or bankruptcy, the decision maker may not be willing to make a decision based on the expected value criterion. Instead, he or she may select an outcome that has a lower expected benefit, but provides better protection against the risks involved. One such criterion chooses the 'best' decision on the basis of a probabilistic threshold for the outcomes. In particular, the decision maker may eliminate any actions from further consideration if the probability of not achieving a certain minimum benefit or of exceeding a certain maximum cost is larger than a given threshold value. For instance, when comparing several mutually exclusive risky investment opportunities, the decision maker may eliminate any which have a probability of 5% of leading to a loss of more than a certain amount. The actions passing the threshold are then evaluated using a secondary criterion, such as maximizing expected benefits or minimizing expected costs.

Unfortunately, for many real-life complex and sequential decision situations, determining the probability distribution of the final outcomes may be difficult. **Risk analysis** — a topic briefly discussed in Chapter 17 — is one attempt to overcome some of these difficulties.

If there is a high degree of uncertainty about the outcomes and, furthermore, some may also involve serious adverse consequences, the decision maker may select the decision which offers the best protection against the worst outcomes. The probabilities are completely ignored. Such a criterion may be appropriate if some of the possible outcomes involve disasters, such as loss of life, serious injury, or irreversible damage to the environment, or if the outcomes are partially controlled by a vicious adversary who is out to get you. In a business context, a firm may resort to this criterion in order to avoid any possibilities of going bankrupt. Discussion of this and similar criteria are the subject of **decision analysis** (Chapter 18) and **game theory**.

EXERCISES

1. One of the major causes of uncertainty listed in Section 15.2 is ignorance about or a lack of complete understanding of a given phenomenon. It is then conceivable that ultimately uncertainty will disappear since advances in science will allow us to understand all phenomena perfectly. Critically discuss this view.

2. A recent court case found a local council negligent for allowing the complainant to built a house in a 50-year flood plane. Although the council had actually informed the complainant of the danger, the court awarded him considerable damages, based on the fact that, within the first five years after completion, the house was inundated in three of these years. The judge's verdict stated that the council's assessment of the flood risk clearly was in error, given that in three out of five years flooding occurred. Assume that the council's assessment of the house being in a 50-year flood plane was correct. Discuss the validity or otherwise of the judge's reason for siding with the complainant.

3. An analyst asked an economist about whether or not he should collect additional data to have a more reliable basis for finding the best policy for a decision problem under uncertainty. The economist's answer was: 'You should collect additional information until the marginal cost of obtaining it is less than the marginal gain of improved decision making.' (This follows the principles developed in Chapter 11.) Why is this a rather naive recommendation?

4. In your own words, not exceeding one page, summarize the major finding of the research by Tversky and Kahneman reported in the article reproduced in the Appendix. Use examples from your own experience as illustrations. Do not simply paraphrase parts of the article, but give your own digested understanding of what they say.

5. Consider the article by Tversky and Kahneman (in the Appendix). For each description listed below, identify which of the heuristics discussed by these authors was or is likely to be used and the potential error or bias it could introduce.
    (a) Discussing politics, Mike says to Sue: 'You can't trust a politician - they are all liars!'
    (b) Instead of using the 5-point assessment procedure for finding a decision maker's utility function for the monetary outcomes of a project, the analyst presents the decision maker with the graph depicting the utility function for a risk neutral person and asks the decision maker to adjust that function in either a risk averse or risk seeking direction until the shape feels right for her.
    (c) Five of John's friends recently won sizable sums in scratch lotto. John's aunt asks him whether the chances of winning in scratch lotto are good. He responds: 'Oh yes, just look how my friends are doing!'
    (d) Andrew goes to the supermarket. In the car park, raised on a slanted platform, is a beautiful cabriolet sportscar - the latest model, offered as the first prize for a nationwide raffle organized on behalf of the Red Cross. He falls in love with the racy car. He has the firm feeling that if he buys a book of tickets for $10, he will win it.
    (e) Margaret got five A+'s and three A's in her first year at university. The head of department of her major subject is overheard making the following remark to one

of his colleagues: 'I bet Margaret will top her class next year too!'

REFERENCES

Armstrong, J.S., *Long-Range Forecasting: From Crystal Ball to Computer*, Wiley, 1985. Extensive coverage. Armstrong is a provocative writer.

Bross, Irwin D.J., *Design for Decision*, Macmillan, 1953. The date of publication makes this a classic. It is a classic! Humorous, insightful discussion of many issues associated with uncertainty. My discussion in parts of this chapter has been strongly influenced by this book. The relevant chapters are 1 to 5.

Hogarth, R.M., and Makridakis, S., 'Forecasting and planning: an evaluation,' *Management Sciences*, Feb. 1981, 115-38. This seminal paper first reviews some of the psychology human judgment, followed by a review of reported applications of formal forecasting methods. It finds that the latter are prone to similar problems as the former. It then concludes with some suggestions for overcoming some of these problems.

Tversky, A., and Kahneman, D., 'The framing of decisions and the psychology of choice,' *Science*, Jan. 1981, 453-8. A popular follow-on article to 'Judgment under uncertainty' that shows preferences and, hence, decision choices are highly dependent on how the problem in question is presented or framed.

Tversky, A., and Kahneman, D., 'Rational choice and the framing of decisions,' *Journal of Business*, No. 4, part 2, 1986, S251-8. The more academic version on the same theme as their 1981 paper above.

Appendix to Chapter 15 — Judgment under Uncertainty: Heuristics and Biases

by A. Tversky and D. Kahneman

reprinted with permission from *Science*, vol.185, 1974, pp.1124-31
Copyright © by the American Association for the Advancement of Science 1974

Abstract

Many decisions are based on beliefs concerning the likelihood of uncertain events such as the outcome of an election, the guilt of a defendant, or the future value of the dollar. These beliefs are usually expressed in statements such as 'I think that ...', 'chances are ...', 'it is unlikely that ...', and so forth. Occasionally, beliefs concerning uncertain events are expressed in numerical form as odds or subjective probabilities. What determines such beliefs? How do people assess the probability of an uncertain event or the value of an uncertain quantity? This article shows that people rely on a limited number of heuristic principles which reduce the complex tasks of assessing probabilities and predicting values to simpler judgmental operations. In general, these heuristics are quite useful, but sometimes they lead to severe and systematic errors.

The subjective assessment of probability resembles the subjective assessment of physical quantities such as distance or size. These judgments are all based on data of limited validity, which are processed according to heuristic rules. For example, the apparent distance of an object is determined in part by its clarity. The more sharply the object is seen, the closer it appears to be. This rule has some validity, because in any given scene the more distant objects are seen less sharply than nearer objects. However, the reliance on this rule leads to systematic errors in the estimation of distance. Specifically, distances are often overestimated when visibility is poor because the contours of objects are blurred. On the other hand, distances are often underestimated when visibility is good because the objects are seen sharply. Thus, the reliance on clarity as an indication of distance leads to common biases. Such biases are also found in the intuitive judgment of probability. This article describes three heuristics that are employed to assess probabilities and to predict values. Biases to which these heuristics lead are enumerated, and the applied and theoretical implications of these observations are discussed.

REPRESENTATIVENESS

Many of the probabilistic questions with which people are concerned belong to one of the following types: What is the probability that object A belongs to class B? What is the probability that event A originates from process B? What is the probability that process B will generate event A? In answering such questions people typically rely on the representativeness heuristic, in which probabilities are evaluated by the degree to which A is representative of B, that is, by the degree to which A resembles B. For example, when A is highly representative of B, the probability that A originates from B is judged to be high. On the other hand, if A is not similar to B, the probability that A originates from B is judged to be low.

For an illustration of judgment by representativeness, consider an individual who has been described by a former neighbour as follows: 'Steve is very shy and withdrawn, invariably helpful, but with little interest in people, or in the world of reality. A meek and tidy soul, he has a need for order and structure, and a passion for detail.' How do people assess the probability that Steve is engaged in a particular occupation from a list of possibilities (for example, farmer, salesman, airline pilot, librarian, or physician)? How do people order these occupations from most to least likely? In the representativeness heuristic, the probability that Steve is a librarian, for example, is assessed by the degree to which he is representative of, or similar to, the stereotype of a librarian. Indeed, research with problems of this type has shown that people order the occupations by probability and by similarity in exactly the same way (Kahneman and Tversky, 1973). This approach to the judgment of probability leads to serious errors, because similarity, or representativeness, is not influenced by several factors that should affect judgments of probability.

One of the factors that have no effect on representativeness but should have a major effect on probability is the prior probability, or base-rate frequency, of the outcomes. In the case of Steve, for example, the fact that there are many more farmers than librarians in the population should enter into any reasonable estimate of probability that Steve is a librarian rather than a farmer. Considerations of base-rate frequency, however, do not affect the similarity of Steve to the stereotypes of librarians and farmers. If people evaluate probability by representativeness, therefore, prior probabilities will be neglected. This hypothesis was tested in an experiment where prior probabilities were manipulated (Kahneman and Tversky, 1973). Subjects were shown brief personality descriptions of several individuals, allegedly sampled at random from a group of several individuals - engineers and lawyers. The subjects were asked to assess, for each description, the probability that it belonged to an engineer rather than to a lawyer. In one experimental condition, subjects were told that the group from which the descriptions had been drawn consisted of 70 engineers and 30 lawyers. In another condition, subjects were told that the group consisted of 30 engineers and 70 lawyers. The odds that any particular description belongs to an engineer rather than to a lawyer should be higher in the first condition, where there is a majority of engineers, than in the second condition, where there is a majority of lawyers. Specifically, it can be shown by applying Bayes's rule that the ratio of these odds should be $(0.7/0.3)^2$, or 5.44, for each description. In a sharp violation of Bayes's rule, the subjects in the two conditions produced essentially the same probability judgments. Apparently, subjects evaluated the likelihood that a particular description belonged to an engineer rather than to a lawyer by the degree to which this description was representative of the two stereotypes, with little or no regard for the prior probabilities of the categories.

The subjects used prior probabilities correctly when they had no other information. In the absence of a personality sketch, they judged the probability that an unknown individual is an engineer to be 0.7 and 0.3, respectively, in the two base-rate conditions. However, prior probabilities were effectively ignored when a description was introduced, even when this description was totally uninformative. The responses to the following description illustrate this phenomenon:

> *Dick is a thirty-year-old man. He is married with no children. A man of high ability and high motivation, he promises to be quite successful in his field. He is well liked by his colleagues.*

This description was intended to convey no information relevant to the question of whether Dick is an engineer or a lawyer. Consequently, the probability that Dick is an engineer should equal the proportion of engineers in the group, as if no description had been given. The subjects, however, judged the probability of Dick being an engineer to be 0.5 regardless of whether the stated proportion of engineers in the group was 0.7 or 0.3. Evidently, people respond differently when given no evidence and when given worthless evidence. When no specific evidence is given, prior probabilities are properly utilized; when worthless evidence is given, prior probabilities are ignored (Kahneman and Tversky, 1973).

Insensitivity to Sample Size

To evaluate the probability of obtaining a particular result in a sample drawn from a specified population, people typically apply the representativeness heuristic. That is, they assess the likelihood of a sample result, for example, that the average height in a random sample of ten men will be six feet (180 centimetres), by the similarity of this result to the corresponding parameter (that is, to the average height in the population of men). The similarity of a sample statistic to a population parameter does not depend on the size of the sample. Consequently, if probabilities are assessed by representativeness, then the judged probability of a sample statistic will be essentially independent of sample size. Indeed, when subjects assessed the distributions of average height for samples of various sizes, they produced identical distributions. For example, the probability of obtaining an average height greater than six feet was assigned the same value for samples of 1,000, 100, and 10 men (Kahneman and Tversky, 1972). Moreover, subjects failed to appreciate the role of sample size even when it was emphasized in the formulation of the problem. Consider the following question:

> *A certain town is served by two hospitals. In the larger hospital about 45 babies are born each day, and in the smaller hospital about 15 babies are born each day. As you know, about 50 percent of all babies are boys. However, the exact percentage varies from day to day. Sometimes it may be higher than 50 percent, sometimes lower.*

For a period of one year, each hospital recorded the days on which more than 60 percent of the babies born were boys. Which hospital do you think recorded more such days?

The larger hospital (21)
The smaller hospital (21)
About the same (that is, within 5 percent of each other) (53)

The values in parentheses are the number of undergraduate students who chose each answer.

Most subjects judged the probability of obtaining more than 60 percent boys to be the same in the small and in the large hospital, presumably because these events are described by the same statistic and are therefore equally representative of the general population. In contrast, sampling theory entails that the expected number of days on which more than 60 percent of the babies are boys is much greater in the small hospital than in the large one, because a large sample is less likely to stray from 50 percent. This fundamental notion of statistics is evidently not part of people's repertoire of intuitions.

A similar insensitivity to sample size has been reported in judgments of posterior probability, that is, of the probability that a sample has been drawn from one population rather than from another. Consider the following example:

Imagine an urn filled with balls, of which 2/3 are of one colour and 1/3 of another. One individual has drawn 5 balls from the urn, and found that 4 were red and 1 was white. Another individual has drawn 20 balls and found that 12 were red and 8 were white. Which of the two individuals should feel more confident that the urn contains 2/3 red balls and 1/3 white balls, rather than the opposite? What odds should each individual give?

In this problem, the correct posterior odds are 8 to 1 for the 4:1 sample and 16 to 1 for the 12:8 sample, assuming equal prior probabilities. However, most people feel that the first sample provides much stronger evidence for the hypothesis that the urn is predominantly red, because the proportion of red balls is larger in the first than in the second sample. Here again, intuitive judgments are dominated by the sample proportion and are essentially unaffected by the size of the sample, which plays a crucial role in the determination of the actual posterior odds (Kahneman and Tversky, 1972). In addition, intuitive estimates of posterior odds are far less extreme than the correct values. The underestimation of the impact of evidence has been observed repeatedly in problems of this type (Edwards, 1968; Slovic and Lichtenstein 1971). It has been labeled 'conservatism'.

Misconceptions of Chance

People expect that a sequence of events generated by a random process will represent the essential characteristics of that process even when the sequence is short. In considering tosses of a coin for heads or tails, for example, people regard the sequence H-T-H-T-T-H to be more likely than the sequence H-H-H-T-T-T, which does not appear random, and also more likely than the sequence H-H-H-H-T-H, which does not represent the fairness of the coin (Kahneman and Tversky, 1972). Thus, people expect that the essential characteristics of the process will be represented, not only globally in the entire sequence, but also locally in each of its parts. A locally representative sequence, however, deviates systematically from chance expectation: it contains too many alternations and too few runs. Another consequence of the belief in local representativeness is the well-known gambler's fallacy. After observing a long run of red on the roulette wheel, for example, most people erroneously believe that black is now due, presumably because the occurrence of black will result in a more representative sequence than the occurrence of an additional red. Chance is commonly viewed as a self-correcting process in which a deviation in one direction induces a deviation in the opposite direction to restore the equilibrium. In fact, deviations are not 'corrected' as a chance process unfolds, they are merely diluted.

Misconceptions of chance are not limited to naive subjects. A study of the statistical intuitions of experienced research psychologists (Tversky and Kahneman, 1971) revealed a lingering belief in what may be called the 'law of small numbers', according to which even small samples are highly representative of the populations from which they are drawn. The responses of these investigators reflected the expectation that a valid hypothesis about a population will be represented by a statistically significant result in a sample - with little regard for its size. As a consequence, the researchers put too much faith in the results of small samples and grossly overestimated the replicability of such results. In the actual conduct of research, this bias leads to the selection of samples of inadequate size and to overinterpretation of findings.

Insensitivity to Predictability

People are sometimes called upon to make such numerical predictions as the future value of a stock, the demand for a commodity, or the outcome of a football game. Such predictions are often made by representativeness. For example, suppose one is given a description of a company and is asked to predict its future profit. If the description of the company is very favourable, a very high profit will appear most representative of that description; if the description is mediocre, a mediocre performance will appear most representative. The degree to which the description is favourable is unaffected by the reliability of that description or by the degree to which it permits accurate prediction. Hence, if people predict solely in terms of the favourableness of the description, their predictions will be insensitive to the reliability of the evidence and to the expected accuracy of the prediction.

This mode of judgment violates the normative statistical theory in which the extremeness and the range of predictions are controlled by considerations of predictability. When predictability is nil, the same prediction should be made in all cases. For example, if the descriptions of companies provide no information relevant to profit, then the same value (such as average profit) should be predicted for all companies. If predictability is perfect, of course, the values predicted will match the actual values and the range of outcomes. In general, the higher the predictability, the wider the range of predicted values.

Several studies of numerical prediction have demonstrated that intuitive predictions violate this rule, and that subjects show little or no regard for considerations of predictability (Kahneman and Tversky, 1973). In one of these studies, subjects were presented with several paragraphs, each describing the performance of a student teacher during a particular practice lesson. Some subjects were asked to *evaluate* the quality of the lesson described in the paragraph in percentile scores, relative to a specified population. Other subjects were asked to *predict*, also in percentile scores, the standing of each student teacher five years after the practice lesson. The judgments made under the two conditions were identical. That is, the prediction of a remote criterion (success of a teacher after five years) was identical to the evaluation of the information on which the prediction was based (the quality of the practice lesson). The students who made these predictions were undoubtedly aware of the limited predictability of teaching competence on the basis of a single trial lesson five years earlier; nevertheless, their predictions were as extreme as their evaluations.

The Illusion of Validity

As we have seen, people often predict by selecting the outcome (for example, an occupation) that is most representative of the input (for example, the description of a person). The confidence they have in their prediction depends primarily on the degree of representativeness (that is, on the quality of the match between the selected outcome and the input) with little or no regard for the factors that limit predictive accuracy. Thus, people express great confidence in the prediction that a person is a librarian when given a description of his personality which matches the stereotype of librarians, even if the description is scanty, unreliable, or outdated. The unwarranted confidence which is produced by a good fit between the predicted outcome and the input information may be called the illusion of validity. This illusion persists even when the judge is aware of the factors that limit the accuracy of his predictions. It is a common observation that psychologists who conduct selection interviews often experience considerable confidence in their predictions, even when they know of the vast literature that shows selection interviews to be highly fallible. The continued reliance on the clinical interview for selection, despite repeated demonstrations of its inadequacy, amply attests to the strength of this effect.

The internal consistency of a pattern of inputs is a major determinant of one's confidence in predictions based on these inputs. For example, people express more confidence in predicting the final grade-point average of a student whose first-year record consists entirely of B's than in predicting the grade-point average of a student whose first-year record includes many A's and C's. Highly consistent patterns are most often observed when the input variables are highly redundant or correlated. Hence, people tend to have great confidence in predictions based on redundant input variables. However, an elementary result in the statistics of correlation asserts that, given input variables of stated validity, a prediction based on several such inputs can achieve higher accuracy when they are independent of each other than when they are redundant or correlated. Thus, redundancy among inputs decreases accuracy even as it increases confidence, and people are often confident in predictions that are quite likely to be off the mark (Kahneman and Tversky, 1973).

Misconceptions of Regression

Suppose a large group of children has been examined on two equivalent versions of an aptitude test. If one selects ten children from among those who did best on one of the two versions, he will usually find their performance on the second version to be somewhat disappointing. Conversely, if one selects ten children from among those who did worst on one version, they will be found, on the average, to do somewhat better on the other version. More generally, consider two variables X and Y which have the same distribution. If one selects individuals whose average X score deviates from the mean of X by k units, then the average of their Y scores will usually deviate from the mean of Y by less than k units. These observations illustrate a general phenomenon known as regression towards the mean, which was first documented by Galton more than a hundred years ago.

In the normal course of life, one encounters many instances of regression towards the mean, in the comparison of the height of fathers and sons, of the intelligence of husbands and wives, or of the performance of individuals on consecutive examinations. Nevertheless, people do not develop correct intuitions about this phenomenon. First, they do not expect regression in many contexts where it is bound to occur. Second, when they recognize the occurrence of regression, they often invent spurious causal explanations for it (Kahneman and Tversky, 1973). We suggest that the phenomenon of regression remains elusive because it is incompatible with the belief that the predicted outcome should be maximally representative of the input, and, hence, that the value of the outcome variable should be as extreme as the value of the input variable.

The failure to recognize the import of regression can have pernicious consequences, as illustrated by the following observation (Kahneman and Tversky, 1973). In a discussion of flight training, experienced instructors noted that praise for an exceptionally smooth landing is typically followed by a poorer landing on the next try, while harsh criticism after a rough landing is usually followed by an improvement on the next try. The instructors concluded that verbal rewards are detrimental to learning, while verbal punishments are beneficial, contrary to accepted psychological doctrine. This conclusion is unwarranted because of the presence of regression towards the mean. As in other cases of repeated examination, an improvement will usually follow a poor performance and a deterioration will usually follow an outstanding performance, even if the instructor does not respond to the trainee's achievement on the first attempt. Because the instructors had praised their trainees after good landings and admonished them after poor ones, they reached the erroneous and potentially harmful conclusion that punishment is more effective than reward.

Thus, the failure to understand the effect of regression leads one to overestimate the effectiveness of punishment and to underestimate the effectiveness of reward. In social interaction, as well as in training, rewards are typically administered when performance is good, and punishments are typically administered when performance is poor. By regression alone, therefore, behaviour is most likely to improve after punishment and most likely to deteriorate after reward. Consequently, the human condition is such that, by chance alone, one is most often rewarded for punishing others and most often punished for rewarding them. People are generally not aware of this contingency. In fact, the elusive role of regression in determining the apparent consequences of reward and punishment seems to have escaped the notice of students of this area.

AVAILABILITY

There are situations in which people assess the frequency of a class or the probability of an event by the ease with which instances or occurrences can be brought to mind. For example, one may assess the risk of heart attack among middle-aged people by recalling such occurrences among one's acquaintances. Similarly, one may evaluate the probability that a given business venture will fail by imagining various difficulties it could encounter. This judgmental heuristic is called availability. Availability is a useful clue for assessing frequency or probability, because instances of large classes are usually recalled better and faster than instances of less frequent classes. However, availability is affected by factors other than frequency and probability. Consequently, the reliance on availability leads to predictable biases, some of which are illustrated below.

Biases Due to the Retrievability of Instances

When the size of a class is judged by the availability of its instances, a class whose instances are easily retrieved will appear more numerous than a class of equal frequency whose instances are less retrievable. In an elementary demonstration of this effect, subjects heard a list of well-known personalities of both sexes and were subsequently asked to judge whether the list contained more names of men than of women. Different lists were presented to different groups of subjects. In some of the lists the men were relatively more famous than the women, and in others the women were relatively more famous than the men. In each of the lists, the subjects erroneously judged that the class (sex) that had the more famous personalities was the more numerous (Tversky and Kahneman, 1973).

In addition to familiarity, there are other factors, such as salience, which affect the retrievability of instances. For example, the impact of seeing a house burning on the subjective probability of such accidents is probably greater than the impact of reading about a fire in the local paper. Furthermore, recent occurrences are likely to be relatively more available than earlier occurrences. It is a common experience that the subjective probability of traffic accidents rises temporarily when one sees a car overturned by the side of the road.

Biases Due to the Effectiveness of a Search Set

Suppose one samples a word (of three letters or more) at random from an English text. Is it more likely that the word starts with r or that r is the third letter? People approach this problem by recalling words that begin with r (road) and words that have r in the third position (car) and assess the relatively frequency by the ease with which words of the two types come to mind. Because it is much easier to search for words by their first letter than by their third letter, most people judge words that begin with a given consonant to be more numerous than words in which the same consonant appears in the third position. They do so even for consonants, such as r or k, that are more frequent in the third position than in the first (Tversky and Kahneman, 1973).

Different tasks elicit different search sets. For example, suppose you are asked to rate the frequency with which abstract words (thought, love) and concrete words (door, water) appear in written English. A natural way to answer this question is to search for contexts in which the word could appear. It seems easier to think of contexts in which an abstract concept is mentioned (love in love stories) than to think of contexts in which a concrete word (such as door) is mentioned. If the frequency of words is judged by the availability of the contexts in which they appear, abstract words will be judged as relatively more numerous than concrete words. This bias has been observed in a recent study (Galbraith and Underwood, 1973) which showed that the judged frequency of occurrence of abstract words was much higher than that of concrete words, equated in objective frequency. Abstract words were also judged to appear in a much greater variety of contexts than concrete words.

Biases of Imaginability

Sometimes one has to assess the frequency of a class whose instances are not stored in memory but can be generated according to a given rule. In such situations, one typically generates several instances and evaluates frequency or probability by the ease with which the relevant instances can be constructed. However, the ease of constructing instances does not always reflect their actual frequency, and this mode of evaluation is prone to biases. To illustrate, consider a group of ten people who form committees of k members, $2 \leq k \leq 8$. How many different committees of k members can be formed? The correct answer to this problem is given by the binomial coefficient $(10/k)$ which reaches a maximum of 252 for $k = 5$. Clearly, the number of committees of k members equals the number of committees of $(10-k)$ members, because any committee of k members defines a unique group of $(10-k)$

nonmembers.

One way to answer this question without computation is to mentally construct committees of k members and to evaluate their number by the ease with which they come to mind. Committees of few members, say two, are more available than committees of many members, say eight. The simplest scheme for the construction of committees is a partition of the group into disjoint sets. One readily sees that it is easy to construct five disjoint committees of two members, while it is impossible to generate even two disjoint committees of eight members. Consequently, if frequency is assessed by imaginability, or by availability for construction, the small committees will appear more numerous than larger committees, in contrast to the correct bell-shaped function. Indeed, when naive subjects were asked to estimate the number of distinct committees of various sizes, their estimates were a decreasing monotonic function of committee size (Tversky and Kahneman, 1973). For example, the median estimate of the number of committees of two members was seventy, while the estimate for committees of eight members was twenty (the correct answer is forty-five in both cases).

Imaginability plays an important role in the evaluation of probabilities in real-life situations. The risk involved in an adventurous expedition, for example, is evaluated by imagining contingencies with which the expedition is not equipped to cope. If many such difficulties are vividly portrayed, the expedition can be made to appear exceedingly dangerous, although the ease with which disasters are imagined need not reflect their actual likelihood. Conversely, the risk involved in an undertaking may be grossly underestimated if some possible dangers are either difficult to conceive of, or simply do not come to mind.

Illusory Correlation

Chapman and Chapman (1967; 1969) have described an interesting bias in the judgment of the frequency with which two events co-occur. They presented naive judges with information concerning several hypothetical mental patients. The data for each patient consisted of a clinical diagnosis and a drawing of a person made by the patient. Later the judges estimated the frequency with which each diagnosis (such as paranoia or suspiciousness) had been accompanied by various features of the drawing (such as peculiar eyes). The subjects markedly overestimated the frequency of co-occurrence of natural associates, such as suspiciousness and peculiar eyes. This effect was labeled illusory correlation. In their erroneous judgments of the data to which they had been exposed, naive subjects 'rediscovered' much of the common, but unfounded, clinical lore concerning the interpretation of the draw-a-person test. The illusory correlation effect was extremely resistant to contradictory data. It persisted even when the correlation between symptom and diagnosis was actually negative, and it prevented the judges from detecting relationships that were in fact present.

Availability provides a natural account for the illusory-correlation effect. The judgment of how frequently two events co-occur could be based on the strength of the associative bond between them. When the association is strong, one is likely to conclude that the events have been frequently paired. Consequently, strong associates will be judged to have occurred together frequently. According to this view, the illusory correlation between suspiciousness and peculiar drawing of the eyes, for example, is due to the fact that suspiciousness is more readily associated with the eyes than with any other part of the body.

Lifelong experience has taught us that, in general, instances of large classes are recalled better and faster than instances of less frequent classes; that likely occurrences are easier to imagine than unlikely ones; and that the associative connections between events are strengthened when the events frequently co-occur. As a result, man has at his disposal a procedure (the availability heuristic) for estimating the numerosity of a class, the likelihood of an event, or the frequency of co-occurrences, by the ease with which the relevant mental operations of retrieval, construction, or association can be performed. However, as the preceding examples have demonstrated, this valuable procedure results in systematic errors.

ADJUSTMENT AND ANCHORING

In many situations, people make estimates by starting from an initial value that is adjusted to yield the final answer. The initial value, or starting point, may be suggested by the formulation of the problem, or it may be the result of a partial computation. In either case, adjustments are typically insufficient (Slovic and Lichtenstein, 1971). That is, different starting-points yield different estimates, which are biased towards the initial values. We call this phenomenon anchoring.

Insufficient Adjustment

In a demonstration of the anchoring effect, subjects were asked to estimate various quantities, stated in percentages (for example, the percentage of African countries in the United Nations). For each quantity, a number between 0 and 100 was determined by spinning a wheel of fortune in the subjects' presence. The subjects were instructed to indicate first whether that number was higher or lower than the value of the quantity, and then to estimate the value of the quantity by moving upward or downward from the given number. Different groups were given different numbers for each quantity, and these arbitrary numbers had a marked effect on estimates. For example, the median estimates of the percentage of African countries in the United Nations were 25 and 45 for groups that received 10 and 65, respectively, as starting-points. Payoffs for accuracy did not reduce the anchoring effect.

Anchoring occurs not only when the starting-point is given to the subject, but also when the subject bases his estimate on the result of some incomplete computation. A study of intuitive numerical estimation illustrates this effect. Two groups of high school students estimated, within five seconds, a numerical expression that was written on the blackboard. One group estimated the product

$$8 \times 7 \times 6 \times 5 \times 4 \times 3 \times 2 \times 1$$

while another group estimated the product

$$1 \times 2 \times 3 \times 4 \times 5 \times 6 \times 7 \times 8$$

To rapidly answer such questions, people may perform a few steps of computation and estimate the product by extrapolation or adjustment. Because adjustments are typically insufficient, this procedure should lead to underestimation. Furthermore, because the result of the first few steps of multiplication (performed from left to right) is higher in the descending sequence than in the ascending sequence, the former expression should be judged larger than the latter. Both predictions were confirmed. The median estimate for the ascending sequence was 512, while the median estimate for the descending sequence was 2,250. The correct answer is 40,320.

Biases in the Evaluation of Conjunctive and Disjunctive Events

In a recent study by Bar-Hillel (1973) subjects were given the opportunity to bet on one of two events. Three types of events were used: (i) simple events, such as drawing a red marble from a bag containing 50 percent red marbles and 50 percent white marbles; (ii) conjunctive events, such as drawing a red marble seven times in succession, with replacement, from a bag containing 90 percent red marbles and 10 percent white marbles; and (iii) disjunctive events, such as drawing a red marble at least once in seven successive tries, with replacement, from a bag containing 10 percent red marbles and 90 percent white marbles. In this problem, a significant majority of subjects preferred to bet on the conjunctive event (the probability of which is 0.48) rather than on the simple event (the probability of which is 0.50). Subjects also preferred to bet on the simple event rather than on the disjunctive event, which has a probability of 0.52. Thus, most subjects bet on the less likely event in both comparisons. This pattern of choices illustrates a general finding. Studies of choice among gambles and of judgments of probability indicate that people tend to overestimate the probability of conjunctive events (Cohen and others, 1972) and to underestimate the probability of disjunctive events. These biases are readily explained as effects of anchoring. The stated probability of the elementary event (success at any one stage) provides a natural starting-point for the estimation of the probabilities of both conjunctive and disjunctive events. Since adjustment from the starting-point is typically insufficient, the final estimates remain too close to the probabilities of the elementary events in both cases. Note that the overall probability of a conjunctive event is lower than the probability of each elementary event, whereas the overall probability of a disjunctive event is higher than the probability of each elementary event. As a consequence of anchoring, the overall probability will be overestimated in conjunctive problems and underestimated in disjunctive problems.

Biases in the evaluation of compound events are particularly significant in the context of planning. The successful completion of an undertaking, such as the development of a new product, typically has a conjunctive character: for the undertaking to succeed, each of a series of events must occur. Even when each of these events is very likely, the overall probability of success can be quite low if the number of events is large. The general tendency to overestimate the probability of conjunctive events leads to unwarranted optimism in the evaluation of the likelihood that a plan will succeed or that a project will be completed on time. Conversely, disjunctive structures are typically encountered in the evaluation of risks. A complex system, such as a nuclear reactor or a human body, will malfunction if any of its essential components fails. Even when the likelihood of failure in each component is slight, the probability of an overall failure can be high if many components are involved. Because of anchoring, people will tend to underestimate the probabilities of failure in complex systems. Thus, the direction of the anchoring bias can sometimes be inferred from the structure of the event. The chain-like structure of conjunctions leads to overestimation, the funnel-like structure of disjunctions leads to underestimation.

Anchoring in the Assessment of Subjective Probability Distributions

In decision analysis, experts are often required to express their beliefs about a quantity, such as the value of the Dow-Jones average on a particular day, in the form of a probability distribution. Such a distribution is usually constructed by asking the person to select values of the quantity that correspond to specified percentiles of his subjective probability distribution. For example, the judge may be asked to select a number, X_{90}, such that his subjective probability that this number will be higher than the value of the Dow-Jones average is 0.90. That is, he should select the value X_{90} so that he is just willing to accept nine to one odds that the Dow-Jones average will not exceed it. A subjective probability distribution for the value of the Dow-Jones average can be constructed from several such judgments corresponding to different percentiles.

By collecting subjective probability distributions for many different quantities, it is possible to test the judge for proper calibration. A judge is properly (or externally) calibrated in a set of problems if exactly 11 percent of the true values of the assessed quantities falls below his stated value of X_{11}. For example, the true values should fall below X_{01} for 1 percent of the quantities and above X_{99} for 1 percent of the quantities. Thus, the true values should fall in the confidence interval between X_{01} and X_{99} on 98 percent of the problems.

Several investigators (Alpert and Raiffa; von Holstein, 1971; Winkler, 1967) have obtained probability distributions for many quantities from a large number of judges. These distributions indicated large and systematic departures from proper calibration. In most studies, the actual values of the assessed quantities are either smaller than X_{01} or greater than X_{99} for about 30 percent of the problems. That is, the subjects state overly narrow confidence intervals which reflect more certainty than is justified by their knowledge about the assessed quantities. This bias is common to naive and to sophisticated subjects, and it is not eliminated by introducing proper scoring rules, which provide incentives for external calibration. This effect is attributable, in part at least, to anchoring.

To select the value of the Dow-Jones average, for example, it is natural to begin by thinking about one's best estimate of the Dow-Jones and to adjust this value upward. If this adjustment - like most others - is insufficient, then X_{90} will not be sufficiently extreme. A similar anchoring effect will occur in the selection of X_{10}, which is presumably obtained by adjusting one's best estimate downward. Consequently, the confidence interval between X_{10} and X_{90} will be too narrow, and the assessed probability distribution will be too tight. In support of this interpretation it can be shown that subjective probabilities are systematically altered by a procedure in which one's best estimate does not serve as an anchor.

Subjective probability distributions for a given quantity (the Dow-Jones average) can be obtained in two different ways: (i) by asking the subject to select values of the Dow-Jones that correspond to specified percentiles of his probability distribution and (ii) by asking the subject to assess the probabilities that the true value of the Dow-Jones will exceed some specified values. The two procedures are formally equivalent and should yield identical distributions. However, they suggest different modes of adjustment from different anchors. In procedure (i), the natural starting point is one's best estimate of the quantity.

In procedure (ii), on the other hand, the subject may be anchored on the value stated in the question. Alternatively, he may be anchored on even odds, or 50:50 chances, which is a natural starting-point in the estimation of likelihood. In either case, procedure (ii) should yield less extreme odds than procedure (i).

To contrast the two procedures, a set of twenty-four quantities (such as the air distance from New Delhi to Peking) was presented to a group of subjects who assessed either X_{10} or X_{90} for each problem. Another group of subjects received the median judgment of the first group for each of the twenty-four quantities. They were asked to assess the odds that each of the given values exceeded the true value of the relevant quantity. In the absence of any bias, the second group should retrieve the odds specified to the first group; that is, 9:1. However, if even odds or the stated value serve as anchors, the odds of the second group should be less extreme, that is, closer to 1:1. Indeed, the median odds stated by this group, across all problems, were 3:1. When the judgments of the two groups were tested for external calibration, it was found that subjects in the first group were too extreme, in accord with earlier studies. The events that they defined as having a probability of 0.1 actually obtained in 24 percent of the cases. In contrast, subjects in the second group were too conservative. Events to which they assigned an average probability of 0.34 actually obtained in 26 percent of the cases. These results illustrate the manner in which the degree of calibration depends on the procedure of elicitation.

DISCUSSION

This article has been concerned with cognitive biases that stem from the reliance on judgmental heuristics. These biases are not attributable to motivational effects such as wishful thinking or the distortion of judgments by payoffs and penalties. Indeed, several of the severe errors of judgment reported earlier occurred despite the fact that subjects were encouraged to be accurate and were rewarded for the correct answers (Kahneman and Tversky, 1972; Tversky and Kahneman, 1973).

The reliance on heuristics and the prevalence of biases are not restricted to laymen. Experienced researchers are also prone to the same biases - when they think intuitively. For example, the tendency to predict the outcome that best represents the data, with insufficient regard for prior probability, has been observed in the intuitive judgments of individuals who have had extensive training in statistics (Kahneman and Tversky, 1973; Tversky and Kahneman, 1971). Although the statistically sophisticated avoid elementary errors, such as the gambler's fallacy, their intuitive judgments are liable to similar fallacies in more intricate and less transparent problems.

It is not surprising that useful heuristics such as representativeness and availability are retained, even though they occasionally lead to errors in prediction or estimation. What is perhaps surprising is the failure of people to infer from lifelong experience such fundamental statistical rules as regression towards the mean, or the effect of sample size on sampling variability. Although everyone is exposed, in the normal course of life, to numerous examples from which these rules could have been induced, very few people discover the principles of sampling and regression on their own. Statistical principles are not learned from everyday experience because the relevant instances are not coded appropriately. For example, people do not discover that successive lines in a text differ more in average word length than do successive pages, because they simply do not attend to the average word length of individual lines or pages. Thus, people do not learn the relation between sample size and sampling variability, although the data for such learning are abundant.

The lack of an appropriate code also explains why people usually do not detect the biases in their judgments of probability. A person could conceivably learn whether his judgments are externally calibrated by keeping a tally of the proportion of events that actually occur among those to which he assigns the same probability. However, it is not natural to group events by their judged probability. In the absence of such grouping it is impossible for an individual to discover, for example, that only 50 percent of the predictions to which he has assigned a probability of 0.9 or higher actually came true.

The empirical analysis of cognitive biases has implications for the theoretical and applied role of judged probabilities. Modern decision theory (De Finetti, 1968; Savage, 1954) regards subjective probability as the quantified opinion of an idealized person. Specifically, the subjective probability of a given event is defined by the set of bets about this event that such a person is willing to accept. An internally consistent, or coherent, subjective probability measure can be derived for an individual if his choices among bets satisfy certain principles, that is, the axioms of the theory. The derived probability is subjective in the sense that different individuals are allowed to have different probabilities for the same event. The major contribution of this approach is that it provides a rigorous subjective interpretation of probability that is applicable to unique events and is embedded in a general theory of rational decision.

It should perhaps be noted that, while subjective probabilities can sometimes be inferred from preferences among bets, they are normally not formed in this fashion. A person bets on team A rather than on team B because he believes that team A is more likely to win; he does not infer this belief from his betting preferences. Thus, in reality, subjective probabilities determine preferences among bets and are not derived from them, as in the axiomatic theory of rational decision (Savage, 1954).

The inherently subjective nature of probability has led many students to the belief that coherence, or internal consistency, is the only valid criterion by which judged probabilities should be evaluated. From the standpoint of the formal theory of subjective probability, any set of internally consistent probability judgments is as good as any other. This criterion is not entirely satisfactory, because an internally consistent set of subjective probabilities can be incompatible with other beliefs held by the individual. Consider a person whose subjective probabilities for all possible outcomes of a coin-tossing game reflect the gambler's fallacy. That is, his estimate of the probability of tails on a particular toss increases with the number of consecutive heads that preceded that toss. The judgments of such a person could be internally consistent and therefore acceptable as adequate subjective probabilities according to the criterion of the formal theory. These probabilities, however, are incompatible with the generally held belief that a coin has no memory and is therefore incapable of generating sequential dependencies. For judged probabilities to be considered adequate, or rational, internal consistency is not enough. The judgments must be compatible with the entire web of beliefs held by the individual. Unfortunately, there can be no simple formal procedure for assessing the compatibility of a set of probability judgments with the judge's total system of beliefs. The rational judge will nevertheless strive for compatibility, even though internal consistency is more easily achieved and assessed. In particular, he will attempt to make his probability judgments compatible with his knowledge about the subject matter, the laws of probability, and his own judgmental heuristics and biases.

SUMMARY

This article described three heuristics that are employed in making judgments under uncertainty: (i) representativeness, which is usually employed when people are asked to judge the probability that an object or event A belongs to class or process B; (ii) availability of instances of scenarios, which is often employed when people are asked to assess the frequency of a class or the plausibility of a particular development; and (iii) adjustment from an anchor, which is usually employed in numerical prediction when a relevant value is available. These heuristics are highly economical and usually effective, but they lead to systematic and predictable errors. A better understanding of these heuristics and of the biases to which they lead could improve judgments and decisions in situations of uncertainty.

REFERENCES

Alpert, M., and Raiffa, H., unpublished manuscript.

Bar-Hillel, M., 1973. *Organizational Behaviour and Human Performance*, vol 9, p. 396.

Chapman, L. J., and Chapman, J. P., 1967. *Abnormal Psychology*, vol 73, p. 193.

Chapman, L. J., and Chapman, J. P., 1969. *Abnormal Psychology*, vol 74, p. 271.

Cohen, J., Chesnick, E. L., and Haran, D., 1972. *Brit J Psychology*, vol 63, p. 41.

De Finetti, B., in D. E. Sills (ed.), 1968. *International Encyclopedia of the Social Sciences*, New York, Macmillan, vol 12, 496-504.

Edwards, W., in B. Kleinmuntz, (ed.), 1968. *Formal Representation of Human Judgment*, New York, Wiley, 17-52.

Galbraith, R. C., and Underwood, B. J., 1973. *Mem Cognition*, vol 1, p. 56.

Holstein, C. A. S. von, 1971. *Acta Psychologica*, vol 35, p. 475.

Kahneman, D., and Tversky, A., 1972. *Cognitive Psychology*, vol 3, p. 430.

Kahneman, D., and Tversky, A., 1973. *Psychological Rev*, vol 80, p. 237.

Savage, L. J., 1954. *The Foundations of Statistics*, New York, Wiley.

Slovic, P., and Lichtenstein, S., 1971. *Organizational Behaviour and Human Performance*, vol 6, p. 649.

Tversky, A., and Kahneman, D., 1971. *Psychological Bull*, vol 76, p. 105.

Tversky, A., and Kahneman, D., 1973. *Cognitive Psychology*, vol 5, p. 207.

Winkler, R. L., 1967. *J. Amer Stat Association*, vol 62, p. 776.

16 Waiting Lines: Stochastic Systems Behaviour

D. C. McNickle
University of Canterbury

As we have seen in Chapter 15, uncertainty about the behaviour of a system can range from knowing almost nothing, to having fairly reliable information in the form of 'objective' probabilities about the various events that may occur in the system. This chapter studies systems where systems behaviour is the realization of a large sequence of random events. Each type of random event can be characterized by a random variable whose probability distribution is known. In practice this means that we either have gathered empirical frequency distributions from past observations for each type of event in question, or have fitted theoretical probability distributions to them as convenient approximations. We shall see that under these conditions a system may exhibit new and interesting types of behaviours — we called them emergent properties in Chapter 3 — behaviours that are not present in deterministic systems.

While in a deterministic system each alternative course of action leads to a corresponding known outcome, in a stochastic system each alternative course of action leads to one of a number of possible outcomes. A priori, we cannot specify which particular outcome will result from a given decision, but only with what probability each of the possible outcomes will occur. These probabilities are usually different for each different course of action. Seen from this perspective, each alternative course of action can be viewed as selecting a given probability distribution for the outcomes. The 'best' decision is the one that produces the most 'favourable' probability distribution for the outcomes. For most OR/MS type problem solving, the most favourable probability distribution is the one with the highest expected benefit or the lowest expected cost. Since we deal with large sequences of one or several types of events, we in fact evaluate the system in terms of its long-run behaviour.

Waiting line situations are ideal for showing some of the emergent properties of stochastic systems, and how the long-run behaviour of such systems is affected by controllable and uncontrollable aspects. The first two sections of this chapter describe the structure of waiting line situations and demonstrate that stochastic systems may exhibit emergent properties that comparable deterministic systems do not have. The mathematics of waiting lines has been studied extensively since 1917. Section 16.3 summarizes some of the most basic results. The remaining sections of the chapter will study in detail a real-life application — the Forest Products weighbridge problem.

16.1 WAITING LINES

We are all familiar with waiting lines or queues. We wait at a bus stop for the next bus, we wait for elevators, we wait at checkout counters in supermarkets, the student cafeteria, or the library until it is our turn to be served. Queueing situations are also a common concern in commercial and industrial situations, leading to important decision problems. For example, ships in a harbour may have to wait for unloading cranes to become available. Every hour of waiting may cost several thousand dollars in operating costs for the ship. On the other hand, each additional crane installed represents a substantial investment. Port authorities do not want to have them sitting around idle. How many cranes should the port authorities operate so as to keep the waiting costs of arriving ships reasonably low, while at the same time keeping the cranes busy much of the time?

The first queueing models, developed by the Danish engineer Erlang in 1917, dealt with telephone exchanges. Communications remains one of the most common areas of application of queueing models. The very first example in Chapter 1 — the TAB telephone betting system — is an application of this kind. We want to know how many telephone lines we need if we want, say, 98% of all punters to be able to place their bets on the first attempt.

Basic Structure

Figure 16-1 depicts the general structure of waiting line situations. Table 16-1 lists a few typical examples. The three major components of a system involving queueing-type behaviour are:

- one or several sources of customers or **arrivals**,
- one or several **queues**, each with its corresponding **queue discipline**,
- one or several **service facilities**.

Arrivals from more than one source may all request service from the same service facility. For example, some arrivals at an accident and emergency clinic may suffer from a life threatening condition that requires immediate attention, while others have some minor accident, whose treatment can be delayed within reason. Each group is viewed as a separate source of arrivals. Similarly, aircraft requesting permission to land may be large commercial airliners or small private planes. In each case, one source may get priority in terms of service over the other source. Furthermore, each source of arrivals may have different characteristics in terms of the kind of service requested or the time interval needed to complete the service.

The sequence in which the server attends to the entities waiting in a given queue is called the queue discipline. In most queues, arrivals are attended to by the server

Figure 16-1:   Waiting line structure

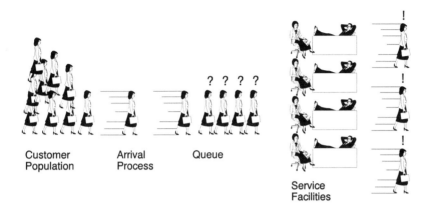

on a first-come-first-served sequence.   There are, however, instances where the service sequence follows a different rule.   For example, some blood banks issue blood for transfusions on a last-in-first-out basis.   The reason for this is that the oxygen carrying capacity of the blood deteriorates with age and hence using the freshest available blood is most effective from a medical point of view.   In other instances, some arrivals satisfying certain criteria are given priority over other arrivals.   For example, some mainframe university computing facilities provide for a ranking of service priority on the basis of the charging rate chosen for a job: the higher the charging rate, the higher the service priority.   However, within each priority class, jobs are processed on a first-come-first-served basis.

Table 16-1:   Examples of waiting line situations

Source of arrivals	Nature of service	Service facility
customers in stores	sales transactions	store attendant
telephone calls	telephone connection	telephone exchange
electronic messages	transmission	transmitter
aircraft	landing and take-off	runway
ships in harbour	berthing	dock
ships berthed at dock	loading and unloading	cranes or/and gangs
cars	sea crossing	ferry
machines	repairs, change-over, etc.	technician/operator
mechanics of shop floor	tools or parts	attendants at counter
computing jobs	hard disk file handling	file server
emergency/accident victims	medical attention	nurses/surgeons
welfare applicants	processing of application	case worker

There may be one queue, several queues, or no queue at all. For example, most banks now-a-days have all customers join a single queue. The person at the front of the queue is first in line for the first teller to become free. On the other hand, in supermarkets each check-out counter has its own queue, while the usual single-line telephone installation has no queueing facilities. If the line is in use by a connection, any other caller gets a busy signal. He or she is not accepted as an arrival put on hold. Each caller has to redial to try for a successful connection. The length of a queue may be limited. For example, a psychotherapist may limit the number of clients waiting for a weekly time slot to become available to at most ten. Any potential clients arriving when the waiting list is full are referred to other therapists. Finally, potential arrivals may balk and depart immediately if they observe that the queue is too long. Some customers already in the queue may also become impatient and depart without service if they expect that the additional waiting time will be too long. Arrivals finding the queue full, or balking and reneging customers are lost to the system. This may result in potential profits foregone.

As the examples in Table 16-1 indicate, the entities in the queues do not have to be at the same physical location, but may be awaiting service in separate locations, such as photocopiers requiring repairs or service, owned or rented by different firms or organizations.

Service facilities may be arranged **in parallel** or **in sequence**. The check-out counters at a supermarket or tellers in a bank operate in parallel. Each service facility performs exactly the same type of service. Customers in the queue require service from only one such facility and may be serviced by any one of them. In contrast, an arrival may require service from several facilities in sequence. For example, a job in a machine shop may have to be cut first on a lathe, then drilled on a drill, and finally finished on a polishing machine. There may be a queue in front of each of these machines.

This brief survey shows that the variety of possible waiting line configurations seems almost unlimited. We shall only study some rather simple situations. Chapter 17 on simulation shows how more complex configurations can be studied.

16.2 WHAT CAUSES QUEUES TO FORM

On the edge of a desert is a small store with a single gas pump. It displays a tall sign warning motorists that this is the last gas station for the next 300 km. As a result, no car ever drives past without filling up. On average, about four cars stop at the service station every hour. Jake, the owner of the store, having seen many cars stop at his station, is never rushed, regardless of how many cars are waiting for gas. If Jake takes a liking to a customer, Jake easily forgets himself and chats away for minutes. On average he takes about 10 minutes to serve each car. Let's study what happens to this simple system under various assumptions about the rate at which customers are served.

Constant Arrival and Service Times

Assume first that cars arrive evenly spaced over time, i.e., the **interarrival time** is constant. With four arrivals per hour, the interarrival time is exactly 15 minutes. We start observing the service station at 8 a.m. No cars are there, so the pump is idle. The first car arrives at 8:04. For some reason, Jake decides that today, he will spend exactly the same length of time with each car, namely 10 minutes. So Jake starts serving the first car immediately upon arrival and finishes serving it 10 minutes later, namely at 8:14. The car departs. Jake goes back to his cup of coffee, kept warm on his stove. The next car arrives at 8:19, exactly 15 minutes after the first car. It gets immediate service, and leaves at 8:29. The third car arrives at 8:34 and Jake completes serving it at 8:44. This regular pattern continues all day long. No car ever has to wait. There is never a queue.

Because there is exactly one interarrival time and one service time for each customer, the service facility is busy a fraction of time equal to the ratio of the service time to the arrival time, or 10/15 = ⅔ and it is idle a fraction of time equal to (1 - [fraction busy]) or 1 - ⅔ = ⅓.

Next day, Jake decides to tell each customer in dramatic detail the story about how this snake had climbed up his pump and he mistook its tail for the nozzle of the pump hose. Hence, each customer has to suffer through an agonizing 24 minutes before Jake finally sends them on their way. We again start observing the station at 8:00 with the first car arriving to an idle pump at 8:04. Jake completes the service at 8:28. In the meantime, the second car has already arrived at the station at 8:19. It has to wait till 8:28 for the service on the first car to be completed before it gets served in turn. The service on the second car is completed at 8:52. By then, a third and a fourth car have arrived at 8:34 and 8:49. Service on the third car begins at 8:52 and ends at 9:16, well after the fifth car has joined the queue of cars waiting. In fact, the number of cars in the queue will slowly but surely increase throughout the day as long as Jake keeps up telling his snake story. No coffee breaks for Jake any more! We conclude that if the service time is longer than the interarrival time, or, equivalently, if the service rate is lower than the arrival rate, the queue length will get larger and larger.

Random Arrival and Service Times

So far both interarrival times and service times were assumed to be constant. What happens when either or both the interarrival times and the service times are random variables, i.e., these times fluctuate randomly? We stick to our previous assumption that the average rate of service is larger than the average rate of arrivals, or that the average service time is smaller than the average interarrival time. We simulated such a system over an 8-hour interval. Figure 16-2 shows graphically how the queue length behaves for three different values of the average service time, s. The average interarrival time is kept the same at $a = 15$ minutes. We also assume that the standard deviations of both random variables are equal to the average times.

Figure 16-2: Queue behaviour for three different average service times and the same arrival pattern with a mean arrival rate of four cars per hour

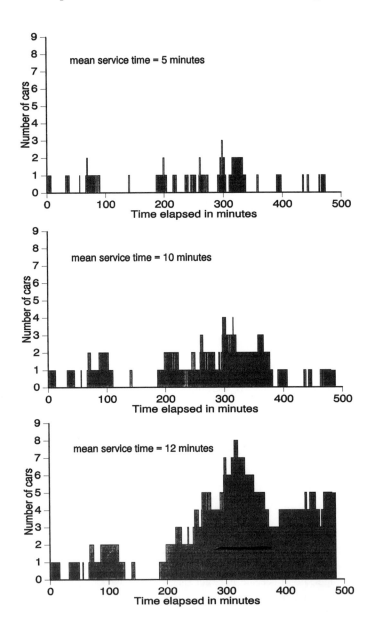

Observe that for $s = 5$, queues occur only on the rare occasion and are usually of no more than 1 or 2 cars. However, as s increases, and gets closer to a, the frequency of queues increases and the length of the queues also tends to increase.

This happens even though, on the average, the service capacity is sufficient to satisfy the service demand. We can compare this with the deterministic case with constant interarrival and service times, where queues only occur if the service capacity is insufficient, but never if the service capacity exceeds the demand for service. Since the deterministic and the stochastic case only differ with respect to the variability in interarrival and service times, the reason for queues forming in the stochastic case can only be attributed to the variability in either or both the interarrival times and the service times. Therefore, we can conclude that, under uncertainty, systems exhibit emergent properties or types of behaviours that are not present in a world of certainty. This is a very important finding.

Another interesting example which you might have experienced yourself is the following. You want to cross a busy highway. If there is a steady flow of cars driving by at equal distances between cars — akin to a constant interarrival time pattern — it may well be impossible to cross the highway safely. However, if cars drive by in a random pattern of inter-distances — some tailgating, others with large distances — sufficiently long breaks between cars will occur for a safe crossing, even if the average number of cars using the highway over a given time interval is the same in both cases.

16.3 FORMULAS FOR SOME SIMPLE QUEUEING MODELS

Mathematical Queueing Models

The study of mathematical models of waiting line systems in known as **Queueing Theory**. Note that *queueing* is supposed to be the word in the English language with the most vowels in a row! Aside from this interesting fact, one of the nice aspects of queueing models is that some of them turn out to have simple formulas for such system characteristics as the mean number of customers in the queue, denoted by L_q, and the mean time that a customer spends in the system, W. If we can determine that one of these theoretical models fits the situation studied reasonably well, then we can use these formulas for studying the performance of the system. This is usually much faster and less costly than determining approximate performance measures by directly observing the operation of the system.

In fact, queues can exhibit such highly variable behaviour patterns that in order to obtain reliable estimates of the mean waiting time and other system characteristics, we may find we have to observe the processing of several thousand arrivals. This may not be possible, both from a technical as well as a cost point of view. Furthermore, if the system studied is still being planned, actual observations are impossible.

The class of simple models we will consider assume that the interarrival times come from a **negative exponential distribution**. That is, that the cumulative distribution function is given by $1 - e^{-\lambda t}$. This distribution is completely specified by a single parameter, the arrival rate, λ, per unit time, e.g., per hour. As we have seen in Jake's gas pump example, the reciprocal of the arrival rate is equal to the average interarrival time, i.e.,

$$15 \text{ minutes } = 1/(4 \text{ customers per hour}), \text{ or } a = 1/\lambda.$$

The standard deviation of a negative exponentially distributed random variable is also equal to a.

For this distribution, very short interarrival times occur more frequently than very long interarrival times. The longer the interarrival time, the less frequently it will occur. When we plot the fraction of interarrival times shorter than a certain time against time (the **sample cumulative distribution**), we get a graph with a slope that becomes less and less positive. This can be used as a rough check that a negative exponential assumption is reasonable. Figure 16-3 plots this for a (small) sample of 40 interarrival times at Jake's service station. Note how there are many more short intervals in the sample than long ones, and hence the typical concave shape to the distribution. The distribution function for a negative exponential random variable with a mean of 15 minutes is also plotted on the graph (the dashed line). While there are statistical **goodness-of-fit** tests available, such as the **Kolmogorov-Smirnov test**, for a more scientific assessment, it appears from the obvious similarity between the two graphs that a negative exponential assumption for the interarrival times at Jake's service station is reasonable.

Figure 16-3: Shape of the negative exponential distribution

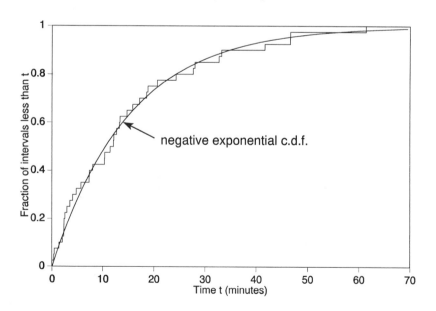

Checking that the assumptions of the mathematical model; the form of the interarrival time distribution, the queue discipline, and the service-time distribution, are reasonable approximations to the characteristics of the actual queue are important steps in validating the mathematical model. In fact because of the highly variable behaviour patterns noted above this may be the only way in which we can validate the model against the actual system.

It turns out that for a surprisingly large number of waiting line situations, a negative exponential distribution is a very good approximation for the interarrival times. This is particularly the case if arrivals are generated independently of each other, such as for instance individual customers or clients requesting some service, or individual machines breaking down.

The most basic queueing model assumes that the service times also follow a negative exponential distribution, with service rate μ, or a mean service time of $s = 1/\mu$. Although this may be an adequate first approximation for some cases, service times more often follow a less variable distribution. Fortunately, the formulas for several important system characteristics of a basic class of models remain valid even if we allow the service time distribution to be of a more general form.

Formulas for the M/G/1 Queue.

A very useful class of queueing models is described by the shorthand notation of M/G/1, where 'M', short for '**Markovian**', refers to the fact that the time between arrivals comes from a negative exponential distribution with rate λ, the service times come from any positive probability distribution with mean s and variance σ_s^2, (i.e., a General service time distribution whose exact form does not need to be specified), and there is a single server.

The formulas listed below assume that the system has been running for a long time. This means that the system is **in steady-state**, i.e., the state of the system no longer depends on the **initial state** of the system, such as how many customers were present at the start. The system's characteristics calculated from these formulas are then valid representations of the long-run behaviour of the system. Note that we are not saying that the waiting time and queue lengths are no longer changing over time, simply that the means of their distributions have stopped changing.

The mean number of customers in the queue will be given by:

$$L_q = \frac{\lambda^2 \sigma_s^2 + (\lambda s)^2}{2(1 - \lambda s)} \qquad \text{provided } \lambda s < 1 \quad (16\text{-}1)$$

λs is called the **traffic intensity**. It can also be interpreted as the fraction of time that the server is busy, and for this class of models as the probability that an arriving customer will have to wait. As was true for the deterministic case in Section 16.2, the traffic intensity has to be smaller than 1, or else the queue will continue to grow indefinitely. Hence, we have the condition that λs must be less than one. Rewriting this condition as $\lambda < 1/s = \mu$, we can see that it is just the condition of requiring that the arrival rate be less than the service rate.

Expression (16-1) rather nicely illustrates a couple of points that, in fact, hold for more models than just the M/G/1 class:

1. The mean queue length (and the other operating characteristics) increase hyperbolically (i.e., like $1/(1-x)$) as the traffic intensity approaches 1.

2. The average queue length (and hence the average delay, as we will show below) depends not only on how busy the server is, but also on how variable the service process is. Thus, for a given traffic intensity we can decrease the average delay by reducing the variability of the service time. Fast food operations, for example, make explicit use of this by limiting the range (and hence variability in preparation time) of the items they sell. The same is also approximately true for arrival processes — the more variable the interarrival times, the longer the average waiting time.

L, the mean number of customers in the system, can be found from:

$$L = L_q + \lambda s \qquad (16\text{-}2)$$

This follows from noting that the mean number of customers in the system must be the sum of the mean number in the queue and the mean number in service — and that the latter is equal to the traffic intensity.

The mean time that a customer spends in the queue, W_q, and the mean time that a customer spends in the system, W, can be found from **Little's Formulas**, which hold for a large number of queueing models:

$$L = \lambda W \qquad (16\text{-}3)$$

$$L_q = \lambda W_q \qquad (16\text{-}4)$$

An elementary proof of Little's Formulas is given in the example below.

Finally, the mean time a customer spends in the system is the sum of the mean time spent waiting in the queue and the mean service time, so:

$$W = W_q + s \qquad (16\text{-}5)$$

An Example

Consider the operation of a small container port. It has only one dock with a single container crane. Hence, only one ship can be unloaded and loaded at the same time. Other container ships arriving while the dock is occupied will have to wait their turn until the dock becomes free. Suppose that a container ship arrives at the port, on average, every five days, i.e., $a = 5$. This implies that the arrival rate is $\lambda = 1/5$ ships per day. It takes $s = 4$ days to unload and load a ship. The standard deviation of the service time is $\sigma = 2$ days. To use the above formulas, we check first that the traffic intensity is indeed less than one: $\lambda s = (1/5).4 = 0.8 < 1$. Since it is, a good estimate of the mean number of ships in the queue is given by expression (16-1):

$$L_q = [(0.2)^2 2^2 + (0.8)^2] / [2(1 - 0.8)] = 2.0,$$

and $$L = 2 + 0.2(4) = 2.8.$$

The average time in days that a ship spends waiting in the queue for the dock to become free can be calculated from expression (16-5) as

$$W_q = L_q / \lambda = 2.0 / 0.2 = 10 \text{ days,}$$

while the average time a ship is in the system, i.e., waiting or being unloaded and loaded, is $W = W_q + s = 10 + 4 = 14$ days.

Suppose that it costs \$8,000 per day to operate a ship while in port. Hence, each ship calling into port incurs a total cost of (\$8,000) multiplied by the mean time a ship spends in the system, W, or (\$8,000)14 = \$112,000. Another measure of interest is the average daily cost of the ships in port. This is given by (\$8,000) times the mean number of ships in port, L, or (\$8,000)2.8 = \$22,400. Both these costs seem to be rather high. Hence, the port operator may wish to increase the unloading and loading capacity, by either installing a second crane on the dock or replacing the current crane with another one of a higher capacity. Verify that if the mean time to service a ship is reduced from 4 days to 2 days with a standard deviation of 1 day, the new system's characteristics are $L = 0.5667$ and $W = 2.8333$. Both measures are reduced substantially. The average cost in port per ship falls to only (\$8,000)(2.83-33) = \$22,667, while the average daily cost of ships in port falls to (\$8,000)(0.5667) = \$4533. A doubling of the service rate results in an almost five-fold decrease in these costs. We see that the performance measures are quite sensitive to changes in the service rate relative to the arrival rate.

We can use this example to demonstrate a proof of Little's Formulas, expressions (16-3) and (16-4). First consider (16-3). We just established above that the average daily cost of ships waiting or being serviced in port is (\$8,000)L. On the other hand your friend works it out this way. Each ship spends an average of W days in port. On any given day, we expect on average λ ships to arrive, each of which is going to spend W days in port. Hence the additional cost, considering only that day's average number of arrivals, is (\$8,000)$W\lambda$. But this must also be the daily cost of all ships in port. Well both arguments are right. Equating the answers, they produce expression (16-3).

16.4 THE NEW ZEALAND FOREST PRODUCTS WEIGHBRIDGE CASE

Description of the System

Every year some 2,500,000 m^3 of cut logs are transported from the forest to a pulp mill operated by the New Zealand Forest Products Company (NZFP). The cartage is done by trucks owned by private contractors. Every truck has to enter the NZFP complex over a single-lane weighbridge. The weight of wood carried forms the basis of the payments to the contractors. The weighing records are also used to monitor fellings in the forest.

When the complex is busy, more than 400 truck-loads per day pass over the bridge. A truck must come to a complete halt on the weighbridge while it is weighed and documents are checked. If a truck arrives to find the weighbridge empty it drives straight onto it. If the weighbridge is already occupied, the next truck in line stops some distance from the weighbridge and, for safety reasons, is only allowed to proceed onto the weighbridge when the preceding truck has completely cleared the weighbridge. A truck forced to wait, therefore, loses additional time by having to drive onto the weighbridge as a separate movement. The resulting move-up time has the effect of slowing down the rate of progress of trucks over the weighbridge. As a result, waiting times observed in 1989 sometimes exceeded 20 minutes per truck. This worried management: had the weighbridge reached its saturation point?

Various options to alleviate this problem were considered. One option was to build a second weighbridge in parallel with the existing bridge. Trucks would form a single queue and move to the first available weighbridge. It is important to note that the weighbridge forms a relatively small component in a very expensive complex, which must be kept supplied at all costs.

Data Collection and System's Parameter Estimation

For analyzing this situation, we needed some data on the movement of trucks. For two days we observed the weighbridge, starting at 5.30 a.m. until the last load was allowed across at 5 p.m. The arrival time, the time of entering the weighbridge and the time of leaving it were recorded for each load. Table 16-2 reproduces a small sample of the data collected. The three numbers listed in each column are the hour, minute, and second at which the corresponding event occurred.

For load 100 the truck was able to drive straight onto the bridge. This follows from the 'arrival time' being equal to the 'time of entry'. Its weighing time was 1 minute 59 seconds — the difference between 'time of leaving' and 'time of entry'. Load 101 arrived 49 seconds after load 100, while that load was still being weighed. Hence, it had to wait for 1 minute 10 seconds for the weighbridge to become available — the difference between 'time of leaving' for load 100 and the 'arrival time' for load 101. It then took the truck 26 seconds to move onto the weighbridge — 'time of entry' less the 'time of leaving' for load 100. Its weighing time was 2 minutes 4 seconds.

Working in this way we can compile a list of interarrival times, move-up times, and weighing times. The averages and variances of these are estimates of the required parameters of the interarrival time and service time distributions.

Table 16-2: A sample of weighbridge observations

Load Number	Arrival Time	Time of Entry	Time of Leaving
..	...	...	...
100	8 22 53	8 22 53	8 24 52
101	8 23 42	8 25 18	8 27 22
102	8 24 45	8 27 56	8 28 36
103	8 26 13	8 28 53	8 29 45
104	8 29 11	8 29 59	8 31 44
105	8 31 09	8 32 08	8 34 34
106	8 36 16	8 36 16	8 37 23
107	8 36 43	8 37 43	8 38 38
...	...	...	...

Generalizing the M/G/1 Formulas to the Weighbridge Problem

Note that the mean and standard deviation of the interarrival times of trucks at the weighbridge are in the same ball park. If truck arrivals are independent of each other, then a mean and standard deviation that are equal or very close in value is a good indication that the interarrival times come from a negative exponential distribution — in this case with rate $\lambda = 1/1.6782 = 0.5959$. Statistical tests confirmed that a negative exponential distribution gave an acceptable approximation for the interarrival times. This discovery certainly increased our confidence in the use of an M/G/1 queueing model for the current operation of a single weighbridge.

Table 16-3: Weighbridge parameters

	Mean (minutes)	Standard deviation
Interarrival Time	1.6782	1.7459
Move-up Time	0.3323	0.2735
Weighing Time	1.2070	0.7309

However there are a couple of places where the system deviates seriously from the assumptions of the M/G/1 model.

1. The weighbridge starts from empty each morning. Hence, the first few trucks tend to experience very small delays. On the other hand, the W_q obtained from the M/G/1 model assumes the system is in steady state. The true average waiting time per truck over the day will therefore be slightly lower than the theoretical steady-state W_q.

2. Trucks arriving when the weighbridge is occupied take some time to move on
to the weighbridge. In some sense the move-up time can be considered as part
of the service delay. However, incurring this additional service delay depends
on whether the bridge is 'free' or not. 'Not free' is taken to mean that a truck
occupies the weighbridge or a truck is moving up Hence, we cannot assume that
the service times are all drawn from the same probability distribution, independent of the state of the queue.

We can analyze the effect that this will cause by considering the weighbridge as
a feedback loop, as described in Chapter 3. (You may wish to review Section 3.8 at
this point.) Figure 16-4 redraws the bottom part of Figure 3-4 to reflect the case of
the weighbridge.

Figure 16-4: The weighbridge described as a feedback loop

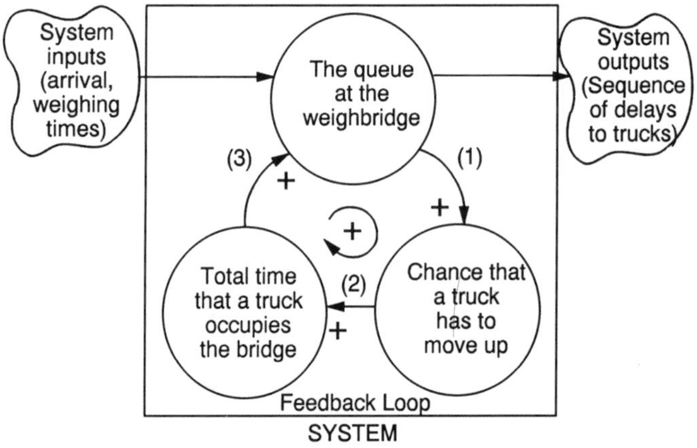

The bigger the queue at the weighbridge, the higher the probability that a truck
will have to come to a complete halt and then move onto the weighbridge (arc 1 in
Figure 16-4). The higher this probability the longer the total time that a truck
occupies the weighbridge (arc 2), and the longer the total time that a truck occupies
the weighbridge, the bigger the queue at the weighbridge will be (arc 3). Thus a
positive change in any of these elements causes a positive effect on the next element
in the loop, as indicated by the 'plus' signs on each arc of the loop. Since all of the
effects are of the same sign the entire loop is clearly a positive feedback loop. As
a queue starts to build up, the process generating the waiting times moves into a
more unstable state, producing longer waiting times, which is only terminated when
the weighbridge becomes idle.

How can we relate the actual characteristics of the weighbridge to those of the
M/G/1 model? Recall that the traffic intensity represents the fraction of customers

who will wait. i.e.:

Fraction of customers waiting = Traffic intensity = λs

In the weighbridge case, the average service time s could be viewed as the average service delay a truck incurs for stopping at the weighbridge. This consists of the average weighing time plus the average move-up time for the fraction of trucks that have to wait. Now we use the interpretation of the traffic intensity as the probability that a customer will have to wait, giving:

s = average weighing time + [traffic intensity][average move-up time]   (16-6)

Putting these two expression together and inserting the known values for λ = 0.5959, the average weighing time = 1.207, and the average move-up time = 0.3323, we get:

Traffic intensity = (0.5959)(1.2070 + [traffic intensity]0.3323)

Re-arranging this equation and solving it for the traffic intensity gives a value of 0.8968. As we have just seen, this is also the proportion of trucks that has to wait and incur a move-up time.

Now we consider the second way in which the actual weighbridge deviates from the M/G/1 model. Although an average of 89.68% of all trucks incur a move-up time, whether or not any particular truck is affected depends on the status of the weighbridge at the time of the arrival of that truck. As we have seen, this effect can be modelled as a positive feedback loop, which provides part of the explanation of the high waiting times. What if we simply ignored this and randomly assigned move-up times to trucks in this proportion? Now all the service delays of all trucks can be treated as if they were drawn from the same probability distribution. This is equivalent to removing arc (1) of the positive feedback loop and hence breaks the entire loop. So this modification suggests that the theoretical M/G/1 formula should underestimate the delay. Note that a systems view has told us this quite valuable piece of information without any further mathematical analysis of the model. W e hope that this under-estimate and the over-estimate produced by the start-up effect will partially cancel each other out.

Evaluation of System's Performance Using the Modified M/G/1 Model

We are now ready to determine the values of the parameters for the M/G/1 formulas. Inserting the estimates of Table 16-3 into expression (16-6) we compute s as

$s = 1.2070 + 0.8968(0.3323) = 1.505.$

For the variance of the service times we use the property that the variance of the sum of independently distributed random variables is equal to the sum of their variances. In fact, we use this property twice — once within the square brackets to get the variance for the delay of trucks that wait and a second time to compute the combined weighted average variance of both trucks that drive straight onto the weighbridge and those that wait, with the traffic intensity and its complement serving as the weights:

$$\sigma_s^2 = (1 - 0.8968)(0.7309^2) + .8968[0.7309^2 + 0.2735^2] = .6013.$$

We now have all input parameters needed for evaluating expressions (16-1) and (16-4). We get $L_q = 4.94$, and $W_q = 8.27$ minutes. The latter agrees quite well with the actually observed value of $W_q = 8.94$ minutes over the two days when data was collected.

Because we have a theoretical model which fits the observed system quite well, we can use it to show what the effect of varying some of the system's parameters would be on the system's performance. It is easy to write a short computer program for calculating values of W_q as a function of the arrival rate of loads. These are plotted in Figure 16-5. Note how the mean waiting time increases hyperbolically as the traffic intensity tends to 1. The situation actually recorded in the two-day survey period corresponds to about 411 loads per day.

So it is clear that the weighbridge is dangerously close to its maximum practical capacity. An increase of only 5% in wood requirements and hence truck loads (the upper line in Figure 16-5) will lead to impossibly long waiting times.

Figure 16-5: The effect of arrival rate on waiting times

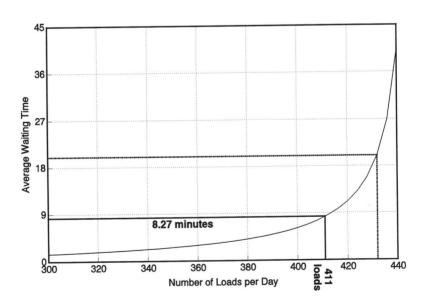

16-5 THE TWO-WEIGHBRIDGE OPTION

The Basic Multi-Server M/M/C Queueing Model

For analyzing the proposed extra weighbridge we will need a theoretical model of a two-server queue. Unfortunately the M/G/2 queue is one of the queueing models which does not have simple formulas for its operating characteristics. If we assume that the service time distribution is also negative exponential with rate parameter μ, however, simple formulas are available for an arbitrary number, C, of servers, i.e., an M/M/C queue. The probability that there are no customers present in the system is:

$$P_0 = \frac{1}{\left[\sum_{n=0}^{C-1} \frac{(\lambda/\mu)^n}{n!} + \frac{(\lambda/\mu)^C}{C!(1-\lambda/C\mu)}\right]} \tag{16-7}$$

Then

$$L_q = \frac{(\lambda/\mu)^{C+1}}{C\ C!(1-(\lambda/C\mu))^2} P_0 \tag{16-8}$$

The other characteristics can again be found from $L_q = \lambda W_q$, and $W = W_q + 1/\mu$.

Expressions (16-7) and (16-8) are quite complex. To evaluate them, especially if they are going to be used repeatedly for sensitivity analysis, the best method is to write a short computer program or spreadsheet macro. The book by Bunday, listed in the references for this chapter, contains programs for this and other models in *Basic*. Alternatively tables of their values are available in many OR/MS books. *Queueing Tables and Graphs*, by F.S. Hillier and O.S. Yu, (Amsterdam: Elsevier/ North Holland, 1979), lists extensive tables for the M/M/C and other queueing models.

The Benefits of Pooling

Before we return to the weighbridge we will use these formulas to demonstrate one of the benefits of theoretical queueing models in a more general case. That is, that they allow us to quantify the effects of alternative system configurations without actually observing the system. The alternative in which we are interested is **pooling**, i.e. combining separate servers into a central facility, as depicted in Figure 16-6.

Is it better to have two single-server queues, each serving a separate stream of arriving customers, or to combine the separate facilities, and the two arrival streams, into a two-server system, each with a single queue? In recent years banks and post offices have moved to the single-queue system. The reason for this is that it avoids the situation where one or more tellers are idle, while other tellers have customers waiting. It appears likely that there would be some benefit in this change, but how large will it be? In Table 16-4 expressions (16-8) and (16-4) have been used to compare the waiting times for the two systems.

Figure 16-6: Two alternative configurations

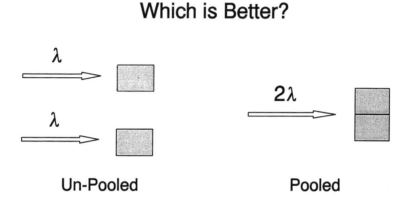

We see that for these models pooling similar service facilities can considerably reduce waiting times, by a factor of about four for low traffic intensities, and by smaller factors when the servers are busier. Provided other factors, such as travel times, or the quality of customer service, are taken into account pooling similar service facilities will always reduce waiting times, often by a considerable amount. (The comparisons in Table 16-4 are valid for any equivalent ratio of λ/μ, even if $\mu \neq 1$.)

Table 16-4: W_q for equivalent un-pooled and pooled systems

W_q (service rate = 1)		
λ	Un-pooled	Pooled
.3	.428	.099
.5	1	.333
.8	4	1.78
0.9	9	4.26

Again this effect can be partially described in terms of feedback loops. In the pooled system, as we move from only one customer in the system to two or more customers present, the service rate will definitely increase as the second server is called into action. Hence the waiting times are partially controlled by a self-regulating negative feedback loop. In the unpooled system the effect will only occur if the customers arrive at the appropriate server, hence the feedback loop may or may not exist.

Evaluation of the Two-Weighbridge Option

Assuming that the service time distribution is also negative exponential implies that the standard deviation of service times is equal to the mean service time. In the weighbridge case, the standard deviation of service times is considerably smaller. From expression (16-1) we see that for the single-server case the larger the standard deviation of service times, the larger the mean queue length and mean waiting time. For multiple-server queues it is also a reasonably safe rule of thumb that the more variable the service process is (i.e., the larger the standard deviation of service times), the greater the average delay. So, using the M/M/2 model will result in overestimating the mean queue length and the mean waiting time. The M/M/2 model provides, therefore, a conservative upper bound on the average delay.

In view of the above reasoning the savings estimated from the M/M/2 model that a second bridge would produce will be smaller than those based on the true variability in service times. The M/M/2 model will thus give a lower bound on the potential savings of a second weighbridge. This is safer than overestimating savings.

Intuitively we should expect that now very few trucks will have to wait. So, our initial approach is to simply ignore the move-up time. If the results confirm that few trucks will wait, then this approximation is suitable. If the fraction of trucks waiting is still significant, then we would have to build a more accurate and hence more complex model.

Using the same arrival rate of $\lambda = 0.5989$ trucks per minute, a service rate of $\mu = 1/1.2070 = 0.8285$, and $S = 2$ servers, the formulas for the M/M/C model give an estimate for W_q of 0.18 minutes. So a good estimate of the minimum reduction in waiting time that will occur if a second weighbridge is built is 8.27 - 0.18 = 8.09 minutes per load. Extrapolated to an average day's number of loads of around 400, this amounts to 400(8.09) minutes or almost 54 hours of truck time per day. This is the equivalent of the workload of about 6 trucks. Hence, the current workload of hauling logs from the forests to the mill could be accomplished by 6 fewer trucks.

Remember that the trucks are paid by the amount of wood hauled. Eliminating most of the time wasted waiting at the weighbridge means that each truck can carry more loads per day. Therefore, NZFP has a good case to negotiate a reduction in the haulage cost per load and still guarantee that each contractor's daily net earnings are at least as high as under the old system. At a running cost of $80 per truck-hour, the reduction in hauling costs for the mill is slightly over one million dollars (54 hours × 250 days × $80) annually. The additional wage bill for staffing the second weighbridge is less than $100,000 per year. The cost of building a second weighbridge is around $400,000. The cost of the second weighbridge can be recovered in the first six months of use. This sounds like a good proposition!

16.6 SOME CONCLUSIONS

It is interesting to see how the models we have used for this problem stack up against the properties of a good model listed in Section 6.3. Certainly they are simple, adaptive, and easy to manipulate. The formulas can easily be evaluated with a small computer program or even a calculator. Do they include all significant aspects of the problem? The assumption that the times between trucks arriving at the weighbridge can be drawn from a negative exponential distribution is critical for the use of simple mathematical models, yet the way the wood transport system operates raises serious questions about the validity of that assumption. In the actual system the trucks each make about 8 round trips per day. Hence it appears that a second weighbridge will change the arrival pattern since the round-trip time will be reduced. The key to resolving this worry is to note that the weighbridge is a very small part of a very expensive mill complex, which must be fed with the required amount of wood at all costs. Hence no matter how the weighbridge operation is altered, the flow of trucks across it will remain dictated by the needs of the mill. Knowing the part that the weighbridge plays in the entire system, we safely conclude that more extensive modeling of the arrival process would be very unlikely to change the recommendation for installing a second weighbridge.

With such great savings, was the second weighbridge built in 1989? The answer is 'no'. As often happens with projects of this sort, by the time the recommendations are submitted to the decision makers or shortly thereafter, other events may change the economic picture. In this case it was a world-wide slump in the demand for newsprint. As a result, the level of operations of the mill was curtailed, reducing the number of daily loads required by the mill slightly. So, the immediate pressure was off. There would be no further increase in wood demand until the market had recovered. The additional bridge was finally built in 1993.

The wood yard manager, however, was able to put Figure 16-5 to good use in presenting a new proposal for a more effective operation of the wood yard in 1989. As Figure 16-5 shows, if the number of loads entering the yard during the time from 5:30 a.m. to 5 p.m. could be reduced to 350, the mean waiting time at the weighbridge decreases to less than 3 minutes. One possible alternative would have been to extend the opening hours of the weighbridge by two hours or so to get the remaining 50 to 60 loads processed during this time. However, that would have required the entire workforce of the wood yard to be present, which would have been rather expensive.

A break-down of the type of wood coming in indicated that about 50 loads per day were thinnings. These were processed at a separate part of the yard employing only two people. The obvious solution was thus to restrict the loads coming in after hours to only thinnings. Hence, the congestion at the weighbridge could be reduced dramatically at a minimum of additional labour cost. Figure 16-5 turned out to be instrumental in judging the merit of this proposal.

EXERCISES

1. A firm operates a 20-tonne crane truck on a job contracting basis. Going through the firm's records over the most recent 100 days shows that 140 requests for jobs were received. They took on average 4 hours or ½ day to execute, including the truck's travel time to the site and back to the yard.
   (a) Define the basic structure for this waiting line system, i.e., what constitutes an arrival, the service facility, and a service.
   (b) If you were to use an M/M/1 model, what assumptions must you make about the arrival and service processes? Indicate why or why not they are reasonable.
   (c) Assume now that the M/M/1 model fits. Find the average number of jobs waiting for the truck, and their average waiting time. What fraction of time is the truck idle? busy?
   (d) If you were to use an M/G/1 model, what assumptions must you make about the arrival and service processes? Are they more likely to be satisfied than those for an M/M/1 model. Why?
   (e) Assume now that the M/G/1 model fits, with a service time standard deviation of 2 hours or ¼ day. Find the average number of jobs waiting for the truck and their average waiting time. What fraction of time is the truck idle? busy?

2. A thermal power station operates its own coal mine. The mine is only a short distance from a barge loading port also owned and operated by the firm. The port consists of one berth with an automatic loading facility which takes 6 hours to load a barge, with a standard deviation of 1.5 hours. Given the distance between the port and the power station, as well as the variable ocean conditions, barges travelling back and forth between the power station and the port arrive at the port in an almost random pattern, with an average of time between arrivals of 10 hours. (The port operates 24 hours/day.)
   (a) Find the fraction of time the port is idle. Compute the average time a barge is in the system, i.e., either waiting or being loaded in port, and the average total time in the system for all barges arriving at the port per day.
   (b) There is a fixed cost of $1200 to operate the port for one day. It costs $1500 to operate a barge for one day. Find the total cost for the port facility, consisting of the port's own operating cost and the cost of the time barges spend in the system.
   (c) The firm is considering upgrading the port's loading facility. The two options available are to decrease the average loading time to 4 hours at a daily operating cost of $1500 or to 3 hours at a daily operating cost of $1800, both with a one-hour standard deviation. Is any one of these options better than the current setup?
   (d) What additional assumption is implicit in your answer to (c)?

3. Consider again exercise 2 above. Assume now that the time to load a barge is deterministic, i.e., the standard deviation of loading times is zero. Re-assess the daily

average cost of each of the three choices of facilities.

4. Compute the average waiting of an arrival for a single-server waiting line system with a service rate of 1 and the following set of arrival rates: 0.1, 0.2, 0.3, 0.4, 0.5, 0.6, 0.7, 0.8, 0.9, 0.95, .099. Show the average waiting times graphically as a function of the arrival rate. (This is a simple 5 minute exercise on a spreadsheet!)

5. Consider exercise 2 again. The power station plans to double its size which will also result in a doubling of the number of barges that will transport coal from the mine to the power station. Management wishes to evaluate three possible options for upgrading the port facilities. Option 1 calls for the building of a second port at a new site that offers easier access and better shelter. This would mean that the firm would operate two separate ports, each handling half of the volume. So barges would arrive at each port on average every 10 hours and each barge would take on average 6 hours to load. The new port would have a daily operating cost of $1000, while the cost of the existing port would remain unchanged. Option 2 calls for the building of a second identical loading facility at the existing port. Barges would arrive on average every 5 hours and then be loaded by the first berth becoming available. However, due to some economies of scale, the two facilities together would have a total daily cost of only $2000. Option 3 calls for the replacement of the current facility by a completely new facility which can load a barge in 3 hours. Its daily cost would be $2000. Barges would again arrive at that facility on average every 5 hours. So, all three options have the same total capacity of being able to load 8 barges per day. Assume that the service times for all three options follow a negative exponential distribution.

   (a) For each option, determine the average time the port facilities would be idle and the total average time in the system of all ships arriving for loading per day. Note that for Option 2 you will have to use expressions (16-7) and (16-8).

   (b) Cost out each option. Which one is the cheapest one?

6. (This problem is a follow on to the weighbridge project with move-up time.) Customers arrive according to a negative exponential distribution at a single-server queue with unlimited waiting space. The mean time between arrivals is two minutes. 30% of the customers require a service of exactly one minute and the remaining 70% require a service of exactly two minutes. The customers are randomly mixed in the arrival stream, i.e., the chance that the next customer will require a service of one minute is always 0.3.

   (a) Calculate the steady-state probability that an arriving customer does not have to wait.

   (b) Calculate the mean number of customers in the queue and the mean time that a customer spends in the system.

7. Consider the TAB problem of Section 1.1 in Chapter 1. Exercise 9 in Chapter 4 asked you to develop an influence diagram depicting which inputs, decisions, and systems variables affected the net profit of the operation. Two of these systems variables are: the number of punters who are successful in placing bets, and the number of punters who are lost to the system (due to busy lines). Can either of these two systems variables be determined on the basis of the formulas listed in this chapter? Why or why not? You need to carefully check whether the assumptions underlying these formulas are approximately satisfied by the TAB situation to answer these questions.

REFERENCES

Gross, D. and C. M. Harris, *Fundamentals of Queueing Theory, Second Edition,* John Wiley, 1985. There has been a vast amount of work on theoretical models for queueing systems. This is the best general reference on them.

Kleinrock, L., *Queueing Systems, Volumes I and II,* Wiley-Interscience, 1975. Another very comprehensive general reference on the theory of queueing models. Many interesting applications of waiting lines are concerned with computer/communications systems. Volume II concentrates on them.

Bunday, B. D., *Basic Queueing Theory,* Edward Arnold, 1986. Easier coverage of the simpler theoretical models than Gross and Harris.

McNickle, D. C., and Woollons, R. C., 'Analysis and simulation of a logging weighbridge installation', *N.Z. J. Forestry Science,* 20, 1990, 111-9. The elementary analysis of the weighbridge.

McNickle, D. C., 'Estimating the average delay of the first N customers in an M/Erlang/1 queue', *Asia-Pacific J. of Operational Research,* 8, 1991, 44-54. The final theory that was actually used.

17 Event Simulation

D. C. McNickle
University of Canterbury, N.Z.

In Chapter 16 we studied systems behaviour under uncertainty with the aid of theoretical mathematical models of waiting-line systems, namely queueing theory. If the problem situation can be captured adequately by fitting a theoretical model to it, this clearly is the preferred approach.   However, there are many problem situations where either no suitable theoretical model exists or the problem is so complex that a theoretical model cannot represent the interrelationships properly. In such cases the management scientist often has recourse to simulation.

What is simulation? *Webster's Ninth Collegiate Dictionary* defines simulation as 'the imitative representation of the functioning of one system or process by means of the functioning of another'.   A film or a play is a simulation.   In OR/MS, simulation is used to explore the dynamic behaviour or operation of complex commercial, industrial, or technical systems or subsystems.   We do this by building a descriptive mathematical model of the system's behaviour over time.   This model would need to include all aspects of the system that have been identified as essential to trace how the state of the system changes over time.   It is then used to record in exact chronological order of **simulated time** (= assumed or imitated time) each and every change in the state of the system that would have occurred had the actual system been operated in **real time** over the same time interval.   At the end of the time interval simulated, various measures for analyzing the performance of the system are computed from the system's state changes. (You may have to read this paragraph again to get its full meaning!)

Would it not be more accurate to observe the real operation directly?   This may be true.   It may though neither be economically, nor technically feasible.   It may take years of actual observations to accumulate reliable performance measures for a given mode of operation, let alone alternative modes.   Any answers derived may be of little or no relevance by then.   Even if observations can be done in a reasonable time interval, this may be too disruptive of the actual operation if alternative decision rules need evaluation.   Finally, the system studied may still be on the drawing board.   The simulation may be done precisely to finalize which of various options should be implemented.

On the other hand, a simulation study may be able to be completed in a few days, weeks, or months, depending on the complexity of the system in question.   For all these reasons, a simulation may be a far more effective approach for studying the problem.

Through simulation the management scientist has at her or his disposal a laboratory technique for experimentation on systems, similar to the experimental methods available in medical, biological, and earth sciences. It is clear that it was the availability of faster and faster computers which allowed simulation to become a powerful OR/MS modelling tool. With the help of ever more friendly computer simulation software, the viability of proposed operating policies for existing and proposed systems can be explored and compared with ease.

This chapter is devoted mainly to one type of simulation, called **event simulation**. Changes in the state of the system are triggered by events, such as the arrival of a customer, the start or end of an activity, and so on. Event simulation is particularly suitable for the study of the dynamic behaviour of complex waiting line situations which are beyond representation by theoretical queueing models.

Event simulation may also be used to verify if a queueing model used for modelling a waiting line situation that does not satisfy all assumptions of the theoretical model is a sufficiently good approximation. For example, in the weighbridge problem we incorporated the move-up time as a random component of the service time and argued that this will tend to slightly underestimate the true waiting times. Any reduction in waiting time for the two-weighbridge option would therefore be on the conservative side. A simulation that models the move-up time properly could be used to verify if our argument is correct.

Section 17.1 demonstrates how a simulation is executed. The example used is the weighbridge problem. Nowhere in OR/MS modelling is the systems view as evident as in simulation. Section 17.2 uses systems concepts to look at the basic structure of event simulation. Section 17.3 discusses some strategic and tactical aspects of running simulations. Section 17.4 briefly describes other types of simulation approaches, such as fixed-time updating and risk analysis. The last section discusses some of the pitfalls of simulation.

17.1 THE WEIGHBRIDGE PROBLEM REVISITED

This section will demonstrate the process of simulation. We will use the original situation for one weighbridge. With simulation there is no need to approximate the move-up process. We can easily model the real-life situation.

A Detailed Record of Processing Trucks at the Weighbridge

Table 17-1 is a detailed reconstruction of how the first 20 trucks arriving at the weighbridge on a given day were processed. (Ignore for the time being columns 9 through 12 of the table.) All times are expressed in seconds of time elapsed since the opening of the weighbridge. The first truck apparently is more or less waiting when the weighbridge opens. Its 'arrival time' is recorded as '2' seconds (column 1). Since the weighbridge is unoccupied, there is no 'move-up time' (columns 2 and

Table 17-1: Simulation of truck processing over weighbridge

Column	1	2	3	4	5	6	7	8	9	10	11	12
Truck arriving	Arrival time	Move-up starts	Move-up time	Weighing starts	Weighing time	Weighing ends	Time in system	Waiting time	Interar-rival time	Random number	Random number	Random number
1	2			2	38	40	38	0	2	0.0166	0.0474	0.1064
2	23	40	61	101	59	160	137	78	21	0.1916	0.9531	0.3418
3	87	160	60	220	78	298	211	133	64	0.4706	0.951	0.5582
4	238	298	10	308	30	338	100	70	151	0.7756	0.4001	0.0113
5	506			506	54	560	54	0	268	0.9297	0.6985	0.2832
6	568			568	98	666	98	0	62	0.4603	0.8185	0.7864
7	584	666	28	694	48	742	158	110	16	0.1468	0.7524	0.2143
8	707	742	15	757	90	847	140	50	123	0.7059	0.5264	0.6932
9	717	847	22	869	82	951	234	152	10	0.0963	0.6721	0.6023
10	731	951	38	989	85	1074	343	258	14	0.1276	0.8513	0.6435
11	828	1074	16	1090	92	1182	354	262	97	0.6181	0.5496	0.7197
12	832	1182	13	1195	107	1302	470	363	4	0.0434	0.4808	0.8895
13	1308			1308	89	1397	89	0	476	0.9911	0.8391	0.6838
14	1387	1397	5	1402	53	1455	68	15	79	0.5412	0.2189	0.2785
15	1432	1455	42	1497	58	1555	123	65	45	0.3571	0.8806	0.3362
16	1435	1555	19	1574	77	1651	216	139	3	0.0259	0.62	0.5482
17	1442	1651	60	1711	115	1826	384	269	7	0.0627	0.9505	0.9785
18	1623	1826	9	1835	91	1926	303	212	181	0.8337	0.3561	0.7126
19	1867	1926	11	1937	74	2011	144	70	244	0.9114	0.4248	0.5106
20	1901	2011	9	2020	73	2093	192	119	34	0.2894	0.3669	0.5002
Average			26.13		74.55		192.8	118.25	95.05			

3 are blank). 'Weighing starts' immediately at time '2' (column 4). The 'weighing time' is 38 seconds (column 5), hence 'weighing ends' at time '40' (column 6), and truck 1 leaves the weighbridge, i.e., leaves the system. Truck 2 arrives at time '23'. It finds the weighbridge occupied, hence it has to wait until truck 1 leaves the weighbridge at time '40'. At time '40', the truck starts moving up to the weighbridge (column 2). This takes 61 seconds (column 3). As a result, weighing starts at time [40 + 61] or '101' (column 4). Weighing takes 59 seconds and truck 2 vacates the weighbridge at time '160'. In the meantime, truck 3 arrived at time '87', finds the weighbridge occupied, waits until time '160', when it starts moving onto the weighbridge, and so on.

I suggest you check your understanding of the process by verifying the various times for the next 4 or 5 trucks. Note that trucks 5 and 6 find no trucks ahead of them and hence do not occur any move-up times.

Column 7 records the total time each truck spends in the system, i.e., the difference between its departure time from the weighbridge and its arrival time. Column 8 shows the unproductive time each truck waits in the queue and moves up to the weighbridge. The time truck 1 spends in the system is simply equal to its weighing time, namely 38 seconds. Its unproductive time is zero. Truck 2 spends 78 seconds of unproductive time, namely the entry in column 4 minus the entry in column 1. Its total time in the system is 137 seconds.

These detailed records allow us to determine some overall measures of performance. For example, the average of column 7 tells us that each truck spends on average 192.8 seconds in the system. 118.25 of this is either waiting in the queue or moving up to the weighbridge (average of column 8). The weighbridge was busy 71.2 % of the time. The latter figure is the ratio of the 'weighing ends' entry for truck 20 and the sum of the weighing times of all 20 trucks.

Generating Random Events

So far we assumed that columns 1 through 8 of Table 17-1 were a reconstruction of how the first 20 trucks arriving after 5:30 a.m. on a given day were processed over the weighbridge. For this reconstruction we needed an exact record of arrival times, move-up times, and weighing times for each truck.

What if we do not have such detailed records, but only have summary statistics on the arrival and processing pattern as shown in Table 16-3 of Chapter 16? Could we construct a table similar to columns 1 through 8 of Table 17-1, that represents a good imitation of what might happen at the weighbridge at the start of a typical day? The answer is 'yes'. All we need is a method for generating for each truck an artificial but typical triplet of times consisting of an interarrival time, move-up time, and service time. These times should be consistent with what we know about their corresponding probability distributions. This is what simulation is all about! It is simply an imitation of the real process, based on artificially created times for the various activities and events that typically occur in the real thing.

How do we generate such artificial activity and event times? With the aid of

random numbers. Random numbers are lists of the digits from 0 to 9, such as would be obtained by repeatedly drawing one ball at random from an urn that contains ten balls numbered 0 to 9. Each ball drawn is immediately returned to the urn after its number has been recorded, and the balls thoroughly mixed before the next draw.

We may need many thousands of random numbers for a single simulation, so sequences of numbers that have similar statistical properties to those of random numbers are usually produced by a computer program, a so-called **random number generator.** Since all computer systems now-a-days contain at least one random number generator in their library of subroutines or procedures, there is little need for you to know the details of the computations involved. All modern spreadsheet programs have a function that generates a random number, expressed as a decimal fraction between 0.000000 and .999999. Columns 10, 11, and 12 of Table 17-1 are lists of 25 such **random decimal fractions** each, rounded to 4 significant digits. In EXCEL, LOTUS 1-2-3, and Quattro Pro the random decimal fractions are generated by the function RAND.

Random decimal fractions can be transformed into random numbers that have any desired distribution — so-called **random variates or deviates.** Consider the weighing times at the weighbridge. According to Table 16-3, the weighing time has a mean of $\mu = 1.21$ minutes or 72.6 seconds and a standard deviation of $\sigma = 0.73$ or 43.8 seconds. Assume that the weighing time is normally distributed. Then the first random decimal fraction listed in column 12, $u = .1064$, can be transformed into a normal random variate v as follows:

$$v = \mu + z_{u\text{-}0.5}\, \sigma \tag{17-1}$$

$$= 72.6 + z_{(0.1064\text{-}0.5)}\ (43.8) = 72.6 + (-1.25)(43.8) = 17.85,$$

where $z_{u\text{-}0.5}$ is the z-value from the normal distribution table corresponding to the table entry $u\text{-}0.5$. (Remember that if $u\text{-}0.5$ is negative, then you look up the z-value for the absolute value of $u\text{-}0.5$ and make the z-value negative. This is the case in the above example. Since $0.1064\text{-}0.5 = -0.3936 < 0$, we look up the z-value closest to 0.3936, which is 1.25. Hence, $z_{(-0.3936)} = -1.25$. The z-value measures how many standard deviations the value of the normal variable is away from the mean, either in a positive or a negative direction.) EXCEL has a function, called NORMINV which performs this transformation for you.

For some probability distributions, the transformation can be done algebraically. For example, a random variate that is uniformly distributed over the range of, say, $a = 28.8$ and $b = 116.4$ seconds, can be produced as follows, using again the first random decimal fraction listed in column 12, $u = .1064$:

$$v = a + u(b\text{-}a) \tag{17-2}$$

$$= 28.8 + .1064(116.4\text{-}28.8) = 38.12 \text{ seconds.}$$

Sometimes we may have an empirical frequency distribution, compiled from observations of an actual process. In such instances, the preferred approach is to use this distribution directly for generating random variates, rather than some theoretical approximation to it. Assume that we have the following frequency distribution:

Observed value	0	1	2	3	4
Frequency	0.23	0.39	0.19	0.13	0.06
Cumulative frequency	0.23	0.62	0.81	0.94	1.00

Say, the random decimal fraction to be transformed has the value $u = 0.7692$. We find the first cumulative frequency which is just larger than 0.7692. This is 0.81 in the above list. Its corresponding observed value is 2. This is the random variate associated with u. Had u been equal to 0.8100, then according to the above rule, 0.94 would have been the cumulative frequency just larger than 0.8100, with an associated random variate of 3.

Figure 17-1 depicts this transformation graphically. It shows the graph of the cumulative frequency distribution for the above example. Note that the vertical axis goes from 0 to 1, while the horizontal axis lists the values of the random variate. We first locate the point on the vertical axis corresponding to the random decimal fraction (0.7692), then go across until we meet the graph. Next we drop a vertical

Figure 17-1: The Cumulative Distribution Function

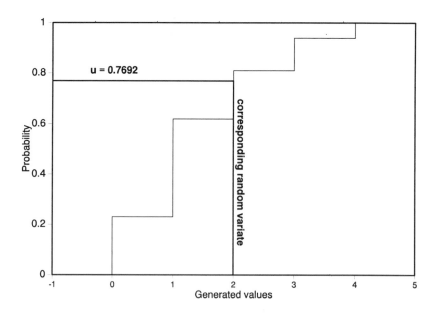

line down to the horizontal axis. This will identify the corresponding value of the random variate. Because we use the graph in this inverted way the method is known as the **inverse transform method**. It is the basis of most methods for generating random variates from empirical distributions, as well as from discrete probability distributions. EXCEL has Macro functions for inverse transformations of this sort.

In this example the random variate had only three possible values, but clearly the same look-across and then look-down process would apply to distributions with more values, and even, in the limit, to continuous distributions. For a few specific random variables, notably negative exponentials, the mathematical inverse of the distribution function is known. Suppose that we want to produce random variates from a negative exponential distribution with mean a, and u is the random decimal fraction we have generated. Then the value of the random variate which we produce is v, where

$$u = 1 - e^{-v/a}$$

or
$$v = a[-ln(1-u)] \qquad (17\text{-}3)$$

ln denotes the natural logarithm to the base e. Thus a simple logarithmic operation transforms a random decimal fraction into a random variate with a negative exponential distribution. Figure 17-2 illustrates this process for generating the interarrival times of trucks at the weighbridge.

According to Table 16-3, the mean interarrival time of trucks at the weighbridge is $a = 1.68$ minutes or 100.8 seconds. So, applying expression (17-3) to the same random decimal fraction as before, 0.7692, produces an interarrival time of 147.79 seconds, as depicted in Figure 17-2. You should check your understanding by verifying that the first random decimal fraction in column 10 of Table 17-1 (0.0166) transforms into an interarrival time of 1.69 seconds.

Most computer system subroutine libraries allow the user to specify a so-called **starting seed** for the random number generator — so-to-speak the first n-digit random decimal fraction used to start off the sequence of random numbers generated. It is though important to realize that for a given starting seed and generator, exactly the same sequence of random numbers will be generated. Most spreadsheets, for example, have a built-in starting seed. So every new session when the spreadsheet is started up will always begin with the same seed. As a result it will produce exactly the same sequence of random numbers each time. This is obviously a serious trap for the unwary, although as we shall see in Section 17-3, there are situations where this can have considerable modelling benefits.

Simulating the Weighbridge Operation

For each truck we have to generate an interarrival time, a move-up time if the truck has to wait, and a weighing time. Table 16-2 shows that the standard deviations of the truck interarrival times and move-up times are very close to their corresponding averages. If this is the case and each occurrence is independent of all other events,

Figure 17-2: The Inverse Transform for a Negative Exponential Distribution

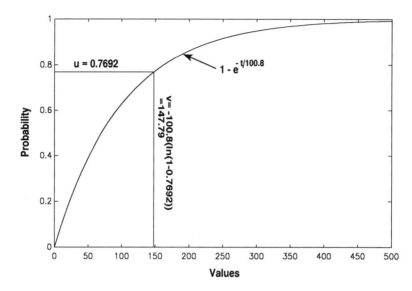

then the negative exponential distribution is often a good approximation. The inter-arrival time is thus assumed to have a negative exponential distribution with a mean of 1.68 minutes or 100.8 seconds, while the mean move-up time has a negative exponential distribution with a mean of 0.33 minutes or 19.8 seconds. (Note that for the negative exponential we use the observed means as the only parameters of the distributions, since the standard deviations are equal to the corresponding means!)

The weighing time, on the other hand, seems to follow a different, but unknown distribution. A tempting choice would be an approximation by a normal distribution with a mean of 1.21 minutes or 72.6 seconds and a standard deviation of 0.73 minutes or 43.8 seconds. However, given the relatively large standard deviation in comparison to the mean, very small random decimal fractions could easily result in negative weighing times, which is impossible. So we have to choose a different ap-proximating distribution.

In a real application, the preferred approach would be the compilation of an empirical frequency distribution, based on a sample of some 100 observed weighing times. It would then be used directly to generate corresponding random variates, as depicted in Figure 17-1. Since we ultimately wish to use a spreadsheet for simulating the weighbridge problem, such an approach is computationally rather demanding. Hence, we will use a somewhat rough approximation, based on a uniform distribution. The range is chosen to correspond to $a = \mu - \sigma = 72.6 - 43.8 = 28.8$ and $b = \mu + \sigma = 72.6 + 43.8 = 116.4$ seconds, i.e., one standard deviation on either side of the mean. Although the true distribution is likely to be skewed, with a fairly long tail for high values, this approximation should   underestimate the average waiting times. From a modelling point of view this is preferable. We do not want to represent the current situation as worse than it is in reality, and thereby produce a bias in favour of a change.

Consider again Table 17-1. The simulation starts at simulated time '0'. We now generate the first arrival. For this we need an interarrival time. For the first truck this is the time between the start of the simulation and the truck's arrival time. We use the random decimal fractions in column 10 to generate interarrival times. The first entry in column 10 is 0.0166. This is the number you used above in expression (17-3) to generate a random variate from a negative exponential distribution. You got a time of 1.69 seconds, which is rounded to the nearest integer. So the first interarrival time is 2 seconds. This is the entry shown in column 9. Hence truck 1 arrives 2 seconds after the start of the simulation (the entry in column 1). Since the weighbridge is empty, no move-up time has to be generated. The next random variate needed is the one for the weighing time of truck 1. We use the random decimal fractions in column 12 for that. The first entry is 0.1064, which we used above in expression (17-2) for demonstrating how to generate a uniformly distributed random variate in the range of 28.8 to 116.4. We got a time of 38.12 seconds, which we round to 38 (entry in column 5).

We now create the arrival of the second truck. Using the second entry in column 10, 0.1916, expression (17-3) gives an interarrival time of $100.8(-ln(1-0.1916)) = 21.44$ seconds which we round to 21 (column 9). Truck 2 arrives at simulated time $[2 + 21] = 23$ seconds (column 1). It has to wait. So, we now generate a move-up time from a negative exponential distribution with mean 19.8 seconds, using the random decimal fractions listed in column 11. The second entry in column 11, 0.9531, by expression (17-3), transforms into a move-up time of $19.8(-ln(1-0.9531)) = 60.58$ seconds which is rounded to 61 seconds (the entry in column 3). Note that if a truck does not have a move-up time, we simply skip the random decimal fraction reserved for this calculation in column 11. This was the case for truck 1. The second entry in column 12, 0.3398, gives a weighing time of $28.8 + 0.3398(116.4 - 28.8) = 58.57$ or 59 seconds (column 5).

This process continues until the simulation is stopped. To test your understanding verify the generation of random variates in the simulation for another few arrivals. In this example, the simulation was stopped after 25 truck arrivals. A more common **stopping rule** is to run the simulation until the simulated time reaches a specified time, such as a whole working day for the weighbridge problem. Table 17-1 is in fact the first 40 minutes of simulating a full working day at the weighbridge by a spreadsheet. So the lists of random decimal fractions in columns 10 to 12 were produced by the random number function of a spreadsheet program.

17.2   THE STRUCTURE OF SIMULATION MODELS

In the terminology of event simulation, the components of the system are called **entities**. An event simulation traces the behaviour of entities through the system.

There may be several types or **classes of entities**, such as people, machines, goods, or pieces of information, interacting with each other. For example, consider the simulation of a job shop, where various jobs arrive for processing on one or a sequence of machines. The sequence may be different from job to job. The jobs form one class of entities. Each group of interchangeable machines forms another class of entities.

Some types of entities may be **permanent**, such as the machines in the job shop. They remain part of the system throughout the entire simulation run. Others are **temporary** entities, such as the jobs. They are created at the time they arrive and then cancelled or destroyed at the time they have finished all processing.

Entities engage in **activities**. For example, a job and a machine engage jointly in an activity, separate, and then may join another entity for a new activity, or become idle (for machines) or leave the system (for jobs).

The exact sequence of processing a given job in the job shop example is called an **attribute** of the job. This is an example of a permanent attribute. The machine on which a job is processed at any given point in simulated time is another attribute of the job — a temporary attribute in this case, since it changes once the processing at that machine ceases. Machines also have permanent and temporary attributes, such as the speed of processing, and whether a machine is idle or busy.

At any given point in simulated time, the system has a given configuration, defined by the ongoing activities of the entities and the value(s) of the various temporary attributes of each entity. This is the **state** of the simulated system. A change in the state of the system is referred to as an **event**. For instance, in the job shop system the arrival of a new job, the start of processing a job on a machine, or the end of processing a job on a machine, are all events.

Some events may be imposed on the system from outside, i.e., they may be specified as an input into the system by the analyst. A typical example is the event that causes the simulation to stop, such as the value of the simulated time signalling the end of the simulation run. Other events are generated by the simulation itself, either by the completion of an activity or by another event. For example, in the job shop the event 'machine X starts processing job K' may be the consequence of the event 'machine X finishes job L', with job K waiting for processing at machine X (a temporary attribute of job K) or the event 'job K arrives at machine X', with machine X being idle at that time (a temporary attribute of machine X).

The Weighbridge Simulation Structure

The weighbridge is a permanent entity. The weighing time distribution is its permanent attribute, while 'waiting for a truck to move-up' and being 'busy' are its temporary attributes. The trucks are temporary entities. Their permanent attribute is their arrival pattern, as indicated by the interarrival time distribution. 'Waiting in the queue', 'moving-up', or 'being weighed' are their temporary attributes.

Trucks engage in three activities. They 'arrive', 'move-up', and are 'being weighed'. The weighbridge engages in one activity only, namely 'weighing'.

However, it is standing by while a truck 'moves-up'. During that time the weighbridge is blocked — a sort of pseudo-activity it goes through if a truck has been 'waiting' when it finished a 'weighing'. A truck engages in the activities 'arriving' singly, while for 'moving-up' and 'weighing' it also requires the presence of another entity, namely the weighbridge. So a truck and the weighbridge engage jointly in the activities 'moving-up' and 'weighing'. The events are 'the arrival of a truck', 'the start of moving-up', 'the end of moving-up', 'the start of weighing', and 'the end of weighing'. So, most events are associated with the start or end of an activity. There are two more events present in each simulation, namely 'the start' and 'the end of the simulation'.

Some activities and events can only occur if the state of the system satisfies a given condition. For example, the activity 'moving-up' can only start when two conditions are satisfied, namely a truck must be waiting and the event 'weighing has been completed'. On the other hand, once the truck has completed 'moving-up', it and the weighbridge unconditionally engage in the joint activity 'weighing'.

Entity Life Cycles

Each type of entity goes through a sequence of activities and changes of temporary state attributes. For example, a truck first 'arrives', 'waits in the queue', if the weighbridge is 'busy' or 'waiting for a truck to complete moving up'. Sooner or later the truck 'moves up', followed immediately by 'being weighed', and finally leaves the system. Alternatively, if a truck arrives while the weighbridge is in state 'idle', it goes through 'wait in the queue' without stopping and immediately engages in 'being weighed', and then leaves. So each truck goes through a **life cycle** of activities and inactivities or queues. This can be depicted graphically. Figure 17-3 shows the two paths for the truck life cycle. Activities are depicted as rectangles and queues as circles. The source and the sink of temporary entities are depicted as clouds.

This entity cycle diagram has a special feature, namely alternative paths that a truck could take, depending on whether or not the weighbridge is 'free' at the time of its arrival. A diamond is used to depict this switching mechanism. (Note that different authors may use different diagramming conventions.)

The entity weighbridge also has a life cycle, as shown in Figure 17-4. Since it is a permanent entity it repeats that life cycle for each truck it processes. As for trucks, the path involves a switch, depending on whether or not the queue of trucks is empty. Say the weighbridge is 'idle' which can only happen if no trucks are 'waiting in the queue'. Then it remains 'idle' until a truck 'arrives'. At that point the weighbridge engages in 'weighing' (right-hand side of diagram) and then returns to the switch. If in the meantime one or more trucks have 'arrived' and are 'waiting in the queue', then the switch sends the weighbridge onto the left-hand path where it first 'waits for truck to complete move-up', after which it 'weighs' the truck, and returns again back to the switch for a new cycle.

Note that we show 'idle' as a queue. If there is only one weighbridge, it may

Figure 17-3: Life cycle diagram for truck entities

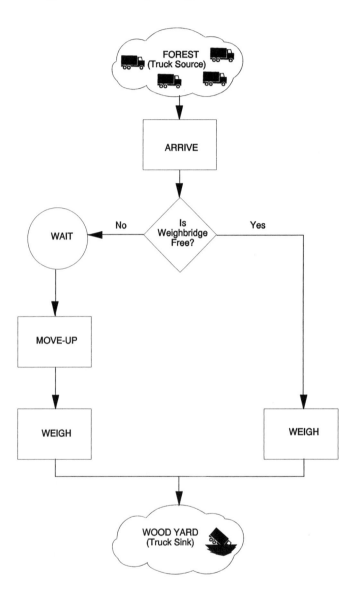

not seem so obvious that 'idle' has the nature of a queue.   In state 'idle' the
weighbridge is waiting for a truck to arrive.   If there are several weighbridges that
could be in the state 'idle', it becomes immediately clear that this is in fact a queue
structurally no different from the queue 'wait' for trucks.

To show the interactions between the two types of entities we combine the two

Figure 17-4: Life cycle of weighbridge

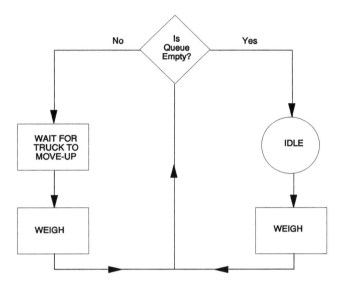

life cycles, such that they coincide for activities engaged in jointly by a truck and
the weighbridge. This is shown in Figure 17-5. Since 'moving-up' and 'waiting for
truck to complete move-up' always occur in parallel, in other words jointly, nothing
is lost by referring to both as 'moving-up'. The two cycles merge for 'moving-up'
and separate again after 'weighing'.   For the alternative path, a truck and the
weighbridge only join for 'weighing'.

Note that if trucks do not need to go through a 'move-up', but can directly enter
the weighbridge once it becomes free, there is no need for a switch mechanism for
either the truck or the weighbridge. In this case each has single, unique path for its
activity cycle. After 'arriving', a truck 'waits' until the weighbridge becomes 'idle'
and then immediately joins with the latter for 'weighing' before departing.   The
weighbridge also remains in the queue 'idle' until a truck arrives, at which point it
joins the truck for 'weighing' and returns to 'idle'.   If another truck is already
waiting, it simply zooms through 'idle' and immediately starts another 'weighing'.

I suggest you draw the combined activity cycle diagram for this simpler
situation. The model used for the weighbridge creates the truck entities coming from
the forest and then cancels them after weighing. In reality, the trucks are involved
in round trips, picking up logs in various forests, bringing them to the mill over the
weighbridge, unloading them in the wood yard, and returning to the forest, starting
another round trip. Given that the weighbridge operation occupies only a small part
of each round trip, we used this as justification for separating it out from the round
trip. However, any time lost waiting at the weighbridge will reduce the number of
round trips a truck can undertake per day. As long as the congestion at the weigh-

Figure 17-5: Truck and weighbridge life cycles combined

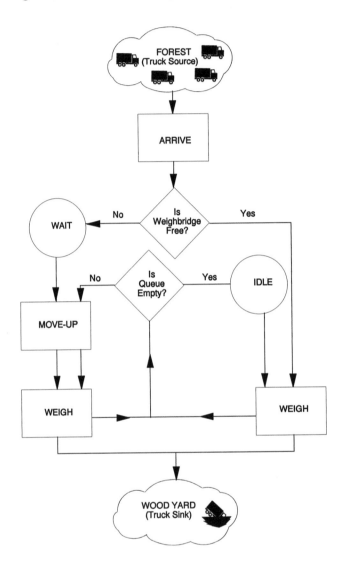

bridge remains minor, the reduction in round trips will be negligible. If the waiting times become excessive, say longer than 15 minutes, the effect may become significant.

A better approximation might be to model the round trips explicitly. In this case, the trucks also become permanent entities, executing several new activities and queues, such as 'trip to forest and back', 'travel from weighbridge to wood yard', 'waiting for unloading', and 'unloading of logs'. Additional permanent entities, such as log unloaders, may have to be introduced. The life cycle diagram for trucks then becomes also a closed loop. (Such a simulation would be very difficult to program for a spreadsheet solution. A proper computer simulation program would be essential.)

As we discovered for influence diagrams, entity life cycle diagrams have a number of uses. They are a powerful display device for facilitating communication between the problem owner and the analyst of the system simulated or between analysts. They clearly show the interactions between entities and therefore facilitate better understanding of the complexities of the system. They can serve as a first step for writing a computer simulation program. In fact, several computer simulation packages explicitly or implicitly view event simulations in the form of entity life cycles. Some require the input to be organized and submitted in this form.

17.3 HOW IS A SIMULATION PLANNED AND RUN ?

So we have developed a computer simulation program for a given system. This program could use one of the powerful computer simulation systems, such as GPSS, SIMSCRIPT, SIMULA, SLAM, CAPS/ECSL, or simply a spreadsheet, like we did for the weighbridge problem. How do we best use this program to get useful and reliable results? This is a rather tall question. So do not expect a comprehensive and definitive answer, if one even exists! We will just point out some of the more basic and obvious rules to follow and pitfalls to avoid.

Measures of Performance

The analyst has to be very clear what kind of measures are needed to judge and compare the performance of alternative systems, such as one weighbridge versus two weighbridges. The simulation program has to be capable of collecting the informa-tion for compiling these measures. For instance, in the weighbridge problem we are interested in such measures as the average time a truck spends in the system, as well as how that time is made up, such as waiting, moving-up, and being weighed. In a spreadsheet simulation, these measures can be computed from the details recorded. Other simulation packages may require setting special accumulators to capture this information. Management may also wish to know what percentage of trucks has to wait longer than, say 3 minutes. Hence, the data collected may have to be organized in a different form, such as a frequency distribution, rather than the simple cumulative totals needed for averages.

The performance of the real system usually varies over time. For example, in the weighbridge operation, there will be days when everything moves smoothly over the weighbridge, with few long delays. On other days, the congestion at the weighbridge may be very bad, with many trucks delayed up to 20 minutes. So the average waiting time per truck varies from day to day. A good simulation of the weighbridge operation should, therefore, exhibit a comparable pattern of daily performance measures. Table 17-2 lists the results of 64 simulation runs, each for one day's operation covering about 400 truck arrivals. These results were obtained using the spreadsheet format of Table 17-1. With the help of a simple macro program, all 64 runs were made in succession, taking less than 6 minutes on a 386 PC with a numeric co-processor.

The average time trucks spend waiting in the queue and moving up varies widely from a minimum of 172 seconds for day 21 to a maximum of 1084 seconds for day 40. In fact, each run is one observation on a random experiment. Hence, the times listed in Table 17-2 are 64 observations of the random variable 'average waiting time per truck'.

Table 17-2: Sum of waiting and move-up times for 64 days

Day	Time	Day	Time	Day	Time	Day	Time
1	426	17	173	33	405	49	560
2	915	18	278	34	582	50	835
3	327	19	641	35	302	51	317
4	954	20	199	36	400	52	329
5	782	21	172	37	426	53	350
6	330	22	394	38	325	54	241
7	289	23	331	39	607	55	308
8	475	24	386	40	1084	56	459
9	256	25	333	41	677	57	558
10	242	26	279	42	603	58	325
11	330	27	615	43	243	59	347
12	432	28	392	44	627	60	183
13	589	29	277	45	342	61	186
14	316	30	655	46	705	62	524
15	729	31	449	47	875	63	372
16	601	32	258	48	517	64	545
		Average	452.9			Standard deviation	207.8

Variability of Simulation Results

In contrast to most OR/MS models, the inputs to a simulation model are often sequences of random variates (such as the sequence of truck arrival times), rather than the single parameter estimates we might need for a theoretical queueing model. For example, although we based the generation of interarrival times on an average of 100.8 seconds, the observed average for the first 20 interarrival times shown in Table 17-1 is, in fact, 95.05 seconds. Hence the output measures of systems performance collected from the simulation model will also reflect this variability. Figure 17-6 attempts to capture the problem we now face. We want the variable inputs in order to have a valid model. However, as a result of this, we can expect to observe variable output measures, such as waiting times in a queue. As we have seen in the example above, the variations observed may be surprisingly large. To get a sufficiently reliable picture of the long-run performance of the system simulated, it is, therefore, essential to make a sufficiently large number of simulation runs. This will not only give better estimates of the average values for all performance measures, but also allows us to estimate their variation, such as their standard deviations. These can then be used to specify interval estimates for the performance measures of interest. Narrow interval estimates give more confidence in the reliability of the results. It is essential that the presentation of simulation results always includes some measures of the variability of the results as an indication of their reliability.

Figure 17-6: Variability of simulation results

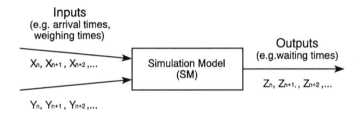

For our example, the overall average for the 64 days is 7 minutes and 32.9 seconds. This is fairly close to the values predicted by the theoretical model in Chapter 16. The standard deviation of average waiting times is 207.8 seconds. We can thus specify a 95% confidence interval on the average total time waiting of 400.9 to 504.9 seconds (i.e., $452.9 \pm 2[207.8/\sqrt{64}]$; see a statistics text for details on how to find confidence intervals). Note that this is a rather wide interval. Unfortunately, the number of runs needed to get confidence intervals that bracket the overall average by just a few percent can easily be in the hundreds or thousands.

Much of the more sophisticated simulation methodology is, in fact, concerned with reducing some of the variability in the simulation output measures. Let us briefly touch on one of those, namely the use of common random numbers.

Simulations are usually done to explore how crucial performance measures are affected by different operating options or configurations, such as one or two weighbridges. If each option is simulated with a new set of random numbers, then the simulation results are affected by two sources of variability. The first is the variability inherent in the operation itself. That variability we want to measure. The second is the variability introduced by using different sequences of random numbers. That second variability we would rather do without. Fortunately, in many instances, this second variability can easily be eliminated. The secret is to use for a given type of activity or event the same sequence of random numbers for each configuration.

This can be achieved by taking advantage of the property of random number generators mentioned in Section 17.1, namely that for any given starting seed the random number generator will always reproduce exactly the same sequence of random numbers.

Let us demonstrate this for the weighbridge example. There are three types of random activities: the arrival of trucks measured by the interarrival time between consecutive trucks, the move-up time, and the weighing time. All we need to do is to make sure that for the two-weighbridge simulation the times used for each truck arriving are identical to the ones used for the one-weighbridge simulation. This will eliminate the variability that would be introduced, had we used different times generated by the use of different random number sequences. (In a spreadsheet simulation, the simplest way to guarantee this is to generate the required sequences of random numbers prior to the start of the simulation proper and store them somewhere in the spreadsheet for later use.)

Intuitively, what we are doing is just what you would do if you were running an agricultural experiment to determine the difference between the yields from two brands of carrot seed - you would ensure that as many as possible of the inputs (water, sunlight, fertilizer) to the two plots were the same, in order to reduce the variance of the difference of the outputs. In terms of Figure 17-6 we could say that we now have two models, SM_1 and SM_2, producing outputs Z_n^1, Z_{n+1}^1,... and Z_n^2, Z_{n+1}^2,... respectively. By ensuring that as many as possible of the inputs X_n, X_{n+1}... and Y_n, Y_{n+1},... are the same for the two models we hope that Z^1 and Z^2 will be positively correlated. If this is true then the variance of their differences will be less than the sum of their variances. Thus when the objectives of the model are taken into account, what initially appeared in Section 17-1 to be a serious defect of random number generators is indeed often exploited to produce more accurate model results.

Length of Simulation Runs

In the weighbridge system, the system starts at 5:30 a.m. every working day with an empty queue. No trucks arrive after 5:00 p.m., but any trucks waiting at that time will still be processed. There are many real-life applications with this daily or periodic pattern, with each period starting and ending with an empty system, i.e., with no temporary entities present. For periodic operations of this type, the system's performance is measured with respect to that period, e.g., a day.

In the job shop example, the operation is also interrupted at the end of each working day. However, the system starts each new day in exactly the state it was stopped the previous day. Any temporary entities in the system simply resume their life cycle at the point the system was interrupted at the end of the previous day. Hence, the operation does not go through a regular daily cycle, but continues on indefinitely.

Figure 17-7 shows how the performance measure for the cumulative average waiting time in a simple queueing model behaved in an simulation run of 1,000 arrivals. This is an M/M/1 queue with a mean time between arrivals of 15 minutes and a mean service time of 10 minutes. Because the first simulated customer arrives to an empty queue the average waiting time also starts from zero. Although initially it rapidly increases towards the steady-state value of 20 minutes (calculated from formulas (16-1) and (16-4)), it is clearly affected by the initial empty state of the system. This effect is referred to as the **transient effect**. Note that even after the transient effect becomes small, the average waiting time continues to fluctuate up and down, although the magnitude of these fluctuations becomes smaller.

Figure 17-7: Behaviour of waiting time with run length

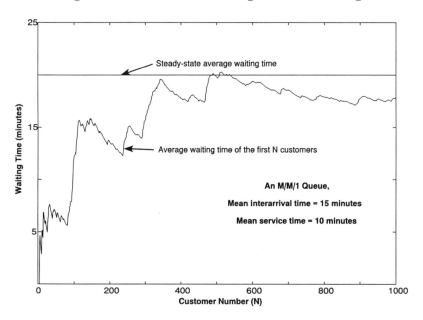

You should also note that often in simulations we are observing highly correlated random variables, such as the waiting times of successive customers in the queue or successive trucks at the weighbridge.   If the 300th truck has to wait for an abnormally long time then there is a good chance that the 301st truck will also be abnormally delayed. (You may like to look at the graphs in Figure 16-2 to help confirm this point.) It is often this **positive serial correlation** that accounts for the very slow convergence of system characteristics towards their steady-state values, both in simulations, or in actual systems.

In view of this long-run behaviour, how should the length of a simulation run be chosen if we want to estimate long-run characteristics of the system? The answer to this question is not simple. The stronger the initial transient effect is, the longer it takes for the system to settle down, and the longer the simulation must run. If we could start the system in an initial state which reflects the system's long-run behaviour, the transient effect would disappear or become negligible.   As a consequence, the length of the simulation run could be shortened without affecting the accuracy of the performance estimates obtained.

Note that the fluctuations for the cumulative average waiting time in Figure 17-5 tend to decrease the longer the run. This means that the accuracy of the estimates obtained from each individual run increases with the run length. There is a second reason why the accuracy of the estimates increases with the run length. This has to do with the fact that actual frequency distributions of the various random variates generated tend to get closer to their corresponding theoretical distributions. As we have seen in Table 17-1, the average interarrival time over the first 20 arrivals was 95.05. As the run length increases, the resulting average will get closer to its theoretical value of 100.8 seconds. Hence, the simulation results become more representative.

But long runs also take more computer time to execute. Furthermore, measures of the variability of the results become more reliable if they are based on a sufficiently large number of runs. So, the accuracy of the final results can be increased by either increasing the run length of each simulation or the number of runs. Which strategy is more effective is hard to tell. There is a trade-off between the number of runs and the length of each run. As a rule of thumb, the number of runs should be at least 10 for small sample statistics to give acceptable results in terms of reliability. Similarly, most analysts would chose a run length for each simulation covering thousands of periods, say days, rather than just a few hundred.

Initial Conditions

We saw above that, for some problems, a natural initial condition for starting the simulation is with no temporary entities present and all permanent entities in their natural 'parked' position. Such systems also end in the same 'empty state'. Hence, each simulation run starts with an empty state.

For other situations an empty state may occasionally occur too at random points in time. However, if used as a starting point, it may result in a long transient period before the performance measures settle down around their long-run averages. Getting rid of this transient period gives more accurate results even for shorter run lengths. In some situations, the analyst may be able to guess a suitable initial state for each run which shortens the transient period substantially. For example, setting the number of temporary entities in various queues equal to or close to their long-run average may have the desired effect.

A favourite trick used is to set the initial conditions for a simulation run equal to the ending state of the preceding run. This relieves the analyst from having to manually set initial conditions.

Another method that helps to eliminate the transient effect is to exclude all data for an appropriately chosen initial interval of the simulation, sometimes called a **warm-up period**. Data collection only starts after that interval. A good length for this initial interval can be found by some experimentation.

Computer Simulation Packages

Most simulations are performed by computer programs. A number of commercial computer simulation packages or languages are marketed. For all but the simplest types of simulations, recourse to one of these packages is recommended. Although spreadsheets can do rudimentary simulations, they lack not only many of the facilities needed, but also can only handle simple systems where each temporary entity can be processed through all operations with reference to event times of only the just preceding entity. This is the case for the single weighbridge problem. For the two-weighbridge problem, the two weighbridges may not necessarily process two trucks that arrived consecutively, but trucks that were separated by other truck arrivals. Writing spreadsheet macros to deal with this complexity would be tricky, increasing the computational time many fold.

Computer simulation packages have facilities to generate random variates from many distributions with up to 10 individually controlled random number generators. They automatically keep track of the state of the system and properly execute all events at their scheduled time. They automatically collect performance measures on all queues and allow the programmer to specify other statistics to be collected, including frequency distributions for various passage times, like waiting times. They

Figure 17-8: GPSS/H Queueing Program

```
         GENERATE       RVEXPO(3,100.8),,,,,1PH

         ASSIGN         EMPTY,F(BRIDGE),PH

         QUEUE          WAITQ

         SEIZE          BRIDGE

         DEPART         WAITQ

         TEST G PH(EMPTY),0,EMPT

         ADVANCE        60,FN(MOVUP)

  EMPT   ADVANCE        60,FN(WEIGH)

         RELEASE        BRIDGE

         TERMINATE

         GENERATE 41400

         TERMINATE 1
```

contain automatic checking for errors in the simulation logic. They also allow the creation of output reports in the form needed for submission to the problem owners. The input into many of them consists simply of the various entity life cycles. Programming time is therefore reduced to a fraction of what it would take to use one of the general purpose computer languages, like *Basic* or *Pascal*.

To give you an indication how simple such a program may be, Figure 17-8 lists the core of a GPSS/H program, representing the combined activity cycles of Figure 17-5 needed for simulating the weighbridge problem. The entire program consists of only 37 lines. It was run on a 80386 PC. To run 100,000 hours of weighbridge operations, however, took over eight hours of computer time. The computer run times for using such packages may thus be quite long.

The report on the simulation runs should indicate what choices the analyst made for the various points discussed above, and the reasons for these choices.

17.4 OTHER SIMULATION STRUCTURES

Fixed-Time Incrementation

Event simulation is particularly suitable for queueing and sequencing situations of all sorts. Simulated time is always updated to the time when the next most imminent event is scheduled to occur. For some situations it is more appropriate to update simulated time in equal discrete time intervals, such as a day, a week, or a month. Recall the production scheduling problem for the CRYSTAL SPRINGS MINERAL WATER COMPANY in Chapter 14. There we traced out exactly what would happen over time for a given shift level and production schedule. In fact, we simulated the response of the system to various policies, trying to identify the best policy. We did not refer to it as a simulation, but it was a deterministic simulation, where time was updated in monthly intervals.

This type of time updating is called **fixed-time incrementation**. It is a suitable modelling approach if some events occur regularly in each period and it is not important to record exactly at which time within each period any event occurs or this has little effect on costs. All events are assumed to occur either at the beginning or the end of a period. Consider for example the production/inventory control situation, like the one described in Chapter 6. A simulation of the behaviour of the inventory level over time would assume that any replenishments arrive in stock, say, at the beginning of a day, while all stock withdrawals to meet customer orders occur at the end of each day. All costs would be assessed as of the end of each day.

Fixed-time incrementation is also used as an approximation for simulations of continuous systems, such as the operation of a series of hydro storage reservoirs. In such systems, some water flows in and out of each reservoir constantly. The control variables are the rate of water release for electric power generation. We do not have entities and events in the sense discussed in Section 17.2. Although a number of computer simulation packages, like SIMULA and DYNAMO, are capable of modelling the continuous flow rate nature of such situations, we often approximate the behaviour of such systems by fixed-time incrementation. Inflows and outflows of water are assumed to occur at constant rates over each planning subperiod, say, an hour or a day. Any changes in rate also occur only at the beginning or end of a period. The inflow rate may be generated randomly from a theoretical probability distribution or an empirically obtained frequency distribution. With these assumptions the state of the system, such as reservoir levels, generators in use, and so on, at the end of each period can be assessed exactly. Each simulation run might cover a year and is repeated for different randomly generated inflows 30 to 50 times for each set of alternative policy rules.

Monte-Carlo Simulation and Risk Analysis

For investment decisions, the exact amounts of various future cash flows are usually not known with certainty. They are random variables. Conventional methods of investment evaluations approximate these random cash flows by their expected values or some other conservative estimates.

Consider the following investment project. A firm is considering the construction of a large recreational facility, such as a new ski-field. Based on initial but fairly comprehensive investigations it has accumulated information about

- construction costs, including various contingencies;

- operating costs for various levels of patronage and number of skiable days;

- share of the region's skiing market for various levels of day user fees;

- future levels of patronage for the region's skiing market over time;

- number of skiable days in the region based on records over the past 15 years for neighbouring ski-fields.

The level of revenues and costs in any given year will be affected by the value assumed by each of the various factors listed above. They are therefore random variables. We could extract from this information single annual estimates of revenues and costs for each level of day fees over the entire planning horizon. Discounting these to the present will give us a single number on which to judge the 'worth' of the project for each alternative level of day fees. Although this may be useful information of the project's success or failure 'on the average', it provides no information on the risk involved in the project. Before the firm makes a firm commitment it would want to get some feel for how risky the venture is. For example, how likely is the firm to go bankrupt due to adverse conditions? Answering such questions requires more than a single estimate of the venture's net present value. We need a distribution of the net present values which reflects all possible combinations of the various factors influencing revenues and costs.

What if we simulate the sequence of annual cash flows that results from the joint effect of the various factors, using a randomly generated value from the probability distribution of each factor? The net present value obtained would be one observation of what might happen. If we repeat this experiment a thousand times, each with a different set of random numbers, we can generate a frequency distribution for the net present value which reflects the uncertainty in each random factor included in the analysis. This frequency distribution would provide us with the answers about the riskiness of the venture. This is essentially what risk analysis does.

Risk analysis is a very effective method for generating a frequency distribution of the outcomes of sequential experiments where the events occurring at various stages in the process are random and possibly conditional upon the value of previous events. It is highly demanding in terms of the inputs required. We need to define a probability distribution for each random event. Some of these distributions may be conditional.

Using the above example, assume that the number of skiable days ranges from 16 to 20 weeks. We approximate this random factor by a simple five-value probability distribution, one for each week from 16 to 20. For each level of skiable weeks we need a probability distribution of the region's patronage for each year in the planning horizon. Some of these, particularly in the later years of the planning horizon may be the same, but it could be as many as 60 different distributions. For each level of patronage and each year we then need a probability distribution for the field's market share. These are highly subjective. Say, they are identical for all levels and all years. To simplify things further, assume that yearly operating costs are a deterministic function of the number of person ski-days in each year, which can easily be determined from the values for the number of skiable days, the level of patronage, and the field's share of the market. Finally, we also need probabilities for the construction contingencies — again subjective guesstimates. Even with all these simplifying assumptions, we end up defining up to 62 different probability distributions. This requires a massive data collection and analysis effort. Admittedly, many distributions will be discrete with only few possible outcomes, others will be based on the assumption of normality. Many will be subjective distributions, expressing the beliefs of the decision makers and experts.

In spite of this massive data collection effort and the difficulties associated with it, risk analysis is a valuable tool for quantifying the degree of risk involved in such projects. Once the basic model structure has been developed and programmed for computer analysis, extensive sensitivity analysis will indicate the importance of each factor in the outcomes. This in turn allows the analyst to direct the data collection effort into these crucial areas. Armed with this information, the decision maker will be able to make a more informed decision, rather than one largely based on intuition, gut feeling, and some measure of wishful thinking.

This analysis can be performed on a spreadsheet, using macros. There are several spreadsheet-based commercial risk analysis packages available for PCs.

17.5 SOME CONCLUSIONS ON SIMULATION AS A TOOL

Simulation, especially computer simulation, is sometimes described as a last-resort technique, to be used when attempts to fit some kind of analytical model have failed. While this may sometimes be true in practice it is not a particularly good way of thinking about the place of simulation in the range of OR/MS tools. As we have seen above the use of simulation models in no way reduces the data requirements or the need for a thorough understanding of the system that is being modeled. This latter point is often vital, as starting to build a simulation model before the system has been fully understood may lead to excessively detailed modelling of unimportant parts of the system while crucial parts are overlooked. As well, the analyst is faced with acquiring simulation software which is often very expensive, learning how to use it, and writing and debugging the simulation program.

A better way of thinking about simulation is that it is a technique that may require large inputs; data collection, study and understanding of the system being modeled, knowledge of the simulation software, and knowledge of the special statistical problems that occur in the analysis of simulation output. On the other hand, a simulation model (a) may produce detailed output on performance measures for various parts of the operations, (b) be a flexible model that can include aspects of the system for which no easy analytical model is available, (c) has the ability to easily test the effect of varying system parameters, and (d) if a system is used that can produce visual displays of the behaviour of systems entities, be seen by management as more convincing than one based on formulas.

For the weighbridge problem we can compare the simulation model with the approach using queueing formulas discussed in Chapter 16. Among the advantages of using simulation are:

- The move-up time can be easily allowed for by a line in the GPSS simulation program which assigns an arriving truck a parameter equal to the number of trucks waiting ahead of it. If this is non-zero the truck is delayed for a randomly generated move-up time.

- The simulation can be started with an empty queue and stopped at the end of a (simulated) day. There is no need to use steady-state formulas.

- It is easy to model the two-weighbridge situation because the computer package specifically provides for multiple servers.

- It is easier to convince management that we have a 'solution' to the problem because a fancier version of the program makes little trucks move across the computer screen. (In fact this version of the program is far too slow to be of any practical use, and the extra programming required to produce the visual display makes logical errors in the program that much more likely.)

While the simulation model is easy to program and works well, its distinct disadvantage is the length of time which each simulation run requires. Because the queue is so sensitive to slight variations in its parameters the simulated daily mean waiting time can vary from 3 to 25 minutes. A run of 10,000 days is required to reduce the standard deviation of the mean daily waiting time down to 0.05 minutes. This takes over eight hours of computer time on a 80386 PC with a numeric co-processor. For management, the most valuable part of the original study using the theoretical queueing model was the sensitivity analysis for the number of loads that could be carried per day (Figure 16-5). Doing this analysis by simulation would have required eight hours of computation for every point.

We can consider the two approaches in terms of the criteria for a good model listed in Section 6-3. Both approaches could be classed as **appropriate**. They produce the required economic information for management to make the decision about the second weighbridge at very small cost. We would probably conclude that while the simulation model is superior on the completeness and simplicity criteria for a good model, it is distinctly inferior to the queueing formulas for ease of manipulation, being easy to communicate with, and adaptivity. Some of the guidelines for modelling listed in Section 6-4 can also be related to the weighbridge problem. In particular the ability to adequately model the arrival process of trucks at the weighbridge by assuming that the interarrival times were sampled from a negative exponential distribution is vital for the use of simple queueing models and also results in a much simpler simulation program. Here we are using the guideline characterized as **Ockham's Razor** in Section 6-4, of excluding aspects, such as the fact that the trucks actually made round trips, that do not contribute to the predictive power of the model. Our argument for this exclusion can be found in Section 16-6.

Where the simulation model proved vital was in validating the queueing formulas that were used in the final report. These are slightly more complex than the ones shown in Chapter 16. (What is in Chapter 16 is, in fact, our first attempt to produce a quick approximate answer to the problem. This was later refined into a more elegant method which turned out to give very similar answers. Thus we were also following the advice given under **An Iterative Process of Enrichments** in Section 6-4.) By determining that the simulation and formula results are in close agreement for a few selected input values we can reasonably assume that the formulas will be correct for intermediate values, hence saving a substantial amount of computer time and data analysis. Management appeared to be happy with this validation study and found the results of the analytical models acceptably accurate.

EXERCISES

1. Develop a spreadsheet similar to Table 17-1 to simulate the behaviour of the weighbridge and simulate the arrival and processing of 80 trucks. Determine statistics for the amount of idle time of the weighbridge and the total waiting time for the first 80 trucks.

2. The table below is a partial simulation of ships arriving at a port for unloading and loading. The average interarrival time between ships is 48 hours. Interarrival times follow a negative exponential distribution. It takes on average 12 hours to unload a ship. The unloading time also has a negative exponential distribution. The loading time is uniformly distributed between 8 and 32 hours. There is only one berth in the port. Thus only one ship can be unloaded and loaded at a time. Loading commences immediately after unloading has been completed. At the start of the simulation, no ship is in the port. This system is to be simulated for 12 ship arrivals, using the table format below. Note that the first 2 ships have already been processed to indicate the pattern.

(a) Define the structure of this system, i.e., the permanent and temporary entities, the activities, and associated events. What would you use to define the state of the system?

(b) Draw a combined life cycle diagram for the entities.

(c) Simulate the behaviour of this system by hand for 12 arrivals. Round all times to the nearest hour. The following set of uniformly distributed random decimal fractions should be used:

[.0196][.0674][.1064][.1584][.6801][.9531] .4418   .1916   .7706   .6510   .5582
.0112 .9296   .6985 .2832 .4603 .8185 .7864 .1268 .7524 .2143 .7059
.5264 .6932 .0963 .6721   .8095 .4541 .6392 .1983 .8791 .5023 .1276
.8512 .6435 .6181 .5496 .7197 .0434

(those used already for the first 2 ships are shown bracketed — simply continue with the next relevant uncrossed entry.)

ship num- ber	inter- arrival time	arrival time	un- load time	start un- load	end un- load	load time	start of load	end of load
1	1	1	1	1	2	12	2	14
2	8	9	14	14	28	42	28	70
3								

(d) What is the waiting time for ship number 3? What is the total time the berth is idle, exclusive of the initial period at the start of the simulation?

3. A firm uses the following policy to control its inventory: Whenever the stock on hand has been reduced through sales to 8 units, a replenishment of size 24 is placed. This replenishment arrives at the firm's premises in the morning of the third day after it has been placed and becomes immediately available to meet customer demands. If the demand on a given day is larger than the stock on hand, then the amount short is lost, i.e., the customer goes elsewhere. The daily demand pattern is as follows:

Demand size	0	1	2	3	4	5	6	7
Frequency	0.25	0.20	0.15	0.12	0.10	0.08	0.06	0.04

Simulate the behaviour of this system by hand for an interval of 30 days. Use a table format that has one row for each day and appropriate columns for the amount of stock on hand at the beginning of each day, the demand generated using the set of random numbers listed above, the stock level at the end of the day, the amount of goods on order (stock replenishment orders are placed at the end of the day after sales have been processed), and the amount of lost sales. To generate the random demands you need to use the scheme described in Section 17.1, in particular the method demonstrated in Figure 17-1.

4. A product is assembled on a two-station assembly line. Station A assembles the first part (Part A) of the product, while Station B finishes the assembly of the product (Part B). Station A takes any time between 40 and 50 seconds to assemble one unit of Part A. The time is uniformly distributed. Station B takes on average 46 seconds to finish

the assembly of one unit of Part B, with a standard deviation of 9 seconds. The distribution of the Part B assembly time is approximately normal. Station A starts assembling a new Part A immediately after having completed the previous unit. Any completed units are put on a counter within reach of the operator at Station B. Station B also starts a new assembly (Part B) after having completed the previous assembly, provided there are any Part A units ready (waiting) on the counter for completion at Station B. If no Part A units are available, then the operator at Station B is temporarily idle until the next Part A has been completed at Station A. Assume that the work day begins at 8:00 a.m. and Station A starts the first Part A assembly. Station B starts work as soon as the first Part A has been placed on the counter.

(a) Define the structure of this system, i.e., temporary and permanent entities and their attributes, the activities, and the various events. How would you define the state of the system?

(b) Draw a combined life cycle diagram for the entities.

(c) Set up a computer spreadsheet and simulate this system for 60 assemblies. It should show when each event occurs. Use a new row for each new assembly started. Round all times to the nearest second. Use the following approach for generating approximate normal random variates with a mean of 0 and a standard deviation of 1: generate 12 uniformly distributed random decimal fractions and compute their average. (This needs to be repeated for each normal random variate.) You want to collect statistics for the length of time taken to complete the assembly of 60 complete items, as well as the fraction of time each of the two stations are idle during that time. Do not include the time at Station B at the beginning of the work day when Station B is waiting for the first partially completed assembly to be released by Station A as idle time.

(d*) Write a spreadsheet Macro that allows you to repeat this simulation for 20 different runs, each one using a different set of random numbers. Compute the average of the statistics and a measure of the variation of the 20 runs.

5. An inner city service station has one pump and only space for 2 cars in total, i.e., the one being served and at most one waiting. Any potential customer intending to tank up at that station and seeing both spaces taken (i.e., two cars in the service station) will not enter and simply drives by to go to some other service station. These potential customers are thus lost to the system. Potential customers arrive at the service station at a rate of 10 per hour, or on average every 6 minutes. Given that each potential customer makes the decision to tank up or not independently, a negative exponential arrival distribution is a good assumption. The service takes on average 5 minutes. It is uniformly distributed over the range from 1 to 9 minutes. Service is on a first-come/first-served basis. The service station owner would like to determine the effect of the limited space available to serve customers, in particular the average number of customers lost due to lack of space. On average, each customer buys about 25 litres of petrol on which the service station earns $3.75. The owner would also like to know a number of other performance measures that could be of interest or useful. Think carefully about which performance measures you want to observe.

(a) Define the structure of the system, i.e., the temporary and permanent entities, the activities and the events. What would you use to describe the state of the system?

(b) Draw a combined life cycle diagram for the entities.

(c) Develop a computer spreadsheet and simulate this system for a total of 40 potential arrivals. Round all times to the nearest minute. It should enable you to collect/observe all performance measures of interest. List the formulas used for every cell in the row of your spreadsheet for the second arrival.

(d*) Write a spreadsheet Macro that allows you to repeat this simulation for 10 different runs, each one using a different set of random numbers. Compute the average of the statistics and a measure of their variation for the 10 runs.

6*. Consider a simplified version of the TAB telephone betting system described in Section 1.1 of Chapter 1. Assume that a given TAB office has two telephone lines. If a punter calls, and both lines are free, line 1 answers the call. If one of the lines is busy, the other line answers the call. If both lines are busy, the call is lost. During the hour just prior to a given race, calls arrive at a rate of 1 per minute. It is reasonable to assume that interarrival times have a negative exponential distribution. It also takes an operator 1 minute to process a call. Assume that the processing time is uniformly distributed between 20 and 120 seconds.

(a) Draw a combined life cycle diagram for all entities involved. Note that the two entities for the operators/lines follow the same life cycle pattern. Hence, one life cycle for them needs to be shown.

(b) Develop a computer spreadsheet and simulate the arrival of 60 calls. Round all times to the nearest second. Collect statistics on the amount of idle time of the two operators/lines together, and the number of calls lost.

REFERENCES

Banks, J., Carson, J. S., and Sy, J. N., *Getting Started with GPSS/H,* Wolverine Software Corporation, 4115 Annandale Road, Annandale, VA 22003-3910. The introductory manual for the GPSS/H package mentioned in Section 17.3. It includes a functioning version of the software.

Hoover, S. V., and Perry, R. F., *Simulation: A Problem-Solving Approach,* Addison Wesley, 1989. Covers the complete use of simulation as a MS/OR technique and includes introductory material on three of the best-known commercial simulation packages.

Kreutzer, W., *System Simulation: Programming Styles and Languages*, Addison-Wesley, 1986. A discussion of the different programming styles that can be applied to computer simulation problems.

Law, A. M., and Kelton, W. D., *Simulation Modelling and Analysis*, McGraw-Hill, 1991. A very good reference for details of data analysis, modelling strategy, and output analysis in simulation, co-authored by a leading practitioner.

Pidd, M., *Computer Simulation in Management Science, Third Edition,* John Wiley, 1992. A readable, general introduction to simulation either using packages or general-purpose (Pascal, Basic) programs.

18 Decision Analysis

The preceding two chapters explore dynamic systems behaviours where uncertainty can be captured by theoretical probability or empirical frequency distributions. System behaviour is affected by a large number of random events occurring individually at random points in time. It is then appropriate to study the system's long-run behaviour. Its effectiveness can be judged on the basis of its average performance over a long period or a large number of trials or experiments.

In contrast, this chapter studies situations where uncertainty about future outcomes deals with a single event or a relatively small sequence of events. The problems analyzed are often unique situations, where the decision maker has only one chance to get the decision right, such as the introduction of a new product or the acquisition of a new, but risky venture. Uncertainty is often expressed in the form of subjective probabilities about future events. What the future holds in store is called the **state of the future** or the **state of nature**. The benefits and costs associated with the decision choices may be different for each possible state of the future. Furthermore, being one-shot deals, each situation is 'played' only once. There is no long-run behaviour to be observed.

What is an effective and insightful way for modeling such situations? What criteria are suitable for finding the 'best' alternative course of action? This chapter attempts to give partial answers to these questions. They are part of the vast topic of **decision analysis**. Our purpose for studying aspects of decision analysis is not to give you a working knowledge of this set of tools, but rather to let you gain further insights into systems modeling and decision making under uncertainty.

Although the focus of this chapter will be on unique and independent decision situations, there are some recurrent decision problems which have the same basic structure. A fast food stall or cafeteria daily faces the problem of how much of each of various dishes to prepare in anticipation of the coming day's sales. Similarly, 6 to 12 months prior to the start of the new clothing season a fashion goods manufacturer has to decide what assortment, in terms of sizes and materials, to produce. Usually only a single run is made. So it is important to get it right the first time.

Section 18.1 sets the stage with a simple, but by no means trivial decision situation that captures the basic aspects of decision analysis. The problem is borrowed from the fascinating book *Quick Analysis for Busy Decision Makers* by R.D. Behn and J. W. Vaupel (New York: Basic Books, 1982), Chapter 2. Sections 18.2 and 18.3 study a more conventional situation which involves risky monetary outcomes. They demonstrates the general approach of finding the 'best' solution and the kind of insights that can be gained from the analysis. Sections 18.4 and 18.5 explore approaches for dealing with situations where the monetary value of a risky outcome is not a true reflection of the intrinsic worth of the outcome.

18.1 SETTING UP A DECISION PROBLEM

Ollerton Watt, a busy executive, must make one of the most important decisions of
his life. It has nothing to do with his job. Olly suffers from *angina pectoris* — chest
pains often caused by hardening of the coronary arteries. This deprives the heart
muscle of blood when the heart needs to pump harder in response to physical
exertion, excitement, or stress. Medication prescribed to Olly relieved some of the
symptoms, but was not successful in clearing the problem. So Olly has just had a
complete cardiac examination. His doctor now sets out the options available to him.
He can continue with his medication, taking it easy, and suffer the occasional angina
attack. These are painful and frightening. He can elect to have bypass surgery.
This will almost surely be successful in relieving the problem completely. There is
only a small chance that the pain is not totally eliminated. However, the doctor also
informs him that, in view of his age and previous medical history, there is one
chance in ten that he could die on the operating table — more than twice the average
death rate for this type of surgery! The doctor also explains to him that there is
currently little medical evidence suggesting that surgery increases the patient's life
expectancy. Olly could live as long with angina pectoris as with surgery, provided
he took it easy. Should he decide to have surgery or not?

Olly's problem is far from unique. There are millions of people all over the
world facing similar decision problems. Not all of them involve life-and-death decisions. Many may simply involve other risky outcomes, such as whether or not to
accept the job offer in a new city, or getting into a stable relationship with a partner,
or possibly large monetary gains and losses.

Structuring the Decision Problem

A **decision tree** lays out sequential problems of this sort in a schematic form by
decomposing it into simple single stage components. It clearly highlights the
chronological structure of the problem and its sequential, conditional logic.

Figure 18-1 is a graphical representation of Olly's decision problem. This
decision tree is read from left to right. It begins with a **decision node** — whether or
not to undergo surgery — depicted as a square (labelled 1). The two branches
leaving the square denote Olly's two decision choices 'Surgery' and 'No surgery'.
The top branch 'No surgery' leads to the outcome 'Live with angina'. The bottom
branch leads to a **chance node**, denoted by a circle (labelled 2). Each branch
leaving the circle denotes one of the possible outcomes. In our example, there are
two possible outcomes: 'Patient dies during surgery' and 'Patient survives'. The
bottom branch 'Patient survives' leads to another chance node (labelled 3), also with
two branches: 'No pain' and 'Some pain remains'. The 'Surgery' decision thus
leads to one of three possible outcomes.

The branches leaving a chance node lead to uncertain outcomes. We associate a probability (subjective or objective) with each outcome. These are shown in parentheses next to the branches. Since one of the outcomes must occur, the probabilities attached to the outcome branches originating at a given chance node add up to one. For example, according to the surgeon, there is a 10% chance that Olly dies during surgery. Hence, there must be a 90% chance that he survives. So we attach a probability of 0.1 to the top branch and a probability of 0.9 to the bottom branch. Similarly, Olly is told that if he survives the odds are 1 in 200 that 'Some pains remains'. Hence the odds for 'No pain' are 199 in 200. The probabilities attached to these two outcome branches are 0.995 and 0.005.

Figure 18-1: Decision tree for angina pectoris problem

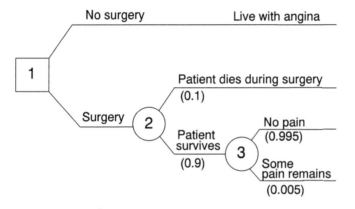

Evaluating the Decision Choices

We will initially ignore the small likelihood that, although Olly survives the surgery, some pain will remain. Surviving surgery is now assumed to mean 'surgery is successful'. With this small approximation, Olly faces a choice between a certain outcome 'Live with angina' if he decides on 'No surgery', and an uncertain outcome if he decides on 'Surgery'. That uncertain outcome — either 'Surgery is successful' or 'Patient dies during surgery' — is equivalent to participating in the following gamble with 'nature'. An urn contains 90 white and 10 black balls. If Olly decides on 'Surgery', 'nature' draws one ball at random from the urn. A white ball means 'Surgery is successful', a black ball means 'Patient dies during surgery'.

Whether or not Olly should choose 'No surgery' or 'Surgery' will depend on Olly's assessment of the three possible outcomes. Clearly, he will view 'Surgery is successful' as the most preferred outcome, while 'Patient dies' is the worst outcome.

'Live with angina' will be somewhere in between these two outcomes on his preference scale.

Olly could express these preferences on an arbitrary **point scale**. This point scale would be highly personal and subjective, reflecting Olly's preference structure with respect to this particular situation at this point in time. It would be different for another person. For instance, Olly might assign the most preferred outcome 100 preference points and the least preferred outcome zero points. He would then assign 'Live with angina' more than zero but less than 100 points. If he judges it as only a little bit better than dying, he may assign it 5 points on his preference scale. On the other hand, if he views 'Live with angina' as a condition he is willing to live with, he may assign it 80 points.

A low preference point value for 'Live with angina' will push Olly towards 'Surgery' and willing to accept the gamble this option entails. A high point value will tip the scale towards the 'No surgery' option. For example, he might prefer 'Live with angina' to the gamble if he positions 'Live with angina' at 25 points, but prefer the gamble if it is only 10. So as the point value decreases from 25 towards 10 his preferences switches from 'Live with angina' to the gamble. Somewhere on his preference scale there is a **switch point** where he will be indifferent between the two options.

In the above discussion we assumed that the probability of dying was given and known. An alternative way of looking at this problem is as follows. Assume that the proportions of white and black balls are not fixed yet. It is a fair guess that if the proportion of white balls is low, say only 50%, Olly like most people would opt for 'No surgery'. This choice may remain the same if the proportion of white balls increases to 70%. On the other hand, a very high proportion of say 95% would lead him to choose 'Surgery'. His choice would not change any more if the proportion were even increased to 99%. So, we see that as the proportion of white balls increases, there comes a critical level where Olly switches from the riskless 'No surgery' option to the risky 'Surgery' option. In our example, this critical level must be higher than 70%, but less than 95%.

This critical level V is called the **switch probability** or the **indifference probability**. If the proportion of white balls is just equal to V then Olly would be indifferent between the two options. Neither is preferred over the other — he could let the decision be made by the toss of a coin. The two options are equivalent to each other in terms of their degree of preference. One could be substituted for the other. However, if the proportion of white balls is less than V Olly prefers the riskless 'No surgery' option; if it is more than V he prefers the risky 'Surgery' option.

Viewed in this way, Olly's decision rule would be: choose 'No surgery' if the proportion of white balls is less than the indifference probability, choose 'Surgery' if it is more than the indifference probability, and flip a fair coin, with 'heads' meaning 'No surgery' and 'tails' meaning 'Surgery', if it is equal to the indifference probability. Finding this indifference probability is no simple matter. We will postpone this task to a later section.

What is the effect of having approximated the original risky option 'Patient survives surgery' with 'Surgery is successful'? 'Patient survives surgery' leads to another uncertain outcome, namely 'Surgery is completely successful' and 'Some pain remains'. Clearly, 'Surgery is completely successful' is preferred to 'Surgery is successful', since the latter outcome, in fact, also includes a low chance of 'Some pain remains'. I leave it to you to determine how this changes the indifference probability.

The discussion in this section captures most of the conceptual features of decision analysis. It has given us some important insights. First, decision makers are able to rank final outcomes, even of a non-pecuniary nature, in order of their preference, from the least preferred outcome to the most preferred outcome. If the outcomes can be expressed in dollars and cents, the monetary values may well reflect the ranking order. In other instances, particularly highly risky situations, such as large financial gains or losses, or situations involving emotional, aesthetic, ethical, or environmental concerns, it may be possible to express the preferences along an arbitrary point scale. It is then possible to compare a riskless option with a risky option in terms of this scale.

Second, faced with three outcomes, A, B, and C, where A is preferred to B and B is preferred to C, we can compare an (assumed) riskless option B with a risky option involving outcomes A and C in either of two ways. We could find the switch point for which the decision maker is indifferent between the riskless and the risky option. If the valuation of B is higher than the switch point, the riskless option of B is preferred to the risky option, and vice versa. Alternatively, we could find the indifference probabilities for A (the most preferred outcome) for which the decision maker is indifferent between the riskless option B and the risky option involving A or C. If the best assessment for the probability for A is higher than the indifference probability, then the risky option is preferred to the riskless option and vice-versa. At the switch point or the indifference probability, the riskless option is equivalent to the risky option.

The importance of this discovery is that it allows us to substitute a riskless option for a risky option in any further comparisons. We shall make use of this property in Section 18.5.

18.2   A DECISION PROBLEM WITH MONETARY OUTCOMES

A Situation Summary

Barry Low, the founder and major shareholder of FIRST SOFTWARE (FS) has just been informed by his lawyer, Debbie Deft, that the Ying-Yang Computer Software House (YY) has informed her through their lawyer that YY plans suing FS for copyright infringements by FS's EASY-OPT What-If Solver Release 2.1. YY claims damages of $500,000 and triple punitive penalties of $1,500,000. Debbie Deft also tells Barry Low that YY's lawyer has hinted that YY would be willing to settle out of court by granting FS retroactively a flat-fee licence for using the software in contention for 2 million dollars. This would allow FS to continue selling Release 2.1. Barry Low estimates that the future revenue potential for Release 2.1 amounts to roughly 3 million dollars. If FS chose to defend the law suit and lost, these sales would also be lost. Debbie Deft estimates that the cost of defending the law suit will amount to $600,000. If FS wins, YY will have to refund FS about $500,000 of this. Similarly, if FS loses, it will have to refund YY an equal amount of costs.

Development of EASY-OPT Release 3.0 has just been started. With its completely new format, it will definitely not run any danger of infringing copyrights. Its development can be accelerated. This will allow Release 3.0 to be introduced four to eight months earlier than currently planned, provided it is initiated within a month. The difficulty is that without some preliminary analysis no prediction can be made by how much. Such a preliminary analysis has a cost tag of $100,000. Accelerating the development will also increase the cost by $200,000 for a 4-months early release to $400,000 for an 8-months early release. However, FS would recoup about $300,000 of the potential loss on abandoning Release 2.1 for every month of early introduction. Upon questioning Debbie Deft, Barry thinks that YY would be willing to accept an out-of-court settlement for $600,000 in compensation for past copy-right infringements, if FS immediately stopped marketing the Release 2.1. He also thinks that YY would be willing to accept a licence fee of $1,250,000 if Release 3.0 is introduced 8 months earlier and $1,600,000 if it is introduced 4 months earlier.

Debbie impresses on Barry that he has at most 5 to 6 weeks available to make up his mind whether or not to accept an out of court settlement. Once YY has initiated the court case, there was little chance that they would still be interested in a deal.

There are two major uncertainties in this situation. What are FS's chances of successfully defending a court case? And, how much earlier can Release 3.0 be marketed if FS decides to accelerate its development? Debbie's subjective assessment is that FS has about a 70% chance of winning the case. Prior to a preliminary analysis, the EASY-OPT development leader estimates that there is a 60% chance of being able to complete Release 3.0 8 months earlier and a 40% chance of being able to complete it only 4 months earlier.

Setting Up a Decision Tree

What is the sequence of decisions and uncertain events? Within 5 weeks, Barry has to make up his mind whether to abandon marketing Release 2.1 immediately, accept a licence agreement with YY, or defend the case in court. Which one of these decisions is 'best' may well depend on whether or not Barry decides to accelerate development of Release 3.0. Indeed, acceleration or no acceleration must be Barry's first decision. This is the decision node labelled 1 in the decision tree depicted in Figure 18-2. While 'Do not accelerate' has no immediate cost, 'Accelerate' incurs an immediate cost of $100,000. This is shown as $-$0.1 (in millions).

Figure 18-2: Decision tree for Barry Low's copy-right infringement problem

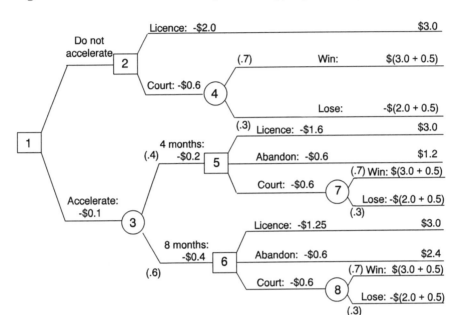

'Do not accelerate' leads to decision node 2. Since it is quite obvious that abandoning Release 2.1 without acceleration is a very unattractive option in comparison to taking out a 'Licence', there is little point in showing it as one of the decision alternatives. Hence, the two alternatives left are taking out a 'Licence' or going to 'Court'. The first results in a licence fee of $2 million (shown as −$2.0), but will also generate revenues of $3 (million). The second incurs cost of $0.6 (million). It leads to a chance node 4 with branches 'Win' and 'Lose', with probabilities of 0.7 and 0.3, respectively. A 'Win' results in revenues of $3 (million) plus a refund of $0.5 in court costs, while 'Lose' means penalties and court costs paid to YY totalling $2.5 (million). (Remember that costs are shown as negative amounts!)

'Accelerate' leads to chance node 3. It has two branches: Release 3.0 is ready '4 months' earlier at an additional cost of $0.2 (million) with a probability of 0.4, and Release 3.0 is ready '8 months' earlier at an additional cost of $0.4 (million) with a probability of 0.6.

Each one of those branches leads to a new decision node, labelled 5 and 6, respectively. Both have the same choices, namely, take out a 'Licence', 'Abandon' Release 2.1 immediately, or go to 'Court'. Taking out a 'Licence' from node 5 has a cost of $1.6 (million) and will generate revenues from sales of $3.0 (million). 'Abandon' causes costs of $0.6 (million). With Release 3.0 ready '4 months' earlier, lost sales of $1.2 (million) can be recovered. Going to 'Court' has exactly the same structure as for the branch leaving decision node 2. Can you figure out the net cash flows and probabilities from decision node 6 on?

Evaluating the Decision Tree by Backward Induction

What is Barry's 'best' choice of decisions? Before we can answer this question, we need a criterion for 'best'. One criterion mentioned in Chapter 15 is to identify the decision or alternative course of action that **maximizes the expected monetary return**. For Barry this is the expected value of net cash flow. But 'wait' you may interject! 'Does it make sense to base the decision for a unique non-repetitive situation on an expected value concept?' It can indeed be shown that, under assumptions considered reasonable by most people, choosing the action that maximizes the expected value of the outcomes is a rationally consistent criterion. What the expected value criterion implies is that the decision maker is willing to 'play the average' even for one-shot deals — the argument being that averaging over a string of unique decision situations is not necessarily different than averaging over recurrent decisions. This does not mean that this approach sits well with everybody. Section 18.4 considers other criteria for selecting the 'best' action.

The first step in evaluating the decision tree is to find the cumulative net cash flow associated with each end point of the tree. We will refer to this as the **payoff** associated with the chain of actions and events leading to this end point. This is simply equal to the sum of the monetary outcomes attached to all branches on the path from the origin — node 1 — to each end point. For example, the path from node 1 to the top end point in Figure 18-2 goes through the branch from node 1 to node 2 ('Do not accelerate') and the branch labelled 'Licence'. The dollar amounts associated with these two branches are $0 and ($-2.0 + 3.0) million. Their sum is $1.0 million.

Figure 18-3 reproduces the tree of Figure 18-2. Instead of showing the detailed cash amounts associated with each branch, it only lists the payoff for each end point of the tree. So, the top end point shows $1.0 (million).

The second end point consists of the path from node 1 to node 2 to node 4 and branch 'win'. Figure 18-2 lists the sum of the cash flows associated with this path as ($-0.6 + 3.5) or $2.9. Check the payoff associated with the remaining ends in Figure 18-3! For evaluating the tree we only work with these payoffs. The cash flows associated with individual branches are now ignored.

Using the expected value criterion, we find the best action by evaluating the nodes in the decision tree in reverse order. Evaluating a chance node means computing the expected value of the outcomes associated with all branches originating at that chance node. Take node 8. It has two branches. The top branch has a payoff of +$2.4 with probability 0.7 and the bottom branch has a payoff of $-3.6 with probability 0.3. The expected value is equal to the sum of the products of the payoffs and the corresponding probabilities. For node 8 this is (+$2.4)(0.7) + ($-3.6$)(0.3) = $0.6 million. We insert this result above chance node 8 (shown in the small rectangular box).

Evaluating a decision node means finding which of the decision branches originating at that node has the highest monetary value. Consider decision node 6 in Figure 18-3. It has three decision branches. 'Licence' has a payoff of $1.25 million. 'Abandon' has a payoff of $1.3 million. We just computed the expected payoff for 'Court' at node 8 as $0.6 'Abandon' has the highest value of $1.3 million. This is the amount inserted in the rectangle above node 6. Hence, at decision node 6, the best action to take is to 'Abandon' Release 2.1 immediately and wait for Release 3.0 to become available. To signal that this is the best decision, the other two actions are blocked off (shown by the two cross-bars).

Figure 18-3:   Evaluating the decision tree by backward induction

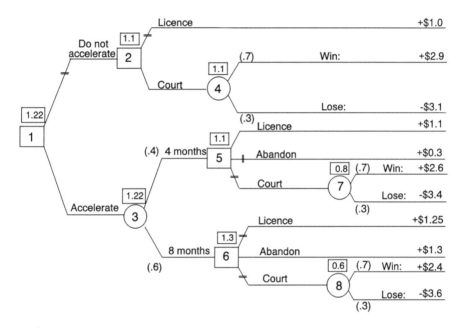

Note that we used the expected payoff we computed for node 8 as an input into finding the expected payoff for the 'Court' branch at node 6. In fact, if we had not already evaluated node 8, we would not have been able to determine the expected payoff for 'Court' and hence evaluate node 6. Since we need the results of all successor nodes, if there are any, for evaluating a given node, the tree has to be evaluated by starting at the end and working backwards to the beginning — hence the term **backward induction**.

Verify that for chance node 7 the expected payoff is $0.8. Hence, for decision node 5, the three decision choices offer $1.1 for 'Licence', $0.3 for 'Abandon' and $0.8 for 'Court'. The best decision is 'Licence' with a value of $1.1 million — the amount listed above node 5 — while 'Abandon' and 'Court' are blocked off. With nodes 5 and 6 both evaluated, we can now evaluate chance node 3. This is again the expected value over the two branches originating at node 3, namely, ($1.1)(0.4) + ($1.3)(0.6) = $1.22, the amount listed above node 3.

Before decision node 1 can be evaluated, decision node 2, and hence chance node 4 needs to be evaluated. Verify the results shown. At decision node 1, decision 'Do not accelerate' has an expected payoff of $1.1, while 'Accelerate' has an expected payoff of $1.22. Hence the best decision is to 'Accelerate'. 'Do not accelerate' is blocked off.

We now have the best sequence of decisions. It is to 'Accelerate' development of Release 3.0. Then, if the results of the preliminary analysis indicate that only four months can be gained, Barry should take out a 'Licence'. On the other hand, if 8 months can be gained, then he should 'Abandon' Release 2.1 immediately. One of two possible final outcomes will occur: $1.1 million with probability 0.4 or $1.3 million with probability 0.6. The average of these two outcomes, weighted by their probabilities is $1.22 million.

Note that only the first decision is firm. The second decision, taken either at node 5 or 6, is conditional on what happens at the chance node 3. So we see that, under uncertainty, the best alternative course of action is not a single decision, but a sequence of conditional decisions. This is referred to as a **strategy**. Nor do we know what the final outcome will be. All we have is a list of possible final outcomes. Their corresponding probabilities can be inferred from the path of branches that leads to each final outcome, as the product of the probabilities of each chance branch. In contrast, in deterministic situations the best alternative course of action can be specified as a firm single decision or a firm sequence of decisions. We will know exactly what will happen and what the final outcome will be.

Sensitivity Analysis

Remember that much of the input to Barry's problem was based on educated guesses. Would YY really settle out of court for the amounts used on the decision tree under the various options of abandoning Release 2.1 right away, 8 months or 4 months early? And what about the probability of winning the case or of introducing Release 3.0 several months earlier than originally scheduled? Let us analyze what happens as the probability of winning, p, becomes larger than 0.7.

Verify that when the probability of winning increases to 0.72, 'Do not accelerate' also has an expected payoff (at chance node 4) of $(0.72)(2.9) + (0.28)(-3.1) = 1.22 million. (Note that an increase in p does not change the best choices at decision nodes 5 and 6.) So, as this probability increases beyond 0.72, the preferred sequence of decisions is 'Do not accelerate' at decision node 1, followed by go to 'Court' at decision node 2. These decisions are unconditional, however, the final outcome is still either $2.9 million with probability $p > 0.72$, or $-$3.1 million with probability $1 - p < 1 - 0.72$. The best current strategy is, therefore, quite precariously poised on the probability of winning. A small increase in it will tilt the balance towards a different alternative course of action. If Barry is even a bit of a gambler he may well decide to go to court regardless.

18.3 THE EXPECTED VALUE OF PERFECT INFORMATION

Debbie Deft suggests that Barry Low consult with this famous soothsayer, who, it is said, has a perfect record in predicting the future. Unfortunately, this person does not come cheap. How much should Barry be willing to spend as an upper limit for acquiring a 'perfect' prediction on which state of the future will become true? Knowing which future state will eventuate, Barry can plan exactly what he has to do to get the best result for that future state. However, prior to receiving such perfect information Barry can only make contingency plans about which strategy is best for each possible future state. Then, knowing the probability for each future state, he can compute an expected payoff associated with his contingency plans. Comparing the expected value of his contingency plans, based on receiving perfect information, with the expected value of the best strategy without such information, Barry can then see how much better off he will be with perfect information.

The states of the future are given by the various combinations of the two types of events, i.e., the outcomes of the court case and the acceleration of Release 3.0. The four possible combinations of events are listed under the heading 'Joint state of nature' in Table 18-1. The probability of each of the combinations occurring is given by the product of the corresponding probabilities of each type of event. For example, based on the currently available (subjective) information about the future, the probability of the joint outcome 'win' and '4 months' is the equal to the probability of winning (0.7) times the probability of accelerating Release 3.0 by 4 months (0.4) or 0.28. Verify the remaining three joint probabilities, listed in the bottom row of Table 18-1. Note that the joint probabilities for the four combinations of outcomes must add up to 1, since one of them will occur.

Table 18-1: Payoff table for combined actions and joint states of nature

STRATEGY EVENT	JOINT STATE OF NATURE			
Acceleration result	4 months	4 months	8 months	8 months
Court outcome	win	lose	win	lose
A: Do not accelerate & get	$1.0	$1.0	$1.0	$1.0
B: Do not accelerate & abandon	$0.4	$0.4	$0.4	$0.4
C: Do not accelerate & go to	$2.9	-$3.1	$2.9	-$3.1
D: Accelerate & get licence	$1.1	$1.1	$1.25	$1.25
E: Accelerate & abandon	$0.3	$0.3	$1.3	$1.3
F: Accelerate & go to court	$2.8	-$3.4	$2.4	-$3.6
Best strategy for state of nature	C	D	C	E
payoff	$2.9	$1.1	$2.9	$1.3
Probability of state of nature	0.28	0.12	0.42	0.18

The six strategies are listed in the first column. In terms of Figure 18-2, each path from the initial node to an end point in the tree is a separate strategy. The entry at the intersection of each strategy and each state of nature is the payoff (in millions of dollars), as listed at the end points in Figure 18-3 — hence the name **payoff table**. Note that for some strategies, such as 'A: Do not accelerate & get licence' the monetary outcome does not depend on the state of nature. Hence, it is the same for all states.

For each state of nature, the best strategy can now easily be identified. It is given by the strategy with the most favourable monetary outcome of its column of payoffs. For example, for 'Acceleration result is 4 months and court case outcome is win', the strategy with the highest payoff is 'A: Do not accelerate & get licence'. Its payoff is $2.9. Check out the other three states.

So, prior to receiving this perfect information, the expected value of the payoffs for the best strategies is given by the sum of the products of these payoffs with their corresponding probabilities, or

$2.9(0.28) + $1.1(0.12) + $2.9(0.42) + $1.3(0.18) = $2.378 million

Again, the actual payoff will be one of the four payoffs, not their weighted average.

Without getting any information about the true state of the future, all Barry can expect is a weighted average payoff of $1.22 million associated with the optimal strategy developed in Figure 18-3. Getting perfect information, the expected payoff goes up to $2.378 — a gain of $1.158 (million). This increase in the expected payoff is called the **expected value of perfect information**. It represents the upper limit that Barry should be willing to pay to get perfect information. Naturally, the perfect predictor does not exist, and imperfect information is worth considerably less.

So we get a new, albeit not unexpected, insight into decision making under uncertainty. It may pay to acquire better information about the true state of the future. Furthermore, we can put an upper limit on how much the decision maker should be willing to spend for better information.

The decision maker may be able to obtain better information through various means, such as market research and test markets (i.e., trying out the product on a small, reasonably well self-contained market), additional scientific research to gain a better understanding of the underlying principles and causes, or by having recourse to expert advice, e.g., through a Delphi study.

18.4 CAPTURING THE INTRINSIC WORTH OF OUTCOMES

In many situations, the intrinsic worth of an outcome can quite often be adequately measured by its monetary outcome. This is particularly so for routine type decisions, where the monetary outcome falls well within the decision maker's normal range of experience. However, for strategic or unique decisions the monetary outcomes are usually outside this range. Furthermore, the outcomes usually involve a high degree of uncertainty. In such instances, few decision makers are willing to 'play the averages'. Other factors, such as the decision maker's financial ability to absorb large losses or the personal likes and dislikes of engaging in risky situations, may well influence how such uncertain outcomes are viewed.

You can easily check this out by imagining the following situation. It is the 20th of the month and you have $80 left for food and other necessities to carry you through the end of the month, when you get your next sustenance payment. You have no other means to get money. A 'friend' takes you to a party where you are invited to participate in a game. At a cost of $60 you are asked to flip a coin. If it falls heads you win $360, tails you get nothing. If you take the offer, you end up with either $380 or $20 in your pocket. The expected value of your financial situation is (0.5)($380) + (0.5)($20) or $200. Given that you right now have just barely enough to get through the remainder of the month, would you be willing to participate in this game? If you are like most people, you would decline. The great majority of people in such a financial position would rather have $80 in their pocket for certain, than a 50-50 chance of $20 or $380.

Similarly, most of us carry insurance on our cars and other property. Some of us buy lottery tickets or gamble at the races. Clearly, these decisions are not based on a simple criterion of maximizing the expected monetary outcome. How else could insurance companies or lottery and gambling operators cover their operating costs, their pay-outs on claims or wins, and at the same time also make handsome profits? Should we infer from this that decisions to buy insurance or to gamble are not made on a rational basis? Far from it! It simply means that factors other than simply monetary outcomes affect how decision makers view outcomes that involve a great degree of uncertainty.

Furthermore, for many decision situations the outcomes can often not be measured in monetary terms alone without introducing rather questionable value judgments. This is clearly so for Olly's problem. What is the monetary equivalent for 'Living with angina' or 'Dying in surgery'? Similarly, for many decisions in the public sector the outcomes of various courses of action could be the preservation or the destruction of scenic beauty, wilderness areas, or other important sites of public interest, changes to public safety, public health, or equity, and so on. Assigning monetary values to such things is fraught with controversy.

For example, a proposal to build a third international airport for London in the late 70s would have destroyed a Norman church built in the 11th century. The analysts valued the church at its fire insurance value (to be ridiculed in the public hearings held)! In such cases, a simple criterion of maximizing expected monetary values will not do. Some of the approaches discussed in this and the next section may help. In other instances, decision criteria that explicitly consider multiple conflicting objectives may have to be invoked. Dealing with multiple conflicting objectives is the topic of the next chapter.

To measure the intrinsic worth or desirability of highly risky outcomes outside our normal range of experience we have to go beyond monetary values. This section discusses two approaches which are not based on 'playing the averages'. The next section gives a short introduction to **utility theory** — an approach to express the intrinsic worth of outcomes along a numeric scale that expresses the decision maker's world view, her or his personal value judgment and attitude towards risk.

The Minimax Criterion

Consider again Barry Low's problem, but with an additional twist. Losing the court case means that Barry's firm goes bankrupt. Barry is not so much of a gambler to run that risk. So any action which runs this risk is excluded. In fact, Barry is even more of a risk averter. He really wants to play it safe. So he wants to choose a decision strategy that guarantees him at least the best of the worst outcomes possible over all alternatives, no matter what happens. In this example, this means finding the strategy with the maximum lowest payoff. This decision rule is known as the **minimax criterion** (derived from **mini**mizing the **max**imum loss; when dealing with benefits, it is also referred to as the maxmin criterion, derived from maximizing the minimum benefit).

Finding the minimax strategy could be done on the decision tree. However, since we have already summarized the information in the decision tree in the form of a payoff table, it is simpler to work directly with this table. Table 18-2 reproduces those parts of Table 18-1 we need for this evaluation. We find for each strategy its worst outcome or payoff. This is the number entered in the last column of the table. For example, for strategy 'C: Do not accelerate & go to court' the worst payoff is -$3.1, obtained for two of the states of nature. Verify the remaining entries in the last column.

Table 18-2: Payoff table for combined actions and joint states of nature

STRATEGY EVENT	JOINT STATE OF NATURE				Worst payoff for action
Acceleration result	4	4	8	8	
Court outcome	win	lose	win	lose	
A: Do not accelerate & get	$1.0	$1.0	$1.0	$1.0	$1.0
B: Do not accelerate & abandon	$0.4	$0.4	$0.4	$0.4	$0.4
C: Do not accelerate & go to	$2.9	--$3.1	$2.9	-$3.1	-$3.1
D: Accelerate & get licence	$1.1	$1.1	$1.25	$1.25	$1.1
E: Accelerate & abandon	$0.3	$0.3	$1.3	$1.3	$0.3
F: Accelerate & go to court	$2.8	-$3.4	$2.4	-$3.6	-$3.6

The best of the worst outcomes or, in our case, the maximum of the minimum payoffs is $1.1 million, obtained for strategy 'D: Accelerate & get licence'. Strategy D is therefore the **minimax strategy**. Interestingly, the minimax strategy for Barry is the same as for maximizing the expected payoff. But this is by coincidence rather than by rule.

Note that at no point did the probabilities of the various outcomes at chance nodes enter into the decision process. So even if the chance of losing the court case is, say only one in a 1000, or 1 in a million for that matter, the minimax criterion will choose the same strategy. This seems to be rather unreasonable. In business, conservative decision makers of that sort end up accepting only riskless ventures. But most riskless ventures are also low-return. They miss most good opportunities. Their businesses stagnate and ultimately will be squeezed out by competitors who are willing to assume some reasonable risks.

On the other hand, if the decisions involve ethical, safety, or environmental aspects, such as life-and-death outcomes, or the possible destruction of unique ecological or scenic areas, a minimax approach may be more appropriate as a decision criterion than maximizing the expected payoff.

A Risk Threshold Approach

In this approach, any decision choices that carry a probability of certain specified adverse outcomes larger than some critical level are eliminated. The 'best' alternative course of action is then chosen from the remaining ones, based on some other criterion, such as maximizing the expected net cash flow.

For example, assume that Barry is not willing to run a risk of more than 1 in 5 of going bankrupt. Any strategy which has a probability of more than 0.2 of resulting in bankruptcy is eliminated. 'Do not accelerate' followed by 'Court' has a probability of 0.3 of bankruptcy. Hence it is ruled out. This leaves only 'Licence' to follow 'Do not accelerate', at a net cash flow of $1.0 million. 'Accelerate' can lead to bankruptcy for both chance outcomes at node 3 if 'Court' is the follow-on choice. However, using an expected value criterion, 'Court' is not a contender. The 'best' follow-on choices for 'Accelerate' have a zero chance of bankruptcy. Based on that reasoning, the expected net cash flow for 'Accelerate' is $1.22 million (as for the original problem situation). This turns out also to be the best strategy under the constraint of a probability of bankruptcy of at most 0.2.

Sensitivity analysis on the subjectively imposed limit for going bankrupt will give additional insight into how critical that 'constraint' is in terms of its effect on the expected outcome of the best decision strategy. If the expected value is highly sensitive to the constraint, this may lead the decision maker to review and possibly change that 'constraint'.

Rather than impose a 'constraint' on the probability of a certain type of outcome, the 'constraint' could be imposed on the maximum possible loss.

The risk threshold approach has considerable appeal. It formalizes the intuitive decision behaviour used by many decision makers. This lends it to a more rational analysis, particularly when coupled with systematic sensitivity analysis. Its major difficulty is that it may become quite intractable for complex decision situations with a large number of possible combinations of decision choices and random events.

The literature on decision analysis discusses a number of other criteria. Most are mainly of academic interest, with little or no practical use for real-life situations.

18.5 UTILITY ANALYSIS

In 1944, Von Neumann and Morgenstern, a mathematician and an economist, proposed an index designed to quantify the personal subjective worth of a risky
outcome to a given decision maker, valid for a particular decision situation at a
particular time. They called it **utility** — a rather unfortunate choice, given the
traditional usage made of this term in economic theory. For this reason, some
authors prefer the term **preference theory.**

A **utility function** expresses a decision maker's valuation of risky outcomes on
a numerical scale. We already used this concept for capturing Olly's preference
structure. The scale used is arbitrary; it could cover a range from 0 to 1, or 0 to
100. The lower limit reflects the worth of the least desirable outcome, the higher
limit the most desirable outcome, with all other outcomes in between.

Basic Forms of Utility Functions

Figure 18-4 shows three different shapes for such utility functions. The horizontal
axis measures the monetary outcomes of the decision problem. The vertical scale
shows the intrinsic worth of that outcome on the arbitrary scale chosen — in this case
the range from 0 to 1. The straight line in the middle represents the utility function
for a person who is **risk neutral.** Such a person does not need to have recourse to
a utility function — the 'best' decision will be the same if it is based on maximizing

Figure 18-4: The three basic shapes of utility functions

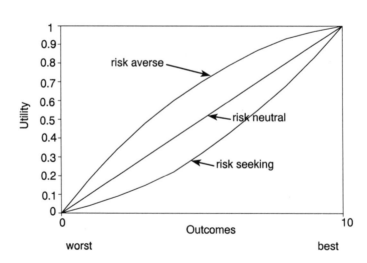

expected monetary outcomes. Most of us are risk neutral when we deal with outcomes which are clearly within our everyday range of experience. This may be a few dollars for an individual, but could be in the hundred-thousands for large business corporations.

The concave curve above the straight line is the general shape of the utility function for a decision maker who is **risk averse**. Consecutive equal increments in the monetary outcome result is smaller and smaller increments in utility. Most people exhibit some degree of risk aversion, particularly for large monetary gains or losses in their private and professional life.

The convex curve below the straight line depicts the utility function for a person who is a **risk taker**. Doubling the monetary outcome increases the utility more than proportionately. Few people exhibit such a pattern for outcomes of important business and private decision choices. The exception is the pathological gambler. However, all of us occasionally are risk takers when we are looking for thrills or fun, such as gambling at the races or playing cards.

So, we see that the same person may make some decisions from a risk-neutral position, others from a risk-averse position, and a few from a risk-seeking position. Each position is perfectly rational within its proper context and consistent with the person's world view.

A Five-Point Assessment Procedure

Recall the insights we gained from Olly's problem situation. We concluded that, given a risky option with outcomes A or C, we can construct an equivalent riskless option with outcome B, where A is preferred to B which is preferred to C, such that the decision maker is indifferent between choosing the risky or the riskless option. The equivalent riskless option can be constructed by either adjusting the value of B or by adjusting the probabilities of the risky option. Indifference between the two options implies that their intrinsic worth is the same. These surprisingly simple ideas form the basis for finding the utility function for a given decision situation.

We will now demonstrate the procedure with Barry's problem. We start out by assigning the worst outcome in Barry's problem an intrinsic value or a utility of zero, and the best outcome a utility of 1. The choice of these values is arbitrary. It will not affect the relative ranking of the various decision strategies open to Barry. In Barry's case, the worst outcome is –$3.6 million (i.e., a loss of $3.6 million), the best outcome a gain of $2.9 million.

We now offer Barry a choice of two options: (1) a 50-50 gamble involving the best and the worst outcomes, and (2) a riskless option involving a net cash flow somewhere in between the worst and the best outcomes. The technical term for the gamble is **reference lottery**. We could start out with a cash flow exactly half-way, i.e., –$0.35 million. (Keep in mind that negative outcomes represent losses!) Knowing that Barry is risk averse, we expect that he will prefer the sure payoff of –$0.35 million to the gamble. This is indeed the case. So we know that his utility for –$0.35 million is higher than the utility of the gamble. We now lower the monetary value of the riskless option. Say we reduce it to −$2.0 million. We again ask Barry to rank the original gamble and the sure outcome of −$2.0 million. He now says that he prefers the gamble. This implies that his utility for −$2.0 is lower than the utility of the gamble. Our next try is a value between −$0.35 and −$2.0 million. We continue presenting Barry with a choice of the original gamble and a sure outcome of X dollars, increasing the value of X if Barry prefers the gamble and decreasing it if he prefers X. After a few more trials, Barry finally settles on a value of −$1.5, for which Barry is indifferent between the gamble and the riskless outcome. Indifference between the original gamble and the sure thing of −$1.5 implies that these two options have the same intrinsic worth or the same utility. But we know what the utility of the gamble is. It is equal to the expected utilitiy of the outcomes of the gamble. For a 50-50 gamble this is (0.5)(1) + (0.5)(0), where 1 and 0 are the arbitrary utility values assigned to the best and worst outcomes. So, the utilities of the gamble and of the riskless outcome of −$1.5 million are both 0.5.

We now repeat this procedure a second and third time. But instead of choosing a 50-50 reference lottery involving the worst and best outcomes, we replace either the worst outcome or the best outcome with the value −$1.5 million just found. So the second reference lottery is given by a 50-50 chance of −$1.5 and $2.9 million. Again we know what the expected utility of this reference lottery is, i.e., (0.5)(1) + (0.5)(0.5) or 0.75. After a number of trials Barry agrees on an equivalent riskless option of $0.4 million. Hence, an outcome of $0.4 million must have a utility of 0.75, the same as the second reference lottery. For the third round we set the reference lottery to a 50-50 chance of −$3.6 and −$1.5. Verify that the expected utility of this reference lottery is 0.25. After a few more trials Barry settles on an equivalent riskless option of −$2.8 million. Hence, −$2.8 must have a utility of 0.25.

We now have determined the utility of five outcomes in the range from the worst to the best outcome for this particular decision situation under uncertainty. They are depicted in Figure 18-5 by the solid squares. Fitting a smooth curve through these five points yields a good approximation to Barry's utility function for this problem. As expected, Barry is clearly risk averse. His utility function is everywhere above the straight line representing a risk neutral utility function.

Finding the Best Decision Using Utility Functions

For outcomes measured along a monetary scale the 'best' decision strategy is based on an expected monetary value criterion. If the intrinsic worth of outcomes is measured by utilities, the 'best' strategy is the one that **maximizes the expected utility**. We simply replace the net cash flows at all end points in the decision tree by the corresponding utility values, and then proceed to evaluate the tree by backward induction as before. I suggest that you read off Figure 18-5 the utility values corresponding to all end point net cash flows, insert them into Figure 18-3, and evaluate all nodes again. Note that the 'best' strategy using an expected utility criterion does not change. However, the best action at the blocked-off node 2 switches from 'Court' to 'Licence'.

Figure 18-5: Barry Low's utility function

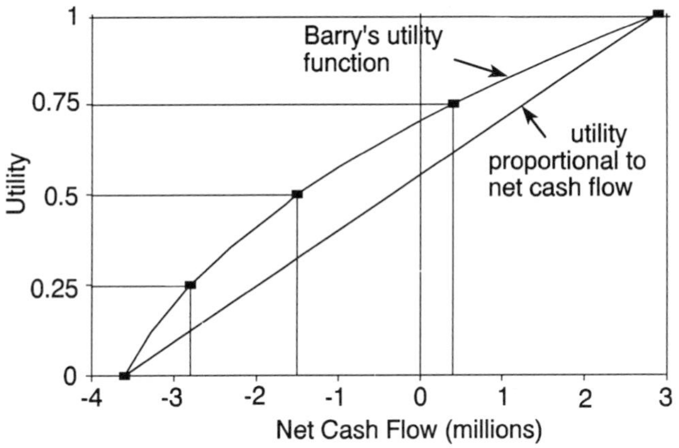

Some Reflections on Utility Measures

It is important to stress that the utility measures obtained in this manner not only reflect the decision maker's valuation of outcomes, but also the attitude towards risk. So these utility functions are not valid for decisions that do not involve uncertainty. Furthermore, they are valid for the particular situation for which they were assessed at a particular point in time. Each new situation needs to be re-assessed anew. Similarly, a decision maker's attitude towards risk may change over time.

The procedure can also be easily adapted to situations that do not involve monetary outcomes, such as is the case in Olly's problem. In fact, there have been serious efforts made since the early 80s to introduce utility-type concepts into decision situations in the health fields.

The method for assessing approximate utility functions is surprisingly simple. Increased accuracy for drawing the curve can easily be obtained by finding equivalent riskless options for additional utility values between the ones assessed in the five-point procedure. It may also be possible to fit algebraic functions to the points assessed. Given the simplicity of the procedure, why have utility functions largely remained an academic curiosity, and this in spite of the fact that this topic has been part of the curriculum of most college and university business courses since the early 60s?

There are a number of reasons. Although the procedure is simple, most decision makers find it difficult to think in terms of reference lotteries and equivalent riskless options. Hence, they are reluctant to be pinned down to definite answers. Their answers may not be consistent, requiring a delicate process of re-assessment. In fact, it needs a fairly skilful analyst to get results which the decision maker feels truly reflect her or his preference structure for the problem situation in question. Up to now few real-life applications outside academic institutions have been reported.

Research by M. McCord and R. de Neufville ['Lottery equivalents': Reduction of the certainty effect in utility assessment, *Management Science,* Jan.. 1986, pp. 56-60] and by P. Delquié [Inconsistent trade-offs between attributes: New evidence in preference assessment biases, *Management Science,* Nov. 1993, pp.1382-95] indicates that the utility functions derived may differ depending on the exact sequence and form of assessments made, the framing of the assessment, as well as other unexplained factors. Hence, this sheds serious doubts on their validity.

However, even if the utility functions derived are never explicitly used in finding the 'best' decision strategy, the process of assessing such utility functions will enhance the decision maker's awareness of her or his preference structure and thereby lead to better and more informed decision making.

EXERCISES

1. Sally Smart is planning how to survive, in financial terms, the 1994-95 academic year. The way matters stand right now, she will lose her government assistance since her parents have just joined the class of 'nouveau riche' created by the conservative government to raise the moral of the country's population. With another brother struggling to finish his engineering degree, chances are nil that her parents will be able to support her with more than an occasional carrot cake. She has a number of choices:
    *   She could drop out and join the ranks of the unemployed. Using her skills in present value calculations recently acquired in MSCI 101 she calculated that the NPV of her lifetime loss in earning power would amount to $25,000 if the finance minister's ECON 101 policies continue to depress the economy, while the loss would only be $5,000 if the prime minister finds the courage to sack her with most of her Treasury advisers. Sally figures that the chance that the prime minister can find the necessary courage is only 25%.
    *   She could take out a loan, finish her degree and then pay it back over the next 5 to 10 years. The NPV cost of that action is $15,800 with the present finance minister remaining in office and $12,400 if she is replaced.
    *   She could enter into a marriage of convenience with another student and then automatically retain her government assistance. With the cost of the parties her friends would insist she throw for both 'tieing the knot' and 'cutting it again after graduation', as well as the potential 'intangible' costs associated with this action, she figures that the net cost to her would be $4000 with the present finance minister remaining in office, but $16,000 without her (due to having gotten married without really any need for it).
    (a) Develop a decision tree, attaching costs and probabilities to the various branches. Using this tree find the best action for Sally based on monetary considerations only.

(b) Using the method of Section 18.3 determine the value of perfect information.

2. After making her choice, Sally decides to sleep on it for a few days before taking any irrevocable action. On the second morning, it dawns on her that the minister of education might stumble on the marriage of convenience scheme. She figures that there is in fact a 40% chance that the Government would introduce a questionnaire asking embarrassing personal questions about the civil state of the applicants for government assistance. She might then have incurred the expense of getting married ($4,000) only to find out that she does not qualify for assistance anyway, given her marriage is one of convenience only. She would then be back to the drawing board, but obviously still could settle on one of the first two choices above. (The $4,000 would then have been incurred in addition to the cost of these choices.)
   (a) Draw up a new decision tree for this problem and find the strategy that minimizes expected costs now.
   (b) Using the method of Section 18.3, determine the value of perfect information.

3. In the mid-70s a small car was blown off the access road to a ski-field in the Southern Alps of New Zealand, resulting in a fatality. The car's owner had in fact ignored warnings not to use the road during gale force winds that had sprung up in the early afternoon. Several other cars had close shaves during other storms. The management of the ski-field was faced with the dilemma as to what action to take, if any, to prevent further accidents of that sort. Three alternatives were investigated: (1) Relocation of the road away from exposed areas at a cost of $2.5 million, completely eliminating any further danger. (2) Erection of protective wind barriers at a cost of $1.5 million, which would prevent any vehicle from being blown off the road, except under the most severe storm conditions. The chance of such a storm occurring over the next 10 years was estimated at 20%, but, since the road would be closed to traffic if such a storm was predicted, the chance that a car would actually be caught in such a storm was only 10%. If, however, an accident would happen, the ski-field company would be liable to punitive damages and possible loss of income due to adverse publicity to an amount of $4.2 million. Furthermore, the company would have little choice but to relocate the road then. (3) Do nothing, but close the ski-field whenever there was the slightest danger of any winds in excess of 20 knots. This would not involve any immediate costs, but would lose considerable revenues. These are estimated at $1 million. Furthermore, there still remained a residual 10% chance of a major accident due to the inability to predict the often sudden weather changes in the region. An accident would have the same financial consequences as for option (2), i.e., punitive damages and the cost of relocating the road. Assume all amounts are already expressed in present values.
   (a) Develop a decision tree for this problem, attaching costs and probabilities to the various branches.
   (b) Determine the action with the lowest expected cost.
   (c) Using the method of Section 18.3, determine the value of perfect information.

4. The British Columbia tourist industry has experienced a drop in tourist tour bookings of over 25%. According to the latest forecast, the tourist trade is unlikely to pick up significantly before the middle of next year. In fact, one of the tour operators, Green Tours, using The Airport Château has just notified Michel d'Hôtelier, the Quebec born manager, that they might cancel their bookings for the coming year. Green Tours

booked on average 20 rooms for 250 days of the year (i.e., 5000 room nights). Michel thinks that this may be a ploy to get reduced room rates. He expects that there is a 50-50 chance they will renew the contract if he reduces the room fee from $150 per night to $130 for 1994. If Green Tours abandons their bookings, it will be too late to fill the empty rooms by arranging a contract with another tour operator. However, he thinks that there is a 75% chance he will be able to negotiate a contract with another tour operator for 5000 room nights for 1995 at a price of $140. This alternative will however incur a $20,000 cost, regardless of whether the negotiations are successful or not. If Green Tours continue their bookings for 1994, Michel is 80% certain that Green Tours will renew their contract for 1995 at the old price of $150. If not they would certainly do it again at the $130 price. If no firm contracts can be arranged with a tour operator, then all Michel can expect is to sell about 1000 room-nights per year on a casual basis to individual tourists at a room rate of $180 per night, leaving some 4000 room-nights empty.

Michel can also look for alternative business for 1994/5. By far the most reliable business is in so-called 'air-crew contracts', where an airline books a fixed number of rooms every night at a fixed contractual sum for the entire year, regardless of whether the rooms are used or not. Michel has already been approached by Bamboo Airlines, which serves the lucrative tourist trade to South East Asia, with a contract proposal for 20 rooms for a two-year period at a fixed contract sum of $1,200,000. This averages to about $82 per room per night, considerably less than the price paid by tour operators, although it is guaranteed for the entire two years. Unfortunately, he will have to make a decision on the Bamboo Airlines contract before being able to conclude the negotiations with Green Tours for 1994.

In any case he expects that by 1996, his Airport Chateau will again be fully booked out with tour operators. The hotel's operating costs are obviously dependent on its occupancy rate. If Michel clinches any deals with tour operators or the airline, he will need a full staff complement. The hotel's annual operating costs will be $300,000 higher than if it only relies on casual tourist traffic.

(a) Develop a decision tree for this situation. Show the revenues and costs associated with each branch, as well as any probabilities. Also show the cumulative cash flow associated with each end point of the tree. You do not have to use discounting on the cash flows.

(b) Use the tree developed under (a) to find the best strategy. What is the best strategy and its expected profit?

(c) Using the method demonstrated in Section 18.3, determine the value of perfect information.

5. A recording company is faced with the decision as to whether or not to record and market an album for a promising, but so far unknown and untested local rock band. The usual method to reach a decision is as follows: Two songs of the group's repertoire are recorded in the firm's studio. These are then submitted for appraisal to a consumer panel. These two steps have a cost of $3000. The panel is asked to rate the songs as 'potential hits' or 'questionable'. The talent scout and the music director of the firm agree that from what music they have heard of the group and the perceived current preference patterns of the potential buyers, the probability that the panel will rate the songs as 'potential hits' is 0.7. If the panel rates the songs as 'questionable', the firm normally decides not to go ahead with any further recordings of the band. If

the panel rates the songs as 'potential hits', the firm will record a full album and prepare its release on the market. This has a fixed cost of $50,000. The decision to be made then is whether to make an initial production run of a combined total of 10,000 or 40,000 disks, records, and cassettes. Two months after the release, the market response will be evaluated. It is either 'success' or 'failure'. "Success" means all disks, etc., will be sold at a gross unit profit of $7. 'Failure' means that the majority will have to be dumped at a heavy discount, at an average gross profit of $1.50 if 10,000 are made and $0.50 if 40,000 are made. Past experience shows that out of 10 cases where the panel rated the songs as 'potential hits', 8 turned out to be 'success'.

(a) Draw a decision tree for this situation, attaching costs, gross revenues, and probabilities to the various branches.

(b) Find the best action for the firm for this particular band.

(c) Find the payoff table corresponding to this problem and determine the value of perfect information.

6. A firm has just placed an order for a special-purpose machine. Since this is one of a kind, it is cheaper to also order some essential spare parts for the machine at the time when the original order for it is placed, rather than wait until later when they might be needed. Consider a particular part. If ordered with the machine, each part has a cost of $2,100. If ordered later on at the time of an actual breakdown, the cost of the part is $6,000. In addition, the loss in profit due the machine being down for several weeks amounts to another $4,000. Past experience with similar machines indicates that the probability of needing n spare parts over the machine's productive life is as follows:

number of parts needed	0	1	2	3	4
probability	0.1	0.3	0.3	0.2	0.1

Any parts remaining unused at the end of the machine's productive life have only a scrap value of $100. (Ignore the fact that various cash flows may occur over a span of several years.) The decision is the number of spare parts to be included in the original machine order. Develop a decision tree for this situation and find the best action.

7. A bookshop is considering how many copies of an exclusive connoisseur art calendar to buy. The purchase price is $240 per copy. They would be sold for $440 each. From past experience the owner predicts the following probability distribution for the demand for this calendar:

Demand	4	5	6	7	8
Probability	0.4	0.3	0.15	.1	0.5

Any calendars not sold are disposed of below cost for $50.

(a) Draw a decision tree depicting the decision choices and associated outcomes for this problem. Show the revenues and costs associated with each branch and the probabilities associated with all branches issuing from chance nodes.

(b) Use the decision tree to determine the optimal number to procure and find the associated expected profit.

(c) Interpret the meaning of the expected profit in terms of the possible outcomes.

8. Consider again the decision tree developed for the ski-field case in exercise 3 above. Find its corresponding payoff table and determine the minimax strategy. Note that in this case it is the strategy that minimizes the maximum cost.

9. Consider again the decision tree developed for the recording company in exercise 5 above. Find its corresponding payoff table and determine the minimax strategy.

10. Assume that your mechanic just told you that there is a 50-50 chance that your beloved BMW's motor will seize within the next 6 months. If this happens, other major damage will occur to your motor. The total repair bill will amount to about $2000. He advises you to have the motor overhauled now at a fraction of that cost. What is the maximum amount that you personally would be willing to spend on an overhaul, such that you would just be indifferent between the 50-50 chance of the motor seizing and the overhaul? Using the other steps of the five-point assessment procedure, determine the approximate shape of your personal utility function for expenditures on your BMW.

REFERENCES

Behn, R. D., and Vaupel, J. W., *Quick Analysis for Busy Decision Makers*, Basic Books, 1982. A fascinating book dealing with a wide range of close-to-real-life decision situations under risk and uncertainty. The aim is to convince current and future decision makers of the usefulness of decision analysis and make it easily accessible to the lay person. No mathematics background required.

Cooke, Steve, and Slack, Nigel, *Making Management Decisions*, Prentice-Hall, 1991. Chapters 6 and 7 cover the topics of decision analysis and utilities at an elementary level.

Hill, Percy H. et al., *Making Decisions - A Multidisciplinary Introduction*, University Press of America, 1986. Chapters 7 to 10 deal with decision analysis at a level similar to this text.

Keeney, R. L., and Raiffa, H., *Decisions with Multiple Objectives*, Wiley, 1976. Authoritative treatment of utility functions and their use, particularly for multi-attribute outcomes. Chapter 4 deals with single-attribute utility functions.

Samson, Danny, *Managerial Decision Analysis*, Irwin, 1988. Comprehensive treatment of decision analysis at an introductory level, including the use of the Arborist decision analysis package for PCs. Contains numerous fully worked out examples, case studies, and real-life applications.

19   Decisions with Multiple Objectives

So far we assumed that for any given decision problem the decision maker pursues a single objective. Often that objective was minimizing costs or maximizing net benefits. You will rightly point out that, in real-life decision situations, most decision makers attempt to satisfy a variety of objectives and goals simultaneously. Some of these objectives or goals are fully or partially conflicting. Multiple conflicting objectives and goals are an integral part of each person's Weltanschauung — a word you have not heard for a while! It is not just politicians who promise to deliver the 'maximum benefits' to the 'largest number of people' at the 'least cost'. Few business people are so single-minded as to only look for maximum returns on their investment. Most also wish to provide high quality products or services, maintain the best customer services possible, keep a happy and cooperative workforce, and achieve the largest market share possible. Similarly, most decisions dealing with environmental and social issues strive to meet multiple and usually conflicting goals. On a personal level, have you not allowed yourself to dream of that ideal job that offers daily challenges, involves a variety of interesting duties, has responsibility and prestige, has excellent promotional opportunities, has a pleasing work environment, is high paying with lots of fringe benefits, and involves extended stays on the French Riviera? In each instance, the actual decision taken is usually a compromise. It does well on some objectives or goals, worse on others.

But even our daily life is a sequence of compromises between conflicting goals and objectives. This means that we must in fact be experts in decision making with multiple objectives! And we do this without any support of a formal approach. So why should we need such support in a managerial or planning context? In part, it is for the same reasons that led us to have recourse to formal decision models when we ignored all but one objective, namely as a means for overcoming at least in part the complexity of the situation. Remember our discussion in Section 15.7 on people's limited cognitive abilities for processing complex, multi-faceted relationships? This is not only a reality when faced with decision making under uncertainty, but becomes even more pronounced when faced with weighing several partially conflicting objectives.

There are other reasons. A formal approach allows a fuller exploration of the solution space, thereby providing deeper insight into the problem — one of the prime aims of OR/MS. The joint performance of the objectives in response to the various potential decision alternatives can be observed, compared, and weighed. This may reveal that certain objectives are much more sensitive, while the performance of others is hardly affected, no matter what action is taken. The decision maker is thus provided with a more effective basis for finding the most preferred compromise. It may lead to a partial or complete re-evaluation of the importance of the various objectives and ultimately to better, more defensible, and wiser decision making.

This chapter will only lightly scratch the surface of this vast topic. To set the stage, we will summarize three real applications reported in the literature. Section 19.2 reviews how 'traditional' OR/MS methods deal with multiple objectives. Sections 19.3 and 19.4 give a brief overview of the difficulties and aims of multi-criteria decision making, commonly abbreviated as MCDM — not a roman numeral — and the approaches to MCDM suggested in the literature. The discussion is largely restricted to the case where the choice has to be made from a set of discrete alternatives. This sidesteps the rather more complex situation of continuous decision variables, for which multiple objective mathematical programming techniques, similar to linear programming, have been invented. Sections 19.5 and 19.6 then apply one of the simplest MCDM approaches to the selection of the 'best' venue for a conference of a software users' group.

19.1 THREE REAL MCDM PROBLEM SITUATIONS

Multiple Land Use Planning

The Federal Land Policy and Management Act, passed by the 94th U.S. Congress in 1976, gives the following mandate to the Bureau of Land Management (BLM) for the management of the over 400 million acres of federally owned land under its control: Land management is

- to be on the basis of multiple use and sustained yield;
- to protect the quality of scientific, scenic, historical, ecological, environmental, air and atmospheric, water resource, and archaeological values;
- where appropriate, to preserve and protect certain public lands in their natural condition;
- to provide food and habitat for fish, wildlife, and domestic animals;
- to provide for outdoor recreation and human occupancy and use.

Many of these objectives are in direct conflict with one another. For some areas, the BLM will be under fire from different pressure groups to have their vested interest prevail. These groups include farm lobbies who want more grazing land, mining companies who want prospecting rights, and conservation groups who want to keep some areas in their natural state. How does the BLM resolve these conflicts?

Assume that a BLM district officer has to develop a multiple-use land program for an area which at present is used mainly for grazing. Geological surveys indicate the potential for oil or gas deposits of possibly economic significance. The area's recreational value is mainly for big game hunting and winter use by snow-mobiles. BLM's current procedure roughly consists of compiling detailed inventories of the area's topography, soil, vegetation, other physical features, and of its existing uses. This is followed by a detailed assessment of the area's unlimited potential for each possible use, without regard to any other uses.   Independently of this, a socioeconomic profile is compiled that provides relevant information on attitudes of current and prospective users of the area, on special interest groups, and on the economic importance of exploitable natural resources. Armed with these documents, the area manager has to develop a compromise solution that reflects both the best intrinsic uses and relevant socioeconomic factors. This is a very difficult task of weighing conflicting objectives against each other.

A pilot study by K.F. Martinson at the University of Colorado 1977, implemented on a trial basis by some BLM districts, demonstrates how a multiple-objective linear programming approach can be used to gain deep insights into how the various objectives respond to each other, leading to more effective and more defensible management plans. (Section 22-5 in H.G. Daellenbach et al., *Introduction to O.R. Techniques*, Allyn and Bacon, 1983, shows a simple, but detailed example of this approach.)

The Mexico City Airport Development

One of the more publicized examples deals with the Mexico City airport development, done in 1971 for the Ministry of Public Works (MPW) of Mexico by two MIT professors, H.R. de Neufville and H. Raiffa. As in many other large urban centres, the growth in the volume of air traffic, the difficulties of further expansion of the existing major airport, with its take-off and landing flight patterns largely over built-up areas, lent considerable urgency for providing an acceptable airport service development strategy over the next 30 years.   The existing Texcoco airport is sandwiched between the remains of Lake Texcoco to the east and the sprawling city expanse to the west. Upgrading Texcoco on the highly unstable former lake bed or by displacement of large populations would make construction and maintenance very expensive. The continued increase in air traffic that this would allow would further aggravate the current noise problem and increase the danger of serious air accidents with potentially numerous casualties among the residents in the densely populated surrounding areas. The advantage of upgrading Texcoco was its close proximity to the city centre.   The most attractive alternative sight was at Zumpango, an undeveloped rural area some 25 miles north of the city. It would not suffer any of Texcoco's problems, but would increase travel times to and from the city substantially.

Based on a consensus of the directors of the MPW, a partial list of objectives included:

- minimizing total construction, maintenance, and operating costs;
- minimizing travel times to and from the airport;
- maximizing airport operating safety;
- minimizing the effect of air traffic noise pollution;

- minimizing social disruption and displacement of the population; and
- raising the air traffic service capacity for Mexico City.

There were many uncertainties associated with any decisions. For instance, what will be the future growth in air traffic? What will be the noise levels of future aircraft engines? What safety standards will IATA and international pilot associations impose for future airport operations?

Faced with the multiple objectives and these uncertainties, how should the MPW go about developing a strategy that is 'best' in terms of social, economic, safety, and political considerations? After attempts by the MPW to 'solve' this problem using traditional cost-benefit analysis (a version of the project evaluation method of Chapter 10 adapted for public projects), the two professors, together with the senior staff of the MPW, applied a form of decision analysis based on multiattribute utility functions to come up with a set of recommendations. This method develops individual utility functions for the performance on each objective. These are then combined into a single complex aggregate utility function which is used for comparing various development strategies. (See R.L. Keeney and H. Raiffa, *Decisions with Multiple Objectives*, Wiley 1976, for a detailed account of that study, as well as several other case studies. Chapter 22 of the text by Daellenbach, listed above, contains a fairly elementary demonstration of this approach to a search and rescue service.)

Blood Bank Stock Management

Blood banks maintain stocks of the various blood products, including fresh blood, for use in emergencies and scheduled operations. Unfortunately, fresh blood has a limited shelf life of anywhere from 28 to 49 days, depending on the type of preservatives added. Any unused blood past its limited shelf life is outdated and has to be destroyed. Blood bank managers try to avoid two types of undesirable events: (1) running short of blood needed for emergencies and scheduled operations, and (2) outdating of unused blood. The first may have serious consequences or require expensive remedial action, such as calling up suitable emergency donors, the second is a waste of a valuable product. If donors give blood without compensation, outdating of blood is morally undesirable. Avoiding both shortages and outdating of blood are the major objectives of fresh blood management. Cost considerations usually do not enter into the picture.

Relatively large stocks of each type of blood will help to keep shortages to low levels. On the other hand, outdating can be kept to a minimum by keeping low levels of blood stocks. The achievement levels of the two objectives vary thus inversely with each other. The solution must be a compromise. Naturally, most managers will view blood shortages as more serious than outdating of blood. They will thus risk more outdating of blood in order to keep shortages to acceptably safe low levels.

In the 70s and 80s a lot of research has been devoted to this problem. The policies derived from the models developed have led to a reduction in outdating of blood from well over 25% of all blood collected in the early 70s to below 5% currently, without an increase in the rate of shortages.

19.2   TRADITIONAL OR/MS APPROACH

The traditional approach for modeling multiple objectives is to optimize what is considered the most important objective, while meeting minimal performance targets on all other objectives. For instance, for most issues involving safety, such as the operation of various means of transport or plants, like a nuclear power station, an acceptable 'solution' is obtained by minimizing operating costs, subject to meeting certain safety standards. Usually, cost minimization is considered to be the most important objective, while safety and other objectives are subordinated to it.

In this approach the lesser objectives are replaced by minimal performance targets that have to be met, i.e., by firm surrogate constraints. Therefore, they restrict, in fact, dictate the best level of achievement that is possible for the most important objective. In other words, this approach first guarantees that the targets on the lesser objectives are satisfied, before it allows any look at the most important objective. So, by a rather ironic twist, the most important objective becomes subordinated to the less important objectives.

Mind you, when dealing with safety issues, this may be all the better. However, there are many situations where this inadvertent reversal of priorities is more questionable. In particular, these minimal performance targets on the lesser objectives may involve a considerable degree of arbitrariness, nor do the performance targets chosen have the inviolate nature of physical constraints. They are often the result of a policy decision. They reflect what is seen as a reasonable or a desirable level of achievement — both rather fuzzy and highly subjective notions. It is, therefore, important that the OR/MS analyst does a comprehensive exercise of sensitivity analysis with respect to all these surrogate constraints. The decision maker should be presented not simply with the 'optimal' solution, but also with the insights gained from the sensitivity analysis.

The traditional approach is a fairly arbitrary ad hoc procedure. It really shirks the fundamental issues in MCDM. The next two sections look at some of these.

19.3   SOME BASIC ISSUES IN MCDM

A New Meaning for 'Optimal Solution'

Finding the optimal solution with respect to a single objective has a precise meaning. It identifies that solution which either achieves the maximum or the minimum outcome for the objective, whichever is the aim of the optimization. What is the meaning of an optimal solution in the presence of several objectives?

Clearly, it cannot be a maximum or a minimum of something. Only by coincidence will all objectives take on, for instance, their maximum outcome simultaneously for the same decision choice. The objectives are then not conflicting and the problem is trivial in this respect. In general, one decision choice does better with respect to some objectives, while another fares better for other objectives. By necessity, the decision chosen as the 'best' one is a compromise. It may achieve the optimum outcome for some objectives, but falls short to various degrees on others. So, rather than refer to the solution finally chosen as 'the optimal solution', it makes more sense to call it the **most preferred** solution.

Dominance

Some decision choices can be ruled out as potential candidates for the most preferred solution. If a decision choice A performs no better than another decision choice C with respect to all objectives and worse for at least one, then A is **dominated** by C. A can be eliminated from further consideration. A rational decision maker will never consider A as a potential candidate for the most preferred solution (provided the objectives used capture everything that counts about the decision choices).

Figure 19-1 depicts the concept of dominance graphically for the case of two conflicting objectives. Each axis measures the achievement level on one objective. The higher the level, the more desirable it becomes. The joint achievement levels on both objectives for each decision choice represent a point in the positive quadrant.

Figure 19-1: Dominance and efficient solutions

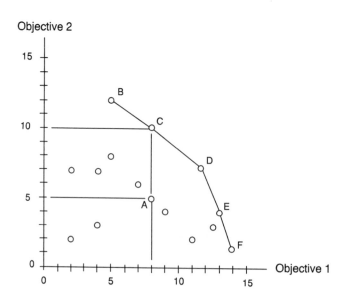

For example, alternative A achieves an outcome of 8 on objective 1 and 5 on objective 2, while alternative C achieves 8 on 1 and 10 on 2. A is no better than C for objective 1, but worse for objective 2. Hence, A is dominated by C. On the other hand, alternative B with outcomes of 4 on objective 1 and 12 on objective 2 does not dominate either A or C and is dominated by neither.

The solid line in Figure 19-1 from B to F connects all those alternatives that are not dominated by any other alternative. They are referred to as **efficient solutions**. They should be the only candidates for the most preferred solution. (In economics, the concept of dominance is also referred to as **Pareto optimality**.)

Measuring Outcomes for Objectives

The performance of an alternative decision choice is measured by a set of outcomes, one for each objective. The outcomes for some objectives may readily be measured in terms of some natural physical unit, such as dollars or number of people. For others, such as beauty or convenience, no natural measuring scales exist. Ultimately, the various decision choices must be compared with one another in some way. This comparison is either made indirectly in terms of some 'overall' performance derived from the individual outcomes over all objectives, or on a holistic basis in terms of a ranking of alternatives from best to worst. In the latter case, the outcomes achieved for the objective need not be measured along a cardinal scale.

Sometimes the measurement units used for different objectives can readily be compared. For example, the overall performance of a blood bank can be expressed in terms of the average number of pints of blood that have to be destroyed over a given time interval because the blood has outlived its useful life, i.e., pints of blood outdated, and in terms of the average number of units of blood requested for transfusions which cannot be delivered, i.e., pints of blood short. Although the consequences of outdating and shortages of blood are vastly different, the two measures can readily be compared.

Contrast this to a safety problem, where the outcomes of any decision choice are expected total cost and the expected number of injuries of various severities and deaths. How can dollars be compared with numbers of people injured or numbers of deaths? Economists would suggest that we express injuries or deaths in terms of the loss of future income. However, that ignores all intangible aspects, such as the pain, potential loss of life enjoyment, or the emotional personal loss of relatives of a dead person. Furthermore, how can we even measure such intangible aspects in a meaningful way?

The commonly accepted way out of many of these difficulties is to express outcomes in terms of a **score** along an arbitrary scale from say 0 to 1 or 0 to 100. The worst possible outcome may be given a score of 0, while the best possible outcome is given a score of 1 or 100. All intermediate outcomes are scored inside the interval selected.

This approach is used for all objectives. For outcomes with a natural unit of measurement the scores are simple linear transformations. For example, if the range of monetary benefits runs from $10,000 to $260,000 over the various alternatives, the maximum outcome is assigned a score of 100, with all other scores proportionately less. $20,000 then gets a score of 4. For intangible objectives, the scores assigned are, by necessity, highly subjective to the person doing the scoring. The scores assigned are not valid for another person, nor may they remain the same over time.

The difference in the scores achieved by pairs of alternatives for a given objective reflects the differences in desirability. For example, if alternatives A, B, and C have scores of 10, 50, and 70, then a switch from A to B is interpreted as twice as desirable as a switch from B to C, since the gain in the score is 40 for the first and only 20 for the second. The same conclusion is reached if the three scores are 20, 60, and 80. It is not affected by the initial choice of a score of 10 or 20 for A. It only depends on the difference between scores. However, the ratio of two scores is not assumed to have any meaning. So, the ratio of scores for B and A of $50/10 = 5$ cannot be interpreted as B being five times more desirable than A. That ratio is affected by the initial choice of the score for A. It reduces to 3 if A is scored at 20 and B at 60, while the difference between them remains at 40.

If the scores range from 0 to 100, then each score may also be interpreted as the percentage achieved on a given objective by the alternative in comparison with the highest scoring alternative.

The Decision Maker's Preference Structure

How decision makers value various outcomes forms part of their **preference structure**. The latter reflects their world views. It is therefore highly personal to each decision maker. Naturally, it also enters into the valuation of outcomes for single-objective decision making, as we have seen in the discussion on utility functions in Chapter 18. However, in MCDM a new dimension is added. It is now not simply a question of valuing outcomes of individual objectives, but also a question of the relative importance of each objective. In order to assess the relative worth of an alternative we need a measure of both. Only then can the alternatives be ranked from best to worst.

Multiple Decision Makers

Situations with more than one decision maker raise a new difficulty. Each decision maker brings her or his own personal preference structure into the evaluation. These may result not only in different scores assigned to the same outcome by the various decision makers, but also in differences in relative importance of the objectives. As a result, each decision maker may end up with a different ranking of the alternatives. However, the group as a whole will ultimately have to agree on a common single ranking. This calls for at least a partial reconciliation of the individual preference structures. A discussion of suitable processes for resolving such conflicts goes beyond the scope of this text. The bibliography to this chapter lists some references.

19.4 THE PROCESS OF EVALUATING CHOICES

The two predominant approaches for finding the most preferred of a set of discrete alternatives are **aggregate value function methods**, principally used and developed in the U.S., and **outranking methods**, originating in France and Belgium.

Aggregate value function methods in their most basic form assume that

(1) a favourable outcome for one objective can be traded off with a less favourable outcome on another objective; and

(2) the overall or aggregate score of an alternative is a function of the outcome scores and the weights of the relative importance of the individual objectives.

Usually, the weights are normalized such that their sum adds up to 1. So each weight is a number larger than zero and less than 1.

An example may help. To keep things simple, I use a linear aggregate value function. This means that the overall score is equal to the weighted sum of the individual scores, with the relative importance serving as the weights. Say, there are only two objectives X and Y. Objective X is considered the less important and objective Y is viewed as 3 times more important than X. X is therefore assigned a raw weight of 1 and Y a raw weight of 3. The sum of the raw weights is 4. For normalizing the raw weights we simply divide them by the sum of the raw weights. Hence, objective X gets a normalized weight of $1/(1+3) = 0.25$ and Y one of $3/(1+3) = 0.75$. Their sum adds up to 1 as desired. Assume further that alternative A achieves outcome scores of 90 and 60 for objectives X and Y, while alternative B has outcome scores of 75 and 65. The overall scores are then

$$\text{Alternative A:} 0.25(90) + 0.75(60) = 67.5$$

$$\text{Alternative B:} 0.25(75) + 0.75(65) = 67.5$$

They are the same. If a choice is made exclusively on the basis of the overall scores, the decision maker would be indifferent between the two alternatives. So we can conclude that a loss of 15 score points on objective X from 90 to 75 is compensated by a gain of 5 points on objective Y from 60 to 65. In other words, score points of one objective can be traded off for score points on another objective, such that the aggregate score remains unchanged.

Outranking methods assume that the decision maker is unwilling or unable to define trade-offs between objectives. This implies that no aggregate value function can be derived. Any ranking of the alternatives has to be done on the basis of pairwise comparisons of alternatives. These comparisons indicate that one alternative is preferred to the other, that the two alternatives are indifferent to one another, or that the comparison is inconclusive. These relationships are derived from indices based on the outcome scores and the relative importance of the objectives for each pair of alternatives. The end result of this process is a partial or complete ranking of the alternatives. The various methods offer little theoretical justification for how these indices are computed. In contrast, the theoretical justification for the aggregate score of aggregate value function methods is based on utility theory.

19.5 SELECTING A CONFERENCE VENUE — AN AGGREGATE VALUE FUNCTION APPROACH

The Alternatives

Nancy Clare, the promotions manager of XL SOFTWARE has to decide on the venue for next year's European XL Users' Group conference. Such meetings are always preceded by one or more workshops for new users of XL's products. Geneva has been chosen as the location for that conference. Nancy visited the four potential venues on the short list and made the following brief comments:

Venue A: A first class airport hotel, well-known for hosting international meetings, with experienced, helpful and flexible staff, good conference facilities, all-round good accommodations, reasonable catering, social meeting places limited to its several busy restaurants and bars, direct access to airport and railway station, fairly expensive.

Venue B: A luxury city centre hotel, extensively used for international conferences of all sorts, with experienced, helpful, but overworked staff, well equipped modern conference facilities, including computer networking, luxury accommodations, good but rather expensive catering, a wide choice of in-house and close-by social meeting places, fast and easy access from the airport and the railway station, but very expensive.

Venue C: The university conference venue, used mainly for scientific and cultural conferences; its staff somewhat bureaucratic and not known to be helpful; with a wide choice of good, but somewhat stark conference facilities, including computer labs, modest, barely adequate accommodation and catering, few attractive close-by social meeting places, a nice park-like environment, reasonable access to transport means, and cost-wise by far the cheapest.

Venue D: A newly renovated chateau in a near-by village, overlooking Lake Geneva with the Alps as a backdrop, a recent new-comer in the scene of conference venues with limited staff experience, reasonable facilities for small conferences, excellent modern accommodations, famous for its catering, good social meeting places on its facilities and in the several small restaurants in the village, access from the airport and the railway station would have to be organized by bus, still reasonably priced. equal.

Nancy recently studied Prof. Val Belton's tutorial on MCDM (in L.C. Hendry and R.W. Eglese, [1990]) which demonstrated various aspects of the use of MCDM on exactly the type of problem Nancy is facing now. She wants to give the simple multi-attribute value function approach a trial.

Selecting Objectives

The first step is to come up with a list of objectives considered important for evaluating each alternative venue. In fact, this step has to be done before making up a list of possible venues. It tells the analyst(s) what aspects to look out for and what information to collect about each venue.

In consultation with the conference director and the pre-conference workshop leaders, Nancy develops the following list: (1) low overall cost of the facilities, (2) easy transport access, (3) a wide range of top-quality conference rooms and other conference facilities, (4) high quality of accommodations, (5) outstanding catering for conference meals, (6) a high level of staff experience and helpfulness available to organizers and participants, (7) a wide range and high quality of informal social meeting places and restaurants easily accessible to the participants, and finally (8) a congenial, pleasant overall environment of the venue.

These objectives fall into three groups: (a) those associated with the 'Location' of the venue, (b) those associated with the 'Facilities' offered by the venue, and (c) its 'Cost'. They become the **first level objectives**, while the original list with the exception of 'Cost' is referred to as the **second level objectives**. It is conceivable that even some of the latter might already be groupings of third level objectives. This **hierarchy of objectives** is depicted in Figure 19-2. Objectives that are not broken down further are called **end objectives**.

Figure 19-2: Hierarchy of objectives for evaluating conference venue

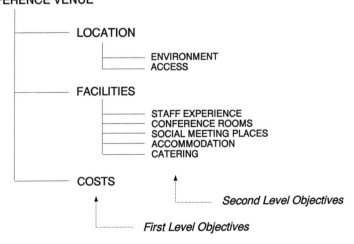

Setting Importance Weights

The next step is to assess a weight of the relative importance of each objective. These are numbers between 0 and 1. They are usually chosen so that the weights of the first-level objectives add up to one, and similarly the weights of the second level objectives associated with each first level objective also add up to one, and so on for third level objectives. This is demonstrated in the second and third columns of the spreadsheet printout in Figure 19-3. Note that column 2 sums to one, and similarly the weights for each grouping of second level objectives also sum to one. Again, Nancy settles on these weights after two animated sessions with the conference director and workshop leaders. These may not be the final weights, but serve as a good starting point.

Figure 19-3: Spreadsheet evaluation of conference venues

CONFERENCE VENUE SELECTION						
	WEIGHTS		SCORES FOR VENUE			
OBJECTIVES	level 1	level 2	A	B	C	D
Location:	0.35					
Environment		0.50	0	25	40	100
Access		0.50	100	80	35	0
Facilities:	0.45					
Staff experience		0.10	100	80	40	0
Conference rooms		0.30	75	100	50	0
Social meeting places		0.15	25	100	0	75
Accommodation		0.20	80	100	0	90
Catering		0.25	60	70	0	100
Cost	0.20		5	0	100	60
EVALUATION						
	Facilities		67.5	90.5	19.0	54.3
	Cost		5.0	0.0	100.0	60.0
	Overall		48.8	59.1	39.9	53.9
	Rank		3	1	4	2

Setting weights that truly reflect the importance a decision maker attaches to the various objectives is no easy task. The decision maker may well be prone to similar biases as in the assessment of subjective probabilities (see the article by Tversky and Kahneman, Appendix to Chapter 15). Naturally, being aware of these biases is the first step towards overcoming them. However, it is essential that the analyst performs extensive sensitivity analysis with respect to these weights, which should be fed back to the decision maker. The latter may well then wish to re-ssess these weights in the light of their effect on the aggregate scores.

Assessing Achievement Scores

Assessing the scores achieved by each alternative for each end objective is step 3. Since Nancy is the only person who has inspected the facilities, this task falls exclusively onto her shoulders. After much agonizing and a few phone calls to Geneva, she comes up with the scores in the last four columns of Figure 19-3.

For all end objectives with the exception of 'Cost', the higher the level of achievement of a given venue the more attractive it becomes. Hence, the highest achievement level is assigned a score of 100, while the lowest achievement level gets a score of 0, with all other scores in between. On the other hand, the higher the cost of a venue the less attractive it becomes. The highest cost is therefore given a score of 0 and the lowest cost a score of 100.

These scores are relative only with respect to the four alternatives. Adding other alternatives may require some scores to be re-assessed. Say, we add a new venue E that does better for 'Accommodation' than venue B which previously had the highest score of 100. Then venue E would get a score of 100, while all other venues, except the one with the score of 0, would have their relative scores adjusted down. A similar re-adjustment could occur if an alternative is dropped. Although these re-adjustments may be a nuisance, relative scores based only on the alternatives included are generally easier to assess.

Another approach is to use scores for each end objective that are relative to arbitrary worst and best reference achievement levels. For example, the scores for 'Catering' could be with reference to the Paris Ritz and a typical university student cafeteria. Adding or deleting alternatives would then not require re-adjustments of any scores. Such **absolute scores** require considerably more effort to derive, since a suitable set of reference pairs has to be selected for each objective. This effort is, however, well justified if we are dealing with a repetitive decision problem. For example, if XL has several such conferences in different parts of the world every year, then an absolute scale could well be preferable.

Evaluating the Alternatives

Armed with this information, we can now compute a weighted overall score for each alternative. The steps are similar to the roll-back procedure in a decision tree. We first determine a weighted score for each grouping of end objectives. These weighted scores become an input into the next higher level in the hierarchy of objectives, until we can determine the weighted score for the first level objectives. In our case, we have only two levels. So, using the second level objectives that make up 'Location' and 'Facilities' we find the weighted scores for these two first level objectives. For example, for venue A the weighted score for 'Location' is equal to $0.5(0) + 0.5(100) = 50$ and for 'Facilities' $0.1(100) + 0.3(75) + 0.15(25) + 0.20(80) + 0.25(60) = 61.8$. The first level score for 'Cost' is simply its score of 5. The first level scores are shown under 'Evaluation' at the bottom of Figure 19-3.

With all first level scores computed, the 'Overall score' can now be obtained. Again, for venue A it is found by summing the products of the first level weights and the first level scores, i.e., 0.35(50) + 0.45(67.3) + 0.2(5) = 48.8.

As a first cut, the four alternatives are ranked from best to worst in the order of B - D - A - C. The city centre hotel scores highest, with the chateau coming in as a respectable second. However, this ranking should not be taken as the final answer. It should be used as a catalyst for discussion and for learning more about the problem. But more on this in the last subsection of this chapter!

Graphical Representation

As usual, representing the results in graphical form may allow the decision maker to gain a better 'feel' for them. Figures 19-4 and 19-5 show two different charts for the first level objectives. Similar charts can be constructed for the second level objectives making up a given first level objective.

Figure 19-4 shows a profile of the performance of each alternative on the first level objectives. The three objectives are spaced along the x-axis. Their scores are measured along the y-axis. Each line connects the scores on the three objectives for a given alternative. Such a chart shows whether a given alternative dominates another alternative. But even if no strict dominance occurs, it reveals whether such dominance is close. In our example, no venue dominates, although Venue B comes close. It is just better than A for 'Location', far outstrips A for 'Facilities', and is just marginally worse than A for 'Cost'. On this basis, Nancy Clare may well eliminate Venue A as a serious contender.

Figure 19-4: Performance profile of alternatives

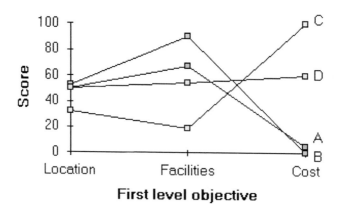

Note though that first level objective dominance does not imply dominance over all end objectives, as defined in Section 19.2. First level scores may be weighted averages over end objectives farther down the hierarchy. (Just compare the scores for 'Environment' and 'Access' of A and B. There is no dominance there, although the weighted score for 'Location' of B is better than for A.)

The graph also helps clarify the overall pattern of performance of an alternative. Is it a good all-rounder or does it have significant weaknesses? A good all-rounder may be an attractive choice, even if it does not achieve the highest overall score.

In our example, Venue D comes close to being a good all-rounder — its 'Facilities' score being a minor weakness. The chart also clearly highlights that 'Cost' is the major weakness of venue B — our highest scoring venue.

Figure 19-5 contrasts the overall score of the alternatives and how each breaks down into first level objectives. Each first level objective score has been scaled by its corresponding weight. This reveals the relative weighted contribution of each objective towards the overall scores. An alternative's weakness with respect to a particular objective, as revealed in the performance profile chart (like Figure 19-4), may be viewed as less damaging if the importance weight of the objective is relatively small in comparison to all other objectives.

In our example, the striking features are the high contributions made by 'Facilities' for venue B and 'Cost' for venue C, amounting to more than 50% of their overall scores. Contrast this with the much more even distribution of venue D. It now has an even more pronounced image of a good all-rounder.

Figure 19-5: Composition of overall performance scores

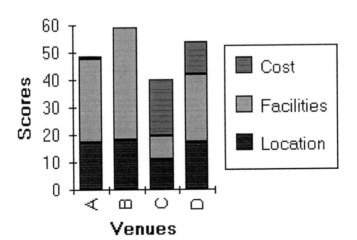

19.6 SENSITIVITY ANALYSIS

Subjectivity of MCDM Methods

As for decision analysis, personal subjective judgments play a much more important role in MCDM. In fact, every step requires some subjective inputs. The choice of objectives, their grouping into a hierarchy, the choice of importance weights for the objectives, the assessment of the end objective scores for each alternative all involve subjective judgments. Even the choice of the evaluation criterion is in part subjective. In the conference venue example we used a criterion for maximizing the weighted overall score. An alternative criterion could have been to maximize the lowest weighted score on any first-level objective (similar to the minimax criterion in decision analysis). Given this high degree of subjectivity it is essential to perform extensive and thorough sensitivity analysis, at least for those aspects that involve numerical inputs, such as the importance weights and the end objective scores.

Sensitivity Analysis with Respect to Importance Weights

Table 19-1 shows the results of sensitivity analysis on the importance weights. The first set of three rows shows the response of the overall score distribution as the importance weight for 'Location' decreases from 0.45 to 0.25 in steps of 0.1, with the weights of the other two objectives increasing by 0.05 at each step. The second set of three rows decreases the weight for 'Facilities' from 0.55 to 0.35, the third set the weight for 'Cost' from 0.3 to 0.1, while adjusting the other two weights accordingly. The striking feature of this analysis is the fact that the overall score for Venue D only changes marginally, in contrast to the scores for the other three venues. The performance for D is thus very robust, reenforcing its quality of a good all-rounder. However note that B remains the highest scoring venue as long as 'Facilities' has a relatively high importance weight.

Table 19-1: Sensitivity Analysis for Conference Venue Selection

| Weights | | | Venue | | | |
Location	Facilities	Cost	A	B	C	D
0.45	0.40	0.15	50.2	59.8	37.2	53.2
0.35	0.45	0.20	48.8	59.1	39.9	53.9
0.25	0.50	0.25	47.4	58.4	42.6	54.6
0.30	0.55	0.15	52.7	65.5	35.2	53.8
0.35	0.45	0.20	48.8	59.1	39.9	53.9
0.40	0.35	0.25	44.8	52.7	44.7	54.0
0.30	0.40	0.30	43.4	52.0	47.4	54.7
0.35	0.45	0.20	48.8	59.1	39.9	53.9
0.40	0.50	0.10	54.1	66.3	32.5	53.1

Firming up the Preference Structure

When embarking on such an analysis, the decision maker(s) may often have somewhat vague ideas about the relative importance of the various objectives. In other words, the preference structure is not yet clearly defined. Helping the decision maker(s) to firm up the preference structure is frequently an essential and integral part of an MCDM analysis. Access to an appropriate spreadsheet template or a dedicated MCDM computer package will facilitate this task.

In our example, notice the relatively subdued response of the scores to major changes in the relative importance of 'Location', as revealed by the first three rows in Table 19-1, in contrast to the much stronger response to major changes in each of the other two weights. 'Location' is a less discriminating objective than either 'Facilities' or 'Cost'. This could well lead Nancy to re-appraise the importance she initially attached to 'Location'. She might settle for the weight distribution in row 3 of Table 19-1. Although this does not change the relative ranking, it reduces the difference between Venues B and D further, with the all-rounder D becoming even more attractive.

EXERCISES

1. Consider the Deep Cove project discussed in Section 1.1 of Chapter 1. Define a set of three to four suitable objectives, goals, or targets which any option chosen should either meet or achieve as well as possible. These have to be chosen such that appropriate measures for their performance levels can be determined, either using a natural or a point scale. Indicate how each would be measured.

2. Consider the Breast Cancer Screening project discussed in Section 1.1 of Chapter 1. Define a set of three to four suitable objectives, goals, or targets which any option chosen should either meet or achieve as well as possible. These have to be chosen such that appropriate measures for their performance levels can be determined, either using a natural or a point scale. Indicate how each would be measured.

3. Consider the CIA problem situation described in exercise 4 of Chapter 4. Define a set of three to four suitable objectives, goals, or targets which any option chosen should either meet or achieve as well as possible. These have to be chosen such that appropriate measures for their performance levels can be determined, either using a natural or a point scale. Indicate how each would be measured.

4. Consider Sally Smart's problem described in exercises 1 and 2 of Chapter 18. Indicate why a single objective approach dealing with monetary outcomes alone may not really capture all essential aspects of the problem situation. Define a set of three to four suitable objectives, goals, or targets which any option chosen should either meet or achieve as well as possible. These have to be chosen such that appropriate measures for their performance levels can be determined, either using a natural or a point scale. Indicate how each would be measured.

5. Consider the following hierarchy of objectives, associated importance weights, and achievement scores for selecting a location for a factory:

objective	weights level 1	level 2	A	B	C	D
locality	0.5					
transport access		0.6	0	60	100	50
water availability		0.4	80	100	0	50
Cost	0.5					
construction		0.3	100	30	0	50
operating		0.7	70	0	100	50

Using a weighted average scoring approach, which location is the highest scoring one? Is there a close second? Show your results in performance profile graphs.

6. The manager of a BLM district office has been asked to come up with a management plan for a 16 square mile area in southern Colorado. The area consists of two mesas with adjoining gullies and deep canyons. The vegetation consists of low brush, junipers, and other bushes that thrive in the semi-arid low rainfall area, with a few stands of pines and other trees in sheltered parts. The few open places on the mesas are currently used for sheep grazing at a very low stocking rate. The current runholder would like to get permission for clearing brush and increasing the stocking rate The mesas and canyons get the occasional visit from backpackers. One of the gullies between the two mesas contains an abandoned silver mine which was worked in the late 19th century. It has the potential for being developed into a tourist attraction, as have the interesting rock formations in the canyons. The area has considerable wildlife, particularly deer and various big birds. The deer stalkers' association would like the area preserved for hunting excluding all grazing by domestic animals which severely compete for the limited fodder available. No human habitation is currently in the area. Seven management options have been put forward by various interest groups. The district manager would like to select the option which best achieves the intrinsic values and characteristics of the area. He has captured these by four objectives: (A) preservation of scenic beauty, (B) recreational potential, (C) economic potential, (D) watershed protection, each being a first level objective. (There are no second level objectives.) All objectives are to be maximized. The table below lists the seven management options and their achievement scores for each objective:

Option	A	B	C	D
Exclusive intensive grazing of mesas*	50	0	$50,000	30
Exclusive 4-wheel vehicle recreation*	30	80	-$40,000	0
Exclusive hunting*	90	60	$40,000	90
Tourism in canyons, grazing of mesas	60	80	$100,000	50
Tourism in canyons, 4-wheel use of mesas	40	100	$30,000	20
Continuation of current usage	70	40	$20,000	70
Exclusive wilderness area use	100	30	$0	100

The options marked by an asterisk assume that most of the current other low intensity recreational use would continue.

(a) The district manager, after extensive consultation with various experts, comes up with the following set of importance weights: A - 0.2, B - 0.4, C - 0.15, D - 0.25. Which option would you recommend on the basis of an aggregate value function approach? Note that to apply this method you will need to convert the economic achievement levels into a suitable point scale. Show your results in a performance profile graph.

(b) Perform some sensitivity analysis, increasing and decreasing the weight of each objective individually by 0.15 at the expense or benefit of the other three objectives. How does this affect your conclusion derived under (a)?

REFERENCES

Belton, Valerie, 'Multiple criteria decision analysis - Practically the only way to choose', in L.C. Hendry and R. W. Eglese, *Operational Research Tutorial Papers 1990*, Operational Research Society, Neville House, Waterloo St., Birmingham B2 5TX, England, 1990, 53-102. This is an elementary, but highly instructive introduction to the basics of MCDM, similar in level to the coverage here, but rather more extensive. It also has an extensive up-to-date bibliography.

Keeney, R.L., and Raiffa, H., *Decisions with Multiple Objectives: Preferences and Value Tradeoffs*, Wiley, 1976. The classic text for multi-attribute utility analysis, with several extensive reports on actual case studies done by the authors. Demanding in parts, both mathematically and conceptually.

Goicoechea, A., Hansen, R.R., and Duckstein, L., *Multiobjective Decision Analysis with Engineering and Business Applications*, Wiley, 1982. One of the less technical texts, with comprehensive coverage up to the date of publication.

20 Conclusions

It is now time to take stock of the vast and rugged landscape of quantitative decision making we have traveled through, to highlight its most prominent features and put them into perspective. The first part of this final chapter is devoted to this.

Section 20.1 contrasts the 'traditional' view of the OR/MS methodology with the brand advocated in this text. Section 20.2 will then elaborate on some aspects of the difference between these two views and at the same time highlight the important features of the methodology developed in the first eight chapters of this text.

Section 20.3 will briefly visit another dimension of OR/MS, largely neglected so far in our treatment, but underlying any decision making process and any professional activity, namely ethics. The process and the recommendations derived will not just be judged on elegance, efficiency, and effectiveness, but also on their ethical implications.

The second part examines the place the OR/MS methodology assumes in the much wider context of decision making processes. Section 20.4 contrasts the OR/MS approach with so-called **soft systems methodologies** and gives a brief overview of the basic tenets underlying them. The best known of these, the Checkland methodology, is then studied in a bit more detail in Section 20.5 to give the general flavour of these approaches.

By briefly studying soft systems methodologies, I hope that you will gain a better appreciation of the rightful place OR/MS should occupy as a decision aid, for what type of decision situations it is most suitable, how it should be used, and what its limitations are. You will then be able to judge which types of problem situations are best left to alternative decision making approaches. Hopefully this will entice you to devote some time and effort to studying such alternative approaches.

20.1 TRADITIONAL VIEW OF OR/MS METHODOLOGY

The philosophy of the OR/MS methodology promoted here is fundamentally different from the cut-down 'run-of-the-mill' versions that you will find in most OR text books — Churchman's 1957, Ackoff's 1968, and Daellenbach et al.'s 1983 texts are the exceptions. Most authors will proclaim that the OR/MS methodology is an adaptation of the scientific method of the natural sciences. Although there may be statements to the contrary, the OR/MS methodology presented is a technical process, largely devoid of any human aspects. The main emphasis is on building a suitable mathematical model for the 'problem' and finding its 'optimal solution'. The stated aim of OR/MS is to find optimal solutions to problems.

The underlying assumption is that 'the problem' has essentially been identified, i.e., the objective function is known and the range of decision choices are known, and that it is sufficiently well insulated from the wider system to which it belongs. Some lip-service is paid to the systems approach, interpreted as meaning 'systematic' rather than 'systemic'. It is pointed out that model building is an iterative process, without ever demonstrating how. What more can you expect in 6 to 10 pages? And then the texts launch into an exhaustive review of a dozen or so OR techniques and the mathematics of their solution techniques. It is therefore no wonder that many students of OR/MS have a completely wrong view of OR/MS as an aid to real-life decision making. Too often projects, analyzed with such a techniques-focused world view, never see 'their optimal solution' implemented and for good reasons. Here are some:

- The problem solved was not the real problem.

- Although the real problem was studied, and the model developed was technically brilliant, unfortunately it was inappropriate, or not credible, or not relevant any more, i.e., too late.

- The model ignored the human aspects underlying the problem situation.

20.2 ALTERNATIVE PHILOSOPHY OF OR/MS METHODOLOGY

OR/MS Methodology ≠ Scientific Method of Natural Sciences

Even a cursory reading of the first eight chapters of this text should have made it obvious to you that the traditional view only forms a small part of the decision aiding process and maybe not even the most important one, although it may be the one that causes the most excitement for the analyst. The philosophy underlying the OR/MS methodology developed in this text is not devoid of human aspects. It recognizes explicitly that the possibly conflicting world views of the stakeholders in the project cannot be ignored, nor should the analysts be under any illusion that their own world views will not affect various aspects of the project. The methodology is thus not a version of the scientific method of the natural sciences. It is not objective, but subjective. In almost all instances it cannot be replicated by another analyst under exactly the same conditions — one of the important attributes of scientific research. It is unique, relevant for a specific situation at a given point in time. It is not aimed at furthering scientific knowledge, but at solving real-life problems in most of their complexity. This real world cannot be neatly isolated in a laboratory. It has to be studied in its dynamic context — context which usually is an important aspect of the problem situation.

Another consequence is that few projects have a clearly identifiable data collection phase as is the case in the scientific method of the natural sciences. In OR/MS projects, different types of data are collected at several stages of the process. For example, in the LOD project we needed some preliminary data on costs and the distribution of the demand for assembling a situation summary or rich picture of the problem situation. More detailed data was needed during the modeling phase for estimating the potential savings that the model could achieve. The major data collection effort did, however, only occur during the implementation phase of the full-scale study. Finally, more data had to be obtained for the final audit report. So some data collection occurred throughout the entire life of the project.

The Aim is Insights, not Optimality

The major aim of the methodology is not to produce 'optimal' solutions, but provide insights to the decision maker. OR/MS is seen as a decision aid for situations that lend themselves to quantitative type analysis. The concept of optimality is always relative to the scope of the system explicitly modeled. What may be optimal for some narrow system, may only be suboptimal for the wider system. The concept of optimality thus loses some of its gloss. Most of the time, the analyst is content with achieving some degree of improvement over the previous situation.

With the aim on providing insights into the problem situation, the emphasis of the analysis shifts to an exploration of the solution space. How does the system's performance measure respond to changes in the inputs, both in terms of resource availabilities, as well as input parameters and coefficients, such as costs, benefits, or technical aspects? What is the effect of deviations from the 'optimal' solution? How do errors in the input data affect the solution? Hence, sensitivity and error analysis become integral parts of the methodology, and are not simply theoretically interesting afterthoughts.

Remember the weighbridge problem in Chapters 16 and 17? The recommendation to build a second weighbridge was not implemented at that time. Rather, the insights gained from the project helped management to understand that a 10 to 15% reduction in the arrival rate would reduce the average waiting time to a few minutes only. So, an imaginative solution was found for rescheduling thinnings and processing them at a separate yard — very much cheaper than building a second weighbridge.

Problem Situations, not Problems

The occasional project starts out in a relatively well-structured form. This means that some of the hard work of identifying the issues has already been done. For example, in the LOD project a decision as to which products to produce and stock had been made well before the study was started. The project was only concerned with finding the best stocking policy. Similarly, some projects are concerned with exploring specific well-defined options as input into strategic decisions, such as evaluating various possible production configurations for a proposed plant. Again these options will be relatively well-structured. The Heinz logistics problem of Chapter 11 is a case in point. The analysis there was used as input into a policy decision about whether or not to replace the railcars.

Most of the projects, however, begin life as vague feelings of dissatisfaction or concern about the current state of affairs.   Although this is not the way it was discussed in Chapter 9, the Mushrooms Galore project was of this nature.   Bob Moss, the general manager, was dissatisfied with the current rate of production.   If he wanted to fully develop various export markets, he had to find ways for increasing total annual output.   But the situation was made more complicated by the fact that these export markets were much more volatile due to competition than the stable local market.   Hence, expansion involving substantial investments could put the firm into a highly vulnerable position.

So most of the time what the OR/MS analyst faces is not a problem, but a problem situation, involving usually complex human factors, that need sorting out. We have seen that the best way of doing this is to start out the project with assembling a comprehensive situation summary.   This is then used to identify various possible issues and the relationships between them.   Only then is one of them chosen as the subject of a project.   It is a crucial and highly critical phase of any project.   The seeds of success or failure are quite often sown here.   Homing in on a 'problem' without first seeing it in its full context can be costly.   The issue that gives rise to the feeling of dissatisfaction may not be the real 'problem' or can only be tackled once one or several other issues have been resolved.

There is a telling story about the operation of a bank of elevators in a high-rise office building.   For several years, the management of the building was inundated by complaints about the long waiting times in the main lobby.   Several teams of operations researchers were asked to investigate the 'problem of excessive waiting times' over these years.   A number of 'solutions' were tried out, such as having some lifts operate exclusively for the lower floors, while others were express lifts to the higher levels.   But each project team reached the conclusion that waiting times could only be reduced effectively by installing additional lifts — precluded by the horrendous cost of this.   Each team basically took the problem as it was defined by management, namely one of excessive waiting times, except for the last team.   One team member suggested studying why people objected to waiting for lifts in the main lobby.   They discovered that it was mainly boredom.   So if boredom could be overcome, then complaints about excessive waiting times would to a large extent disappear.   The same team member suggested that they install mirrors along all the walls in the main lobby.   This would surely alleviate boredom.   Some people would take advantage of the mirrors to make last minute checks on how they looked and put on some finishing touches, others could observe people standing around without being too obvious about it.   This was the essence of his argument, although he put it rather more bluntly by stereotyping people by gender.   This surprisingly cheap solution was implemented and complaints almost completely disappeared.   The lesson of this story clearly is that it pays to go slowly initially and look at the problem situation in very broad terms, rather than launch immediately into the 'problem' that may have triggered off the study.

Emphasis on 'Systemic'

When formulating a relevant model, it is essential to identify first both the narrow system of interest and the wider system of interest relevant to the problem situation. The OR/MS methodology is based on a systems approach precisely because it views the problem within a systems context. It identifies the system boundaries, the major system components and their interactions, and how the system transforms inputs into outputs. One of these outputs is the system's performance measure, which must at least in part be affected by the control inputs. Some of the system's outputs are planned and desirable outcomes, others may be unplanned and undesirable, particularly from the point of view of the wider system. One of the reasons for focusing on a systems approach is to be better able to identify all outcomes. Chapters 1 and 2 list a number of examples that demonstrate the importance of taking a systems view.

However, the analyst does not claim that the system he or she constructs does in fact exist in this form in reality. The system is what he or she finds a useful and relevant image of the operation or process. Again, it is not objective, but subjective to the analyst. Another analyst may view the system differently. There is not one unique system for a given problem situation, but a range of possible systems views. What is the most appropriate view depends on many things, such as the purpose of building a system, the likely benefits and costs associated with the project, the resources available, the time frame within which the analysis has to be done, and last, but not least, the background and training of the various stakeholders and, in particular, the analyst.

Diagrammatic Aids for the Problem Formulation Phase

Various diagrammatic aids prove useful during the formulation phase. A rich picture is very effective in capturing the essential aspects of the situation summary and, in particular, highlighting the relationships between various aspects of the situation. It is an ideal vehicle for discussion, as well as for allowing analysts to verify their understanding of the problem situation. It helps analysts and problem owners define which issue or problem needs to be tackled first. If kept up-to-date, it also provides a record of how the view of the problem situation changes as the project progresses.

Influence diagrams, material and/or information flow charts, decision flow charts, and precedence diagrams help clarify the system structure. Again they are ideal means for communication and clarifying aspects of the issue under study. They often provide a first step towards formulating a mathematical or quantitative model.

The Process of Building a Quantitative Model

As is the case for the system defined by the analyst, a model is also a conceptual device. There is no implication that what happens inside the model in any way reproduces the physical and relational aspects of the problem. It is simply a device for transforming the inputs to the system into outputs, via control inputs. Some simulation models, such as the simulation of an assembly line, may come fairly close to what happens physically on the production floor. On the other hand, most queueing models are fairly theoretical abstractions of the physical processes that can be observed in the real world.

We have seen that building a quantitative model is a process of successive rounds of enrichment and enhancement. We start out with a simple model and ascertain how much of the system is captured in a satisfactory manner. We then add enhancements to this model to incorporate additional aspects. If the model is judged satisfactory in capturing all significant aspects of the system, we stop. Otherwise we start the process again with a more complex model, by either expanding the previous model, such as going from a one-variable model to a two or several-variable model, as we did in the LOD problem, or starting from scratch with a completely different model type, such as going from a queueing model to a simulation, so as to capture aspects that cannot be represented realistically in a queueing model.

Again, this process is largely subjective. It depends on many factors, such as the time and resources available for the analysis and the training and experience of the analyst. I was once involved in a manpower scheduling problem, where my colleagues were strongly in favour of building a sophisticated integer programming or network model, coming from a background of mathematical programming, while my preferred route was to build a simple spreadsheet-type interactive model that allowed a quick and easily understood graphical exploration of various possible alternative schedules, but would not guarantee finding the optimal solution. Its main advantage was simplicity, validity, and credibility — three of the important properties of any good model.

Sensitivity Analysis

We have seen how important it is to carefully explore the solution space and perform extensive sensitivity analysis of the optimal solution with respect to various input parameters. Both the decision maker and the analyst gain valuable insights into the 'behaviour' of the problem, as formulated. It leads to the identification of the critical aspects of the problem. It tells the decision maker the cost or penalty incurred for deviations from the 'optimal' solution. All this leads to better and more informed decision making.

Sensitivity analysis is always with respect to a given model. It is only as good as the model itself. If the latter is a distortion of the real problem, then no amount of sensitivity analysis will overcome that deficiency. Little valid information may be gained, except perhaps some indication of which aspects included in the model and relevant for the problem may possibly be critical.

Implementation

Implementation is not something tacked on to the end of a project. Implementation must begin with the first contact between the problem owners and the analysts by establishing good communications and a sense of mutual trust. It must remain an underlying concern for both analysts and problem owners throughout all phases of the project. Only through implementation can the benefits of the project be realized.

Implementation requires not just technical and planning skills. It usually involves people. Therefore, people skills are an important ingredient. Although implementation is a two-way street, the greater onus falls on the analysts to manage the lead-up to the physical implementation effectively. Many decision makers are far too busy to devote much attention to this aspect of a project. Their involvement in a project is only a small part of all their activities. Hence, the attention devoted to it is also small. They rely on the analysts to manage all aspects of the project, including implementation.

An Iterative Process

It is a rare project that sails through all phases as a simple progression of the eleven steps of the methodology. Most will require some backtracking to earlier steps at one stage or another. There are forward linkages. All along the analyst will look for data needed in later stages. Considerations of implementation are ever present. It is not only in the nature of complex problem situations that new aspects and relationships are discovered as the analysis proceeds, leading to changes and revisions of the model, but it is also that few of us are that perfect. So the methodology is iterative. ·The analyst will sometimes have to backtrack and revisit previous steps and look forward to later steps to assess data needs and implementation aspects. Furthermore, iteration is inherent in the process of enrichment and enhancement in model building.

Report Writing

Most projects require some or all of the following reports: a project proposal, a project report, including users' manuals, and a final audit. These are the prime documents that the other stakeholders of a problem situation will see. They sell the project. They advertise the skills or otherwise of the analyst. They largely establish her or his credibility. Without credibility, no analyst will survive long in this business. It is therefore very important that the analyst develops good report writing skills. Would you trust an analyst who cannot develop a logical line of argument or write coherent logical sentences, and who submits a report full of grammatical and spelling mistakes?

Interpersonal and Interviewing Skills

OR/MS project usually deal with people — problem owners and problem users. People skills are therefore important: being a good listener; putting people at ease; and coming across as interested in the issues and the people and as willing to learn.

Similarly, a good interviewing technique will facilitate obtaining all the relevant information. Both these skills can be learned. For example, doing a TA 101 — the basic course in transactional analysis, offered periodically in most major cities — is a good start.

Technical and Subject Skills Needed by Analyst

Since much of the data for projects, at least those of a commercial or industrial nature, come from accounting records, the analyst should have a good grounding in the nature of various costs and benefits and how accountants collect and process such information. For many projects, the form needed for such data is in terms of marginal costs and marginal benefits, rather than averages. My experience is that the best form of the data is raw, unprocessed data, associated with individual transactions or events, rather than processed data. For example, instead of getting average unit costs of production, it will be more useful to have total costs of production for various output levels. The analyst can then use statistical tools for determining fixed and marginal costs.

This point also indicates that data analysis is usually an integral part of any OR/MS project. Basic statistical data analysis skills are indispensable.

The analyst needs to be conversant with the basics of financial mathematics, i.e., discounting and so on. In fact, the analyst with a good background in finance and investment analysis will have the edge over those who do not.

Most real-life situations involve some degree of uncertainty. The degree of uncertainty may require that the model explicitly recognizes this aspect. So some training in probability and stochastic processes will be highly useful.

Finally, most projects involve intensive calculations at some time in their life. These can only be done efficiently with the use of computers. The analyst should have some basic computer skills. In particular, being fully conversant with the use of some advanced spreadsheet package, like EXCEL, LOTUS 1-2-3, or QUATTRO PRO, is an absolute must. More complex projects may require some basic programming. Many project involve handling large data bases. Hence, exposure to database management systems is an advantage. Graphical interfaces, although they still have a fair way to go, will become more and more important.

20.3 ETHICAL CONSIDERATIONS

Ethics is the code of moral principles and values that govern the behaviour of a person or a group of people with respect to what is judged right or wrong by the society they live in. The difficulty is that there are genuine conflicting views among people and societies about what constitutes ethical behaviour and what is not, and that we are highly selective and inconsistent in choosing which ethical principles to apply or ignore in various decision situations. Furthermore, different societies and subgroups of society will tend to abide by different ethical standards. What is acceptable behaviour for one group of society, may be very objectionable for another. Nor do such standards remain static over time. Even religious moral principles acquire new interpretations over time. Certain generally accepted industrial practices in the 19th century are now viewed as morally detestable.

Ethics has occupied philosophers and religious leaders for as long as humanity has existed in the form of organized societal structures. The discussion that follows will therefore hardly scratch the surface of this fascinating subject.

Ethics as a Basis for Decision Making

Ethics is relevant for decision making in at least two ways. First, it goes without saying that ethical principles should form the basis for all human decision making. Without following some ethical principles, decision making will degenerate to become opportunistic, self-centred, inconsistent, and destructive to all stakeholders involved. What forms a minimal set of ethical norms has been the concern of philosophers, from Pythagoras (6th century B.C., better known for his mathematical discoveries) to Bertrand Russell (1872-1970). Its discussion goes beyond the scope of this text. However, what is relevant is that in recent years a number of people have developed decision making methodologies that are largely based on ethical considerations. They consist of check lists for evaluating the decision process, the decisions, and the outcomes and their effects on all stakeholders. The paper by K. Goodpaster (1988) is an example of this. Although interesting, this is not our concern here.

Personal Ethical Considerations for Analysts

But even within the OR/MS methodology, ethics and ethical considerations must concern OR/MS analysts at a personal and a professional level. At a personal level, analysts have a moral responsibility for the effects of their own involvement in a project on the various stakeholders, in particular the problem users and problem customers, i.e., third parties that benefit from or are the victims of the results of the project, such as certain segments of a given population or society. For example, the project may involve increasing the efficiency of personnel use, such as the nurses and doctors in a public hospital, which, depending on the decisions taken, could result in a considerable number of nurses losing their jobs, potential increases in waiting lists for elective surgery, and possibly increases in risks to patients. Or the project deals with the siting of a nuclear power station or the extension of an airport runway, adversely affecting large numbers of people.

How should analysts deal with such situations? If an analyst has personal, moral or environmental objections to the possible outcomes of the project, then clearly he or she should decline participation in the project. At the least, the analyst should make a full disclosure of her or his moral objections to the project or its possible outcomes, or other possible conflicts of interest (such as possible personal gain or loss), and leave it up the problem owner(s) to make a judgment about whether her or his involvement in the project should continue. If the involvement is continued, then the analyst must confront the issue of how these moral objections could influence the analysis and the results, and attempt to keep the analysis as far as humanly possible free of these personal biases.

The analyst must also be aware that in public advocacy processes he or she cannot assume both the role of modeler and advocate of vested interest without having the role of unbiased modeler put into serious question. For example, assume that you are a member of the official publicly funded project team modeling an environmentally controversial project. This team is supposed to take a neutral view. You would put both the model and your own credibility in question when you then also become an advocate for some vested interest, such as an environmental lobby group or the mining company who would benefit from the project.

This does not imply that the analyst may not draw the problem owners' attention to any adverse consequences. In fact, this should be their responsibility, regardless of their own personal views of the project.

But even if the analyst is personally neutral or favours the outcomes, there still remains the ethical responsibility not only to point out the positive aspects of the expected outcomes, but also fully disclose the negative consequences without belittling them. It is not the analyst's place to judge these consequences as to their desirability or otherwise, but to provide the decision maker with a relevant basis for making a fully informed decision.

Professional Ethics of the OR/MS Analyst

The second level of ethical concerns is on a purely professional level. The analyst must make sure that the analysis performed is not flawed from a professional point of view. To a large extent this means following scrupulously the guidelines given in Chapters 4 to 8 about how to approach and execute an OR/MS project, such as:

- Disclose any vested interest in the project or its outcomes.

- Approach the problem situation from the world view of the problem owner(s) as far as this is possible. Become aware of your own biases.

- Keep the problem owner(s) regularly informed about the project and immediately report any aspects discovered that may call for a re-assessment of the project or its directions.

- Fully document the model, such that any other analyst of similar training can understand and verify it. This must also include recording of any assumptions, simplifications, and known omissions made, data ignored or discarded, as well as the proper justification of these things.

- For any data used as input into the analysis, record their sources, keep data specifically collected for that purpose in raw form, or save operational data that in the normal course of events will be destroyed after some limited time period.

Without such data it is impossible for a third person to verify or reproduce the analysis done.

- Verify and validate the model. Perform sufficient sensitivity analysis to evaluate the robustness of the model and its recommendation. Establish ranges of critical input parameters for which the recommendations are not affected.

- Provide the problem owner(s) with a report on the project, the analysis done, and its recommendations, at a level appropriate and agreed upon beforehand. This is in addition to the full documentation of the model used itself which is intended more for other analysts. This report should cover what was accomplished by the study, as well as, even more importantly, what was not accomplished, and any possible weaknesses and limitations of the analysis done.

- Scrupulously observe any ground rules about confidentiality for the disclosure of data and any reports produced, as laid out at the inception of the project. This should also cover what material may be removed and by whom from the premises of the sponsor.

These points just cover the most important ethical considerations. There are other obvious rules of moral conduct that are not unique the OR/MS projects, such as

- Do not undertake a project that requires you to rubber stamp a conclusion or decision already reached or do it only with the clear (written) understanding that you are in no way bound by prior decisions or conclusions.

- Do not omit aspects (such as data, alternatives, sensitivity analysis, weaknesses, limitations) that you know will weaken your case. The temptation to do that may sometimes be quite strong.

- The report and its analysis should be written in such a manner that neither can be easily misrepresented or used to imply more than it should.

If the analyst is involved in a public advocacy process, full disclosure of all inputs, assumptions, simplifications, etc., is even more important.

20.4 OVERVIEW OF SOFT SYSTEMS METHODOLOGIES

The Domain of 'Hard' Methodologies

The protagonists of soft systems methodologies refer to OR/MS and similar approaches as **hard methodologies**. Their claim is that they are suitable only if

- the problem has been clearly defined, implying that
  - the objectives of the decision maker are known, and there exist criteria to ascertain when they have been achieved,

- the alternative courses of action are known, either as a list of options or a set of decision variables,
- the constraints on the decision choices are known, and
- the input data needed are available;

- the problem is relatively well structured, meaning that
  - the relationships between the variables are tractable,
  - they can be expressed in quantitative form, and
  - the computational effort for determining the optimal solution is economically feasible;

- the problem can be sufficiently well insulated from its wider system; and

- the problem is of a technical nature, largely devoid of human aspects.

They claim that, although such problems exist, the majority of the real-life problem situations in business, industry, and government violate many, if not most of these assumptions, and that OR/MS is thus largely dealing with rather simple and unimportant problems.

As we have seen in Section 20.1, many OR/MS texts and particularly much of the scientific hard-core OR journals do a pretty good job in confirming this impression. But, as this text and a few others indicate, this is a rather narrow view of OR/MS as a problem solving methodology. One almost gets the impression that the proponents of soft systems methodologies feel the need to strengthen the case for their approaches by deliberately narrowing the scope of OR/MS to the image conveyed in the more mathematically oriented scientific literature. Unfortunately, not enough of the scientific literature in OR/MS is, in fact, dealing with problem solving. Much of it is strictly devoted to the mathematics of OR, with little concern for the practical relevance or practical use of the techniques and algorithms presented — one of the unplanned for and undesirable systemic consequences of the 'publish-or-perish' policy imposed (self-imposed ?) on academics at many universities. Most practising operations researchers largely ignore this portion of the literature. Their approach to problem solving is much more along the line of what has been presented in the first eight chapters of this text. The above list is thus a far cry from good OR/MS practice.

There are some notable exceptions to, and efforts to counterbalance, the emphasis of the mathematics of OR. *JORS*, the official journal of the U.K. OR Society, and *Interfaces*, jointly publishes by ORSA, the OR Society of America, and TIMS, the Institute of Management Sciences, have regularly run accounts of real-life applications since the late seventies. One issue per year of *Interfaces* is devoted to the six finalists of the annual Franz Edelman award competition for achievement in management science practice, rewarding outstanding examples of professional OR/MS practice that have been implemented. Since 1986, *Operations Research*, the official journal of ORSA, includes one or two accounts of implemented applications of OR/MS work in each issue.

Experienced analysts do not deal with problems, but problem situations. They realize that different stakeholders will appreciate and perceive the problem situation differently — interpreted through their own Weltanschauung. They help the decision maker to determine suitable objectives and develop effective new alternative courses of action. They investigate the systemic content of the hierarchy of systems involved and overcome difficulties associated with lack of or inadequate data sources. They take human aspects of problem solving into account in the type of models considered and in the difficulties associated with their implementation. Nevertheless, out there in the real world, there are many more problem situations of high importance and complexity where the issue in not so much finding a 'best' solution, however we define that term, but finding a satisfactory solution, or simply clarifying vague, fuzzy issues, involving interpersonal conflicts of all sorts. Furthermore, OR/MS is only suitable if the problem lends itself to being quantified. So there are real limitations on the domain of applicability of OR/MS.

Properties of Soft Systems Methodologies

Soft systems methodologies are approaches to deal with complex problem situations, which are messy, ill-structured, ill-defined, not independent of people, in other words, where different stakeholders with different Weltanschauungen have different, possibly conflicting perceptions about the problem situation and the major issues, and where there may be no agreement about the appropriate objectives. These methodologies are characterized by

- structuring the problem situation, rather than by problem solving;

- facilitating dialogue between the various stakeholders with the aim of achieving a greater degree of shared perceptions of the problem situation, rather than providing a decision aid to the decision maker;

- 'What' questions, more than by 'How' questions, i.e., 'what is the nature of the issue?', 'what are appropriate objectives?' given the various world views of the stakeholders, 'what is the appropriate definition of the system for the issue considered?', 'which changes are **systemically desirable** and **culturally feasible**?', and only then 'how are these changes best brought about?'.

- eliciting the resolution of the problem from the stakeholders themselves, rather than from the analyst; and

- changing the role of the 'problem solver' to one of becoming a facilitator and resource person who relies on the technical expertise of the stakeholders.

Note that 'how' questions, i.e., which means are the best for achieving the desired objectives, must ultimately also be addressed by soft systems methodologies. But they are often an anti-climax, almost obvious, rather than being centre-stage as in most OR/MS projects.

There are currently more than half a dozen soft systems methodologies, some being true methodologies, others having more the character of a method. Here are some of them (the number in parentheses gives their approximate date of birth): **the strategic assumption surfacing and testing method** (Mason and Mitroff, 1969/ 1981), **the viable systems model** (S. Beer, 1972), **Checkland's soft systems methodology** (P. Checkland, 1972), **the social system science** (R. Ackoff, 1974), **robustness analysis** (J. Rosenhead, 1980), **strategic choice approach** (J. Friend, 1978), **strategic option development and analysis** (C. Eden, 1983), and **the total systems intervention** (M. Jackson, 1991).

20.5 CHECKLAND'S SOFT SYSTEMS METHODOLOGY

Peter Checkland's soft systems methodology or SSM is without doubt the most researched, the most rigorously based in terms of its theoretical premises and philosophical reasoning, and the most widely applied, with well over a thousand known applications, many of them documented in the literature. It is a fair assessment that its track record is reasonably good. Based on an action research programme at the University of Lancaster, started in 1969, the methodology slowly evolved, using itself as a learning system to grow and develop. Although in their latest book, Checkland and Scholes (1990) profess a somewhat more flexible use, its best known version is the one presented in Checkland's 1981 book *Systems Thinking, Systems Practice*, a text that any serious student of management science should study carefully. It is a seven-stage process, as shown in Figure 20-1. We shall now briefly review these seven stages. The intention is not to give you a full understanding of the methodology, but rather a flavour of the ideas underlying it.

Checkland sees problem solving within a management or social systems context as a never-ending learning process. It begins with one or more people viewing a situation as problematical, with its own history and various stakeholders, all having possibly different perceptions of the situation and different world views. Similar to the OR/MS methodology summarized in Chapter 5 (see Figure 5-1), the first two stages are to assemble a **situation summary**, or **rich picture**, which then leads to the identification of various possible candidate issues and the ultimate choice of one of them for further investigation.

Although this is what any self-respecting OR/MS analyst would do, Checkland's methodology formalizes these two stages. They have been largely adopted as part of the OR/MS methodology presented in this text.

At stage 3, several different systems views are developed for the issue selected. Note that Checkland views systems definitions as intellectual constructs. There is no implication that the various components and relationships necessarily exist, or should exist, in the real world. Each relevant systems view is expressed as a succinct unambiguous statement, a so-called **root-definition**, specifying the owners of the problem, the transformation process to be achieved and by whom, the Weltanschauung that makes that transformation a meaningful activity, the customers (victims and beneficiaries) of the system, and the environment of the system. The reasons for formulating several root-definitions, and hence corresponding systems views, are to gain deeper and more varied and contrasting insights into the problem, each possibly reflecting a different Weltanschauung.

Figure 20-1: A flow diagram of Checkland's SSM

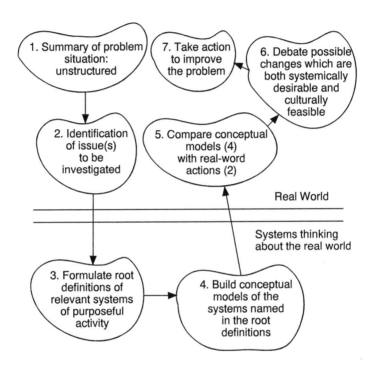

Root definitions can either be **issue-based** or **primary-task** based or a mixture of both. For example, consider the operation of a hospital blood bank, briefly described in Section 19.1 of the preceding chapter. The major concerns raised are the potential shortages of blood products and the wastage of fresh blood through outdating. An issue-based root definition could be as follows:

> 'A system which allows the director of the blood bank to reconcile the conflict of potential blood product shortages versus outdating of fresh blood so as to derive a medically defensible policy for managing limited shelf-life blood stocks, collected from voluntary donors and needed for transfusions to patients in emergency and scheduled operations and for conversion into blood components administered to patients with blood deficiencies.'

This root definition specifies the problem user or actor (director of the blood bank), the problem customers (director, patients, donors), the transformation process (reconcile conflict), the Weltanschauung (medically defensible), and aspects of the environment (demand for blood and blood products, limited shelf life). The problem owner is not stated explicitly. By implication it is the board of management of the blood bank or its director.

At stage 4 a so-called **conceptual model** is developed for each root definition. This model shows the logical relationship between all systems activities needed for the transformation defined in the root definition to happen. This conceptual model is usually expressed in the form of six to ten verbs, connected to each other in a logical influence or precedence sequence. Figure 20-2 is a possible version of the conceptual model associated with the issue-based root definition for the blood bank management problem above.

Figure 20-2: Conceptual model for blood bank problem

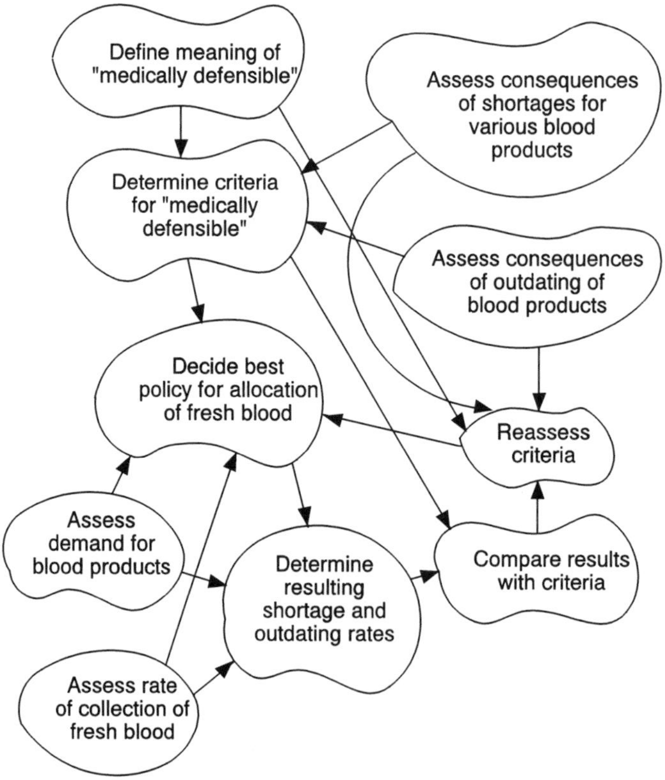

Some activities may be decomposed further into subactivities at a higher level of resolution, such as 'Decide best policy for allocating fresh blood'. Some, such as the one just mentioned, could well lead to the construction of a suitable OR/MS model.

As is true for systems, conceptual models do not pretend to represent the real world or some ideal system. They simply show what activities of the system described by the root definition need to occur for the system to achieve a particular transformation process. So each conceptual model must be derived solely from its corresponding root definition. It should include activities which monitor the performance of the system in terms of the stated transformation process.

Stage 5 compares the conceptual models with the rich picture, i.e., with what is perceived to exist in the real world. The aim is to develop an **agenda of discussion topics** with the stakeholders of the problem for stage 6. So we look for similarities and differences between conceptual models and the real world. The emphasis should be on 'whats', e.g., 'what activities are missing or problematic?', rather than in terms of 'hows', such as 'how is this activity done in the real world?' There may be several 'hows' to achieve a given 'what'.

The **debate** at stage 6 should, whenever possible, involve all types of stakeholders. The purpose of this debate is to subject the implications of possibly conflicting world views to the collective judgment of the group in an open and non-defensive manner. The aim is to develop new ideas for change in the real world that are systemically desirable and culturally feasible. Regardless of whether any changes are implemented or not, each completed cycle of this process will transform the original problem situation into a new one. The new situation should find the stakeholders with a shift in perception and at a higher level of understanding. That new situation becomes then the starting point for another learning cycle, i.e., the methodology cycles back to step 1. By involving all stakeholders in the process, it is hoped that change or **implementation** (stage 7) is facilitated.

It is also interesting to look at the focus of these various steps. Stage 1 and 2 clearly relate to the real world. Stage 3 and 4, on the other hand, focus on systems concepts. They are in the imaginary world of systems and in terms of systems language. Stages 5 to 7 return to the real world, comparing the systems view with the real world.

Note that nowhere in this short description of the process was the analyst mentioned. In fact, ideally, there is not one analyst, but the various stakeholders or a subgroup of them are the analysts themselves. If there is an analyst, her or his role is largely one of offering advice about important 'do's' and 'don't's' at various stages. As the stakeholders become more confident with the process, the analyst becomes superfluous.

Some Concluding Remarks

Some of the reasons for choosing Checkland's SSM as an example of a soft systems methodology are that it is the best documented one, that it is the most formalized one, consisting of a sequence of steps and rules that evolved from an extensive consultancy practice, rather than from theoretical considerations alone, and that this makes it eminently teachable in contrast to other methodologies.   I would like to let John Naughton (*Soft Systems Methodology*, p. 52, 1984) have the last word:

> '. . . it tackles both the *intellectual* problems of interpretation, analysis and synthesis involved in conceiving ideas for change, *and* the practical problems of facilitating the change process itself. Thus it uses powerful ideas — like the concept of system — to generate insights into a problem situation, but only in conjunction with a process of inquiry and debate which incorporates people in discussion of the implications of these abstract ideas. In that sense, the approach . . . is a unique blend of theory and practice.'

REFERENCES

Ethical aspects of OR/MS:

Hill, Percy, et al., *Making Decisions, A Multidisciplinary Introduction*, University Press of America, 1986. Chapter 4 deals with Ethical Decision Making, largely viewed as a decision making approach. Highly interesting and recommended reading.

Operations Research, ORSA journal, September 1971. Guidelines for the Practice of OR. The entire issue is devoted to guidelines operations researchers should follow in the pursuit of their profession, with emphasis on professional ethical standards, particularly relevant for public advocacy processes. Two actual cases are discussed in detail, both dealing with hearings held in 1969 in US Congress subcommittees. Pages 1127-37 list in detail professional guidelines.

Gass, S. I., 'The many faces of OR,' *J. of the OR Society*, January 1991, 3-16. Thought provoking address given to the UK OR Society Conference 1990. Pages 10-15 deal with ethical issues.

Goodpaster, K., 'Ethical frameworks for management,' in *Policies and Persons*, by J.B. Mathews, K. Goodpaster, and L. Nash, McGraw-Hill, 1988. An example of guidelines to ethical decision making in business.

Soft Systems Methodologies:

Checkland, Peter, *Systems Thinking, Systems Practice*, Wiley, 1981. Chapters 6 and 7 give a detailed account of his soft systems methodology. The whole book covers interesting and thought provoking material.

Checkland, Peter, and Scholes, J., *Soft Systems Methodology in Action*, Wiley, 1990. Shows the further development of Checkland's methodology and gives nine detailed case studies, emphasizing various aspects and new developments of the methodology.

Friend, J. K., and Hickling, A., *Planning under Pressure: the Strategic Choice Approach*, Pergamon, 1987. Devoted entirely to this highly successful method.

Jackson, Michael C., *Systems Methodologies for the Management Sciences*, Plenum Press, 1991. A comprehensive and critical review of all major strands of systems methodologies with emphasis on soft systems methodologies, as well some of the more recent developments in critical methodologies and their theoretical basis in sociological theories. A complete bibliography to 1990.

Naughton, John, *Soft Systems Analysis: An Introductory Guide*, (T301 Technology course: Block IV: The Soft Systems Approach), The Open University Press, Walton Hall, Milton Keynes, MK7 6AB, England, 1984. This is my preferred exposition of Checkland's SSM. It demystifies it, brings it to a level any beginner can grasp. There is also a workbook with additional examples with it.

Rosendhead, J., *Rational Analysis for a Problematic World*, Wiley,. 1991. A brief overview of the important properties of soft systems methodologies, followed by a detailed account with case studies of several methodologies, written by various contributors. This is probably the best starting point to get the 'basics' of and a 'feel' for these approaches.

Index